OILER BLUES

The Story of Pro Football's Most Frustrating Team

BY JOHN PIRKLE

SPORTLINE PUBLISHING
HOUSTON · SAN FRANCISCO
2000

OILER BLUES
The Story of Pro Football's Most Frustrating Team

Copyright © 2000 by John P. Pirkle
Published by Sportline Publishing
3346 E. TC Jester Boulevard
Houston, Texas 77018

All right reserved. Printed in the United States of America. No part of this book may be used or reproduced without prior permission except for the purpose of critical review. For information contact Sportline Publishing.

Cover Design:
    Stephanie Zelman (Boston)
    Modifications by Gladys Ramirez (Houston)

Photographs:
    Metropolitan Research Center
    Houston Public Library

    Private Collections
    Joel Durate
    Carter Smith

Distribution arranged by: Midpoint Trade Books, 27 West 20th Street, Suite 1102, New York, NY 10011. Telephone (212) 727-0190.

Oiler Blues is not licensed, authorized or endorsed by any league, player or players association, nor is it authorized or endorsed by Bud Adams, the Houston Oilers, Tennessee Oilers or Tennessee Titans.

Publisher's Cataloging-in-Publication
(Provided by Quality Books, Inc.)

Pirkle, John.
    Oiler blues : the story of pro football's most
frustrating team / by John Pirkle. -- 1st ed.
    p. cm.
    Includes bibliographical references and index.
    LCCN 99-72809
    ISBN: 1-891422-01-4 (softbound)
    ISBN: 1-891422-00-6 (hardcover)

1. Tennessee Titans (football team)--History. 2. Houston Oilers (football team)--History. 3. National Football League--History. 4. American Football League--History.   I. Title.

GV956.T45P57 2000
796.332/64/0976819   QBI99-1201

DEDICATION

In the early 1970s, a kid living in Houston named Carl won a contest sponsored by a radio station. The prize was fabulous — a trip for two to the Super Bowl.

Carl, however, was troubled. The source of his dilemma was his love of the Oilers. Like countless other Houstonians, he was a diehard fan. Carl had Columbia blue flowing through his veins. He lived for the day his team would make the big game. But the Oilers of the early '70s were about as far away from the Super Bowl as a team could get. Thus Carl had mixed feelings about going even though it was all free.

Enter Carl's father who came up with what seemed to everyone at the time like a workable solution. The father would take the contest trip (which included seats on the 40-yard line) and, in exchange, would pay the cost for Carl to attend the first Super Bowl the Oilers made. Plane, hotel and game tickets — whenever and wherever.

I do not know what became of Carl. But I am sure about one thing, his father never had to pay for that trip.

This book is dedicated to Carl and Oiler fans everywhere who all have a little bit of Carl in them.

ACKNOWLEDGMENTS

I am grateful to all those who helped bring this, my first book, to print. They include but are not limited to Rochelle, Linda, A.J., Stephanie, Jeff, Joe, Jean-Louis, Carter, June, Nicole, Amanda and my loving and supportive family Faye, Twila, Tom, Kimberly and Sara.

Additional thanks go out to those who helped me compile the bulk of the research — namely the Reference Room of the Houston Public Library — and all the wonderful photographs — especially the Metropolitan Research Center of the Houston Public Library. Special thanks goes to Joel Durate and for his individual attention and assistance with the photos.

CONTENTS

THE BEGINNING 11

ONCE THEY WERE CHAMPIONS

1960: Opening Season 21
1961: Their Finest Moment 27
1962: Three's A Charm? 34

THE FIRST DARK AGES

1963: The Transition 41
1964: Who Needs A Playbook? 45
1965: Like Sophia Lauren Does A Bikini 51

WALLY AND THE DUKE

1966: The Odd Couple 59
1967: From Last To First 68
1968: An Eventful Year 77
1969: On The Brink Of Greatness 87

THE RETURN OF THE DARK AGES

1970: The Death Of Wally World 87
1971: Hughes He? 90
1972: As Bad As It Gets 94
1973: About That Lifetime Contract 99
1974: The Turning Point 103

LOVE YA BLUE

1975: A Winning Season 111
1976: Letdown 118
1977: Rebirth 123
1978: The Tyler Rose 130
1979: The Second Best Team In Football 144
1980: It Should Have Been Their Year 158

THE THIRD DARK AGES

- 1981: Some Big Boots To Fill 171
- 1982: For Whom The Bell Tolls? 176
- 1983: The Bell Tolls For Thee 181
- 1984: Trading Heroes 186
- 1985: Cuz' When You're Talkin' Houston,
  You're Talkin' Super Bowl 194

THE GLANVILLE YEARS

- 1986: The Rule Of Five 199
- 1987: Suckers Such As You 210
- 1988: The House Of Pain 224
- 1989: Exit Stage Left 235

THE PARDEE YEARS

- 1990: Enter The Run 'N' Shoot 251
- 1991: Finally 260
- 1992: People Will Take This Game
  To The Grave 271
- 1993: The Effective End
  Of The Houston Oilers 284
- 1994: Turn Out The Lights,
  The Pardee's Over 300

WAITING TO EXHALE

- The Life And Death Of The Bud Dome 313
- 1995: Is Bud a Capitalist or a Socialist? 319
- 1996: All My Ex's Live In Texas 331

THE SHORT LIFE OF THE TENNESSEE OILERS

- 1997: Requiem For The Memphis Oilers 343
- 1998: On To Nashville 353

CONCLUSION 359

BIBLIOGRAPHY AND READING LIST 361

INDEX 363

About The Author 367

PREFACE

I WROTE THIS BOOK to record and recognize the heroes and highlights of Oiler football. I grew up with this team. They are a part of me and always will be. I wanted to share that history.

I wrote this book because the story of the Oilers is so rich and full. As the book title and dedication suggest, the team's record is fraught with disappointment. Indeed, the Oilers are synonymous with unfulfilled expectations, broken dreams and heartache. Nonetheless, writing this book has been a heck of a journey, one full of colorful characters, humor and intrigue. The Oilers got under your skin. They got under mine. They were impossible for me to ignore.

I wrote this book because the Oiler tale never generated much national attention. Houston, like San Diego or Seattle, is a geographically isolated big city. Unlike those places, however, it is not a tourist center. Nor is it a media center. Thus, even though Houston can compete with any large city on a daily basis in terms of business culture, crime, traffic and high rises, any news generated there, including sports news, has a tendency to remain local. But the Oiler story is one the rest of the world should know, because it has much to tell the rest of the world.

I wrote this book to put up a defense for the fans in Houston. The team's departure left them with a black eye. The NFL and national media called them nonsupportive. They blamed the team's departure on this false premise. The facts will refute that tag. At the same time, I will explain why, despite Houston's passion for the Oilers and football in general, not many tears were shed when Bud Adams loaded up the truck and moved to Tennessee.

I wrote this book so Tennessee Titan fans can share in their team's past. No doubt, they have been at least a little curious as to why Houston did not put up a better fight keep the Oilers. Moreover, as time goes by and team owner Bud Adams' actions leave them confused or angry, they will be able to consult this book for perspective and reference.

I wrote this book because I did not think anyone else would.

I wrote this book in a season-by-season, chronological order. My original goal was to let the story speak for itself, just state the facts. I found this impossible to accomplish, but have tried to keep editorial comment to a reasonable minimum.

The usual sports book is written by a sports reporter. Benefits accrue accordingly to his or her newspaper or magazine. The general public, however, does not share in this benefit if those reporters compromise their objectivity by being part of the story. In Houston, sports journalists were often part of the story. Sometimes, as will be seen, they *were* the story.

I wrote this book to present a complete picture by including the perceptions of both reporters and fans. Certainly, fans' perceptions of their team are colored by what they read in the local newspaper. While this is less true today with cable TV and the Internet, it was very much the case for most of the Oilers' existence in Houston. The point is, to understand Houston's attitude about the Oilers, it is necessary to consider the opinions of the influence peddlers. In this book, the spin doctors of sports are an integral part of the plot.

Long-time fans will enjoy recalling the individuals and events that made Oiler football what it was from specific players to particular seasons or games and even to certain plays in the Oilers' 39-year history. Despite the overall tone of underachievement that has nagged the franchise, there have been plenty of instances of individual and team greatness.

While new fans are and should be most concerned with where their team is going, this book will allow them to learn how their team got where they are.

—JOHN PIRKLE
1999

TABLE OF ABBREVIATIONS

The book contains several abbreviations most of which will be know to average football fans.

AFL	American Football League
NFL	National Football League
NCAA	National Collegiate Athletic Association
TD	Touchdown
FG	Field Goal
PAT	Point after touchdown or extra point

OFFENSE

QB	Quarterback
RB	Running back
TB	Tailback
FB	Fullback
WR	Wide receiver
SE	Split end
FL	Flanker
OG	Offensive guard
LG	Left offensive guard
RG	Right offensive guard
OT	Offensive tackle
LT	Left offensive tackle
RT	Right offensive tackle
C	Center
TE	Tight end
H-back	A second or motion TE who lines up anywhere
K	Kicker
P	Punter

DEFENSE

NG	Nose guard in a 3-4 alignment
NT	Nose tackle in a 4-3 alignment
DT	Defensive tackle
DE	Defensive end
LE	Left defensive end
RE	Right defensive end
LB	Linebacker
MLB	Middle LB in a 4-3 alignment
ILB	Inside LB in a 3-4 alignment
OLB	Outside linebacker
LOLB	Left outside linebacker
ROLB	Right outside linebacker
WSLB	Weakside LB playing away from TE
SSLB	Strongside LB playing on TE
DB	Defensive back
CB	Cornerback
LCB	Left cornerback
RCB	Right cornerback
FS	Free safety
SS	Strong safety

CHAPTER 1

THE BEGINNING

The story of the Oilers begins in the 1950s. While some look back at this era as boring and homogenous, the 1950s were a portent for change. One of the most significant was a big increase in leisure time for average working Americans. New products from freezers to credit cards were altering lives. With the extra time, families headed outdoors for playing with boats and swimming pools and indoors for living with air-conditioning and television.

The influence of television has arguably been the most pervasive. As TV sets became more affordable, they helped transform a generation of Americans and their successors from one of doers to one of watchers, and in the process sounded the death knell for small-time entertainment. Why would people pay to see a no-name production when they could watch better entertainers for free? This included local sports such as minor league baseball, immensely popular then. People did not want go sit outdoors in the heat and mosquitoes to watch marginal talent when they could sit in the comfort of their home and watch the pros

Television also fostered the wane of regionalism. In the world of sports, fans wanted nationally competitive professional leagues. In the late 1950s, NBC had the big-ticket item of the day, college football, and led the growth of network sports departments. CBS was a distant second, while ABC did not have sports.

The NFL Title game in 1958 between Johnny Unitas' Colts and Frank Gifford's Giants in New York is said to be the game that connected the nation and its television sets to professional football. The Colts won the classic battle 23-17 on an Alan Ameche overtime touchdown. Some called it "the greatest game of all time." It was the first OT championship and the first watched by millions.

Among the growing fan base were people of means who wanted to participate. They saw potential in football's growing gate receipts and television revenues. But getting in this game would not be easy.

BIRDS OF A FEATHER

Around the time of the Colts' championship, the NFL Cardinals, Chicago's first professional team, were in financial trouble. The family that controlled the Cards wanted out of direct competition with George Halas and the Bears, aka the Monsters of the Midway.

These were the two teams whose broadcast market covered Texas. In need of a relocation, the Cards cast a lustful eye towards the state and its burgeoning population and wealth. Texas was already a hotbed of high school and college football talent and excitement.

Cardinal brass looked first to Texas' largest city. Houston had no big league team of any sort, but appeared to have a big appetite for football as indicated by attendance at local college games. Texas' only Ivy League quality school, tiny Rice University (then Rice Institute), had a student population of under 1,500 but a 70,000-seat football stadium that regularly filled. During the 1958 season, attendance at Rice home games ranked third nationally behind only Michigan and Ohio State.

In 1958, Cardinal brass contacted one of Houston's rich young oilmen, Kenneth Stanley "Bud" Adams, Jr. The 36-year-old Adams was already recognized as a sports promoter. He had pushed AAU basketball, been a part of a syndicate trying to bring professional baseball to the city and co-promoted an NFL exhibition game. Adams recognized the ridiculous fiction of the Chicago teams being considered Houston's home teams. He knew Houston had the appetite and size for its own team. But the deal fell apart when the Cards would not let him have a controlling 51%.

The Cardinal people then turned their attention to Texas' second largest city and one of the country's wealthiest families. Like Adams, young Lamar Hunt wanted a pro team where he lived. That deal also ended over controlling interest.

In March of 1959, Hunt flew to Houston for a meeting with Adams. Over dinner at the Shamrock Hilton Hotel, they shared their mutual frustrations over the Cardinals and equally frustrating attempts to get the NFL to expand. They agreed Texas was a natural for the pro game. They also knew the old men of the NFL like George Halas and Art Rooney, who were just beginning to make big money, would never willingly expand or share NFL wealth with newcomers. Hunt mentioned that in his pursuit of a team, he found enough interest in other cities to form a league.

Bud said later, "I picked him up at the airport and we had dinner. We finished eating and he finally asked me if I would be interested in having a football team in a new league." Adams' response was, "Hell yes."

Their idea was not novel. There had been other leagues, but the NFL survived. There were even three failed American Leagues. The last, the All-American Conference, only made it a few years.

This American League would make it. Looking back from the 1990s, Adams said, "I never thought pro football would grow to the extent it has reached today. But I was convinced that it would work in Houston because there are so many football fanatics in this area."

Kenneth Stanley "Bud" Adams, Jr. circa 1960

SEEDS OF FORMATION

When word leaked out that these two young oil millionaires wanted to start their own league, they were invited to Chicago for a visit with the Papa Bear. At the Bears' offices in July of 1959, George Halas told Adams and Hunt that a new league was no good because it would cause the costs to go through the roof for everyone.

He offered expansion franchises to each if they would drop the idea. After a conference, they agreed, but on one condition. They wanted it in writing. Halas stammered and coughed. He promised he would follow through at the right time. Adams and Hunt had heard promises like that before. They turned him down on the spot. Halas was furious with what he saw as their arrogance and threatened a financial blood bath. When they left Chicago, the two young men knew they had a big fight on their hands.

A few days later, they made their announcement. The press conference came on August 3, 1959, from Adams' ostentatious bunker below his oil company offices in Houston. Reporters heard the rival league would begin play in 1960 in direct competition with the NFL. Adams and Hunt were the first two franchise holders in an 8-team league with a 14-game schedule. They claimed the unnamed teams would be Texas' first professional sports franchises.

The names and locations of the other owners were announced later. They were Bob Howsam of Denver, Barron Hilton of Los Angeles, Harry Wismer of New York and a group headed by Max Winter in Minneapolis. They each put up $25,000 supplemented by a performance bond of $100,000. The bond was both clever and necessary. It bound the early founders in a way the earlier rival leagues failed to do.

LOCAL REACTION

This news ambled slowly around the country. It was a different era. The United States was smaller. Most say it was a more "innocent time." Every home in America did not yet have a television, and things like cable television, CNN, ESPN and the world wide web were not even pipe dreams yet. Most Americans got their news from the local paper. Every big city had at least two.

In Houston, there were three — the *Chronicle*, *Post* and *Press*, but the August 3 announcement was not front page news in any of them. The *Chronicle* had nothing about the story on its cover and the *Post* only had a one-liner at the bottom. The big news in those days revolved around President Dwight Eisenhower, Vice-President Richard Nixon, the Red scares in Cuba and Laos and labor union corruption. Even a story about a Rockefeller marrying his housekeeper received regular front-page coverage over news of the AFL.

The sports page was much smaller and covered mainly professional baseball and college football. Stories regarding the NFL were gaining space, while the NBA received only minor notice. Local participatory sport and leisure events such as softball tournaments, bowling, golfing, and hunting and fishing were big stories. What space the news from the Adams' Petroleum Center got was small compared to competing tales of individual accomplishment like the skin diver who speared a 432-pound jewfish, the South Texas family who hunted for rattlesnakes at night with slingshots and the man who dragged an 8-foot hammerhead shark in by the tail from the shallow waters off West Galveston beach.

Most people were skeptical of a new league's chances. Adams said, "To the guys on the street, it was a big gamble. I was going to sell some interest in the team, but I couldn't get anybody to take it."

BOOM TOWN

Houston was a city on the move. Growing by over 300,000 in the 1950s, it was well over 1 million by 1959. It was sixth largest in the United States and closing.

Unlike overcrowded East Coast cities where people lived on top of each other, growth in Houston went out. Families lived in detached houses with yards and driveways instead of apartment buildings. While Houston grew, urban centers in the East decayed. Nor did it suffer the same levels of crime or racial strife. The public school system, fourth largest, began desegregating in 1960 without incident.

Houston grew because of a good business climate. It was the oil capital of the world. Its port was second largest to New York. The medical center was one the world's finest. Throw in agriculture and cattle, banks and insurance, restaurants and television stations, and you had a boom town. Everything was new and modern. There were not any "old" buildings to tear down to make room for the new ones. The oil companies which headquartered there tried to outdo each other by erecting ever taller office buildings. People poured out of the rotting conditions in Detroit, New York, Cleveland and Philadelphia in search of jobs and better conditions. Eventually, so many Northerners would occupy the 44-story Humble Building, the South's tallest office structure, that locals referred to it as "Yankee Stadium."

Despite the size, newcomers were greeted by friendly and hospitable natives. They quickly learned Houstonians did not live up to their Hollywood stereotypes. There were no Cadillacs with longhorns on the hood; the city was not overrun with loudmouths in cowboy hats; the bars were not filled with debutantes; and Texas Rangers did not patrol the streets on horseback.

At the end of the decade, Houston was the largest city in the country without a pro sport franchise, but things were coming together. In 1957, Craig F. Cullinan, Jr. formed the Houston Sports Association ("HSA") for the express purpose of bringing professional baseball to Houston. Cullinan sold shares in the syndicate to 27 men, all civic-minded and associated with oil money, names such as Bracewell, Elkins, Allen, Cullen, Kirkland, Scurlock, Robertson and Adams. This group had deep roots in Houston and looked for ways to make it grow and thrive. They believed a pro team would show the world Houston had arrived as a large city.

To have one, however, they had to have a stadium. In 1958, Harris County voters approved a $20 million bond package to build the requisite sports complex. Part of the success of that vote was due to the public's confidence in the individuals who made up the HSA.

The summer of 1959 was equally eventful. First came news of an outlaw baseball league (the Continental) that would put a team in Houston. Shortly afterward, the rival football league appeared, proposing to do the same. These moves made both MLB and the NFL wake up and give Houston some attention. As a result, the city confronted the 1960s with much excitement and momentum.

THE NFL'S FORMAL POSITION

Formally, the NFL took the position that it would do nothing to inhibit the birth of the AFL. Somewhat ironically, it was NFL Commissioner Bert Bell who first publicly announced a new league was forming while testifying before a congressional subcommittee on antitrust practices in sports. Bell's testimony flushed out Adams and Hunt, resulting in the premature press conference. Bell pledged cooperation. A few even believed it.

THE REAL STORY

There was a more sinister side than what met public scrutiny. Bell was more or less a puppet. Halas directed NFL policy behind the scenes. Unlike many pro sports owners who used the pro leagues as a place to put money in lieu of giving it to Uncle Sam, Halas and Pittsburgh's Art Rooney were in it to make money. Halas privately opposed both the AFL and NFL expansion. He believed he built the league and deserved the profits that were finally coming. He sure did not want to share with a pair of rich young Texans. He started a secret war to undo the new league before it ever started.

His immense influence showed when national writers wondered aloud if there were enough players to sustain more teams. The AFL was the "outlaw" league.

The NFL even had political clout in Houston where county officials planning the new stadium publicly stated that they were considering making it a baseball-only facility. Some Houstonians feared they were only making the NFL angry and would never get a team. *Chronicle* columnist Dick Peebles editorialized that the city would be wise to wait for NFL expansion. Through the controversy, however, Adams and Hunt stuck together. They said the NFL had been promising expansion for years and doubted it would really happen. They even suggested the AFL would expand into Chicago.

Later in August 1959, Halas and Rooney came to Houston for a Bears-Steelers exhibition game that was ironically co-sponsored by Adams and Cullinan. From Adams' backyard, they announced plans to expand the NFL into Houston and Dallas starting in 1961. After the pronouncement, the *Chronicle* predicted the AFL would suffer the same fate as the All-American Conference. Public sentiment was being divided.

Adams and Hunt remained unfazed. They suggested the NFL's actions were anti-competitive and said they were going forward by adding two more teams from among Seattle, Buffalo, Miami, Louisville and Atlanta. Halas denied the antitrust implications, saying the NFL's sudden desire to expand was not due to the AFL but to the culmination of plans that "had been under consideration for five years."

Unable to sway Hunt or Adams, Halas then dangled franchises in front of different groups in Dallas and Houston. Bud's HSA buddy Cullinan led the Houston group. Unlike the AFL announcement, the NFL's offer to Cullinan did make the local front-page headlines. The *Chronicle* caption blared, "Houston Offered National League Grid Franchise." The press urged Adams to team up with Cullinan and bring in the NFL; suggesting that if he did not, "It will be an opportunity missed forever." Adams refused, saying, "We're going ahead. I've been hearing a lot of expansion talk for a long time but won't believe it until I see it." Times were tense as the two groups battled for the one absolute requirement, a stadium lease.

A TURNING POINT IN HOUSTON HISTORY

The NFL's toughest condition was that all teams had to have "suitable" stadiums. That meant a minimum of 50,000 seats. In pre-Astrodome Houston, that meant Rice Stadium. Located in a beautiful tree-lined neighborhood not overrun by Houston's malignant mascot, the billboard, Rice Stadium seated over 70,000. But Rice officials were philosophically opposed to football as a profession. They did not want their facilities used by mercenaries who openly took money to play a game the colleges invented. Coach Jess Neely clung to the romantic ideal of football. The pro game had already taken over cities like New York and Chicago at the expense of the colleges. Besides, times were pretty good for Rice football and attendance was high.

In October Adams locked up the major high school facility, Jeppesen Stadium. Unable to land a deal with Rice, Cullinan announced in early November that the issue was forcing him to give back the franchise. Thus, it was Rice University, and more specifically, Jess Neely, who effectively kept the NFL out of Houston.

A few years later, Rice would change its mind and rent to the Oilers. Many a Houstonian can look back to November 1959 as the first of several missed opportunities to have a pro football team operated by someone other than Bud Adams.

HALAS' LAST DITCH EFFORTS

Dallas was another story. The NFL awarded a franchise to businessman Clint Murchison, who had failed in his earlier attempt to land an expansion team. That city failed to support its one prior entry into the NFL, the Texans in 1952. Unlike Rice, SMU games did not draw big crowds. Nonetheless, Dallas was looking at the prospect of having two pro teams. Halas was determined to squeeze the AFL in the home of the league's founder and its home offices. His political clout showed again when the Texas State Fair Commission determined it could not let Hunt and the Texans have the Cotton Bowl to themselves, but would have to share with the NFL team.

Halas continued to offer Adams and Hunt franchises or parts of franchises up to and even past the inaugural AFL draft. Despite the pressure, they persevered. All of the AFL owners did except one. The mutiny occurred in Minnesota. Showing the Texans what they thought of loyalty, the Winter consortium took the NFL club previously earmarked for Houston.

In Minneapolis for the announcement, Halas made one last run at Adams, offering him a franchise for $650,000 if he would bolt with the Minnesota group. Adams refused, saying he would honor his word to Hunt.

THE FOOLISH CLUB

Obviously, the original owners were an eclectic lot. Houston had Bud, whose father, KS "Boots" Adams, Sr. was the Chairman of Phillips Petroleum. Boots set his son up in Houston after World War II. At age 23, Bud formed Ada Oil Company with $17,000 he described as his "entire life savings." By 1959, Ada was the largest branded oil distributor in the country and among the top three oil brokers. By then, Bud not only was chairman of the Adams Petroleum Center, Independent Oil

Terminal, and Tidelands Service Company, but also sat on the board of a local bank.

He also had an uncle who was a great chief of the Cherokee Nation in Oklahoma, which gave some of the players cause to later refer to Bud as "Crazy Horse's Revenge." Adams has a fat, round face and uneasy smile. He is a person prone to grand gestures like wearing a cowboy hat and a full-length leather coat to games in the Houston heat. He used to throw team events at his ranch serving Black Forest stag and barbecued goat.

In October 1959, he announced that he had named his team the Oilers for "sentimental and social reasons." He had earlier sponsored a local basketball team known as the Ada Oilers. He later said he intended the name to honor his father.

In 1959, Lamar Hunt was 23-years-old, barely out of college and worth $50 million. He had a confidence that came from a daddy who was even richer than Boots. HL Hunt reportedly earned $200,000 a day. When someone asked HL how long Lamar might last with the new league if he lost $1 million, he replied, "Oh, about a hundred years." Yet Lamar was as frugal as they come. He drove a beat-up old car and possessed only one pair of shoes at a time, the soles of which he always wore down. He wore off-the-rack suits and flew second class. He made a comical picture signing athletes to million-dollar contracts with holes in his shoes. Mickey Herskowitz, who would eventually establish himself as Houston's best sportswriter, noted that "the difference between Adams and Hunt was that Lamar might go several days without mentioning money." Lamar played fourth string at SMU and was loyal to the school and the city. He cultivated the image of an unselfish person who wanted to promote sports and bring pro football to his hometown. He named his team the Texans.

Former Cowboys GM Tex Schramm, who competed with Hunt for Dallas, has a very different opinion of him. He complained that Hunt was a shameless self-promoter. This is from a man who brought us the Dallas Cowboy cheerleaders.

Baron Hilton of the Los Angeles Chargers, 32, was heir to hotel magnate Conrad Hilton, and was once a stepson to Zsa Zsa Gabor. He headed the Carte Blanche credit card program, which he said contributed to the name of his team ("If Buffalo has the Bills, Los Angeles gives you ... ") Although a strong presence early in the league, outside pressures pulled him away. He lost about $1 million the first year, then wept when he announced the move to San Diego. He did make sure the financially strapped AFL clubs had a roof over the heads while on the road.

The Howsam family of Denver owned a minor league baseball team in the days before television killed that sport. Somewhat out of his element, he was soon replaced by Calvin Kunz, who actively sought to move the team.

Harry Wismer of the New York Titans was the most well known. He was an ex-sportscaster and the league's most visible pitchman. He was also cash poor and ran the team out of his apartment. He helped negotiate the first television contract.

Prior to the first draft, the AFL had added two more clubs. The front man for the Boston Patriots was Billy Sullivan, who had been a PR guy at Notre Dame and Boston College. He was well-connected to the Irish elite. He also had cash problems, and consequently, trouble signing draft picks.

Ralph Wilson, a Detroit insurance and automobile man, ended up with a team in Buffalo, New York. His first choice was Miami, but when he was unable to lease the Orange Bowl, he settled on Buffalo sight unseen. Who knows where that franchise might have ended up if Wilson had traveled to Buffalo anywhere between November and March? The venue decision aside, Wilson was more presentable, refined and dignified than any of the other owners.

The Oakland club had a life of its own. After the Minnesota group sold out after the draft, Atlanta and Seattle were the first choices, but Hilton pushed for another California team to save expenses and give a geographic rival. Oakland received the franchise even before anyone had expressed interest in owning a team there. The original Oakland teams were very bad because of this late start. It did not help their image that the original team name was the "Señors" with plans for serape-draped cheerleaders on the sidelines wearing sombreros with footballs on top. Fortunately, someone soon figured out that the plural of señor was señores and they became the Raiders. The first team did not look very tough in the green uniforms they borrowed from the University of the Pacific. Behind the scenes the real savior was Ralph Wilson, who violated the league's bylaws by secretly kicking in $250,000 through his father's Detroit company.

The secret Wilson deal revealed how close-knit the league owners were. Other than the Minnesota defection, they stuck together. The togetherness would serve them well in the face of coming financial struggles and the tremendous heat brought by the NFL. For all the trouble they went to and risks they took, they nicknamed themselves the foolish club.

THERE WAS A TIME WHEN TEAMS PAID FOR (AT LEAST PARTS OF) THEIR STADIUMS

Of all the details involved with starting a league, the most pressing was finding a stadium suitable for professional football.

The Patriots were stuck in Fenway Park, a baseball stadium. The Titans found their soul mate in the Polo Grounds. Both the team and the stadium were falling apart. As the Polo Grounds' grass wore out, Wismer could not afford to replace it, and simply painted the dirt green until he could no longer afford the paint. In Dallas, both the Texans and the Rangers (later Cowboys) were in the Cotton Bowl where bats lived in the lightless end zones. The Chargers were equally embarrassed by the 17,724 who showed up for their first game, which made the cavernous 100,000 seat LA Coliseum look empty. Rams games there averaged about 75,000 in 1959.

The Oakland team had to settle for pathetic old Kezar Stadium located in San Francisco's Golden Gate Park, and said to be held together by seagull guano. Kezar was then replaced by Candlestick Park, but they had to share it with the hated 49ers. In 1963, they opened Frank Youel Field, a simplistic pipe rack stadium that would shake with the crowd. Construction was so basic that a port-a-can had to be welded to the exterior of the upstairs press area.

In Houston, the Oilers settled on an old high school facility named Jeppesen Stadium located near the University of Houston campus. Bud was so happy about the NFL not getting a foothold in Houston that he agreed to finance the expansion of Jeppesen to 36,000, including 300 to 500 "air-conditioned" seats. Clearly, he was counting on his yet-to-be-signed first draft pick to fill some seats.

Still, it was difficult to disguise Jeppesen. Called by some "an open sewer," the moldy old arena had one constant — the smell of urine. Prevailing wind direction determined the choicest seat. It was cramped and unnecessarily uncomfortable. Adams tried to make it more cheery by painting it his favorite color, Columbia blue. It did not help the smell.

The field condition was another story. Sporting that well-worn look after Thursday and Friday night high school contests, the ground was usually as hard as concrete. "Poorly laid concrete," according to Hank Stram. That was the case unless it was raining. When the ground was wet, only pigs and George Blanda were happy. An Oiler lineman once stepped into a Jeppesen puddle and sunk down to his shin. By the time he pried his foot out, his shoe was gone. The trainer had to fetch another. The first was never found.

From a fan's viewpoint, two things made Jeppesen bearable. First, the Oilers were a competitive team from the start. Second, a domed stadium was on the drawing boards. For the seven home games in 1960, a season ticket package sold for as low as $31.50.

A WHITE KNIGHT

By late 1959, the AFL had named a commissioner and had held a draft. It also had eight committed teams and a schedule. Nonetheless, many knowledgeable people predicted it would not survive. They believed the NFL would simply pick up the best teams when the league collapsed, as had happened in 1950 when the NFL added the 49ers and Browns of the All-American Conference. Halas said, "That damn Mickey Mouse league doesn't even own a football," employing the same insult effectively used against the AAC.

Things would be different this time. For one, the AFL had several very wealthy owners who had more staying power. They also put a clause in their constitution that any owner jumping would not only forfeit the franchise, but also all the player contracts, which would stay with the league. This prevented the best teams from leaving, which is what happened to the AAC.

The main reason the AFL made it, however, was good timing. It piggybacked the increasing role and power of television. In 1959, the NFL was collecting $200,000 for its television package, but all indicators pointed skyward. It appeared that if the AFL could field its teams and simply survive for a couple of years that it too could catch the updraft.

With CBS and the NFL in bed together, the other networks wanted a piece of the sizzling professional sports pie. The linchpin came when the AFL signed a 5-year television deal with ABC worth $2.5 million in the summer of 1960. That contract singularly gave the AFL a fighting chance. In the end, what Halas and Rooney failed to recognize was that the country's appetite for the game had grown to such an extent that the NFL's 12 teams could not satisfy it. Ultimately, it was fan hunger that fueled the television deals which fed everything else.

AFL Commissioner Joe Foss pooled the television rights and spilt them evenly among the teams. Explaining the reasons for pooling, Adams cited the lopsided financial power in baseball held by the New York Yankees as "an example of how to ruin a professional sports league." Some things just do not change.

THE FIRST OILER

Forming a league was easy compared to finding players. For the Oilers, this job fell to John Breen, who became the first Oiler employee on October 18, 1959. A long-time scout with the Chicago Cardinals, Breen was a good evaluator of talent and a clever operator. Officially, he served as the team's first player personnel director, but did much more than the title indicates. The NFL had spent a lot of energy over the years convincing Americans that there was only enough talent to go around for its teams. It was up to Breen to shed the light of day on that tired old myth.

Breen, who Oiler QB George Blanda later called "one of the few competent football executives that Adams ever hired," got the Oilers off to a fast start by finding players and negotiating contracts while most of the other teams were still trying to determine their colors and line up stadiums. His initiative would reap big rewards in the early years. Blanda also said that while hiring Breen was "one of the first truly intelligent moves" Adams ever made, it was also "one of the last." John Breen bucked tremendous odds, holding out 17 years under Adams.

THE FIRST DRAFT

The AFL set its initial draft for November 22, 1959, purportedly a week before the NFL draft but the NFL had already held a secret draft. The AFL held a second draft on December 2. At least half the teams were not ready, so Breen and the GMs from the Chargers, Broncos and Texans (later the Chiefs) pooled all the information on the college players.

The first round was by territory with Houston getting the rights to players from Rice, UT, UH, Texas A&M, LSU and Baylor. Dallas got the rights to players from SMU, TCU, Texas Tech and the like. The idea was that each team would receive one regional or national star who would become both a building block and box office draw.

John Breen

For the rest of the draft, the general managers decided the top 8 players at each offensive position (which is how all players were listed in those days). Thus, the first eleven choices were to be by position to assure balance.

A CANNON SHOT ACROSS THE BOW OF THE SS NFL

Houston's first pick was Heisman Trophy winner Billy Cannon of LSU. Cannon was player-of-the-year, a unanimous All-American and the most sought after of all the collegians. A legend at that level, he had size, strength and speed. Most importantly, his high profile would provide the AFL some much needed credibility. He was also the number one pick in the NFL draft.

Bud, who did the negotiating, worked the phone lines between Houston and Baton Rouge in pursuit. Cannon, however, was hiding in the backwoods because he had already agreed to a deal with the NFL's Rams and received $10,500 in checks from them. He appeared at the NFL draft and LA publicly announced he would play there. However, once word got to Billy that Bud would beat any NFL offer, Cannon surfaced with a big grin, saying, "Mr. Adams, I've been trying to get a hold of you." Cannon soon agreed to his second pro deal while still playing for the Tigers.

In a signature Adams' gesture, the signing was set for the moment his undergraduate career ended under the south goal post of the Sugar Bowl following the LSU-Mississippi game. When the Rams smelled a rat, they hurried their young General Manager, Pete Rozelle, to Bourbon Street to keep Cannon in the fold. Understandably, the Ole Miss players were not impressed with all the shenanigans and hammered Cannon and the rest of his team. Billy signed with Bud's attorney under the goal as advertised.

In a bad omen for Bud so far as PR went, the newspapers barely covered it. Although the *Chronicle* had reporters in New Orleans to cover the game, full details did not appear for five days. None published the picture of Billy and Bud's rep under the goal posts. On the other hand, articles on a proposed third baseball league (one that did not happen) filled all three local papers on a daily basis.

Nonetheless, LA felt the repercussions. When Pete Rozelle reached the postgame dressing room, he put an arm around him and said, "Well Billy, its going to be awfully nice having you with us in Los Angeles." He replied, "But I just signed with the Houston Oilers."

A dejected Rozelle took the last plane for the coast. Soon, he filed an injunction in federal court seeking to enforce his deal. That contract, it turned out, was undated and signed before the Sugar Bowl. Billy returned the Rams' checks uncashed and said he did not feel what he signed was a valid contract. Bud tried to take the moral high ground, saying, "I don't think any court would rule in favor of any professional team that tried to get a boy to break the amateur rules right before the biggest game of his career."

Adams' call on the lawsuit was correct thanks to home court advantage — a Louisiana judge. Cannon went on to play solidly, occasionally spectacularly for several years with the Oilers. However, the immediate symbolic significance to the "Mickey Mouse League" of signing the best-known player in college football far transcended his subsequent performance. The Oilers turned some heads. It made a skeptical national press sit up and take another look. It also showed the NFL it was serious. More than any other single event its first year, the Cannon signing showed the AFL was for real.

BILLY CANNON
Halfback

THINGS GOT A LITTLE NASTY

The AFL lost most other marquee names. Highly regarded QB Don Meredith of SMU was Hunt's first choice. But he signed with the expansion NFL Dallas Rangers before that team was approved by the owners. The message was delivered. It would be tough sledding for the AFL.

The AFL did sign a number of All-Americans and a couple of future Hall of Famers in OLs Ron Mix and Jim Otto. However, for the most part, the NFL got the best players from the big schools while the AFL got the better players from places like Ripon, Heidelberg and Panhandle A&M. Lawsuits flew around the country, because like Cannon, many players were signing contracts with both leagues.

Because of John Breen, the Oilers did a little better than the other clubs. He signed the first two Oilers on December 8 — Don Hitt and Tony Banfield, both of Oklahoma State. He signed 9 of the Oilers' first 11 picks, beating out the Giants for LB Doug Cline of Clemson, the Cardinals for QB Jacky Lee of Cincinnati and the Colts for DE Don Floyd of TCU.

The draft competition was a tempest brewing. Once the details of Rozelle's dealings became public due to the Cannon lawsuit, college officials vehemently complained. Rozelle's Rams were singled out by the Penn State coach for secret meetings with some of his players. Players had no agents in those days. The pros were seen as taking advantage of kids by conning them into things that might jeopardize their college careers. LSU drew a chuckle saying it was going to look into whether Cannon had forfeited his eligibility and possibly all the team's victories.

Rozelle's tactics violated both the NFL's bylaws and NCAA rules on contact. The AFL and Joe Foss threw that as well as Halas' attempts to smash the AFL into a $10 million antitrust lawsuit against the NFL.

A SHORT FALL TO THE TOP

The NFL held its January meeting in Miami after the Colts beat the Giants again in the NFL Title game. They voted in Dallas for 1960 and Minnesota for 1961, over the sole opposition of Redskins owner George Preston Marshall. A successor to Bert Bell, who died, was also named after several deadlocks. In a surprising compromise, tall and tan Pete Rozelle emerged as the new commissioner. As GM of the Rams, Pete made so many bad trades that the Rams went in the tank, causing coach Sid Gillman to be fired. He also got egg on everyone's faces over Cannon. Naturally, they promoted him. The owners thought they could easily control him due to his youth. To his credit, one of his first acts was fining George Halas. As time went by, he rose to the position.

WELCOME LOU RYMKUS

On January 3, 1960, Adams hired as his first coach Lou Rymkus, who had been an assistant to Sid Gillman in LA. Lou was a serious man who had geared his entire life toward becoming a head coach. The new league was his ship coming in. Fate presented him the head Oiler job. Fate would also soon prove to have a cruel sense of humor.

Rymkus was 40 and was coming off a solid pro career. The former lineman was still quite fit. His huge square-jawed face seemed to stick out unnaturally from his tall frame. His eyes were usually in a tight squint. All together, he looked sort of like a giant bird of prey.

A Notre Dame graduate, he viewed athletics as a noble pursuit that built character and strong values in men. Born of Slavic descent, he was one of the many non-Irish Fighting Irish. Indeed, he was straight out of one of those old "Win One for the Gipper" movies. He even named his twin boys Pat and Mike. To Lou Rymkus, football was more than a game, it was a holy mission. Winning meant everything. He told his guys that "football was mother and father and home and family to me. I want you players to think the same way I do." While the merits of Lou's sophomoric techniques used on professionals is debatable, his first team's success is not.

Rymkus was a throwback. Unfortunately, that is what Bud Adams did with him sooner than later. He was not Bud's first choice. That was Giants' assistant Tom Landry, who decided not to take a chance on a new league. Nor was Lou his second choice; that was Oklahoma's Bud Wilkinson. While he was Bud's third option, Rymkus was the first choice of the Chargers and Texans. Talk about your life-altering choices. The coaches those teams hired, Sid Gillman and Hank Stram, stayed put until the merger. Despite winning the first championship and Coach of the Year awards, Rymkus only lasted until the fifth game of his second season. Every tradition must have a starting point, and Bud Adam's nagging propensity to fire coaches started with Lou Rymkus.

WANTED: ONE ARM WITH EXPERIENCE

Breen realized that, besides a seat-filling name like Cannon, his team needed experience at certain positions. "My first thought was if you're going to play in a new league, go get the best-throwing quarterback you can find and have him put the football in the air, because it will be a year or two before anyone can get the kind of defensive backs that will be able to stop him." There were only two available to fit that job descrip-

Lou Rymkus

tion: George Blanda and future politician Jackie Kemp. Breen was familiar with Blanda from his Chicago days.

Blanda had a strange NFL career and even stranger relationship with his coach, George Halas. In 1954, he led the league in completions. At the time, Halas called him "best quarterback in football."

But Blanda never started again. Halas, known for stockpiling QBs, kept George buried on the bench for most of ten years, using him only as a kicker. Ironically, the two men had similar poor immigrant backgrounds. Maybe they did not like looking at themselves when they looked at each other. When Chicago fans clamored, "We want Blanda," Halas told George, "You better get up in the stands, they want you." As Blanda approached 30, Halas' treachery caught up with him.

Approaching the 1959 season, George's option year, Halas came up with an illicit scheme to pay Blanda not to come to camp with the promise of possibly adding him to the roster later. This kept Halas from having to act on the option and kept Blanda out of the clutches

George Blanda with Bud and the ever gracious Nancy Adams in happy times.

of competitors. Blanda naively went along, not realizing he was had until the season was well under way. Bell attempted to persuade Blanda to retire. Backed into a corner, Blanda came out suing, but soon realized the time required would mean whatever was left of his career. Luckily, at least for George and the Oilers, Commissioner Bell dropped dead, affording them all a window of freedom. The interim commissioner released George on condition that he "retire" from the NFL. He could sign with the AFL, but Halas thought it was going to disappear. Thus, George Blanda turned into an ironic birthday present from Halas to the AFL.

THE SHADOW KNOWS

Thanks to timing, Blanda's career did not die at the end of a cold bench at Soldier Field. John Breen had been following the Halas-Blanda saga closely, and quickly made him an offer. All clubs eventually did, including the Chargers' Sid Gillman. Believing many AFL teams were on shaky financial ground, Blanda narrowed his choice to the Oilers and Chargers, who he felt were putting together the two best organizations. If the AFL did collapse, they had the best chances of being merged into the NFL.

Gillman, like Blanda, was not exactly Mr. Congeniality. The bow-tie wearing coach has been described as "a dowdy Jewish uncle — which he was — but he could be an ogre." After spending some time with Sid, Blanda decided he would just be another Halas. He liked Lou Rymkus. He also liked Houston's fast-paced growth, which he hoped would provide business opportunities in the off season. His original deal was for $20,000 and was the most significant to the success of the early Oilers.

Gillman was not happy about losing the best veteran QB available to his old assistant. In the first of many episodes of bad blood between Sid and Oiler personnel, he publicly attacked Houston over the Blanda signing before the league had seen its first game. It did not work and he settled on NFL and CFL-reject Kemp, who went on to be the All-League QB the first year.

NOW THAT'S A LOT OF TOUCHDOWNS

Blanda must have wondered if he made the right choice after his first Houston appearance. The team's excited management called a press conference at the Cork Club. With Adams, Breen and Blanda in attendance, the spokesman told the local media how George led the NFL in pass completions one year and held the record for consecutive extra point kicks at 156. After some questions about how a 31-year-old QB might hold up, one of those moments arrived that tends to define a relationship. A member of the Houston press stood, cleared his throat and asked, "Were all those extra points in one season?" Blanda looked perplexed, Adams looked self-conscious and Breen looked at his shoes.

CHAPTER 2

ONCE THEY WERE CHAMPIONS 1960-62

Having survived a defection, negative press reports and their own doubts, AFL owners turned toward their inaugural season. By the summer of 1960, they were a real league with uniforms, helmets, jock straps and everything. Contrary to what George Halas said, they even had a few footballs.

Blessed with an experienced NFL personnel man, the Houston Oilers got off to a fast start and became an early powerhouse. They were so good that, as difficult as it is to believe today, they were once champions. It was a lot of fun for Houston fans. Unfortunately, it was all downhill from there.

1960: OPENING SEASON

Coach Rymkus quickly completed his staff with assistants Walter Schlinkman, Fred Wallner, Wally Lemm and Mac Speedie with Bobby Brown as trainer. Adams appointed himself general manager, saying, "I figure the only way to learn pro football is to be intimately associated with it. You just can't get much closer than general manager, so I decided to take the job."

The rest of the front office included Don Suman, Jack Scott and Carroll Martin. This group was really something. Suman was once Rice's head basketball coach, but when Bud picked him up, he was serving as their concessions manager. Originally an administrative assistant, he became Oilers VP and later GM, even though he had no football experience. UH publicity man Scott took the same role with the Oilers. Martin was a former pipe salesman who had moved up through Bud's companies. He was the ticket manager. It was a Kremlinesque existence as the various parties plotted to advance around the others.

1960 TRAINING CAMP

The first Oiler training camp alternated between Buff Stadium (minor league baseball) and a vacant lot next to the UH campus. In what was most likely God's last attempt to warn the people of Houston not to let these guys into their hearts, it rained like hell for several days at the start of camp. When the thunderstorms finally passed, the humidity and mosquitoes stormed in. The most prized recruit was the one receiving the most repellent. Conditions were deplorable. There was no air-conditioning. The locker rooms flooded every time it rained. It stank. Giant cockroaches were everywhere. Players alternately passed out from the heat and stink. The Oilers sprayed jerseys with ammonia to keep from fainting, but the remedy backfired as the potent combination of ammonia, sweat and insect repellent felled even the strongest man.

There were few well-known names outside Blanda, Cannon and ex-NFL receiver Johnny Carson. They had Jacky Lee, who had just thrown six TDs in the annual North-South all-star game. They also had All-Americans FB Bob White of Ohio State, DE Dan Floyd of TCU and DL Dan Lanphear of Wisconsin. The majority, however, were unknowns like Bob Talamini from Kentucky, Bill Groman of Heidelberg College, Dave Smith of Ripon, and Charley Tolar and Charley Hennigan, both from Northwestern State College (Louisiana). The Oilers even talked one guy out of law school, former Rice DT Orville Trask.

The first Oilers were Oklahoma States's Don Hitt and Tony Banfield. Banfield was an all-star (1961-63) until slowed by a knee injury.

The hottest commodities were players with NFL experience. AFL teams waited like lions in the bush for the cuts coming out of NFL camps up to and beyond the season opener. Breen and the Chargers were the most successful at this game. Breen's old NFL sources tipped him off on cuts. On Tuesdays, he could usually be found in the Dallas airport trying to lasso players making connections on their way home after being released. "I didn't have to play Sherlock Holmes. I recognized the players at the airport," Breen said. "A player might have been a cut victim in the NFL, but he was still good for our league."

NFL rejects arrived weekly. They included future wrestler Wahoo McDaniel for a short stay and ex-Lion Jim Norton, who stayed for a long time. Each team has its characters and Houston had Al Jamison, a closet-academic from Colgate with a mischievous grin. As an OT, he was known as a "masterful holder." His propensity for fighting earned him the nickname "Dirty Al." They also had Julian Spence, one of the original African-American Oilers, who was a 153-pound former army sergeant playing safety. Spence was best known for his brilliant Bud Adams imitation complete with cowboy hat, blue tinted glasses and full length white leather coat.

In total, 150 players passed through camp that first summer. Among the entire group, there were two dominant personalities — the grizzled veteran Blanda and the tough Rymkus. Coach Lou worked his players hard. His philosophy was that everyone was equal, even the golden boy. He said to Cannon, "Until you prove yourself on that football field, you're just another football player to me." After landing behind the unheralded Tolar in camp, Rymkus added that Billy was "no standout among the backs we have." Such commentary was not exactly music to the ears of the player-of-the-year or the man who went to so much expense to sign him.

But Rymkus was uncompromising to a fault. His stubbornness would not mesh well with his coaching dreams.

THE GREAT PLASTIC PIMPLE

On August 20, plans for the world's first domed stadium were unveiled. Blanda called it "the great plastic pimple on the plains." Another nickname was the "Big Blister." The plans had been under wraps for some time as county officials waited until it looked fairly certain they could fund the bond revenues (i.e., have rent-paying tenants). As of August, 1960, it appeared Houston would have both pro baseball and pro football.

STUMBLING OUT OF THE BLOCKS

Meanwhile, the city, players and coaches were becoming excited about their first home game, an exhibition match with the Dallas Texans. There was just one small problem: In a signature move, the first home game in Houston Oiler history was held in Tulsa, Oklahoma. What they meant was that the game would be near *Bud's home* of Bartlesville. He was out to make sure that everyone was aware from the outset just whose team it was (his) and whose it was not (Houston's).

Tulsa, for its part, was happy. Many folks showed up for the players' parade. If only the Oilers had. Their motorcade got lost. Missing a parade route in Tulsa in 1960 had to be a challenge. But that was not all of it.

Once the team found the stadium and tried to suit up, it discovered many jerseys were missing. They cried theft but no one had any suggestions about who might actually want them. To play, they borrowed the Texans' other set of jerseys. Thus, the Oilers took the field for the first time as patriotic as any team ever with their home blue pants, the Texans' blazing red home tops and their white helmets. They figured not much else could go wrong until the public address system broke. To top it off, they lost 27-10 as Cannon fumbled twice and Blanda threw two interceptions. And thus it came to pass that not only did the Oilers lose their first game, but they were also booed by their *home* fans.

Most exhibition games were on the road in those days. A more color-coordinated Oilers team later beat the New York Titans in Mobile, Alabama. In attendance was a ninth-grader named Ken Stabler who was there with his dad. The younger Stabler preferred the AFL's wide-open style. He went down on the field after the game and got George Blanda's autograph.

In their first exhibition game at Jeppesen (18,500), they beat the Broncos, who wilted in the humidity. Before the season, they were pushed around again by Dallas before 51,000 in the Cotton Bowl, where Billy Cannon was the crowd favorite. Hank Stram's Texans, mindful of their fight with the Cowboys, went 6-0 in the exhibition season.

The AFL had accomplished a lot in a short time. It would begin play approximately one year after its first press conference. Interest in Houston was increasing as all the papers began regular coverage. They even had daily televised reports from camp by Houston Heights product Dan Rather of KHOU-TV.

THE 1960 REGULAR SEASON — EARLY SUCCESS

The Oilers went into the regular season with many doubts after a 2-3 preseason record. Major weaknesses were the secondary and OL, the latter of which caused great pain for their ex-lineman head coach. Rymkus remedied part of the problem by activating 31-year-old assistant coach Fred Wallner who had not played since the 1956 Pro Bowl. Breen partially fixed the other problem by grabbing NFL-cut Jim Norton.

The regular season opened in San Francisco against QB Tom Flores and the Raiders on September 11, 1960. Starting on offense were Blanda, Cannon, Dave Smith at FB, Johnny Carson and Charley Hennigan at WR, and John White at TE. Houston won 37-22. The first Oiler TD went down as a 43-yard pass from Blanda to Hennigan. The first rushing TD in Oiler history came on an 8-yard scamper by Smith, who also became the first Oiler to rush for 100 yards. Blanda threw 4 TDs and one interception. Attendance at Kezar was a disappointing 12,703 even though Houston had some recognized stars. They had hoped for 40,000.

The Oilers then had four consecutive home games. September 18 saw the home opener. With folding chairs on the field to bring capacity to 20,000, an overflow crowd braved the heat and smell to see the LA Chargers, who had more veteran players than any other team. Unreserved seats were available for $2. The pregame festivities lasted almost as long as the game. There were long speeches and even a presentation of the first Miss Houston Oiler. The lucky local beauty was *rewarded* with heat-stroked roses and a big kiss from Mr. Adams. The Oilers won a thrilling game 38-28, rushing for five TDs. Little could the crowd have known, but those five were a team record that would last forever. In an anomaly, Blanda ran for three of them. He also hit a FG and 5 extra points, accounting for 26 points. Of a less jolly note, there was a small pregame protest regarding the segregated seating at the city-owned stadium.

They next lost to Oakland 14-13 thanks primarily to an Achilles heel secondary. Attendance was 16,421. They then beat New York 27-21 in a game of great tragedy as Titan Howard Glenn broke his neck and died in the dressing room. A distressed Bud nervously counted just 16,151 paying customers.

Let the record reflect that on October 13, 1960, he publicly threatened, for the first time, to move his team. The Oilers responded by winning their fourth game in five, beating the Dallas team who owned them twice during the preseason. The crowd of 19,026 seemed to cheer Bud up at least until Rice drew 73,000 the following Saturday for its game with Texas.

The Oilers were on a roll. They moved to 6-2 two days before John Kennedy slipped past Richard Nixon to become president. Success, however, did not close the credibility gap. Some fans at local weekly luncheons asked: "When are we going to get a pro football team in Houston?" The one they had just kept winning. They had also become a good draw. In Boston, they moved to 8-3 before the AFL's top crowd of 27,123.

The defensive front of Davla Allen, Dan Floyd, Orville Trask and George Shirkey came together to stop most rushing games, but the secondary with CBs Chuck

Coach Rymkus (6'4) gets eye-level to congratulate Charley Tolar (5'5) on his first touchdown.

Kendall and Mark Johnston and safeties Spence and Norton were getting toasted. Mickey Herskowitz of the *Post* wrote, "Houston's weekly question is whether Blanda can throw more touchdown passes than the Oiler secondary gives up."

But that was true of every AFL team, and the Oiler offense was better than most as they dominated the Eastern Division at 10-4. Average attendance was 20,019. Home attendance figures would never be lower, including the awful early '70s and lame duck 1996-97 campaigns. Their opponent in the first championship would be the Chargers, who were also 10-4, proving correct Blanda's earlier analysis of the AFL's top two teams.

THE 1960 AFL TITLE GAME — LOS ANGELES AT HOUSTON

Sid Gillman, QB Jack Kemp and RB Paul Lowe led the Chargers. Gillman was a great offensive coach. He was also intense and had a quick fuse. That anger got him into physical confrontations with Rymkus and even the man himself, one-time collegiate OL Bud Adams. It all made for good drama and helped foster the two teams' spirited rivalry in the early going.

A crowd of 32,183 was on hand January 1 at Jeppesen. Rymkus took personally any match with his ex-boss. He dug deep into his bag of cornball Notre Dame motivational speeches for this one. Lou first heard the Great Northern Buffalo speech in college by the great Frank Leahy, who paraphrased the great Knute Rockne before one of those frozen, snowy northern games. Although no snow clouds were near southeast Houston at game time, the coach amazed his players with the story of the heroic northern buffalo which faces adversity head on. It seems that when the really cold weather comes, the northern buffalo turns his large neck and frame so that he faces directly into the cold wind. The smaller southern buffalo, on the other hand, turns his skinny rear to the wind. Rymkus concluded with, "Now get out there and show them you are Great Northern Buffaloes! Don't stick your asses to the wind like puny southern buffaloes!" The effect of the speech is debatable, the outcome not so.

Blanda to Groman was the top deep threat in either league in 1960. Bill had 1,473 yards on 72 receptions to lead all receivers. He also has a good year with the tooth fairy.

Billy Cannon, the 1959 Heisman Trophy winner, was MVP of the 1960 AFL Championship on the basis of his game-clinching 88-yard TD. Houston beat the Los Angeles Chargers 24-16 before 32,183.

The game was close and entertaining with many fights and ejections, including Oiler safety Spence and part-time wrestler Hogan Wharton. The lead switched hands three times. It turned in the fourth quarter with the Oilers up 17-16 and facing a third-and-nine from their own 12. Blanda called a play requiring Hennigan to take the defending CB with him across the field and cut behind Cannon, who would be coming out of the backfield on a slant. It worked as Hennigan and the corner momentarily separated Cannon from the assigned safety. Blanda hit the former Heisman winner at the Houston 35. A two-step cushion was plenty as Billy galloped 88 yards for a 24-16 lead.

Later, the Oilers missed on fourth-and-goal from the one, allowing Kemp and Lowe (165 yards), one more chance. The AFL's first MVP almost brought them back as the game ended with the Chargers deep in Houston territory.

The Houston Oilers were champions. Blanda threw for 301 yards, three TDs and no interceptions. Cannon was the game's MVP, seemingly justifying all the trouble that went into signing him.

In the locker room, Blanda cast a few stones. "This is my first championship. I've waited all this time for one," he reflected. "The damn Chicago Bears never won one during my ten years. Maybe if Halas had let me play, they might have." In his euphoria, he praised both owner and coach, saying, "Bud Adams pays a man what he's worth," and "Coach Rymkus treats you like a man. I'm going to enjoy getting used to both in the years ahead." Finally, he offered the customary prophecy, "This is just the first of a lot of championship teams in Houston." Even though a poor prophet, Blanda was justifiably proud of his first year. Rymkus said, "if that wasn't as good a brand of football as they play in the other league, I'll kiss your ass."

The others were content with their winners' shares of $1,016.42, determined by gate receipts. For his part, the team owner promised diamond rings to everyone on the AFL's first championship team. He did not deliver, at least not this decade.

OVERVIEW

While John Breen deservedly got credit for allowing the Oilers to field a competitive team (12 of 22 opening day starters had been through other teams' camps) and Blanda for scoring enough points, Lou Rymkus designed the offense — the key to which was the line blocking. Lou had learned both OL and DL positions playing for Paul Brown, who invented modern pass protection schemes. Under Brown, Rymkus blocked for the legendary Otto Graham. As soon as he took the Houston job, Lou immediately began installing Brown's system.

A proud Bud Adams with the championship trophy flanked by an artist's sketch of the proposed Harris County Domed Stadium.

He molded the team in his image, tough and hard-hitting. As their record indicated, the OL, although injured much of the time, was the AFL's best. Their pass protection gave Blanda the time to find Groman, Carson and Hennigan. The OTs were Al Jamison and Rich Michael, the OGs Bob Talamini and player-coach Wallner, and the center George Belotti. Michael, Dave Smith and Bill Groman made the All-AFL team. Rymkus was AFL Coach of the Year. He got carried away later with standard Fighting Irish hubris ordering drinking glasses with his likeness etched in the sides. He gave away thousands of "Lou's mugs."

Both Cannon and Blanda came on as the season progressed. Blanda was unquestionably the team leader. At 6'2 and 215, he was built more like a FB. The 33-year-old's main asset was managing to stay healthy. He said his durability came from habitually working out and watching the diet. In the offseason, he ran, golfed and played handball. He also drank and smoked a little. Those within earshot say his real specialty was cussing. Always competitive, he frequently took other players' and even management's loose change on road trips in card games.

He was always more of a short range passer than a bomber. With the patchwork line that had only Dirty Al Jamison start all the games, he became famous for unloading the ball quickly. Breen said, "Blanda runs backwards faster than most quarterbacks run forward."

The quick delivery frequently left his uniform clean. To keep the line from getting lax, the old pro used to smear dirt all over his pants to leave the impression that he was getting hit.

Houston's passing game was a TD machine averaging over 36 points per game. For the season, George threw for 2,413 yards and 24 TDs (all-AFL QB Jack Kemp had 3,018 and 20). The Oilers' offensive philosophy could be summed up by noting George was last in completions but second in TD passes. They went for it. He also attempted 34 FGs. WR Bill Groman, who got his steel nerves working on the kill floor of a meat packing plant, became a true deep threat. He led the team in receptions with 72 and 12 TDs. His rookie receiving record of 1,472 yards has never been topped. Cannon was the leading rusher with 644 yards, just beating Dave Smith's 643. Both made at least one of the all-star teams.

The defense was another story, more of a tale of two cities. For the rush defense, it was the best of times as they allowed only 1,027 yards for the season (73 per game), a team record that would last for over 30 years. On the season, they allowed only 6 rushing TDs. For the pass defense, it was the worst of times. The secondary gave up 3,784 yards (270 per game). Incredibly, this mark also proved to be a long-time team record that lasted over 30 years. Trask, Mike Dukes, Dennit Morris, Julian Spence and Mark Johnston made all-star.

Ken Hall, the "Sugar Land Dandy," had an incredible 31-yard average on kickoff returns which would be the best ever for an Oiler. His highlight came against New York when he returned one 104 yards for a TD.

1961: THEIR FINEST MOMENT

The AFL and its champions got no respect. A *Sports Illustrated* article read: "No player on the Houston Oilers could break into the starting lineup of any of the top four teams in either division of the NFL, and only one or two could break into the starting lineups of any team in the NFL." John Breen, who had scouted the NFL for years, disagreed. He felt the Oilers, Chargers and Patriots could hold their own against the average teams of the NFL, such as Pittsburgh, Washington and the Cardinals (now in St. Louis).

It was a tough sell. The NFL's formidable propaganda machine was hard at work trying to convince everyone that the AFL was bush league. Commissioner Rozelle refused to mention the AFL by name. He would have no part of a championship game or common draft. CBS, the NFL's television partner, did not give AFL scores during telecasts. At the widely

**The First HOUSTON OILER Football Team and Coaching Staff
AFL Champions — 1960**

First Row: (L to R) Jim Norton, Bobby Gordon, Tony Banfield, Billy Cannon, Dennit Morris, Charles Tolar, Julian Spence, Gary Greaves, George Shirkey and Allen Hurst, Assistant Trainer

Second Row: (L to R) John Carson, Ken Hall, Bob Talamini, Charles Kendall, Bob White, Hugh Pitts, Al Witcher, Jacky Lee, Dave Smith, Bill Groman, and Don Floyd

Third Row: (L to R) Coach Fred Wallner, Charles Milstead, George Belotti, Mark Johnston, Hogan Wharton, Charles Hennigan, Doug Cline, George Blanda, Rich Michael, Phil Perlo, Trainer Bobby Brown and Coach Walt Schlinkman

Fourth Row: (L to R) Head Coach Lou Rymkus, John White, Dalva Allen, Al Jamison, John Simerson, Jerry Helluin, Mike Dukes, Dan Lanphear, Coach Mac Speedie, Coach Wally Lemm and George Greene, Equipment Manager watched Senior Bowl, announcer Lindsey Nelson lost some respect for giving only the NFL team a college player signed with, while refusing to mention the AFL.

To inflict maximum damage, Rozelle began televising two NFL games in whatever AFL cities had home games. This move would have long-lasting meaning in Houston. Once the domain of the Bears-Cardinals network, Houston began receiving regular feeds of Cowboy games. Pete loved sticking it to Bud.

The poor Oilers could not even win on the homefront. *Post* writer Jack Gallagher championed backup QB Jacky Lee all season. Even after Blanda took the team to the league's best record and championship, Gallagher called for a replacement. Nor did the championship game make the front page.

MONEY

All AFL teams lost money, primarily because of stadium expansions. New York was in the worst shape where cash-strapped owner Harry Wismer had to go head-to-head with the popular Giants. Some Titan games only drew 2,000 fans. To fill up the Polo Grounds for television, the Titans would open the gates to neighborhood kids. They promptly ran over the handful of paying fans with uniquely New York City charm. Eventually, the Titans became so bad that even the street kids stopped going. Titan television crews had to go to canned cheering.

In Dallas, the Texans were having a tough time in direct competition with the Cowboys. The Raiders were not even playing in Oakland and there was much discussion of moving that team. The Chargers could not handle the heat from the Rams and cut a deal with San Diego. The financial problems hurt them with the draft.

In Houston, in spite of Adam's protestations, the Oilers led the AFL in attendance. His total payroll was $375,000. The highest paid player was Billy Cannon at $30,000. Bud said that with the Jeppesen refurbishing costs and Cannon legal fees, his loss was over $700,000. In the 1990s, he revised that figure down to $445,000.

THE 1961 DRAFT

Although NFL took 155 of the common draftees to the AFL's 18 in 1960, the NFL was still not happy about Cannon. NFL owners tried to use the 1961 draft to kill the AFL.

Drafts were much earlier then than they are today. The AFL's was cloaked in secrecy. An unannounced telephone draft began in mid-November while the colleges were still playing. It was a tricky business with the competition for players tempered by the issue of their eligibility. In response to criticism from the colleges, the NFL moved its draft to December 27 after the close of the collegiate season. But it was just more propaganda as NFL teams pursued seniors all over the country before that date.

For the second year in a row, Houston was competing with a powerful NFL club for the rights to their first pick. This time it was the Bears for Pit's talented tight end Mike Ditka. After losing so much money the first year, Adams was gun-shy about getting into a bidding war with Halas, who was stinging from the way the Blanda deal turned out. Houston never even got the chance to make Ditka an offer because the Bears hid him. Iron Mike signed with Chicago for $15,000 and a $4,000 bonus with Halas gloating they had "beaten" the Oilers.

While Ditka went on to a Hall of Fame career as he redefined the tight end position, Bud had a card of his own up a sleeve. Two days after the Bears' announcement, he signed Chicago's starting end Willard Dewveall. SMU graduate Dewveall was the No. 8 leading receiver in the NFL and second team All-Pro. The native Texan was more than happy to escape the frozen tundra and became the first player to jump from the NFL to the AFL. His contract called for both the usual: a $15,000 salary, and the unusual: Adams' purchase of a big insurance policy from Dewveall's offseason insurance business.

The Papa Bear said, "Adams' stunt is typical bush-league and characteristic of him. The biggest mouth west of the Mississippi has spoken again, and as usual, nothing has come out but hot air."

Hiding players was the modus operandi of the day. Because of its superior size and organization, the NFL was much better at it than the AFL. Besides Ditka, the NFL also signed Herb Adderley, Fran Tarkenton, Tom Matte, Bob Lilly, Deacon Jones, Ben Davidson, Billy Kilmer and Norm Snead.

One AFL team, however, stood out. Barron Hilton had turned over the management of his team to football veterans. Sid Gillman's staff, led by scouting director Don Klosterman and assistant coach and ex-college recruiter Al Davis, knew how to play the game. The Chargers landed DE Earl Faison, RB Keith Lincoln and gargantuan DT Ernie Ladd, who once knocked out Deacon Jones four times in one game, out of the Oilers' backyard.

Ladd (6'9, 312) played high school football at Beaumont Charlton Pollard and later at Grambling. It was slick Al Davis who lured the Big Cat onto the Charger plane to "play cards" after their game in Houston. Then he told the pilot to start the engines, saying, "Oops, too late, Ernie, you have to go with us." The Chargers were willing to do whatever it took. This 15th round pick would haunt the Oilers for years.

The Oilers at least drafted to weakness with 13 linemen in their first 15 picks. The problem was that Adams and Suman lost 4 of their top 6 to the NFL. They did sign their second- and third-round picks, OG Tom Goode and OT Walt Suggs, both of Mississippi State, as well as TE Bob McLeod of Abilene Christian. The biggest miss was 270-pound DT Houston Antwine, who they drafted in the 8th round but let go to the Patriots. In Boston, he started as a rookie, played 12 seasons and made the AFL all-time team.

HOW THE OILERS SAVED BASEBALL FOR HOUSTON

A few weeks after the championship game, Harris County was back before voters with a new $22 million general bond package designed to replace the $20 million revenue bond package passed in 1958. The power brokers began to fear that the HSA, which was to get a 30-year lease, could not fund the revenue bonds.

Revenue bonds are paid by the profits of that specific use. Taxes may not be used. General obligation bonds, on the other hand, are tax backed, and accordingly, enjoy a lower interest rate. Officials said they were after the lower rate, but the possibility of available tax revenues to service the bonds was there. It was thought to be such a tough sell that the election was hastily put on the ballot for January in the hopes that it could ride the Oilers' coattails. Watergate special prosecutor-to-be Leon Jaworsky led the drive.

A National League baseball franchise had been formally awarded in October 1960. Play was to begin in 1962. The baseball folks, like the NFL, demanded a suitable major league stadium. If the election failed, the baseball team's start would have been at least temporarily delayed if not rescinded and given to another city.

It passed in a close vote. Good timing was a key. The football vote pushed the measure over.

Officials said the Harris County Domed Stadium would be ready by the start of the Colt .45's first season in 1962. Construction, however, did not begin until 1963.

In hindsight, the scheme revealed a remarkable lack of foresight by Houston's leaders. At the time, baseball was still considered the national pastime. Judge Roy Hofheinz and the Chamber of Commerce types were obsessed with getting the big league game for status. In their lust, they lacked the vision to see another trend that was just beginning to sweep the country.

The signs were there already in the gate, television contracts and success of the rival league. Football was ready to eclipse baseball as the nation's No. 1 spectator sport. In this sense, Houston's fathers missed the boat. To the extent Houston is more a football than a baseball town, something polls have long supported, it would suffer in the long run for the deals made back in the early '60s.

The Dome was designed and built for baseball. The needs of the football team were secondary. The baseball team got the master lease. All others had to sublease. Eventually, this situation would play a role in the Oilers' exodus from Houston.

1961 TRAINING CAMP

Things were relatively quiet with the team except for the Dewveall signing, about which the working-class Rymkus asked: "Why doesn't Adams buy a policy from me? I'm coach of the year. I've proved what I can do." Lou would have been wise to just be happy to have such an experienced player and keep quiet.

About the only negative news going into camp was the resignation of Wally Lemm, who went home to Illinois and entered the world of sporting goods sales. But even dead Houston fans know that peace and tranquillity do not rest long in the Oil Patch. The bell rang in March when Adams announced that, after opening at Ellington Air Force base, camp would move to Hawaii.

Bud thought it would be a nice gesture. He even suggested that the 1962 camp be held in Spain with exhibition games in bull rings. Rymkus was not amused. While Big Lou could hold his own in any bar, he fretted about his players. "When we go to training camp, a new year starts," he lamented. "We're just last year's champions, but when a tropical moon is out and the palm trees are swaying and you can hear the surf crashing against the beach and you know that the restaurants and bars are full of horny schoolteachers from Iowa and it's 10:30 p.m., how in the hell can I convince the players that they ought to go to bed?"

He also knew he would be at a disadvantage because he could not fly out NFL camp cuts for tryouts. This premonition rose to bite him in a hurry. WR Carson quit. Center Belotti and safety Spence were cut. Starting LBs Hugh Pitts and Al Wichter left for various reasons. Dewveall would later hurt his knee and have to go on injured reserve.

Frustrated and perhaps feeling somewhat untouchable, Rymkus began to criticize management for not bringing in replacements. He suggested Hawaii was just "a way for Mr. Adams to entertain his big-shot oil company friends." Rymkus also became hard on the players, so much so that rookies Tom Goode and Walt Suggs, both from one of the team's identified weaknesses, the OL, left for Mississippi.

It was not all Bud or Suman's fault that Lou did not have enough players. That year, Oakland offered Rymkus center Jim Otto for punter/third string QB,

Charley Milstead. But Lou liked the ex-Aggie too much to let go. Otto would go on to make every All-AFL team and the Hall of Fame, while Milstead was out of football by 1964.

Rymkus was right about his players. When the Raiders and Chargers flew to Honolulu for exhibition games, the Oilers played as if they had been on a tropical vacation. Trailing the Chargers 39-0 at halftime, Rymkus and his nemesis Gillman had a verbal sparring match as the teams were leaving the field at the half. Rymkus carried it into the dressing room, berating his players, "If you sons of bitches want to tell your children you were members of the first pro team ever to get beat 100-0, you go out and play the second half just the same way you played the first half." They rallied but fell 46-28.

He let up briefly, turning his players loose for 3 days. Three rookies promptly rolled their jeep in an irrigation ditch. Another player was hurt jumping out of a window to avoid an irate husband. In general, bar bills piled up and the 6-to-1 female-to-male ratio in Hawaii kept the switchboard lit. A few days later, they regrouped and beat the Raiders 35-17. Climbing on the airplane the next day with his sunburned and worn out troops, Lou's days were numbered. But if he knew it, it did not show. Grabbing the intercom, he decreed there would be "no more pinching of the hostesses. If there is any pinching to be done, from now on the coaches will do it."

THE 1961 REGULAR SEASON — CURIOUS BEHAVIOR FOR A MILLIONAIRE

Safely back in Houston, Coach Rymkus cracked down with hard practices. It seemed to work as the Oilers opened their second season at Jeppesen by crushing the Raiders 55-0 in the swirling winds preceding Hurricane Carla. Lou said, "It couldn't be helped. They got caught in a whirlwind." Blanda threw 3 TDs and kicked 2 FGs and 6 PATs.

Rymkus told his men that it was the worst performance he had ever seen. He frequently said things like, "This is the way we did it with the Browns," or "Paul Brown always said ... " The players felt they were never good enough in his eyes. It took its toll. Lou began to lose some players.

The Oilers then lost three close games in a row. The unrest grew. In one of the losses, facing a hopeless situation late in the fourth quarter in the rain, Cannon looked around the huddle and asked, "I wonder what would Paul Brown do here?"

With each loss, Houston's newspapers grew increasingly impatient. The widely circulated Jack Gallagher was particularly venomous. Before the Oilers, he had to write about minor league baseball and high school sports. Instead of acting grateful for the ride to the big leagues, he claimed the AFL would fail and said Houston should wait for an NFL team. As time passed and the AFL survived, he did not give in and spent much effort trying to prove he was right.

He regularly clobbered the AFL, the Oilers, its owner, management and some of the players, especially Blanda. A crafty, frequently eloquent proponent of his cause, his hatchet jobs often had teeth. They sank in with many fans and maybe even Bud Adams.

Rymkus was an early victim. After the three losses, he called for a new coach. That was three close losses *after* a championship. He tried to get at Bud asking whether the team could "attract a big gate [for the upcoming Dallas game] if Lou Rymkus brings in a team that has lost four in a row? A switch in coaches would serve to hypo the box office."

With that seed sewn, the team flew to Boston. Rymkus was last to drag off the plane. By now, he knew his job was on the line. It did not help that some of the players might have been eager to help their hard-driving coach out the door. To top it off, the game was on a Friday the 13th. Out of desperation, he benched Blanda, Cannon and a few others.

QB Jacky Lee had a field day with over 450 yards. Hennigan caught 13 passes for 272. As AFL games frequently went, however, it was not enough and the Oilers trailed 31-28 with 10 seconds left when Rymkus sent in Blanda to kick a game-tying and possible career-saving field goal. The benched warrior trotted out in his characteristic black "three-quarter" hightops. In the huddle, Cannon urged, "Miss it, George. Teach the son of a bitch a lesson he'll never forget." But Blanda made it to leave an ambiguous glow over the trip home.

As former Houston sportswriter Wells Twombly put it in *Blanda, Alive and Kicking* (1972): "Adams is getting ready to do something that he will repeat over and over again through the years — deal from panic, curious behavior for a millionaire."

In a signature event, Adams fired the defending Coach of the Year the next day just five regular season games after winning the first AFL championship. He claimed he had no choice because "Lou and the players *clashed*." He said his decision was also based on his review of the game film in which he "questioned some of [Lou's] strategy." He was at least smart enough not to face Rymkus (6'4, 220) directly. He made Suman do it. For Lou Rymkus, life did not turn out like it did in those old Notre Dame movies that used to make him cry.

On the morning of October 16, after firing his first coach over breakfast, Bud hired quiet, unassuming sporting goods salesman Wally Lemm over lunch. Short and stocky, the square-jawed Lemm did not look like a football player. He did not play pro ball or big time college ball. But he had the intangibles that made for a good coach, which was good since two of Rymkus' coaches quit, leaving Lemm only Walter Schlinkman and Joe Spencer (who originally replaced Lemm).

Lemm was experienced and bright. He quickly let up on the boot camp atmosphere. He also brought back Julian Spence. The two other personnel changes on that side of the ball that made a difference occurred under Lou with Freddy Glick added to the secondary and Ed Husmann added to the line where he joined Trask, Allen and Floyd. He made no radical scheme changes other than adding LB blitzes or red dogs.

On offense, Wally installed some double- and triple-wing formations which were essentially improved versions of the offense Pop Ivy ran with the Cardinals when Lemm was an assistant there. The improvements were designed to better protect the ball and set Billy Cannon free. Primarily, however, Blanda and Schlinkman ran the offense.

The three coaches had a huge job to get ready in one week for the big game with the Texans. Lemm stayed with Lee who had put up the big numbers the prior week. But once the Oilers fell behind 7-0, he called on Blanda on a "hunch." To the chagrin of Jack Gallagher, the crowd cheered his appearance. Blanda called it his warmest Jeppesen memory. "That was the only time I ever heard so much cheering for me in Houston," he wrote. "They gave me a standing ovation. No booing, only cheers. It never happened that way again." He brought the Oilers from behind to humiliate Hank Stram's team 38-7. Blanda remained the starter the rest of the season as Lemm's hunch unleashed an offensive juggernaut.

Blanda next punished the Bills 28-16 with 464 yards, an Oiler record that would last until Warren Moon broke it in 1991. Hennigan accounted for 232 yards. Lemm's softer touch was working. He also added a new offensive innovation for each opponent. Ed Husmann, cut by the Cowboys because of Bob Lilly, was making a difference on defense.

They won their fourth in a row over the Mike Holovak-coached Patriots before an AFL record of 35,649. That total outdrew three NFL games on the same day. As a result, AFL expansion talk heated up with Atlanta and Miami mentioned as possible sites.

In mid-November, they blasted the Titans 49-13 as the resurgent Blanda had 7 TD passes to set another record. The Jeppesen crowd of 33,428 was second largest in AFL history. They beat Denver the next week with 582 net yards.

That set up a showdown with the 11-0 San Diego Chargers, who had beaten the Oilers 34-24 in September on 6 interceptions. San Diego was so good that some believed they needed to play the NFL for competition. They had assembled their own fearsome foursome led by rookie-of-the-year Faison and Ladd (now 6'9¾ and still growing). "The measurements of Ladd, San Diego's answer to King Kong," wrote Gallagher, "are becoming as celebrated as Jayne Mansfield's." In the earlier game, Ladd threw Cannon around "like a paper cup." Blanda said trying to pass against them was "like throwing out of a well."

This time, however, Bob Talamini handled big Ernie and Houston ended San Diego's win

When Wally Lemm took over in 1961, he said, "Whether it's junior high school or professional, football should be fun for the players. Pro football players, like anyone else, do their jobs better when they like their work. And that's how I'm going to handle this ball club; by getting the most out of players because they're enjoying their work." That is trainer Bobby Brown behind him.

The Oiler offense in 1961 was one of the best of all-time led by league MVP George Blanda, who had one of the greatest seasons of any quarterback ever with 3,330 yards and 36 touchdowns. The TD mark is an NFL single-season mark for a 14-game season.

streak 33-13 before another record crowd of 37,845. Blanda threw 4 TDs and had 3 FGs in a gusty wind, including a record 55-yarder. Charley Hennigan, frequently open because of double and even triple teams on Groman, caught 10 passes, including 3 TDs. In a scene indicative of the times, Charley was so swamped by autograph seekers after the game that the PA announcer had to politely ask that he be excused so "the boy can go take a shower."

Billy Cannon took over the next game in New York, accounting for 330 all purpose yards. He scored 5 TDs, 3 rushing and 2 receiving while setting an AFL single-game rushing record with 216 yards. They closed out their Cinderella run by smacking the Raiders 47-16.

The Oilers finished 10-3-1 and won the Eastern Division again. Ironically, the tie in Boston that cost Rymkus a job gave the Oilers the Division title by half a game over the Pats. Blanda's refusal to intentionally miss that kick further cemented the wily veteran's position as the team leader. When Wally took over, they were in last place. They did not lose a game under him, winning nine in a row. He was the AFL Coach of the Year.

THE 1961 AFL TITLE GAME — HOUSTON AT SAN DIEGO

There was no time to celebrate as the Oilers had to face the great Charger team again for the AFL Championship Game. A capacity crowd of 29,566 showed up on Christmas Eve in Balboa Stadium.

It was a train wreck. "I've never been hit so hard," Cannon said. "The toughest game I've ever been in," echoed Blanda. In all, 13 players left the game. Twelve teeth were knocked out with Willard Dewveall, coming off an early season knee injury, losing two. In a particularly cruel blow, Houston lost its splendid wideout, Bill Groman, who went down with a knee injury from which he would never fully recover. It would take a decade to replace him.

Deviating from the usual AFL fare, defenses controlled the game. Neither team had 100 yards rushing. Ladd seemed to take up residence in the Oilers' backfield and harassed Blanda all day. The two teams combined for 7 fumbles and 10 interceptions, 6 of which were Blanda's. With all the fights, there were also 174 yards of yellow flags.

Blanda and Cannon again combined for the game winner, a 35-yard broken pass play for the only TD.

Blanda's partners in crime for the aerial bombardment were (above left) Charley Hennigan, Bill Groman, Willard Dewveall, Bob McLeod and John White. Most defenders only knew their backsides. According to Hank Stram, the tandem of Hennigan and Groman led directly to his invention of the zone defense.

Leading just 10-3 late, Spence intercepted Kemp to seal it. It was sweet revenge for the Rymkus cut victim.

The Houston Oilers were champions for a second time. This time the *Post* deemed the event worthy of a one-line mention at the bottom of the front page. Cannon received another MVP award. The winning players' individual shares reached $1,724. In the dressing room, Bud again promised championship rings. Players rolled their eyes.

In an ugly postgame incident, Sid Gillman, upset over his team's ten penalties, knocked the field judge to the ground with a stiff forearm. He then cussed him out while standing over him. When the man tried to rise, Charger players surrounded him and threw him to the ground again. He was knocked to the ground a third time before he could finally escape by way of police escort. Joe Foss' fines were on their way.

OVERVIEW

The Oilers again proved they were the best team in the league. They had a lot of carryover of talent, and their attitude and self-confidence were better because they had been there before. They had the quiet confidence of a defending champion.

Wally Lemm got much of the credit, even though he did not change much other than adding more blitzes. Primarily, he changed attitude.

He took a negative situation on defense and melded it into a more professional one with everyone working together for the same goal. It was what he did best and was what Cannon meant when he said Wally "could incite a team to riot."

Jim Norton, who led the team with 9 interceptions, compared the two championships as follows: "Lou instilled in everyone the desire to be the best team in the league. The team was willing to pay the price to be champions ... [but we] still felt inferior.

"[In 1961] the talent carried over ... and [the team] had more composure. We knew we were getting better. The team was down 1-3-1 [when Rymkus was replaced]. Lemm really didn't change anything. He improved the pass rush. Red dogged a lot. Winning it all meant more the second year because I knew we had a better team."

The offense was the best all-time in Houston and one of the best ever in the pros, although they are rarely recognized as such. Weak AFL secondaries took the blame.

They averaged 449 net yards per game. During the win streak, they averaged 41 points a game. The biggest difference from '60 was the play of the line. The only change was Bob Schmidt at center. Mostly, they were more lucky with injuries. A healthy Talamini at OG was crucial. Jamison was arguably the best OT in the league while the other tackle, Michael, made second team All-AFL (first team in '60).

With good protection, George Blanda put up huge numbers with 3,330 yards and 36 TDs. No passer had ever thrown for that many touchdowns. Over the 9-game win streak, he threw for 30. It took a while for Gallagher to fully digest his words. The team as a whole had 48 TD passes and scored an incredible 66 TDs overall. Of George's 362 attempts, 22 were intercepted. He called them "occupational hazards." He also kicked 16 FGs, scoring a total of 112 points with his foot alone. He was the unanimous player-of-the-year.

Naturally, it was also a record-setting year for the WRs. Bill Groman caught 17 TDs while Charley Hennigan had 12. During one stretch, Groman caught TDs in 8 consecutive games and finished the year with 18, a team record that stood until Earl Campbell broke it in 1979. Hennigan was the main weapon as Groman was heavily defended. He caught 82 for a record 1,746 yards, breaking Bill's yardage record from the previous year.

In attempting to visualize how dominating these two WRs were, it helps to look at when and how their records were broken. None fell until 16-game seasons and liberal passing rules. Charley's single season mark did not fall until 1995 to Jerry Rice (1,848 yards) and Isaac Bruce (1,781). Groman and Hennigan's combined yardage of 2,921 was broken by the Lion's tandem of Herman Moore and Brett Perrimen (3,174) again in 1995.

Lemm's double and triple wings also helped Billy Cannon have his finest season, winning the league rushing title with 948 yards. He had a 4.7 yards per carry average and set the single game rushing record with 216. When Rymkus was fired, he had barely 200 yards through 5 games. Lemm's offenses also allowed him to lead all RBs in receptions and set an all-time team record for combined yards with 2,043 (948 yards rushing, 586 receiving, 509 on returns). Charley Tolar finished fifth in the league in rushing.

The Oilers placed an extraordinary 13 players on the various all-star teams led by official All-AFL (by the coaches) first teamers Blanda, Cannon, Hennigan, Groman, Jamison, Floyd and Banfield. Second teamers were Tolar, Talamini and Schmidt. The other all-stars were Husmann, Johnston and Norton.

There was talk of an Oiler dynasty. Some feared the Oilers were too good and that was bad for the rest of the AFL. One of the main reasons the All-American Conference failed was because it had just one dominant team, the Browns. While those fears would prove to be premature, 1961 was the Oilers' finest offensive effort of all time.

1962: THREE'S A CHARM?

The most significant event for the owners was simply surviving to see 1962. With a few big names, an exciting wide open game and a television contract, this league was in better shape than those that preceded it. Talk of the Mickey Mouse league was still prevalent, but more people were noticing them. The owners enjoyed being asked when their league would expand. The AFL was beginning to make for a good story.

Attendance numbers were up everywhere except Oakland and New York. The Titans were a special case. The owner was insolvent. He took it out on those around him. Wismer fired coach Sammy Baugh for not having a playbook. Slingin' Sammy's response was that, "Before you can have a playbook, you first have to have paper."

For Houston, 1961 season ticket sales rose to 6,737. Attendance climbed from 280,356 to 316,381, which not only led the AFL again, but was also better than four of the 13 NFL clubs.

Before the 1961 Title Game, Bud announced the team would break even, the first AFL club to do so, and might show a positive cash flow. "It's very encouraging and actually it puts us a year ahead of what we hoped for when we projected the AFL in Houston over the first four years." In the 1990s, he contradicted himself, saying, "In 1961, we took in $755,000 but lost $418,000," adding, "We had a TV deal that paid each team $185,000 the first year, and we thought that was great. But it was based on the ratings, which weren't very good. So we only got $125,000 each the second year."

OVER IN THE NFL

The NFL had other problems besides the AFL. When Rozelle became commissioner, the old league was not very competitive. A few strong teams dominated. The reason was the league had no control over broadcast rights. The strong teams stayed strong because they could sell local television packages. Other teams had no television deal at all.

Rozelle received credit for the idea to centralize the package and give equal revenues to all teams. In reality, he was simply mimicking the AFL (which copied the NBA). The socialistic idea was not popular in New York, but it worked. The 1962 contract with CBS was $4.65 million for one year. The next one, done by competitive bidding, was $28 million over two. Ultimately, this concept fueled the NFL's growth into the monster it is today and made Rozelle a legend.

Pete was also a good lobbyist. In 1961, he obtained a limited antitrust exemption from Congress, paving way to pool the television revenues. He later obtained another legislative concession that allowed the merger to go forward. That deal was helped by two key Louisiana congressmen. Coincidently, New Orleans got an expansion team around the same time.

THE 1962 DRAFT

It was to be another rough signing year for the AFL. The CBS contract allowed the NFL to offer signing bonuses, big salaries and no-cut contracts.

AFL Commissioner Foss gave into pressure from the colleges and moved their draft back to December 2, two days before the NFL draft. But AFL owners held a secret telephone draft beginning November 12 without Foss' knowledge. Roman Gabriel was the first pick by Oakland. Denver took Merlin Olsen. The Oilers drafted next to last and tabbed UT standout James Saxton. When word leaked out, an embarrassed Foss canceled the whole thing and scheduled another to start December 3.

The Saxton pick exposed the Oilers' amateur approach. He was the leader of a great team, but had limited pro prospects. Given the fresh start, all the teams made the same selections except Houston. The Oilers switched to lineman Ray Jacobs of Howard Payne, another surprise pick. That he signed two days later gave the appearance that Bud was more concerned with PR than talent.

Most teams of this period did not have sophisticated systems. Combines were a foreign idea. A handful of progressive teams had begun to put together packages of player profiles, scouting reports and even crude computer programs, but Houston was not among this group. Here again, Bud Adams marched to the beat of a different drummer.

Although he had promoted George Suman to GM the previous May, the Oilers' scouting and draft preparation had Bud's fingermarks all over it. For 1962, he personally attended the national college coaches' convention in Chicago. There, he poured coaches drinks for several days in his penthouse atop the Hilton. Each night he asked the attendees to fill out cards with the top five pro prospects on their teams. Bud then drew out the "winning" $100 responses.

By way of contrast, Don Klosterman set up a thorough system for the Chargers. He had thick files on all players arranged in large binders with individual photos of each. Houston reporters often had to contact him for information about Oiler picks. For the record, he liked Jacobs. But he liked Lance Alworth and John Hadl a lot better.

The Oilers, who drafted in front of San Diego, thus had two chances at Houston-native Alworth and missed him both times. Chargers assistant Al Davis signed the Arkansas back under the goal post of the Sugar Bowl. The man known as "Bambi" would go on to be the best WR in the history of the AFL. With Klosterman, Gillman and Davis, and an owner who kept out of their hair, the Chargers were well on the way to supplanting Houston as the AFL's best.

Another backyard player they missed was Tom Sestak from Gonzales (Texas) via Baylor and Texas A&M. Taken in the 17th round by Buffalo, he turned into the AFL's best DT. Two other need positions they missed filling were MLB, where Nick Buoniconti went to the Pats in the 14th, and center, where the Vikings inked undrafted Mick Tingelhoff. He would play 16 years in Minnesota.

If Adams was a bumbler, the Cowboys' Tex Schramm was tactless. His people pursued common pick Ray Jacobs into his hospital room and pestered the youngster until 3 a.m. when he finally gave in and signed with Dallas too.

The Oilers drafted 7 OLs with their first 9 picks but only signed two. Including DE Gary Cutsinger (4th) and DB Bobby Jancik (19th), they took 4 of 28 selections into August. After Jacobs was hurt, they carried only Cutsinger and Jancik in 1962. They were losing this battle.

On the overall front, the NFL was outsigning the AFL 3-1 on the top players. The NFL got 6 of the AFL's 8 first-round picks, including Gabriel and Olsen to the Rams. Of the NFL's 14 first-round picks (including Minnesota), the AFL got two, both of which Klosterman signed. Though the NFL liked to flaunt its success ratio with common picks, the numbers were somewhat misleading because the NFL teams always contacted the players of the earlier drafting AFL and would not draft players who had already signed.

NOT AGAIN

Despite the draft failures, the team had a nucleus of good players and a coach to whom the players responded. Lemm had even installed a positive defensive mentality, something sorely missing from the first team. With Adams' thirst for exotic training camps apparently quenched, all was well in the Oil Patch. That, of course, meant trouble was near. Like an out-of-town guest who realized he had overstayed his welcome, prosperity showed itself the door.

The offseason boiled. First, Gallagher fired up controversy by writing and suggesting that Blanda should retire. Then in February they lost Wally Lemm, a move that would have lasting implications.

Lemm was supposed to re-sign, but Adams was slow to lock up his undefeated coach of the year. While Bud fiddled, Lemm's old team the Cardinals called. Their coach, Pop Ivy, had just quit. Lemm agreed to a deal while Adams was vacationing in Florida.

When he heard the news, Bud said not to worry. "As long as the material is there, any team can win," he noted. "Player personnel is 80 percent responsible for any team's success. Coaching is 20 percent."

Hindsight has given him a different perspective. He later recalled Lemm had the Oiler contract in hand when the Cardinals contacted him. He said Wally signed the contract "on a Sunday and left it on his dining room table. That night he got a call from (the Cards), offering him the head coaching job. If he had mailed the contract back, I think Wally would have been our coach for at least the rest of the decade. That would have kept us from hiring four or five coaches right there."

Bud did not offer an explanation as to why it took him so long to work out the terms of the relatively simple deal or why he did not have someone hand deliver and pick it up. His response was predictable.

Ten days after Lemm quit, Adams hired Ivy. It sort of worked out like a trade. Ivy was the Oilers' third head coach in three years. No other team in either league behaved like this.

WELCOME POP IVY

After playing and coaching in the NFL, Frank "Pop" Ivy coached the Edmonton Eskimos of the CFL to three Grey Cups in four years. He coached the Cardinals from 1957-61 during the period Adams and Hunt were trying to acquire that club and was in Chicago as the Blanda-Halas saga unfolded. He was credited with turning that team around and his resignation was unforced. He said he just felt it was time to go. The nickname was a thoughtful gift from a college teammate at OU who felt his hairline was receding somewhat prematurely.

Pop saw a good team pronouncing, "I was really surprised how good a team we had. We had a number of players like George Blanda, Billy Cannon, Ed Husmann, Charley Hennigan and Charley Tolar, who could have played in the NFL. The big difference in the squads in the two leagues was depth. The last five or six players on the rosters of the NFL teams were better than those on AFL rosters."

The Oilers did have a solid core of veterans. The problem was the lack of new blood. The older guys knew they had to carry the load. Some grew restless.

Some had an attitude brought on by consecutive championships. It is hard to three-peat in any sport. The national press was only reluctantly beginning to acknowledge the eye-popping offensive statistics coming out of the AFL. It was the names of Oilers showing up in the record books. They got some deserved attention. Some got the big head. It is here that the seeds of discontent were planted for future nurturing.

Besides his propensity for hats, Ivy had one other immediately noticeable personal characteristic — a soft voice. It was so delicate that it made some, including a few roughneck football players, uneasy. Communication would become an issue.

1962 TRAINING CAMP

The 1962 camp was held in its entirety at Ellington Air Force base outside Houston. At first, it sounded better than Buff Stadium. That was until someone figured out the place did not have a football field. Practices were held on a shrapnel field. Twisted ankles and rusty cuts made the organization look more like a MASH unit than two-time defending champs. The players' quarters were old wooden barracks giving the place a charm described as "something in early prisoner of war." It did have one uncanny similarity to Jeppesen: it smelled bad.

There were a number of roster changes. Trask and Shirkey were lost in a special draft designed to give the league more balance. TE John White and DE Davla Allen were traded. Rattlesnake collector Dennit Morris and fifth-round pick Rice were early cuts. Spence quit. The newcomers for 1962 would be Cutsinger, Jancik, Baylor center John Frongillo ('61, 28th round) and free agent WR/track star Charley Frazier of TSU. Also returning to the team were DL Dan Lanphear, after being out a year, and the two Mississippians, Walt Suggs and Tom Goode. Ed Culpepper, an NFL vet, replaced Shirkey for a total of 8 new faces in 1962.

On defense, the line was small but would play well. The DEs were team captain Husmann plus the marginal Culpepper. Cutsinger was backup. Lanphear replaced Allen at DT beside Floyd. The LB crew was a weakness with Gene Babb and Mike Dukes but OLB Doug Cline would come on. In the secondary, they were in good shape at safety with Norton and Freddy Glick (replacing Johnston), but having just one good CB in Banfield would cost them big time.

It was offense where Pop Ivy considered himself an innovator. He planned to use many of the same double- and triple-wing formations of Rymkus and Lemm, but with some new wrinkles that were supposed to get the ball to Cannon more on sweeps. Sometimes, his formations left no one back to block for the QB. The odd formations created two divisions inside the Oil Patch: (a) Pop is ahead of his time, or (b) he had lost his mind. Cannon was of the latter school of thought and unhappy. He did not recognize the sets as modified versions of Lemm's offense which had set him free. Like he had with Rymkus, Cannon openly complained about the coach. Unlike Cannon, his backfield mate, "fireplug-shaped fullback," Charley Tolar, was quiet. He was so because he could see the future and he was in it.

The most serious early injury was a thyroid problem that developed with Blanda in July. He had surgery to remove three small growths from his neck. He would attempt to come back too soon and the condition would affect him all season.

Pop Ivy

A MISSED OPPORTUNITY

Meanwhile Bud Adams' feud with Roy Hofheinz, who had taken over leadership of the HSA, was spilling over into the public. The HSA wanted the Oilers to agree to play in Colt Stadium, the temporary home of the Colt .45s. Bud, whose season ticket sales were up to 10,000, wanted to remain in Jeppesen. In what would become a pattern with Bud, when they could not work out a deal, it became personal. The HSA looked to the NFL.

In the heat of this battle, an opportunity arose that might have changed the course of Houston history. Bud offered to sell the Oilers to the HSA for $2.5 million just to avoid a situation like they had in Dallas with two teams. Like so many other points along the Oiler time line, it was close but no cigar.

THE 1962 REGULAR SEASON — ALMOST

The Oilers opened at Buffalo against the improving Bills on September 9 while John F. Kennedy was in Houston inaugurating the Space Center. With Blanda starting, Houston got off to a 28-3 lead. The *Chronicle* called his first half "an artist at work." But not the second. In a dark foreshadow for the remainder of the season, the Oilers did not attempt a punt the entire game.

The reason was not many of George's passes hit the turf. He either threw a completion or an interception. His 6 interceptions nearly let Buffalo back in as Houston held on 28-23. Tolar, the "pocket-sized atom bomb," started off his best year with 113 yards.

Blanda threw 4 more picks the next week in Boston as the Pats ended the Oilers' 11-game win streak 34-21. That set up yet another showdown with San Diego where Ernie Ladd's legendary shoe size had grown to an 18 D. The 5'5 Tolar said "the shoes" was all he ever saw of him. Ernie responded that defending Tolar was "like trying to tackle a manhole cover." Other Chargers had become obsessed with OT Al Jamison's blocking technique, saying, "He never hit anyone before the whistle in his life." They thought about it so much they psyched themselves out as Houston smoked the talented Chargers 42-17 on Billy Cannon's 3 TDs.

The game cost both teams. For San Diego, Sid Gillman tried to sneak injured QB Jack Kemp through waivers, but lost him to Buffalo. Kemp would later begin his political life there. For the Oilers, Billy Cannon hurt his back in the game and would never be the same as a RB. Blanda was also hurting. The new offensive sets resulted in some broken ribs. That injury combined with the thyroid condition and relentless blitzing resulted in many bad passes. Jack Gallagher and his old college roommate and fellow sportswriter, Steve Perkins, were having a field day at George's expense.

One thing that could always cheer him up, though, was New York on the schedule. He murdered the pathetic Titans with 6 TD passes, the same team he burned for 7 in 1961. As a team, the Oilers had a shameless 8 TDs and 56 points. Nonetheless, at midseason, they were just 4-3 and in need of another long win streak.

It happened. After losing to the Texans 31-7 at Jeppesen, they ripped off 7 in a row, starting with a 14-6 win the next week in Dallas. They beat Oakland next on a

Fullback Charley Tolar came into his own in 1962, becoming the Oilers first 1,000-yard rusher with 1,012.

54-yard Blanda field goal. That was followed by an important win over the Pats before 35,250 as they took over first place despite 4 Blanda interceptions. In late November, they trailed San Diego 27-19 only to win 33-27 on a 98-yard TD pass from Jacky Lee to Willard Dewveall. Adams missed the longest pass play in Oilers history locked in the men's room. He said he knew something good had happened because he could hear the cheering. They won their fifth straight over Denver 34-17 in the mud and a heavy rain. The teams combined for 97 pass attempts and 13 interceptions. The 8 by Houston's defense overcame 5 by George.

They closed the season by pounding Oakland (32-17) and New York (44-10) to finish 11-3 and slip by Boston (9-4-1) again for the Eastern Division crown. It would be the best record in team history in terms of winning percentage (.786). They beat every team in the league at least once. Their third straight division title set up football's longest day.

THE 1962 AFL TITLE GAME — DALLAS AT HOUSTON

Jeppesen Stadium hosted its second AFL Title Game on December 23. The largest AFL crowd to date of 37,981 crammed in, exceeding its enlarged capacity by over 1,000. The Oilers opponents this time were Hank Stram's Dallas Texans. It was the matchup dreamed of when the league first formed: Dallas vs. Houston for all the marbles.

Hank Stram was a good college coach when, at age 34, he was hired by the then twenty-something Hunt to lead the Texans. The son of a circus wrestler, Stram was shaped something like the bottom figure on a totem

The Oilers won their final 7 games in 1962 to finish 11-3 (.786), the best winning percentage in team history. The pass defense was one reason, allowing opponents to complete a league low 43.8% of their passes. Here, Doug Cline (31), Freddy Glick (27) and Jim Norton (43) break up a Denver pass on a typical rainy, muddy December day at Jeppesen. Houston won 34-17.

pole. An uptight Catholic, he went so far as to have a priest on the sidelines of big games. He was also a "groomer" who made his team travel in blazers with the team emblem with gray slacks, white shirts and black ties. Facial hair and sideburns were also forbidden. They lined up for the national anthem. They reflected their coach and city well.

They were also 11-3. As a coach, Stram was an innovator generally credited with inventing the moving-pocket, and double-tight-end and I-formations. He is credited by some with the zone defense, which he claims he invented specifically to counter the Oiler duo of Groman and Hennigan. Bill Walsh and Ed Hughes were among his assistants.

During the season, the Texans were led by player of the year Len Dawson who, like Blanda, was an NFL reclamation project. For the big game, Stram surprised Houston by de-emphasizing Dawson. He threw just 7 passes in the first half. The confused Oiler defense let Dallas amass 124 rush yards by the half. The Texans also played a smothering defense. They led 17-0 at halftime on two TDs by rookie-of-the-year Abner Hayes and a FG by Tommy Booker. Booker was already somewhat notorious in Houston. In 1960, he kicked the field goal that let Alabama tie Texas 3-3 in the Bluebonnet Bowl.

On the other side of the ball, the Oilers were looking old. Jamison's back was out and Blanda kept blowing scoring opportunities by completing passes to the wrong team. The most deadly came after driving to their 9.

At the half, Blanda rededicated himself with the assistance of Willard Dewveall, who grabbed his jersey to say, "Listen you SOB, you better throw to me this half. I've been wide open all day." It worked. Early in the third quarter, Blanda hit Dewveall with a 15-yard TD. After no receptions in the first half, Dewveall had 7 in the second. The defense also figured out what Dallas was doing. They continually gave the offense good field position through a combination of 43 yards worth of sacks and a poor Dallas punting game. In the fourth, Blanda kicked a FG, and with 5:58 left, Tolar tied the game with a 1-yard score. With under 3 minutes left, what would have been Blanda's game-winning 43-yard FG was blocked. They were that close to winning their third in a row.

The first OT championship game since the 1958 Colts-Giants game was about to unfold. Throw in an overly analytical coach, a rookie out of North Texas State and the Oilers, and you have more twisted history being made. In what would become their second nature, the Oilers came out on the wrong side.

Stram sent in NTSU's Hayes to call the coin flip. Before he left, Stram filled his head with too much strategy. He told Abner that there was a strong wind blowing towards the stadium clock and both defenses were playing tough. He did not think the Oilers could move the ball so they should take the wind and kick off. He said, "The way the wind is blowing we'll only want to kick toward the clock." If Houston were to kick off with the wind, Blanda would put it into the end zone. Not believing his team could move that far, either, he did not want them to have to punt into the wind. Stram thought Blanda could then win it on a short FG. "Got that, Abner?" Stram asked. Right, boss.

His head spinning, Hayes trotted onto the field to commit what was known as one of "football's most unforgettable blunders." The fly in the ointment was that Hayes won the toss. Dutifully, he said, "We'll kick to the clock." The ref was not sure if Abner was trying to pull a fast one, so he said, "Look, young fella, either you get the wind or the ball but not both." Still hearing Stram's words, he said, "We'll still kick." Oops. Blanda replied, "Then we'll run toward the clock," and trotted off the field. Thus, Houston got both the ball and the wind and Hayes got a lifetime of abuse. It was not fair considering how the Oilers responded.

Despite being spotted so many advantages, they could not score and the game went to a sixth period. This time, the Texans correctly took the wind, but Houston got the ball and George took them to the Dallas 36 where they could almost taste the victory champagne. With Blanda afraid to kick into the wind from there, they went for one more first down. On second down from the 35, he looked for old reliable Billy Cannon, but the ball fluttered in a gust and was intercepted by a rookie defensive lineman who ran it back to the 50. It was his fifth on the day. The defense, which did not give up a first down in either OT until then, finally broke. Dawson got them to the Oiler 18 where Bama's Booker kicked the winner this time.

It was the longest professional game in history ending with 2:52 gone in the sixth period. It even got its own nickname — *The Longest Day* — from a popular war movie by that name playing at the time.

In the dressing room, Al Jamison, tears steaming down his face, was laid out with a bad back that ended his playing career. Cannon blamed himself for not catching the last pass. He announced he was headed for Oakland via trade. Blanda took it in his customary manner, by cussing. "I was horseshit," he concluded.

The exciting game focussed more attention on the AFL. It looked like real football these guys were playing after all. While most still considered the product of lesser quality, it was competitive, hard-hitting and fun to watch.

The 1962 AFL Title Game set up the matchup dreamed of when the league was formed—Houston vs. Dallas. The Jeppesen Stadium crowd of 37,981 and a growing television audience saw the longest game in professional football at the time. It was a tale of two halves as the Texans scored 17 in the first half, followed by 17 from Houston in the second. It ended with 2:54 gone in the sixth period, or second overtime, on a 25-yard field goal by Tommy Booker (above) as the two-time defending champions fell 20-17. It was the last game for the Texans as they moved to Kansas City for the 1963 season and became the Chiefs. Little did Oiler fans know, but it was as close as they would ever come to another championship.

OVERVIEW

The 34-year-old Blanda overcame broken ribs, a thyroid condition, the loss of Groman and the double-teaming of Hennigan to attempt more passes than the previous two seasons with 418 (vs. 362 and 363). He managed 27 TDs and 2,810 yards on 197-of-418 passing. The linchpin was an almost unbelievable 42 interceptions. In judging QBs, a ratio that allows a quick comparison is TDs to interceptions. Two-to-one is a good ratio. While George's interception rate had always been high (25/22 in '60 and 36/22 in '61), he went off the charts in 1962 (27/42). Taking the interceptions into account raised his completion percentage from 47 to 57%. Jack Gallagher mentioned most if not all.

Cannon, who was having a great year until his injury, should have sat out eight weeks to recover. However, with Dave Smith also injured, the team was down to just two RBs and he had to play. He had more carries than in 1961, but less yardage. The press was not understanding. Cannon would have been better able to use his skills at TE, but by the time they figured this out it was too late. Charley Tolar seized his chance to become the team's first 1,000-yard rusher (1,012), third best in the league. He added seven TDs and 30 receptions.

With Groman out and Hennigan smothered, no WR finished in the top 5. Hennigan made first team All-AFL (picked by the players) along with Talamini. Jamison, Blanda, Tolar and Schmidt each made at least one all-star team.

The defensive standouts were CB Tony Banfield and DE Dan Floyd, who made first team All-AFL. DT Ed Husmann made first-team UPI and AP. S Jim Norton and OLB Doug Cline also made all-star. The major weaknesses were slow LBs (Babb and Dukes) and DBs. The defense did manage to intercept 35 passes with the University of Idaho's Norton leading the way with 8. The turnovers on defense and Blanda's determination to get into the end zone (the team had 32 passing TDs) are what held the team together.

Despite all the positives, there were problems bubbling just below the surface. The offseason departures of the popular Shirkey, Trask, Allen and Morris made some veterans unhappy. Moreover, as vets disappeared, they were not replaced. Only two '62 draftees, Cutsinger and Jancik (who led the league in kickoff returns), were on the active roster. With the '63 draft already upon them, it was about to get worse. As for Ivy, his soft-spoken voice and bad communication skills had undermined his ability to lead. Cannon, for one, said he would never play for Ivy again.

CHAPTER 3

THE FIRST DARK AGES 1963-65

Whether he appreciated it or not, Bud had a pretty good thing going. His team had been in every championship to date. They led the league in attendance in each of those embryonic seasons and were the biggest road draw. In 1962, they participated in 12 of the AFL's top 17 attended games, including No. 1 (Title Game — 37,981) and No. 2 (Pats — 35,250), both at Jeppesen, plus No. 4 (at Denver — 34,496) and No. 6 (at Boston — 32,276). While not yet up to NFL standards, they were solid numbers, showing both that the AFL had a good base and that it was making up ground.

For Houston fans, the fun was just about over. The initial advantage gained with the early organizational start and John Breen was wearing off. Bad management and turmoil, the two hallmarks of Adams' teams, were about to catch up with them. Within two years, the Oilers would go from the penthouse to a great place for reading.

1963: THE TRANSITION

In terms of significance, most of the important events or changes that occurred in 1963 came off the filed. Some involved the Oiler organization, some did not.

THE SUBPLOTS

While the Oilers were heading south, steps were being taken in Oakland that would later turn that team into the AFL's best. Al Davis left his assistant's post under Sid Gillman to become the Raiders head coach and general manager. While he was not the first choice, he turned the league's worst into a 10-4 club in his first year.

From there, he would go on to become AFL Commissioner and play a crucial role in the merger. Davis later became one of the more powerful owners and had a significant impact on the direction of the NFL. Always a maverick, it was his stance toward franchise moves that paved the way for the Oilers' exit from Houston.

As of 1963, however, he was just another 33-year-old head coach. His first game would be in Houston.

In Dallas, meanwhile, there was a tempest brewing. In their zealousness to defeat the AFL before it got off the ground, the NFL put an expansion team in Dallas hoping the Texans would fail financially and take the rest of the AFL with it.

The Cowboys hired a coach and GM before the NFL voted to expand. At coach, they hired ex-Longhorn star and Giants assistant, Tom Landry, who had already turned down Bud Adams. At GM, they hired a guy from California named "Tex."

Hunt had the first option on the Cotton Bowl which forced the Cowboys to play on Fridays and Saturdays, angering the high school coaches. Competition was intense if not comical. For example, the Texans had a game day promotion that let in any teen with a ticket stub from a Friday high school game. For their part, the Cowboys brought in the King of the Cowboys, Roy Rogers, for a promotion. Cowboy fans threw ice at poor Roy.

The two organizations went head to head like that for three years. As of the end of the 1962 season, the Texans were the better team and were coming off an

AFL Championship. Attendance figures were close, but both sides were losing money. Dallas was not big enough for two teams. Also looming on the horizon at the time was a contemplated change in federal tax law which would prevent teams from deducting their losses. The change was compared to stealing the millionaires' punch bowl.

Accordingly, Hunt went looking around. He liked New Orleans, but Tulane opposed any move onto their turf. Kansas City offered a good deal, including the promise to sell 25,000 seats. On May 14, the move was announced and the Dallas Texans became the Kansas City Chiefs. Ironically, it was the Texans' on-field success that made them attractive.

The Chiefs' first year was rough. In a preseason game with the Oilers, one Chief, Stone Johnson, was paralyzed after a hit and died from the injury about a week later. The team never recovered from that shock. Just one year after their championship, they were 5-7-2 and out of the playoffs.

Things would eventually improve. As players drafted or acquired by the Chiefs replaced Texan players, the fans came around and the Chiefs became a success story in Kansas City.

In New York, the number-one television market, the AFL languished. The Titans were 19-23 over 3 years. During the 1962 season, they averaged 5,166 at the Polo Grounds. The Giants owned the city, having played in four of the previous five NFL title games. The Titans went into receivership in March of 1963.

The team's failure would have a silver lining, though. A rich syndicate headed by Sonny Werblin bought the assets out of bankruptcy. Werblin would prove to be not just a breath of fresh air for the New York franchise, but for the whole AFL as well.

Former MCA executive Werblin handled dealings with some of the more established stars of the day, such as Andy Williams and Ed Sullivan. According to George Blanda, he was a "bright and clever, a superannuated bar mitzvah boy." He understood the power of celebrity and saw the link between sports and entertainment. That understanding helped the Jets land Joe Namath, who would go on to make history for the AFL. The Oilers were a part of that history, but alas, only as a footnote. In addition, Werblin would help the AFL land a fat television contract that would give the league the ammo to sign better players and eventually force a merger.

In Houston, a lot of people were still trying to figure out how the Oilers managed to lose that last championship game. It occurred to some that since George Blanda liked to gamble on cards and horses, he might also bet on football games. It made for an easy explanation for all the interceptions. Rumors spread that George was into point shaving and throwing games.

Both the league office and the Houston Police Department's vice squad investigated George. Both came up empty. The rumors, however, would continue to dog him. Blanda denied it, saying: "It may sound corny, but I love football too much to ever risk damaging it. Hell, if it isn't for football, I'm a schoolteacher in Somerset, Kentucky, or I'm working for the Robertshaw thermostat company in Youngwood, Pennsylvania." He added, "Besides, I'm too honest to throw games or shave points."

1963 TRAINING CAMP

Adams gave Pop Ivy a new two-year contract in February. He also made him the GM. Cannon took it hard, but would remain an Oiler through 1963. Ivy exercised some of his new power by moving preseason camp to Colorado Springs. He said that after three division titles, the players deserved a break, but many assumed he was just getting away from Bud.

The fourth new training camp location in four years turned into another one of those Oilers-only stories. While they escaped the Texas heat, they caught Colorado in the midst of its worst drought in 36 years. There was no fresh water. The practice field at Colorado College had to be irrigated with sewer water. Every scratch became an infection. The morning routine included lining up for antibiotics.

The team had holes. Walt Suggs replaced Jamison at OT to solve one problem, but the draft offered no help. Although they had 11 picks in the first 9 rounds and 29 overall, they would carry only 2 into September. They stuck with regional picks, thinking they would be easier to sign. The first 10 picks included players from Arkansas, LSU, Texas, Auburn, Texas A&M, TSU, Clemson and Mississippi State.

The No. 1 was Arkansas LB Danny Brabham. Considering who they passed over (Lee Roy Jordan, John Mackey, Walt Sweeney, Ed Budde, Dave Robinson, Bobby Bell, Marv Fleming, Andy Russell), this was one of their all-time worst selections. Brabham quickly signed (to a no-cut contract), and so, for the third time in four years, Bud could claim he signed his first pick. The only other was LB Johnny Baker (8th round). They would later sign junior Don Trull (14th) of Baylor as a "future" choice.

They made some good picks, but just failed to sign them. For example, WR Homer Jones of TSU (5th) ended up with the Giants as a 20th round pick. From 1964-70, he was one of the NFL's top deep threats, a position Houston could not fill over that period. LB Leroy Caffey (4th) played 10 solid years, OG Don Chuy played 7,

DE Lionel Aldridge 11, DB Jim Burson 6 and DB Tom Brown 6. All in the NFL.

With Brabham not ready and Baker injured, Babb and Dukes stayed in the lineup. Another Cowboy cast-off, Jim Meredith, replaced Culpepper at DT. They were also light at DE, CB and safety. Groman was traded, leaving a big hole opposite Hennigan. Tolar was again basically alone in the backfield with the oft-injured Dave Smith and Cannon, who reported overweight.

At QB, Jacky Lee, the reigning QB of the future, had been riding the bench behind Blanda for 3 years and was frustrated. Blanda, a fierce competitor, never let up for a moment. Whether it was the starting position, cards, golf or horseshoes, George won. Jacky developed a complex. Worst yet, the veterans were loyal to Blanda and did not put out the same effort when Lee was in the game. Then came Trull, who set national passing records at Baylor. Lee asked for a trade.

Probably the most frustrating aspect the 1963 season was Ivy's personnel decisions. Deciding to hang onto some marginal veterans, he cut three youngsters who went on to start for Denver. DL Ray Jacobs ('62, 1st round) played 7 years there. LB Jerry Hopkins ('63, 4th) lasted 6 years in the league. And in one of the worst moves in team history, Ivy cut free agent CB Willie Brown. He was a special case.

An undrafted end from Grambling who never played defense, Brown would be starting by midseason in Denver. In 1964, he set a record with 4 interceptions in one game and made the All-AFL team. He played 16 seasons and had 54 interceptions as one of the best corners to ever play. Brown made all-league 7 times, the all-time AFL team and the Hall of Fame. He single-handedly invented bump-and-run coverage.

None of those cuts made sense, considering the Oilers went into the draft looking to fill the exact positions (DT, LB, CB). The Oilers would founder for years at Brown's CB position. The only explanation was Ivy felt pressure to win right away.

Finally, the players loved Colorado. They played around a lot and did not practice hard. They took advantage of Pop. Once the season started, they were out of shape and the coach did not have full control of the team.

THE 1963 REGULAR SEASON — THE ROOTS OF UNDERACHIEVEMENT

Going into the season, the *Chronicle* stated, "The team may have a hard time gaining its fourth straight division title," but noted the "defense is sound." Season ticket sales were at 11,000, about the same as '62. As the season opened, Blanda got to read of himself described by Steve Perkins as the "ageless grandpappy." He hated that kind of talk, something Perkins knew well.

Proof that the great Willie Brown was once an Oiler

The Oilers opened with the Raiders at home in Al Davis' debut. They could be forgiven for taking the Raiders lightly, as that club had been a bad comedy routine going 2-12 in 1961 and 1-13 in 1962 under a coach named Marty Feldman. A crowd of 24,749 braved rain, wind, thunder and lightning to see the Oilers lead 6-0 at the half. Although the defense held Raider QBs to a 13-of-46 day, they could not overcome Blanda's 5 interceptions and 4 team fumbles and dropped a 24-13 decision they should have easily won. To top it off, they lost Cannon to torn ankle ligaments.

Without Cannon or Smith most of the season, Blanda led them to win 5 of their first 8. For a while, they were calling him the "genius behind the unguided missile."

But the poor running game caught up with them in Boston. With Tolar exhausted, they had an all-time team low 19 yards rushing and no rushing first downs. With Blanda benched, Lee had 3 interceptions. The Patriots won 45-3 for their worst defeat in history. They also lost Dan Floyd to a broken jaw, which helped the rush defense collapse.

Nonetheless, after beating New York 31-17 with a furious fourth-quarter rally, they moved to 6-4 and into first place in the Eastern Division with 4 games left. Only San Diego had a better record.

Then came an unscheduled break. On November 21, approximately 300,000 Houstonians greeted President John F. Kennedy and Jackie along the route of the presidential motorcade. After a ceremony, he left for Dallas, where he was assassinated the next day. The AFL postponed its games that weekend. The NFL did not.

The Oilers needed more than an extra week. They were racked by injuries, including Floyd, Cannon, Wharton, Smith and Michael. With no running game, defenses blitzed at will. Blanda had to rush his passes. On defense, LB play was atrocious. A discipline problem developed.

Long faces on the sideline, something of an Oiler tradition, made their debut in 1963.

With Ivy's personality wearing thin, the flimsy power structure of the organization was exposed. In one game, Ivy called for a FG and sent in Lee as the holder, but Blanda waived him off. Lee turned around and headed to the bench, only to be waved back in by Ivy. It was an unusual sight as Lee stood between the huddle and bench not knowing who to obey. Blanda prevailed and went for the TD. George took heat in the press for trying to run the team.

Going into the San Diego game, the *Post* called the Chargers the Oilers' "favorite patsy" and reminded fans that Houston had won 4-of-6 regular season games and both championships from them. Sid Gillman posted the article in the dressing room and San Diego undressed Houston 27-0.

After being blasted a second time by the Pats 46-28, they stood 6-6 but amazingly could still win a fourth-division title by winning the last two against the Chargers at home and the Raiders on the road. Lee started but was awful, and had to be replaced by the injured ageless grandpappy in the second quarter. Throwing from the shotgun the entire game, Blanda went 17-of-32, but fell just short of a miracle comeback. Afterwards, they bitterly complained about a bad call on the goal line that took away a Dewveall TD. The whole season turned on that one call — missed by the 3 referees employed in those days (today there are 7).

The final game in Oakland was a letdown. The Oilers took a three TD lead late, causing the Raider faithful to bail for the exits. Once they got to their cars, they could only listen on their radios as the Oilers collapsed. When the dust settled, the teams had combined for 101 points in Oakland 52-49 victory. The win left Al Davis at 10-4 as he won Coach of the Year honors.

Despite losing twice to the Raiders, the Chargers won the Western Division. They went on to win their first AFL Championship over Boston in front of 30,127. Green Bay beat Cleveland in the NFL Title game before 54,921.

OVERVIEW

The Oilers finished 6-8 and out of the playoffs for the first time. Led to believe the team performed below its capabilities, the boo birds came out. Some booed Ivy. Some Blanda. Some Cannon. Early promise and high expectations followed by a midseason collapse ending in disappointment, trademarks for many Oiler seasons to come, made their first appearance in 1963.

The offense averaged 3 TDs a game, but it was not enough. Blanda threw for over 3,000 yards for the second time on 224-of-423 passing. He had 25 TDs and 24 interceptions while kicking 9 field goals. He took the brunt of the blame from fans. Through the first few years, Jacky Lee had always been the choice of some, but three consecutive championship game appearances behind George left the movement looking foolish. With the team now missing the playoffs, that element became more vocal.

Charley Tolar led the team again, but this time with just 659 yards and 3 TDs. The team finished next to last in rushing. Billy Cannon's statement in '62 that he would not play for Ivy again came true in an ironic way as a bad back basically ended his career as a running back. He lost his characteristic explosiveness and ran timidly, often backing into the line of scrimmage or running out of bounds. It looked like he was afraid to take a hit and the crowd turned on him.

Fred Glick led the AFL with 12 interceptions, and the entire defense had 36 picks. But, on the whole, the defense lost the focus it gained under Lemm, giving up over 26 points a game. The rush defense collapsed, finishing next to last.

Jim Norton summed up their first losing season some years later saying, "We didn't know what to do. You could chart the decline starting with the offensive line. It fell apart. It had some talent but not the same attitude. The players were not as alert or concerned with details. Apathy developed just when the championship game was bringing good money.

"We missed Wally. The loss to Dallas [in the 1962 Championship] was disheartening. The team did not have the same spirit. It was not the same as when Wally was there who convinced us we were winners. Pop was more critical. Plus, the defenses began to catch up with the offenses."

Ivy lamented a bad draft. Brabham was the only pick on the roster and he did not play. Pop added, "I should have pressed the players more. They were out of shape. They had been division champions three years in a row and thought nobody could beat them. I thought I'd let them go until they lost and then get on them. But it was too late."

His problems ran deeper, though. He was not the players' coach Lemm was. His worst sin was failing to assert himself or take command in front of the players. He waffled. The Jacky Lee incident was the most public. It hurt him in the eyes of many of the players. By the end of '63, he had antagonized most of them.

Still, he might have been a success with a little organizational support. But Houston's front office was out of their league. Once, when Frank Gifford's name came up, one of them asked, "Who is Frank Gifford?"

Indeed, the organization's problems ran back to the 1961 championship — it came with a price. Hindsight shows that Adams' decision to replace Rymkus five games into the season was the shot the team needed to become repeat champions. However, the more remedial and long-lasting effects of his itchy trigger finger would affect the team into perpetuity. It was like he sold his team's soul to the devil for the 1961 AFL championship.

Blanda summed up as follows:

> When Lou left it started a landslide. They saw coaches come and go and they started getting the idea, 'Well, fellows, if we don't like this guy, we can get rid of him in a hurry. All we have to do is lose a few.' That's an unhealthy attitude, maybe the most unhealthy attitude a football team can have. The Oilers got off to a great start. Maybe if Lou could have held onto his job and they had put a football man in charge of the front office operation, they might still be on top today.

From *Blanda, Alive and Kicking* by George Blanda and Wells Twombly (1972).

1964: WHO NEEDS A PLAYBOOK?

As of the end of the 1963 season, Pop Ivy took the unrest in stride. He thought his team was not far from being playoff caliber and believed the main problem was that he was too slack on them in the preseason. He was optimistic. He had another year on his contract and the Oilers had signed their number-one pick.

THE 1964 DRAFT

The pressure was on. Houston acquired no starters from the last draft and only two marginal ones from the one before. In 1964, they had 7 picks in the first 5 rounds (Nos. 6, 9 and 13), which were the equivalent of 3 first round NFL picks.

In a predraft interview with Oiler secretary Dania Fisher intended as a fluff piece, she was asked whom *she* would draft first. "Paul Warfield is the best player," she calmly replied. Asked about linemen, she quickly answered, "Carl Eller."

Unfortunately, Dania was not the GM. They not only passed on Warfield (Eller was not available) but Mel Renfro, Leroy Kelly, Roger Staubach, Bob Brown, Paul Krause, Bob Hayes, Jethro Pugh, Matt Snell, Gerry Philbin and Lloyd Voss, as well.

Sticking with their theme, they took All-American DL Scott Appleton off the Longhorn national championship team. Bud landed him after battling the Cowboys and Steelers. The inflated deal included a big signing bonus, cattle and a service station.

Appleton was good PR because he was the top lineman in the country. He made it four of five number-one picks signed, and let them beat the Cowboys again. But PR was all they got, as he did not make it as a pro.

Again, they missed the better ones, including ASU back Charley Taylor (2nd round), LSU tight end Billy Truax (2nd) and Oregon LB Dave Wilcox (6th). Each made a fine pro, especially Taylor, who would be NFL rookie-of-the-year at RB. In 1966, he switched to split end where he played for 12 more years and became the NFL's all-time leading WR. Truax had a 10-year career while Wilcox became one of the greatest strongside LBs of all time. He played 11 years, making the Pro Bowl 7 times. An entire chapter of Oiler history would be very different today had they signed these three picks.

They inked Mississippi State RB Ode Burrell (4th round), Texas A&I RB Sid Blanks (5th), DB Pete Jaquess (20th) and QB Don Trull from 1963.

The Oilers were not alone. Not only was most of the AFL getting creamed, but also they had to pay more for the ones they did sign. AFL owners again called for a mutual draft. Rozelle, who was still not acknowledging the AFL, was not about to go for that or the championship game, or even a proposed all-star game to benefit the JFK Library.

THE RACE CARD

One of the reasons the Oilers failed to sign some picks in this period was race baiting by the NFL. The other league told black athletes that the Oilers were prejudiced and would not give them a fair chance.

While the Oilers were not formally segregated like the NFL's Redskins who refused to draft black players, they at least gave the appearance that some criticism was fair. For example, only two members of the 1960 championship squad were black. While this was not unusual in 1960, as time went by, they stuck with that original 1960 backfield of White, Cannon and Tolar in the face of the overwhelming trend towards backs with lateral moves such as Abner Hayes, Paul Lowe and Cookie Gilchrist. The same went for their defensive backfield, which was mostly white, mostly slow and mostly costing them games.

Overall, public integration came to Houston faster and smoother than other cities in the Southern part of the US. For example, when a boycott threatened the 1964 AFL All-Star in segregated New Orleans, it moved to Houston. Then again, it was behind other parts of the country in this sense. UH did not sign its first black scholarship athletes until Elvin Hayes and Don Chaney in 1964. Perhaps Adams had a notion that he needed a mostly white team to keep the mostly white ticket buyers coming back. His big-name high-draft picks of the day lend support to this theory (Cannon, Ditka, Jacobs, Gros, Brabham, Appleton, Elkins, Neely, Anderson, Nobis, Hindman), as does the list of those passed over (Ladd, Bell, Buchanon, Warfield, Renfro, Leroy Kelly).

If it was true, it appeared to be over or at least ending with the '64 draft. Nonetheless, the NFL propaganda machine did not stop. Besides losing Taylor in '64, they would lose 6 of 8 African-Americans drafted in 1965. Moreover, if true, it is another example of how Bud's questionable judgment hurt his team. All fans wanted was players who played with a purpose and gave their best efforts. They would have paid to see a team of one-legged Communists from New Jersey had they given 110%.

WELCOME SAMMY BAUGH

There were additional explanations why Houston was unable to sign players. One was reputation. Many players were simply avoiding what they saw as a circus environment in Houston with its amateur front office and revolving door head coach policy. These two traits would dog the team forever.

One of the strangest Oiler tales began in May of 1964 when Sammy Baugh was in Houston to attend his son's graduation from Rice. He met with Bud, the two spent 24 hours together "talking cattle" and the next thing you knew, Slingin' Sammy was an Oiler assistant. Baugh had been an All-American QB at TCU and star in the pros. As a passer, he was legendary — often called a "one-man team." He was not as successful as a head coach. The Oilers used his last team, the New York Titans, as their personal punching bag. But Sammy could speak Bud's language and Bud thought it would be great if Sammy could school the Oilers' young quarterbacks.

Ivy was not concerned because they needed a replacement for Walt Schlinkman who quit to join Wally Lemm. Plus, all Baugh really cared about was his ranch. He said he wanted to be a part-time coach so he could spend the most time in Rotan.

Maybe Pop would have worried had he known Schlinkman quit out of frustration. Or that he slammed Pop to the owner on his way out of town. Or that Adams offered Schlinkman the job on the spot. Another signal came with the announcement that Cannon would be the split end for the '64 season. Word of that decision came from the league meetings which Bud attended and Ivy did not. As was his custom, Adams also complained about money. He said the team lost money (barely) in 1963. He blamed bonuses, a claim openly challenged by Jack Gallagher, who wrote that Adams exaggerated the amount of the bonuses, and besides, not that many picks ever signed.

All Ivy directly heard regarding his performance came at the end of '63 when Adams said he was "satisfied with the job done by Pop." Then, a few weeks after Baugh arrived, Pop encountered one of those uniquely Bud experiences.

Heading to work on a Monday morning in early June, Ivy made his way down into the subterranean part of the Adams Petroleum Building on Fanin where the Oiler offices sat next to Bud's office. Bud's *office* was the Taj Majal of bunker complexes complete with lily pond, bubbling spring, singing birds, barbecue pit, walls of Indian murals and a desk large enough to sleep on. As Pop rounded a corner towards his office, one of the secretaries was there to greet him. She was carrying the contents of his desk drawer and a message from the boss. Just like that, Sammy Baugh became the Oilers' fourth head coach in its five-year history. Never mind that camp was about to open.

"Our fans just didn't seem to believe Pop could cut the mustard," Bud explained. "Pop's popularity hit bottom (in 1963). The fans demonstrated their feelings by writing letters and not buying tickets. If we're going to

Slingin' Sammy Baugh.

have pro football, we have to have the fans in the stands." While it was true that '63 attendance was down, revenues were up, courtesy of higher prices. Pop was the second winning coach Bud fired. Ivy went 17-12 while Rymkus was 12-7-1 (Lemm was 10-0).

Cannon had a little extra bounce in his step, but Blanda called him "one of the best coaches I played under," even though, "his personality wasn't real hot." George wrote in his book: "I wasn't really surprised ... Nothing that happened in Houston really surprised me. Everything was getting pretty goofy there. We never thought a coach would last more than a year with the Oilers, not the way Bud Adams operated."

Speaking of goofy, Adams named Carroll Martin as GM to replace Pop. Martin used to sell oilfield pipe for Adams. Like Adams and Suman before him, he had no pro experience

THE REST OF THE LEAGUE IN 1964

By early 1964, the AFL had already seen the Chargers and Chiefs move, Denver and Oakland change ownership, and the Titans' face bankruptcy. In addition, the signing wars were escalating beyond reason. For example, to keep him away from Houston, rookie Billy Truax got a contract worth more than the great Jim Brown's.

The AFL took another gut shot when CBS beat out NBC for the new NFL contract worth $28.2 million over two years. At the time, the AFL still had another year to go with ABC at $2.3 million. It could have spelt doom but for the quick work of the new Jets owner and NBC.

To the benefit of the entire league, Sonny Werblin was generating some excitement in New York. The Jets beat the Giants to a couple of draft picks. Season ticket sales rocketed with their move to Shea Stadium, which was just being completed over a garbage dump. Werblin was well-connected in the entertainment field. After announcement of the NFL-CBS deal, he quickly huddled with NBC, and on January 29 a new 5-year deal between the AFL and NBC was announced. It was worth $36 million over 5 years beginning in 1965.

When averaged out over the NFL's 14 teams and the AFL's 8, the contracts were comparable with NFL teams getting about $1 million per year compared with $900,000 per year for each AFL team. The original ABC/AFL deal called for $180,000 for each team annually.

This was the silver bullet that, according to Bud, "put to rest any doubts about the AFL's survival." More than survive, they could thrive with "war chests" to compete for players. It was an arranged marriage. CBS had a stranglehold on the NFL. NBC wanted in pro sports. To do so, the AFL had to survive. As of 1964, the league and network were joined at the hip. The president of NBC Sports said, "Our dollars will help the AFL buy players and we will help underwrite expansion."

NFL owners got the message. Soon, they began secret negotiations to discuss the possibility of a merger. The original discussions took place between Ralph Wilson and Carroll Rosenblum. Wilson said, "I met with Carroll behind the scenes in 1965. We met in Miami on a number of occasions, but the deal fell through because several owners still were against it." The talks would be rekindled after another crazy draft.

1964 TRAINING CAMP

Baugh's first act was to bring in his old friend John Strebler as an assistant. His main function was to give Baugh a dominos partner. Baugh's second act was to bring in his old friend Hugh "Bones" Taylor as another assistant. Taylor was Baugh's receiver from their Redskin days. His main function would be understood at the end of the season.

Camp moved back to Houston at a new facility at Fanin and Braeswood. Going in, the Oilers had some serious problems on the line with Wharton and Michael coming off injuries, which made new GM Carroll Martin's first act a head-scratcher. He traded starting center Bob Schmidt, an all-star in each of his Oiler seasons (1961-63). It was the beginning of a seemingly never-ending series of bad trades by the Oiler organization.

Then realizing the team was desperate for linemen, Martin traded Billy Cannon to Oakland for OL Sonny Bishop and two others. Cannon reported at 230 pounds and got in Baugh's doghouse by twice missing curfew. Sam fined him $3,000, the largest fine in football at the time. The Raiders had the wisdom to move him to TE. In 1964, he had 34 catches and 5 TDs. Billy played there another 6 seasons and was still making the Pro Bowl at the end of the decade. After retiring, he started a dental practice in Baton Rouge. His story had a bad ending as he eventually filed for bankruptcy after going to prison for counterfeiting.

Martin also sent away one of Baugh's supposed pupils. In an odd transaction, Jacky Lee was "temporarily" traded to Denver for two years. The Oilers got 36-year-old DT Bud McFadin, another Texas grad, and Denver's No. 1 pick in the next draft. The trade was supposed to help Denver as well as let Lee finally play. Fans did not like it.

The turnover was significant. Gone from the '63 team were 18 players and 3 coaches. Among the new faces were 9 rookies. That was a large percentage of the 34-man roster (over 25%) and represented the largest number of rookies to make an Oiler team. They were Appleton (1st round), Blanks (5th), Odum (10th), Nelson (12th), Jaquess (20th), Trull ('63, 14th) and Faulkner ('63, 21st). RB Ode Burrell (4th) was hurt in the college all-star game and put on season long IR. The top two rookies were not from the draft. TE Willie Frazier and defensive back WK Hicks were signed as free agents.

New starters (and the player replaced) were Sonny Bishop at RT (Michael), John Young at RG (Wharton), John Frongillo ('61, 28th round) at C (Schmidt), Sid Blanks at right HB (Cannon), Frazier at TE (McLeod), Scott Appleton at left DE (Cutsinger), Bud McFadin at left DT (Meredith), Danny Brabham at LB (Dukes), Johnny Baker at LB (Babb), Pete Jaquess at CB (Banfield), WK Hicks at CB (Jancik) and Benny Nelson at safety (Norton). The best back in 1963, All-AFL corner Tony Banfield, hurt his knee early and went on IR. With Hicks, Jaquess and Nelson, the secondary would be faster but very green.

The trades and release of Dave Smith left only 8 originals (Blanda, Tolar, Hennigan, Talamini, Floyd, Cline, Norton, Banfield). That group represented the team leaders. With each new subtraction from their ranks, those remaining grumbled louder. But the moves were justified as the majority of those traded or released would not be playing the next year. Nevertheless, there was quite a bit of dissension at the time.

The local writers either chose to ignore the signs of trouble or simply did not understand was happening with the team. Wells Twombly of the *Post* wrote, "They generally have better personnel than any other club in their Division." He predicted an Oakland-Houston championship game. Dick Peebles wrote, "By the end of the season, the Oilers could easily be the strongest team in the division. The rookies will have had valuable experience, the veterans will have mastered Sammy Baugh's system and recovered from injuries. The Oilers could easily capture their fourth division championship in five years." Jack Gallagher told fans there was a 50-50 chance they would win the division if they started Don Trull. Jack called Don and the Chiefs' Pete Beathard the "faces of the future" in the AFL. Fans bought into it hard. Crowds of up to 8,000 showed up for practices at the new facility.

Adams played it both ways. On the one hand, he encouraged the expectations to sell tickets. He also called it a rebuilding year, saying, "I hope the fans will bear with us because I intend to go along with Sammy no matter what happens. I imagine that we will lose a few games this season, but this is a long-term proposition." As if speaking directly to Gallagher, he added, "Sam's my coach and that's it."

THE 1964 REGULAR SEASON —
THE BEGINNING OF THE DEMISE OF THE OILERS

The Oilers opened at San Diego with 6 rookies starting, including 5 on defense. The Chargers won 27-21. Blanda was 27-of-47 and Sid Blanks caught 13 passes coming out of the backfield. They beat Oakland 42-28 the next week with Blanks gaining 127 rushing yards. Oiler publicist Jack Scott came up with a release, stating, "Oilers fired their Cannon and shot their Blanks at Oakland." They next beat Denver 38-17. The *Post* gushed that "Blanks gives the Oilers the most exciting backfield in their five year history."

Blanda and Hennigan were also having a great year. One thing Coach Baugh knew about (maybe the only) was the passing game. He threw out the double and triple wings and installed the pro set. He also tried an old T formation, hoping to give Blanda some protection. The *Post* wrote, "Baugh has convinced a lot of people that he's the head coach Bud Adams has been looking for all these years."

Baugh, however, had a chaotic coaching technique — one that did not take long to master. Slingin' Sammy did not believe in playbooks or game plans. None were printed. The ones they had were left over from Wally Lemm. Sam figured they were as good as anything he could come up with. Nor did he believe in reviewing film of opponents. Mainly, what Sammy did was play dominos with Strebler. Blanda said that his "real ability as a coach was his skill at hitting a bucket ten feet away with a chaw of tobacco." That spittoon in his office never caught on with the secretaries.

The combination of inexperience, disgruntled vets and no game plan was a potent one. They also suffered through 9 knee injuries.

After starting off 2-1, they lost 9 in a row. They were an embarrassment on the field. Just two seasons after winning their third straight division crown, the Oilers were the laughingstock of the league. One of the main culprits was the breakdown of the OL. They had no system. When the ball was snapped, the linemen simply looked ahead and blocked whoever was near them.

Blanda drew plays in the dirt during huddles. He said, "It was like a touch football team." He was pressured on almost every down. Always a drop back passer, never a scrambler, George was susceptible to blitzing. But he and Hennigan kept airing it out. In a game against Buffalo, who would go on to win the championship, Blanda attempted a record 68 passes, completing 37 for another record. Hennigan caught 12 of those. They finally won again in mid-December, beating the Jets 33-17 behind Blanks' 179 yards.

The season mercifully came to a close on December 20, which would also be the last game for Jeppesen Stadium with the Oilers set to move to the Harris County Domed Stadium in 1965. With the season they had, one might expect a quiet finish. Things just do not happen that way with the Oilers.

Citing Rotan, Sammy Baugh quit before the game. The announcement came several games after Adams announced he was extending Baugh's contract. Bud's response to the news was to apologize for not letting Sam pick his staff.

Then there was the matter of the game with the dirty Broncos, a team who counted 3 starters cut by Houston. It was an unusually spirited game with many fights.

One highlight befitting the stadium that housed two of the first three AFL championships involved Charley Hennigan. Once a blocking back for Charley Tolar in college, the skinny and long-armed Hennigan tied and then broke the all-time single season receiving record with his 100 and 101st catches. Sid Blanks also had a magnificent 91-yard TD run. Even the ageless grandpappy had a 6-yard run for a TD, earning a sarcastic standing ovation.

There were also some low lights. After a Dan Floyd interception, a Denver player desperately clung to Dan's pants, causing Floyd to run right out of them. Then came *the kick*. Former Oiler Jerry Hopkins had been knocking Blanda down all day. He was clearly enjoying himself. After being splattered by Hopkins on a very late hit following a PAT, George looked up from the turf to see the young Aggie doubled over in laughter. Someone should have warned him that George was also the punter at Kentucky. As Hopkins walked away, Blanda stood, caught up from behind and punted him in the butt with all he had. The crowd gasped and then applauded. After Denver mugged George on the ensuing kickoff, the bench-clearing melee was on. It was a fine way to cap a rotten season and send Jeppesen out with some fireworks.

OVERVIEW

The Oilers had fallen a long way in a short period. The 1960-62 teams were not the most talented, but they believed they could win and that attitude carried them. By 1964, the team had lost its edge. It was a team just going through the motions. The winning spirit disappeared. A self-defeating culture had consumed them.

Trainer Bobby Brown called 1964 the turning point. He termed it "a fiasco. The team was in utter turmoil. It was the beginning of the demise of the Oilers."

George Blanda said it started with the blundering front office and trickled down. "When it became ap-

Charley Hennigan's 101 catches in 1964 (over 7 per game) were a record that lasted 20 years. No one ever had more in a 14-game season. His 1,546 yards are still ninth all-time.

parent in 1964 that the club wasn't really serious about signing the truly outstanding rookies," he wrote in *Blanda, Alive and Kicking*, "I think a lot of the veterans kind of gave up, because they knew help wasn't on the way. A lot of us got this feeling of hopelessness, as if the core of Oiler veterans would have to carry the club until they dropped dead on the field."

Safety Jim Norton said, "I came back from the all-star game and Sammy benched me. I think this was the year the graph hit the bottom. There were so many changes — a change in the system and a change in the coaching staff. Everything was terrible. Nothing was right. We were 4-10. I don't want to talk about it anymore."

Baugh got the job just before camp and threw a staff together. His approach was casual, doing just enough to keep management off his back. For example, after their opening loss to San Diego, he was happy because they "kept it close." These were not exactly inspirational words, especially compared to someone like Lou Rymkus, who used to yell when they won. Baugh's "losing-close-was-good-enough" attitude permeated the team.

There was also trouble in the front office where Bud had installed a rookie GM who apparently felt obliged to do something to justify the promotion. After trading away the starting center, he shipped out Billy Cannon. Meanwhile, behind his back, the PR man conspired to get his job. Publicist Jack Scott got the ire of the players by referring to them as "dumb jocks." True or not, it was not what the PR man needed to be saying, and showed the poor judgment that permeated Oilertown.

After the naive preseason buildup by Peebles, Twombly, et al., fans felt cheated. The unsinkable Gallagher quickly metamorphosed from booster to heckler, and from Lee-lover to Trull-touter. He focused fan frustration on George. Many in the stands bellowed for native-son Trull.

Despite the problems, there was one main highlight, Charley Hennigan. His 101 catches in a 14-game season would be a record that would stand for eternity. Even with 16-game seasons and more liberal offensive rules, it lasted until 1995. He was quite a story. He and Charley Tolar were both NFL cut victims in 1958. Hennigan was teaching high school when the AFL formed in 1960. After hearing of the new league, they drove together to the first Oiler tryout camp in a car that probably could not have made the return trip to Shreveport.

In the preseason, Hennigan did not make the transition to WR easily, dropping most of the balls thrown his way. He lost confidence, and it looked as though he might have to cash his last teaching paycheck, which he had taped to inside of his helmet for inspiration. But Mac Speedie fought hard to keep him. He also gained inspiration from a book fellow WR Johnny Carson gave him, *The Power of Positive Thinking*. He made the team and did not look back. Today, with a master's and Ph.D., Dr. Charley still resides in Houston.

Hennigan's records outshone some otherwise notable performances of his offensive mates. The passing game moved the ball all year despite having no play books, no film review, no integrated blocking schemes and no game plans. The Oilers had the second-best offense in the league. Blanda later admitted it was "a lot of fun." He had 3,282 yards (1,546 to Hennigan) on an amazing 505 attempts (36 per game). He completed 52% of his passes, but managed only 17 TDs. Under season-long pass rush pressure and lacking mobility, he tossed 27 interceptions to the improving AFL defenses.

Each Oiler possession had a higher statistical probability of ending in either a score or interception than a punt. For the season, the team punted only 54 times or less than four a game. That is lowest amount of punts ever by an Oiler team in one season. Bobby Jancik also led the league in punt returns.

Rookie Sid Blanks had 756 yards (4th in AFL) and came in second in rookie-of-the-year balloting. He was also fourth in the NFL receptions with 55. TE Bob McLeod saw his streak of 33 consecutive games with a reception dating back to 1961 end. Hennigan and Talamini made first team all-AFL. Blanks and Bishop also made the writers' teams.

While many of the games were exciting, the team wound up with a 4-10 record, good enough for last place. Injuries, including 8 knee surgeries, hurt, but the main problem was the defense gave up 25 points per game to the offense's 22. While safety Fred Glick made first team all-AFL with 5 picks and rookie CB Pete Jaquess had 9, it was frequently death by bomb as missed assignments often left opposing WRs wide open.

1965: LIKE SOPHIA LAUREN DOES A BIKINI

Once again, the Oilers ended one season and began another with turmoil in the coaching ranks. This type of disorganization had a double edge in the 1960s because of the earlier drafts. It not only affected their ability to make personnel decisions, but the lack of a staff severely hampered their ability to find and sign the players they did select.

The 1965 AFL draft was held in late November 1964. At that time, the Oilers were led by an uncommitted, disinterested coach who was about to quit. It resulted in their greatest draft failure.

THE 1965 DRAFT

On paper, the Oilers were in great shape. The silver lining for having the worst record in the league is that you get to draft first. Plus, they owned Denver's No. 1 from the Lee trade, the second pick overall. They also had two 2nd round picks, making their first 4 picks the equivalent of four 1st round picks in the NFL draft. Considering they had finally joined a joint scouting combine, the future looked bright.

There were many great seniors. The most exciting was Bear Bryant's QB at Alabama. In a secret early draft, the Oilers selected Joe Willie Namath. Bud had his sleuth, Red Dog Ettinger, probe Joe to find out if he was willing to play for the Oilers. Red Dog said he would not. That put the Oiler brain trust in a pickle.

The Jets were there ready to help. They selected so-called passing wizard Jerry Rhome of Tulsa in 1964 as a hardship selection. The hardship draft was for players who had been in school for four years, but who because of injury or other reasons had played only three. Those players could either turn pro or stay in school another year. The NFL's Cowboys had also drafted Rhome and were hot after him.

The Jets told Oiler GM Martin they could not sign him, and asked, "How would you like to stick it to the Cowboys?" The Jets knew the Oilers were still steaming over the way Dallas had escalated the bidding for Scott Appleton. It was too easy. With Baugh's approval, they sent the first pick to New York for the rights to Rhome. This decision by Baugh, along with his earlier one to turn down the Bill's offer of QB Daryle Lamonica and a DE for Gary Cutsinger, would haunt the Oilers for a decade.

Furthermore, Rhome pulled an Appleton. He accepted a deal from Houston, then marched over to Dallas to get them to beat it. Angry and feeling used, the Oilers announced they were pulling out of the bidding. The whole charade was confusing, considering that the Oilers already had Blanda and two college passing wizards in Trull and Lee (due back in 1966).

What the Jets were up to, however, was no mystery. They selected Namath with the Oilers' choice. They sent assistant coach Chuck Knox to baby-sit Joe through the Orange Bowl (his No. 1 ranked Tide lost to Texas). Shortly afterwards, the young QB from Beaver Falls, Pennsylvania signed with Sonny Werblin and New York. Werblin, light-years ahead of Adams in understanding the drawing power of a star, forked out a record $425,000 (including $10,000 each for Joe's sister and two brothers) in the biggest contract ever given to a football player. Namath was immediately tabbed "the $400,000 quarterback." But he was also a winner and would pay many dividends.

With their second pick, the Oilers took WR Lawrence Elkins, Trull's old battery mate at Baylor. He was also a first-round pick of the Packers, but the Oilers hustled and quickly inked him. Unfortunately, he would turn out to be like Brabham and Appleton, more sizzle than steak. After an early knee injury he never lived up to his billing.

It got worse. In the second round, they took Rice OL Malcolm Walker and Oklahoma LB Ralph Neely. The lost both to Dallas, but not without a fight. The Oilers went hard after Neely with the new television money and signed him. Then he said he would rather play in Dallas and signed with them, too.

This one would bounce around in the courts for years, but the most immediate impact on Neely was playing with the Cowboys in 1965. Adams had to eat crow for years as he turned into an all-star OT for 13 seasons, an area of constant need for the Oiler offense over those years.

The third round was no better. The Oilers took UT fullback Ernie Koy (6'2, 220). They needed him, as Tolar had been going it alone since 1962. At the time, most NFL teams were weary of going head-to-head with the Oilers, who had the reputation of overbidding for players, especially the ones from Texas (6 of their first 9 picks in '65 were from Texas). So the Giants waited until the 11th round to select him.

The Oilers thought this one was in the bag as no kid from Bellville, Texas, would want to live in New York. They believed that up to the moment he signed with the Giants. It was quite an insult that a local product would make that kind of sacrifice just to avoid the Oilers. To top it off, he was signed by Giants' assistant Pop Ivy, who was still on the Houston payroll at the time. Pop crowed and crowed.

Of their top 5 picks they signed one, and he would be a bust. Even without Namath, those 5 choices could have been from among Dick Butkis, Gayle Sayers, Otis

Taylor, Mike Curtis, Fred Billetnikoff, Lance Rentzel, Roy Jefferson and Miller Farr.

The Oilers signed only 2 of their top 10, and in direct competition with NFL teams, lost 18 of 20. Individually, Dallas beat Houston to Rhome, Neely, Walker, and Rice LB Russell Wayt (18th round) in one month's time, prompting the *Post* to say, "The Oilers lose draft choices as steadily as they lose football games." They also lost out on eighth-round pick Roy Hilton, who played 11 years at DE for the Colts, and 16th round RB Junior Coffey, who played 7 years.

Management was perturbed by the double-dealing Rhome and his father, who used them to leverage a better deal out of the Cowboys. Rhome's dad said that Oiler players advised them not to sign with Houston because of the "turmoil in the organization." One of the jokes around the league was that the Oilers had a "coach of the year plan."

And they were still missing the top players in their backyard. In 1965, Don Klosterman beat them to the great Otis Taylor. He not only drafted the Houston Worthing and Prairie View product out from under Bud's nose, but outfoxed the NFL in signing him. During the signing period, he found him in a Richardson, Texas (outside Houston) motel room guarded by a group of NFL thugs. Klosterman smuggled him out under the dark of night, flew him to KC and immediately inked him. Taylor reciprocated by almost single-handedly carrying the Chiefs to the first Super Bowl.

The poor Oilers even eventually screwed up the few good things to come from this draft. Example number one was LB Bobby Maples from Baylor (3rd round). He played solidly after being converted into a center until the Oilers unceremoniously dumped him in one of their notorious early 1970s housecleanings. Maples played 9 more seasons. In the eleventh round, they selected CB Kent McCloughan, but traded him to Oakland. He was an all-star by 1966 and first team all-league by 1967.

Finally, OT Norm Evans from TCU (14th) rode the bench for a year and was then allowed to go to Miami in the expansion draft. He played through 1978 (including 3 Super Bowls) and made the Pro Bowl twice. Through all those years, tackle would be an Oiler weakness. As of the '65 draft, they had the building block OTs they needed right in their hands in Neely and Evans.

WELCOME BONES TAYLOR

Slingin' Sammy Baugh hung it up as the Oilers' head coach five games after Adams had extended his contract. Blanda wrote: "This way Sammy [could] spend more time kissing his horse back in Rotan." Baugh said he thought he had the time to be an assistant coach, just not a head coach. Strebler took the first boat back to Abilene.

After an exhaustive search lasting nearly 5 days, Adams hired Hugh "Bones" Taylor on December 22, but only after first offering the job again to Walt Schlinkman. In another record, he was the third head coach in 6 months. The saddest thing about this choice is that the AFL was a hotbed of coaching talent. If Adams had been less parochial, he would have found the following AFL assistant coaches: Bill Walsh in KC, John Madden and Chuck Knoll in San Diego and Chuck Knox in New York. In the CFL, Bud Grant was willing. Even big-name Baltimore head coach Don Shula could be had, as Miami proved a couple of years later.

Instead, Bud went with Bones, whose nickname came from his tall, skinny frame. He became the fifth Oiler coach as the team headed into its sixth year. He called it the "realization of his greatest ambition," and he quickly charmed the local press with his folksy humor. The *Post* called him "an expressed exponent of organization."

Bud promised he would not do to him what he did to Baugh — hire his coaches for him. Not long after that statement, Bud hired assistants Walt Schlinkman and Lou Rymkus. Big Lou, a crowd favorite because of his bluntness, was assigned to the OL. That hire was a transparent attempt by Adams at placating angry fans. Sammy Baugh was also retained as an assistant. Thus, Bones Taylor, who had no previous pro head coaching experience, was nonetheless in the unusual position of having two former head coaches as his assistants and a third who had been offered the job twice before.

OTHER CHANGES

Although Pete Rozelle, among others, was still consumed with burying the AFL, the new league was eking out some progress. In 1963, CBS started giving AFL scores. Attendance was increasing in most AFL towns. In New York, fans began to abandon the Giants for the Jets as Shea Stadium and Namath gave the AFL a good fan base in the country's major media market. In August 1965, the AFL awarded its first expansion franchise to Miami to be jointly owned by entertainer Danny Thomas and Joe Robbie. In the ultimate insult to Rozelle, AFL cuts were beginning to show up on NFL rosters.

The country around them was also changing. In 1965, there was major rioting in Los Angeles and other major cities. On the lighter side, Beatlemania began sweeping the country, and men began growing their hair longer. In Houston, a student was kicked out of high school for letting his hair grow, drawing a protest by a group of Rice professors and students. Women's skirts, in the

Hugh "Bones" Taylor was a disciple of Sammy Baugh and employed many of Sam's coaching techniques.

meantime, were going in the opposite direction. By 1965, skirts had made it to the thigh and would turn into full-fledged miniskirts the next year. Over at the University of Houston, Bill Yeoman hired a young defensive coach named OA Phillips.

READY FOR THE MOVE TO THE DOME

Going into summer camp, the Oilers had multiple problems, not the least of which was a terrible image. Topping it all off was Bud Adams. Adams' name had always been mud with the NFL types. By 1965, even the other AFL owners doubted him. Just when things could not get much worse, a new blip appeared on the Oiler radar.

Across town, HSA head man Judge Roy Hofheinz had changed the name of the baseball team to the Astros and of the stadium to the Astrodome. Roy called it the eighth wonder of the world. Critics said it housed the ninth wonder of the world — the ninth place Astros. Cynics called the one-million-plus fans who paid to see them the tenth wonder of the world for being the largest crowd to watch a loser in baseball history. Bud thought the lease terms the Judge wanted were yet another wonder.

In spite of its detractors, the Dome was a big hit. People were coming from all over the world to see it. Together with NASA, it was putting the city on the international map. It was a glimpse of the future with a $2 million exploding scoreboard, artificial turf, bouffant-haired waitresses in polyester minidresses and groundskeepers who wore fluorescent orange astronaut suits. For the wealthy, there were fancy VIP suites with a bowling alley and even a chapel.

In December 1964, the local papers reported a completed lease between HSA and the Oilers. Football fans looked forward to escaping humidity for air-conditioning. Season ticket sales roared to a new high.

In June, negotiations fell apart. It seems that Roy felt no gratitude towards Bud and the Oilers for saving his pet project. He played hardball, squeezing Adams over parking and program concessions, and even exhibition game promotion. Roy figured Bud did not have many options. The situation was tense.

Adams would not be bullied. He surprised Hofheinz by negotiating with Rice University. General Manager Carroll Martin learned that his former employer would consider reversing its earlier position and make its stadium available. Circumstances had changed at Rice. The football program was in decline and the money did not sound so bad anymore.

According to Dick Peebles in *From Cannon to Campbell*, it was touch and go. Adams was ready to move the team to Atlanta. "Rice's surprise decision ... saved the Oilers as far as Houston was concerned," wrote Peebles.

It was a turning point in several ways with far-reaching significance. If Rice had taken that position in 1959, the Oilers might not have survived the competition of an NFL entry. The entire AFL might have followed. Football history would have been different. Furthermore, without the surge in the vote from the football-delirious voters, Houston would probably not have had the Astrodome, at least, not by 1965. Without the Dome, there would have been no baseball team, again, at least not at that time.

Fans who purchased season tickets with the reasonable expectation of nice cushioned theatre seats in the Astrodome were not happy campers. It was their vote that swayed the bond election, but now they would not be able to enjoy it. County officials called for an investigation.

Nor was the AFL happy. They planned to use the first Dome football game to put the world spotlight on the league. The situation with the Houston franchise had become a liability for all of them. Whispers made the rounds that maybe the Oilers and the AFL would be better off with different ownership. The name John Mecom surfaced.

Mecom was the leader of one of the city's wealthiest families. Unknown to most Houstonians at the time, Mecom tried to buy the Oilers in 1964, but Adams refused. Making it more tense, Pete Rozelle sent NFL officials to scout the Astrodome.

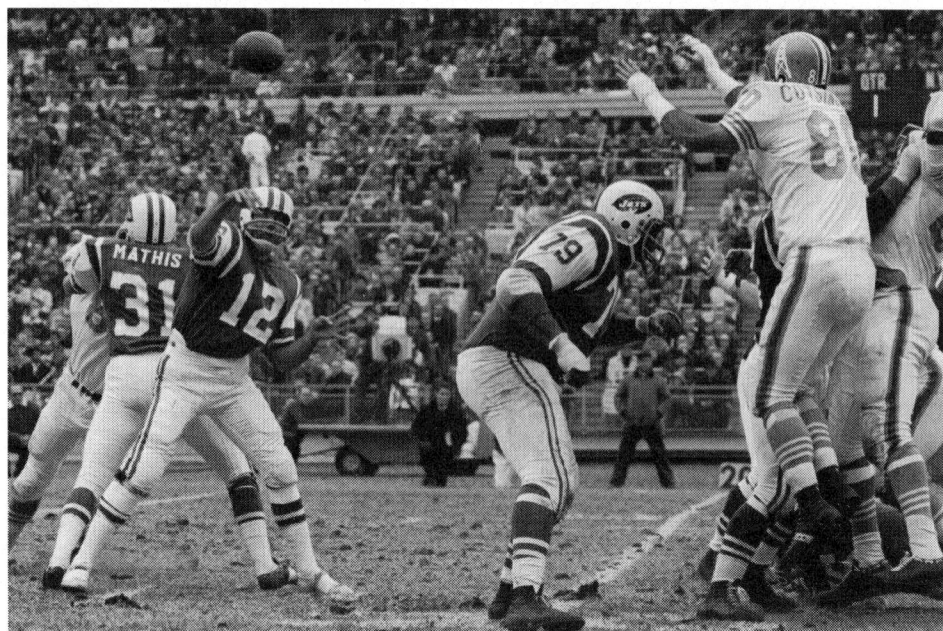

What might have been. One of Sammy Baugh's last acts as head coach was one of the worst moves in football history — trading away the draft rights to Joe Namath. A few months earlier, he had turned down an offer from Buffalo of QB Daryle Lamonica, asking why he needed another QB? At left, Joe completes a TD pass against the Oilers at Shea Stadium on November 21, 1965. Photo © Corbis/Bettman.

1965 TRAINING CAMP

On the heels of that disaster, the Oilers would suffer yet another in Federal Court in Oklahoma in the Ralph Neely case. The Oilers signed him before the season was over. Once word leaked out, the Sooners had to drop their All-American just before their bowl game. That drew the ire of college coaches and commentators from around the country. While it was a fairly common practice at the time, Adams was the first since Rozelle to publicly admit that his team was jeopardizing college careers and games.

After all that, Neely signed with Dallas. In court, Bud testified that Neely wanted to sign before the January 2 game so he could put the signing bonus on his '64 income tax return. The undated contract was prepared at Neely's request and to accommodate him. Neely said he considered the contract a letter of intent. The court ruled against Adams and invalidated the contract. Neely went to Dallas. The decision, like the Cannon one before it, was wrong in terms of contract law, and the Oilers would eventually win on appeal. By that time, Neely was well ensconced in Dallas.

Being an Oiler was like living through a soap opera. After the offseason drama, the players and coaches filed into training camp in the middle of a very hot Houston summer. Considering the preceding season, the lack of good rookies, and more new coaches to get used to, the players were not exactly brimming with optimism.

For a team in need of some radical change, Bones Taylor made few. He did make some switches on defense away from zones and to more man-to-man coverage in the hope of bettering the rush defense and putting pressure the passer. His offensive scheme was Baugh's.

There were multiple problems on the personnel front. Of the handful of players from the previous few drafts — Brabham, Baker, Appleton, Burrell — none had played a full season. Nor was there any help on the horizon. They took fewer rookies to camp than any team in either the AFL or NFL. Six rookies made the team and just 4 of those were draft picks, led by Elkins (1st round) and Maples (4th). Then Elkins hurt his knee in the first preseason game.

Hennigan's "retirement" exasperated that injury. After his record-setting performance, Hennigan wanted a pay raise. When Bud refused, he quit. Blanda, fully aware of who buttered his bread, talked him into coming back. Hennigan not only failed to get more money, but also was fined for showing up late.

Then first-year sensation Sid Blanks blew out a knee. Blanks not only led the Oilers in rushing in '64 with a terrific 5.2 yard average, but he also caught 55 passes. They definitely could have used Neely, not to mention Namath, in camp.

Another problem was mileage on veterans. While today's game has large rosters and "situation" players, players in the '60s went the whole way. Many of the key position players for Houston were still the original models.

That summer, the Chargers offered two all-stars, Earl Faison and Ernie Ladd, for Hennigan. Both were big, rugged DLs, while the Oilers had a woefully undersized line. Starting DTs Bud McFadin and Ed Husmann weighed 260 and 245, respectively, while DEs Gary Cutsinger and Dan Floyd were both 245. Opponents frequently ran over them. DE Faison was 270, while DT Ladd was around 300. Furthermore, the Oilers already

On their way down, the Oilers passed several teams on their way up, namely the Oakland Raiders who would become the biggest bullies on the block for the rest of the decade. Here, second-year free agent TE Willie Frazier held on and went on to make first team all-AFL.

had a promising trio of young WRs with Larry Elkins, Charley Frazier and Willie Frazier. But they turned it down.

In an attempt to appease fans, management had the coaching staff approach the exhibition season with a vengeance. As if there was any choice, the coaching staff played veterans throughout the exhibition season.

The theme of camp was Taylor's honeymoon with the Houston press. He charmed them. He cajoled and bamboozled them. Veteran Dick Peebles wrote, "It looks like the Houston Oilers hit the jackpot when they named Bones Taylor (coach)." Mickey Herskowitz gushed that Taylor, "was beginning to look like the real article, a guy who may be here to stay."

The constant stream of purple prose got fans excited. The *Post* called them the "best coached and directed of all Oiler teams." Peebles wrote, "A simple definition of a successful coach is one that wins. Bones Taylor fits that description like Sophia Lauren does a bikini." Jack Gallagher told fans that "indications (were) bright" and that "the defense had improved." The *Post* promised "a vastly improved running game," this even though they went into the season relying on Ode Burrell (5'10, 185) as the main ball carrier.

As a result, the Oilers opened the exhibition season in front of 30,142, their biggest preseason crowd ever. They won all 5 preseason games. Going back to 1964, that was 7 wins in a row.

Wells Twombly was the only Houston writer not sucked in. He noted that the team had gone undefeated in the preseason with no trades and no rookies. It was the same team. He asked how they could be better than 4-10. "Common sense tells you that the Oilers are not a very good football team." Trying to explain the win streak, he wrote, "They are an enigma, wrapped in a puzzle, surrounded by a mystery."

The real warning came from San Diego, where Taylor had been observed up close while on the Charger staff. Writers there elected him the "hands down winner of the least-likely-to-succeed-as-a-head-coach poll." When a Charger player was asked about Bones as an assistant, he replied, "Bones hands out papers at the meetings."

But Houston was sold. GM Carroll Martin claimed, after the 5-0 start, he not only hired Bones but Rymkus, Baugh, Schlinkman and Spencer as well. Martin told Adams, "If this staff doesn't get the job done then it's my fault."

THE 1965 REGULAR SEASON — THE PITS

Playing the name game, the 1965 CBs were WK "Contact" Hicks and Pete Jaquess, while the safeties were Jim "the Blade" Norton and Freddy "Pinocchio" Glick. McFadin, Husmann, Cutsinger, Floyd and Appleton shared the line. The LBs were Danny "the Arab" Brabham and Johnny "Ringo" Baker with Doug "Don Juan" Cline moved to MLB.

The OL had Suggs, Michael or Norm Evans at OT, Talamini and Bishop at OG and John Frongillo at center. The split end was Charley "the Razor" Frazier and Charley "Hands" Hennigan was flanker. The TEs were Bob "Hayseed" McLeod and Willie Frazier. The backfield consisted of Charley "the midget" or "the mouse" Tolar and Burrell. Soon to be 37-year-old Blanda came out to start his sixth season. Bobby "the cat" Jancik was the kick returner.

Game one was with the Jets at Rice Stadium. Originally intended as the AFL showcase premiering both Joe Namath and indoor football, it instead was played in 100-degree heat with Joe on the bench. The largest

It is a part of Oiler folklore that George Blanda (16) drew plays in the dirt during the Baugh-Taylor regime. Addressing claims that he took over the team, he wrote in his book, "If there's a wishy-washy coach and a strong quarterback, it's going to look like the quarterback is taking over."

Oiler crowd to date of 52,680 (and largest AFL crowd of the year outside New York) happily watched them beat the Jets 27-21. Don Trull, the most popular man in Houston, came off the bench to throw 3 TDs.

Blanda came back the next week and the Oilers drummed a good Boston team 31-10 before 32,445 in the rain and mud. George Blanda became the first AFL passer to go over the 15,000-yard mark. He was both booed and cheered.

The Patriot win made it nine in a row going back to 1964. Taylor bellowed, "There is no team in pro football, either league, that we can't beat;" and "This team has the right mental attitude. It has the spirit of a high school or college team. Winning all 20 games has been our goal right from the start." *Post* writer Herskowitz chimed in with this forgettable line, "The Oilers are what's happening baby."

It was a facade. Twombly was right. They were still the same team of the last few years that had no solution to the LB blitzes that started coming en masse in 1962. With no changes in personnel or scheme, the immobile Blanda was said to wear Boston LB Nick Bounicotti around his neck "like a wine keg on a St. Bernard." Hennigan was double-teamed and would be all season. On defense, they were bad all over.

In late September, they had Oakland beaten with a 17-14 lead and the ball with under 1 minute remaining. But a Trull fumble on their 17 resulted in a sobering 21-17 loss. It cost them a 3-0 record. They fell to 2-2 the next week as the Chargers pounded them 31-14 behind John Hadl. Taylor took a lot of heat for continuing to start Blanda as a QB controversy engulfed an entire city.

Things came to a head the next week against Denver. After leading 14-0, they lost 28-17 behind 5 Blanda interceptions and a blocked Jim Norton punt returned for the winning TD. At 2-3, they were two plays away from 4-1. The Blanda-Trull controversy was the main newsline, but the fissure was much deeper. The team was in disarray. Taylor had lost control. During the game, LB Johnny Baker refused to leave the field when ordered to do so. Norton also unilaterally decided to make a run for it on fourth and 15.

GM Martin, reasonably concerned for his job by this time, fined Norton, Baker and Bobby Jackson for deviating from the game plan. At that point, the leader of the veterans stood up and told Martin the fines were unfair because there was no game plan or playbooks, for that matter. They had not had any since Pop Ivy. George was backed up by defensive captain Ed Husmann. It should not have been a surprise. Taylor apprenticed under Baugh. If there was ever a team that looked like it played without the benefit of playbooks, it was the 1964-65 Oilers. Not even all the coaches could get along with Taylor and Baugh forming one group, Rymkus and Spencer another, with Schlinkman in the middle.

Martin cracked down on Taylor, ordering him to devise both a game plan and a playbook. Bones resented Blanda for ratting him out and stopped talking to his starting QB. The sports headlines blared that Trull would start the next game. On the surface, it appeared Bones gave into the public pressure. It was the first time Blanda had been benched since Rymkus sat him down in the fifth game of 1961.

So Don Trull, the $300,000 man, got his first start against the Chiefs. It was not much of a favor, however, because the Chiefs were the "meanest team in the league." With Trull running for his life, KC took a 17-0 lead at the half led by rookie QB Pete Beathard. Taylor, who Blanda referred to as "the Oilers' coach-of-the-year for that year," sent Baugh over to tell George he would start the second half. Humiliated, the ornery Blanda demanded a personal request from Taylor. Bones gave in. The stage was perfectly set for the old warrior to make a point, which he did with flair.

Taking the field in a smoking rage, he had the best second half by any Oiler QB ever. He connected for touchdown passes the first 4 times he touched the ball and 5 TDs total. His performance caused the Chiefs to dump their own wunderkid Beathard in favor of their own old vet, Len Dawson, who had them ahead 36-35 with two minutes left. But that was plenty of time for Blanda on this magical day as he calmly moved the offense for a clinching FG and a 38-36 victory. The 38 second-half points were a record. Blanda bathed in the attention. Herskowitz wrote, "No one has ever faulted George for leadership. He is the sort you see shouting orders into the teeth of a typhoon or above the roar of guns."

In the locker room, the surly old man told the reporters they could "go f— themselves." It brought up one of the oddities of the day among Houston's newspapers. George spoke to reporters from the *Chronicle* after games but not the *Post*. Accordingly, on Mondays, the *Chronicle's* game story was always different and more accurate than the *Post's*. It was George's way of getting back at people like Gallagher and Perkins for years of abuse.

The afterglow of the Chiefs game carried the Oilers over first place Buffalo as they ended up at a competitive 4-3 halfway through the season. Fan optimism rekindled, but it did not last. In the second half of the season, they lost to injury Baker, McFadin, Glick, Tolar, Frongillo, Jancik, Charley Frazier and Willie Frazier. They collapsed. Carroll Martin started making halftime visits to yell at the players, but it did not help.

They followed an O-for-November by going O-for-December to finish 4-10 again. The Bills, who the Oilers beat in October, won the AFL championship over the Chargers for the second straight year.

If Bud Adams possessed a sense of timing, it was for bad timing. On December 5, at the halftime of a 29-18 loss to Buffalo, Adams announced that he was giving "Lazy Bones" Taylor a new three-year contract. For a team with many low moments, this had to be one of the lowest. It was Oiler purgatory

OVERVIEW

Jim Norton thought Taylor "did a good job early and had the respect of the players. We won all five exhibition games and our first two games. I don't think we had much different personnel. This was the year Billy Cannon was traded off but the talent was still there. Then we started losing and there wasn't anybody to weld the talent together. [There] were too many changes."

Blanda was the main scapegoat — pilloried in the press and booed from the stands. He was the hottest topic in Houston. Some said he was running the team. Others thought he was past his prime. One of the favorite sayings around Houston was, "I'll start going to games again when they get rid of Blanda."

George, who finished his career a Raider, is quoted in *Blanda, Alive and Kicking*:

> There was talk that I 'took the club over' [under Baugh/Taylor]. Well,

someone will assume leadership responsibility on a team. If there's a wishy-washy coach and a strong quarterback, it's going to look like the quarterback is taking over. In Oakland, the 'team' is everything. If you aren't a good team man, you're gone. In Houston, it was a matter of survival. You had to survive somehow in order to play pro football because of the crazy circumstances. There really was no 'team' after the Ivy years. Nobody cared about the team during the Baugh-Taylor years. Everyone was concerned about keeping their jobs.

Gallagher and the boo birds overlooked the fact that, statistically at least, the offense was second in the league. Blanda threw a remarkable 442 passes (31 per game), completing 186 (42%). He hit for 2,542 yards (second to John Hadl) and 20 TDs (second to Len Dawson's 21). Joe Namath threw for fewer yards (2,220) and TDs (18), but made the all-star team and was rookie of the year. Trull played more and more as the losing season went along. On the other hand, Blanda also had 30 "occupational hazards." For comparison's sake, Warren Moon's worst year was 1986 with 26 interceptions while Ken Stabler had 28 in 1980, both in 16-game seasons.

It was not only unfair to lay all the team's woes at Blanda's feet, but not even all the interceptions were his fault. There were many contributing factors. First was the annual breakdown of the OL that left him under intense pressure with no time to throw. Second, Hennigan played with a hurt leg and had a subpar year. Double- and even triple-teamed, he caught 41 passes, 60 fewer than in 1964. Perhaps distracted over his failure to get a raise, he uncharacteristically dropped a large number of catchable balls. In addition, the running game was lousy. The featured back, scrappy Ode Burrell, had just 528 yards and 3 TDs. With no running threat, defenses pinned the ears back and came after George all game long.

Finally and perhaps most significant was the defense. They were the worst (last in total defense and rushing defense). Indeed, the 1965 Oilers were one of the worst defenses in the history of football, giving up over 30 points per game. The rush defense surrendered over 5 yards per carry. It is hard to win ballgames that way. Blanda had no choice but to pass even though the other teams knew what was coming. With Hennigan not having the same year, Charley Frazier still not ready, it made for tough going.

One bright spot was TE Willie Frazier, a unanimous all-league selection along with OG Bob Talamini. Also making various all-star teams were Hennigan (6th consecutive year), OG Sonny Bishop, RB Burrell (4th in league in receptions with 55) and corner WK Hicks (led AFL with 9 interceptions).

With the solid guard play out of Talamini and Bishop, the Oilers would have been in good shape had they brought in Ralph Neely to join Walt Suggs and Norm Evans at OT. With Bobby Maples about to emerge as a center, the line would have been on the brink of solidifying, which would have done wonders for the running game and given a QB time to pass.

CHAPTER 4

WALLY AND THE DUKE
1966-69

After over a half decade at the wheel, about the only thing Bud Adams had convincingly established was that he was not born to manage a football franchise. From such a bountiful start, he had driven his franchise into the dirt. As the '65 season closed, things were not well. An unimaginably bad draft would bring it to a head. Without the merger, it is doubtful the Oilers would have survived in Houston.

But a merger did come, and along with it, a sudden willingness by Bud to finally let someone with experience take over. The changes he made in 1966, although they would not bear fruit for another season, put the team back on solid footing. The transformation would be remarkable. With a legitimate QB and some patience, the team assembled in the latter part of the decade could have really made some noise. Alas, before they could do so, Bud Adams' unyielding focus on the short term would get the best of him and them.

1966: THE ODD COUPLE

The middle 1960s were a time of monumental events and changes in the United States. In 1966, news from Vietnam shared the front pages with news of rioting, which had spread from the big cities to places like Wisconsin. This was when Martin Luther King, Jr., tried to take his freedom march out of the deep South into the North, but was rebuffed. In sports, Texas Western (later UTEP) became the first team with a majority of black players to win the NCAA basketball tournament, upsetting the heavily favored all-white Kentucky Wildcats.

The City of Houston was still busy growing and building. Unfortunately, the local sports teams were a poor reflection on its "can-do" spirit.

Attendance in 1965 at Oiler games dropped from over 52,000 for the opener to 24,000 for the last game. Rumors of an NFL team in the Dome resurfaced. That kind of talk made both Bud and NBC nervous.

Instead of negotiating better terms for the Dome, Adams resorted to his form of guerrilla warfare. He loved backroom stuff. One of his favorites was starting rumors. For this, he relied on a reporter at the *Chronicle*. When Bud wanted to "leak" some news, he secretly called the reporter late at night from his River Oaks home. He did it to test the waters on his ideas before he acted. When the scoops made it into print, he acted disappointed that there was a leak in his organization. Poor Carroll Martin had to scurry around and try to find the source.

Bud used this system during the '65 season to float another threat to move if attendance did not improve. Other rumors surfaced, including a purported feud between Blanda and Taylor that fueled speculation about whether they would be back. Despite the contract extension, Taylor appeared to be in trouble. Wally Lemm was also rumored to be considering leaving the Cardinals, while Don Klosterman was said to be on the outs in KC. Nothing would happen before the Oilers mismanaged another draft.

THE 1966 DRAFT

The competition for players would peak with the 1966 draft. The money from the AFL's new TV contract created an untenable situation for everyone. Owners of the most marginal teams were pushed to the brink.

Houston again had a lot of good picks. Jack Gallagher applied the pressure writing that Bud "owes it to the public to sign some high draft picks." Adams promised money was no object and that, this time, he would get his men. With an amateur front office and more turmoil among the coaching staff, he was hardly in a position to deliver.

Their top pick was All-Universe LB Tommy Nobis of Texas. Like Appleton, he was the Outland Trophy winner. He was also the No. 1 pick in the NFL draft selected by the expansion Falcons. Recognizing his team's desperate need for top-flight defensive help, Bud personally handled negotiations. He ponied up $650,000, plus a handsome pension plan to compete with the NFL's. The offer was roughly 9 times what it cost to sign Cannon just six years before.

Nobis wanted to play near home. He also wanted to play in the NFL. To the dismay of the NFL, the Houston-based crew of Gemini 7 sent a message from space encouraging Nobis to stay in Texas. With the help of his "friends in high places," Bud thought they had a deal and grandly suggested the signing occur in his company airplane while high above Memorial Stadium in Austin. The papers blared, "Nobis to Be Houston Property By Dark." But the theatrics did not sit well with the conservative Nobis. Bud's last proposed stunt sent him to Atlanta. Other NFL clubs chipped in so the Falcons could afford him. Nobis turned into another great one that got away. Adams called the loss "one of the low points of my career as an owner."

The hits kept coming. Bud attempted to pacify fans, saying losing Nobis "will free money to sign Hindman." Ole Miss All-American OG Stan Hindman was Houston's No. 2 pick. He signed with the NFL, too. Then, when Boston appeared ready to lose its first pick to the NFL, they traded the rights to LSU's All-American OT Dave McCormick to Bud. Adams promised McCormick would sign. He did, but with the NFL.

It got worse. Adams then guaranteed he would sign All-American HB Donnie Anderson of Texas Tech who the Oilers selected in the 1965 redshirt draft. Bud flew Anderson and a friend to Houston and put them up at the Warwick, the hotel where the Duke of Windsor stayed when at the Medical Center. This time, Bud offered a gargantuan package with a Rivers Oaks home, a $36,000 swimming pool, a car, 16 gasoline stations and even a job and car for Donnie's father. The total deal came to a whopping $887,000.

To Adam's chagrin, Anderson was decidedly noncommittal, as if stuff like that went on all the time in Lubbock. He and his buddy used the time in the hotel to pursue women around Houston. The next thing Bud knew, Donnie was in Green Bay negotiating with the Packers, who were offering only $600,000. It was the ultimate insult that Donnie would even consider an offer $250,000 million less. Bud lowered his offer. When word reached Anderson, he immediately signed with Green Bay.

Adams said his "confidence in American youth is just about shattered." Anderson said that several Green Bay players called to urge him to sign, while several Houston players advised him not to sign with Houston.

The Oilers did manage to sign two tackles, Glen Ray Hines of Arkansas (redshirt from 1965) and George Rice of LSU (3rd round). They also got Mississippi FB Hoyle Granger (5th). Otherwise, this draft was no help.

The money was out of hand. Anderson's deal was the largest rookie deal in history. It dwarfed the Namath contract from the year before, supposedly the be-all and end-all, and Anderson was no Namath.

Adams was hurting. After shocking the world with Billy Cannon in 1960, he would never again recapture the old Mojo, suffering a spectacular string of public failures from Ditka to Namath to Taylor and Wilcox to Neely and Koy, to Nobis, McCormick, Hindman and Anderson. This was a man who loved pomp. He once had a shinny red antique firetruck remodeled and drove it around River Oaks, ringing its bell. Someone who does things like that can *almost* be forgiven for thinking all it took to sign good players was money.

As the 1960s unfolded, the Oilers, Chargers, Bills and Patriots, who had the best early teams, gradually fell back because they were no longer signing the best players. The Chiefs, Raiders and Jets were the ones doing what was needed to get to the top. Some of the teams that fell back did so because they were unwilling to spend even with the new TV contract. Bud did not fall into that group, however, as he showed with his offers to Brabham, Appleton and Anderson.

Nor was Houston's problem player evaluation. They annually drafted good players who would have solid careers, including Ditka, Suggs, Antwine, McLeod, Gros, Case, Cutsinger, Aldridge, Baker, Caffey, Jones, Chuy, Burson, (Tom) Brown, Namath, Taylor, Truax, Wilcox, Neely, Koy, Maples, McCloughan, Evans, Coffey, Anderson, Hines, Hilton, Nobis, Hindman, Granger and Long — plus free agents (Willie) Brown, Frazier and Frazier.

Taking money and scouting out of the equation reveals that most players simply did not want to play for the Houston franchise of the AFL. Their reputation was the pits. The Oilers were the Oilers' worst enemy.

Billy Cannon, who re-emerged as an all-star at TE in the late 1960s, said years later, "I spent a lot of frustrating years with the Oilers, and I blame it all on the basic incompetence of the front office. I don't think they ever knew what they were doing. The happiest day of my life was when I stepped on the plane and left Houston."

BUD MOVES TO COUNTER THE UNPRODUCTIVE DRAFT

Pete Rozelle caused more worries when he visited Houston to discuss expansion with John Mecom. Even the other AFL owners not so secretly wished the team were in less flamboyant hands. Bud was desperate.

Enter Operation Cross-Check. Bud had always been convinced there was undiscovered football talent missed by the scouts. He once found a kicker from Argentina working as a bartender and gave him a private tryout at midnight at Jeppesen.

Operation Cross-Check was cloaked in secrecy. It was Bud's answer to the Cold War. It was also expensive, involving "spies" and a phony team in Arizona run by loyal scout Red Dog Ettinger. It gave Bud something to tell disappointed fans — "We may have lost Tommy Nobis and Donnie Anderson but Red Dog signed 54 free agents today." Some consolation.

The result was that 127 players showed up for training camp unannounced to the coaching staff. Not one made the team. It was grand waste of time, energy and money.

MORE UPHEAVAL

During this period, the Oilers were making news every day. Rumors flew around about Klosterman and Lemm. On January 10, Wally Lemm and the Cardinals formally parted ways. Carroll Martin was in touch with him right away.

On January 13, Adams made a bold move, hiring Don "the Duke" Klosterman as Oiler GM and executive vice president. He had grown bored with life on the plains. His crack that "Kansas City is not heaven or hell, but more like purgatory," got him canned. He was generally credited with building both the Chargers and Chiefs into powerhouses. Showing Bud that finding a talented GM really was not that hard, Hunt quickly replaced him with Bobby Beathard.

The move came after the draft and after Adams had already lost most of his picks to the NFL. Clearly, the '66 draft took it out of him. It was a long, painful trip, but Bud finally did it. He finally hired someone who knew something about football to run his team.

Seeing the handwriting on the wall, publicist Jack Scott quit. For all he had done, Carroll Martin was promoted to vice president and director of operations. John Breen became director of public relations. Klosterman immediately stepped into a crash course on the state of the Oilers.

His first day on the job, the Duke woke up to a *Chronicle* story about a brewing feud between the head coach and starting QB. Taylor purportedly called Blanda a "bad influence," and said he would not coach again if "evil" George was still around.

On his second day on the job, he caught an earful from Sid Gillman. Sid accused Bud of tampering. In December, Adams had slipped into the San Diego dressing room uninvited after the game at Rice. He approached DLs Ernie Ladd and Earl Faison, who were playing out their options. Bud said he would pay them well once their options expired. Although they were technically free agents, there was nothing free about their status. Moreover, this type of contact was improper, and Bud was hardly stealth in the locker room. When Gillman found out, he was livid and vowed revenge.

After the season, the Oilers traded for the two players. For dramatic effect, the deal was prematurely announced at halftime of the AFL all-star game in Houston. It was hailed as Adams' greatest success, instantly turning the Oilers into contenders. Ladd and Faison were happy, but Gillman took heat for giving away two all-stars for three average players (Baker, Jaquess, Cutsinger). At the press conference, he sprang his surprise, not only reneging on the deal, but also turning Bud into the league for tampering.

On January 19, Joe Foss agreed. He had little choice. He not only nullified the trade, but also censored and fined Bud. Gillman was ecstatic. "I've done it! I've done it!," he roared. "I've finally screwed the fat Indian."

Meanwhile, Bones was busy backing away from the remarks about Blanda. Adams stated the decision was up to the Duke, but no one believed it. Taylor calmly pointed to his contract extension in December.

Soon thereafter, another one of those anonymous rumors appeared in the *Chronicle* to the effect that Taylor had never actually signed the extension. Adams had done it again. This time he fired a coach through the media.

WELCOME (BACK) WALLY LEMM

On January 29, Wally Lemm was named head coach. Wally was a little surprised to find Klosterman in as the GM and Martin, who had hired him, upstairs. Another surprise was that Taylor had already hired a new OL coach, FA Dry.

Taylor moaned about mistreatment all the way to Pittsburgh, where he was forced to take a pay raise from $14,500 as a head coach to $18,500 as WR coach for the Steelers. Baugh was let go, with Bud promising there would be no more part-time coaches. He ended up even farther away from Rotan as a Lions' assistant. Rymkus ended up with the Colts.

Looking back at Oiler history, it is difficult to definitively state the lowest point of all time. No doubt the Baugh/Taylor era ranks down there somewhere. It was not all their fault. They had a lot of help. In the words of Jack Gallagher, "The Oilers started with everything in a new league and by incredible mismanagement turned it into nothing."

THE ODD COUPLE

While some argued over whether Lemm should be counted as one Oiler coach or two, there was no argument over his popularity. The Cardinals wanted him to stay, but could not agree on terms. The Bills also offered him a position, while the AFL Commissioner wanted him to take over the expansion team in Miami. Then Martin called and he decided to return to Houston to become the Oilers' sixth head coach in the team's seven year history.

Lemm and Klosterman made quite an odd couple. Lemm was stocky, quiet and unassuming. Klosterman has been described as "psychedelic." He wore hip clothes and rode in limousines painted to match his eye color. He was friends with movie stars and governors. He converted the front office from discount cowboy to colors and incense. At a time when football was becoming popular with celebrities, Klosterman was the perfect fit. Wells Twombly in *Blanda, Alive and Kicking* said he was "in Houston to straighten the Oilers out. He's the swinging, sideburned prophet of something nebulous he calls the New Era."

The New Era was his PR campaign designed to win back fans. With his crew cut, thick glasses and European immigrant clothing, Lemm was not exactly the poster boy for a New Era. But the two men worked things out. They had to. Operation Cross-Check was on the way.

Klosterman could not salvage the draft, but immediately started making deals. He obtained LB Ron Caveness, who had been an All-American at Arkansas and first-round pick. He completed the deal for Ernie Ladd, surrendering all-star TE Willie Frazier and DB Pete Jaquess. He re-signed Jacky Lee and Bill Groman, and picked up 35-year-old FB John Henry Johnson. His best player acquisition that offseason was a large DL from the CFL named Pat Holmes.

His most significant transaction came during the season when he finalized the Ralph Neely situation. The Oilers eventually won the case on appeal, but Neely was already playing. Dallas, making its first move into the playoffs,

Yet another press conference announcing yet another new head coach. This one, occurring January 29, 1966, was the sixth such event as the Oilers headed into their seventh season. At left, Wally Lemm (seated) is shadowed by (from the left) John Breen, Bud Adams, Don Klosterman and Carroll Martin. The decorations are Klosterman's. Note also the possible subliminal communication indicated by Bud's pants legs.

wanted him to remain. To keep him, the Cowboys gave up $150,000, their 1967 first- and second-round picks, two mid-rounders and an agreement to play the Oilers. Dallas had been avoiding them for years. The first of three preseason games, which became known as the "Ralph Neely Bowl," would begin in 1967. John Hollis described the settlement in *From Cannon to Campbell* as "a total surrender by the Cowboys."

The acquisition of Ladd and Holmes allowed the Oilers to move Bud McFadin to a coaching position. Lemm also retained Fry and rehired Walt Schlinkman. He added Hugh Davore, Wayne Robinson and Joe Childress to complete the coaching staff.

A LEAGUE COMES IN FROM THE COLD

By early 1966, AFL owners were pushed to the brink. The war had reached a critical stage. For the 1965 season, both leagues spent about $25 million signing picks. AFL teams usually had to outbid the NFL teams to win a draftee.

There was also a new threat. Pete Rozelle reversed the so-called Bell Blackout Rule, which prohibited football from being televised in the city of a home game. That switch, to begin in 1966, scared the poop out of NBC.

AFL owners met privately and decided to make one more aggressive push. That meant saying good-bye to Joe Foss. Foss had a nice face and was good for PR, but he was too ethical for this deed. To oust him in a publicly acceptable way, they feigned anger over losing expansion site Atlanta to the NFL. Unhappily settling on Miami gave them the excuse they needed.

They knew they needed a strong replacement. Out of stalemate, a compromise candidate rose. Al Davis was not exactly Mr. Popular, not even in Oakland. Raider owner Wayne Valley recommended him, causing speculation that Valley just wanted Al out of his hair. With crucial support from Ralph Wilson, Davis made it by one vote. The owners thought he would be more of a figurehead with only nominal authority. Davis took over as the Commish on April 7.

ANOTHER HIGHLIGHT IN OILER HISTORY

The announcement came from the Shamrock Hotel in Houston during an executive committee meeting. Like Don Klosterman a few months before, Davis had no idea what he was about to step in. On April 8, with Davis presiding over his first league affair, Jack Gallagher appeared with a photographer for pictures. Bud was fresh in from the ranch and still dressed in his cowboy duds. Spying Gallagher, he said, "Hello skinhead." Gallagher suggested they take two shots, one with Cowboy Bud in it and one without. Adams replied, "Go ahead, sonny boy, get your picture," and turned away.

Jets owner Sonny Werblin, who thought the remark was directed to him, asked, "What did you say?" Bud loudly replied he did not mean him, but that "Irish son of a bitch over there."

Irish he was. Outweighed by 100 pounds, Gallagher nonetheless stepped forward with a beet-red bald head and raised fists, saying, "If you are going to do something, go ahead and do it."

It was over quickly. Adams landed three punches while Jack threw a Buddy Ryan-like jab. Davis and Ralph Wilson had to pull off Bud. As they held him, he tried to kick in Jack's face. The *Post* photographer ended up with some good material, while Gallagher ended up with a swollen nose and a trip to the hospital.

THE AFL'S SWAN SONG

Al Davis set up shop in New York, taking Mickey Herskowitz with him. His primary weapon initially was a media blitz prepared by Mickey and the other PR flunkies. They tried to scare the NFL by threatening to sign their best players.

It was the NFL that cast the first stone when the Giants signed Bills' kicker Pete Gogolak. While legal, there was an unwritten rule against such moves. Several NFL owners were not happy because they knew what was coming. Vince Lombardi called it "stupid."

Davis responded by going after the NFL's quarterbacks. AFL recruiters, including Klosterman, beat the bushes. On May 26, the Raiders signed the Ram's Roman Gabriel to a 3-year deal. Klosterman signed John Brodie to a $250,000 contract to begin in 1967. Seven NFL QBs were rumored to have signed. The Oilers even inked their old friend Mike Ditka.

Davis and Rozelle, who were still against any merger and believed the AFL would fold, became arch enemies. Al believed just as strongly that the AFL was beginning to get the upper hand. In his PR, he claimed the AFL signed the better players from the past two drafts and was on the verge of becoming the dominant league. History shows he was not just blowing smoke.

What neither knew was that owners' reps were meeting secretly. Wilson and Rosenblum's 1965 discussion was followed by another in February 1966 between Lamar Hunt and Tex Schramm, who secretly met in a parked car at the Dallas Airport. By late May, a proposal neared agreement. The main sticking point was the "indemnity" the AFL would pay for the " invaded" territories (New York and San Francisco). It was later settled at $18 million over 20 years.

On June 8, 1966, the leagues held a joint news conference at the Warwick Hotel announcing the merger.

Rozelle wept when he learned of the vote. Davis felt betrayed. He said he "thought the AFL had lost the war." But he was smart enough to take credit, saying, "What brought the NFL to the table was the fact that we were goin' after their quarterbacks. What got it done was when [I] said 'Look, we're gonna take their f—in' best players.'"

Some people saw it as an NFL victory, believing it got the merger mostly on its terms, since it still had the prestige of having the players worth raiding. Only Oakland and Houston signed any NFL players, and the Gabriel and Brodie contracts were rescinded. In addition, the NFL was to receive some large payments.

But the AFL, on the strength of its NBC contract and some wealthy owners who had already been through a lot together, won where others had tried and failed. They could point out that the NFL only had a couple of very strong teams while others were having problems.

The 33-year-old Rozelle became commissioner of the combined league, earning the nickname the "boy czar." Davis wanted the job and would always hold a grudge against Rozelle because of it. Nonetheless, he made out like a bandit. With the position of AFL commissioner eliminated, he was out of a job. Luckily, the Oakland owner felt indebted to him for not allowing the 49ers to force the Raiders out of Oakland. He made Davis the GM and a part-owner for cheap, making him an instant millionaire. He took the title of "managing general partner" and has not looked back since. Hank Stram had this unflattering comment, "Al's new position is second guesser. He's the greatest second guesser in the world."

The terms of the merger provided for a common draft starting in 1967. The new league would expand to 26 teams with the NFL adding a city in '67 and the AFL adding one in '68. Realignment (Colts, Browns and Steelers moved for compensation) and a common schedule would occur in 1970. The championship game would begin immediately.

Adams has given contradicting statements about the merger over the years. In 1971, he said, "If the war had lasted much longer, I would have gotten out." He complained he barely broke even that year. No doubt, he was paying for some bad management at the time. In 1971, he owed large back salaries to several ex-Oilers, including Ladd ($300,000), Cannon ($200,000), Holmes ($200,000) and George Rice ($150,000), plus the indemnity payments. Over the next few years, he would owe even more to Ed Hughes, Ed Peterson and Sid Gillman.

Time has changed Bud's memory. In 1995, he claimed he never considered selling. "It was starting to be a bloody mess for the NFL," he said. "I think 1966 was the bloodiest year because it was the last year of having a separate draft. We were giving some players $700,000 and $800,000 contracts, which was huge in those days. But by then, we had good crowds and I couldn't see any down side to it. The league was going to make it. If anything, I felt we merged with the NFL too soon. We paid $2 million per team to be paid in $200,000 installments over 10 years with no interest. But I guess that was a pretty cheap entry fee."

1966 TRAINING CAMP

Going into their seventh summer camp, the Oilers had seen 6 head coaches, 14 assistant coaches and 5 GMs. It is from this type of organizational consistency that ideas like Operation Cross-Check arose.

Since Red Dog and his operation were shrouded in secrecy, Lemm had no idea what was about to hit. It was July, it was Houston and already 100 degrees. Then, the Cross-Checkers started showing up all over the place. No camp in the history of football had ever seen 127 rookies at one time.

The first week was chaos. There was no coaching. Mostly, it was like Army processing. "At the end of the first workout, I called for all the wide receivers to line up for wind sprints. They covered the field," Wally recalled. "I never saw such a mob in my life." There were 29 cuts the first day alone. Nine did not get past their physicals and two of those sued. The majority disappeared by the end of the first week. Blanda said it was the first time he had seen "a team cut by the busload."

With new players and coaches to synthesize, Lemm did not need the distraction. He lost valuable time and never recovered. Always the company man, he did not complain. Mindful of his miracle year in 1961 and aware that such expectations with this club would be harmful to everyone, Lemm tried to dampen enthusiasm. He would have none of the bravado of Baugh and Taylor. About the most committal he got was saying, "This isn't a bad football team." He identified the top problem as the OL, noting a need to improve both pass protection and the worst rushing offense in the league. Close behind were rush defense and pass defense, which were also the worst in the league. The best he could muster about his LBs was "adequate." Wally was low key and did not single out individuals. He believed in his players. His major task, he said, was to "change attitude."

Somewhat ironically in light of the boos, the one area Lemm did not need to radically improve was the passing game. It was the only consistent aspect of the team. Despite poor blocking, injuries, susceptibility to blitzes, an immobile QB and constant double teams, Houston moved the ball through the air. That Blanda was able to overcome those obstacles and lead was remarkable, even more so because he was singled out as the cause of all the other team problems. Wally knew that if he could get better protection and a running threat, the touchdown-to-interception ratio would improve.

Lemm named Blanda as the starter early to circumvent controversy. The rumor was it was going to be George's last season. Against Oakland in the preseason, fans let their feelings be known. As his name was announced in the pregame festivities, Blanda was showered with boos. It was ugly. After the game, the old warrior quietly left the stadium without showering.

The Oiler QB question swallowed up the city. Klosterman noted, "I was in town only two weeks when I found there are three names you could mention and get an immediate response. Those names are Judge Hofheinz, Percy Foreman and George Blanda."

Starting Blanda "is a case of turning disaster into catastrophe," wrote Gallagher, who was out of the hospital and breathing fire. "Are the Oilers really progressing by losing with the same old face every season? ... If Blanda is producing, then every oilman in Houston should reevaluate the dry holes he has dug and hire the Oilers coaching staff as consultants."

Literally the biggest change was the addition of Holmes and Ladd, who joined Floyd and Cutsinger to convert the DL from the smallest to the largest in the league (271-pound average). At LB, they added Caveness to Baker, Cline and Brabham. Ernie Ladd's uncle, Garland Boyette, was a nice addition alternating between LB and DE. The secondary had one good player, Hicks, and another good but slow player, Norton, who probably would have been the best punter in the league if he did not have to play safety. Rounding out the secondary were Glick and Jancik. The starting OL was the same with Hines and Rice providing depth. At WR, fans heard for the third year in a row how former track star Charley Frazier was finally ready to start making plays.

Among the cuts were Bill Groman and Tony Banfield, neither of whom recovered from knee injuries. Also cut were Bobby Maples ('65, 4th round) and Hoyle Granger ('66, 5th), but they later re-signed. The Maples and Groman cuts were particularly unpopular.

The lack of change was not lost on Gallagher, who wrote, "It is time the Houston Oiler management stopped dreaming and faced the facts of pro football life. Twenty of the 22 starters who participated in three successive losing seasons are still on the roster."

Not every writer was as caustic. Others predicted they could make a run at the title if they stayed healthy and picked the Oilers to finish second. The tireless Klosterman's "New Era" billboards littered the landscape.

THE 1966 REGULAR SEASON — THE NEW ERROR

Staring down his 39th birthday, Blanda came out for his seventh straight year as Oiler QB, and together with the defense, pasted Denver 45-7 before 30,156 at Rice. He was 13-of-25 for 210 yards, 3 TDs and no interceptions. It was the most points the offense had scored since '63. Even more impressive, the defense limited the Broncos to 26 total yards and no first downs for the game. It was the first time in 24 years that a team was held without a first down.

Next was Oakland, which was on the verge of becoming the AFL's best team. On this day, Blanda was anything but impressed, going 17-of-34 for 202 yards and 2 TDs. Houston fans were so loud that the Raiders could not get a play off, which resulted in an Oiler penalty

Cowboy Bud had a big 1966. He temporarily settled his grievance with sportswriter Jack Gallagher the way men did in those days. He hired another coach and GM, scared off Tommy Nobis, implemented Operation Cross-Check, beat the other Cowboys in court over the rights to Ralph Neely and came close to being run out of town by the NFL.

which caused cups, cushions and even folding chairs to be tossed onto the field. The Oilers wasted them 31-0. It would be their last victory over the Raiders for a very long time.

The Jets crashed the party the next week, winning 52-13 before 54,681 at Shea Stadium. Namath had 5 TDs, but the real story was Jets' coach Weeb Ewbank who had a spy in Houston to watch practices and record plays. The Oilers made it easy by practicing in front of an open field. It worked. On the way back to the huddles, Houston's WRs kept hearing that they were running the wrong patterns. The complaints were coming from the Jets' DBs.

Then came a dark day in Buffalo. Tied at 20 with under a minute to go, the Oilers were looking to move to 3-1 with the ball at the Bills' 34 under some dark skies. Blanda later wrote, "God is about to be merciful and cover Buffalo with a layer of snow, so that no one can see the smoldering neighborhoods, the corroded downtown." Instead of going for the long FG, he threw his 53rd pass of the game. It was an eerie scene. The simple 5-yard curl to TE McLeod was intercepted and run back for a TD and a Buffalo victory. The Bills crushed George on the run back and he lay face down in the snow for several minutes. He needed help to stand.

That hit in Buffalo really racked the old man, who was already playing with a bum arm which required cortisone shots and daily treatments at the Medical Center. He did not throw during the week, but made trainer Bobby Brown promise silence. Only Brown and Lemm knew the extent of the pain. Fans did not know or seem to care. They wanted blood. No Houston sports figure has ever heard such boos before or after.

Next they lost to Denver 40-38 on a FG with 37 seconds left. The Oilers had no rushing offense. Blanda had 300 yards and 5 TDs after another cortisone shot, but his season and Oiler career were just about over.

At 2-3, Lemm started making changes. He brought back Maples and Granger. Maples would soon replace Frongillo at center while Granger found a home at FB. Neither would give up his starting position for awhile. Glen Ray Hines replaced Michael at OT while Appleton replaced Ladd at DT. Big Ernie's leg problems were causing an inconsistent year. George Rice later replaced Appleton. Caveness replaced another Oiler original, Doug Cline, who was released. Unlike past teams, this one agreed with the changes.

The next week, they put together their best effort of the year to get some revenge on the Jets 24-10. Sitting at 3-3, they were just a few plays away from 5-1. But that was the end of the ride. Injuries to Hicks, Glick, Hennigan, Ladd, Floyd, Brabham and Blanda proved fatal. The win over the Jets was the last of the season.

Jack Gallagher encouraged fans to boycott the games and said management did not listen to them, or him. He kept telling them that Trull was the answer. He would live to see that theory tested.

On October 30, Houston was mauled 48-23 by the Chiefs, who were making their Super Bowl run. Lee started, but gave way to Blanda. It was George Frederick Blanda's last game at QB for the Houston Oilers.

Lee's injury opened the door for Don Trull, one of Gallagher's "faces of the AFL's future." They lost all 5 of Trull's starts.

By the end of the season, the Oilers were a team divided. The last game summed it up well. They lost to Miami 29-28 to become the first team in history to lose twice in one season to an expansion team. Trying to get out of town, the Oiler airplane choked and sputtered. After a delay for repairs, players were told the craft was fine but they could find alternative transportation if they chose. The troops split. One mostly white faction led by Trull voted to stay in Miami, while a mostly black faction led by Ladd voted to go home. Another group tried to get back through New Orleans. The Oiler plane made several stops along the way, with the Ladd group ending up stranded in Oklahoma. It came to final rest in San Antonio with players scattered between there, Miami, Tulsa and New Orleans. It was an appropriate ending to a 3-11 season and last-place finish.

The long ride home gave Wally some time to reflect. Upon landing he vowed, "We may lose [next year] but it won't be with the same people."

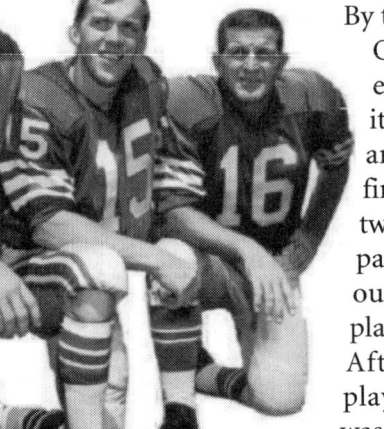

The Oiler QB trifecta of Don Trull, Jacky Lee and the venerable Mr. Blanda was back together for the 1966 season.

OVERVIEW

The worst record in team history was somewhat misleading. Four losses came in the last minute; otherwise, they would have been a respectable 7-7. Most games were close, with 7 of 11 losses coming by 7 or fewer points. After Baugh and Taylor, this was tangible progress.

Again, the pass offense was the only impressive function. Despite arm problems and decreased PT, Blanda led the team, going 122-of-271 for 1,764 yards, 17 TDs and 21 interceptions. Many of those, according to Lemm, were due to Hennigan running the wrong patterns or cutting his routes short. Charley, who played with a torn leg muscle, caught just 27 in his last year as an Oiler. Charley Frazier, at long last, flourished to lead the team in receiving with 12 TDs and 1,129 yards on 57 catches, fifth best in the league.

He was a John Breen project. A track runner in college who had not played football, he was 4 years behind from the outset. Breen had to talk him into a tryout. He learned behind Hennigan, and it paid off in 1966 with a berth on the all-star team. Breen and Al Davis both recognized the changing face of football. A Davis prophecy from 1966 fit Frazier well. African-Americans, Davis said, "will dominate because speed is it now. If a [black player] doesn't have a good coaching background the pros have no choice but to compensate for that with patience."

The woes of the running game showed in Ode Burrell's team-leading 406 yards, which was not good enough to land him in the top 10 of a 9-team league. There was one step forward in the backfield as they finally found a FB, something missing since 1962. Rookie Granger survived being cut to come back for 388 yards and an impressive 6.9 yards per carry average. With Hoyle, you got what you saw. Asked if he preferred *GRAN-ger* or *grawn-GHAY*, he replied, "It don't make no difference to me." And there you had it.

While the offense scored 335 points, the defense gave up 396 (over 28 per game). The DL put up a meager pass rush and the backs were torched. The defense gave up an astounding 50 TDs, including about 35 over the Jancik (injured) side of the field. The Oilers were last in team defense, second worst in pass defense and worst in TD passes surrendered.

Once upon a time, they had the difference makers they needed on defense. In Oakland, Kent McCloughan was AFL defensive player of the year. In Denver, Willie Davis was an all-star CB. In Boston, Houston Antwine was first team all-league at DT.

OG Bob Talamini was the only Oiler to make first team All-AFL. OT Walt Suggs and LB Johnny Baker each made at least one other all-star team as second-teamers while Blanda made it as a kicker. Gary Cutsinger had a good year and was team MVP. The biggest disappointment besides Ladd was the play of No. 1 picks Elkins and Brabham.

THE FIRST SUPER BOWL

The participants in the last two AFL Title Games, Buffalo and San Diego, peaked a little early. Hank Stram, Otis Taylor and Len Dawson were right on time. They whipped Buffalo 31-7 to earn a berth in Super Bowl I.

Over in the NFL, the hated Cowboys made the post season for the first time. Actually, they were not that hated in all parts of Houston, courtesy of Rozelle's television flood. When combined with the Oilers' regimented decline,

---

Even by today's standards, 6'9, 300-pound Ernie Ladd was a big man. In the 1960s, he was a giant. Blanda said trying to pass over the Chargers' fifteenth-round pick in 1961 was "like trying to throw out of a well." By the time he arrived in Houston, leg problems had slowed him considerably. But fate was kind. After leaving football in 1969, the Big Cat was able to parlay his natural good looks into a fine career in professional wrestling.

Dallas had gained quite a foothold by 1966. The NFL Title game set up a possible showdown between the two teams that battled it out for Dallas. But the Cowboys had to first get past the Packers, something they could not do.

The big game was on January 15 in Los Angeles. Seats were $6-12 and the stadium was one-third empty. Television rights were worth $2 million via a joint telecast by NBC and CBS. Winners' shares were $15,000. Officially it was known as the World Championship Game. However, Lamar Hunt came up with the term "Super Bowl" after his daughter made a ball out of some play dough and called it a super ball. The press loved it.

The Packers were an insulting 13-point favorite on the neutral field. By this time, the AFL believed it had proved itself, but the media said they were still second rate. The Chiefs were "a so-so team from the Mickey Mouse League." Some Green Bay fans even wore Mickey Mouse hats to the game.

The Pack was led by Vince Lombardi, who had done wonders with the once hapless team. After promoting fourth stringer Bart Starr to QB, they won 5 league championships. They were fairly simple, with two offensive formations and one defensive alignment. They also had Starr, Paul Hornung and Jim Taylor. They just lined up as if to say, "Here we are, beat us."

It was 14-10 Green Bay at the half. In the second half, Lombardi uncharacteristically switched defenses and blew it open to win 35-10. It kept the AFL in its place. Lombardi added to the perception by saying the Chiefs did not compare to the top NFL teams.

1967: FROM LAST TO FIRST

Bud Adams was feeling relief on at least two fronts. First, John Mecom got an NFL franchise for New Orleans where voters had already approved a domed stadium. The price was $8.5 million. Second, he no longer had to compete for draftees.

By no means, though, was he suddenly well-loved by his peers. His willingness to spend and sue, the scorn he showed the NFL's elders and his flamboyance probably made him the most resented owner in the AFL. The speculation was that Rozelle would try to force him out.

Meanwhile, Wally Lemm was disturbed by his club's psyche. "The team had been losing and had that just-get-by attitude," he decried. When asked how many players the Oilers needed to become champions, he replied, "We'd have to replace 15 or 20." They would have a chance to do that with 10 picks in the first 5 rounds and 21 overall.

THE 1967 DRAFT

Arriving too late for the 1966 draft, Don Klosterman was eager to put his mark on this team. He revamped the scouting system. He also eliminated their masochistic tendency of taking the big names from the still mostly segregated Southwest and Southeast Conferences. To facilitate this process, he hired former Grambling assistant head coach and track coach Tom Williams specifically to scout the black colleges.

The Oilers under Klosterman were innovators. Before the first combined draft, which was pushed back to March, they took advantage of Houston's mild winters

Tough guy Don Floyd was typical of the early Oilers. Hailing from Midlothian, Texas, the one-time Southwest Conference star at TCU was first team all-AFL in 1961-62, while making other all-star teams in 1963-64. At a maximum of 6'3, 245, he began to wear down in the middle '60s in the face of larger OLs. One of the last of the originals, he played through 1967, eventually suing Bud Adams over a wage dispute.

to bring in seniors for personal evaluations. Both Lemm and the college coaches enthusiastically supported this program. Week after week, the Oilers reviewed a parade of players, including Gene Upshaw, Willie Lanier, Lem Barney and Pete Barnes. It gave them a big leg up on the competition, until they were ratted out, that is. Naturally, the Cowboys were the rats. After they called Pete Rozelle, he told Houston to stop, even though there was nothing in the rules of either league to prevent it. This rare Oiler innovation led directly to the scouting combines of today.

The Oilers had two firsts, two seconds and 21 picks overall in 17 rounds of a very deep draft. With rosters enlarged to 40, they were in great shape to turn the team around with one class. They needed help across the board, but especially speed in the secondary and at LB. Maples' move to center and Boyette's play at MLB saved valuable picks at those positions.

Although they ended up in a last-place tie with Miami with their worst record in history, the Oilers had to draft behind Rozelle's NFL trio of Baltimore, Minnesota and Atlanta, as well as the Dolphins. After watching the Colts take Michigan State DL Bubba Smith No. 1, Houston took Bubba's teammate George Webster at No. 5. He would be one of the team's best picks ever. Others available were Gene Upshaw, Mel Farr and Alan Page.

With the first Dallas pick, they selected OG Tom Regner. In the second, they took QB Bob Davis and FB Roy Hopkins of TSU. Of those three picks, Regner and Hopkins would stick, but the choices could have been Hall of Famers Willie Lanier (one pick after Hopkins) and Lem Barney (four picks after Davis), plus Willie Ellison. However, the rest of their draft was superb.

Seven of the first ten picks were on defense, including CB Larry Carwell, DT Carel Stith, S Pete Johns, DT Willie Parker, CB Zeke Moore, LB Pete Barnes and safety Kenny Houston of Prairie View (9th round). They also took RB Woody Campbell.

The 1967 draft was without a doubt the team's best to date, and probably the best ever top to bottom. They got one Hall of Famer (Houston), an AFL all-time team member (Webster), plus multiple starters.

John Breen was a little sentimental. He said, "It wasn't as much fun as it was when everybody had players hidden all over the country." The same could be said for negotiations. Before agents, owner and player went one-on-one. One story that made the rounds was of a player who had received the club's final offer. The player said, "Gee, I don't know, I'll have to call my wife and see if it's okay," to which the owner replied, "In that case, I'll have to call my wife to see if it's okay to offer you that much."

NO LONG GOOD-BYES

Lemm and Klosterman continued the changeover after the draft. The holder of all team receiving records and many longtime AFL/NFL records, Charley Hennigan, was traded to San Diego. Leg injuries in '65 and '66 cut into his production. He retired instead.

Klosterman stole talented CB Miller Farr from Denver for Appleton and Baker. It was rare for the Oilers to be on the good side of a deal like this. Lemm called it "one of the best moves we ever made." He also signed free agent TE Alvin Reed and would later sign WR Lionel Taylor, whose single-season reception mark of 100 was the record Hennigan broke in '64.

Doug Cline was cut in '66 and Fred Glick retired. Then on March 19, 1967, the Oilers put out a small press release noting a few more players had been cut — John Henry Johnson, Rich Michael, John Frongillo, and oh yeah, George Blanda. It was one last slap at old George.

At the end of the season, he talked to Lemm about coming back as a kicker and assistant coach. Blanda wanted to do it and they had a basic understanding, but nobody from the team ever contacted him. He learned of being cut by reading the newspaper.

It was a low-handed even for Adams. Blanda had led them to 3 division titles and 2 championships. When asked whether there would be any type of ceremony, Klosterman replied, "No." When asked whether some of the guys like Blanda, Hennigan and Tolar, who carried the team in the early years, would have their jerseys retired, he asked, "Why?"

It was petty. The Raiders claimed George but had to compensate Houston. "We got a player for him," said Lemm, "a tackle. Nice guy named George something-or-other." In Oakland, Blanda would again defy the odds. In 1970, at age 43, he became a national celebrity after he saved Oakland's season with a string of miracle comebacks.

He would play through 1975, retiring at 48 as the oldest to ever play. He is in the Hall of Fame and still holds the NFL's all-time scoring record (2,002 points). He also holds career records for PATs (943) and FG attempts (638), and is ranked 13 in TD passes (236). His 1961 mark of 36 TD passes represents the most ever in a 14-game season.

With the Oilers, he was the first 15,000-yard AFL quarterback. His single-season marks for attempts (505 in '64) and yards (3,330 in '61 and 3,282 in '64) are team records for 14-game seasons and were not broken until Warren Moon went to the Run 'N' Shoot in 1990. He still holds the all-time career records for points (596), field goals (91), longest field goals (55 vs. San Diego in '61; 54 vs. Oakland in '62) and PATs (299). He also holds the single-season records for points (115 in '60) and PATs (64 in '61).

1967 TRAINING CAMP

Going into camp, Wally Lemm was just dreaming of getting back to .500. He strove to get his players off to a fast start. In this regard, the Oilers led the way again in 1967 with another innovation. They brought in all their draft picks as soon as classes were over. No one else did this at the time. By working with them until camp officially opened, the rookies had a much better grasp of the system. Eventually, this idea evolved into the mini-camp.

Wally also wanted them out of the city to help their focus, and no more Cross-Checkers. He got his way. Camp moved to Kerrville, set in the bucolic Texas Hill Country. The town of 15,000 was happy to have them. It was a good situation all around.

There were plenty of roster changes. Along with Blanda, Hennigan, Michael, Frongillo, Cline and Glick, Charley Tolar retired after offseason knee surgery. The increased roster limit caused by the merger allowed them to add 12 rookies, or more than twice as many as made the team the year before. They were Webster, Houston, Campbell, Moore, Regner, Davis, Barnes, Johns, Hopkins, Carwell, Stith, Parker and Alvin Reed. It was a great group. Of 21 picks, 5 became starters.

Webster was the brightest star. Anointed an early starter, he had 15 unassisted tackles in his first game. Lemm called him "a once in a lifetime rookie."

One of the most notable areas of improvement was the OL, thanks to Lemm keeping Dry. FA's best job was converting Bobby Maples into a functional center. Maples, waived and recalled in '66, was originally a QB following Don Meredith out of Mt. Pleasant High (Texas). At Baylor, he backed up Don Trull, but moved to LB because he kept growing. He was still growing when the Oilers moved him to center. Another key to the line was the addition of Reed (6'5, 228). The line jelled with Maples, Reed, OTs Suggs and Hines, and OGs Talamini and Bishop. Depth was found in rookies Regner and Stith.

In the backfield, Granger was pressed by Hopkins, who Lemm felt could have started on most teams. Blanks was back at HB, but pushed hard by rookie Campbell. WR was a weak link. Little Ode Burrell, who was a good receiver out of the backfield, moved to flanker because Lemm wanted bigger RBs. Without question, the biggest weakspot was QB where Gallagher's heroes, Lee and Trull, were joined by the rookie Davis. Trull went into camp the number one, but Lee came out the starter.

There were changes all over the defense. Tragedy struck early as '66 team MVP Cutsinger hurt his back in camp and would not play all year. He was a leader and tough player. Holmes moved to DE while Rice ('66, 3rd) filled Holmes' DT spot beside Ladd. The other DE was Don Floyd. Boyette was the MLB. The OLBs were Webster and Brabham. Among the DBs, Norton, Hicks and Jancik returned to battle Farr and rookies Houston, Moore, Johns and Carwell. It was definitely the most talent Houston had ever seen in the secondary.

The combination of the infectious excitement of so many rookies and the isolated but cozy camp worked wonders. Going in, Lemm wanted to improve attitude and add speed in the secondary. He did both. The attitude adjustment showed in the preseason against the defending AFL champion Chiefs. Powerful rookie Willie Parker broke through the line on an offsides to clobber Len Dawson. He quickly got in a wrestling match with the protective KC linemen and came out of the pile with a helmet. Time seemed to stand still as Willie was surrounded by some big Chiefs. He instinctively swung the helmet to keep them at bay. His teammates rose to the occasion, both benches emptied and a massive fight ensued. Houston lost the game, but gained a sense of identity and togetherness that had been missing from the last several teams.

On a lighter note, one of the more appreciated events occurred when Sonny Bishop, the only full-blooded Sioux in football, did a rain dance in full gear to end a 5-month drought. He was a hero. Acquired in the Cannon trade, Bishop was a loyal Oiler. An undersized OG (6'2, 245) who did not play high school football, he made up for his shortcomings through studious research of his opponents. He worked off about 18 pounds a game.

There were two other notables from the exhibition games. They lost to the Raiders 24-7 with Blanda tossing a TD pass. On September 2, 1967, they met Dallas for the first time outside a courtroom. The Rice crowd of 53,125 seemed to favor Dallas at the outset. While Dallas won 30-17, Houston's inspired play had the home crowd behind them by the end. The highlight was Webster running down Olympic sprinter Bob Hayes from behind in the open field.

Lemm was cautiously optimistic going into the season. He said they might go 7-7. In the preseason, he got better line blocking, a good defensive effort and a better attitude. His depth was much better. Moreover, Bud was keeping his mouth shut and staying out of things. He let Klosterman and Lemm manage the team. Considering they went 0-4 in the preseason, it was remarkably out of character.

"The biggest trouble," Lemm warned, "is at quarterback." He named Lee the starter over Trull. Fully aware of all the past controversy, he stated, "We can't satisfy

THE ORIGINAL DREAM TEAM?

In general, Oiler history leaves fans dreaming about what might have been. This period is a particularly good time to stop and dream. In 1967, several solid players were added, including Webster, Houston, Farr, Moore, Parker, Barnes, Regner, Campbell and Reed. Adding to that team the players the Oilers drafted but failed to sign, plus a couple of trades they were offered but did not take, results in a very talented team.

The following list indicates the team they reasonably might have had. HOF means that player has been elected to the NFL Hall of Fame. ATAFL means that player was recognized on the all-time AFL team. Otherwise, the years a player made Pro Bowl or one of the various all-star teams are shown.

OFFENSE

- QB: Joe Namath (HOF)
  Daryle Lamonica (offered for Cutsinger)
  George Blanda (HOF)
- SE: Charley Taylor (HOF)
  Homer Jones (1967-68)
  Charley Frazier (1966)
- FLKR: Charlie Joiner (HOF, drafted '69)
  Jerry LeVias (1969, drafted '69)
- RB: Woody Campbell (1967)
  Donnie Anderson (1968)
- FB: Hoyle Granger (1967-68)
  Roy Hopkins
- TE: Mike Ditka (HOF)
  Willie Frazier (1965, 67, 69)
  Alvin Reed (1968-70)
- RT: Walt Suggs (1966-69)
  Norm Evans (1972-74)
- RG: Sonny Bishop (1964-65, 68-69)
  Pete Case
- C: Jim Otto (HOF, offered for Milstead)
  Bobby Maples (1967-68)
- LG: Bob Talamini (1961-67)
  Tom Regner
- LT: Ralph Neely (1966-69)
  Glen Ray Hines (1968-69)
- KR: Jerry LeVias (1969)

DEFENSE

- LDE: Pat Holmes (1967-68)
  Lionel Aldridge (1963)
- LT: Ernie Ladd (1961-65)
  Willie Parker
  Tom Domres (drafted '68)
- RT: Houston Antwine (ATAFL)
  George Rice
- RDE: Elvin Bethea (1969, 71-75, 78-79, drafted '68)
  Roy Hilton
- WSLB: George Webster (ATAFL)
  Leroy Caffey (1965-66)
- MLB: Tommy Nobis (1966-68, 70, 72)
  Ron Pritchard (1970-71, drafted '69)
- SSLB: Dave Wilcox (1966-73)
  Pete Barnes (1969)
- CB: Miller Farr (ATAFL)
  Zeke Moore (1969-70)
- CB: Willie Brown (HOF)
  Leroy Mitchell (1968, acquired '69)
- FS: Jim Norton (1961-63, 67)
  Kent McCloughan (1966-67, 70)
- SS: Ken Houston (HOF)
  WK Hicks (1965-66)
- P: Jim Norton (42-yd. avg. over 8 seasons)
- K: George Blanda (HOF)
  Roy Gerela (1972, 74, drafted '69)

The 1967 version of this dream team would have had great players all over the field with 7 Hall of Famers (5 offense, 2 defense) plus 3 all-time AFL defensive team members. With another Hall of Famer-to-be on the way in 1969 and most of the others of all-star quality, they probably would have dominated football through the merger.

It is not as farfetched as it looks. All but 6 of the 25 defensive players noted were on the roster. Of the 25 offensive players named, 17 were on the team. Of the ones they missed, *all* were in Adams' sweaty palms at one time. For example, Namath says that, contrary to what Adams and Red Dog reported, he would have signed with the Oilers if the price was right (he signed with NY for $400,000 in 1965 while Adams offered Donnie Anderson over $800,000 in 1966).

One thing for sure, it would have been a lot of fun watching Namath throw darts to Charley Taylor, Homer Jones and those great tight ends. And pity the DBs once Charlie Joiner and Jerry LeVias arrived. On defense, that group of LBs and DBs would have been second to none. And with Klosterman in charge, there was no reason for it to stop.

everyone. The first thing for coaches is to keep morale of the players up — not the morale of the fans who may like a player they went to college with at Texas, Houston or Baylor."

THE 1967 REGULAR SEASON — ROOKIE CITY

The Oilers opened with the Chiefs, with whom they brawled in August. Houston was an embarrassing 14-point home underdog to the defending champs, generating a disappointing gate. The ones there saw a great effort out of the determined Oilers. Although the Chiefs squeaked by 25-20, Houston easily could have won. The Big Cajun — Hoyle Granger — gained 101 yards and Blanks added 79. The crowd, which had grown accustomed to seeing Oiler teams of the past few years lay down, gave them a standing ovation.

They had to face the defending Eastern Division champion Bills in Buffalo the next week. Despite 26 passing yards from Lee, they broke their 13-game losing streak, winning 20-3. The Oilers continued to develop and rely upon their running game. The DL played well with Rice at DT. New faces were Houston, who replaced Jancik for good in the Chiefs game, and Reed, who took over as a starter at TE against the Bills.

The lack of a passing game caught up with them against a tough Charger team who put everyone on the defensive line. The Oilers tried to take advantage, but no fewer than 5 sure TD passes were dropped by the WRs as they lost 13-3. On the plane home, Lemm was angry. "If some of our [expletive deleted] receivers had caught the ball we'd have won," Wally lamented. Looking across the aisle to see a middle-aged woman, an embarrassed Wally apologized, "Sorry ma'am, no offense." She coldly replied, "I noticed."

Next was a Denver team "full of drunks and cast-offs." The Broncos were so lousy that their punter was the team MVP. Nonetheless, with rookie Bob Davis at QB, the offense could manage just 10 points. Fortunately, the defense and Granger (138 yards) were just

The Oilers thought George Blanda was too old at 39 when they released him in the spring of 1967. He played 9 more seasons. He finished with 26,920 passing yards and 236 TDs while kicking 335 field goals and 943 PATs. Selected to the Hall of Fame in 1981, he is still the NFL's all-time leading scorer with 2,002 points. With Houston, he led the AFL in passing yards in 1961 and 63, and attempts and completions in 1963-65. His 36 TD passes in 1961 are the most ever in a 14-game season. He had team long-field goals of 55 and 54 yards. On the other hand, he threw 189 interceptions in the Columbia blue (27 per season) and finished with a career QB rating of 60. Of his Oiler days, he wrote, "In Houston, it was a matter of survival. You had to survive somehow in order to play pro football because of the crazy circumstances."

good enough for a 10-6 win and 2-2 record heading into bye week.

The off week gave Klosterman and Lemm a chance to assess where they were. Things were looking up. The offensive and defensive lines were playing solidly and they were getting a pass rush. They were not getting killed by the bomb anymore and team spirit was good. Holding them back was a lack of production from the QB. The Oilers had scored just 33 points over 3 games.

Before anyone could say George Blanda, Klosterman contacted the Chiefs about Pete Beathard. The Houston papers told fans Pete was "regarded as the best number 2 quarterback in the league." The Duke had a personal stake in the matter, having drafted him out of USC after he led the Trojans to the national championship as a "running quarterback." But a wily Hank Stram sensed desperation and held out for high ransom. The deal went down, but it took a toll.

The Oilers gave up Ernie Ladd, Jacky Lee (the first player they traded twice) and their 1968 No. 1. Losing Ladd seemed a big blow at the time. After a disappointing '66 season when he came in at over 315 pounds and had leg problems all year, Big Ernie came in a svelte 287 in 1967 and assumed a leadership role. The loss of that leadership would be costly as would the draft pick. Losing Lee left 3 originals — Floyd, Norton and Talamini.

Beathard arrived in Houston on Tuesday and moved in with Lemm. He studied the playbook every day and night to get ready for the Jets game at Shea the following Monday.

New York was the preseason favorite to win the division, and at 3-1, was the hottest team in the league. Broadway Joe and the Jets were hogging all the headlines. In Houston, they called them "the University of Texas at Broadway," because they had more Texans on the roster than the Cowboys and Oilers combined (including Don Maynard, Pete Lammons, George Sauer, Jim Hudson, Winston Hill and Curley Johnson).

The Oilers had not won there since '62 (the Jets had never won in Houston). With Parker (6'3, 275) in for Ladd, the defense rattled Namath for 6 interceptions (the papers said they gave "Joe the willies"). Farr and Houston scored TDs. The last pick was by Hicks with 5 seconds left. He ran 40 yards before lateralling to Ken Houston, who lateralled to Carwell, who was somehow stopped by Namath with a game-saving tackle inside the Jets' 4. The defense scored 3 TDs total to force the 28-28 tie which would have a big impact on team attitude and the final standings. They proved to themselves that they could win the division.

The following week, they traded Trull to Boston, officially ending Houston's QB trifecta. Ironically, Blanda would still be playing after Lee and Trull were long gone from the league.

Beathard then paid dividends, beating his old mates in KC 24-19. Defeating a Super Bowl contestant was another huge boost as they climbed to 3-2-1. Klosterman never rested. During the week, he signed WRs Lionel Taylor and Glenn Bass.

Next, they beat the defending divisional champion Bills again. The game ended with Jack Kemp on the Oiler goal line just like old times. Webster, Holmes, Parker and Boyette led the defense. The left side (Webster/Holmes) was so formidable that teams stopped going that way. The right side was weak, especially after another injury felled Floyd. A partial solution was already on the roster in the form of rookie Pete Barnes of Southern, who was ready to take over at LB. In an uncharacteristic mistake, Lemm refused to play him. Barnes would be an all-star by 1969, but for another team.

They stumbled against Boston 18-7 as the lack of offense killed them. Charley Frazier, in particular, seemed to drop everything. One more loss and they would be back at .500.

With the pressure on in Denver, the defense again saved the day and perhaps the season by scoring in the 4th quarter for a 20-18 victory. Woody Campbell had worked his way into the lineup as both he and Granger had over 100 yards rushing. It was a big win and left them at 5-3-1 with the next four games all at home.

Meanwhile, there was a strange sound coming out of the APC — silence. Adams did not have any Nobis's or Anderson's to chase around, and with the team winning, there was no coach to fire. No one believed Bud could stay that way, and he would soon prove them correct.

But first they suffered another setback when starting right OG "Sioux Sonny" Bishop fell off a hay wagon at a weenie roast. Then the wagon rolled over him. Tom Regner replaced him. The Oilers prevailed over Boston 27-6 despite Beathard hitting just 9-of-23 for 87 yards and throwing 2 interceptions. Granger had 124 yards and the defense allowed Boston inside the 20 just once with no TDs. They were still chasing the Jets by a game.

It all came together the next week. What seemed impossible before the season became a possibility. Houston beat Miami (on Campbell's 100 yards) and New York lost, bringing the teams into a tie. Not everyone enjoyed the turn of events. For example, a writer in Boston called the Oilers "nobodies" and wrote that the thought of Houston in the Super Bowl was "sick." Apparently, he was no fan of defense. Houston's was top ranked. They needed it because Beathard had the lowest completion rating of all starting QBs.

It set up a showdown of first-place teams Oakland (10-1) and Houston (7-3-1). The Raiders were the highest scoring team in the league. Blanda and Cannon were the top two scorers on the team. Coming out of the

Rice tunnel, George hoped fans might be a little forgiving. He was wrong. They started booing before he stepped on the field.

The Oilers played tough and led 7-0 at the half and late into the 3rd quarter until Blanda started hitting FGs. With George accounting for 13 points, the Raiders won 19-7. The Oiler offense gained just 53 yards in the second half. Beathard, the man who replaced the men who were supposed to replace Blanda, was 10-for-27. The good news was the Jets lost, too.

That brought up the Chargers, who the Oilers had not beaten since 1962. In a sign that Roy Hofheinz was throwing in the towel on getting an NFL team, he offered the Dome (which was also his home) up for practices. The Oilers won 24-17 to take over first place at 8-4-1 and clinch at least a tie as New York lost. It was the

An injection of youth and the return of Wally Lemm caused a dramatic turnaround in 1967. It was led by the defense, which was the first to allow fewer than 200 points in one season. The biggest change was an improved secondary. Below, the first of three consecutive Hall of Fame quality players drafted by Don Klosterman, rookie strong safety Ken Houston, brings the wood against the Chargers. The rest of the secondary that gave up only 10 TD passes on the season are second-year CB Miller Farr (20), third-year CB W.K. Hicks (33), and FS Jim Norton (43). Also pictured is MLB Garland Boyette (52). Another significant personnel change was the addition of AFL rookie of the year George Webster at OLB. At left, George (90), second-year DT George Rice (72) and LB Olen Underwood (56), welcome old friend Don Trull to Rice Stadium.

first time they led the Jets all season. Granger had 107 yards to break Tolar's single-season rushing record.

With his team in first and a legitimate shot at the Super Bowl, a newcomer might think Bud was a content man. Not so. On December 22, one day before the final game, he went off. The papers again blared with his threat to move. This time it was Seattle. "This is strictly business," he said, "if the fans of Houston want a team, they'll support it. Why should I lose $300,000 a year to go out and watch seven home games?"

While attendance might have been below what could be expected for a first-place team, fans had been put through the ringer. It went back to the Jeppesen Stadium days when they had to drive through colossal traffic jams just to sit in the heat, stink and mosquitoes of an old high school facility. Then, instead of the cushioned seats of the much ballyhooed Dome, they got the wooden bleachers and outdoor conditions of Rice. They put up with the coaching merry-go-round, miserable draft failures and a front office that was said to operate "with all the dignity and purpose of a Marx Brothers movie." It was no wonder.

The players focused on the prize. Despite Beathard's weak 79 yards passing, they crushed Miami 41-10.

Granger had 135 yards to miss the league title by 22 yards. In a signature moment for the '67 team, Granger asked Lemm to put in Hopkins with the game out of reach, saying he did not care about such things. "Winning is the big thing," Hoyle said. Farr also got his

The 1967 offense was not the equivalent of the defense, but did lead the AFL in rushing. Below, second-year FB Hoyle Granger (32) follows OG Bob Talamini (61), rookie OG Tom Regner (60) and second-year OT Glen Ray Hines (78). Granger finished second in the league in rushing with a team record 1,194 yards. QB Pete Beathard (right), acquired for Ernie Ladd and a No. 1 draft pick, was the catalyst. While no better a passer than Trull or Lee (41% completion rate and led the league in interceptions), he was very mobile and averaged 4.2 yards per carry. In the most important statistic, the team won 7-of-10 games after Pete arrived. Still, with a better passing attack and a little luck, the youthful 1967 Oilers might have had enough to overtake the Raiders and make Super Bowl II.

league-leading ninth and tenth interceptions off Bob Griese.

Suddenly there were only four teams left standing, and a possible all-Texas Super Bowl existed as Dallas made the playoffs again with Green Bay.

The plane trip home from Miami was decidedly different from the one a year before. Despite Adams' outburst, a large crowd greeted the team at Hobby Airport. The mayor proclaimed it Oiler Day. There was a renewed enthusiasm all over town. They had hope based on the fact that Raider QB Daryle Lamonica, who beat out Namath and Hadl as league MVP, did not throw a TD pass on them in the first game. Houston's defense was in a league of its own, setting the record for fewest TDs allowed in a season at 18 (vs. old record of 25). They also gave up the fewest TD passes ever with 10 (vs. 13). They were the first team to ever surrender fewer than 200 points (199). Tragically, the offense also managed only 199 points. The explanation for the won-loss record was defensive TDs.

THE 1967 AFL TITLE GAME — HOUSTON AT OAKLAND

An AFL championship game record crowd of 53,330 showed at the Oakland-Alameda County Stadium. The game was close and hard-fought. After Blanda missed a FG in the 1st quarter, the Oilers drove to the Oakland 44 where Reed took a Beathard pass and rambled to the Raider 19 but fumbled. A short while later, Kenny Houston dropped an interception that would have gone for a sure TD. Oakland led 3-0 at the end of the first quarter.

On the first play of the second, Norton whiffed a tackle on Hewritt Dixon at the 46 and Dixon took it 69 yards for a 10-0 lead. Later in the second, a Hicks' interception was knocked away by the goal posts on third down. Looking at a 13-0 halftime deficit, the Oilers felt they still had a chance. However, Oakland faked the field goal for a TD, pushing the lead to 17-0.

In the third quarter, Zeke Moore took the kickoff and headed for a TD, but fumbled as the Raiders took a commanding 24-0 lead. The offense lacked the firepower to mount any comeback against such a solid defense. The final was 40-7. Blanda hit 4 FGs again. DT George Rice led the Oilers with 18 tackles.

The Raiders won by stacking the line and daring Houston to throw. While Charley Frazier had 7 receptions and 1 TD, the league's top running game generated only 38 yards. Granger had 19. On the other side, Dixon had 145 yards and Pete Banazak 116. It was the most points the Oilers gave up all season.

Another big crowd braved some very cold weather and an overdue flight to welcome their plane at Hobby.

Rice said, "We'll be back. We're a young team and we're going to get better. They haven't heard the last of us." Hicks called it a "taste of honey. We had a taste of honey. After our bad season last year, we needed it. We needed to find out what it was like winning the Eastern Division and playing for the championship. Now we can go to training camp and let the younger guys know what a taste of honey is like."

SUPER BOWL II

Dallas did not make it, either, after losing to Green Bay. No one remembers the Oilers were not that far away from facing the Pack. For the big game, fan interest picked up as a crowd of 75,546 showed up in Miami to see the Raiders and Packers.

The 14-1 Raiders dominated the AFL, outscoring opponents 468-233, yet many thought they did not stand a chance. Green Bay was the NFL's flagship team. They had dominated the league throughout the 1960s. The attention given their win over Dallas in Ice Bowl II weeks before seemed to trivialize Oakland. They were two TD favorites.

It was close early, with the Raiders trailing only 13-7 late in the first half and Green Bay punting from deep in their territory. But the Raiders fumbled and Green Bay took a 16-7 lead at half. They won 33-14 before an estimated 60 million television viewers.

On the surface, the outcome confirmed the views of most of the nationally syndicated sports writers who were heavily biased towards the NFL. The reality was that the Packers were better than all the teams from both leagues and after them the leagues were even. History would bear this out as the AFL would win the next two Super Bowls and an AFC team would win nine of the first ten after the merger.

OVERVIEW

The Oilers won their first division title since 1962. In so doing, they became the first team to go from last to first and the first AFL team to win 4 division titles. Norton, Talamini and Floyd played on all four. The turning points in the season were the tie with the Jets and the win at Denver. With Beathard, they went 7-2-1.

A lot went into turning a 3-11 last place team into a 9-4-1 divisional champion. Moving the camp to was a master stroke. The veterans seemed to catch the enthusiasm of the many rookies and a good team spirit resulted, which was one of Lemm's primary goals. In addition, Wally was a good planner and he was thorough. His teams were prepared every week.

The acquisition of Beathard was a key. They went 7-3-1 after Pete arrived. Thrown into a new system, he managed only 1,114 yards on 94-of-231 passing (41%) with 9 TDs. He also had an AFL-high 14 picks.

For comparison's sake, the much maligned Mr. Blanda averaged 2,734 yards and 24 TDs over 7 years. Had they retained George, they probably would not have given up Ladd and their No. 1 pick in '68 for Beathard. But there is no telling what other effects may have been felt. Likewise, things would have been a lot different with one of the Joe's — Namath or Kapp — or Dayle Lamonica at QB. As it was, the Oiler passing game was worst in the league.

Beathard was better known for his non-passing attributes, like scrambling ability and averaging 4.1 yards per carry. He also had the habit of constantly vomiting on his center. He blamed it on a defective uvula. "I'd go back to the huddle," Maples remembered, "and Sonny Bishop would look over at me, make a face and say, 'Phew!'"

The sensation of '66, Charley Frazier, forgot how to catch in '67, managing just 23 catches and one TD. The veteran Taylor was a good stopgap pickup as he finished second among WRs with 18 in just half a season. On the whole, the Oiler offense scored the fewest points in their 8-year history, averaging 14 per game.

Granger broke Tolar's team record with 1,194 yards, which would be the last time an Oiler RB would gain 1,000 yards until 1978. He added 31 receptions for 300 yards. Woody Campbell was perhaps the biggest surprise of camp. He had 511 yards, was a good blocker, and could catch out of the backfield. He would have received rookie-of-the-year consideration if he had gotten into the lineup earlier. The other good surprise was the play of free agent TE Alvin "Tanglefoot" Reed.

Lemm was a superior defensive tactician ranking right up there with Buddy Ryan and Bum Phillips. The improved play started with the secondary, which surrendered a shocking 20 fewer TD passes than 1966. It all started with the acquisition of Farr. One of football's greatest strong safeties, Ken Houston, began his career during the first game, which allowed Twiggy Norton to move to FS. The experienced Norton made good calls.

He had leeway on the calls because of a good group of LBs led by Webster. Boyette played well at MLB and the line got some pressure. Holmes played much better at DE in '67 than he did at DT in '66. Rice and Parker were a good set of DTs when Willie was motivated. The line play was outstanding in light of the losses of Ladd, Cutsinger and Floyd.

The bottom line was Lemm cleaned house (20 changes from '66 to '67), then convinced them they were good. He let his rookies play early and get experience. All together, the team was able to overcome its horrid past. Players making the various all-star teams were Webster (the only rookie on the first team), Suggs, Talamini, Maples, Granger, Holmes, Farr and Norton.

Jim Norton said it all went back to Lemm. He said everyone was glad in 1966 when he came back. "He inherited a situation of low morale. It was a big problem. We won our first two games (in '66), then something happened. I don't know what. We tried to find out what was wrong all season. Wally's hands were tied. He couldn't do anything about the situation until the season was over. Most of us felt he would come up with the answer and he did.

"Even before we went to (in '67), I felt things would be better. Everything was right in camp. The team was together. There wasn't anything to worry about until we got back to Houston except football. We got more things accomplished than in any other camp. Everybody was willing to sacrifice ... We lost exhibition games playing rookies. But for the first time since '62, I felt we had the basis for a winner. It would all turn on whether the rooks would hold up ... We made fewer mistakes — even with so many rookies. We figured it was only a matter of time before the offense came around."

1968: AN EVENTFUL YEAR

During this period, there was a lot happening outside football, much of it tragic. Both Martin Luther King and Robert Kennedy were assassinated. There were large riots in Cleveland and Washington, D.C. The looting was so bad in Detroit that it took Federal Troops to regain control of the streets.

A turning point in American history occurred when the North Vietnamese Army surprised the US Army, president and public with the Tet offensive. Things would never be the same as a president lost credibility. Anti-war protesting heated up on college campuses, but then ran into an ideal-shattering brick wall in Chicago at the Democratic National Convention.

At the Mexico City Olympics, sprinters John Carlos and Tommy Smith did not face the US flag during the national anthem. Instead they bowed their heads and raised clinched fists high in the air. Their defiant stand was in stark contrast to that of Houstonian George Foreman, who gleefully waved two small flags after winning the boxing gold medal.

On the lighter side, individual expression was the buzz. Hippies and miniskirts were "in." In pro sports, individuality took the form of beards, sideburns and longer hair. Not everyone was impressed. A billboard in Amarillo read, "Beautify America, get a haircut."

In the AFL, Cincinnati received an expansion franchise which would be led by Paul Brown, the man Art

Modell ran off from Cleveland. On January 8, 1968, the NFL Players' Association registered as a labor union.

Houston saw its share of notable sporting events in this period. After two pro bouts in the Dome, Mohammed Ali took up residence in Houston. January 20 brought the biggest event to date to the Dome. That is when the No. 1 ranked and undefeated UCLA Bruins played the No. 2 ranked and undefeated University of Houston Cougars led by Elvin Hayes. Lew Alcindor & Co. were riding a 47-game winning streak. The teams had met the previous March in the NCAA tournament with Hayes outscoring and outrebounding Alcindor, but UCLA winning. The match drew the biggest crowd ever to see a basketball game in person (52,693) or on television, and no one was disappointed. The Big E led the way in the Cougar win with 39 points to the future Kareem Abdul Jabbar's 15. Jabbar is still making excuses.

Getting himself back in the headlines, Bud announced on February 11 that he was moving to the Astrodome. With the Division Title, talk of forcing him out quieted. Sick of hosting bull fights and polo matches, Judge Hofheinz conceded he was stuck with Bud. He said, "The HSA and Oilers expect to be together for a long, long time."

1968 TRAINING CAMP

One of the first things to come out of Lemm's mouth at camp was, "Elvin's a stud." That was in reference to third-round pick Elvin Bethea (6'3, 255) of North Carolina A&T, who would be one of their best draft selections ever. Originally slotted for the OL, Elvin would start as a rookie, play 15 years and should be in the NFL Hall of Fame as a DE. Although no projected defensive player was taken until the seventh and the only one to stick was DT Tom Domres from the tenth, the Bethea selection alone made the 1968 draft a success.

They took three big receivers in the first four picks: WR Mac Haik (6'2, 202), TE Bob Longo (6'4, 210) and spilt end Jim Bierne (6'2, 198) of Purdue, where he was Bob Griese's battery mate. Former No. 1 Lawrence Elkins was released. Ironically, his old college QB Don Trull was cut by the Patriots the same day. Haik and Bierne would each have a few solid years. However, the WR they missed was Harold Jackson (12th round), who played 16 years and had over 10,000 yards. At TE, they missed both Bob Trumphy (also from the 12th), and the great Charlie Sanders (7 Pro Bowls). The most significant lapse with regard to the passing game was selecting Haik instead of QB Ken Stabler late in the 2nd round. A successor to Joe Namath at Alabama, Stabler was also a 2nd round selection of the Astros as a pitcher.

On defense, they looked to the return of Gary Cutsinger to shore up the right side. In a bad move, Pete Barnes ('67, 6th) was allowed to go to San Diego. The Oilers, who were hurting on that side, said he could not cover. The Chargers said coverage was the thing he did best. He made Pro Bowl in 1969.

Overall, however, they looked pretty good, especially since Beathard would now have the benefit of a full camp and the new receivers. The Oilers went 4-1 in the preseason, losing only to Dallas. Houston was favored to win the Division.

Then, towards the end of camp, things turned bad in droves. The cruelest of all was the loss of all-AFL CB Miller Farr, who caught hepatitis. Next, RB sensation Woody Campbell was drafted (the other draft) and would soon be spending his weeks at Fort Sam Houston. He, Boyette and Reed, who were in the reserves, lived with the possibility of being shipped to Vietnam. Then, Bob Talamini held out for a raise. After getting nowhere with Bud, he quit. With Houston's papers calling him "over-the-hill," the 7-time all-star ended up with the Jets (and in a Super Bowl).

The success of the season would be defined early as the Oilers had games with the beasts from the West: the Chiefs, Raiders and Chargers. Newspaperman John Hollis told fans: (1) the passing game had improved ("the bomb has been restored to the Oiler arsenal"); (2) the right side of the defense was "much improved;" and (3) there was more depth on the OL. He said the OL had one "great tackle" in Suggs, one "good guard" in Bishop (who returned from his second-place finish in the fight with a hay wagon) and a center "poised on the brink of greatness" in Maples. While underappreciated by Hollis, Glen Ray Hines was probably the best lineman. The other starter at OG was Tom Regner.

THE 1968 REGULAR SEASON — MY KINGDOM FOR A QUARTERBACK

The Oilers and Chiefs ushered in the 1968 season with the first game in the Astrodome and first Monday night football game. Not everyone waited with open arms. American institution Johnny Carson was particularly bent out of shape, afraid it would cut into his ratings. Football fans did not mind missing the Carson monologue for this wild affair.

After posting Houston to a 7-3 lead, Pete Beathard had a chance to put the Chiefs away early. With the ball on the KC 4, he lofted a deadly interception. It allowed a huge momentum shift as the Chiefs built a 26-7 lead in the second half by pounding away at that supposedly improved right side of the defense. Up to that point, Beathard was 4-of-16 with 2 interceptions. Then he caught fire. Two TD passes to rookie Mac Haik cut the lead to 26-21 at the 4:51 mark. After the defense forced a punt, Blanks was heading for the winning score when he was caught from behind on a saving tackle at the KC 18. From there, another interception seemed to seal the Oilers' fate. However, the defense held again and Beathard got them to the Chiefs' 11 with 37 seconds left. With the sellout crowd whipped into a frenzy, the Oilers died at the 9. Beathard ended up 23-of-48 for 412 yards and the 2 TDs.

Despite the loss, fans were solidly behind the team. But the injuries continued to mount as Burrell broke his ankle. Trull was re-signed and added to the cab team.

They punched out Miami 24-10 six days later with the defense holding the Dolphins 4 times inside the Houston 10. NFL-reject Jim Norton became the career AFL interception leader, snagging his 44th. But they could not establish any momentum, losing in San Diego for the sixth straight year. That brought up the Raiders and a rematch of the AFL Title game.

Another sellout saw Beathard take the opening drive for a TD. Then, like the Chiefs' game, Houston blew a golden opportunity to get ahead early and let their defense dictate. On the next possession, Charley Frazier dropped a bomb in the clear that would have resulted in a 14-point lead. Instead, Beathard forced an interception that let Oakland gain a 7-7 tie. After the defense scored a safety for a 9-7 lead, Beathard again had them in Raider territory, but threw another interception. A Blanda FG gave Oakland a 10-9 halftime lead. In the 3rd quarter, a Norton interception resulted in a missed FG, a frustrating event that would plague them all year. After bungling a fake FG from the Raider 26, they trailed 24-9. But they kept coming and cut the lead to 24-15 with 6:35 left after missing a 2-point conversion. With one last gasp, Campbell took a pass and headed for paydirt, but was caught by the last man.

The Oilers were that close to having a good record. Then Suggs, Hines and Hicks all went down with injuries, and Beathard was hospitalized with appendicitis. With the team desperately needing a win to stay close to New York, QB Bob Davis could not get the job done and the Oilers lost to Miami 24-7 on 8 turnovers.

The defense was playing well, but could not single-handedly win games like it had in 1967. They did shut out the Patriots 16-0 in Boston, where the Oilers had not won since 1961, to set up an important game with the 3-2 Jets in the Astrodome.

With Beathard and Granger out, the defense again rose to the challenge. So did the Jets. At the half, New York had 33 yards and 2 first downs to the Oilers' 29 and none. Namath's first 10 pass attempts fell incomplete. Wally almost bottled some lightning late in the game. Trailing 13-0 in the 4th, Lemm replaced Davis with Trull to the great relief of 51,710 fans. As if according to script, he threw two quick TDs to take a 14-13 lead with 4:10 left. That was too much time for Joe.

Namath slowly and methodically picked his way down the field, using up all the remaining time for a 20-14 Jets' victory. It was another killer in a season of killers.

Trull then took them to wins over Buffalo and Cincinnati, his first wins as a starter. Although the season began with high expectations, 4-5 was not bad, considering the injuries and the fact that 11-of-22 starters were first- or second-year players. Among that bunch was rookie Elvin Bethea, who moved to defense. He started his first game at right DE on November 3 against the Bengals, and would not come out until the 1980s. The Oilers got one more shot at the Jets, but were blown out 26-7 as New York sealed up the Division.

Meanwhile, the AFL was gaining new fans all the time with its exciting brand of ball. Leading the pack were the defending champion Raiders and Jets. In November, these two were involved in the infamous Heidi game.

In that shoot-out, New York took 32-29 lead with 65 seconds left. With Oakland in Jets' territory, NBC cut to a commercial at a time-out. It was 7 p.m. and time to air the previously scheduled children's' movie *Heidi*. After much hand-wringing at NBC studios, *Heidi* began nationwide. On the next play, Lamonica threw a 43-yard TD pass. Would Namath have enough time? For a brief moment, the country was turned on its ear. Fans clogged the phone lines to no avail. The scene was somewhat surreal as NBC flashed updates at the bottom of the screen at the same moment that Heidi's partially paralyzed cousin, Klara, attempted to walk. The typeset continued to scroll past as the Jets fumbled the ensuing kickoff, which the Raiders recovered for the TD and 43-32 victory. In one of the greatest travesties of televised sports, NBC had lost all sense of priority and ruled in favor of the children of America.

The Oilers, of course, could only watch. By November 17, both Beathard and Granger were back and the Oilers played better the rest of the way, winning 3-of-4 to finish at 7-7 and securely in second place. After the lucky 1967 campaign with few injuries, the wheels came off the wagon in 1968. Still, they knew they were not that far away and looked forward to 1969.

THE 1968 PLAYOFFS

The Jets-Raider games were turning into one of the great rivalries in sports. In their second game, the Raider defense broke Namath's jaw. Joe took that shot and went on to become the first QB to ever throw for 4,000 yards.

The 1968 AFL Championship Game was another classic. In an earlier mini-playoff game, the Raiders plastered the Chiefs 41-6 and seemed ready for another trip to the Super Bowl. However, the title game was in New York because of the rotation. It was very cold. Broadway Joe and Lamonica put on a show throwing 96 pass-

The Oilers moved into the Astrodome, Roy Hofheinz's Eighth Wonder of the World, in 1968. Bud Adams called the lease terms Judge Roy wanted the Ninth Wonder. But he did not mind the sellouts, which began immediately.

es between them at a time when most teams did not throw that much. Nationally syndicated sportswriters called it the first important AFL Championship Game (read — the first one in New York). While the Raiders stuck with their plan of intimidation, giving Joe a concussion and dislocated finger, he still took them to a 27-23 victory and shot in the Super Bowl.

Over in the boring NFL, the Baltimore Colts and coach Don Shula lost only one game all year and beat up the Cleveland Browns for the NFL championship. The oddsmakers were not kind, figuring the Jets were the weakest AFL Super Bowl representative yet. The Colts, on the other hand, had an awesome record against supposedly superior competition and an imposing line-up of stars. Their defense was called "the greatest in the history of pro football." The Colts were 17- to 20-point favorites. *Sports Illustrated* writer Tex Maule, who had been a roommate of Oiler-basher Jack Gallagher at Texas, predicted a 41-10 Colts' victory.

SUPER BOWL III — VINDICATION

The Jets had a few things going for them. They were coached by Weeb Ewbank, who had previously coached the Colts to two NFL titles before being ousted for Shula. They also had the unerring confidence of Joe Willie, who "guaranteed" a victory to the national press. Most people laughed and called the game "Joe Namath's first professional football game." His detractors pointed to a high interception ratio and the purportedly bad AFL defenses.

Weeb and Joe had a surprise waiting — they ran. Bob Talamini and the rest of the OL opened up enough holes for Matt Snell to gain 121 yards as New York won 16-7. The vaunted Colts had to slink back to Baltimore as the first NFL team to lose to the Mickey Mouse league.

The win shattered the myth of NFL superiority and let the air out of the Tex Maule's of the world. Joe was tabbed *the* savior of the AFL. That view shortchanged many others, including those players and coaches who were unable to break into the NFL. The AFL opened up the game with the pass. AFL coaches were innovators, from Hank Stram, Sid Gillman and Ewbank down through assistants Chuck Knox, Al Davis, Joe Collier, Bill Walsh, Chuck Noll, John Madden and Walt Michaels. These men understood that wide-open, high-scoring games would keep their league alive.

Theirs were quite a contrast to NFL offenses. In the late 1950s and early '60s, the Giants dominated the NFL. Whatever the Giants did was copied. All teams ran a two-formation offense and a 4-3 defense with man-to-man pass coverage. If you saw one team, you had seen them all. It was copied because it was successful. The Giants' scheme was preserved long after the Giants themselves declined because of former Giants' assistants.

Heading that list was Vince Lombardi, who became coach of the Packers in 1959. His teams picked up where New York left off as the Packers dominated the league for the next 8 years. Lombardi's reign was aided by some good timing, as the NFL had been drained of talent by expansion and competition from the AFL. Nonetheless, the NFL as a whole followed a predictable pattern by mimicking Lombardi's version of Giants football. The idea was simple, run the ball and if you got in trouble, throw it. For NFLers, football was a running game designed to wear down the opponent.

Not so in the AFL. Most of its coaches came from the colleges and were not pre-programmed to follow the NFL model. Many of their schemes were originally ridiculed as odd. That activity stopped with Super Bowl III.

OVERVIEW

Oiler defenders had to grit their teeth watching the Jets run over the Colts in the Super Bowl. New York could not run like that on Houston. Overall, the Oiler defense missed being No. 1 in the AFL by 12 yards. They set a team record for total defense, giving up just 248 yards per game. The pass defense was the AFL's best, giving up just 119 net yards per game, also a team record. In particular, Miller Farr came back to give up only 2 TD passes all season.

Although Granger had only one 100-yard rushing game, he came in fourth in the league with 848 yards. His per carry average dropped from 5.1 to 4.2, but the team had a record 16 rushing TDs. Alvin Reed led all receivers with 46 catches for 746 yards and 5 TDs. His catch total was second best among TEs.

The bugaboo once again was QB. Beathard had 1,559 yards on 105-for-223 passing. He threw for 7 TDs versus 16 interceptions.

Beathard was due some slack because in his first year he practically had to learn the playbook on the run, and in his second, he had the untimely appendicitis attack. Still, many in the organization believed they had a playoff quality team in most other respects. Klosterman was sensitive to the criticism since he drafted Beathard and orchestrated the trade.

Lemm diplomatically said that what hurt them the most was a " lack of fluidity at quarterback." He said the season came down to the first 4 games, "We were in every one of them. A couple of missed field goals, a few bad breaks ..." It was true. The Oilers played the Jets, Raiders, Chiefs and Chargers tough. Then there was the Dolphin game. "The thing that hurt us all season was the Miami loss," Wally said. "We lost Beathard. We turned the ball over 8 times. When you lose early like we did, when you fall behind, it hurts your morale." He also knew that injuries played a major role. Looking forward, Lemm thought the areas for improvement were (1) the mental part of the game, (2) pass rush, and (3) fewer interceptions.

The other AFL coaches liked his team, too, as 7 Oilers were named starters in the all-star game: Hines, Reed, Granger, Farr, Webster, Houston and Parker. The papers called it "giving recognition to Houston Oiler potential." Webster and Farr were both consensus All-Pros on the first combined team, but the two best seasons were arguably had by Prairie View products Ken Houston and Reed. Suggs was team MVP. Other youngsters to come on were Bethea, Regner, and Tom Domres, who replaced Rice. Bethea came in third in rookie-of-the-year balloting. Haik played well early, but had to have knee surgery.

Hoyle Granger breaks through the line against Denver in the Dome (note the turf). Houston won 38-17, but finished a disappointing 7-7 overall. Hoyle was second in the AFL in rushing in 1967, fourth in 1968 and third in 1969.

1969: ON THE BRINK OF GREATNESS

Bud Adams seemed to cool his jets with the increased attendance in the first year of the Astrodome. The average was 41,875, which was an all-time high replacing the previous record of 32,979 set in 1965.

1969 TRAINING CAMP

Wally Lemm said he had "the best talent" he had ever had. Besides the 7 all-star game starters (Hines, Reed, Granger, Farr, Webster, Houston, Parker), he had several others playing well at their positions (Holmes, Suggs, Maples, Hicks, Bishop, Rice, Boyette, Bethea).

He added four more good players in the draft — LB Ron Pritchard (6'1, 235), SMU receiver/KR Jerry LeVias (5'9, 177), Grambling WR Charlie Joiner (5'11, 188) and K Roy Gerela. The good results were partially due to Klosterman squeezing $200,000 out of Bud to improve the scouting department. He and scouting director Charlie Hall set up the best system in team history. Although they passed over Ted Hendricks, Calvin Hill, Carl Garrett, Mercury Morris and Gene Washington, Klosterman nonetheless produced a third straight Hall of Fame quality player. This time it was Joiner.

Added up, it meant Lemm went into camp with 19 solid football players. Klosterman made it 20, picking up Leroy Mitchell from the Patriots (for C. Frazier, Blanks, Carwell, Caveness) to join Miller Farr at CB. That solved one weakness. Combined with safeties Houston and Hicks (replacing Norton), it left them with an all-star secondary. They also had enviable depth in Zeke Moore, Pete Johns and Johnny Peacock ('69, 5th). Norton, the last of the originals, retired before camp. He left with the AFL record for interceptions (45) and would be the first Oiler to have his jersey retired.

Pritchard addressed another weakness as he pressed then replaced Olen Underwood at OLB. They carried 4 DTs, including Parker and Domres. Parker came in late and fat. With a weight limit of 275, he showed up at 327. Once in, he starved himself to get the weight down, trying to live off grapes and vitamins. This, of course, adversely affected his strength. The DEs were Holmes and Bethea. Gary Cutsinger retired.

The OL was the same. WR looked the best it had in years with Haik and Bierne joined by game-breakers Joiner and LeVias. In the preseason, Charley was making Beathard look like a Pro Bowl QB as assistant Fran Polsfoot fought off the defensive coaches to keep him at WR. They also thought Gerela solved the kicking game woes. In 1968, they missed 17-of-29 FGs.

Besides simple inexperience, the major weaknesses were QB and the lack of a breakaway runner. They basically had no HB with Woody Campbell looking at a tour of Southeast Asia. One of the summer projects was attempting to make one out of FB Roy Hopkins.

Of 49 roster players, 29 or nearly 60% had fewer than 3 years' experience, making this team younger than the '67 team. Lemm compared his roster to that of an expansion team. Since they came on board in 1966, he and the Duke had orchestrated a 100% change of personnel with 15 new players in '67, 10 more in '68 and 11 rookies in '69.

Lemm sensed he was sitting on a gold mine. He said, "This group, as a group, is the finest, from the standpoint of guts, potential and as a representative of the city, on and off the field, I've ever had the pleasure to work with." He added, "We feel we have the potential to be a strong contender and possibly champion of the American Football League." All they had to do to win their division was beat the World Champions.

Unfortunately, the '69 team would be hamstrung by hard luck all year. It started in with knee injuries to Johns and Underwood. Then Joiner broke his arm. The worst was losing Leroy Mitchell to a broken neck in a freak injury. That mishap began Zeke Moore's long Oiler career as a starter.

THE 1969 REGULAR SEASON — I COULDN'T WATCH

The season opened with a tall order — the Raiders in Oakland. The Raiders were the defending champions of the Western Division, the toughest division in either league. Houston played well and led 17-14 with 6:25 left due to 3 missed FGs by George Blanda. They lost 21-14 on 2 Beathard interceptions. Rookie Jerry LeVias missed a sure TD in the open that might have been a game winner.

They snapped back to beat Buffalo 17-3, Miami 22-10 (on a team record 5 FGs by Gerela) and Buffalo again 28-14 (sixth straight). Another Dome sellout enjoyed watching the defense hold rookie sensation OJ Simpson to 27 yards. At 3-1, they led the division and the AFL in total defense and pass defense.

Then injuries and inexperience caught up with them. On October 12, they fumbled 8 times in the rain to lose 24-0 at KC as the Chiefs established who had the best defense in the league. It was their first shutout. That game started a bad string that saw the Oilers go 1-2-2 over their next 5, highlighted by a 24-0 loss to the winless Pats. After drumming Miami 32-7 to go to 5-4-2, they blew a good chance to move within striking distance of the 8-3 Jets by losing to the Chargers 21-17. Much like the earlier Raider game, and the Raider and Charger games in 1968, the Oilers led 17-14 with 7 minutes left, only to lose on a Beathard interception.

It took a lot of luster off the upcoming match with the Jets. They played hard and limited Namath to 52 yards passing, but lost 34-26 before 51,923 at home. They beat Boston in the last game 27-23 to finish at 6-6-2 in second place behind the 10-4 Jets.

THE UNFORTUNATE PLAYOFFS

Unfortunately for Houston, the AFL expanded its playoff format in its last year to include the second-place teams. They did it for TV dollars. It meant the injury-decimated Oilers had to play at the Western champion Raiders. It was unfortunate, because it set in motion one of Bud Adams' patented over-reactions that would set the Oilers back almost another decade. The Oilers were 14-point underdogs to the 12-1-1 Raiders. While the Chiefs had the best defense statistically, Oakland's led the league in sacks and was the most intimidating.

December 21, 1969, is one of those dates, like January 3, 1993, that will forever live in Oiler infamy. An inexperienced Oiler follower might see the 10 yards net rushing by Oakland and think good thoughts. A seasoned follower would ask, "How many total yards did they have?" The answer was 412.

It was over early. The Raiders led 28-0 at the end of the first quarter. Lamonica bombed them to death with 6 TD passes. Houston did not score until late in the 4th quarter. Oakland won 56-7. Beathard was 18-of-46. It was the worst defeat in Houston Oiler history.

Blanda said, "Thank god for Mr. Bud Adams! He did me the greatest favor in the world when he released me. It was the best thing that ever happened to me." The Raiders had made the playoffs every year since Blanda joined them.

Blanda's victory party was short-lived, however, as the Chiefs, who upset the Jets 13-6 in the other playoff, upset the Raiders to gain a berth in the Big Dance. It was another heartbreaker for the Raiders. They had been the most dominant team in the AFL for the last 3 years, losing only 4 regular-season games over that period. They led the AFL in sacks each year with their '67 team setting the single season sack record at 67, a mark not broken until the 1985 Bears. Losing each time to the eventual Super Bowl champ, they developed the reputation of choking in the big games.

The NFL representative was the Minnesota Vikings led by tough guy Joe Kapp. The public was still not convinced that the AFL was for real and the Vikings were inserted as 14-point favorites. But the Chiefs won convincingly 23-7 to cast aside any lingering doubts that the New York victory was a fluke. The AFL was on top and not only had the best team, but probably the top three (Raiders, Chiefs, Jets).

Oiler fans who thought all their team really needed was a QB could again point to their friend in the NFL Commissioner's Office. CFL quarterback Kapp agreed to a deal with Don Klosterman back in 1966, but Rozelle later voided it. That deal alone probably would have avoided the storm that was about to blow.

A LONG FLIGHT HOME

It was a long 3-hour plane ride home from Oakland. Star pupil George Webster sat with the head coach and they discussed what went wrong. The team played hard all year, but there was a lack of unity. It was not the same team that came together in Kerrville in 1967. There was some dissension, but the two men could not put their finger on it. One thing for sure, not everyone was giving his best. Lemm would soon address that issue.

One problem was a letdown in an area of strength, the secondary. With Mitchell lost for the year and Johns out for most of it, unproven Zeke Moore had to play corner and was toasted. When safety Hicks was hurt, he was replaced by rookie Peacock who was also toasted. A poor pass rush did not help those players. By the Oakland game, the stage was primed for a big day by Lamonica. Even the usually reliable Farr was overwhelmed. Many passes were completed over him in 1969. In 1967, the defense held opponents to just 14 points per game. That rose to 16 a game in 1968 and 20 in 1969 (279 points). With the offense scoring 278 points, a 6-6-2 mark seems laughably accurate.

While Beathard had his best year as an Oiler going 180-for-370 (48%) for 2,455 yards, he still threw 21 interceptions to just 10 TDs. In 6 years as a pro, Pete never had a completion ratio above 50%. It did not help that Joiner broke his arm early and LeVias, who came in third in rookie of the year balloting, suffered a detached retina. Still, the Oilers placed three WRs (Reed, LeVias, Bierne) in the AFL's top 10 led by Reed's 54 catches. LeVias caught 42 and had 5 TDs. He was even more valuable as a kick returner where he set an all-time AFL record for combined yards.

They passed more because the defense gave up more points and the running game was under stress. With opponents well aware of their poor passing attack, they stacked the line. Granger's numbers dropped to 740 yards and just 3 TDs. They were hurt by poor guard play and no breakaway threat. Roy Gerela was one bright spot with a team record 19 FGs.

SEE THE FUTURE, BE THE FUTURE

On a different part of the airplane home from Oakland sat Don Klosterman. Of all the people involved with the Oilers, he was the one to take something positive out of the humiliating loss. While everyone else was sulking, hiding or searching for excuses, he looked forward. The Duke was gifted with clarity of vision and he liked what he saw.

He set out for any reporter willing to listen how he saw the state of the team. "I still don't think we're that far away from being a very good team. Whenever you have a young football team — and this team is younger than our 1967 team — you have to pay for their mistakes and their inconsistencies," said the Duke. "We have a nucleus of very fine football players. They were soundly defeated on Sunday, but they never quit." Indeed, over half the team made one of the all-star teams, including an all-time team record 10 Pro Bowlers (Hines, Reed, Webster, Bethea, Houston, Farr, LeVias, Moore, Boyette, Bierne). Suggs and Bishop were the other two all-stars.

To put things in perspective, Don reminded everyone that the Chiefs had lost 40-7 to the Raiders in the playoffs in 1968, but won the Super Bowl in 1969. "There's not that much difference in their score and ours," Klosterman argued.

He was right. Many cities with good teams were grumbling about their situations. In Dallas, where years of bad performances had been replaced by an inability to get through the playoffs, people were saying they got rid of the wrong team. In Oakland, they had an even better team, but always lost the big game. Minnesota fans, momentarily delirious, did not yet appreciate just how frustrating it could and would get. Then there were places like Denver, which had not had a winning season in their entire existence.

THE FOUR-YEAR CYCLE

Regardless, it was very tough on fans who found it hard to see progress after losing 56-7. Among the most disgruntled was the team owner. "I couldn't watch," he said, claiming he turned his television off early. Bud said he did not travel with the team because he "had a hunch it would be a bad scene." He navigated with the usual finesse: "Our boys don't want to win badly enough. They're too lethargic ... Some of them are only interested in picking up their pay checks. We can't get rid of all of them because we can't play all rookies. Besides, if you trade nothing, you'd only get nothing in return. Other teams are probably more aware of our players who aren't producing than we are."

He was not finished. "You can't tell me they weren't loafing in the first half. They need somebody to light a fire under them," Bud lamented. "They need a leader. If the talent wasn't there I wouldn't say anything, but the talent is there."

Then he singled out the main villain. "Pete Beathard is the best quarterback we have but I don't think he's the answer," Bud concluded.

The papers ran with the outburst. The *Chronicle's* December 23 sports headline read, "Bud Adams Wants New Oiler Quarterback." The byline below quoted Bud saying, "We'll never win with this type of quarterback."

Houston was in turmoil again over football. Dick Peebles of the *Chronicle* agreed that a lack of leaders led to the team's demise. He pointed to Ladd as the missing leader on defense. The deal to send him for Pete was a Klosterman deal. The comments had the unmistakable smell of an Adams' manipulation.

Peebles was wrong. Recurring leg troubles forced Ernie out of football after the '68 season. Moreover, Klosterman had built a talented team. When the Beathard deal transpired, the team was desperate for a QB — a position not easy to acquire. While giving up the high pick hurt (although the '68 first round was not deep), Beathard did lead them to the Division Title, which would be their last for two more decades. What no one wanted to discuss was that it was not Klosterman who ran Blanda out of town. If George had still been around, they might not have been so desperate at the time of the Beathard deal. Nor was Klosterman responsible for giving away the draft rights to Namath, or

In 1969, the Oiler offense was second in the league in passing and fifth in rushing but just seventh (out of 10) in scoring. Although Pete Beathard had career highs in completions (48.6%) and yards (2,455), he ruined their chances with 21 interceptions to just 10 touchdowns.

The defense played tough again in 1969, surrendering only 3.6 yards per carry. The pass defense was ranked second. However, they continued to give up more points. After leading the league in 1967 at 14.2 points per game, they gave up 17.7 in 1968 and 19.9 in 1969 (fifth). The major culprits were injuries and turnovers by the offense. Here, George Webster (90) and George Rice (72) drop the Pats' Jim Nance for a loss.

not accepting Dayle Lamonica in the trade offer. He had Joe Kapp signed up, but lost him.

John Hollis of the *Post* had followed Adams long enough to sense the big man was about to make one of his infamous reactionary moves. In a December 29 column, he wrote, "Bud has been known to create controversy where none existed. He appears to run in a four-year cycle. Wasn't it four years ago that he (a) hired a cocktail waiter as a kicker; (b) was nailed by Joe Foss for tampering with Ernie Ladd and Earl Faison; and (c) verbally agreed to give Bones Taylor a new contract, then permitted him to be fired weeks later?"

Hollis contrasted Adams with fellow founder Lamar Hunt, who had the patience to leave the football team to the people he hired for the job. "Bud keeps getting his corporate wires crossed and one of them always seems to lead to a panic button," he penned. "One wonders if Bud realizes that since Hunt moved to Kansas City, they have won their division only once. With all *that* talent."

The ruckus resulted in a 4½-hour powwow on December 30 between Adams, Klosterman, Lemm and John Collins, who was Bud's chief bean counter. What came out of that meeting was amusing at best, a disaster at worst. In a one-year period that saw Neil Armstrong walk on the moon, Richard Nixon move into the White House, the women's movement take off, and Charles Manson direct others to murder for him, the Oilers did their part by coming up with the most idiotic team structure in the history of football.

HOW TO SAVE $40,000

At the meeting Lemm learned why Klosterman had acted somewhat distanced from him most of the season. While he had received a 2-year contract extension at the end of 1968, Klosterman had not. His was allowed to expire at the end of 1969.

Even though Klosterman had turned it all around, Adams was unhappy with his use of the expense account. Bud assigned Collins to watch him. John Collins was a non-football man who was the team's administrative VP and assistant to the president. He was an officer in many of Adam's 27 other businesses. He was a 1960s version of Mike McClure. John Breen said, "One day [in 1968] we got a letter ... from Adams authorizing Collins to be boss of everything. It wasn't surprising. Bud needed a buffer. He always had somebody."

In 1968, Klosterman had fought for more autonomy in his contract renegotiations. He wanted his power and responsibility described so he could avoid more clashes with Collins. When Bud refused, the writing was essentially on the wall.

There also had been a more minor rift between Klosterman and Lemm ever since the Beathard trade. Lemm liked Beathard, but thought Ladd and the No. 1 were too high a price. Lemm wanted a final yes or no vote on moves of that magnitude.

In the end, Klosterman was headed to the Colts, with whom he had already received permission to speak. The announcement came on January 6, 1970, although Klosterman began looking for a new job well before the end of the season. The Oilers' half of the announcement was handled calmly. Adams could not be reached for comment, causing someone to say it "had to be a record." History shows that the Colts would soon win the Super Bowl while the Oilers were headed for a different bowl.

For the kicker, the reorganized Oilers would have no GM. This way Bud could save Klosterman's $40,000 salary. Team duties were split among Lemm, Charlie Hall, John Breen and John Collins. Adams called it "bringing sound business practices to football." Collins would have "overall responsibility for the Oilers." Lemm was responsible for the team. Hall was the director of player personnel and would "handle contracts." Breen, who had always wanted to be GM, would stay on as director of public relations and take on the "added responsibility of the preseason schedule." He was also put in charge of the Oilers Speakers' Bureau, which was about as glorious as it sounds. So much for loyalty.

Relying on his unique sense of timing, Adams had season ticket packages mailed out between the Raider loss and the team's determination that it did not need a GM. The packages required season ticket holders to buy tickets to all preseason home games for the first time. Folks did not exactly jump for their checkbooks.

LONG LIVE THE DUKE

In looking at all the bad moves by Bud Adams, getting rid of Klosterman ranks right up there. Even without hindsight, his evaluation was easy.

When he took over the Oilers, the team's image was at its worst. Things were so bad that there was open talk of the team being moved due to fan apathy. He rekindled the old spirit and negotiated the move to the Astrodome. Since that move, the team played before capacity crowds at most games. Klosterman saw support grow to the extent that hordes of fans greeted the team planes in 1967 at the airport after winning the division in Miami and even after the tough loss in Oakland in the AFL championship game.

He revamped the scouting system, and by 1969 it was one of the best in football. He made smart use of Houston weather to bring in prospects for tryouts before the draft. His 3 drafts were the best in history, producing an average of one Hall of Fame quality player per year (Webster, Houston, Bethea, Joiner). That is a great record by any measure. Those responsible for the post-Klosterman Oiler drafts would not come close to matching that record. His drafts also produced the likes of LeVias, Gerela, Regner, Haik, Hopkins, Moore, Pritchard, Domres, Parker, Campbell, Barnes and Bierne. He signed Reed as a free agent while trading for Farr, Mitchell and Ladd.

The whole story was a little too weird. Adams was one of the risk-taking founders of the league. He had made a fortune in a rough and tumble world where the operators are hardly known for austerity. He hired one of the flashiest men in football to save his team. And he does it. In what was supposed to be Bud's main goal, he put cheeks in the chairs. The team was profitable in the Dome even though the '68 and '69 seasons were disappointing.

Assigning a guy with a management degree from the University of Houston who did not know anything about football to look over Klosterman's shoulder was a dubious strategy. It is true that Klosterman freely used his expense account. One of his first fetes upon arriving in Houston was to take all the local media on a get acquainted trip to Las Vegas. He also ran up high advertising expenses with his "New Era" campaign in '66. He played many rounds at Champions Golf Course. But he was the team's ambassador.

With the merger, the business of pro football had become idiot proof. Soon, the owners would be receiving $1.6 million a year from television alone. In such circumstances, rounds of golf and drinks, a few bill boards and even a trip to Vegas were nickel and dime stuff. But Adams did not get the nickname "Bottom Line Bud" for nothing.

Hal Lundgren wrote, "Armed with a refreshing smile, a crisp wit and a winning way," the Duke gave the Oilers a much needed new image. "Don Klosterman enjoyed the company of astronauts rather than crop dusters. He realized that the Oilers only played football 3 hours a week. Between kickoffs, he tried to win as many friends for the team as he could."

THE DECADE IN REVIEW

The 1960s had seen some big changes in sports. Major league franchises reproduced like rabbits. By decade's end, just about every sizable city had a big league team in something.

As of 1969, major league baseball had jumped from 16 teams and an annual draw of 16 million to 24 teams and 27 million. The NHL had doubled in size to 12 teams. Pro basketball had gone from a sideshow to 25 teams in two rival leagues. Pro football led the way. By 1969, the combined league was up to 24 teams.

Television contracts were the key. They multiplied the income of leagues and owners several times over. In an era when the rest of the US economy boomed, athletes finally hopped aboard the train. Rookies were getting signing bonuses several times more than the highest salaries of some of the greatest sportsmen of all-time.

In a couple more years, Pete Rozelle would have the three major networks committed to a combined $142 million contract. The staggering growth prompted Dallas Owner Clint Murchison to describe Rozelle as "the greatest salesman in the history of the world."

Houston joined the big leagues with a football team followed quickly by a baseball team. An NBA team was on the way. Although things looked bleak for football fans after the loss to the Raiders, the decade had not been that unkind.

The Oilers won 2 championships, 4 division titles and appeared in the league championship game 4 times. They made the playoffs 5 of the AFL's 10 years. Maybe it would have looked different to fans had they known that this was as good as it was ever going to get.

CHAPTER 5

THE RETURN OF THE DARK AGES 1970-74

As a new decade began, the team that did not need a general manager would now decide personnel moves by committee, one dominated by an 800-pound bean counter named John Collins who had no experience evaluating football talent at any level. For the point of keeping a record, Collins' co-conspirators on what was supposed to be his side of the team's affairs were Ticket Manager Dan Downs, Finance Manager Wayne Fisher and Business Manager Lewis Magnum. The three with the most power in terms of influencing the football side of things were Collins, Downs and Tom Williams.

This situation signaled the start of the greatest exodus of talent in the history of the NFL as the team quickly returned to the bottom of the NFL food chain. If the talent level on the Oilers was charted on a graph, 1969 would be the high point just before a steep decline.

Over the next three years, multiple management teams would have traded away or simply dumped Glen Ray Hines, Alvin Reed, George Webster, Ken Houston, Miller Farr, Charlie Joiner, Jerry LeVias, Leroy Mitchell, WK Hicks, Bobby Maples, Hoyle Granger, Roy Gerela, Willie Parker and Ron Pritchard. These players represented the heart of Klosterman's "nucleus." The point is worth emphasizing. Among these 14 were two Hall of Famers and two members of the all-time AFL team while each one of the others already was or would soon become an all-star. The lone member of the "nucleus" to remain was Elvin Bethea, and he begged to be traded just about every year for the next 10.

It is one thing to trade away your best players for value, but an entirely different matter to do so and get nothing in return. However, this is what Houston would do in almost every case.

1970: THE DEATH OF WALLY WORLD

Lemm said later that, in light of what was going on with the front office, he would have left with Klosterman if he had not felt they could win the division. Plus, he wanted to stay around for the first interdivisional competition and a chance to beat his old team — the Cardinals.

The team knew it was not in as bad a shape as the score from Oakland indicated. The Raiders were not 49 points better. Even Blanda admitted they played "over their heads," although he smiled when he said it.

The Oilers were actually on the verge of being a good team. With improvement at a few positions, they could win the first AFC Central title. They obviously had to have a QB. Also needed were a speedy RB, OG, MLB and pass rusher. Overall, they needed depth on both lines. Most of all, this team needed experience.

On January 21, Lemm announced he had acquired his old QB from St. Louis, Charles Johnson. Wally hoped (a) they would be able to get the ball to the WRs ("We haven't been able to throw the ball to the outside since George Blanda"); and (b) Johnson would provide leadership. The 10-year vet was definitely bright enough, having already earned his Ph.D. in chemistry. But he was also injury-prone. DB Bob Atkins came with him. The Oilers gave up Pete Beathard and Miller Farr. Before the draft, they let go of another scapegoat from the Oakland game, sending WK Hicks to New York for a draft pick.

1970 TRAINING CAMP

As usual, Wally was optimistic. They seemed to address their other needs with offensive guards Doug Wilkerson (1st round) and Ron Saul (5th), DTs Leo Brooks (2nd) and Ed Duley (5th), DB Benny Johnson (6th) and RBs Bill Dusenberry (2nd) and Joe Dawkins (10th). He would also have Woody Campbell back from Uncle Sam and Jerry Rhome at backup QB.

Then life threw Wally a curve. In June, the NFL Players Association voted to strike. It hurt.

Lemm was the type who put everything into his job. He was a motivator. He was prepared. Tough guy Walt Suggs once said, "If Wally says the moon is made of green cheese, then believe it because he has already checked it out. He is a very thorough man." He was protective of his players, careful not to criticize individuals in public.

Consequently, he considered himself a "players' coach." Wally was confident *his* men would come in when the time came. Several veterans told him that strike or no strike, they would report on time. When the time came and passed with no veterans in sight, he was crushed. He took it personally. When they did show in August, their relationship with their head coach had been forever altered. They were at odds. Neither side could understand the other.

The problems began to compound. When Willie Parker shuffled in overweight and late again, Lemm cut him. Fellow DT George Rice retired after offseason knee surgery, while rookie Leo Brooks never recovered from his. Joiner broke his arm again — the same one he broke in '69. John Douglas, who had been acquired from New Orleans to take over one of the vacant CB positions, had back surgery.

Lemm's plan to slowly groom Wilkerson to replace Sonny Bishop fell apart when Bishop retired. Even though the scouts said Wilkerson was "a better athlete than Bethea," the coaches were afraid to start him on offense. While the line had OTs Suggs (9th year) and Hines (5th), and center Maples (6th), OG would be a problem all season.

The other second-round pick, RB Dusenberry, was cut in camp, although he did inspire one of the all-time great Oiler quotes. When originally defending the selection, Tom Williams said, "He's like Gayle Sayers only faster."

The highlight of the preseason was beating Dallas for the first time 37-21 on three LeVias TDs. Cowboys Owner Clint Murchison was so angry he refused to attend the postgame ceremonies for presentation of the "Governor's Cup." He left it to a red-faced Tex Schramm, who said, "I don't know whether or not we're going to be able to continue this series." Everyone's hopes rose for the regular season except Lemm's.

Wally was so disgusted he decided to quit. He turned in his resignation in August to be effective at the end of the season, but did not tell the players. "The game belongs to the players and owners now," he said. "The head coach is just a title with a whistle around its neck." Years later, he added, "The player strike outweighed everything. It changed my whole outlook ... there's a place for an association but not a union. And no place for strikes. They can bargain completely through contracts. An association could get the other benefits."

THE 1970 REGULAR SEASON — ODE TO ASTROTURF KNEE

The Oilers started out a respectable 2-2, including a 19-7 win over Pittsburgh and a 4-point loss to the eventual Super Bowl champion Colts. But any shot at a winning season ended in the second Steelers game. Besides losing 7-3, they lost Dr. Johnson to a broken collarbone when he tried to make a tackle after an interception.

In addition to Jerry Rhome finally taking over at QB, new faces appeared everywhere to replace the injured Oilers. Regner, Granger, Boyette and Campbell all went down early. Hopkins, Haik and LeVias followed them. Suggs played in terrible back pain. In early November, the Oilers lost Webster to another knee injury and lost to the Cards 44-0. At that point, Lemm told them of his resignation.

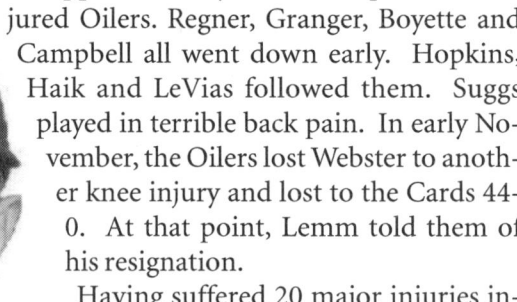

Having suffered 20 major injuries including nine knee injuries, the broken collarbone and a separated shoulder, the Oilers had the unpleasant task of facing the Cowboys in the final game led by a lame-armed Rhome. It was not pretty. Tom Landry showed no mercy as Dallas whipped them 52-10 amid laughter in the Cotton Bowl. They lost seven of

Don Klosterman's staff signed TE Alvin Reed as an undrafted free agent out of Prairie View in 1967. Soft hands helped place him among the top 10 AFL receivers in 1968, and the top 5 in 1969 and 1970.

"Elvin's a stud," is what Lemm said after a few practices in 1968. No kidding. The third-round pick out of North Carolina A&T would be the team's top defensive performer for the next decade.

eight to finish 3-10-1. Lemm said, "A long time ago, I thought coaching football would be a lot of fun. I found out the hard way this is not true." He gave no speech after the game, dressed in private, and departed.

The misery in Houston was compounded by events in Oakland. With Raider QB Daryle Lamonica regularly injured and backup Ken Stabler away for the year, 42-year-old Oiler cast-off George Blanda was busy enjoying his third life in professional football. Nine years older than his coach, he came off the bench to lead the then 2-2-1 Raiders to five miraculous wins in a row, becoming an idol to the so-called *Geritol Generation* in the process. The whole country cheered George. There were television appearances, magazine articles and a book. George said he did not understand why it took so long for him to be discovered. He would be named AFC player of the year and AP male athlete of the year as fathers all over Houston had to try and explain to their sons why the Oilers released him.

The Colts, Don Klosterman and line coach Lou Rymkus won the first AFC Championship Game 27-17 and went to the Super Bowl against Dallas. It was supposed to be a game for traditionalists matching two old-NFL teams. But they had nothing to be proud of as the game included eight fumbles, three interceptions, 14 penalties, a missed FG and a blocked extra point to earn the nickname "The Blunder Bowl." Dallas lost 16-13.

OVERVIEW

There were not many Oiler highlights. Despite the broken collarbone, Johnson led the team with 1,652 yards, 7 TDs and 12 picks. Charley had it rough with Houston, suffering through five operations in his two years. LeVias added 41 catches and 5 TDs while Reed tied for second in the AFC with 47 for 604 yards. Rookie FB Joe Dawkins (10th round) led the team with 517 yards rushing and 2 TDs. Gerela hit 18 field goals.

The offense averaged only 15 points a game, while the defense surrendered 25 (second worst in the league). It all added up to the worst record in team history.

The uncanny string of serious injuries played a major role. Bobby Brown was one of the few pointing to AstroTurf as a cause, but not many were listening. No doubt Lemm's brooding also contributed to the bad record.

Even though things did not look so good, the Oilers still had a lot of good players. Steeler DT Mean Joe Greene said some years later, "When we played Houston for the first time in 1970, I thought they had the best team in our division."

Lemm later said that potential at least made him consider staying. But, in light of the front office and remaining bitterness over the strike, he followed through with the resignation. In his second term with Houston, he oversaw a great transformation. The one overriding deficiency he could not overcome was a succession of has-been or never-were QBs. Without that, he might have won another championship. He left football to become a successful homebuilder in the Houston area. His record from 1966-70 was 28-40-4 (38-40-4 overall). Just one other would top Lemm's five-plus years as Houston coach.

1971: HUGHES HE?

Focus again shifted to a new head coach. Some wondered if Adams would try to run the team without a head coach to save that salary, aka head coaching by committee, another Oiler first. Bud said he did not think it "important to have a coach by draft day."

The papers said the leading candidates were Schlinkman, Polsfoot and Dry. One prospect said, "I don't think I did very well. I did not give very intelligent answers. Then again, I wasn't asked very intelligent questions."

WELCOME ED HUGHES

On January 21, 1971, Adams showed up for his now customary new coach's day sporting some hip clothes and a new pair of long side burns. He named Ed Hughes as the Houston Oilers' seventh head coach going into their twelfth season. Ed arrived for the press conference by helicopter. The first question was, "Who's he?" People are still wondering.

Hughes had been a San Francisco assistant for 11 years, a job his brother-in-law, head coach Dick Nolan, gave him. The 49ers were a playoff team in 1970. Adams was not worried, though, because the trusted John Collins handpicked Ed, saying, "We selected Hughes only after what was probably the most thorough, exhaustive search ever conducted in the history of football." He got a five-year contract.

Schlinkman (RBs) and Polsfoot (WRs) were retained. Dry left for Tulsa University. Collins dismissed McFadin, Childress and Davore. Ernie Zwahlen was hired for the OL, Burnie Miller for the DBs, George Dickson for LBs-special teams and Walt Yowarsky for the DL. Of that group, the one who asserted the most influence was Zwahlen. Many felt he ran the team under Hughes.

RELEASE THE HOUNDS

In the interim, the Oilers were completely rudderless without a coach or GM. That did not keep one-time production clerk John Collins from acting. Five days after the season, he traded 1970 No. 1 Doug Wilkerson to San Diego for former Oiler TE Willie Frazier.

Wilkerson came from a small college and was unprepared. He was talented, but had not been properly coached. The Oilers put him on defense ostensibly to give him some game experience. The Houston papers picked up on an assistant coach's comment that he could only dive block and constantly repeated the line. Another bad rap was that he was too dumb to play offense. Lemm said he opposed the trade. Collins apparently relied upon the newspaper columnists instead. In San Diego, Wilkerson was immediately put on offense and earned a starting spot. He would eventually play his way into the Pro Bowl at OG, indicating that maybe it was not Doug who was the dumb one.

That trade was just the beginning. On January 25, Collins traded the team's all-time rushing leader, Hoyle Granger, and a No. 2 pick to New Orleans for Ken Burrough (who dropped the "s" at the end of his name after college) and DT Dave Rowe (6'7, 280). Granger was one of many who hurt his knees during 1970, playing in only five games. The Oilers felt the play of Joe Dawkins made him expendable.

Just as things were heating up, Bud got cold feet. After letting his team run without a GM for over a year, he surprised everyone by naming one. On February 14, he hired Bob Brodhead. On April 2, Brodhead quit.

According to Brodhead, he flew to his first NFL meeting with Adams and Collins in Miami. The trio went to the first meeting together only to learn that each team was allowed only two representatives. The new GM was left sitting in the hallway. That was all he needed to know. Brodhead was so desperate to get away that he moved to Cleveland, the "jewel of the rustbelt," and joined Art Modell.

A month later, Bud finally rewarded John Breen, naming him Oiler GM. It had been a long journey. His second rise started with the promotion of Collins, which concurrently began the decline first of Klosterman and then of Lemm. Once Collins hired Hughes, Breen lobbied all out for the position.

Collins was not thrilled, though, and ordered that there be no press conference to make the formal announcement. Breen later said that the power structure was the same and he had no real authority. Adams ap-

Bud Adams named Ed Hughes as his new coach on January 21, 1971. But note the expression on Ed's face. This photo is from another press conference held later that year. See below to learn what was behind that look.

parently just grew tired of being laughed at for not having a GM and wanted a live body in the position.

To show he was not growing sentimental, Bud fired long-time trainer Bobby Brown over a purported "conflict of interest." The conflict was that Brown allowed his name to be used in association with a health club. Bobby had become something of an institution in Houston. Blanda called it the "1,372nd dumbest thing Bud Adams ever did."

THE 1971 DRAFT

The team went into the draft about as disorganized as it is possible to be. They had the No. 3 pick and 16 choices overall.

They went with QB Dan Pastorini of Santa Clara. Dan had a cannon for an arm and impressed everyone in a college all-star game. He was the third QB taken following Jim Plunkett and Archie Manning. The Oilers did not have a second, missing a shot at Jack Ham, Dan Dierdorf and Phil Villapiano. In the third, perhaps not trusting themselves, they drafted another QB, Lynn Dickey of Kansas. They said he was too good to pass up. That choice could have been Lyle Alzado, Dave Elmendorf or QB Ken Anderson.

The Oilers also selected OG Larron Jackson (4th round), CB Willie Alexander (6th) and LB Floyd Rice (9th), passing on Harold Carmichael, Ernie Holmes, Bob Chandler and Randy Vataha.

1971 TRAINING CAMP

The exodus continued through camp. The change on the OL was dramatic. Zwahlen wanted his "own men." Having already traded Wilkerson, they sent OT Glen Ray Hines and two second-rounders ('72 and '73) to New Orleans for DT Mike Tilleman. Hines was an all-star, but in Zwahlen's opinion "lacked the necessary agility." He was, however, by far the quickest Houston lineman off the ball.

Then, 28-year-old center Bobby Maples was released outright. Pittsburgh immediately picked him up for the $100 waiver fee. Bobby played eight more years, including a Super Bowl season in 1978 with Denver. Zwahlen also attempted to unload Tom Regner, but Adams had seen enough and prevented it.

DT Tilleman temporarily joined fellow former Saint Dave Rowe on the DL. They were starters, but for a bad team. The extroverted Rowe, who made the Pro Bowl in '68, was a pass rusher. After the Oilers beat the Bears in the preseason, he proclaimed, "This is the greatest team I've ever seen. We can do it all." That sort of infectious enthusiasm was just what the doctor ordered for a team with a morale problem.

Naturally, he was sent packing. The deal came only after someone realized that, after Maples, they did not have another center. Rowe was the price for New England center Tom Funchess. The Patriots were one of the few teams worse than the Oilers. Rowe wondered what he did wrong after getting ratcheted down from the Saints to the Oilers to the Pats.

The OL purge also cost them Jerry LeVias who was sent to San Diego for OT Gene Ferguson and Ron Billingsley. LeVias was the most exciting player in team history. He was their only game breaker and accounted for a third of the offense. He led them in TD passes the last two years and was very popular. This one was on

New QBs Dan Pastorini and Lynn Dickey generated the most fan interest in 1971.

Breen. He said the "performance of Joiner sealed the deal." Jerry vowed, "They are going to regret it."

Jerry "He's No Joe" Rhome was cut, and then, in another classic boneheaded move, so was Roy Gerela, the most accurate field goal kicker in the history of the team. Hughes claimed he "wasn't emotional enough." Like Maples, the Steelers picked him up for $100. In Pittsburgh, he developed a loyal following known as Gerela's Gorillas and went to three Super Bowls. He played another nine seasons.

LB Olen Underwood was traded for OG Bob Young, who was so excited about joining Houston he disappeared. Starters Peacock and Mitchell were dumped.

Hughes and Collins also went through an amazing series of draft picks for busts. Dave Olerich cost them a fourth-round choice, Cleo Johnson a fifth-, Gordie Sellars a seventh and Worthy McClure a fifteenth. They cut them all before the opener. The acquisition of Span Musgrove caused Lundgren to write, "Contrary to rumor, Span Musgrove is not a rain forest near Madrid. He's a Houston Oiler." Not for long. He, too, was cut. So was LB Ken Mendenhall, who was soon starting for the Super Bowl champion Colts.

The young QBs generated much attention. When Dan Pastorini first came to Houston, he met the WRs for some pitch and catch. The receivers ran sideline patterns where they habitually looked down to make a little stutter-step before going out of bounds. Apparently they had not heard about his arm. One of his first tosses hit a receiver square in the face mask as he came up from his juke move. He buckled at the knees as his eyes filled with tears. Dan did not have any more trouble getting their attention.

But QBs were to be endangered species behind Zwahlen's new OL where every position had a new face. Willie Frazier was the TE (for Reed who was called into the reserves). The new RT was Gene Ferguson (for Suggs) and the new LT was Sam Walton (for Hines). Bob Young went in at LG for Regner who replaced Drungo at RG. Suggs was the center, but would soon be hurt and replaced by Jerry Sturm. Tom Funchess, who cost them Rowe, could not crack the starting lineup.

The season opening QB was Charley Johnson, but they would go through most of the season with no true No. 1. Campbell started at HB and Dawkins at FB. Roy Hopkins hurt a knee. Ditto for Mac Haik.

The DL had Tilleman and Billingsley at DT with Holmes and Bethea at DE. The OLBs were Webster and Pritchard with Boyette in the middle. The Houston defensive backfield was now down to one legitimate star in Kenny Houston, plus Zeke Moore, John Charles and rookie Willie Alexander. Bob Atkins was the backup at all four positions. Farr, Mitchell, Hicks, Carwell and Jaquess were all starting for different teams.

The Oilers lost the annual Cowboys exhibition again, but the game did have its moment when the large scoreboard lit up with: "Welcome Dallas Mayor Wes Wise." A lusty booing filled the Dome for minutes.

Hughes gave conflicting accounts of his team. On the one hand, he said winning was not his "immediate goal." On the other, he predicted they would win the division.

He had a fan in Hal Lundgren. After the Rowe trade, Hal wrote, "Coach Hughes has the audacity to make trades such as this one ... he has to be admired for it. When they feel a trade will improve the club, they make it ... Dave Rowe got in the way of improvement." About Maples, he wrote, "Again, Hughes' conviction has to be admired." Rowe and Maples would both play through the 1978 season.

Lundgren's season forecast was just as suspect. He predicted the division: "With the regular season now nine days away, the house is in good order. One reason is that Mr. Hughes is making the decisions." With Lundgren's daily drum beating and deliriously upbeat columns seemingly supported by the 4-3 preseason record, Oiler fans were sucked in again. Good crowds showed for the games, at least the early ones.

ONE PIECE OF UNFINISHED BUSINESS

Bud had a little housecleaning of his own to complete a few days before the season. After overseeing the biggest transformation in the history of the Oilers where some 25 players off the 1970 team were disposed of, John Collins left in September. Talk about the head rat jumping ship. Fully half of the 1971 team was new. Gone were LeVias, Wilkerson, Granger, Maples, Hines, Mitchell and Gerela, who joined the 1970 list of Farr, Parker, Hicks and Beathard. Also missing were second-, fourth- and fifth-round picks in 1972 and a second and third in 1973. After all those moves, the team was much worse.

Shockingly, what happened between Adams and Collins had nothing to do with the destruction of the team. Collins was in charge of Bud's $7 million investment in a sports/nutrition drink called Quick Kick. Had that venture been more successful, Collins might still be playing fantasy league football with the Oilers.

THE 1971 REGULAR SEASON — FUTILITY IS US

If a season can be summed up in a single play, the first play of the 1971 regular season would be that play. In Cleveland, Charley Johnson took the first snap and fell down — unassisted. The Oilers could not block, tackle or run and lost 31-0. To make matters worse, George Webster re-injured his knee. Even old reliable Walt Suggs, who had not missed a game in nine seasons, succumbed to torn knee ligaments.

The Chiefs were next before a SRO Astrodome crowd of 46,498. They booed Johnson. Pastorini almost brought them back in the second half, but fell short 20-16. Many were excited by the Oilers' play in spite of the loss. For example, Jim Beirne said, "We came of age today." He was a little premature.

Going into the third week, Hughes still had not found a replacement for the "unemotional" Gerela. He finally settled on Mark Moseley. In Dickey's first start, they tied the Saints 13-13 but Houston was atrocious.

Next, they lost to the Redskins even though the Washington offense did not score a TD. Houston's offense failed to convert 15 consecutive third downs. Washington won on 5 FGs and run back of a ball Charley Johnson was throwing away after his WR fell down. The stinky RFK Stadium dressing rooms made for a fitting commentary on Oiler fortunes as an aching Johnson sat dejectedly in a pool of runoff.

Hall of Fame WR Charlie Joiner spent most of his career with the Oilers either hurt or stretching out for poorly thrown passes. His best season out of four was 1971 when he caught 31 for 681 yards (22-yard average) and 7 TDs.

In mid-October, Pastorini wrecked his car on the way to his first start. Later, he nearly cut his finger off making a sandwich. Against Detroit, Houston recovered the fumbled opening kick deep in Lion territory. They went backwards. Then Moseley missed the kick. Houston lost 31-7. That made it 50 straight games without beating a team with a winning record. Dick Peebles wrote, "With the Oilers, it seems the game is over from the time they trot onto the playing field."

The offense was one of the most disorganized in the history of the game, and it took down the defense. Coach Zwahlen's men were not working out. The QBs were getting killed. They had no running game. The only backs left standing were Robert Holmes and Dickie Post. On the rare occurrence that the offense did make a good play, it was called back by a penalty.

Peebles wrote: "Never in their history have they been the disorganized outfit they are this season." Even Lundgren turned on them, saying "[they] don't play hard."

Then things really got weird. After being blown out in Oakland to fall to 1-7-1, Adams hung around and read the *Tribune's* account of the game the next morning. It drew an ugly picture of the Oilers' OL. Based on that article, he called Breen, who was already on poor terms with Hughes, and made him fire Zwahlen. Hughes, who had no previous line coaching experience, took over those duties. "I felt Zwahlen had control of the team, and that Ed was only the head coach in title," explained Adams. "I think if we had our offensive line that we had last year, to go with our defensive team we have this year, we'd have a helluva ball team...But, that line of ours couldn't block Westbury High out there on a running play." The Oilers were one of only three teams to average under 100 yards rushing per game.

So inspired, the troops went out and lost to Cincinnati 28-13 as Boyette was benched for poor play. They led Cleveland at the half the next week 17-13, only to lose 37-24.

Just when all seemed lost, they rose to pound the Steelers 29-3 and knock them out of the playoffs. They followed that with a 20-14 win over Buffalo and then closed the season by mashing San Diego 49-33. The last game included a remarkable performance by Ken Houston who returned interceptions for TDs on consecutive John Hadl passes. It is difficult to imagine that record ever being broken.

OVERVIEW

The Oilers finished 4-9-1 and in third place. In spite of losing Webster, the defense was ranked sixth. Bethea and Houston made the Pro Bowl. Ken Houston set an all-time record with 4 interceptions returned for TDs in one season. He had 9 interceptions total.

The offense was an unmitigated disaster. Pastorini led the trio in passing with 1,702 yards, going 127-of-270 (47%). It was the first of nine seasons in a row Dan would lead the team in passing. The rookie had only 7 TDs to 21 interceptions. That was the worst ratio in club history although many were the result of him being hit. In one game, he was sacked 15 times.

Photographing the mauling of Oiler QBs became a profession within a profession. The favorite shot appeared to be Dan landing on his neck with his feet in the air. He and Dickey were lucky to have lived through those first few years.

Robert "Tank" Holmes led the team in rushing with a hilariously low 323 yards. That would be the lowest total for any team rushing leader ever.

1972: AS BAD AS IT GETS

Over the years, Houston fans' expectations had diminished from another championship team to a winner to simply a competitive team to finally just a team that was not a complete embarrassment on and off the field. When the Oilers' performance was combined with that of the Astros and the newest member of the Houston's pro sports losers club, the Rockets, it was enough to give any city a complex.

Texas being a "football state," the decline of the Oilers hurt most. The ascendancy of the Cowboys, whose games were a weekly anchor in Houston on CBS, did not help. They made the Super Bowl again in 1971, and this time they won. Texas' largest cities were competitive by nature. By any other form of comparison, whether size, national stature, museums, business climates, symphonies, schools, even number of trees, Houston had the edge — all except one and that one mattered.

NO PLACE BUT HOUSTON

While the Cowboys were battling through the playoffs, the Oilers were busy discombobulating. What transpired this time was almost beyond belief.

Bud Adams, who personally fired an assistant coach during the season, said, "I'm not a know-it-all but I have some idea about what needs to be done." He criticized Holmes and Boyette ("weren't championship athletes"), Reed ("we'll also need a top tight end unless Reed decides he wants to block someone") and Burrough ("did nothing for 13 games"). He opined that Drungo would be better at OT than OG, that Haik should be tried at FS and that RB Dickie Post be tried at WR. Adams also

The Oilers' top offensive threat in the early 1970s was the Pastorini punt. He averaged 40.6 yards on 75 punts in 1971.

wanted to "get some of those $100 players," in reference to Gerela and Maples.

Hughes was a fair match. Without Breen or Bud's knowledge, he fired defensive coach Walt Yowarsky at midseason, then asked him to stay until the end of the season. He complained that he was promised a "compatible" GM but did not get one. He even blamed the players for "fooling" him into believing he had a good team.

Near the end of the season, he fired Walt Schlinkman and popular equipment man Johnny Gonzales. No longer speaking to John Breen at the time, he informed the GM of the moves by leaving a note in his chair.

Schlinkman replied, "Ed Hughes told me he was relieving me of my duties ... because I have not made a contribution to the offensive game plan this year. I am pleased that Coach Hughes made this statement because I want the public and fans to know that I am not responsible for the Oilers' offensive game plans nor offensive performance this year."

Rumors swirled. Jimmy the Greek made Sid Gillman a 7-5 choice to take over, to which Breen replied, "No chance." Many of the players supported Hughes.

From out of this fog, Breen began looking for a new coach while Hughes dangled. He did not look far. Whether lazy or parochial, he literally looked down the street.

Bill Peterson came to Rice from Florida State where he gained the reputation of an offensive innovator. Actually what Peterson did was bring a pro style offense to college. Because the schoolboys were not used to seeing it, Pete was able to compete with the big dogs with lesser athletes. His first year at Rice, he went 3-7-1. Why this impressed Breen so much is a mystery. His nosing around got the Rice alumni stirred up.

Pete agreed to a deal so long as Hughes left. Not until this point did Bud sit down to evaluate Hughes' season. Only Adams could have decided to keep him after all of this, but he did, on the condition that he rehire Gonzales and fire the trainer.

The trainer was long-time Zwahlen friend Warren Ariail. Somehow, Ariail managed to create a rift on the team that lasted all season. Its cause depended on who you asked, but it helps to keep in mind that this was a different time. Drugs were new, mostly unregulated, and readily available. Bowls of pills could be found sitting openly in many NFL dressing rooms. In Houston, Breen said he "confiscated" over "$9,000 in "pills and dope" from the training room."

In any event, Hughes agreed to Bud's ultimatum, and the Oilers called a press conference. Bud told Pete the news and gave the Broncos permission to speak with him. This really angered the Rice people, who had Pete under contract for four more years. Nonetheless, Pete struck a deal with Denver to become their head coach and GM. A Bronco official was quickly on a plane to Houston, contract in hand.

However, on the day of the scheduled press conference, Hughes had a change of heart and surprised Adams by refusing to fire Ariail.

Bud immediately said he was going to hold Pete to the conditional contract. The Denver official was turned around at the airport and sent home. The news conference originally called to announce Hughes' retention instead became the vehicle to name his successor — and it was done while Hughes was still there. The event was a circus. Rice and the Broncos threatened to sue.

Only in Oilerville could it come to pass that a head coach, popular with many players, was chased off after one season over a dispute regarding an equipment man and trainer. In any event, with Ed Hughes still under contract, the Oilers named Bill Peterson their eighth new coach on December 30, 1971.

The question of whether he was fired or quit, which had a bearing on the four years left on his contract, would go to Pete Rozelle for resolution.

Breen claimed he was never sold on Mr. Ed Hughes. He said, "Hughes applied for every head coaching job that came open. He was a good man and a fine football man but no head coach."

Pastorini said Hughes got a "rotten deal." He claimed the Oilers would "never win the championship so long as Bud Adams was the owner. He fired Ed Hughes without ever really giving him a chance . . . It's going to be the same damned confused thing next year. It just makes me sick."

BY WAY OF CONTRAST

Pastorini was one of the few to openly say the emperor had no clothes. In just one year with Bud, he recognized that Adams refused to hire real football people to run the team, or in the rare instance when he did, he would not leave them alone to do so.

The story of the Miami Dolphins presented a striking contrast. After their first four years, the Fish had won only 15 games and did not draw well. Some of the owners dropped out, but Joe Robbie stayed the course. Once he had solidified control, he fired the coach and asked the NFL Colts permission to speak to their coach, Don Shula. While Colts' owner Carol Rosenbloom was away on his honeymoon, Shula surprisingly accepted Miami's offer. Upon his return, an angry Rosenbloom appealed to Rozelle and eventually received the Dolphins' No. 1 pick in 1972. But Robbie got his man. Then he let him do the job.

Shula recognized that despite their record, the team had a nucleus of good players in Bob Griese, Larry Czonka and a slow WR from Houston named Howard Twilley. Instead of remaking the team in his image, he went with what they had and addressed specific areas of need. For example, he traded another No. 1 for speedy WR Paul Warfield. With an owner who was not competing for headlines or micromanaging his expense account, Shula went 10-4 that first year and would be in the Super Bowl the next.

WELCOME BILL PETERSON

At the press conference, Adams announced that he was "tired of looking for coaches, that's why we signed him to a lifetime contract." Breen estimated that in Budtime, that meant "about three years." According to Giles Tippette in *From Cannon to Campbell*, the contract was for five years at $75,000 a year plus bonuses.

Without a doubt, the best thing about Bill Peterson as a coach was that he was funny. At the press conference, he said he was "looking forward to the draft. I've known Jess Thomas and Tom Brown for years." The references were to Oiler Scouting Director Jess Thompson and Player Personnel Director Tom Williams. He also pronounced Breen as "Breem" and Billingsley as "Billingee" or "Billinger."

At Florida State, he passed a player in the hallway and said, "Everything okay, son?" To which the kid replied, "Yeah, coach." "Are we gonna work everything out?" asked Pete. To which the kid replied, "Yes, sir." "So, you gonna sign with us?" inquired the coach. "I already play for you," said the kid, who had been on the team two years.

Another instance had Pete leading the FSU players in the Lord's Prayer before a big game. He had the players drop to a knee, bow their heads and close their eyes. Then he began, "Now I lay me down to sleep ..." Upon hearing a few snickers, he said, "Cut that out, I'll be damned if I am going to have any atheists on my team!" When someone finally told him it was not the Lord's Prayer, he paused, and then replied, "It's not? Well, why didn't someone tell me? I can't do everything around here."

He once told the Oilers before the national anthem to "Stand on your helmets and put the sideline under your arms."

Hal Lundgren of the *Post* happily wrote that the Oilers had acquired "one of offensive football's most fertile minds."

1972 TRAINING CAMP

Coach Peterson hired assistants King Hill, Dan Henning, Jackie Simpson and Don Breaux. Joe Madro drew perhaps the toughest duty with the OL. One constant in camp was Bud Adams. He made many appearances and spoke frequently with Peterson.

One of Pete's first acts was to institute a "grooming code." This did not sit well with the children of the '60s. His rah-rah college attitude offended others. In general, college coaches were viewed as inferior and not allowed to make the jump. That the Oilers were pioneers in this regard (or any) made fans very nervous.

The changes continued. The biggest trade was Charley Johnson and OG Larron Jackson to Denver (where they joined Leroy Mitchell, Bobby Maples and Tom Domres). They acquired former Chiefs No. 1 Scott Lewis for a second-round pick, but he was damaged goods. They traded tackle Gene Ferguson for 4 draft picks, but Rozelle voided the deal.

Mac Haik quit and would go on to become a successful businessman in Houston. A bad knee forced Walt Suggs to retire after 10 seasons. The strong man was an all-star from 1967-69. Willie Frazier, Woody Campbell and Mark Moseley were also gone. Moseley kicked for another 15 years, making the Pro Bowl several times.

Bill Peterson

Skip Butler was the new PK and backup punter. They added Hoyle Granger, cut from the dreadful Saints. They did that because Pete cut Andy Hopkins, saying he was "too fast for my offensive line." Hopkins went to the CFL and led his division in rushing. He also waived starting OG Bob Young, who made the Pro Bowl three times after he left.

The draft generated little reason for optimism. The Oilers had already traded (or given) away three of their top five selections. The only pick of note was first rounder Stanford DE/OT Greg Sampson (6'6, 243)(passing on Franco Harris and Willie Buchanon). The team felt replacing Pat Holmes was a priority.

The Oilers had a preseason record of 2-3-1, losing to the Cowboys again (26-24). The most memorable game came on August 24 against St. Louis when Lynn Dickey suffered a severe hip dislocation. As he lay motionless on the turf of a silent Astrodome, Oiler physician Dr. Gray Freeman made the diagnosis and decision to put the hip back in place on the field. He is credited with keeping Dickey from becoming an invalid. To his credit, Adams paid the expenses to fly him to Boston for surgery and treatment. Although Dickey's playing career was thought to be in jeopardy, he would be back a year later.

The lineup was similar. Former college LB Kenny Houston was still prowling the defensive backfield where he was joined by John Charles, Zeke More, Willie Alexander and Benny "Jabbo" Johnson ('70, 6th round). The LBs were Webster, Boyette and Pritchard, although they experimented with Pritchard in the middle and second-year player Floyd Rice on the outside. The DEs were Bethea and Holmes, who were backed up by the rookie Sampson. The DTs were Billingsley and Tilleman.

Without Johnson or Dickey, Pastorini was the man on offense. His backups were a colorful cast of no-names. The uninspiring RBs were the recycled Granger plus Tank Holmes, Al Johnson and rookie Willie Rodgers (12th round). WR had Joiner, Burrough, Beirne and rookie Rhett Dawson (10th). Reed was the only TE. For the third straight year, they had a 100% changeover on the line with Calvin Hunt or rookie Guy Murdock (16th) at center; Saul, Regner or rookie Solomon Freelon (3rd) at OG; and Ferguson, Levert Carr or Funchess at OT. Drungo was lost to preseason surgery. Weakness at OG and center kept the QBs dancing. It came as no comfort that Bobby Maples (center), Doug Wilkerson (OG) and Larron Jackson (OG) were all starting elsewhere.

Hal Lundgren was back spinning opening day tales: "Peterson put together a stronger football team than Houston had one year ago. He has done it by being open-minded, but not letting his imagination go berserk." Not even Hal predicted a division title. Dick Peebles wrote, "They definitely look like a better ball club than last year. For one thing, they look like they know what they're doing out there."

THE 1972 REGULAR SEASON —
STILL NUMBER ONE WITH FANS

The Oilers opened against a Denver team full of ex-Oilers that was still looking for its first winning season. That combination must have made smashing the Oilers 30-17 quite fun. Next, they lost to Miami 34-13. It was a familiar story line: no running game, no blocking and a QB with no time to throw. After holding up well in 1971, the defense caved in.

About the only interesting issue was whether they would be the first winless team since the 1960 Cowboys. Fans complained that the expansion teams, filled with the bottom of other teams' rosters, were not this bad. The Dolphins and Bengals both went 3-11 in their first seasons. Houston's 1970 record was worse than that and things had gotten worse since.

Then came the feast or famine Jets. After Houston won 9 of the first 11 contests, Namath arrived and they lost 7 of the next 8. This time, with Pastorini toughing out a hyperextended knee, Houston surprised everyone, including themselves, winning 26-20. It was their first victory over a winning team in 68 games.

The season highlight (or lowlight) came on October 9 with Oakland on Monday Night in the Dome. Fans hated the thought of exposing their embarrassing little secret to a national audience. Blacked out in Houston, it was a game ABC would never forget.

In the first quarter, the Oilers blocked a punt that bounced around at the Oakland 2. Although he could have run it in, Greg Sampson fell on it and was mobbed by the rest of the defense. From the 2, the immobile Pastorini first ran the option for a 1-yard loss. On second down, he was dropped for a 14-yard loss. After an incompletion, Butler missed the FG. Skip hit one later to tie it at 3-3, but the Raiders were offsides. Peterson took the penalty and called for a fake on the second try. They did not even get the pass off.

Houston's secret weapon was that they were so bad, teams sometimes played down to their level. For three quarters, the Raiders fell into the trap. The Oilers trailed just 10-0 well into the third quarter. It was an atrociously played game. Houston had 4 pass completions for minus-1 yard. For the game, they had 89 total yards, 5 interceptions and 7 first downs.

Near the end, Howard Cosell suggested that they "take the film of this game and show it to high schools as an exercise in futility." After Oakland woke up long enough to build a 34-0 lead, ABC cameras panned the thinned-out stands converging for a close-up of a crusty, disgruntled old fan. As Cosell was telling the country, "A look at this fan tells the story," the man slowly recognized that he was on camera and gave America a one-finger salute. Don Meredith had the only comeback: "He's telling us his team is still number one."

Pittsburgh plastered them the next week 24-7. The Oilers had 7 first downs and zero yards passing. Joe Greene said, "Every game against them, it seems we're up against new linemen. You just can't keep changing them and expect to win."

The joke started going around town that, as to Pete's lifetime contract, Bud might have him declared legally dead. The team was beyond bad. Everyone in town knew the call on third down: the screen or the draw. If it was third and really long, Pastorini might go with their best play — the quick kick. Pete took heat for many things, including not playing rookies. For example, he steadfastly continued to start 32-year-old Boyette with two first-year and two rookie LBs on the bench. Of 11 rookies, he only started one, center Guy Murdock, and he got in only due to Calvin Hunt's broken leg.

Among their many strategic blunders during the early 1970s, the worst may have been dismantling the offensive line. More than just stagnating the development of their talented young QBs, it left them literally fighting for their lives every Sunday. The joke about Dan Pastorini was that, with his strong arm, he could be one of the greatest QBs who ever lived — if he lived. What happened to Lynn Dickey (below making a dramatic return to the Dome) was no joke. At the time of his injury, doctors were not sure he would walk again. He not only recovered, but also played 13 seasons, lasting longer than Dan.

One of the few things that kept fans tuning in and going to games was Pastorini's promise. He had some decent young WRs. If he could just get some protection and a semblance of a running game, this offense could really take off. But fans were also predisposed by this point to expect management to screw up even the slightest ray of hope.

They did that after losing to Cleveland 23-17 in late October. Bearing the weight of last place and a 1-5 record, the front office made two more questionable trades. They sent Charlie Joiner and Ron Pritchard to Cincinnati for RBs Fred Willis and Paul Robinson, and George Webster to Pittsburgh for malcontent WR Dave Smith. Peterson called it "quality for quality."

Sending Joiner was one of the bigger blunders in team history. He was a great compliment to Burrough, who was becoming one of the scarier deep threats in the game. It was Charlie's presence that had made LeVias trade bait. But he was more than a great WR — he was also a good guy. Besides graduating with honors from

Grambling, he did great work in the community. Players this talented and well-rounded do not come around that often. Had the Oilers not panicked, Pastorini-to-Joiner might have been one of those memorable combinations like Bradshaw-to-Swann, Montana-to-Rice (or Fouts-to-Joiner). Elected to the Hall of Fame in 1996, Joiner retired at 39 as the most productive receiver of all time with 750 catches over 18 seasons.

Although overshadowed by the departure of Joiner, Pritchard, too, would be missed. He was flaky. His off-season wrestling job caused Breen to label him a "clown." But he was not a troublemaker and fans liked him. Like many of Adams' economics-driven selections, Pritch probably did not deserve to be a No. 1 pick. But he was a good athlete and played solidly if not spectacularly at times. Paul Brown was happy to take them both while getting rid of Willis, 24, who was in his doghouse and Robinson, 27, who was damaged goods. Breen did not offer who the new LBs were supposed to be.

Webster might be the best athlete Houston has ever known. He was such a force that he made the all-time AFL defensive team at age 24. Ken Houston, who was from the same draft, said George had "the greatest skills" of any player he had ever seen. The Oilers said his bad knee made him a question mark, but he was still the best LB on the roster. He played four more years. Pittsburgh was unloading a head case in Smith. While gifted, teams never knew when he was going to show up ready to play.

The departure of three of the better starters Houston could put on the field had a predictable effect. They lost all their remaining games. Mutiny was in the air. Assistant Jackie Simpson benched Willie Alexander, John Charles and Zeke Moore for the final three games.

In mid-December, they lost their finale 61-17 to the Bengals with Joiner and Pritchard. It was the most points they ever surrendered. The Oilers lost 13 of 14. The Jets must have felt pretty bad.

OVERVIEW

Statistics confirmed what fans already knew: the Oilers were the worst team in football. The offense ranked dead last. The amazing thing is that the Oiler brain trust was surprised. For whatever reason, it was not obvious to Adams and Breen that Peterson would not enjoy the same advantage he did in college; *i.e.*, he would not be able to sneak up on the pros with the pro set.

Promising young QB Dan Pastorini hit 48% of his passes for 1,711 yards. Despite having Burrough, Beirne, Reed and Joiner for part of the year, he managed only 7 TDs. The team as a whole had just 10 passing TDs, an all-time low. He did cut his interception total from 21 to 11, which was amazing considering that, in many games, he was hit every time he threw. He also had a 41-yard punting average on 82 punts, not surprisingly the most in the NFL. Willis led all rushers in his partial season with 461 yards but nary a TD.

The defense was third from the bottom as the Oilers were down to two good players, Pro Bowlers Ken Houston and Elvin Bethea. DE Pat Holmes was inspired to retire at 32, saying, "We're right at the bottom, and it will take a long time to come back. We had a bad year in 1966 and won the championship in 1967. But I don't think anything that spectacular will happen here. Having three coaches in three seasons has just about wrecked the program."

Hal Lundgren wrote: "This football team appears to be years away from contending. Possibly years away from a .500 season." Despite telling fans earlier that Pete was "one of offensive football's most fertile minds" who had "put together a stronger football team," he openly chided management for its party-line optimism.

1973: ABOUT THAT LIFETIME CONTRACT

The Oilers were a bad joke. Their last winning season was 1967 and things had really gone sour since 1970. After consecutive records of 4-10 and 1-13, fans were looking for any relief. They would have to wait.

THE 1973 DRAFT

At the end of the '72 season, the Oilers turned down an intriguing offer from KC for Pastorini. The Chiefs offered their first rounder (No. 19) plus any two of their OLs. As much as Houston needed players, it must have been tempting, but they turned it down.

Having already traded away their second-round pick, they gave up their No. 3 and Tom Regner for center Bill Curry, whom the Colts just wanted to unload. On the surface, it seemed like a good deal, as Curry was arguably the best center in the AFC. But Bill had things on his mind other than playing football for Houston. He would soon become a leader in the labor movement.

The Oilers then acquired Atlanta's first (No. 14) for Mike Tilleman, whom they had acquired the year before for two second-round picks. Tilleman was one of the best players on defense.

Houston had the No. 1 overall pick. No doubt the front office felt pressure not to screw it up. They almost got three starters for it (the Rams' Isiah Robertson, Tom Mack, Willie Ellison), but the deal fell through. What they failed to recognize was how bad the Colts wanted Bert Jones, the top player in the draft. They could have named their price. In the end, they held the pick and the Colts traded with the Saints at No. 2.

Taking the offer from KC would have opened many possibilities. With Bill Curry and two KC starters, all they would have needed for a serviceable line would have been for two from among Sampson, Saul, Hunt, Drungo, Funchess and Carr to step up.

And they still would have had three first-round picks (Nos. 1, 14, 19). They could have set the offense for a long time with QB Bert Jones, WR Isaac Curtis and OT Leon Gray. Or they could have waited on QB Dan Fouts in the third, taking OG John Hannah, Gray and a RB from among Otis Armstrong, Cullen Bryant or Greg Pruitt. Alternate choices included RB Chuck Foreman (Pete's favorite), TE Billy Joe DuPree, DB Mike Holmes, TE Charle Young and DL Derland Moore. The possibilities were endless.

But this was a team that, outside of the Klosterman years, had never shown any vision. Bud probably would have choked at having to pay three first-round salaries, even though the Oilers turned a profit each of the last five non-winning seasons.

So they kept Pastorini and the top pick looking to replace Tilleman. The two top DLs were Dave Butz and John Matuszak. Butz would have been a good choice if for no other reason than the Purdue student chants: "We may lose a game now and then but nobody beats our Butz."

They went with mountain-man Matuszak (6'8, 285) from the University of Tampa. Breen called him "the most exciting lineman in the country. He was my first choice." But it was Butz, of course, who turned into an All-Pro and played 16 seasons.

They really choked on the Tilleman choice with Iowa State QB George Amundson, who they intended to convert into a RB (conceding the Joiner trade was a bust). Not only did Amundson barely hang on for three seasons, but they also passed up RBs Greg Pruitt, Cullen Bryant and Terry Metcalf to get him. John Breen was a hard worker but he blew the 1973 draft.

In the third, they got to watch Dallas reload, taking DE Harvey Martin with Houston's pick (acquired from the Saints). The Oilers did not make a good choice until the fourth with Purdue LB Gregg Bingham. That was it. The rest were WR Edesel Garrison (5th round), whose name reminded people of Dusenberry, TE Ron Mayo (6th), OT Shelby Jordan (7th), DB Joe Blahak (8th) and CB Larry Eaglin (11th).

ENTER EL SID

Things had not been going well for Bud for some time. In three years, he had gone from having one of the better young teams around to the bottom of the barrel. Everything the team did went wrong. Fan apathy peaked. Losing seemed a Houston birthright.

Peterson did not appear to be the answer. Adams knew he had to do something radical. Only a despondent Bud would turn to an old enemy like Sid Gillman. Sid and Bud had clashed for years going back to the early days of the AFL. The Oilers' first (and only) two championships were both at the expense of Gillman-coached teams. Sid turned Adams in for tampering and they reportedly once had a fist fight.

Sid sat out the '69 and '70 seasons on doctor's orders. He came back in '71, but did not make any new friends and was replaced. He ended up in Dallas as an assistant. When Adams asked for permission to speak with him, Tom Landry refused. So did Tex Schramm. So much for helping your poor 1-13 neighbors.

According to league rules, the only way Houston could hire Sid away from Dallas was to promote him. That left few positions. To make it happen, Breen stepped down as GM, the job he had coveted for so long. He felt guilty over Peterson.

Adams later recalled: "Sid was sitting up there at Dallas as a kind of offensive consultant. I knew him as a forceful guy who would do whatever was needed to straighten us out. I saw it as a quick fix. He had the ability and know-how to make quick decisions."

Sid Gillman was officially hired March 2, 1973. Like he had done to Klosterman in '66, Adams hired him too late to help with the draft.

Gillman was tough, crusty and abrasive. He was a control freak, and most people thought that he would run over Bill Peterson. They were right. He started right away to remake the team's image. He hired two more assistants and two more scouts. He said, "I predict that within two years we will sell every ticket on a seasonal basis. There will be the day when you can't buy a ticket for an Oiler home game."

He wasted no time dealing. He sent starting DT Ron Billingsley and backup QB Kent Nix to New Orleans for TE Dave Parks, LB Tom Stincic and backup QB Edd Hargett. He obtained DL Al Cowlings (better known as the driver of the white Ford Bronco) for a '74 No. 2. He traded away their 1974 Nos. 1 and No. 3 for former Dallas No. 1 Tody Smith plus Billy Parks. He traded Leo Brooks for Bob Greshham, New Orleans' leading rusher from '72 but a fumbler. He picked up return man Alvin Haymond for a '74 No. 5. In three weeks, he had traded away four of the Oilers' first five picks in the 1974 draft. Sid said the scouts had told him '74 would be "a very poor one in the draft."

The big one came on May 15 when Sid sent All-Pro Ken Houston to Washington for five players: OT Jim Snowden (31-years-old), WR Clifton McNeil (32), DE Mike Fanucci (28), TE Mack Alston (26) and safety Jeff

Severson (24). "It's a heck of a good trade when you can get five-for-one," was the best Coach Pete could come up with, that and pronouncing Fanucci as "Fasoochi." Although Alston was a decent TE and Severson a fair safety, the deal was a huge bust.

1973 TRAINING CAMP

It was to be an unusual camp in Kerrville. In the off season, Dan Pastorini wed buxom British actress June Wilkinson who was at least nine years his senior. Her major role had been an appearance in Playboy in the early '60s. Bud Adams toured Europe in search of a soccer-style kicker and came back with a Norwegian named Finn Seemann. Finn brought his coach with him. He went straight to the cab team.

Stincic refused to report, saying he was going to get his master's degree. Dave Smith was sent home for "insubordination." Billy Parks retired and then un-retired. It was hard to keep up with the receivers. They had Dave Smith, Dave Parks and Billy Parks.

FS Bob Atkins hurt his knee. OL Elbert Drungo lost his quickness due to knee surgery. Former KC No. 1 OT Sid Smith was put on the IR, as were WR Clifton McNeil and return man Alvin Haymond.

The 61-year-old Gillman rode around practices in a golf cart sticking his nose into everything. This did not exactly endear him to the coaches. Sid's motives were altruistic. He wanted the team to shed its losing ways. He did not understand why his experience was not appreciated.

Jets owner Sonny Werblin once said, "In Sid Gillman, the milk of human kindness has turned to yogurt." But a dictator was what the Oilers needed at the time.

But fans responded positively to Sid. Although lost today on people like Paul Tagliabue, coming off a disastrous 1-13 campaign, the Oilers played before SRO crowds for each of four home preseason games. The highlight was a 27-24 victory over the Cowboys. Billy Parks and Dave Parks each caught TDs. The win broke a 14-game losing streak and gave the Oilers their second victory in 10 against Dallas. Fights broke out all over the Dome between Oiler and Cowboy fans.

There were changes all over. The most positive was the DL with Bethea, Tody Smith, Al Cowlings, John Matuszak and Greg Sampson. The secondary was weak. Ken Houston left behind safeties Charles and Severson and CBs Moore and Alexander.

LB was a chore to track. They started with Floyd Rice, Phil Croyle, Richard Lewis and Gregg Bingham (who allowed Boyette to be cut). By the end of the year, it was Bingham, Paul Guidry, Ralph Cindrich, Guy Roberts, Brian McConnell and Dick Cunningham. The mistake was getting rid of Rice, who was a solid OLB. A good late addition was Ted Washington, plucked off waivers. He held onto a cab team spot.

Looking for the next Charlie Joiner, they picked up former first rounder Eddie Hinton. Gillman also put Lynn Dickey on the taxi squad. Dickey was none too happy.

With the Oilers so hungry for players, a staggering list of ex-Oilers littered the NFL landscape. The Super Bowl champion Dolphins had Norm Evans; Cincinnati had Joiner and Pritchard; Pittsburgh had Glen Ray Hines, Gerela and Webster; Washington had Ken Houston and Alvin Reed; Denver had Bobby Maples, Leroy Mitchell, Larron Jackson, Joe Dawkins, Charley Johnson and Tom Domres; New England had Dave Rowe; San Diego had LeVias, Tank Holmes and Wilkerson; KC had Pat Holmes, Willie Frazier and Beathard; the Jets had Julian Fagan; and the Raiders still had Blanda and Willie Brown. In the CFL, Peterson camp-cut Andy Hopkins was leading his division again in rushing. Put them together and you had a decent team, at least one better than 1-13.

Going into the 1973 season, Glen Ray Hines was the starting RT for the Steelers. He noted the Oilers only had two players (Bethea and Moore) left from when he was there last in 1971. Asked to compare his new to his old one, he said, "This is a super football team. I've never seen so many athletes. I just can't believe the organization from top to bottom. Chuck Noll is the reason. It's all happened since he came to Pittsburgh. He's an excellent coach. He's got the athletes. They're young. Morale is high ... They've got the darndest running backs up here you've ever seen ... I've gotten some of the worst blocks I've ever had, and yet these backs broke them for yardage. They don't need much room.

"Winning can't be as difficult as losing. I remember 1967 and how fast it went by. It's a lot easier winning. Losing takes a lot out of you."

THE 1973 REGULAR SEASON — WE'RE NUMBER 26

The new Oilers looked like the old ones losing to the Giants (34-14), Cincinnati (24-14) and Pittsburgh (36-7). It frustrated the University of Houston to no end that the losing Oilers could still outdraw the winning Cougars by over 10,000 a game.

As he did in 1972, Coach Peterson still appeared on his weekly phone-in talk show co-hosted by Channel 13's Dan Lovette. Pete earned the nickname "Captain Courageous" for bravely standing in the line of fire. The "Pete and Dan Show" received a constant barrage of questions about the pathetic running game, erratic kicking game and Pastorini's latest injury. When asked when he was going to resign, Pete shot back, "Sir, I have no intention of ever quitting. In fact, I figure I'm going to be around Houston longer than you will." Then he hung up.

But his team was No. 13 in passing and No. 13 in total offense in a 13-team conference. Something had to give. Soon, his GM would re-enter coaching. The October 4 *Post* headline read: "Sid Gillman Takes Command of Oilers' Lackluster Offense." A "tired and subdued" Peterson said, "Our offense has looked so bad that I've asked Sid to give us a lift and he's agreed. That's why he's dressed the way he is (coach's windbreaker, shoes and shorts)." The *Post* ran an amusing string of Gillman quotes going back to March 2, when he said, "I hope to help build the Oilers but I won't be doing any of the coaching," followed by an August 7 quote: "You know, it's very difficult to stay away from coaching," and finally, one from October 3: "No, I wouldn't call it offensive coordinator. I'm just going to help Pete with the offense."

The Oilers played better the next week, but lost to the Rams 31-26. They also lost starting center Bill Curry, who somehow broke his shin bone and tore ligaments.

On October 13, they lost to Denver 48-20 in the Dome on four Charley Johnson TD passes. That was it.

Sid fired Pete on Monday. "We are in a winning business. There is no excuse for failure. It was necessary for us to relieve Bill Peterson of his duties as head coach and I think the reason is obvious. His record is 1-18," was Sid's report. He indicated he would coach the rest of the season and then seek a replacement.

Peterson handled it well. "I think this team can win in the NFL, but it is young and it is going to take some time," he said. "I guess time just ran out for me."

So Gillman became the Oilers' ninth head coach. The incident brought to mind the December 31, 1971, press conference when Adams, sporting a Rolex, bow tie, mustache and fat Cuban cigar, announced, "We've hired our last coach for some time to come. We have to get along with Pete. He'll be on our payroll a hell of a long time." Indeed, Pete would continue to receive monthly checks for the next 3½ years.

Sid lost his first game 42-13 to Cleveland as the offense generated four first downs and 106 total yards. Next they lost to Chicago 35-14, leaving them 0-7.

Then the improbable happened. They won a game (31-27 at Baltimore on a Dickey to Willis screen pass with less than one minute left). The shocker broke an 18-game regular season losing streak. It was such a rare occurrence that local TV crews did man-on-the-street interviews. Houstonians did not know how to react to an Oiler victory. They did not have much experience with that sort of thing.

It was just a blip, though, as the Oilers lost 32-0 to New England at home before 27,344. Bud said, "I'm not that worried ... I think we're doing pretty well."

They were doing well enough to lose the rest of their games, although they almost surprised the Raiders again in December. Trailing 10-6 with the ball on the Oakland 2, RB Lewis Jolley took a hand-off and was headed for glory until big-hitting safety George Atkinson rattled his teeth and knocked the ball loose. Oakland won 17-6. Approached for comment after the game, George Blanda said, "F— Houston."

Gillman said, "I've never seen anything like it. Everything that can possibly happen to a football team has happened to the Houston Oilers this year. We've had it all. You name it, it happened."

GM Sid Gillman made a lot of changes upon taking the reins in 1973. Most did not pay off. One that did, Tody Smith (left), cost them first and third round draft picks in 1974 which Dallas converted into Ed "Too Tall" Jones and Danny White.

They lost the last two to Pittsburgh 33-7 (8 fumbles, 83 yards of offense) and Cincinnati 27-24 before a Dome banner that read: "We're Number 26."

OVERVIEW

Elvin Bethea's 16 sacks were the highlight. He made the Pro Bowl. So did Ken Houston, Norm Evans, Charley Johnson, Willie Brown, George Blanda, Roy Gerela, Charley Taylor and Dave Wilcox.

The offense was the most inadequate in football. Fred Willis led rushers (579 yards, 4 TDs) and receivers (57 catches). Pastorini had 1,482 yards and 5 TDs to go with 17 interceptions. While his interceptions were up, so was his completion percentage to 53% on 154-of-290 passing. It at least showed improvement over the 47% and 48% of his first two seasons. He was hit so many times that he led the entire league in fumbles with 17. Speedy Ken Burrough caught 43 passes for 577 yards, but dropped many of Dan's best efforts.

The Oilers also set a few team records — number of fumbles in one season, most yards penalized and total yards on kickoff returns.

The pain of another 1-13 season was not eased by the fact that the Cowboys were back in the playoffs, and for a while, looked as if they might be in the one Super Bowl held in Houston (Miami beat Minnesota at Rice Stadium). Traveling across the country, the state or even the city, fans had to handle attacks on their team as if they were personally responsible. Yet if they chose to agree with the criticisms, they were called lousy, nonsupportive fans.

The malady did seem peculiar to Houston. The Rockets had traded away their one marquee player, hometown hero Elvin Hayes, and had foundered ever since. Likewise, the Astros traded away their best players, including Joe Morgan, Mike Cuellar, Dave Giusti, Rusty Staub and Jimmy Wynn. The previous summer, the only great Astro, Cesar Cedeno, was involved in an "accidental" shooting that killed a girl in a hotel room in the Dominican. Maybe it was the Houston water.

The players suffered, too. Bethea said that when he went home to North Carolina in the off season, "Every conversation begins with 'what's wrong with ... '" He asked for a trade.

1974: THE DICTATOR WHO RESTORED RESPECTABILITY

Another year opened with another search for another new head coach. The players wanted Sid Gillman to remain, as witnessed by a petition Fred Willis circulated in December that was signed by all. At the conclusion of the season, Sid said, "I've coached my last game. Coaching is a young man's game."

He was in charge of the search. When asked who would replace him, he agreed it should not be another college coach. He said the new coach would come "with the capacity to work and with intelligence." It would soon be seen who fit this bill.

WELCOME (BACK) SID GILLMAN

The suspense was over January 17 when Sir Sidney named himself coach. He said he liked the young talent on the team and thought they could turn the corner with a few more players. He added that he "just happened to be the best coach available."

He did not want the job permanently and said he would coach one more year, then turn it over to a bright young assistant. He promised continuity, meaning the new coach would come from the Oiler ranks. Speculation centered on King Hill, who played QB for 12 years in the NFL, and scouted and coached for the Oilers.

He also announced Dan Downs, an original Klosterman hire, would be the assistant GM and Jim McLem-

The best addition to the 1973 club was fourth round pick ILB Gregg Bingham. Gregg was a warrior who stayed 12 seasons leading the Oilers in tackles every year but once. Bum Phillips said, "To keep him out of the game you'd have to cut off his head and hide it."

ore would take over as Director of Public Relations. George Blackburn took over as head of scouting. A staff addition was OA Phillips hired as the DC. Phillips served in the same role under Gillman in San Diego. Gillman, who had given Al Davis and Chuck Noll their first jobs in pro football, would eventually add another feather to his cap with Phillips.

THE SUMMER OF '74

Pro football was in turmoil in the Summer of 1974. The latest new league, the WFL, signed several NFL players to futures contracts and took quite a few top collegians in their draft. Then, on July 1, NFL players went on strike.

It was a contentious event, and the Oilers were in the middle of it. Training camp, now in Huntsville (north of Houston), was filled with rookies and free agents. Some of the veterans picketed the practices wearing, "No Freedom, No Football" T-shirts. Center Bill Curry became a vocal president of the players union. Fred Willis was one of the strike leaders. Elvin Bethea was the Oilers' representative.

The players were divided. Steve Kiner, who Sid obtained for a ninth-round choice, said, "I know who pays my bills and where my loyalties lie and it's not with the Players Association." He called the Association president a "redneck a—hole from Georgia. Now who is Bill Curry, really? He's some guy from Georgia who went to George Tech and the NFL and the coach happened to think he had some ability and he developed him. His whole life revolved around the fact he's been a successful athlete and now at the end of his 11-year career he's going to sit out there and tell everybody nobody did anything for him. As long as he wants to deceive those kids and keep them out (of camp) he can go ahead. But all he's doing is jeopardizing their careers."

Even Fred Willis had to agree that the idea of football players picketing in the little town of Huntsville, known mainly for its large state prison, was not "the proper thing to do. It just wouldn't be quite right to go walking through the prison wearing 'No Freedom' T-shirts."

On this issue, Adams and Gillman united. They despised strikes. "You can't get into condition carrying a six-ounce sign," said the head coach. It started to break up in late July as veterans began to trickle in. The Union called a "cooling off" period beginning in mid-August, but it had lost this round.

LAND OF THE FREE AND HOME OF THE BRAVE

By the time the full complement of players arrived, their coach was in a foul mood. Sid has been described as "short on patience, intolerant of imperfection and capable of purple rages." When the vets returned, he announced, "This team is going to be a dictatorship ... and I'm the dictator." There were plenty of retaliations and demotions. He immediately released a load of veterans, including strike promoter Curry, Tom Funchess, Mike Fanucci, Eddie Hinton, Joe Blahak, Finn Seemann and Lee White. About the Curry retaliation, Ed Garvey said, "There is no place in football for Sid Gillman. He is the symbol of what we are fighting against."

Whatever love there was between coach and players the previous December was lost. Just as this mess was beginning to settle down, John Matuszak sprang a leak. Even though a disappointment on the field, his size and notoriety made him the Oilers' poster boy. The team had preprinted thousands of glossies for the upcoming season. But on August 28, after being demoted to second string by Gillman, he signed a WFL contract with the Houston Texans.

The WFL was hoping for a '70s Billy Cannon. Rumors were that he received a $1 million contract. Because he was under contract with them, the Oilers were easily able to obtain an injunction which was served on Big John by an army of deputies on the Dome field during the second quarter of his first Texans game.

It was an odd situation with the mountain-man playing for two teams in two leagues in two games in two nights. He wore *parts* of the same uniform. He played one series. It was the usual Oiler circus.

The Texans then went to court to challenge Matuszak's NFL contract on antitrust grounds. They promised they had found a loophole. They asserted the standard NFL players' contract was unfair and even un-American. It was all very melodramatic, with Matuszak pouting for the television cameras saying he was carrying the flag for the enslaved masses and "striking a blow for freedom." He portrayed Gillman as the Gestapo.

The WFL provided Matuszak with an expensive attorney, but things did not go well. With the Tooz on the stand, it came out that his Texans contract was only worth $50,000 a year for five years, or roughly $3,750 more than his original Oiler deal, but without any pension or medical benefits. He was so bad as a witness that about the only thing the Tooz established was that he may have lacked capacity to sign anything. When asked if he read his Oiler contract before signing, he replied: "No sir. It was obviously a form of coercion. You either sign it or don't play at all ... (the Oilers) had the sole right to me and if I didn't agree to terms I wouldn't be

The 1974 Oiler draft was a waste except for one small exception — Billy "White Shoes" Johnson (No. 84). He was perhaps the only player of his day who could make everyone in the stadium stand whenever he touched the ball. Gillman was against the selection, saying he "didn't want any midgets" on his team. To their credit, scouts Walt Schlinkman and Bob Kebric talked him into it.

allowed to play in my country. I love my country as the land of the free and the home of the brave."

The Texans put Gillman and Adams on the stand, but most of the other 100 Oiler players and staff subpoenaed did not testify. They wasted away the day in the hallway to the amusement of court personnel. In the end, the WFL did not have the silver bullet and the poor masses remained enslaved for the time being. Not long afterward, a more successful attack would be made by different attorneys in a different court. The Texans soon moved to Shreveport, became the Steamer and then ran out of steam.

1974 TRAINING CAMP

There were a few positives that came out of all of this. The coaches got to take a look at several players who might not have otherwise made the team, including Ronnie Coleman, CL Whittington, James Foote, Ted Washington and Ed Fisher. Steve Kiner, not hurt by his stance on the strike, won a starting ILB position. It helped these players that rosters were expanded to 47 in an attempt to ward off the WFL.

They also had few rookies to compete with. While Peterson's plan was build through the draft, Gillman went for the quick kill. He traded away their first three choices in '74, including the No. 1 overall pick (Dallas took Ed "Too Tall" Jones with it). Houston had 11 selections over 17 rounds — three fewer than any other team. It was a risky strategy and ironic in the sense that this was the first year in several when the Oiler front office and scouting department were in place sufficiently in advance to conduct a cohesive draft.

Only one draftee paid off, but he was the steal of the draft — KR/WR Billy Johnson (5'8, 170) of Widener in the 15th round. After so many failures, the Oilers had to get lucky eventually. They got lucky with Johnson.

Gillman also traded for RB Vic Washington. Sid thought the one-time 49er great was the answer, so much so that he gave up another first-round choice (1976) and a third (1975). This move ranked right up there with the Kenny Houston trade.

The defense was sporting a new scheme. New DC Bum Phillips switched to the 3-4 when the 4-3 was standard fare. He did it, he said, because he had only one good lineman and lacked Dick Butkis at MLB. "It takes four real hosses — and another at middle linebacker — to make the 4-3 work," he said. The best feature would be an improved run support brought on by the extra LB. Unlike DLs, the four roaming LBs would not be clogged up at the line. It also allowed for more coverage packages since it had eight cover guys instead of seven. The main criticism was a weak pass rush. Bum said you still get a rush because the fourth rusher could come from anywhere.

The Oilers went 3-3 in the preseason, riding free agent QB Foote to the victories during the strike.

They faced a big task. To turn it around, the Oilers had to first face themselves. For example, there was a poster in a training camp dorm room of the Maharishi Maharesh Yogi, an ancient Eastern religious figure. The Yoga was seated in the lotus position revealing his wrinkled face, long white hair and beard. Handwritten at the bottom were the words: "This man has been a Houston Oiler ticket holder since 1970. He is 26-years-old." Their record over that period was 9-45-2.

THE 1974 REGULAR SEASON — FROM THE VERY BOTTOM

The Oilers opened against Dan Fouts and the Chargers before 29,709 in the Dome. With Pastorini and Willis out, Dickey and Coleman got the start. The Oilers won 21-14 for their first opening day win in four years.

Coleman had 123 yards while FB George Amundson added 2 TDs.

That brought up the Oilers' personal jinx — the Browns. Houston had lost all 8 games to them. The Browns won 20-7 as Vic Washington fumbled 3 times on 8 carries. Coleman had 2 yards on 10 carries while Dickey threw 3 interceptions.

That started another downhill roll as they lost to KC (17-7), the Steelers with Joe Gilliam and Preston Pearson (13-7) and then the big one at Minnesota (51-10) as former Oiler Joe Blahak gave away the Oilers' defensive sets, allowing easy scores.

Bum Phillips's 3-4 took the blame and Sid had him switch back to a 4-3. The next week against St. Louis, the offense played well enough to win, but the defense could not stop them and Houston lost 31-27. Sid had Bum reinstall the 3-4.

The Oilers were in familiar territory at 1-5, but it was not quite the same. They had improved. Outside Minnesota, their losses were by 13, 10, 6 and 4 points. That is how progress was measured in Houston in 1974.

Then came the turning point of the season and decade. The Oilers completed a deal with KC for Matuszak. The Tooz had not played for anyone since the injunction. Hank Stram had his own problems with Curly Culp, who was not happy and signed a future contract to play in the WFL in 1975. The Oilers got Culp and the Chiefs' No. 1 for Matuszak and a No. 3. It would turn into one of the better moves the Oilers ever made.

The Chiefs could not handle Matuszak, either, and Stram would be fired at the end of the season. Matuszak was a wild man. In college, he punched and nearly killed a guy over a woman. While in Kansas City, his wife tried to run him down with her car and he was arrested for drug possession. He also overdosed on alcohol and sleeping pills. In 1976, he was traded to Washington where he was having vodka and Valium for breakfast. He naturally ended his career in Oakland getting a start in a Super Bowl. Later, he made some B-grade movies, but his was the story of a troubled man. He died of a heart attack in 1989 at 38.

Culp immediately replaced Bubba McCollum at NG in the 3-4. He was one of the strongest players in the league, if not the strongest. About the same time, Dan Pastorini returned as the starting QB.

Inspired, they beat Cincinnati 34-21 with old warriors Sid and Paul Brown involved in an amusing feud. After the game, Brown said, "Sid Gillman has really turned it around. Houston won only one game each of the past two seasons and now he's won two. That's a 100% improvement." Sid said Paul was "senile."

They moved to 3-5 the next week, beating the Jets 27-22. New York thought they had it won on a Bobby Howfield FG with 2 minutes left, but Pastorini found Burrough on a 51-yard post pattern to the 1. Willie Rodgers' TD then won it. It was their first consecutive road wins since 1968. Oiler tickets were suddenly hot.

Next, they had OJ Simpson and what was called the finest Buffalo squad ever assembled. Houston won 21-9, holding the Juice to 57 yards and intercepting Joe Ferguson 6 times. The 79,223-strong Polish Army that crammed itself into Rich Stadium threw everything not bolted down, including apples, pink paint, sour cream and obscenities. Coach Gillman was hit by a snowcone. Kiner took some spoiled sour cream down the jersey. Unable to handle success, Bingham and Bethea had a fist fight in the dressing room.

When the Oilers left on their road trip, they were 1-5 and there was some discussion of not allowing them to return. Three road wins later, fans were back in love with them. Like they did with the revivalist Oilers of 1967, fans met the team plane at the airport after the Buffalo game.

That brought back Paul Brown with his top-rated offense run by the robot-like Ken Anderson. They had to limp back to Ohio with a 20-3 loss. The 44,000 demented Dome fans went berserk. They cheered everything that moved, including a standing ovation for the two-minute warning. It was the Bengals' lowest point total since 1970 and Houston's longest win streak since '62. Their two wins over the Bengals knocked Cinci out of the playoffs. Bob Atkins said, "Everybody's together ... the attitude's just great."

It was improbable, but the Oilers were 5-5 and within striking distance of the playoffs. Jimmy the Greek made Gillman the favorite to win coach of the year. He added that if the Oilers finished .500 or above, Gillman should win the Nobel Prize.

Leave it to the team from the Ft. Worth suburbs to spoil the party. The Cowboys had spent years blanketing Texas with television, marketing and great-looking cheerleaders. It was modern hard sell at its disgusting best. The losers of that effort were the Oilers and teams of the Southwest Conference. It seemed like whenever the Oilers showed some small sign of breaking their masochistic tendencies, the Cowboys were there to knock them back down like a mean older brother. So it was on November 17 that Dallas beat the Oilers 10-0 in the Astrodome. The only TD was controversial. Nonetheless, Dallas was still a bit much, holding the resurgent Oilers to an all-time low 81 total yards.

At least it was a respectable showing. The Oilers were no longer the worst team in football. You could almost feel the whole town exhale. An American city's connection to its football team is always an amazing study. Not many things can affect civic pride like the success or failure of that community's NFL franchise. In Houston, after a few wins, players who had been cowering

The 1974 strike was fortuitous for several players, including LBs Ted Washington (59) and Steve Kiner (57), who combine with Bingham (above) to stop Oiler-killer Greg Pruitt. At right, Ronnie Coleman introduced the stiff arm in Houston before it was perfected by another Oiler RB a few years later.

inside their homes for years were suddenly seen all over town. Crowds welcomed home the team airplane. Lines appeared in front of the ticket offices. The sky was blue. Kids played. Dogs wagged their tails. Married couples spoke to one another.

A veteran Oiler watcher could feel in his bones what was about to occur. Just as his team seemed on the verge of breaking out of its long funk, Bud went whining to the press about Gillman. He claimed he went over budget in 1973. He said Sid cost him a $15,000 fine for exceeding the player limit. He said Sid had too many assistants and that he even spent too much on film. What really chafed him was having the seven veterans travel to camp after the strike just so Sid could make his point cutting them when the team had to pay their travel expenses.

Bud said, "If I let Sid spend all he wanted I'd be the greatest owner in pro football. I'd also be the brokest ... I'm very happy about winning games and I don't think you can take any short cuts, but I also think you can win ball games and still make a profit ... You've got to watch your dollars and change and cut out some of the frills ... It embarrasses me to be the owner of the only club losing money in the NFL. It makes me look like a poor owner and I don't want to be the laughing stock of the owners around the league."

Why Bud chose go public with his troubles at this moment, or indeed, why he went public at all, only he can answer. Some say he hated Gillman getting all the press and credit for the turnaround. They were not friends. Adams said they "seldom communicated ... I guess you could say we just co-exist." Without a doubt, Adams did not like Gillman calling him names behind his back. "I've got to have some loyalty," he said. "I grow a little tired of having people come to me, telling me what Sid's called me, like 'That fat bleep,' or 'That fat-bleeping Indian.'" Bud did not appear in the annual team picture.

He had his share of apologists, such as *Chronicle* columnist John Wilson, who wrote in *From Cannon to Campbell* that Bud's "bedrock conviction held that any business, even a sports team, must be run on sound financial principles and that decisions must never evade this responsibility. Gillman had a cavalier attitude toward money. His tendency was to neglect the financial side of management." But others pointed out that the Oilers had been profitable five years in a row when Bud's teams were as bad as any in history. Adams claimed the team was "in the red" in 1973. What he did not freely discuss, however, was how much of the potential negative cash flow was actually caused by his and his family members' salary draws or his continued payments to fired coaches.

Bud Adams presents a curious paradigm. His bottom line had always been about money. The AFL was an idea to make some more just like Quick Kick. The AFL was not formed out of benevolence. Even so, that alone does not explain his conduct. Obviously, he maximized profits when the stands were full. Houston had shown repeatedly that it would respond to a winner or even just a team that played hard. There was an immeasurable layer of latent support in Houston waiting for that spark to send them into mass (ticket and merchandise buying) hysteria. The outpouring of the late '70s would bear this out again.

Yet Adams always seemed to rise at the wrong times to oppose his rare hires who had the skills, vision and drive to do what was necessary to put a team on the

The pivotal point in the Oiler's turnaround was Sid Gillman's acquisition of Curly Culp from the Chiefs. Culp was a natural nose guard in new defensive coordinator Bum Phillips' 3-4 defense.

field that would inspire such support. There were plenty of examples to follow. The Cowboys, Raiders, Rams and Jets did it with marquee players and marketing. The Vikings and Steelers did it with solid organizations, continuity and teams that positively reflected their communities. The Dolphins did it by shrewdly obtaining one of the top coaches in football and then got out of his way.

Adams cited as his motivation the fear being labeled the "laughing stock of the owners around the league" for having the only team losing money. However, he later admitted that the '74 team made money (but only after the Gillman situation was resolved). Perhaps most amazing is that Adams did not appreciate that after back-to-back 1-13 seasons, the coaching merry-go-round and unprincipled series of giveaway trades, his team *already was* the laughing stock of the league and he its laughing stock owner.

For example, a *Pittsburgh Press* article from October 6, 1974, read: "They are the National Football League's garbage can; a disposal for the wretched refuse of 25 other, better football teams. They are the Houston Oilers and they are, in a word, stiffs." Backup center Fred Hoaglin said before the Browns game: "When I was in Cleveland, if you had a bad game (the coach) would threaten to trade you to the Houston Oilers." Vic Washington said about his trade to the Oilers, "I look[ed] at it as a form of punishment."

Gillman did not have much to say. He defended himself against the fines by saying they were not over the player limit "by much." It was actually reasonable considering the uncertainty regarding Matuszak and AWOL safety Tommy Maxwell, who walked out of camp without a word to anyone but later came back. Meanwhile,

Coach Gillman had to get his team ready for the Steelers on the road.

Facing almost certain elimination from the playoffs and a freezing rain at game time, a letdown would have been easy. But the Oilers rose on both sides of the ball for a 13-10 victory over the team that would win the Super Bowl. It was a great effort. The defense held the terrific Pittsburgh offense to minus-12 yards in the second half. Fred Willis also rose from the ashes. Out all year with a purported hamstring pull (more likely post-strike-itis), he carried everyone on his back on a 49-yard, 11-play drive that ended with a 34-yard Skip Butler FG with 2:32 left.

They had an emotional letdown the next week losing in Denver 37-14 after which 63-year old Gillman flew into one of his purple rages and kicked Dan Downs out of the locker room. Downs was just trying to set up postgame interviews. It happened in front of the entire team and caused Downs to quit a month later.

The final game of the season was with Cleveland. The Oilers had not beaten the Browns in nine tries, losing by the scores 28-14, 21-10, 31-0, 37-24, 23-17, 20-0, 42-13, 23-13 and 20-7. The totals were 245 to 98. Hoaglin said, "I know how the Browns regard the Oilers. We used to figure two victories were in the bag."

So the Oilers buried some ghosts on December 15, beating Cleveland 28-24 to end up 7-7 and tied for second. One Dome sign read: "Keep It Shut Bud." Another: "Get Rid of Adams. Keep Gillman."

Pittsburgh won the division at 10-3-1 while the scorned Browns finished 4-10. Buffalo, who the Oilers crushed 21-9, got the wildcard spot at 9-5. Sid, "the dictator who restored respectability," was named AFL coach of the year.

Accepting the award, Gillman said, "This has to be without a doubt the most satisfying season for me. The reason is the response I've gotten from the players. They have given me everything they've got to the limit. I know how this team has improved. They came from the bottom and that makes it very pleasurable. And I mean from the very bottom."

The other half of the Culp trade, John Matuszak, predictably ended up with the Raiders. Photo © F. Carter Smith.

OVERVIEW

The year got off to a strange start with the strike and Gillman's tough stance against it. By releasing seven veterans as soon as they got to camp, he angered both the remaining veterans and the owner who liked to count his chips. Then John Matuszak jumped to the WFL and literally dragged everyone into court. Bethea and Dickey asked to be traded, the trainer quit, and safety Tommy Maxwell walked out of camp after being demoted. After winning the first game, they lost the next five and teetered on the edge.

But the return of a healthy Dan Pastorini and the addition of Curly Culp started a 4-game win streak. After winning 6 games in 3 years and one in each of the last two, they won 6 of 8, including one over the Super Bowl champs and two over Cincinnati. Their 7-7 record was their best since 1968. Along the way, Adams threw a tantrum over money, Kiner chased young *Houston Post* reporter Dale Robertson out of the training facility and Coach Gillman kicked his assistant general manager out of the dressing room.

According to the coach, the turnaround came after the 51-10 loss to Minnesota. In that game, the Vikes had 7 TDs, 502 yards, 4 interceptions and 1 sideline knockdown of Gillman. "The whole season could have collapsed right there." Sid said. "They were whipped dogs and I could have killed them off if I had told them how bad they really were." Instead, he spoke softly and found a few positive things to say. "It was a strain to find them," he said.

Gregg Bingham pointed to the second Pittsburgh game. Going in, they had lost 7-of-9 to the Steelers. "That was the best defensive game we ever had," he said years later. "The Steelers had 96 yards in the first half and minus-12 in the second for 84 total yards. They won the Super Bowl ... and averaged 368 yards a game."

Bum Phillips' defense, although ranked statistically near the bottom most of the year, finished strong, holding Cincinnati to one FG, Dallas to 10 points, Buffalo to 9 and Pittsburgh to 10. Bum was the first to employ the 3-4 on a full-time basis, although Bill Arnsparger used it sometimes during Miami's Super Bowl seasons.

He put it in while at San Diego, but Gillman vetoed it. "Sid thought you could run on it," Phillips said. "Somebody made a first down on us once." With Houston, he insisted that he be allowed to install it before he took the job.

He said the personnel dictated it. After losing DTs Matuszak and Sampson (to the offense), the only good DL left was Bethea. Good LBs were more plentiful. Phillips also said it was easier to teach. "The 4-3 takes time, more than we had," said the coach. "With our defense, you can get by with less overall talent and still play good football."

It all came together with the arrival of Curly Culp who slid between Bethea and Tody Smith. The strong man immediately started drawing double- and even triple-teams which clogged the middle of the line and made it hard to run. As Bum liked to say: "It's not what you line up in, but who you line up." With the big men jamming the line, the LBs were free to pursue and fill holes, and the Oilers' run-stopping ability soared.

To strengthen the pass rush, Phillips blitzed LBs from anywhere at anytime, which is what set Bum's 3-4 apart from Arnsparger's "53." Speed on the outside was key. The Oilers had one good OLB in Ted Washington, who led them with 11 sacks. The other OLB spot would be addressed in the next draft. Bingham and Kiner played tough inside. Gregg led the team in tackles, as he would for the next decade.

On offense, Pastorini had 1,571 yards on 140-of-247 passing (56%), 10 TDs and 10 interceptions. Hard to believe but his completion ratio was a team record. Willie Rodgers was the leading ground gainer with 413 yards and 5 TDs. Burrough slumped to 36 catches for 492 yards and just 2 TDs. Billy "White Shoes" Johnson turned out to be the best kick returner in football and the Oilers' most exciting player since Jerry LeVias.

Gillman reflected later, "I worked them hard. It's the price they have to pay to win. You can't do this job unless you dedicate your whole life, 365 days, 24 hours a day, to it. Give me a coach who goes on vacation and I'll give you a loser."

The return of some measure of prosperity in 1974 was accompanied by a return of Bud Adams to the headlines. This time it was over Gillman's budget. Plus, he said he was tired of being called names by his GM. Among Sid's nicknames for Adams was one that stuck — "Bottom Line Bud."

CHAPTER 6

LOVE YA BLUE
1975-80

Houston was due to catch a break. It had been seven seasons since their football team had had a winning record. Over that period, the Oilers lost 65 games. Since the merger, they averaged barely three wins a year. Fans were ready for some football. A savior was on the way, one wrapped in a different package, but a savior nonetheless. Bum Phillips was the right man at the right time. He would lead them through what can safely be called the Golden Age of Oiler football.

Although his teams never won the big one, Bum Phillips reached the pinnacle of sports popularity in Houston. To this day, some two decades later, only Earl Campbell, Nolan Ryan and Hakeem Olajuwon come close in those terms. For this reason, the treatment Phillips received at the hands of Bud Adams did more than anything, including moving the team, to cement Adams' reputation as the most hated man in Houston.

1975: A WINNING SEASON

Well before the season ended, speculation erupted about whether Sid would stay as coach or GM or leave. His acrimonious relationship with the owner seemed to alternately be repaired and get worse. Sid was cryptic about his intentions.

WELCOME BUM PHILLIPS

The speculation ended January 25, 1975, when Gillman named OA "Bum" Phillips, the Oilers' fifth coach in its last six years. The *Post* described him as "a former Marine fighter and wild bull rider who prefers unstarched collars, cowboy boots and a sorrowful three-chord country song." He promised to keep the team on the path to recovery, saying, "Sid's a little more of a driver than I am. Some people get effort out of players in different ways. My methods will be different but I plan for the results to be the same ... the only pet project I've got is to win."

"I wanted to be a head coach in pro ball. It's where I wanted to be, at the best level. It's what I've been working for all my life ... my family has moved around and made a lot of sacrifices so I could be at this point now. I'm very pleased."

Asked if he played college football, he said: "Well, I thought I did until I looked at some old movies." On his hair, he said, "I don't plan to do a whole lot different now that I'm head coach. I'm not going to let my hair grow out and I don't expect you to go out and cut yours."

"The big problem with the Oilers in the past," said Gillman, "has been so many changes in the organization, changes in coaching, in all phases of the operation. It's just not conducive to winning," he said. "Bum has vast experience and the knack for getting along with folks. He has a mind of his own." Gillman said he would remain as GM: "I'll be around to help if it's needed, but he will be his own boss."

HOW DID HE DO THAT?

In mid-February, Adams announced that Gillman would not return as the club's GM. None of those directly involved commented on it much. Gillman said his "contract was terminated by mutual consent."

There was, of course, more to it than that. Bum agreed to become coach on "a handshake." The details of the contract were not worked out until after the announcement. After Sid sent a contract over to Bum, he asked for a meeting with Bud. The sticking point was over what authority he would have as coach.

According to Adams, "Bum said he would not be able to do the job as coach unless he had it spelled out that he had the authority to run the football team. When Sid had picked Bum as coach I had figured he was putting his man in the job. So Bum was a lot smarter than I had given him credit for ... it kind of surprised me when he wouldn't let himself get in that mousetrap, having to try to coach with Sid looking over his shoulder."

Bud told him to make the changes he wanted and give the contract to Sid. He did, and a in few days, it came back to Adams signed by both Bum and Sid. According to Phillips, they never discussed the changes. Adams said he did not know if Gillman looked at it.

Not long after, Bum began to assert that authority. He asked Sid not to attend the coaches' meetings. Bum felt he could not establish himself as the authority figure if Sid was there all the time. Phillips also asked that Sid's office be moved from the second floor where the coaches were to the third floor where the administrative staff was. Adams had it moved.

Soon thereafter Gillman telephoned Adams from California and said it was time for him to step down. He said he did not think he could help the club under that arrangement. So Adams bought out the remaining two years of his contract.

To be sure, Gillman and Phillips were fond of each other. Bum owed him his big break and appreciated his knowledge of the game. But once he became coach, he could only do it one way. "There were no hard feelings between us. I'm sure he understood what I had to have," Bum said. "And, I think that deep down when he knew he wasn't coming back as the coach that took away a lot of the interest he had in the job." Bum became GM.

Thus ended Sid Gillman's Oiler career. He had done a lot in a short period. Understanding what he did is easier than understanding how he did it.

Clearly, he did not inherit a team rich in talent. Nor did he build through the draft after trading away their 1974 and 76 first-, 1974 second-, 1974-76 third-, 1975-76 fourth- and 1974-76 fifth-round picks. Most of his

Bum Phillips was Sid Gillman's handpicked successor. They made an odd couple, but Sid's faith was there. "I established a good system and hired Bum to maintain it," he said.

trades were unproductive and some were quite harmful. For example, All-Pro Ken Houston was converted into three washed-up players, a backup safety and a blocking TE who did not catch well. The picks for Al Cowlings, Tody Smith and Vic Washington could have been Dave Casper, Jack Lambert, John Stallworth, Rick Upchurch *and* Pat Thomas.

Sid insisted on experienced players. That was the only path to a quick turnaround. He lacked the patience for young players. Was there ever turnover. It seemed as if half the league came through Oiler camps.

They improved on both sides. On offense, the biggest thing was Pastorini matured. On defense, he hired Phillips. His one good trade produced the missing link in Curly Culp.

The biggest thing he changed, though, was attitude. Employing a different technique from Lemm, he got the same result by convincing them that they were better than they had been playing. He somehow convinced them they were winners. By 1974, the team believed it could compete with the Pittsburghs of the world, and that was a major breakthrough.

Willis said, "When I first came here, I was amazed by the situation. You could look around and see in people's faces that they didn't believe in themselves. We'd play the Bengals and knew we were going to lose ... When Sid first came here, he had an unbelievable task, to say the least ... He's got the best football mind I've ever seen. He's a hard worker, one of the hardest workers I've ever seen ... I'd say the biggest single thing Sid has done with the Oilers is he's organized us. When we go on the field we know what our purpose is ... I know I was criticized last year when I said I thought [he] should stay on as coach but he gets us prepared, physically and mentally. He associates with the players and helps motivate our ballclub ... Now we believe in ourselves and in each other."

Perhaps most of all, it was Sid Gillman's burning desire to succeed. He refused to accept failure. Insofar as one person can alter the collective attitude of a large group by nothing more than force of personality, Sid was the man. He is in the Hall of Fame.

THE 1975 DRAFT

The Oilers' draft position was somewhat similar to 1973. This time they had the No. 6 (KC's) and No. 15 (their own) picks in the first round. They had three of the top 40 selections. Gillman had said, "We want the best football player ... We could use a running back, a lineman, a defensive lineman, a linebacker. We could use almost anything of top caliber."

With the Chiefs' selection, they took Walter Payton's roommate at Jackson State, OLB Robert Brazile (6'4, 241). Brazile was a menace in college with 209 tackles his senior year. He had size, strength, speed and aggressiveness. "Brazile hits everyone in his reach and also some who aren't within his reach," summarized his new head coach. This time, the coach's rhetoric was on target, although fans were not initially overjoyed at another no-name small school player. They would learn to love him, however, as Brazile would turn out to be one of the finest outside linebackers to ever play.

With their own first-round pick, they took FB Don Hardeman (6'2, 230) of Texas A&I, who he led to a 13-0 record and NAIA championship. They said he was the best FB on the board. He definitely had a big mouth. At his first new conference, Hardeman said, "I'll make Pastorini All-Pro," and "If I touch the ball seven times, I'll put it in the end zone twice." He quickly gained the nickname "Jaws."

The second round saw another whiz-kid failure at WR, Emmett Edwards (Kansas' all-time receiving leader). The Oilers did not have a pick in rounds 3 through 5. Other picks included TE John Sawyer (11th round) and WR Willie Miller (12th).

The top selection overall was QB Steve Bartowski by Atlanta. Dallas continued its amazing ability to wiggle top picks out of the draft, taking Maryland DL Randy White second. In just two years, the Cowboys had paved their future with DLs White, Ed Jones and Harvey Martin. Two of those three came with Oiler draft picks.

Taking Hardeman at No. 15, they passed on Russ Francis, Louie Wright, Louie Kelcher, Fred Dean and Fred Solomon. Phillips wanted Kelcher who played for him at SMU, but deferred to the scouts since he had only been on the job three days. The scouts badly overrated Hardeman and Edwards. Taking Edwards at No. 40, they passed on Rod Shoate, Rick Upchurch, Rod Perry, Roosevelt Leaks and Rubin Carter. If Phillips had trusted himself more, he could have had Brazile, Kelcher and FB Leaks, who was better than Hardeman.

Before the draft, Gillman stated the Oilers "should be able to get at least three players that will play regularly." As it turns out, they got one, but he was a real good one — Robert Brazile.

1975 TRAINING CAMP

Phillips completed his staff by hiring Ed Biles as the DC and retaining King Hill in the same capacity on offense. He also hired George Rice as DL coach, Fran Polsfoot for WRs, Andy Burgeois for RBs, Joe Madro for the OL, Larry Peccatiello for LBs, Richie Pettibon for DBs, Sam Boghosian for special teams and Joe Wooley as offensive assistant.

Houston fans at this point were not sure what they had yet. They had already seen other assistants like Bones Taylor and Ed Hughes who were unable to make the jump. People were rightfully skeptical. On the other hand, this guy did seem a little different.

His name was Oail Andrew. His father was also an Oail but went by Flip. About Oail, he said, "Can't nobody spell it or pronounce it or anything." It was his sister Edrina who, in her stuttering attempts to say brother, came up with "B-b-b-bum." He said he did not mind "as long as it's a name and not a description."

He played football but not on a scholarship, saying "there was not much demand for 185-pound linemen." He said he was "a fullback but they played me at guard." He saw some action in the war: "Yes I saw combat with the Marines but I never liked to talk about it. It was a great job I had to do. All of us. So we did our jobs." In a lighter moment he said, "I joined the Marine Corps and I learned my lesson. I never joined anything else the rest of my life. I went in as a private and, 31 months later, I came out as a private. I thought they couldn't win that war without me. Then I got in there and I thought they couldn't win because of me. The Marine Corps was real spit'n polish. I wasn't."

His coaching career included all the high school hot spots like Nederland (where he was "90-something and 2"), Port Neches, Amarillo and Jacksonville. He coached at UTEP, UH and one year under Bear Bryant at Texas A&M in 1957. He coached the defense with the Chargers until Gillman left in 1971. He was the DC under Hayden Fry at SMU in 1972 and at OSU in 1973. Gillman hired him as Houston's DC on March 7, 1974.

The man with the crewcut looked at life and football in a refreshing way. "Football isn't everything in life. Sometimes us coaches and players think it is, and sometimes us in football have presented that image. Mistakenly so, in my opinion. But believe me, it's not," said Bum. "And, anyone who thinks so ought to take a walk through Texas Children's Hospital sometime. That'll change your outlook in a hurry on what's important and what isn't."

Although miles apart from Sid Gillman in most ways, he did keep a steady stream of new players coming through camp while giving up draft choices. He acquired a couple of ex-Oilers, Jerry LeVias and Glen Ray Hines. LeVias, who was coming off knee problems, said, "I'll be all right just as soon as I can decipher the meaning of 'June bug on a hot rock.'" Phillips said he was "as happy as a June bug on a hot rock" to get Jerry. Also acquired were DB Charlie Ford, TE Morris Stroud, OG George Daney and TE Bob Adams. Phillips acquired a draft choice from Baltimore for Al Cowlings. OJ's buddy moved to LB, fell behind and lost playing time. Bum also sent RB Bob Gresham to the Jets for DL John Little. The best move he made was for center Carl Mauck from San Diego for the rights to Booker Brown and Benny Johnson, who played in the WFL in 1974.

LeVias was among the final cuts, retiring at 27 because of a bad knee. Another was QB James Foote who had become a fan favorite after leading the strike team to three wins. Bubba McCollum and Vic Washington were also let go.

Bum made a mini Vic Washington kind of mistake, giving Kansas City a fifth-round pick in '76 and a fourth-rounder in '77 for Elmo Wright. Elmo was from UH and had some great seasons with the Chiefs but was past his prime. Phillips cut him before the season started. He sued.

He began to address the poor guard play by releasing Brian Goodman, who started every game in '74, and Soloman Freelon ('72, 3rd round). The middle of the OL was completely revamped with Mauck and free agents Ed Fisher and Conway Hayman. Fisher, who came in as a DE, was one of the players who got a look because of the strike the previous summer. He was probably the most improved player in camp.

In total, 13 new players made the team. The draft picks were Brazile, Hardeman, Edwards, Mark Cotney and John Sawyer. Further frustrating the WR situation, cut victim Willie Miller would end up catching 50 passes for the playoff-bound Rams in 1978.

Several free agents also made the team, a hallmark of Phillips' reign. They were Hayman, LB Ted Thompson (SMU) and CB Greg Stemrick. They also re-signed Tank Holmes from a construction site after a stint in the WFL.

Reports from camp had people wondering what was going on in Huntsville. After calling off practice because of lightning, the coach said, "I've got some influence now, but not *that* much. What if it struck some of our good players, or the head coach?"

THIS IS NOT A COAL MINERS' TYPE THING

The Oilers went 3-3 in the preseason, including Bum's first win as a coach at the first game in the Super Dome and a 17-14 loss to the Cowboys. They averaged 42,019 over the preseason and escaped without major injuries. But first there was more labor trouble on the horizon.

The previous December, a federal judge in California ruled that the "Rozelle Rule," part of the draft, and parts of the standard players' contract violated antitrust law and were illegal. In July, another antitrust suit went to court in Minnesota. Players went to camp without a collective bargaining agreement in place. Ed Garvey attempted to incite the players to strike again.

Oiler player representative Skip Butler said, "I'm 99% sure we wouldn't go along because everybody has a good outlook and it all goes back to one man, Bum Phillips. I don' think there's ever been a man in pro football who treats players so much like men. He's a mainstay. I think the general feeling here is, 'whatever Bum thinks is best for the team we'll do.' If a man like Bum had sat on both sides of the negotiating table last year, an agreement would have been reached before there ever was any strike."

Phillips said, "I like players. It's no secret. But I also have to tell them what I think and I don't think a strike like this is right ... This is not a coal miner's type thing. They're not working for $7 an hour."

ANOTHER GOLDEN OPPORTUNITY LOST

In late September, Bud Adams announced publicly that, after 15 years, he was ready to sell all or a portion of the club to whoever wants it. "It's worn me out," said Bud. "It's just not much fun anymore."

He complained about having to negotiate with agents and lawyers instead of the players and the labor union,

Success in Bum Phillips' 3-4 defense was predicated on speed on the outside. First-round pick Robert Brazile was the perfect fit.

and about being sued by players. He said the players are not "as dedicated." Seemingly oblivious to the hypocrisy of his statements, Bud said, "They're more interested in their accountant, their investment advisor than sometimes they are on the field. It's not all 100% football now ... Now they're trying to tell men who have been in the business for years how it should be run. Most of them are about 23-years-old. What do they know about running a football team? But they might end up running it. Who knows?"

He said, "Since the team was on their way up, I can gracefully step aside now." Asked what he thought the public reaction would be, Adams laughed and said: "Well, there probably would be a lot of cheers."

He backed off before anyone could hold him to it, explaining, "It was an emotional time for me when I said that. There was talk about the players going on strike. But several players have come to me recently and told me they wanted me to keep the club." He did not name the players.

THE 1975 REGULAR SEASON — HOLD THE ROPE

Playboy picked Houston to finish 7-7 and in third place. The front 7 was the same except the addition of Brazile at OLB. Like Bingham two years before, Bob would start in his first game and keep starting for a long time. The problem was the backfield with Moore and Alexander at CB and Atkins (later Whittington) and Germany at safety. The offense had Pastorini, Holmes and Willis in the backfield, although Coleman would later become the HB with Willis moving to FB. The WRs were Burrough and Johnson with Alston at TE. The OTs were Drungo and Sampson, and the OGs were Fisher and Hayman with Mauck at center.

Houston opened with a 7-0 win at New England. Willie Germany scored the lone TD off a fumble recovery. He was a free agent DB coach Richie Pettibon had to talk Bum into keeping. Phillips said, "It was good judgment on my part. I sure like it when one player does all the scoring and he happens to be on your team." It was their first shutout since 1968 (vs. Pats).

They beat San Diego the next week before 33,765. With Coleman replacing Willis, both he and Hardeman had over 100 yards rushing (first time since Granger and Campbell in '67). It was the first time they won two games to start a season since 1966. Curly Culp scored his first-ever TD with Bethea yelling the whole time that he was running the wrong way. During the following week, the Oilers claimed Bubba Smith off waivers.

Then came a pivotal contest at Cincinnati where the Oilers blew the game and the playoffs. Leading 17-7 in the third quarter with a chance to put it away, Pastorini completed a pass to TE Sawyer to the Cinci 16. But old friend Ron Pritchard knocked the ball loose as it bounced all the way to the 1. From there, Bengal Ken Riley ran it back 43 yards and Ken Anderson scored 6 plays later. That was followed by a Pastorini fumble which allowed Cincinnati to take a 21-17 lead. Dan then got them back to the Bengal 1 for the four most frustrating plays of the season. On first down, Dante collided with Jaws. Then on successive plays, Willis and Hardeman were stopped at the 1. With Bum screaming for a time out, Willis was stopped at the goal line. Cincinnati took the safety, which cut it to 21-19. Needing only a FG, Pastorini threw a final interception to seal their fate. It was a killer.

They regrouped to win impressively in Cleveland for the first time, 40-10. White Shoes ran a kick back for a TD. Like LeVias, he made everyone in the stadium stand every time he touched the ball. Bum said, "Billy is an equal opportunity runner. He gives everyone an equal chance to tackle him." When asked about Johnson's penchant for wearing panty hose to guard against injury and the cold, Bum said, "No, I didn't wear them Sunday or any other day. I think I would just go ahead and get cold. But if Billy wants to wear them, I'll help him put them on."

White Shoes' five touchdowns in 1975 allowed him the opportunity to introduce the end zone dance to pro football. Fans loved it. Bum said, "They're all waiting after the games for his autograph. I get on the bus pretty quick. The only question they ask me is, 'When's Billy comin' out?'"

In mid-October, the Oilers beat George Allen, Billy Kilmer and the mighty Redskins 13-10. It was the biggest Oiler victory in a long time and was Houston's tenth win in its last 13 regular-season games. The noise in the Dome was deafening. Ed Biles called fans the "12th man for us" as the defense turned back three scoring threats in the final 13 minutes off a Moore interception, a Bingham stop on fourth-and-one, and a Culp sack in the waning minutes. Brazile was a one-man wrecking crew. Bethea said, "We won't get cocky. We proved what we can do. We proved it to Washington and the whole country. Howard Cosell will see that."

Fans began to believe. Around this time, Phillips came up with his "Hold the Rope," motivational line. It came from a story about a mountain climber who fell off a cliff clinging desperately to his rope. "But, no matter how tight he held on," Bum told them, "it wasn't gonna do him any good if the guy at the other end wasn't holding just as tight." Bum said that if he were hanging over a cliff, he would want "the best possible fellow holding the end of the rope ... and that's the sort of players I want on my team." It was a metaphor for believing in the player next to you, trusting him to do his job so you can do yours.

Fans ate it up. Rope was everywhere for Detroit. They won 24-8 to move to 5-1 and officially enter the horse race with 6-0 Cincinnati and 5-1 Pittsburgh. About White Shoes, the Lions' coach said, "No team should let that man get his hands on the ball."

In early November, Pittsburgh dropped Houston 24-17 on a bad call in an exciting ballgame. With Mel Blount and Billy Johnson wrestling in the end zone for the ball, the officials gave it to Pittsburgh. Replays showed Johnson had it. "I've got no complaints except the score," said the coach. It was the Oilers' bad luck that the AFC Central had turned into the best division in football just as they hit stride. Houston, Pittsburgh and Cincinnati combined were 17-1 against outside teams, including 6-0 against NFC teams. Yet the Oilers were in third place at 5-2.

That brought up a huge game with the Dolphins, winners of two of the last three Super Bowls. Bubba

Ken Burrough (No. 00) was 6'3 and could run a 4.4 in pads. He finally got it going in 1975 to lead the NFL in receiving yards (1,063) and yards per catch (20.1).

The 3-4 is great against the run due to its gap stuffing linebackers. The 1975 team allowed an NFL-low 3.4 yards per carry, and was the AFC's top scoring defense. At right, all four LBs — Washington (59), Brazile (52), Kiner (57) and Bingham (54) meet for a party in the Chiefs' backfield.

Smith got the start at DE, replacing his brother Tody. He played under Shula at Baltimore who he felt had shafted him. Besides providing help on Shula's tendencies, he had 6 tackles and 2 blocked extra points. Except for 4 plays, the defense played well, despite being on the field the entire third quarter. Johnson had his record-tying fourth kick return for a TD. But it took Coleman's incredible multiple-tackle-breaking 7-yard run on the third down to eke out the 20-19 victory.

The Oilers were on top of the world but not their division. And the 8-1 Steelers were waiting for a *Monday Night Football* showdown. But Houston first had to endure the premiere of Dan Pastorini's movie, *Weed*, in which he played a drug smuggler opposite his wife, who was a sexy federal agent. The most polite local critic was Ron Saul, who mustered: "Well, Dan was a heckuva lot better than Joe Namath in *CC & Company*."

Everyone was eager to show they were not the same team that lost 31-of-34 from 1972 through 1974. The mayor and a few other city fathers hoped to erase the image of the last MNF game on October 9, 1972, sometimes referred to as "the one-finger salute game."

Howard Cosell was in their corner. "The Oilers are probably the most underpublicized truly fine football team in my six years of *Monday Night Football*," he said.

"I want the whole country to see how good the Oilers are ... and learn about the Teddy Washington's and Willie Germanys of the world in addition to Billy Johnson." A victory would throw the division into a three-way tie for first.

With all the build-up, a let down was in the cards. The history of the Oilers is either you get a team that, when bad, stinks worse than any in history, or when good, will take you to the brink and then break your heart every time. Pittsburgh led 15-3 at the half, winning 32-9 in a game that exposed a lot of limp rope in the Astrodome on national television. Some said Pastorini's appearances all over town before the game hurt, but the two dropped TD passes bothered him more.

The coach thought they suffered from performance anxiety syndrome. "It's the only time I've ever seen a team too ready to play," he later recalled. "We were so damn intent on killing them, we never did settle down. We charged in there on every play and Pittsburgh called about 25 traps. They ran right past us."

Six days later, they had to play at Cincinnati in the rain. The Oilers did not have it, and lost 23-19, even though the Bengals played a backup QB. The loss would be costly as they fell to 7-4, with all four losses to the Bengals and Steelers.

They regrouped on December 7 to thump the 49ers 27-13 in a game that started with Al Green forgetting the lyrics to "The Star Spangled Banner" and ended with the defense limiting Frisco to 7.2 inches per carry.

Next, they beat the playoff-bound Raiders 27-26 on a Pastorini to Alston TD pass with no time left. It was

The Oiler's 20-19 victory over the Dolphins on November 16 was a watershed game. Bum called Ronnie Coleman's game-winning touchdown "as great a seven-yard run as any back ever made."

their first win in Oakland since 1961 and just Oakland's twelfth home loss in 10 years. Going in, 48-year-old George Blanda needed 4 points to reach 2,000 for his career but fell short, missing a FG, an extra point, and having another blocked by Bubba Smith. They closed the season with a 21-10 win over the Browns to sweep that series for the first time.

Houston finished 10-4, but out of the playoffs. Same for Miami as they became the first two teams ever to win 10 games and not make the playoffs. Cincinnati made it as a wildcard team at 11-3 by virtue of its two victories over Houston. The Colts also made it at 10-4 as Eastern Division champs. Pittsburgh won its second straight Super Bowl, beating Dallas 21-17.

OVERVIEW

The 1975 season was a big step for this team. It was their best record since 1962, and included victories over the powerful Dolphins, Redskins and Raiders. They beat the Chiefs for the first time since 1965, the Raiders for the first time since 1966 and an NFC team for the first time ever, ending that 11-game losing streak. They knocked both Miami and Washington out of the playoffs. They beat the point spread 12 of 14 times.

Some unusual circumstances, namely the WFL and the strike in '74, had come together to get the Oilers to this point. The 1973 No. 1 overall draft choice, wasted on Matuszak, turned into Culp in 1974 and Brazile in 1975 primarily because of the WFL. Former WFLers Booker Brown and Benny Johnson turned into starting center Carl Mauck. Brown ended up a backup in San Diego while Jabbo was a cut. Without the strike, starters Coleman, Washington and Fisher might not have even made the team. Finally, Johnson came out of nowhere as a fifteenth-round throwaway draft choice.

On the other hand, after a 7-2 start, they dropped back-to-back games to division rivals Pittsburgh and Cincinnati to drop out of the race. All that was needed for the playoffs was one win over the Bengals. In general, however, the players, coaches and fans were happy to have their first winning season in eight years.

The defense led the way starting with the front line. In '74, the Oilers ranked 21st (out of 26) against the run. In '75, they led the NFL, surrendering just 3.4 yards per carry. They became well-known for shutting down opposing RBs. Mercury Morris had 6 yards on 9 carries, Mike Thomas had 11 on 17 carries, Don Woods had 60 and Greg Pruitt averaged 44 yards in two games. Only Pittsburgh held the key with 411 yards in two games.

They also forced 38 fumbles and got a good pass rush out of the 3-4, setting a team record with 45 sacks led by Culp's 11½ and Bethea's 10. They were fifth in points allowed (first in the conference) and gave up just one third quarter TD the entire year.

Pastorini threw for 2,053 yards on 163-of-342 (46%) with 14 TDs and 16 interceptions to rank tenth in the AFC (out of 13). The team's 17 interceptions total were an all-time low. Burrough had his best season with 53 catches and was the only player to have over 1,000 yards receiving (1,063). His 20.1 yards per catch average also topped the NFL as he took a place beside Cliff Branch as one of the game's top two deep threats. Coleman was No. 8 in the AFC in rushing with 790 yards on 175 carries (4.5-yard average), the most since Hoyle Granger in 1969. Hardeman added 648 yards, but was injured most of the second half of the season. Even when healthy, he seemed to fall down a lot. Bum liked to say, "His mind outran his feet."

The best-known Oiler was White Shoes, who tied the record for most return TDs (4) and led the league in punt returns. The Oilers placed four on the All-Pro team: Bethea, Culp, Burrough and Johnson. Robert Brazile was rookie of the year.

The season even pleased hard-to-satisfy Bethea, who said, "After the '72 season, I hated to walk out that door. I wanted to wait until everybody in the whole stadium had got into their cars and gone home. Not now. We can all walk out of here with our heads held high. We're going to be home for Christmas, but we don't have anything to be ashamed about anymore."

Adams also quieted down. His team drew a club record 336,458 fans for 7 home games (48,065 average).

1976: LETDOWN

The Oilers appeared to be on their way. But there was trouble just below the surface. The OL was still in sad shape. Depth was very thin. Unfortunately, there would be no relief coming through the draft.

THE 1976 DRAFT

The Oilers had already traded away their first- (Washington), third- (Culp), fourth- (Maxwell), fifth- (Wright) and seventh- (Bob Adams) round picks, and had just 13 choices overall in the 17 rounds. Only George Allen's Washington Redskins had fewer.

The two teams the Oilers trailed in the standings, the Steelers and Bengals, had 22 and 24 selections, respectively. Cincinnati had double choices in each of the first five rounds. Fortunately, it was not a very deep draft.

On April 2, just before the draft, the Oilers traded QB Lynn Dickey to Green Bay for QB John Hadl, CB

Ken Ellis, a fourth-round choice, and some money. The *Post* headline read: "Oilers Strike it Rich," and opined that "the Dickey trade ... should go far in atoning the miscalculations of yesteryear." Hadl, 36, and the NFL's third-leading career passer, would serve as backup and sage to Dante. Ellis was a former All-Pro, and they certainly needed the draft choice.

The Oilers needed help anywhere except LB. They were hoping for a WR. The problem was that tiny Billy Johnson kept getting nicked at that position, and the injuries were interfering with his kick returning. Finding a replacement was imperative.

With their top pick, they took TE/WR Mike Barber of Louisiana Tech. Barber was a risk coming off knee surgery, but had 4.5 speed when healthy. He said the right things, "I just want to get my headgear on and play for Houston because that's where I wanted to go in the first place. I didn't want to go East. I wanted to stay in Texas, but I didn't want to play for the Cowboys. Don't ask me why, but I just never cared much for them."

They used Green Bay's fourth-round pick on WR Steve Largent (5'11, 180) of Tulsa where he played under former Oiler assistant FA Dry. The *Post* said he fit "the mold of the 'possession-type' receiver Houston lacked last year." Other selections were OT Todd Simonsen (6th round), DT Larry Harris (8th), OT Bobby Simon (8th) and LB Art Stringer (9th).

1976 TRAINING CAMP

Camp was back in Huntsville for the last time. Things were very loose, perhaps too loose. Bum did not like to scrimmage or hit in camp. Plus, there were not many rookies or free agents to offer competition. Many players took it easy.

About the slack atmosphere, Bum said: "Most pros are married and they have to spend some time around the house. They have responsibilities to their wives. They're in the honey-do business. You know, honey do this and honey do that. I don't want the players' wives complaining about old Bum Phillips in their pillowtalk all night."

The coaching changes included Ken McCullough of the CFL who replaced Sam Boghosian on the OL. Bum also hired his son, Wade. "Negotiate? There wasn't any negotiating to it," he said. "I just showed Wade the contract and said, 'This is it.' Just like I'd tell him what to eat for breakfast. After all, if he can't trust his 'ol daddy,

Mike Barber

who can he trust?" When someone asked what would happen if he had to fire Wade, he answered: "If I fire him, I gotta fire my wife, my daughter-in-law, and my grandchildren."

Phillips also kept up the horse trading. He acquired veteran safety Mike Weger. He also continued taking pot luck with over-the-hill skills players, sending a '78 fifth-rounder to KC for Otis Taylor. An All-Pro in '72 and '73, Taylor was coming off knee surgery, and like Vic Washington and Elmo Wright, was not the same player he used to be. Reflecting the team's disappointment in Hardeman, Bum picked up ex-Oiler FB Joe Dawkins from the Giants for a seventh-round choice. Later in camp, he traded more draft choices for another one-time great, RB Altie Taylor of Detroit. This Taylor was Detroit's all-time leading rusher, but at the time of the trade, was in a hospital suffering from what was described as "mental exhaustion."

Bum also traded special teams demon LB Guy Roberts for OG Dennis Havig. He sent OG Ron Saul to Washington for a seventh-rounder in '77, a sixth-rounder in '78 and a third-rounder in '79. He also got more choices for Ken Ellis (Miami's 3rd and 4th), who came in the Dickey trade. Although once an All-Pro, he was now a dud beaten out by 32-year-old Zeke Moore.

Altie Taylor "recovered" long enough to fail his physical voiding that trade. He was later signed only to be cut. Other cuts included Billy Parks (one catch in '75), Jim Beirne (for the fourth time), Willie Germany (starting SS in '75), Otis Taylor and Bubba Smith. They also lost Mark Cotney in the expansion draft.

There was not going to be any help from the draft. TE Barber, OTs Harris and Simon, and LB Stringer all ended up on the IR. The IR was a favorite technique of Phillips' to hold onto younger players.

The most painful cut of a drafted player was one that would come back to haunt them many times. Fourth-round choice Steve Largent was released early. Looking for backups for Burrough and Johnson, they chose Emmett Edwards, Otis Taylor, Mike Barber and Melvin Booker. Bum said the early cut was to give him a chance to sign with another club. The word was that he was "too slow." WR coach Fran Polsfoot would later lose his job over this decision. Meanwhile, Taylor turned out to be lame and was cut just two weeks after Largent. Melvin "Home Run" Booker was cut around midseason without ever catching a pass. Edwards was traded. Largent, on the other hand, went on to become the most prolific WR in NFL history. "I've been looking for an excuse

Coach Phillips' meetings were not always as entertaining as his press conferences.
Photos © Joel Durate.

why we traded him ever since. We blew it," Bum recalled later.

Despite the easygoing atmosphere, tempers flared. Beaumont's Bubba Smith was not happy being cut, and claimed Bum first asked him to fake an injury to be put on the IR. He refused and was released. This angered his little brother, Tody, who got into a locker room fight with Bingham in which Smith reportedly pulled a pistol. Both players denied the incident and Bubba was later reactivated.

The Oilers went 0-6 in the preseason, losing to the Cowboys 26-20 in OT after leading 20-3 in the 4th quarter. Oiler publicist Jim McLemore died of a heart attack that weekend.

The losses troubled fans, but not Phillips. Winning exhibition games was not high on his list. The *Post's* preseason football special noted they were stronger, although the only new starter was Weger at SS. Pointing out that the defense that surrendered just 16 points a game was back, as were Johnson, Burrough and Pastorini, the *Post* predicted that with "a steady ground game, the Oilers can roll ... all the way to the playoffs."

THE 1976 REGULAR SEASON — SLACKING

Fans were nervous for the opener with Tampa Bay. It looked like a set-up by the league and another opportunity to add to Oiler mythology by becoming the expansion team's first victim.

Luckily, it was Tampa who made history. They became lost after the warm-ups and could not find the dressing rooms. The whole team, consisting of 45 players, eight coaches and various trainers and equipment men, were wandering around the innards of the Dome. By the time a security guard found them to take them to their dressing room, it was time to start the game. The Bucs could not find the end zone, either, losing 20-0.

Tampa went on to lose their first 26 regular season games, 11 by shutout. They were the only expansion team in history to go without a win its first season, and did not win one until December 11, 1977. Fortunately it was the Saints, not the Oilers, who earned that honor.

The next week, they beat the Bills for the ninth consecutive time 13-3, again holding down OJ Simpson (38 yards). Hardeman scored the only TD and Butler added a 55-yard FG.

They then had a golden opportunity to take over sole possession of first place against the Raiders who were playing without Ken Stabler. In the 1st quarter, Houston blew a first-and-goal settling for a FG. Trailing 7-6 in the 3rd quarter, Brazile had an interception for a TD but stepped out at the Oakland 9. On third down following the interception, Willis was ruled down at the 6-inch line. Instead of kicking for the lead, Phillips went for it and Pastorini was stopped on a sneak. The Raiders went up 14-6 on a bad call when replays showed Cliff Branch was out of the end zone on a TD. Pastorini cut it to 14-13 with a TD to Alston with 7 minutes left. But that is how it ended, as Butler barely missed a 55-yard FG with no time left.

Then there were several changes. Mike Barber had season-ending knee surgery and Emmett Edwards was traded to Buffalo. Edwards had 4.4 speed but could not catch. They also picked up safety Mike Reinfeldt off waivers from Oakland.

They next went to New Orleans and a hockey game broke out. Houston broke open a close game with three 3rd quarter TDs to go up 31-9. With about five minutes left, Saint Tony Galbreath threw elbows at Teddy Washington who was taking his time releasing after a tackle. The benches emptied. Off to the side, Zeke Moore punched Tinker Owens, injuring his eye. Archie Manning and another Saint charged at Moore, and then at an official. Moore and Manning were ejected as Owens was carted off on a stretcher. Ten minutes went by before another play was run. As Moore walked off the field, a fan jumped out of the stands and kicked him from behind. As the rest of the Oilers made their way off the field after the 31-26 victory, the players and coaches were showered with garbage, bottles, cans, fruit and other substances. Photographers caught Bum giving the angry Who-dats the finger.

Next, they beat Denver 17-3, holding Otis Armstrong to 47 yards. Although 4-1, they were in trouble. Mike Weger was lost to knee surgery. Tody Smith, Whittington and Bethea all came out against Denver. Culp, Washington, Johnson, Willis and Burrough were also hurt going into the next game at San Diego. That is where it all collapsed.

With Cincinnati already defeated, Houston was alone in first place for the first time since 1962. It lasted only four hours, though, as they fell 30-27 to the heavy underdog Chargers. Ted Washington and Greg Sampson were lost for the season to knee injuries. Washington was felled by a viscous clip. With him and Smith out, the Chargers ran over the Oilers' left side, ringing up 473 yards against what had been the top defense in football. Countering was Pastorini, who went 25-for-39 for 329 yards and 3 TDs. The Oilers had the game won but for a Charlie Joiner TD that should not have counted. Joiner dove for a quick-out at the Charger 29. After rising to one knee, Ted Thompson slapped Joiner's shoulder. But when no whistle blew, Joiner stood and took off with everyone standing around thinking the play was over. Replays left no doubt that he was downed by contact. The rule had changed that year about when a player was downed. All that was needed was a touch. Apparently the rule was not well understood.

That brought up Cincinnati for the biggest game of the year. In midweek before the game, Pastorini totaled his car around 4 a.m. near downtown. He said he was lost, missed an exit and crashed while trying to put out his cigarette. Miraculously, he not only escaped death, but also came out of it with only a few cuts and a mild concussion. "It was kinda scary, especially when my engine came up and joined me in the front seat," said Dante. Dale Robertson wrote: "Officers were aware that the 27-year-old quarterback had been drinking, a *Post* source said, but he was definitely not intoxicated and no chargers were filed. The police report indicated that no alcohol test had been administered." Dale and Dan would not exactly become the best of friends.

He should have just stayed in the hospital. Trailing 20-0 at the half, they self-destructed on two goal line failures in the third quarter. On the first, an attempted fourth down pass to tackle eligible Elbert Drungo was too high. Three minutes later, with eight minutes left in the third, the Oilers had another first-and-goal at the 1 and a chance to get back into the game. But Pastorini was sacked at the 12 and fumbled. Coy Bacon (Cincinnati acquired him for Charlie Joiner) picked it up and ran 48 yards, then lateraled to another Bengal who ran the final 32. They lost 27-7.

Fans wondered what was up with Pastorini. It was just a year before that he was partying all over town with his movie opening before the biggest game of that year. He was booed. Coach Phillips stood by his man. "That's his business," Bum said when asked about the incident, "I'm sorry it happened but I'm extremely relieved he wasn't hurt seriously. Sometimes it doesn't turn out so good when you're in a car wreck." Bum had his own brush with catastrophe the day of Dante's wreck as his coaching tower blew over and crashed in stormy weather just a few minutes after he climbed out of it.

The next game, the Oilers made it 0-3 on *Monday Night Football*, losing in Baltimore 38-14. After WRs dropped 8 passes, Pastorini yelled at them on the sideline and was promptly benched as Phillips reminded Dan who did the coaching. After the game, Pastorini reminded Bum that he wanted to be traded. Not wanting to be left out, Bethea also asked for a trade. Even Culp began grumbling.

The main problems were injuries followed by an offense that could not move the ball. A crummy punting game did not help. Attempts to replace Pastorini became progressively comical with the likes of Mitch Hoopes, then Skip Butler and Leroy Clark. The defense could not hold together under that kind of pressure.

After losing their fourth in a row to the Browns (21-7), they were in last place. That was followed by a 31-27

loss to the Bengals on a tackle-breaking bomb hauled in by Oiler-killer Isaac Curtis in the last seconds. In the final game, the Oilers had a chance to knock Pittsburgh out of the playoffs, sending their friends, the Bengals, in their place. The defense played tough for one half but later collapsed under the weight of a pathetic offense, losing 21-0. "Ever been to a circus when the bears got loose? The people scatter. That was us out there the second half," said Phillips. At least it meant Cincinnati missed the playoffs, too.

After the 4-1 start, the Oilers lost 8-of-9 to finish at 5-9. Pittsburgh, Cincinnati, Baltimore and Oakland made the playoffs, and after many years of frustration, Oakland finally won the Super Bowl. They did it running Bum's 3-4 defense.

Phillips came clean at the end of the year, saying, "I knew this could happen to us. I knew it before we went to camp. But I certainly wasn't gonna talk about it. We're in the business of selling tickets too."

OVERVIEW

People questioned the team's commitment. Several players made vague comments about camp, referring only to "the activities" going on in Huntsville. Robertson of the *Post* called the 10 wins in 1975 "flukish" and said they did it against "a schedule of moderate difficulty, with a lot of big breaks." As to '76, he said "the Oilers fooled themselves" into thinking they were good by winning 4 of the first 5 against "teams they were supposed to beat."

That was a bit harsh, considering the injuries. Plus, they were not losing to patsies. The Chargers were the only team without 9 wins to beat them. Houston dropped 4 games to 10-4 Pittsburgh and Cincinnati, 2 games to 9-5 Cleveland and a game apiece to 13-1 Oakland and 11-3 Baltimore. "We played some doggone fine teams," Bum admitted, "and they all beat us." In addition, two of the losses were the direct result of erroneous calls on that allowed TDs.

As of 1976, not everyone was convinced that Bum Phillips was the answer.

The moment things went bad was when Tody Smith was hurt against Denver. With Washington already hurt, the left side of the defense collapsed. Even though they beat the Broncos, the Chargers paved the way right over undrafted rookie Al Burton the next week, and it continued that way most of the rest of the year. The other side, the weak side, was very tough with Bethea (14½ sacks) and Brazile (6½).

Phillips managed to tweak more sacks out of his base 3-4 each year. In 1973, they had 27, improving to 40 in '74, 45 in '75, and 50 in '76. Still, the defense gave up more points than it did in 1975, while surrendering fewer yards. In 1976, they gave up 3,967 yards and 273 points compared to 4,137 and 226 in 1975. The rush defense slipped from first in the AFC to seventh. The pass defense gave up 600 fewer yards but had only 11 interceptions, compared to 24 in '75.

The rush offense fell to No. 27. The OL also gave up 39 sacks for 357 yards of losses. RB was by committee. Coleman led with 684 yards and 2 TDs, but a knee injury hindered his effectiveness. Willis added 552 yards while Hardeman had only 114.

Burrough led the team with 51 receptions for 932 yards and 7 TDs. Burrough's 51 receptions placed him fifth in the AFC. He was the only Oiler near the top of any category. Double zero's career average on TD receptions was 50.1 yards per catch. As the major offensive threat, he always drew a double team. Johnson added 47 for 495 yards. Nagged by injuries all season, he did not have any returns for TDs. Coleman added 39 catches for 220 yards.

Pastorini went 167-of-309 (54%) for 1,785 yards, 10 TDs and 10 interceptions. Hadl had 644 yards on 60-of-113 passing. They were both dogged by way too many dropped passes. Alston bobbled a bunch, as did Edwards, who was traded. Booker missed so many that Pastorini yelled at him. Even Burrough and Johnson joined in the dropsies. Meanwhile, Steve Largent was Seattle's leading receiver.

Brazile made All-Pro in his second year, but none of the '76 draft choices contributed. Barber and Stringer showed promise, but could not stay healthy. Of the three tackles drafted (Simonsen, Harris, Simon), none would ever contribute.

"We played hard all year," said Phillips, "as hard as we could. Motivation was never a problem. We just weren't deep enough to overcome our problems. If we hadn't had the injuries, we coulda done a whole lot better, but you can't expect to go every season without getting people hurt." It was true that injuries ruined the season. Motivation was another matter. A poor draft produced no rookies to challenge for positions. Consequently, the veterans took it easy. To his credit, Phillips would not make that mistake again.

1977: REBIRTH

In 1973, the Chiefs offered their No. 1 plus two starting OLs for Pastorini. That would have given them three first-round picks plus two desperately needed linemen. The top college player that season was QB Bert Jones of LSU. Thus, Houston could have had Jones and the two OLs, but also any two from among Isaac Curtis, Mike Holmes, Joe DeLamielleure, Derland Moore, Greg Pruitt, Cullen Bryant, Terry Metcalf, Leon Gray, Dan Fouts, Harvey Martin and Mike Barnes.

They turned it down because they already had Pastorini and Dickey. They took John Matuszak while Jones went second.

At the time, there were not many great QBs. The best of the day was Stabler followed by Tarkington, Griese and Staubach. Bradshaw had not yet arrived. Pat Haden, Roman Gabriel and Steve Grogan were considered good. Charley Johnson was the fourth-rated passer in the AFC. That left many teams needing help and opened up lots of trade possibilities.

While Houston could not have known Dickey would have a hip dislocated or Pastorini would beg to be traded to Los Angeles, Bert Jones was the better fit. It was Jones who married his high school sweetheart, came back to the Louisiana-Texas area every year to go hunting and fishing, and chewed tobacco. Pastorini, on the other hand, married a well-endowed actress and liked to hang with the Hollywood crowd.

Jones and Ted Marchibroda turned the Colts from a two-win team in 1974 to a 10-win team in 1975 that won the AFC East. In 1976, they crushed the Oilers on their way to an 11-3 season. Joe Namath called him the premier QB in football.

Pastorini complained of mistreatment. Dan stated he intended to play out his option in 1977 and move on. He also said if the Oilers were going to keep making him punt, he should have a punter's salary added to his wages.

In April, Pastorini's lifestyle had some dire consequences. He lost control of his drag boat at a competition. The craft careened wildly through the water, and then plowed through a crowd of spectators lining the shore. Two people died.

THE 1977 DRAFT

The Oilers would have another chance to trade Dante before the '77 draft. LA and Don Klosterman, who came over with Rosenbloom, thought Dan was the key to the Super Bowl. But they were not willing to pay the Oilers' price of two first-round picks and two seconds.

It was past time for an infuse of talent. The last six drafts had produced five starters (Bingham, Brazile, Johnson, Sampson, Pastorini). It was the worst draft record in football. Of the 43 roster players at the end of the season, 21 were free agents. The only rookie to contribute in 1976 was free agent Al Burton. The team needed both depth and immediate starters.

For once they had some picks, including a 1st, 2nd, three in the 3rd (Dickey, Ellis and Edwards trades), a 4th (Ellis), and two each in the 6th and 8th (Largent) for 14 picks total. It was a fairly deep draft. The total rounds were shortened from 17 to 12 and the draft was pushed back to May which gave staffs more time to prepare.

"When you only win five games," Bum said, "you can use help everywhere. We're not looking for people to play positions. We're looking for good football players."

The first selection was Missouri OT Morris Towns (6'4, 275) followed by Penn State OG George Reihner (6'4, 263). Bum said, "In order to move the football, you have to get some blocking. Both of these guys are big, fast and agile, and they're from winning teams in good leagues. We know they can play."

Towns was the third tackle taken. They could have chosen Ted Albrecht (a better OT), Raymond Clayborn (UT), Robert Jackson (A&M), Robin Cole, Bob Brudzinski or Stanley Morgan (Tennessee).

Reihner was the second OG taken and eighth lineman overall. Bum said, "The other people who went with offensive linemen in the first round changed in the second. That left us with a real good pick. You couldn't have got a Reihner any later than we did."

They had a great third round with RBs Tim Wilson of Maryland and Rob Carpenter of Miami of Ohio. The *Post* said "Neither is a burner but they do like to block." Bum's assessment was: "We had a couple of chances to get a scooter but how much blocking could they do if we run to their side? No, we wanted blockers." They followed up with TE Jimmy Giles of Alcorn State, who Bum called a "sleeper."

In later rounds, the Oilers again played the WR game with Warren Anderson (4th round), Steve Davis (8th) and Eddie Foster of Houston Kashmere and UH (8th). Had they kept Largent, they would not have been chasing

Maryland's Tim Wilson was one of several good players added in the 1977 draft.

WRs and could have selected Lester Hayes (5th), Joe Klecko (6th), Wilbert Montgomery (6th) and Rod Martin (12th). Houston had to forfeit its fifth-round choice because of a "signing violation." Hayes went to Oakland four choices later. Other Houston selections were DB Bill Currier (9th) and 29-year-old PK Ove Johansson of Abilene Christian (12th).

"We drafted for depth," said the coach. "In the past, it was always for need. You know, that best available stuff. That's like trying to plug 15 holes in the dike with 10 fingers. Instead, we strengthened one side, where we can put 10 fingers in five holes." The most noticeable weakness that went unaddressed was DE.

Although Towns would not start, it was a solid draft. Three picks were named to the All-Rookie team. Six would start at times in 1977 (Reihner, Wilson, Giles, Carpenter, Foster, Currier). The scouts were George Blackburn and Bill Groman.

TURN AND FACE THE CHANGE

In the offseason, the coaching staff and front office were revamped for the umpteenth time. Just since the end of the '76 season, Houston made 20 changes in those two areas alone. It was nothing new. Since 1970, the Oilers had gone through 5 head coaches, 4 GMs, 6 personnel directors, 11 scouts, 23 assistant coaches, 3 public relations directors, 3 photographers, 3 trainers, 2 ticket managers and no championships.

Although Phillips was starting his third season, he was already second behind Wally Lemm in tenure. As remarkable as it sounds, heading into season No. 18, the Oilers had had just one head coach last more than three years.

By way of comparison, the Cowboys had employed one coach (Landry), one GM (Schramm) and one personnel director (Brandt) since 1960.

In 1977, Tom Williams (assistant GM) and Gordon Johnson (ticket manager) were fired. Bob Boen went from assistant controller to controller. Lewis Mangum went from controller to business manager. Wayne Fisher moved from executive vice-president to assistant controller. Bob Ellis became assistant director of public relations. Ladd Herczeg was moved from finance VP to senior VP of Bud Adams Enterprises, Inc. Walt Schlinkman went to the Speakers Bureau. Joe Madro was fired as director of scouting, as was scout Bruce Kebric while scout John Math resigned.

Pat Peppler, who had been Atlanta's head coach in '76, was named assistant GM. WR coach Fran Polsfoot was fired (see Largent). King Hill went from OC to WR coach (see '76 offensive stats). Ken Shipp was the new OC. George Rice was fired as DL coach ('76 rush defense fell from first to seventh) and replaced by Wade Phillips. Ken McCullough was fired as OL coach after one year ('76 rush offense was the second worst in NFL) and replaced by Joe Bugel.

Sportswriter David Casstevens put it like this: "The Oilers ... may lead the league in shortsightedness, infighting and change for change's sake ... Keeping up with the Oiler personnel can be a mind-boggling exercise, like trying to keep straight in your mind the characters of a Russian novel ... If all this is beginning to sound like an old Abbott and Costello routine, then you can understand both the amusement and confusion with which other teams around the league must view (the Oilers), a club on a merry-go-round, going everywhere but nowhere in particular."

1977 TRAINING CAMP

Training camp in 1977 was to be a lot different, as well. First, Houston showed some uncharacteristic chutzpah moving into Dallas Cowboy territory at Nacogdoches on the Stephen F. Austin University campus.

Second, there were many personnel changes. With the draft reduced to 12 rounds, more free agents were available. The Oilers began camp with over 50 rookies and free agents. "Some new guys may start. And others will push veterans to improve," said the one-year wiser Phillips. "The veterans know we've thrown open some jobs, but they won't gripe about it. They don't mind the competition. They're like football coaches. They always think they're gonna win."

Starting TE Mack Alston, the sole remaining player from the Ken Houston trade, played out his option and

Bum in his tower.

was not asked back. Bum also cut three WRs, two LBs and two DLs. "That's eight spots right there." Phillips said. "We want to go with as many youngsters as possible at the backup positions, and I guarantee you, we have the best crop to choose from that I've seen here."

Altie Taylor, Joe Dawkins, John Sawyer, Dennis Havig and the brothers Smith were released. Kicker Johansson was cut. Still looking for that WR, Bum picked up Bob Gaddis and Gary Garrison. They would be cut, as well, as would Phillips' RB project, Horace Belton. Al Johnson and Ted Thompson were cut but re-signed.

Most of the open positions were on offense where they had a new coordinator, a new line coach and 10 of 14 draft picks. The biggest change would come on the line both in terms of position and attitude.

Fiery young line coach Joe Bugel moved almost everyone around. He surrounded Mauck with Elbert Drungo at RG (from RT) and rookie George Reihner at LG. Conway Haymond went from LG to RT. Only Sampson (LT) and Mauck (center) remained at the same positions. Fisher was out for the time being as a starter. The other backups were Kevin Hunt who had started for the injured Sampson in 1976 and rookies David Carter and Mo Towns. First-round draft choice and one-time blubber mountain Towns was said to be "having trouble with his pass blocking."

The idea was to beef up at guard where Houston was getting run over in its division by the likes of Mean Joe Greene. Drungo played at 270 and Reihner at 260 while Fisher was just 245. In addition, he thought Hayman's natural quickness was wasted at guard. Bugel said, "I want big guards on big defensive tackles and I want our quicker people, guys like Conway and Greg Sampson, up against the ends."

On Elbert he said, "By moving Drungo inside, we're taking advantage of his size and adding years to his career." Of Reihner, he said, "I didn't think a guy could come in like he did and pick things up so fast. He's aggressive, a real street fighter." On his center, he said, "Mauck's just a pleasure to be around. He gives you an honest day's work."

Bugel was more than just a tactician; he was also a motivator possessing a Master's degree in guidance and counseling. "These guys had been told for so long how lousy they were that they'd begun to believe it themselves." Joe said. "They were just beaten down. That was the first thing I wanted to correct."

"From the first day he met us," Hayman said. "Joe's been 100% behind us. He said to forget about last year. He didn't care what happened. He said he believed in us." He viewed each side of the line as a team, like a good marriage. It worked in the preseason as the line opened holes and the young backs ran through them. Bum said, "We had two first-round picks this year, Mo Towns and Joe Bugel."

New OC Ken Shipp stated his philosophy as "moving the chains." Shipp came with a good resume of helping young QBs (Jim Hart, Archie Manning, Greg Landry) and building offenses. The scheme did appear to be more diverse, as advertised. Opposing teams had gotten into a habit of double-teaming Burrough, figuring if they stopped him, they stopped the Oilers. Shipp placed less emphasis on bombs and more on establishing the running game and utilization of the TE. Giles would be the starter and Barber the backup.

Pastorini seemed to respond and had a good preseason. Going into his seventh season, he surprised many by staying in Houston during the offseason and working out. "That meant a lot to his teammates," said the coach. "It was his way of telling them he intended to give it his best. Hell, I know he will. But he had to convince some other people."

They had a new starting WR in Eddie Foster, who was described in Oilerspeak as "a good blocker for a receiver," and a revamped backfield with Carpenter and Wilson joining Hardeman and Coleman, who was coming off hepatitis. Willis was out with a knee injury.

On defense, Jimmy Young was added at left DE. "He don't always know where the ball's going," Bum said of the former fireman, "but he's sure as hell interested in finding out." Phillips picked up undrafted rookie Ken

Kennard (6'2, 248) to fill a backup DL role with Al Burton and A&M's Jimmy Dean.

The LBs were the same. CB had Stemrick on one side and Moore and Alexander battling it out on the other. The safeties were Reinfeldt, Al Johnson and rookie Bill Currier with CL Whittington and Mike Weger both hurt. They claimed punter Cliff Parsley off waivers.

Houston went 2-4 in the preseason. The highlight was hammering the Cowboys while rolling up 400 yards of offense.

Naturally, there were problems. The new training sight was one focal point of controversy because of the unbearable heat. The beautiful pine trees around Nacogdoches were so thick they did not allow any wind. It was stifling. Bum blamed the preseason losses on the inability to get in shape because of the heat. It explained why it did not bother Dallas that the Oilers had camp in "Cowboy Country." Dallas trained in California. "It's just hot standing around," Bum said.

Hardeman was another matter. He came in 20 pounds overweight, causing teammates to change his nickname from Jaws to Cheeks.

Culp was also unhappy and Bethea was an early holdout. The new contract the Big E got by complaining so much turned into another Bud legend. Reportedly, to seal the deal, Adams gave him part of one of his ventures — a feed lot. But Elvin's cattle died and he was tweaked. Bud called it "a personal matter ... between him and me" and not part of the standard contract. Bud did not want any part of the mandatory arbitration clause. Some speculated Elvin just wanted to skip camp. Arriving for his tenth season, he said, "I deserve a medal for being here that long."

In August, Adams announced he was considering moving home games back to Rice Stadium. He said Rice might give the team a competitive advantage early in the season. "I don't think teams from the Northeast could stand the heat. We could because we practice in it," said Adams. "They might wilt before halftime. If we make the move, it will be for that reason."

The head coach seemed to support the idea that playing in air-conditioned comfort robbed the team of its home-field advantage. "We have to play Cleveland, Pittsburgh and Cincinnati in the snow up there," Phillips said, "but when they come to Houston, we play them indoors. From a coach's standpoint, I'd rather be outside."

The players thought it was stupid. "Bud's crazy as hell if he does this," said Bethea. "Down in that hole, the temperature has to be 110 degrees (in September). How the hell can that be an advantage? You're too hot to do anything. I don't care if you train outside all summer." Former Stanford player Greg Sampson agreed:

"It's not valid. When you're hot and tired, that's just how you feel. You don't get used to it. In the long run, it might wear us out. You can't play half a season in this heat and not feel it."

Some thought the reason Bud was looking at Rice was because it seats 72,000. During baseball season, the Astrodome seated 44,800, later increasing to 50,000. With an earlier start caused by the new 16-game schedule, the Oilers would have even more home games before capacity could be increased. Furthermore, the rent was cheaper and the team would get parking and concession rights which they did not have at the Dome. Adams went on record saying, "We'll be able to charge less for our tickets."

Many believed he was just trying to renegotiate his Dome lease through the press. The issue would fade away but never fully disappear.

In the meantime, the Oilers prepared for the season opener. A total of 17 new players made the team, including Toni Fritsch who would be signed a week into the season. Ten of 14 draft picks made the team (Towns, Reihner, Wilson, Giles, Carpenter, Anderson, Woolford, Carter, Foster, Currier) and 12 rookies total. New starters for 1977 included rookies Reihner, Giles and Foster. Tim Wilson and Bill Currier would soon be starting, and Carpenter would become a starter by midseason. Free agents starting the first game were NG Kennard (for Culp), DE Young (for Smith), CB Stemrick (signed '76) and safety Reinfeldt (signed '76).

THE 1977 REGULAR SEASON — FROSTED

The Oilers shut out Richard Todd and the Jets 20-0 in the season opener. The score was all the more impressive considering Skip Butler missed three FGs, had another blocked and even missed an extra point. The much maligned Butler was promptly cut and replaced by a 32-year-old balding Austrian named Toni Fritsch.

That brought up Lynn Dickey and the Packers. Green Bay was happy with Dickey's performance. Houston's end of that trade was John Hadl, Tim Wilson, Jimmy Giles and Warren Anderson. The final result would not actually be seen for another year when one of those four would be packaged in a deal for the right to pick a RB playing at the University of Texas. Late in the 4th quarter with the score tied 10-10, Green Bay threatened from the Houston 9. But Willie Alexander intercepted Dickey and ran it back 95 yards for a 16-10 Oiler victory.

They were blown out by Miami the next week as the Dolphins had 21 points before Houston had its second first down. That brought up the Steelers, whose defense from 1974-76 had yielded the fewest points and fewest yards in the NFL. To steal a phrase from John Matuszak, the Oilers "struck a blow for freedom" by shocking Pittsburgh 27-10 in the Dome. Bradshaw had 4 interceptions and broke his wrist, while the Steelers had 9 total turnovers.

The Steel Curtain punished Pastorini, too, and it cost them the next game. With Dante limping on a badly sprained ankle, the Oilers crashed against Cleveland 24-23, despite limiting the Browns to 170 yards of offense.

As of mid-October, all four Central teams were tied at 3-2 as Houston headed for Pittsburgh where the Steelers had won 18 of their last 19 divisional games. Both QBs were in pain. Bradshaw played with a cast over his wrist and Pastorini had a bad back and two twisted ankles. Dante was sacked 5 times, threw 5 interceptions and had 14 yards net passing. Pittsburgh provided balance by fumbling 5 times. It was 7-7 at halftime. With 6 minutes left, the Steelers clung to a 13-10 lead. They poured it on at the end to win 27-10. The turning point in the game came on a fumbled punt by Johnson, his first. Coleman had 114 yards to become only the second back in two years to gain over 100 yards against the Steel Curtain.

Then came the season crusher. Again it was Cincinnati. Injuries were piling up. Stemrick, Reihner and Pastorini were all out as 37-year-old John Hadl took the Oilers to no points through three quarters. With Houston down 10-3, a gimpy Pastorini came off the bench to lead them to a tie. It set up one of the worst calls to ever go against Houston. With 27 seconds left, Steve "the Bomber" Baumgartner recovered the kickoff in the end zone for the winning score. Or it was until ref Vince Jacob ruled Bengal Willie Shelby touched the ball with one foot on the sideline, making it a touchback. If that were true, it would have been the right call, but replays showed Shelby was nowhere near the ball. When questioned after the game, Shelby said, "I didn't touch the ball, I know that ... uh, why? Was I supposed to have touched it?"

In the OT, Pastorini made the wrong call on the coin flip and Chris Bahr soon gave the Bengals a 13-10 victory. When asked why he did not make an onside kick, Bum replied: "As it turned out, we had one helluva onside kick."

Phillips said he was "frosted," and openly criticized the officials. "If I had my choice, I'd like to see full-time officials," said the coach. "If they can cost me my job, I'd like to be able to cost 'em theirs. I'd like 'em to have a little more responsibility. Right now, they can go back to their insurance businesses. I really don't have an insurance business to go back to."

Bum was not fined, as was customary for critical remarks directed at game officials. It was later revealed that Rozelle agreed the call was wrong and personally apologized to Bum.

When more injuries claimed Wilson and Hardeman the next game, they might have thrown in the towel. Instead, their performance in the Bengal game convinced them they were a good team. With Carpenter inserted at FB, they took out their frustrations on Jack Pardee's Chicago Bears 47-0. Burrough caught bombs of 85 and 43 yards and Carpenter had 255 yards rushing. It had been a long time since a Houston team beat someone this bad. Radio announcers Ron Stone and Ron Franklin were so giddy they embarrassed them-

One of the reasons Bum Phillips was a special coach is that he was able to coax maximum performance out of everyone on the roster. At right, undrafted free agent LB Ted "Hi-Yo Silver" Thompson lays it out for his team. Below, one of Bum's jack-of-all-trades, Kenny Johnson, shows Denver's Rick Upchurch why he was captain of the special teams.

selves and apologized to any Bears fans listening. John Breen deadpanned, "Sid really has their offense going." Gillman, who had become the Bears' OC, would have them going in time to make the playoffs.

Against Oakland the next week, they lost Bethea for the season with a broken arm. Since his rookie season, Elvin had started a team-record 135 straight games. Suddenly Culp was surrounded by Ernest Kirk and Ken Kennard. Then they lost Fritsch, leaving Ted Thompson and Pastorini to kick off. Houston gave up field position to the defending Super Bowl champs the whole game and it was the difference. Though leading 29-24 in the 3rd quarter, they lost 34-29. Pastorini was 11-of-27 and had 4 interceptions. On losing Bethea, Bum said, "They're (Bethea and Culp) not the guys who usually get hurt. They're what you call hurters, not hurtees."

They came back and beat Seattle 22-10. In a trademark of Oiler teams of this era, they beat the Seahawks all over the field (432 yards total offense), but could not put them away. On a more positive note, Houston's exciting players (Pastorini, Burrough and especially Johnson) had made them a road attraction. They drew Seattle's biggest crowd of the year.

They were 5-5. The good news was they were just a game behind Pittsburgh. The bad was that even if they won they rest of their games, Pittsburgh had to lose twice because they owned the tie-breaker. The remaining schedule had Kansas City, Denver, Cleveland and Cincinnati.

They beat the Chiefs 34-20, overcoming 5 turnovers by rushing for a club-record 297 yards. According to Coleman, the team had come together: "Things have gone so well the last few weeks that we're just anxious to get back on the field. It's been a lot of fun. You can see the enthusiasm increase with every game." They joined Cleveland and Cincinnati at 6-5, trailing 7-4 Pittsburgh. Denver and the Orange Crush were next.

After 18 seasons of bad teams and losing, the Broncos put together a Cinderella season in 1977. At 10-1, they were looking at the playoffs for the first time ever. They were too much for Houston winning in the Astrodome 24-14 and knocking the Oilers out of the playoff picture.

That brought up another late season game in Ohio. With game time temperature at seven degrees and three feet of snow on the ground, Bum suggested that "we just forget it and play 'em a doubleheader next year." About a possible letdown, Bingham said, "I have started 97 consecutive games for this team and I have never seen this defense let down. We may have a bad series, but never a whole game. Naw, we won't let down. We don't know how." He was right as the defense forced 8 turnovers. They won 19-15.

That set up a rematch with Cincinnati, who had pulled into a first-place tie by upsetting Pittsburgh. They had to beat Houston to make the playoffs. Many in Houston felt it should have been the Oilers battling for the playoffs. Other than Vince Jacob's bad call, the Oilers would have been the ones gunning for a 9-5 record and the playoffs.

Asked if he ever thought of that call, Bum said, "Oh, maybe four or five thousand times." He expanded, "Last year, we couldn't beat Pittsburgh in that last game. We weren't good enough. We had a hard time against anyone, even the teams we were supposed to beat. It's different this season. We have good depth and better people at every position. We're playing young guys who are gonna help for a lot of years to come. We belonged in the division race. We beat Pittsburgh and we beat Cleveland. Now we got a chance to beat Cincinnati. We've been saying that we're as good as they are and we should have beaten them the first time. Well, we have a chance to prove it."

Houston won 21-16. It was defense and white shoes. Ken Anderson had 60 yards on 8-of-23 passing and was

After being decimated by injuries and lack of depth in 1976, the tough defense returned in 1977, allowing just 3.5 yards per carry, third best in the NFL. From left to right: Greg Stemrick, Mike Reinfeldt, Bob Brazile, Steve Kiner, Gregg Bingham, Andy Dorris, Elvin Bethea, Curly Culp and Ted Washington.

A high pain threshold was necessary to quarterback the Houston Oilers. Dante Antonio played through broken ribs, ankle sprains, shoulder contusions, groin pulls and even a punctured lung. From 1971 through 1979, he missed five regular season games.

sacked 5 times. Johnson accounted for 263 total yards on 14 touches. "Up there," Phillips said, "we beat them worse than we did here — except in the final score." It was a satisfying win after which the Steeler players began calling the Bengals "choke artists." The victory sent Pittsburgh into the playoffs for the sixth consecutive year as Houston knocked Cincinnati out of the playoffs for the third time in four years (although in '76, they did it by losing to Pittsburgh in the last game). The Oilers and Bum were popular in Pittsburgh, and Phillips even appeared there in the off season as a banquet speaker.

Finishing 8-6 was a significant improvement over 5-9. They were able to accomplish several things they could not in 1976, or most other years, namely beating Pittsburgh, Cincinnati and winning at Cleveland. And they knew their record could have easily been better. Besides the stolen game, two of their losses came on last-second FGs, and they probably would have beaten Oakland with the services of Fritsch. Thus, although out of the playoffs for the tenth consecutive season, it appeared they had turned the corner.

THE 1977 PLAYOFFS

In the AFC, the Steelers opened at Denver while Bert Jones had the Colts in the playoffs for the third year in a row against the Raiders. The Broncos ended seven years of AFC domination by the Dolphins, Raiders and Steelers as they beat Oakland to earn a berth in the Super Bowl.

It was a different story in the NFC. Since the merger, the AFC had dominated. AFC teams had not lost an interconference series in seven consecutive years. The NFC had the worst teams in the NFL, including such perennial losers as the Packers, Saints, Falcons, Eagles, Giants and Bears. Those teams had a combined record against AFC teams going into the '77 season of 44-77-3. They got murdered again in 1977. To top it off, Tampa Bay was just added to the list.

The Cowboys were the only good team in the NFC. They feasted on NFC teams, making the playoffs every year. In 1977, they opened against the Bears, who Houston destroyed 47-0. Although they probably could not have beaten the Raiders, Steelers or even the Colts, they got lucky and drew Denver with ancient ex-Cowboy Craig Morton at QB. He was no match, and consequently, Dallas won its second Super Bowl.

OVERVIEW

Going into the season, Houston had a lot of uncertainty. They had a new and unproven OL. The secondary was scary even with Weger and Whittington. Fans booed the QB, who wanted a trade. And they had a tough schedule.

The season started out just like the past couple had. They played good defense, bad offense and had rotten luck. After six games, they sat at 3-3.

Things began to change on October 30 in Cincinnati. Trailing 10-0, Dan Pastorini limped into the game to lead the Oilers to two scores in the final eight minutes to tie the game. They lost that game on a bad call and could have folded their tents up for the season. Instead, Dante's swagger in Cincinnati seemed to wake the offense from its deep slumber. The next game, they ran and passed all over Chicago in something of a watershed game. They won 5 of their last 7 games

Pastorini was gaining admirers. "A few years ago, when we were 1-13, I'd look at the game films and I couldn't believe the blows and licks he was taking," said top target Burrough. "You know, a receiver never sees the sacks. But I'd go by Dan's apartment some Mondays and find him asleep on the floor. He couldn't get up to go to bed. The guy took so much punishment ... I mean, he couldn't get back five yards before he'd be creamed. I started getting into my patterns quicker so he wouldn't have to hold the ball ... We have a good line now and don't have to make excuses. But before, we used to say if you put Pastorini behind Oakland's line he'd be all-planet. They talk about Ken Stabler. Dan can throw with anybody and he's a great leader."

Besides Pastorini, Burrough and Johnson stepped up, as did a slew of rookies. They also had better blocking, and consequently, the running game improved. Bugel's troops played better as the year went on. In particular, Sampson and Reihner emerged on the left side. The rushing offense climbed to eighth best. Carpenter had a great second half at FB gaining 652 yards, second most by an Oiler rookie. Coleman's 660 were tenth best in the AFC. Burrough was not in the top 10 among WRs but had the highest average per catch. With Foster starting at WR, White Shoes regained form and led the NFL in punt returns. Pastorini overcame multiple injuries to go 169-for-319 (53%) and 1,987 yards with 13 TDs and 18 interceptions.

The offense was still 13th in the AFC, but it did score more points, averaging 21.3 per game, the most since 1968. The defense gave up just 16.4 points per game. Ed Biles' guys were tough. They ranked fifth overall, seventh against the rush and seventh against the pass.

Culp, Brazile and Johnson made All-Pro and Burrough made second team. Carpenter and Reihner made the All-Rookie team while Currier should have made it.

"In all my years of coaching," Phillips said, "I've never had a more satisfying season." While the '75 team went 10-4, Bum said that team would be no match for the '77 team, which was younger, had more offensive punch and much better depth.

1978: THE TYLER ROSE

For once, all was peaceful and quiet on the Oiler front. While the team was still far from a Super Bowl, they were at least respectable again. It was a big relief to no longer be the laughing stock of the league. With the Houston economy booming, there was all lot of excitement in the air. It was about to peak.

THE 1978 DRAFT

Houston was happy with its last draft. Five draft choices earned starting spots on offense and another one on defense. It was one of the best drafts in team history. The unwritten rule, however, was that it takes two good drafts in a row to make a difference. They had the No. 17 pick in the first round. Speculation was that Houston would take a CB.

Bum got no rest after the season, having to immediately go on a tour of the various college all-star games. On the plane back from the Senior Bowl, he sat with the agent for Earl Campbell and learned that the legendary Texas high school and college back would like to stay near home. The Heisman Trophy winner was regarded as the best player in the draft. Since Tampa took Ricky Bell first the previous year, it did not need another TB. They were looking to deal.

The Oiler rumor hit the press, as did rumors that Campbell was going to Cincinnati or the Rams. The *Post* told readers he was possibly heading to Dallas for Ed Jones and draft choices. That caused jokes that he would change his name to "Camp-*bell*," ala Tony Dorsett.

In mid-April, Phillips called Coach John McKay in Tampa to let him know Houston was interested. McKay said he wanted Giles, 1978 first- and second-round picks, and a third-rounder in 1979. Bum agreed on the spot. McKay said he would speak to the owner and get back to him.

When he got off the phone, Bum said he was standing around with Assistant GM Pat Peppler and PR Director Jack Cherry and "they wondered if they were dreaming."

There was no call from McKay the next day, a Friday. Actually, he did call, but could not get through and left a message with the switchboard operator. She did not

The Southwest Conference's all-time leading receiver joined the Oilers in 1978 along with its all-time leading rusher.

Earl arrives in San Angelo in July 1978 for his first camp. Photo © F. Carter Smith.

give it to Bum until Monday. Phillips called right away on Monday. McKay said they had a deal on one condition. Bum held his breath. McKay also wanted a fifth-round pick in 1978.

They worked out the details and teletyped them to the league office to make it official. Bum said, "I don't think the City of Houston has been the same since."

There were some skeptics, which was natural in light of Houston's draft history. But anyone who had seen Earl play in person knew he was something special, a unique combination of speed, strength and determination. At 6'0, 225-pounds, he stiff-armed his way to the NCAA rushing title. He ran around, over and through would-be tacklers — whatever it took.

Earl was different in a lot of ways. He took his mother to the Heisman presentation. "When I was a kid and in trouble, I used to say 'Mama, I'm in trouble,'" Earl said at his acceptance speech, looking over at her in the audience. After a pause, he added, "So Mama, I'm in trouble. I don't know what to say." The pictures of mother and son made national headlines.

In Houston after the draft, Mrs. Campbell, who spent most of her life growing roses in Tyler and raising 11 kids said, "I was worried about Earl when he went to Austin to school — just a little ol' country boy going to the bright lights. I just told him not to forget the Lord, and I don't think he did. So far, it's paid off. I think he's a pretty good kid." Fans thought so too as Oiler ticket lines immediately filled.

After Earl came Art Still of Kentucky, Wes Chandler, Chris Ward, Terry Miller and James Lofton. With Houston's selection, Tampa took Grambling QB Doug Williams. There was a big drop-off after the first round. Tampa took Brett Moritz with Houston's second pick.

The Oilers took the BYU quarterback, Gifford Nielsen, in the third. Dale Robertson unabashedly called it the "upset pick of the day." Nielsen was one of the top passers in college his junior year, but was injured half of his senior year which was the only reason, according to Robertson, he lasted until the third.

In the fourth, they took TCU receiver Mike Renfro, who was the SWC career receptions and yardage leader. Other selections were defensive back JC Wilson (8th round) and OG John Schumacher (12th). Looking for a replacement for Giles, they took two TEs: Conrad Rucker (6th) and Stephen Young (10th). They took yet another WR, Willie Thicklen, in round eleven.

It was all offense (7 of 9 picks) for the second straight year. Bum said, "Mike broke all the SWC receiving records and Earl broke all the rushing records, so it's been a defensive draft. We ought to be able to keep the ball enough and score enough to keep the defense off the field."

In each of the past four drafts, Houston's defense had been ignored. They took just 5 defensive players out of 16 selections in 1975, 4 out of 14 in 1976, 5 of 14 in 1977 and 2 of 9 in 1978. Brazile was the only defender from those drafts higher than a sixth-round choice. Coach Biles noticed. "Getting Earl was a great deal for the team," he said, "but it made it difficult to get defensive help." Biles then added, laughing, "Bum says with the offense we're gonna have we won't need a defense. I hope he knows what he's talking about."

1978 TRAINING CAMP

Oiler camp in 1978 had a good feel to it. Going into his fourth season, Phillips had established patterns and routines the players were now familiar with. That continuity, a new word in the Oiler vocabulary, bred a certain level of comfort.

The strong finish in 1977 and addition of Earl generated excitement. Season ticket sales jumped. Several magazines were picking the Oilers to win their division.

Reached in Baton Rouge by the *Post*, the Oilers' first Heisman winner, Billy Cannon, had this advice for Earl, "All I can say about Campbell is that I hope Earl gets it all down in writing."

Earl actually came to terms before the draft because he wanted to get a quick start on the house he was going to build for his mother. "It's going to be simple and it's going to be big," said Ann Campbell. "There are nine grandkids already, and there will be more. I want them to have plenty of room when they come see me. The main thing is to have a house that's full of love and a roof that doesn't leak."

Occasionally the winner of the Danceland wet T-shirt contest would show up at practice the next day. Bum justified his curfew, saying, "This town's got a lot of water moccasins."

That contract, negotiated by an inexperienced agent, would come back to haunt Earl. But as of the Summer of 1978, all he wanted to do was play football. At one of his first practices, Campbell approached a jogging Tim Wilson and asked, "Say, do you think I'll make the team?"

Later, a reporter asked Phillips about some trouble Earl had finishing a one-mile run. Bum said, "Well, when we're faced with third and a mile, I won't put him in."

Another bit of early excitement was caused by the addition of former USC All-American Anthony Davis to the Oilers' impressive fold of RBs. Bum picked him up in May for Don Hardeman. Jaws was a huge disappointment. The player Phillips wanted with that draft pick, DT Louie Kelcher, made the Pro Bowl in 1977-78.

Davis was something of a gypsy going from the WFL to the CFL to Tampa Bay. Dale Robertson called the move "a stroke of genius." It showed Bum originally envisioned Earl as a FB and Davis at TB. It did not bother Earl. Davis said, "I talked to Earl and he said, 'AD, you gotta get some of that Skoal in you.' I don't know. Maybe we'll both have a pinch in our mouths before the season's over." But Davis proved to be all hat and no cattle. The only pinch he got was in his leg. On the second day of practice, Steve Kiner broke his leg on a routine tackle: Oiler luck.

The Oilers also traded Nacogdoches for San Angelo, and in so doing traded East Texas for West Texas, sweltering heat for dry heat and Cowboy Country for cowboy paradise.

Real cowboys, not the kind with stars on their helmets, were popular, thanks to the likes of *Urban Cowboy*. That fad coincided with some recent economic clout created by OPEC. San Angelo was riding high in the saddle. The locals fit the stereotype of Texans from the movies wearing boots and hats and big buckles. But while they were a lot more country than John Travolta, they were still bankers, lawyers and other such professionals in boots. The majority of real working cowboys in the area were actually from Mexico.

In any event, Bum and Earl fit in fine. Even California-bred Pastorini did his part to fit in. After bed check, he pulled on a pair of boots and slipped out to Danceland, West Texas' version of a disco. He was one of several Oilers asked to judge the weekly wet T-shirt contest.

The lantern-jawed Phillips still liked to survey the troops from his platform. "You know," he said, "tryin' to run wide on us is like spittin' in the ocean." One reason he felt that way was the play of Ted Washington, about whom he said, "He's wide and slung low. He's just like one of those old cement irrigation tanks. You're not gonna get the ground he's on. He's some stout."

There were problems, of course. Contract squabbles were en vogue. With most athletes represented by agents or attorneys, negotiations were more difficult and holdouts more common. Assistant GM Pat Peppler was assigned to deal with those situations. Billy Johnson held out. Several vets like Bingham, Reinfeldt, Sampson and Drungo were unhappy with their minimal 10% raises. Robertson of the *Post* wrote that "Bingham was given shabby treatment when he sat down to negotiate a new contract," while Pastorini got a sweet new deal.

Dante, who was making a movie in South America when they drafted Earl, inked a six-year, $2.5 million contract in the off season. It was a good raise over the $180,000 he made in 1977. At least it finally quieted his requests to be traded. He seemed more at ease. One day, within earshot of the coaches, he said South America was not his "cup of tea. I don't like being some place where I can't understand the language. Sorta like being around Coach Phillips."

This movie *Naked Sun*, starring Lee Majors, Karen Black and Margaux Hemmingway, had Dan as a sky-diving jewel thief. He ended up eaten by piranhas. The movie folks said any resemblance to the line blocking on Dan's first few teams was coincidence.

Because his team was better, Bum did not have to make as many desperate moves or take as many chances on elder statesmen as he had in years past. But it would not be a Phillips' camp without one of those. He obtained eight-year veteran WR Rich Caster from the Jets for two seventh-round picks.

Camp also means saying good-bye. Phillips kept JC Wilson (8th round) over 12-year vet Zeke Moore after 145 games as an Oiler. Part of the talented '67 draft,

Earl fit in quickly and easily. Number 26 is Rob Carpenter, a player he would at least partially displace in the backfield.

Zeke was the second oldest CB in the league in 1977. He also kept John Schumacher (12th) over eight-year veteran OT Kevin Hunt and Cliff Parsley over 37-year-old Jerrell Wilson.

"I preach to the players that the team comes first, and, if I really believe that, I've got to put myself in the same situation," said Phillips. "We might have sacrificed a little this year by keeping a guy like Schumacher instead of Hunt, but by the end of this year, the young guy will be even, and next year, if you stick him in there, he won't hurt you ... We're building for the future, which is the right way." Regarding the inherent risks, he replied, "There are two kinds of coaches in this business, them that get fired and them that's gonna get fired. We felt we should go with the younger guys as our reserves. Their futures are ahead of them."

Al Johnson also retired. The former college QB was Bum's kind of player, backing up at three positions: RB, WR and DB. A big-hitter who was captain of the special teams, he often led the charge downfield on kicks. He would be missed, eventually rejoining the team in November.

Seven rookies made the team, including six of eight draft choices (Campbell, Nielsen, Renfro, Rucker, Wilson, Young, Schumacher). Only WR Willie Thicklen was cut outright. Bum found free agent Johnny Dirden driving a cement truck. The other new faces were Caster, Davis and jack-of-all-trades Guido Merkins.

The offense had come of age. Seven of 11 starters were former first- (Pastorini, Campbell, Burrough, Sampson, Towns) or second-round (Barber, Reihner) selections. Tim Wilson came in the third and Renfro the fourth. Renfro got the start due to knee injuries to Johnson and Foster. Of all the starters, only Hayman was an undrafted free agent, and he would soon start splitting time with Towns at OT to make room for the return of Ed Fisher to OG. Instead of pouting after his demotion in 1977, Fisher spent the off season in the weight room bulking up. The assembled talent stood in marked contrast to the past when the offense was a patchwork of free agents.

The defense had gone the other way. There was very little new blood, with seven of 11 starters from the 1975 team returning (Culp, Bethea, Brazile, Washington, Kiner, Bingham, Alexander). The only first-round choice on defense was Brazile. Four of the starters were basically walk-ons (Washington, Young, Stemrick, Reinfeldt), as were many of the top backups (Kennard, Baumgartner, Whittington, Thompson, Andy Dorris). Just three defensive players from the previous three drafts were on the team and none were high picks.

Bum admitted "slighting the defense for the sake of the offense," but said it was necessary considering the shape of the offense when he took over. "Now we're strong enough all around to draft for specific weaknesses next year," summed up the coach. Clearly the pressure would be on the offense to perform.

On balance, the state of the team appeared good. Critic Dale Robertson wrote, "In terms of public credibility, Houston's long-suffering National Football League franchise has taken a series of giant steps forward ... The Oilers, within striking distance of a playoff berth last fall, should be over the hump ... they have the personnel to match Cincinnati and Pittsburgh. A victory over either won't be an accident."

The team customarily stumbled through the preseason going 1-3, but no one panicked. After four years, fans believed Phillips when he said those games did not matter. Nonetheless, all home exhibition games sold out. It did not hurt that the one game they played well in was against the defending Super Bowl champion Cowboys, thrashing them 27-13. In a foreshadow of things to come, Earl had 151 yards.

Campbell was first tried at FB with Carpenter at HB. After awhile, they figured out what Fred Akers did the year before, that Earl was a natural TB in the I-formation. Carpenter went back to FB. Wilson would eventually become Earl's primary backfield mate. He was given No. 34, Woody Campbell's old number. His college number (20), was already taken by Currier.

The NFL instituted some changes. The regular season would be 16 games, not 14. One additional wildcard team in each conference expanded the playoffs. In the first round of the playoffs, the two wildcard teams squared off, while the three division winners drew byes.

The new format was a boon to the AFC Central, which had been the toughest division in football for several years. The Oilers' 10-4 but no playoffs season in 1975 helped bring about the change. But what the television committee giveth, the schedule maker taketh away. The Oilers faced an incredibly tough 11-game stretch. It was LA (best defense in the NFC), at Cleveland (where Houston was 2-6), at Oakland ('76 champs), at Pittsburgh (two-time champs), Cincinnati (knocked Houston out of the playoffs in '75 and '77), Cleveland (12-4 vs. Houston overall), New England (now with Chuck Fairbanks), Miami (two-time champs), at Cincinnati and Steelers again.

THE 1978 REGULAR SEASON — OILER CANNONBALL

Fans were cautiously optimistic. Although the Oiler house appeared in order, this was a team that had enjoyed two winning seasons in 10 years and six in its entire 18-year existence. Its last divisional title was in 1967. They insulated themselves with low expectations. The offense's having scored four TDs the entire preseason did not calm nerves, and neither did the sight of half the pickup trucks in Houston flashing "This is Cowboy Country" bumper stickers.

The Oilers opened in Atlanta. The Falcons were on the rise. In 1977, they climbed to respectability by going 7-7, which generated coach of the year honors for Leeman Bennett. But the man behind the turn around was DC Jerry Glanville, whose defense set a record by giving up only 129 points (under 10 per game). They were ranked the number one pass defense, and they created havoc by blitzing on any down.

Led by QB June Jones, Atlanta generated just 171 total yards. But Houston's offense was just as poor. Pastorini kept trying to pass, and ended up getting sacked 4 times and throwing 2 interceptions. He was blitzed on almost every pass play. The Oilers had all the offense they needed in Earl, but did not use him. Atlanta won 20-14 on a TD off a blocked Parsley punt. Dan, the $2.5 million dollar man, defended the game plan, saying they tried to take what Atlanta gave.

Pastorini started in KC the next week despite contusions of the lung. Leading 17-6 in the third quarter, the Chiefs chose to defend against the bomb. That might have worked against Houston in previous years, but in 1978 it opened holes for Earl Campbell, who had 111 yards and 2 TDs, including the game winner with under 2 minutes left. Houston won 20-17.

The 49ers and OJ Simpson were next. Bud Adams bought the final 100 tickets for the sellout, which bumped the Cowboy telecast. Despite limiting OJ to 7 yards, the game was in doubt until the end. With 76 seconds left, Fritsch kicked a 19-yarder for a 20-19 lead. With time expiring, the 49ers missed a 46-yarder. Bum said he was "looking for my pocketknife. I was gonna cut my throat." Earl moved into the league rushing lead.

That brought up the rough stretch in the schedule. Although 2-1, problems showed. They did not put away the teams they were supposed to. The offense was blamed, and more for the play-calling than talent. Second and less publicized, the DBs were getting beat deep. Injuries were also troublesome. Billy Johnson re-injured his knee in his first action back from a contract fight. Pastorini had bruised lungs, and Anthony Davis was lost for the season when he re-injured the same leg. The DL rotation of Dorris for Young, Kennard for Culp and Dean for Bethea was messed up when Dean was lost for the season.

The Rams and the top defense in the NFC were next. It was a big challenge for the Oilers, who thought they were one of the best teams but had not proved it. Here was their chance.

LA gained almost 400 yards of offense but could not score, while the Oiler offense called a terrible game. Earl got few carries. Still the rookie was leaving an impression, especially on LB Isiah Robertson who dogged Earl in the press before the game. At one point, Earl lowered his shoulders and plowed into the all-star's numbers. The hit was so violent that Robertson's helmet popped straight up in the air as he dropped like a rag. Later, Earl flattened Jack Youngblood and carried safety Bill Simpson five yards downfield. Simpson said, "It was like trying to tackle a runaway train."

Late in the second, the Oilers shifted to the I-formation and began to move the ball. They might have won but for a couple of questionable play calls that let the Rams escape 10-6. Twice in the third quarter, Pastorini called dubious third down plays. On third-and-long, he tried a short pass to Carpenter. On a third-and-5 at the LA, 45, he went for the bomb. Finally, midway through the fourth, after moving on the ground to the LA 47, he lofted a deep pass for Burrough on first down that was picked off. The Oilers never got the ball back. Campbell had 13 carries.

Bum tried to put things in perspective. "Four years ago, nobody would have bet we could stay on the field with LA," he said. "Now we lose by four points to a team five straight years in the playoffs, and everybody's mad as hell. I guess that's a compliment."

Jack Gallagher wrote, "It becomes increasingly evident that if the Oilers are to win consistently this year, someone other than Pastorini must call the plays ... [fans] left the Astrodome wondering whether Dan Pastorini can call a square dance let alone a football game."

The next day, Ken Shipp criticized Pastorini in the local papers. That was a mistake. The emotional QB stomped off the practice field rather than "deck the guy." He returned only after a meeting with Phillips and Mauck. Bum told everyone, "We kissed and made up." He paused, then added, "Well, not literally." Pastorini said, "I didn't appreciate a remark made by a certain member of this organization. The calls I made are calls I was coached to make. I'm just doing what I'm told to do out there." In the end, Phillips gave in, saying, "I can find a coach a lot quicker than I can find a quarterback." Shipp soon resigned.

Sitting at 2-2 a full two games behind the Steelers, the Oilers had to travel to Cleveland for a game without Campbell, who had a strained hamstring. Although totally outplaying the 3-1 Browns in the first half, the Oilers still trailed 10-0. They blew three scoring opportunities in the first quarter on a Ronnie Coleman (195 total yards) fumble and two botched QB keepers, including an idiotic end around by Pastorini on fourth down from the Browns 1. But the defense shut down Cleveland in the second half as Alexander, Reinfeldt and Brazile each intercepted Brian Sipe. Pastorini hit Caster with a bomb to tie it at 10 in the third, and then hit Burrough with another to the Cleveland 4. The crowd

Phillips said of Toni Fritsch: "Looks like a Dutch family moved out of the backside of those britches."

stopped the game with a deluge of bottles and debris. A broken beer bottle gashed Burrough's leg. Things were so out of hand that Fritsch's 19-yard FG attempt had to be moved to the other end of the field, the part where the stands were further back. He hit it and Houston won. "No pressure," said Fritsch, shrugging, "no problem."

The next game took them to Oakland to face football's winningest team over the preceding decade. Nursing a 17-7 lead with 5 minutes left in the third, they were poised to blow the game open deep in Raider territory. But Earl was stripped of the ball at the 4 and watched Charlie Phillips run for a 96-yard TD the other way. At that point, even though both Oiler TDs came on long passes (Renfro and Barber), they became conservative, nervously hoping to sit on the 17-14 lead. Twice in the fourth quarter on third-and-long, Carpenter was sent up the middle for no gain. They ended up giving it back to Stabler with too much time. Snake sliced and diced his way 80 yards, hitting a well-covered Dave Casper with the game winner with 42 seconds left. Houston's offense rolled up 373 yards while the defense limited Oakland to 279, intercepted Stabler three times and held Mark van Eeghen, the AFC's second leading rusher, to 33 yards.

Bum defended the conservative play calls. "Remember, we were ahead. The only way we could beat ourselves was to get a pass intercepted and run back," Phillips said. "There's no percentage in taking chances under those circumstances, not when you're leading. We were aware of Oakland's potential for moving the ball and scoring, but they were going to have to do it, which they did. They beat us. We didn't beat ourselves."

"It's a long season," mulled Pastorini. "We've got 10 games left. A lot of things can happen. A lot of good things. We'll bounce back." One bad thing that happened was losing starting left OG George Reihner to a knee injury. Another was losing Billy Johnson again who, while trying to play hurt, re-injured the same knee.

The ending of the Raider game brought back some bad memories. Since 1975, when the Oilers returned to respectability, they had been besieged by just enough bad calls, bad luck and self-mutilating tendencies to keep them out of the playoffs. There was the 1975 Cincinnati game, which eerily resembled the 1978 Raider game. The Oilers led 17-7 when TE John Sawyer hauled in a pass and headed for the clincher, but fumbled at the Bengal 10. It let Cincinnati back in as they eventually won 21-19. The 11-3 Bengals made the playoffs while the 10-4 Oilers stayed home. Likewise, in 1976, the 4-1 Oilers lost to San Diego on an awful non-call on a Charlie Joiner diving catch that turned into an 81-yard TD. Houston tanked after that. Then there was the infamous 1977 game in Cincinnati when they were robbed of a TD, the game and the playoffs.

After beating Buffalo 17-10 for the tenth straight time (17-7 all-time over Buffalo), they were 4-3 and headed to Pittsburgh to take on the NFL's sole undefeated team. Houston had the distinction as the only Central team to have ever won at Three Rivers but had also lost 5-of-6 to them, including three in a row there.

Dan Pastorini took criticism in 1978 for his play calling, but had his best year with career highs in passing yards (2,473) and TDs (16) while completing 54% of his passes.

And this one was on *Monday Night Football*. Houston's 4-game *MNF* history consisted of a 21-0 loss to Cleveland in 1970, a 34-0 loss to Oakland in 1972 (the finger game), a 32-9 loss to Pittsburgh in 1975 (Oilers were 7-2 going in) and a 38-14 loss to Baltimore in 1976. "The main reason we've had problems," a sedate Elvin Bethea reflected, "is that we showed up."

This time they surprised the Steelers 24-17 behind Pastorini's 13-of-19 passing and Earl's 89 tough yards and 3 TDs against the AFC's top defense. Houston led 24-10 in the fourth quarter, but put it away only after turning Pittsburgh back on successive possessions from Houston's 15- and 14-yard lines. It was their biggest win in a long time. In 1977, the Steelers sent Houston players and coaches leather briefcases after the Cincinnati game. In 1978, they sent nothing.

Sitting 5-3 at the halfway mark, they liked their chances with 5 of the remaining 8 games at home. They promptly blew that advantage, losing to the 0-8 Bengals 28-13. In less than a week, they had beaten a 7-0 team but had lost to an 0-8 club. Willie Alexander said, "I guess you can call it our annual screwup." It hurt.

They rebounded, beating Cleveland 14-10 behind 7 sacks by the defense. The next week they trailed New England 23-0 in Foxboro late in the second quarter before Pastorini carried them to a 26-23 upset, dropping the playoff-bound Patriots to 8-3. "That's the same Dan Pastorini everybody's bitched about all these years," said Bum. "But now he has the weapons he needs." Asked what he said at halftime, Bum replied, "I begged a little and I cried a little." The bad news was they lost Carpenter for the season.

At 7-4, they stared down another *Monday Night* showdown, this time with the Dolphins. It was quite a game. ABC still considers it one of its all-time best, and Campbell's performance was voted as the greatest single-game *MNF* performance ever.

The first-half score was knotted at 14 after the teams combined for 335 yards and 23 first downs. After three quarters, it was 21-21. Early in the fourth, Miami sacked Pastorini for a safety to give them a 2-point lead. But Houston came right back on Earl's third TD of the game. Later, after an interception by Kiner, an exhausted Earl took a routine pitch around right end and busted it 81 yards for a memorable TD. The blue and white pompon-waving sellout crowd went bananas, as did Cosell & Co. and a good part of the country. It gave Earl a career high 199 yards as he became the first Oiler since Hoyle Granger in 1967 to gain 1,000 yards (also the last playoff year). Earl characteristically credited his OL. His performance was needed to offset Bob Griese's 23-of-33 passing for 349 yards against what had been the AFC's top defense. Houston won 35-30.

Bum deadpanned that the 81-yard dash "ruined our game plan. We just wanted a first down so we could run out the clock."

At long last, Houston and its team were at peace. The national TV performance was intoxicating. But tranquillity's shelf life in Houston is akin to that of a quart of Blue Belle Ice Cream in Mo Towns' freezer. The following week, Dale Robertson wrote a pair of front sports page articles about Phillips' contract situation. He speculated that Bum might coach out his option and not be with them in 1979. Bum was quoted saying the chances he would be back were 50-50. Bud Adams said he was aware of no problems. It was hard to tell whether the young reporter was being manipulated by Phillips (who Dave Casper once described as a "hoser") or trying to improve his name recognition, but with the team at 8-4 and pushing towards the playoffs, it sent a chill through Houston. It was always something.

After getting some revenge against Cincinnati 17-10, they were 9-4. With Pittsburgh at 11-2, New England at 10-3, and Miami and Oakland at 8-5, Houston was in the driver's seat for a wildcard spot and had an outside shot at the division if they could handle Pittsburgh in the Dome. The Steelers had something different in mind.

Brazile (52) combines with Washington (59), Currier (20) and Reinfeldt (37) to make the stop. The rush defense finished fourth in the AFC in 1978. And, although they gave up 18.8 points per game to the offense's 17.7, the team finished 10-6 and back in the playoffs for the first time since 1969.

"When we play them," Bum said beforehand, "it's not a game, it's a collision. The team with the most Band-Aids wins." This one was a war. Campbell went out with damaged ribs in the first quarter and did not return. Pastorini went out with broken ribs in the third. Renfro ended up on crutches. Willie Alexander left in the first quarter with a jammed jaw. Culp injured a shoulder. Barber dislocated his shoulder in the third. Brazile played through a strained groin. Reihner's knee went out again. Tim Wilson played with a broken rib. With Caster already out with a groin pull, Guido Merkins had to play WR. "It was the toughest I've ever been in — physically and mentally," said Bradshaw. "And I've never seen our football team want to win so badly."

Earl appeared headed for a big day with 41 yards in the first quarter when Donnie Shell sent him out of the game. In the audience was Ann Campbell who had gone to see her son play for the first time as a pro. He called her in the Fingers' Furniture Skybox at halftime to say, "Mama, I'm okay." The rest of the team was not. On its next four possessions, Houston netted minus-10 yards. The defense kept it close and it was just 3-3 at the half. The Steelers finally scored the lone TD late in the fourth quarter, defeating the undermanned Oilers 13-3 before 54,261, the seventh straight sellout and the largest Dome crowd ever to see the Oilers.

After clinching a playoff spot against the Saints, they set their sights on securing home field for the wildcard game against San Diego. With Pastorini and Campbell hobbling, the Oilers came from behind to take a 10-7 lead; came back from 11 points down to cut the halftime deficit to 21-17; and rallied again to cut a 14-point deficit to 31-24. But Dan Fouts was too much as he ripped the secondary for 369 yards en route to a 45-24 shellacking. Houston and the other playoff teams were fortunate that the Chargers, 7-1 over the second half of the season, missed the playoffs at 9-7.

The 10-6 Oilers were in their first playoff since the merger. They were the first team to make the playoffs with more than 4 losses, and would not have made it but for the expanded format. The loss to San Diego meant that to get to the Super Bowl, they had to win 3 road games. Playing on the road, however, did not scare this team. Since 1974, they owned a 19-17 road record.

Joining them as a wildcard team was 11-5 Miami. The division winners were 14-2 Pittsburgh, the best record in football, 11-5 New England and 10-6 Denver. The Raiders missed the playoffs and John Madden soon quit.

The Heisman Trophy winner and number-one draft pick lived up to the accolades and then some. He took the league by storm to win the rushing title. He had the most yards by a rookie in history and was named the NFL's Most Valuable Player, edging out Terry Bradshaw.

THE 1978 PLAYOFFS

The Oilers opened at the Orange Bowl before 70,036 on Christmas Eve. Pastorini had three broken ribs, a strained hamstring, a badly bruised elbow and a knee strain from the San Diego game that put him in the hospital for three days. At game time, he was outfitted like a medieval knight. He wore a military-style flak jacket around his upper torso with a molded plastic shield over the cracked ribs, a compression bandage around his throwing elbow and a bulky knee brace on his right knee. Not to mention his ears were still ringing from the boos in the last game.

Calling it a gutsy effort would shortchange his performance. With Miami determined to stop Campbell in the first half (13 yards on 16 carries), Dante torched their secondary for 261 yards. When Miami switched to defend the pass in the second half, Earl began to exert himself. Pastorini went 20-for-29 for 306 yards, his season high. He put the game away by choreographing two time-consuming fourth-quarter scoring drives as they beat the favored Dolphins 17-9. It was Houston's first playoff victory since 1961. Equally amazing was that it was the largest margin of victory over the entire 17-game season.

Houston was rocking. After the game, hard-nosed center Carl Mauck came out with *The Oiler Cannonball*, a musical praise to his team set to the tune of Wabash Cannonball:

> *Now listen to the blockin,'*
> *The ramblin' and the roar,*
> *As he glides by along the sidelines,*
> *By the hashmarks then the score.*
> *From the fancy passin' Dago,*
> *To the Tyler bowling ball.*
> *Those Patriots can be taken,*
> *By the Oiler Cannonball.*
>
> *From sunny Miami, Florida,*
> *To icy Boston, Mass.*
> *From the Broncos of Colorado*
> *To the iron in the Steelers' masks.*
> *He's mighty tough and rugged,*
> *He's feared quite well by all.*
> *He's the winning combination*
> *Of the Oiler Cannonball.*

The 10-year veteran, in many ways the heart and soul of the team, said it took him 20 minutes to pen. His mates were none too kind. "It's got to be," said his best friend Pastorini, "the worst song ever written."

No one questioned Mauck's toughness. He played smart and he played hurt. Joe Bugel said, "He's a fighter. He never surrenders." Trainer Jerry Meins said, "Mauck would play on a bloody stump." Bum said: "Anybody who doesn't think football is life and death better check with Carl. You step on that field and you're invading his territory." That the song came from this man gave it added meaning.

A large crowd was at the APC as the team left for the airport. They were rewarded with a New Years Day headline that read: "Oiler Cannonball Keeps Rolling." They destroyed the favored Pats 31-14 in Foxboro. Leading 21-0 at half, they never looked back. In the locker room the players were already calling the upcoming match in Pittsburgh "World War III."

In the two games, Dante completed 72% of his passes for 506 yards, 4 TDs and 1 interception. His playoff QB rating was 131.8. Phillips enjoyed playing the I-told-you-so game. "Yeah, Dan sorta rose to the occasion didn't he?" he asked. "He's the toughest kid I've ever seen." Mike Barber emerged as a key go-to guy with 5 receptions for 196 yards and 2 TDs.

Houston exploded. Years of suppressed emotion bubbled to the surface. It had been a long time coming. Never has a team been down so low for so long to come back to so much public love.

THE 1978 AFC CHAMPIONSHIP — HOUSTON AT PITTSBURGH

Once the butt of jokes, the Oilers were now a force. They made an interesting lot from their flamboyant QB to their quiet, record-breaking RB. Leading the parade was the head coach. By the time they reached the AFC championship, even the Eastern press had to pay attention.

Those writers did not know what to make of Bum Phillips. Their instinct was to label him a clown. That hat, those boots, the accent and chewing tobacco. And then there was what he said. Oh my god. The problem with sticking a pejorative label on Bum was that he struck a cord with football fans wherever he went. Joe Fan appreciated his unpretentious nature, bluntness and humor. It was hard not to like him.

The national press types followed him around like puppies. He obliged. He brought Terry Bradshaw a handsome black cowboy hat trimmed with a gold band and left it in his locker the day before the game. Asked what difference Campbell had made, he said, "Earl gave the Oilers a sword to fight with." Asked what he did to motivate players for the road wins, he replied, "I tell 'em I'm gonna leave 'em if they don't win." Regarding the attention, he noted, "I've always said these things. Only when I was at Nederland High, people weren't coming around and asking me questions." About the possibility of an all-Texas Super Bowl match-up with Dallas, he said, "The world's not ready for it. You think we're obnoxious now, you just wait and see."

Steeler and Texas-native Dwight White said, "Texas will file for sovereignty. They'll secede from the Union. Knowin' all the money and influence they've got down there, they'll have the game moved. They'll tell the league, 'the hell with Miami, we're playin' it in Austin!'"

Pastorini enjoyed the bright lights. He showed up in a full-length fur coat and a Columbia blue cowboy hat.

The overachieving Carl Mauck was the living embodiment of Bum Phillips' Oilers. When someone suggested that with his short hair, black shoes and lack of gold chains, Mauck was a throwback to another era, someone else volunteered, "Yeah, the Cro-Magnon era."

After battling injuries for two seasons, TE Mike Barber became a force toward the end of 1978. He finished with 32 catches, and as the season closed and playoffs began, had become a favorite of Pastorini; that is, until taken out by a vicious spear in the AFC championship.

When asked by reporters what he was doing differently in '78, he smiled, nodded in Campbell's direction and replied, "Giving the ball to him."

The game had a lot of interesting contrasts: Campbell vs. Harris, Bradshaw vs. Pastorini, Phillips vs. Noll, Pittsburgh's famous 4-3 Steel Curtain led by down linemen Greene, Greenwood, White and Furness vs. Houston's no-name 3-4 led by Culp, Bethea and Brazile.

Although Pittsburgh won the last meeting 13-3, Houston played without Campbell and Pastorini for most of that game. But the Steelers had another weapon, the weather. Freezing rain and snow flurries were predicted. "There ain't but one guy who can do anything about it," said the coach about the conditions, "and he ain't speaking to us. Not yet anyhow."

At game time on January 7, 1979, icicles hung from the goal posts. It was 26 degrees with a light but continuous rain. Bum had to put plastic around his hat.

The worst part was the slick field. It was partially frozen, icy and wet. Big Earl slipped, slid and fumbled the entire game. He could not make any sharp cuts. On their first play, he took a hand-off and was met head-on by LB Jack Hamm two yards behind the line of scrimmage. The force of the collision cracked Hamm's helmet. Joe Greene told his teammates in the ensuing huddle, "That's the way we're going to hit him all day."

At the end of the first quarter, the Steelers led 14-0, piling up 118 yards to Houston's 12. The blitzing Oiler 3-4 was not blitzing, which made the secondary vulnerable to Bradshaw bullets. Emotion poured over. There was lots of pushing and shoving. At the start of the second quarter, Steeler safety Mike Wagner speared Barber at the knees after an overthrown pass, and Barber was gone for the day, taking away one of Pastorini's primary options. Once back to the sideline, Barber yelled at Wagner and shook his crutches at him.

Late in the 2nd quarter, trailing 14-3, the Oilers were driving and had the Steelers on their heels. Pastorini hit Coleman over the middle for 15 into Steeler territory, but as he was fighting for more, Hamm hit him hard and knocked the ball loose. Bethea described what was about to happen: "It was like we'd put everything we owned in one big basket and then watched the whole bottom fall out. The bottom just dropped out."

Four plays later, Bradshaw hit Swann for a 21-3 lead. Next, Johnny Dirden fumbled the kickoff untouched in the open field and Pittsburgh had it at the Houston 17. Two plays later, Bradshaw hit Stallworth for another score. Then Coleman fumbled on the first play of the ensuing possession and Roy Gerela gave them a 31-3 lead with 4 seconds left in the half. It was 17 points in 48 seconds off 3 fumbles. Coleman said, "The ball didn't feel like a football."

Houston never recovered and lost 34-5. The Oilers had 9 turnovers, losing four of six fumbles and suffering five interceptions, four of the latter coming in the second half which helped keep the score so lopsided. Turnovers led directly to 27 of Pittsburgh's 34 points. The offense generated 168 yards, 10 first downs, no drives over 50 yards and converted 1-of-11 third downs. With Barber out, Burrough was smothered and did not catch a pass.

Fisher said, "No excuses. They just beat the hell out of us." Bradshaw was 11-of-19 for 200 yards and 2 TDs. Of the weather, he said, "It was awful," then adding with a smile, "awful good for us."

"The behinder we got," said Phillips, "the worse it got." As to his halftime speech, he said, "I don't think Billy Graham could have brought us back." He added, "The weather didn't beat us, Pittsburgh did ... They're a

Unfortunately for Earl and the Oilers, they were in the same division with one of the great defenses of all-time. In the conference championship, the Oilers kept running Earl, and the Steelers kept knocking him down on the frozen turf.

splendid football team, better than any of their other teams I've seen ... Their passing game is the best that's ever been, and today they took advantage of the breaks they got ... even if Dallas is from our state, I gotta pull for the team from our conference — and the team that beat us. I hope they're the best. And I think they are."

An admirable respect developed between the combatants. An emotional Barber did the only trash-talking, promising he was "going to get" Wagner. But several Steelers, including Joe Greene and Jack Lambert, visited the Oilers' locker room after the game, shook hands, and tried to soothe some feelings. "They're a great bunch of guys," said Earl, "They're hard-hitting but they show a lot of class and I'll be pulling for them."

Steelers fans were not so great. They pelted the dejected Oilers with snowballs as they left the field. One guy stole Bum's hat off his head. To top it off, the Oilers had to sit in the airport for five hours because of the weather. They had no idea what would be waiting.

THE RALLY

A welcome home party had already been set, win or lose, sponsored by KILT radio and the Dome. It was billed as the "I Love You, Houston Oilers Night." Once they finally landed, a parade of fans followed a team bus from Intercontinental Airport all the way to the stadium. They did not arrive until around 11 p.m. and when they did, they were shocked to find 45,000 screaming, pompon waving fans who had been drinking beer, singing and partying for hours. They were joined by two high school bands and the Derrick Dolls.

Bum had to wipe away tears as he looked around mumbling, "Gawdalmighty." It was hard to hear because the Astrodome sound system has never been good, but nobody cared. Pastorini promised a Super Bowl with this kind of support. Barber said, "This is the beginning of 1979 for us." It was a wild affair that drew almost as many people as the game did in Pittsburgh.

"What people don't realize," said Phillips later, "is there were thousands of people in cars lined up all along the road all the way from the airport to the Dome. People were honking and clapping for our buses all the way there. More people were outside than there were inside."

Later in the week, local columnist Lynn Ashby wrote a "Thanks, Oilers" article trying to explain the moment. "We were not celebrating a loss to the Steelers," he wrote, "but a victory over not caring. Indeed, we were getting so beaten for so long, we couldn't even get excited over our apathy. Now we care. Now almost everyone is an Oiler fan. And, having survived the Long March, having suffered so much for so long, and having so much in common for once, Houston has come up from the deepest valley to the mountainside. Next year, we plant the flag on top."

OVERVIEW

No question that the biggest addition was the Tyler Rose. It was also significant to the team's success that they did not have to give up Pastorini or Brazile to obtain the rights to draft Earl. They did surrender a good TE, but they had two good ones at the time.

Earl set several team records — rushing yards (1,450), rushing TDs (13) and rushing TDs in one game (four vs. Miami). His 81-yarder against Miami was the second-longest rushing TD. He was the first non-kicker to lead the team in scoring. Few rookies have ever had such an impact. He led the league in rushing and was named MVP, rookie of the year and first team All-Pro. It was somewhat unfair to defenders. At just under 6' and leaning over his gigantic thighs, they often did not see him coming through the line until it was too late.

Pittsburgh DE Dwight White said, "Earl represents the Oilers. I mean a lot of teams when they face second-and-seven will go with a draw or a reverse or a screen pass....The Oilers just give the ball to Earl and he gets his five yards. OJ would razzle you for five yards. Campbell just runs smack over your butt ... It's so obvious what he does for that team. He relieves pressure and applies pressure. He demands and commands attention. I don't see how he can get much better. He's the best thing since canned peaches."

Years later Phillips pointed to the 24-17 Oiler win at Pittsburgh on October 23 as "a real turning point for us. Earl was fantastic. He just killed them. Earl was so good that he forced the Steelers out of their overshift defense. They never ran it against us again. I knew Earl had great talent, but I didn't know what kind of heart he had until I saw him on the field that day. Earl was the type of player who was twice as good in the fourth quarter as he was in the first."

Despite being one of the final four teams, the only other Oiler on the All-Pro team was Bob Brazile. The view among many pro scouts was that the Oilers had average to below-average talent. Their success, accordingly, spoke well of Phillips. But the scouts primarily attributed it to Campbell. They said he was so good that he made everyone around him better. The Steelers had four All-Pros — Bradshaw, Hamm, Swann and Mike Webster. Steve Largent, who led the AFC in receptions, also made it, while Ken Houston was named to his eleventh Pro Bowl in a row.

Among WRs, Rich Caster led in TD catches. He split time with Renfro, giving the team versatility. Defenses had a tall order when the 6'5 Caster played opposite the 6'3 Burrough. Rich played both inside and outside, and a tight-flanker in short yardage situations, which led to many of his touchdown opportunities.

Pastorini enjoyed his best season with 2,473 yards on 199-of-368 passing (54%), with 16 TDs and 17 interceptions. Along the way, he transformed his reputation from that of temperamental playboy to one of the top QBs. It was a tortuous journey. His team missed the playoffs his first seven seasons. As late as 1976, they struggled to finish 5-9, and he was a lightning rod for the blame. He was called a bum. He was criticized for the interceptions and refusal to look to secondary receivers. He did not care for the pressure, the boos or the annual bungling by the front office and owner, and wanted out. In 1978, Pastorini finally found some peace.

The weakest link on the team was the secondary, which finished tenth in the AFC (out of 14). Without Johnson, the special teams finished seventh in punt and kickoff returns. The punting game was poor, making Phillips wish he had kept Wilson.

The season was both thrilling and tough. The schedule included games against five of the 10 playoff teams.

Eleven of Houston's 12 victories were still in doubt with three minutes left. The exception, ironically, was New England in the playoffs. All 10 regular season victories were comebacks, and 11 of the 12 wins were decided by seven points or less. Austrian Toni Fritsch, who Bum called his "little austrich," won several games in the fourth quarter and two literally in the last seconds.

The Oilers could have been 0-16 as easily as 16-0. Some of the losses were hard to swallow. They lost 10-6 to the Rams at home, inexplicably giving Earl only 13 carries. They blew a 17-7 lead against Oakland and somehow lost to 0-8 Cincinnati. The opening day loss to Atlanta was another they let slip away.

Injuries also affected the team all year, starting with the loss of Johnson, the best return man in football. The WR position was hurt early with the loss of Foster in the preseason and then decimated as they lost Renfro late in the year, Caster in the playoffs and Barber in the championship. The backfield lost Rob Carpenter in the eleventh game, and the line suffered without OG George Reihner, out at midseason.

They survived because of depth. Bum remade the entire team. Only Pastorini, Bethea, Sampson, Alexander and Bingham remained from the last 1-13 team. Of the 45 players on the '78 roster, 32 had been acquired by Phillips since 1975 and 20 had two years' experience or less. While the perception was that Phillips' teams were entitled to AARP discounts on hotel rooms, the '78 team was grounded in youth. Of the five AFC teams in the playoffs, Houston's was the youngest. According to Bum, the most satisfying surprises of the year were Caster and Mo Towns, who replaced Reihner after spending 1977 on the IR. Earl was not a surprise.

Another reason they survived was simply Phillips himself. The players responded to him. His approach to the game was low-key and easy. The team reflected that attitude. They marched through some tough road games in the playoffs loose and relaxed.

For fans, 1978 was sweet redemption. They had paid their dues with an endless stream of fumbles, bumbles and stumbles that were synonymous with Sundays in Houston in the Fall. The Oilers were beyond bad or disappointing; they were embarrassing and humiliating. No team had ever been so awful as to compile back-to-back 1-13 seasons. But Sid Gillman's hand-picked protégé put together a team that came within one game of the Super Bowl. Arguably, they were the second best team in football. Just two years before, they struggled to make 5-9.

It pulled the city together. Houston was still a toddler in terms of big cities. It was filled with immigrants drawn by employment who had little or no sense of what there was of local history or tradition. Visiting teams often thought they were playing at home. The 1978 Oilers changed that perception. They gave the people something in common. They gave them something to support and cheer together. They bonded them under the rubric of "Houstonian."

The crowd in the Dome was there to make a statement, to let the team know how much they appreciated what they had done, that they supported them win or lose and just that they cared. It was more than for winning and finally making the playoffs. It was as much for how they lost to Pittsburgh as it was for how they beat the odds against Miami and New England. It was for the hard play, the determination and the dedication. It was for the respectful and classy way they did it. It was for losing without whining or making excuses. It was for shaking the victors' hands and wishing them luck. It was for Earl running over everyone in the league without ever so much as spiking the ball and for how he always predicated his success on the play of Bugel's unsung linemen. It was for Bum's honesty, individuality and self-humility. It was for Brazile's athletic excellence and Bingham's relentlessness, for Bethea's years of toil and Pastorini's toughness, for Mauck's no-nonsense approach and Culp's power, for Wilson's sacrifice and Barber's emotion. It was for the Guido Merkins and Jimmy Youngs of the world.

IN THE WORDS OF BUD ADAMS

Bud was given a chance to put the season in his own words in a January 8, 1979, guest column in the *Chronicle*. Here are some excerpts from that piece:

> The Oilers are not "just another football team." It's a team with personality that everyone in America can relate to. We have a host of young people, some veteran players, a group that plays together, and a team that forgets about its injuries and hurts, and defies the odds that are against it every week. They just go out and win.
>
> The City of Houston told the world, "This is our team" and I am proud that the recognition has come, not only to the football team, recognition that they so richly deserve, but also to the people of the city. We are proud as an organization that we have been able to build the club to the point that they have now achieved.
>
> Even though we weren't the victors on Sunday, I firmly believe that we have put together for the City of Houston a team it can rightly be proud of, and a

team that will be in the forefront of the National Football League for many years to come.

There are those who will say that having a sports franchise is not important to the city, nor is the success of a sports franchise important to a city. I know better ...

Perhaps somewhat telling for the future of the team, he did not mention Coach Phillips once, although he did use the word "we" nine times.

1979: THE SECOND BEST TEAM IN FOOTBALL

Despite the bad loss, the Oilers were rocking. They were the hottest ticket in town. They had proven they belonged among the elite of the league because they had beaten most of them. If they could beat the teams they were supposed to, they might make a Super Bowl.

1979 TRAINING CAMP

Camp was back at Angelo State and Bum was back in his tower. There would be tragedy early. Starting left OT Greg Sampson, leader of the line and honorable mention All-Pro, became ill after an undetected injury and had to be life-flighted to Methodist Hospital in Houston. He had a subdural hematoma which was apparently caused by a collision during practice. During emergency surgery to remove a clot on the brain, a small piece of his skull had to be cut away. He was definitely gone for the year and his career was threatened.

That devastating loss was quickly followed by the loss of starting left OG George Reihner whose torn knee cartilage required surgery. Reihner and Sampson were the left side of the line. They emerged together in 1977 when George arrived as a rookie and turned the line play completely around. Besides helping Earl lead the NFL in rushing, the line as a unit gave up the fewest sacks in the NFL.

Phillips moved decisively, acquiring OT Leon Gray from New England. As a Patriot, Gray teamed with OG John Hannah to form the best left side in football. He was one of the two or three best tackles in the game and cost them 1980 1st and 6th round picks. It was a cheap price for a healthy two-time consensus All-Pro. Somewhat ironically, it was Houston's two victories over New England in 1978 that hastened the departure of Chuck Fairbanks and started the housecleaning. The Pats, who had been one of the top teams, went into a long slide after the trade. The Oilers could empathize. Bum said of Gray, "I'd say he's capable of learning our system completely in a short while. In most cases, it's block the feller closest to you."

With five starters injured in camp, Phillips said, "I've got to remind everybody Houston ain't on Houston's schedule." He favored no contact in camp. Finally, Pastorini had what was described as a stress fracture on the ribs that affected his passing. In reality, he had a serious muscle condition, but hid it from reporters. It did not, however, stop Dante from bringing his motorcycle and ski boat to camp.

There were also the obligatory holdouts. Stemrick and Coleman were this year's flavors. It was around this period when agents began using the media as leverage in negotiations. Coleman's agent said his client "was going to play in Canada." The team fought back more subtly. Newspaper articles soon touted the play of twelfth-round draft pick Wayne Wilson. Phillips also picked up Boobie Clark off waivers. Coleman signed before the first game.

Seven of 10 draft picks made the team. They were DT Mike Stensrud (6'5, 280), DE Jesse Baker (6'4, 256), FB Kenny King of OU (could have been Joe Montana), LB Daryl Hunt (6th round), LB Mike Murphy (6th), DB Carter Hartwig (8th) and WR/KR Richard Ellender (9th).

The two tops picks both came with some baggage. Dale Robertson wrote, "Some scouts accused Stensrud ... of lacking intensity and aggressiveness." He noted that rap originated from his college coach. The Stensrud pick could have been DT Fred Smerlas, OT Greg Roberts or DE Mark Gastineau. Dale wrote that Baker "had a bad actor's rap hanging over his head." That choice could have been ILB Bob Golic. As it would turn out, Stensrud held out and then showed up overweight, but Baker would have a fine first year.

From five drafts, Phillips had added 22 players. The remainder of the 45-man squad was made up of 4 acquired by trade, 10 free agents and 9 holdovers. Of the holdovers, 8 were starters and the ninth was Alexander who had just lost his starting spot.

The cuts included ex-Tennessee Vol Steve Kiner, who started at ILB for 5 years, beginning with the 1974 turnaround season. He became an instant celebrity after cussing strike leader Bill Curry and chasing Dale Robertson out of the locker room. He was a Gillman project who had been in trouble over drugs. In Houston, he turned into a dedicated worker never missing a game or practice. Kiner could still hit, but was too slow for coverage. He was replaced by four-year player Art Stringer, who was faster but had not made it through one season healthy.

Unable to get secondary help in the draft, the Oilers outbid several teams for CFL-star Vernon Perry (6'2,

211). Brought in as a corner, he ended up beating out Currier at SS to become the eighth player in six years attempting to replace Ken Houston. He was originally drafted and cut by Chicago where Jack Pardee said he was too slow for the NFL. Left corner was left to JC Wilson who beat out Alexander.

Another change on defense was Andy Dorris starting at left DE for the injured Young. Jesse Baker would also gain playing time at end. The other backups on the DL were Kennard and Stensrud. Dean was cut.

On the OL, Conway Hayman replaced Reihner while Grey replaced Sampson. Mo Towns moved to RT, replacing Hayman. The right OG was Ed Fisher, and Mauck was back at center. Billy Johnson returned at WR, while the rest of the offense was the same. RBs King and Wilson handled kickoffs.

Johnny Dirden, who had an untimely fumble in the last playoff game, was cut and replaced on punt returns by Guido Merkins who also was the third string QB and a backup WR.

Houston would have to deal with new pressures in 1979, the kind that come with success and high expectations. The schedule was tough. With three of their first four on the road against the Redskins, Steelers and Bengals, the possibility of a stumbling start from which they would never recover worried an entire city. They also had road games at Baltimore, Dallas, Washington, Miami, Seattle, and Cleveland for the fifth roughest schedule in the league. The hardest schedules were those of Cincinnati and Cleveland, because they had four games with both Pittsburgh *and* Houston. They went their typical 1-3 in the preseason.

Bingham said the success in 1978 was a boon, not a detriment. "We're a lot more confident," he said. "We won last year because we had good talent, but it took us all season to really believe we were good. Look at what we did. We came back from 23 down to beat New England and then beat them again after we embarrassed them. We beat Pittsburgh in their place. We beat Mi-

Of the tower, Bum said, "A guy's convinced you're up here watching only him." One he could see was Toni Fritsch who liked to take naps on the tackling dummies.

ami twice. That pumps you up. There's a big difference between hoping you can win and knowing you can."

Phillips, too, was content. "I've got a lot to be thankful about," he said. "There's nothing I'd rather be than a head football coach in the NFL. And there's definitely no place I'd rather be than in Houston ... Down here's my home." Asked if he would ever leave Texas, he drew an imaginary line, saying, "I done drew the line. Just like at the Alamo. You're either on one side of the line or the other. I don't want to ever leave Texas again. I don't see moving me and my family someplace none of us want to be. Oh, there are other good places. New Orleans is a good town. Arizona is nice. But I'm never going north of the Mason-Dixon line. I don't want to be living around people I don't know. And don't understand....How 'bout another beer?"

THE 1979 REGULAR SEASON — SUPER BOWL ITCH

The Oilers came out flat in the opener at RFK Stadium against Jack Pardee's Redskins. They threw interceptions and played awful on special teams. Trailing 27-13 late, they ran off 16 straight to win 29-27 behind Big Earl's 166 yards. Afterwards, Earl said he did not want any more (player-of-the-game) watches and asked that, in the future, they be given to his linemen.

Then came the rematch at Three Rivers. Despite a lot of pregame huffing and puffing, Pittsburgh blew them out 38-7 in good weather, limiting Campbell to a career-low 38 yards. Pastorini was 4-of-16 for 16 yards

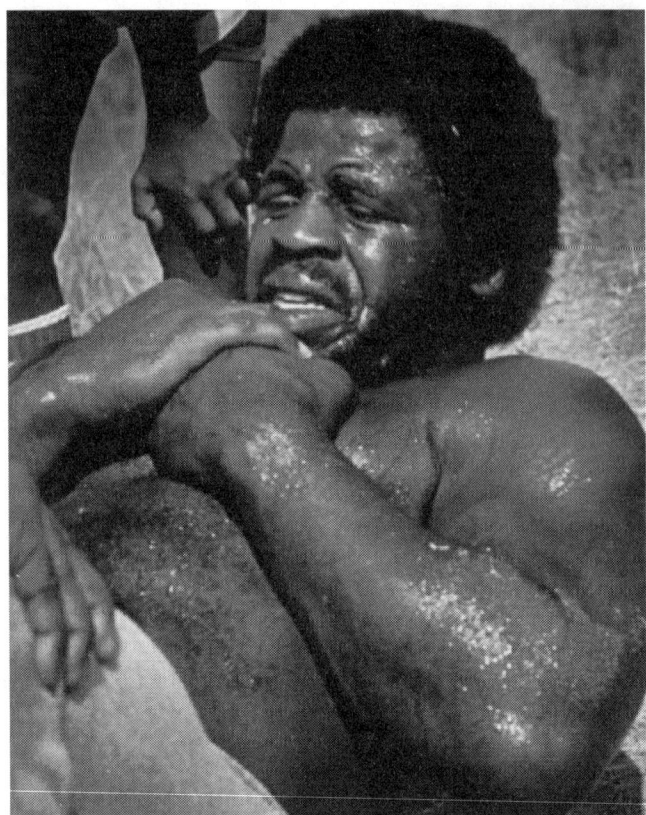

Not surprisingly, Earl Campbell and Robert Brazile were usually the two who stayed after practice and kept working out. Photo © Joel Durate.

and 3 interceptions. He spent most of the day either on the run or his butt. He left the field on a stretcher. With the Oilers trailing 24-0, Billy Johnson hurt his knee again and also left on a stretcher. "What can you say when you get your brains beat out?" asked Mauck.

Earl came back with 131 yards to beat KC without Pastorini, then 158 to beat the Bengals. It was their first win in Cincinnati in five years, and they overcame a 24-point second-quarter deficit to do so. Fritsch hit the game-winner after a Chris Bahr miss in OT. "Those Cincinnati fans were hollerin', but that didn't bother him," said Phillips. "As well as he understands English, he might have thought they were cheering for him." Rookie Stensrud was lost to a knee injury, but Baker was piling up the sacks.

They closed out September by pasting the unbeaten Browns 31-10 behind Earl's 3 TDs. While No. 34 was rolling, Pastorini was in pain. His efficiency rating of 34.4 was worst in the NFL. Despite a 4-1 record, Dan was taking heat again. Barber complained that he was not a part of the offense. Dale Robertson rode him hard in the paper as the feud that had simmered between those two began to boil.

Then the Oilers committed a cardinal sin. They came out flat and lost to 1-4 St. Louis 24-17 at home despite recovering four first half fumbles. There were no excuses and it would cost them. The spat between Barber and Pastorini also expanded. Mauck said they "were acting like little boys." Art Stringer kept his streak alive by hurting a knee and was gone for the year. He was replaced by Hunt, who was good, but not as fast or as experienced.

They bounced back to beat Baltimore 28-16 on Campbell's 149 yards and 3 TDs. The defense allowed 189 net yards, had 3 interceptions and 5 sacks. With Bethea nursing a sore knee, Baker's sack total climbed to 11½ as he learned on the job. Reinfeldt led the league in interceptions with 7 and Stemrick had 4. The Oilers were tied with Pittsburgh, Miami, New England, Denver and San Diego for the best record at 5-2, but all was not well. Pastorini was still playing poorly and reading about how bad a leader he was.

Next, they showed they gained no knowledge from the Cardinal game, losing to the 2-5 Seahawks 34-14. QB Jim Zorn (18-of-25 for 252 yards) and WR Steve Largent (135 yards, 2 TDs) ripped what had been the fourth-ranked pass defense in the AFC. Campbell was injured and had just 4 yards on 3 carries. Penalties, especially holding calls, killed them.

After dropping 2-of-3, the Oilers stood at 5-3 at the halfway point, the same as the year before. Hard-to-explain losses to the underdog Cardinals and Seahawks kept them from having the best record in football.

Around this time, *Post* writer Jack Gallagher wrote a nasty piece on Dante. He compared him to Astro star Cesar "the next Willie Mays" Cedeno, who was also "involved in a fatal accident", and likewise, whose career "appeared in descent." Gallagher said Dan had become an "anti-hero," a type of "high-paid athlete who has not produced as well as expected," only to become an "object of scorn." Pastorini's flaws were that he was injury-prone, overpaid and not willing to accept critical commentary. Coming to the aid of his friend Robertson, he wrote that Dan "reacts like a petulant, spoiled child" by refusing to speak to Dale. Like he had done with Jacky Lee and Don Trull, Jack called for Giff Nielsen, but said Phillips was "resistant to change." He even used the opportunity to drag Blanda's name around as he compared the two QBs, but it was unclear which one he meant to insult the most.

Pastorini did have an explanation. The previous February, he contracted a virus that destroyed a major nerve in his right shoulder. The anterior serratus muscle was paralyzed. He could not raise his arm above his head. The muscle atrophied. Although doctors said the nerve would grow back, his throwing motion was debilitated and he lacked arm strength.

He and Bum decided in camp that the best thing for the team was to keep it quiet. Only a few teammates knew the extent of the injury. Training camp was a charade, a big show as far as Dan was concerned. He went through the motions while trying to avoid straining the shoulder. He played in only four quarters the entire preseason.

Once the season began, he tried to disguise his limitations. Throughout the first 8 games, he had 6 TDs to 13 interceptions while completing just 45%. He told everyone the arm was fine.

"If you had looked real close at that shoulder," said Phillips, "you would have seen how little muscle tone he had. It looked like a woman's shoulder. But we had to keep it a secret ... If word got out, you'd have seen defenses using an 11-man line....They'd have all been up there, licking their chops. We wouldn't have had any choice then. We would have had to set him down."

Clearly, Bum had no faith in the "steal" of the '78 draft, Nielsen. He denied that pressure or high expectations kept Dan in the games. "I wasn't worried about the season. There will be plenty of seasons," said Bum, apparently forgetting who owned the team. "A football player has only one career, and if Dan was throwing his away by trying to play, I would have had to live with that for the rest of my life. The doctors assured me he wasn't hurting himself. They said it would take 7 to 8 months for the nerve to grow back, no matter what he did. I kept him in the lineup because I thought his leadership and experience would carry him until his arm came around." It started coming around at midseason and once it did, he and the Oilers went on a tear.

They beat the Jets 27-24 in late October on a Fritsch FG in OT. "I tell you what," said Bum, "every time I see that kid going onto the field, I thank God for our country's immigration laws." Earl, still hurt, had only 11 carries for 37 yards as he lost serious ground in the rushing race to Walter Payton, Otis Anderson and Tony Dorsett. At practice the next week, Bum said, "Earl's walking better, but he's much more valuable to this team if he can run."

He busted out against Miami on *Monday Night Football* again with 120 yards on 32 carries as Houston won 9-6 on three Fritsch field goals. Pastorini threw just 10 passes, but had 205 yards against Oakland the next week as Houston won 31-17. Earl had 107 yards. It was a trying week as militant Iranians stormed the US embassy in Tehran.

Next, they beat up Cincinnati 42-21. Earl had 112 yards while Pastorini and Nielsen combined for 322 passing yards. It left them tied with Pittsburgh at 9-3 with a Thanksgiving date with the Cowboys in Texas Stadium to look forward to.

Bum tried to play down the significance of the match-up, coyly making reference to "the team up north of here, I can't think of their name." But Dallas had been a thorn in Houston's saddle for a long time. Since 1966, the Cowboys had compiled 12 winning seasons and 3 trips to the Super Bowl. Over that same period, Houston had 4 and none. Cowboys merchandise sold well in Houston, and even about 3,000 Houstonians subscribed to their team newsletter.

The game was like a prize fight with every punch met with a counterpunch. On the fourth play from scrimmage, Roger Staubach hit Drew Pearson on a 56-yard TD pass. But Campbell answered on Houston's first possession with a 61-yard scoring run. After Dorsett gave Dallas a 21-10 lead late in the second, Campbell came back with his second TD to cut it to 21-17 at the half. Two minutes into the third quarter, Pastorini hit Renfro with a 21-yarder to give Houston its first lead at 23-21. After a Dallas FG, the turning point in the game arrived as Houston drove to the Dallas 37 midway through the fourth quarter. On four-and-four, Bum

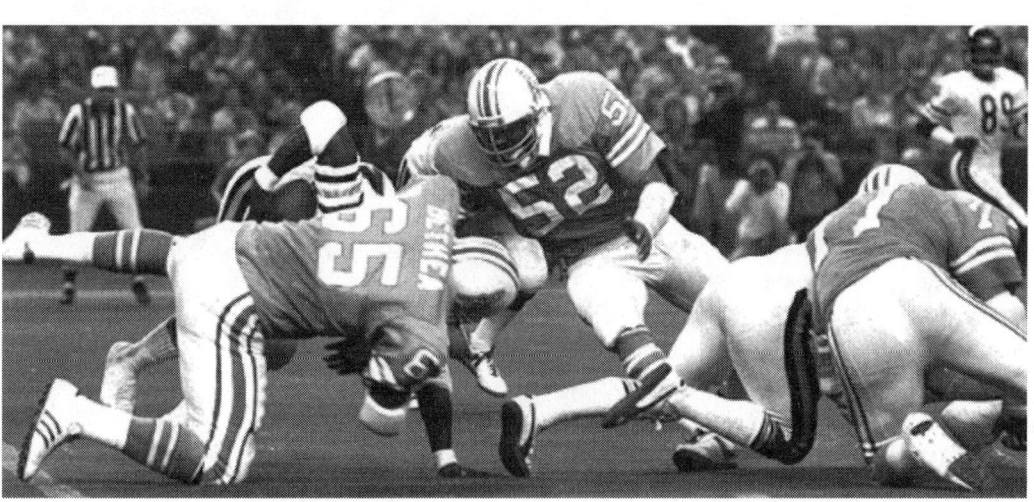

The right side of the Oiler defense was tough. Right OLB Bob Brazile made his first Pro Bowl in 1975, and was a unanimous first team All-Pro in 1978, '79 and '80. Right DE Elvin Bethea made the Pro Bowl eight times: 1969, 1971-75, 1978-79.

elected to punt rather than go for a 54-yard field goal. But Dallas was flagged for having 12 men on the field. Pastorini quickly hit Burrough with a 32-yard TD to make it 30-24 with under 8 minutes remaining.

Staubach (21-of-30 for 287 yards) got the ball back with ample time and took the Pokes to the Oiler 20 on a pass to Hill on fourth down with 2:38 left. Then the defense finally stood up. On first down, Dorsett got 1 yard. Ted Thompson deflected a second-down pass. On third, Hill could not handle a bullet at the goal line. On fourth, all WRs were covered and Staubach's pass went out of bounds. Still, the Oilers faced third-and-three from their own 26 with 1:30 left. To seal the win, Campbell had to literally carry DD Lewis and Cliff Harris 5 yards for the first down.

At the end of the day, Earl had ripped Tom Landry's proud defense for 195 yards. "He's the greatest running back in football," said Harris. "All you can do is close your eyes and hope he doesn't break your helmet." Pastorini was 9-of-17 for 163 yards, 2 TDs and no interceptions.

"If they're America's team," said Bum, "I guess we must be Texas' team and that's better." It was their first regular season victory ever over Dallas. They were tied with Pittsburgh and San Diego for best record in the league. It was their longest win streak in 17 years. "Remember how I told you guys last week that this was just another game?" Phillips asked reporters. "I lied."

Over the five-game win streak, Pastorini completed 58% of his passes for 790 yards. In the wins against the Raiders, Bengals and Cowboys, his efficiency rating was 133. He began regaining arm strength around midseason and his timing was coming back. His WRs agreed. Caster said, "Against the Cowboys, every ball he threw was a bullet. That's the Dan I remember from last year." Renfro said, "He's smelling the playoffs."

Robertson wrote: "For personal and professional reasons, (Pastorini) declined from the start to use his disability as a crutch. He never made excuses. He insisted, as far back as the opener in Washington, that the arm was fine, thank you. It was an admirably stoic approach. But he was so insistent that people — particularly the press — took him at his word. When he failed to deliver, he was criticized, sometimes severely. His reaction was defiance mixed with withdrawal. Some bitterness remains." This story was not over.

One more win and the Oilers would clinch a playoff berth. But the last three were all tough at Cleveland, then Pittsburgh and Philadelphia at home. Cleveland is never a pretty sight, but in December it is about as hospitable as the South Pole. The entire week before the game, the hottest QB in the league was ill with a severe stomach flu that put him in the hospital. Despite Earl's 108 yards, the Browns won 14-7 behind Brian Sipe and Greg Pruitt.

That loss put extra pressure on the showdown with Pittsburgh on Monday night. The Oilers went into the season knowing they could not afford two losses to the Steelers; they already had one. It was the biggest game in the Dome since the '75 *MNF* game when the Steelers buried Houston 32-9, knocking them out of the playoffs. "I hate Pittsburgh" T-shirts were popular in the sellout crowd of 55,293, who were also given 22 x 16 "Oiler Blue" cards. The Dome was swallowed in a sea of blue. It made a colorful sight on television. A hand-painted sign in one corner read "Love Ya Blue." The crowd was very loud. Pittsburgh's incomplete passes drew more noise than a Houston TD normally did.

Houston won 20-17 behind a balanced offense. While Earl had 109 yards, they spread the ball around. "They finally wised up," said Joe Greene concerning the play calling that did not simply run Earl three downs. The victory put them back into a tie with Pittsburgh and San Diego for the best record at 11-4, and assured them home field in the first round of the playoffs.

Keeping White Shoes off the sidelines and on the field was a major concern of the late 1970s. He missed the majority of games in the Oilers' two best seasons, playing in five games in 1978 and two in 1979.

Earl after a score in Dallas on November 22, 1979. Despite 74 touchdowns as a pro, this is his only end zone demonstration captured on film.

Pittsburgh's earlier victory that sewed up the division made meaningless the last game against a tough Eagles team. One Oiler who played with enthusiasm was Earl, who trailed Otis Anderson by 3 yards for the rushing title. The big fella had 134 yards in the first half. With Anderson gaining just 39 in his game, Earl and most of the regulars sat out the second half. Houston lost 26-20 to drop to 11-5.

They finished a game behind the Steelers, closing out the first decade of the AFC Central without ever winning it. While the Oilers proved they could rise for the big games, they were still losing to the patsies. The games they wanted back were St. Louis (1-5 going in) and Seattle (2-5). Had they taken those teams seriously, they could have won the division and had home field throughout. Instead, Pittsburgh won its sixth consecutive divisional title and made the playoffs for a league record eighth straight time.

THE 1979 PLAYOFFS

The Oilers faced Denver in the wildcard playoff game. It was the first ever in the Astrodome and 17 years to the day from the last one in Houston when the Texans beat them for the AFL Championship at Jeppesen Stadium.

The city was wholeheartedly behind the team. The Love Ya Blue era was in full blossom. There were signs in yards, messages on billboards, bumper stickers, clothing and even new songs on the radio like "Super Bowl Itch." It was a magical time.

The Oilers won 13-7 with the defense sacking immobile Craig Morton 6 times. It came at a high price, however. In a one-and-a-half quarter span, they lost Campbell and Pastorini to pulled groins and Burrough to a rebruised tailbone. The bittersweet feeling surrounding the game was captured in Pastorini's defiant yet worried stance on the sideline, sans shoulder pads, with a bag of ice jammed down the crotch of his blood-soaked pants.

All over town, the bands played on. The city could not wipe the grin off its collective face. San Diego was grinning, too. Don Coryell had assembled the greatest passing attack in NFL history with Dan Fouts, Kellen Winslow, John Jefferson and old friend Charlie Joiner. Fouts, the MVP of the AFC, set the all-time single season passing mark with 4,082 yards, just breaking Joe Namath's record of 4,007 yards. At 12-4, the Chargers tied the Steelers for the best record, including a 35-7 pounding of Pittsburgh. They were coming off 12 days' rest to Houston's six. Air Coryell looked forward to the AFC Championship and Super Bowl.

Las Vegas, however, was not so sure. The Oilers had developed a national following with Earl and Bum and their performances in nationally televised games. Thus, despite the fact that Giff Nielsen and Rob Carpenter were starting, Houston was only an 8-point underdog. That all changed when Carpenter sprained an ankle at Thursday practice. When the oddsmakers saw him boarding the team plane on crutches, the game came off the board. Loosely translated, at that point Vegas could not give Houston enough points to make them an attractive bet.

The popular theory was that the Oilers played their best with their backs against the wall. That theory was about to be tested. The hobbled Carpenter set the tone. "I didn't take a pain killer," he said. "I wanted to feel the pain." Houston's confidence was not shaken when the Chargers took their first possession for a TD. It grew when Fouts' second possession ended in a Vernon Perry interception. It grew some more when the next San Diego possession ended with Perry blocking a FG attempt, catching it on the bounce and running it back 57 yards to the Charger 28. Instead of falling behind 10-0, Fritsch cut it to 7-3.

Earl went into the last regular season game of 1979 against the Eagles trailing for the overall rushing lead. By the end of the day, he had 87 more yards than his closest competitor to capture a second straight NFL rushing crown (1,696 yards and 19 touchdowns).

That sequence provided a big emotional boost. In the second quarter, another Perry pick got the ball back and the offense clawed within sniffing distance of pay dirt. In one dramatic moment, Nielsen scrambled 14 yards deep into Charger territory, where instead of going out of bounds, he dove for the goal line only to be violently sandwiched between two defenders. Third-string QB Guido Merkins swallowed hard on the sideline. Mauck screamed at Giff as he writhed on the ground. After he got up, the Oilers cut it to 7-6. That was until Coach Phillips violated one of the golden rules of coaching — he took points off the board on a penalty. He wanted 7. The tactic worked and Houston took its first lead.

The offense, which fought for every inch, kept doing just enough. On one play, Carpenter, who had 67 yards on 18 carries, crawled back to the huddle on his hands and knees after absorbing a bone-rattling hit. The defensive players could not help but be moved to push their own limits. With 2:05 left in the third, Nielsen hit Renfro with a 47-yarder that turned into an inartistic zig zag to the end zone.

Equally inspiring was the effort of Vernon "too slow" Perry, who tied a playoff record with 4 interceptions, the last with 3:18 left to seal the game. He had 3 on the season. San Diego claimed he stole the plays as they were signaled in from the Charger bench. Actually, the Oilers discovered in film study that Fouts tipped off running plays with the position of his left foot. He still had 333 yards on 25-of-47 passing. But the Houston defense stopped him when it mattered most and the Oilers won 17-14. It was the upset of the decade.

It was also a great way to end one. In 1970, being an Oiler was not so great. As of December 29, 1979, it was not so bad. "I'm a Christian, I'm a Mormon and I'm a Houston Oiler," gushed Nielsen, who finished 10-of-19 for 111 yards. "I'm very proud to be all three. I could not be more proud of our team. The Lord was with us today."

The idea of divine intervention did not seem out of the question. There is no way the Oilers should have been able to stay on the field in their condition against such a talented team. The *Post* called it, "The most inspiring and uplifting victory by any of Houston's teams ever ... With the exception of [Perry], it wasn't a game measured by statistics. It was a game measured by resolve and courage." Bum said, "You hear a lot about games being character builders. Well, this was a character finder. Never, in my 31 years of coaching, have I seen one like it."

They were picking up new fans. "I've never rooted for the Houston Oilers in all my life and I didn't think I ever would," said Tex Schramm. "But the courage they displayed in the face of all that misfortune made me root for them." Don Klosterman added, "You could have bet me that I never would have rooted for the Oilers again. But when I sat there and watched them in that game, I had to root for them. Anybody would."

Houston was jamming. It was enveloped in blue. The NFL expansion committee might be wise to take a look at a video clip of what happened during this period.

Bum said throughout the season, "All roads to the Super Bowl lead through Pittsburgh." He was right as the Steelers beat Miami in the other game. He added, "When I die I want y'all to put a P.S. on my tombstone: He'd have lived a helluva lot longer if he hadn't had to play the Steelers six times in two years."

THE DALE AND DAN SHOW

With so much prosperity at hand, trouble had to be lurking behind the next tree. Less than 72 hours before the biggest game in team history, it reappeared.

One of the most frequently cited reasons for the Oilers' foibles over the years has been Bud's ego. The conduit for most of those stories was the writers who covered the team. Many of them possessed the same personality traits as the characters they followed.

Just before the Oilers left for Pittsburgh, there was an incident involving *Post* sportswriter Dale Robertson and Dan Pastorini. This Oiler tale of woe started several months earlier when party boy Mike Barber ended up with one of Dan's ex girlfriends. As the season progressed, Mike did not see many balls his way. He complained. Robertson referenced the girlfriend issue as a possible explanation.

Pastorini already believed he was unfairly singled out for scrutiny of his public and professional life. This time, he cut off Robertson completely, refusing to speak to him. With the shoulder malady and the first half of the year subpar, the relationship festered.

On January 3, it blew. Just before an afternoon news conference with a pre-championship game media horde at the Oiler practice facility, they got into an argument. It was over some tape-recorded quotations Dale used in an article. Dan told Dale not to quote him anymore unless he spoke directly to him. Carl Mauck had to separate them.

A short while later, as Pastorini headed from the dressing room to the conference room to meet reporters, they crossed paths again in a hallway. According to Robertson, he felt it was time "to stand his ground." He

Bum Phillips leaves the field after the 1979 AFC wildcard game. With the offense losing both Campbell (second quarter) and Pastorini (first drive of the second half), the defense had to and did carry the day in the Oilers' 13-7 victory. It was Houston's first home playoff victory since the 1960 AFL Championship.

said he was on his way to tell Phillips "something had to give." As they closed, Dale asked, "Mind if I listen in?" Dan was in no mood. "I've taken enough crap from you," he said. Perhaps intoxicated by the moment, Dale replied, "Yeah, you've really had it rough, you asshole." Pastorini was ready to rumble.

Dan (6'3, 205) grabbed Dale (5'9, 160) and flung him around like a doll in full view of the 20 or so members of the local and national media, including cameramen for the local TV stations. They stumbled through a doorway and came to a rest with an angry Dan on top of a frightened Dale, who was dressed like '60s folk-rocker David Crosby with a frizzy afro, mustache and vest. "If you ever call me an asshole again, I'll kill your ass, you son of a bitch," Dan railed as he released his grip. Unlike Bud's fight with a *Post* writer in 1966, no punches were thrown.

It all happened just as Coach Phillips arrived. Robertson landed at his feet. Bum was stunned. "What the hell's going on here?" he asked as Dan disappeared.

"I later apologized to Bum if I disrupted the preparations for [the game]," said Robertson later, "but I'd just let too many of [Pastorini's] abuses slide." He filed a complaint with the NFL office in New York. That night, he had a police escort home from the *Post*.

The next day, Dan appeared on the practice field in a "Rocky" jersey. Once they all arrived in Pittsburgh, Robertson was the story. Writers actually left Terry Bradshaw and Joe Greene to interview him. Even Steelers players approached him to ask questions.

Dale's timing was certainly suspect. If he hoped to use the notoriety to springboard into a gig at an even larger media market or a television position, it did not work. Although he would later move to the *Chronicle*, the El Paso native remained in Houston.

THE 1979 AFC CHAMPIONSHIP — HOUSTON AT PITTSBURGH

Pittsburgh in January does not exactly conjure up thoughts of Club Med. Even though the skies and water have cleared quite a bit with the closure of the steel mills, winters were tough there before anyone had ever heard of Andrew Carnegie. At game time on January 6, 1980, it was 22 degrees and dropping. A biting wind blew and the field was ringed by a snowbank. But it was not raining or snowing.

The morning of the game, Mike Barber walked onto the field wearing only a T-shirt and shorts. He said, "Who cares how cold it is?"

It started off well enough. Perry picked up where he left off, intercepting a Bradshaw pass and running it back for a 75-yard TD. Houston was up 7-0 before the offense ran a play.

Unfortunately, when the offense did have the ball, it did not do much with it. Houston was determined to stick with the ground game. All day long, Pittsburgh was there waiting with 8 or 9 defenders. They dared Houston to throw on first. Of the Oilers' 8 first down plays in the first half, 7 were carries by Campbell totaling 5 yards. Steelers surrounded him on every play whether he had the ball or not. Earl finished with 15 yards on 17 carries.

After Pittsburgh cut the lead to 7-3, Houston drove the ensuing kickoff to the Steeler 14, but stalled and settled for a 10-3 lead. Bradshaw then got busy with 2 TDs in the second quarter. With 10 minutes left in the half, he found TE Benny Cunningham, who made a leaping catch over Perry on third-and-7 to tie the game. With 3 minutes left, Renfro caught a first down pass, but fumbled. Bradshaw promptly turned it into a 20-yard TD to John Stallworth, who beat Greg Stemrick. Pittsburgh led 17-10 at the half.

Houston's defense laid it all out in the third quarter, holding Pittsburgh to minus-5 yards. However, despite

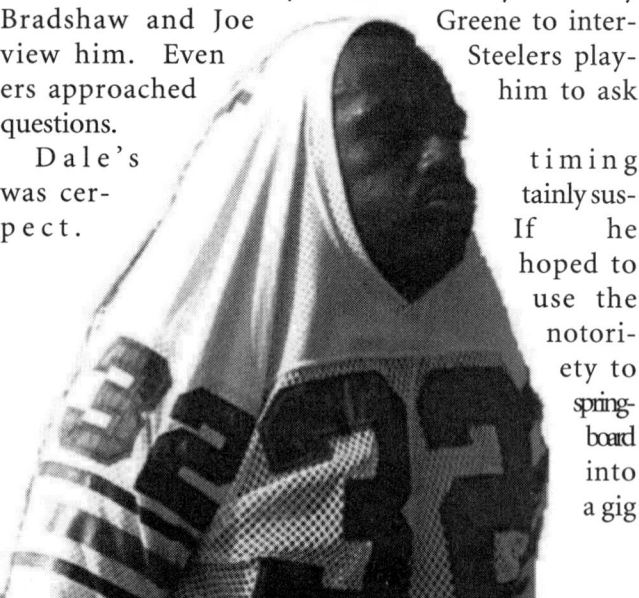

The biggest hero of the Oilers' improbable 17-14 victory over the powerful Chargers in the 1979 AFC divisional playoff game was rookie safety Vernon Perry. Besides a playoff record 4 interceptions off Dan Fouts, he also blocked a field goal attempt and returned it 57 yards. With Pastorini and Campbell on the sidelines, this was one of the greatest upsets in the history of the NFL.

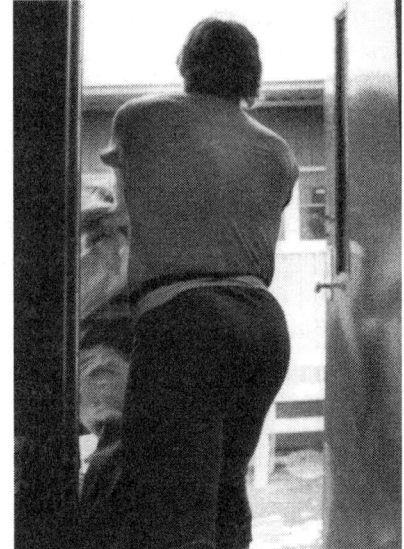

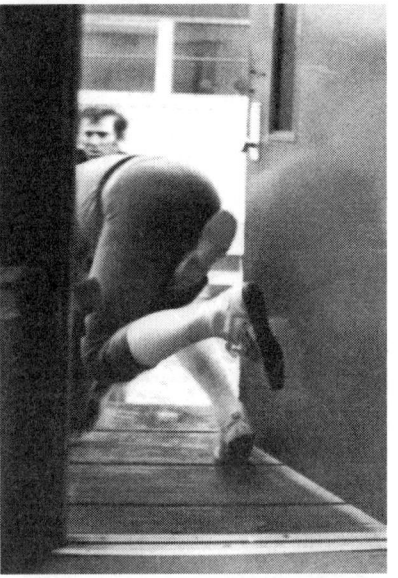

This highlight in Oiler history was captured by photographer F. Carter Smith. Photos © F. Carter Smith.

recovering a fumbled punt at the Steeler 41, the offense could not take advantage.

Late in the third, after a 66-yard Craig Collquitt punt, the Oilers finally mounted a drive starting from their 14. It almost stalled after the refs missed an interference call on Mel Blount 25 yards downfield. But Pastorini found Renfro for 21 and they were in business at the Steeler 6. That set up the play that led directly to the NFL's instant replay mechanism.

On first down, Pastorini lofted one of his patented high, arching drop-into-the-corner-of-the-end-zone passes for Renfro. He was under a hard rush and it initially appeared it would go out of bounds. But the crafty Renfro had other ideas. Steeler CB Ron Johnson, realizing he was beaten, grabbed Renfro before the ball arrived, but there was no call. Renfro did not give up, and like a good rebounder, positioned himself between Johnson and the ball. Then he went up and made an exceptional catch. All Johnson could do was shove him out of bounds. It was close, but he had it. Side judge Don Orr stood there dumbfounded. He looked lost. Then he looked for help. He finally made a weak, incomplete signal and then ran over and huddled with the other officials. No one else had a clear enough view to overrule the call — not to mention they wanted to make it out of town alive. The minutes went by. The call was that although he made the catch he did not have possession at the time he went out of bounds. Johnson's interference was ruled "incidental contact."

Renfro said, "I looked up and saw the official, and his eyes were kind of starry. I knew I was in trouble." Years later, he held to his story. "I know this," he said. "I had complete possession of the football, and I'm positive both feet were in bounds."

The Oilers were furious. Replays to Houston and the rest of the country indicated that, while a tough call, it was a TD. It took awhile for things to calm. Instead of having a 17-17 tie, or at minimum, a first down at the 1, it was second down from the 6. They got no closer than the 5 and had to settle for another Fritsch FG and 17-13 score as the fourth quarter began.

On the next possession, the defense forced a third-and-21 and it looked like they would get the ball right back. But Bradshaw, dropping back at his 20, hit Swann over the middle for 21. Then, on a third-and-6, Harris carried for 6. The drive ended in a 55-yard FG.

Houston's last effort ended in a Guido Merkins fumble at the Oiler 41 with 5:46 remaining, after a first down reception. Pittsburgh rode 33-year-old backup Rocky Bleier to a capping TD with 56 seconds remaining to make the final score 27-13.

"They executed, we didn't," was Ed Biles' take. Others discussed the Renfro catch. Pastorini, who had a huge black and blue bruise on the inside of his upper left leg and blood dripping from a large wound on his left elbow, said, "I saw it. It was in."

"I hate to get beat this way," groaned Mauck. "I'd rather get the hell knocked out of us like we did last year than to lose on a bad call. I'm not saying we would have won anyway, but that changed the complexion of the game completely."

The bad call took some focus away from the rest of the Oilers' game. They had their chances. Twice, they fumbled after first down receptions, both of which led to Steeler TDs. Twice more, they were flagged for delay of game penalties on plays that gained first downs. Dan threw an interception. Four punts averaged 30 yards, while three Pittsburgh punts averaged 51 yards. They gave up 161 yards, rushing mostly right up the gut with a defense guarding against the outside run. The offense converted just 3-of-11 third-down opportunities.

Despite beating Pittsburgh 20-17 in December with a diverse offense, they reverted to their old ways and were held to 24 yards rushing on 22 carries. Houston ran on 11 of their first 13 first-down plays. The results were 1 yard, minus-2, minus-4, 4 yards, 1 yard, 1 yard, 4 yards, 3 yards, minus-1, 2 yards and 2 yards. Pittsburgh threw on 11 of its first 19 first-down plays.

When they did pass, Pastorini was on target. He hit 19-of-28 passes for 203 yards but no TDs, or none that counted. With Burrough out of the game by the end of the first quarter, 14 of Dan's completions were to his running backs.

"It's easy in here to say we should have thrown more," said Phillips from the locker room. "Maybe we should have. But I don't think there was anything wrong with our game plan. We were in it until the end. We had our chances. What we were doing wasn't wrong. We just didn't do it good enough."

Steeler DE Dwight White questioned the strategy. "If you're smart, having a back like Earl Campbell, you work your play action passes," he noted. "You've just got to mix it up because if you don't, you aren't using everything you have." Houston did not and was not. They just kept calling Earl's number. "They've built their whole team around Earl and have a definite pattern to run on certain plays," White said. "With that, you've got to get a lot on first down....Earl's been getting 5 or 6 yards on first down and that gives Pastorini a free down. What we tried to do was turn it around and take away that free play."

Someone stole Bum's hat again. "I have more respect for the guy last year who stole it off my head," he said. "It doesn't take much talent to grab one off a table."

After holding Earl to under 3 yards per carry in the 1978 AFC Championship, the Steelers did it again in 1979, holding the entire team to 24 yards rushing.

Side judge Donald Orr and company huddle after the Renfro catch. One writer compared them to "hens in heat." Renfro said, "I looked up and saw the official, and his eyes were kind of starry. I knew I was in trouble."

THE RALLY — PART DEU

It was another long flight home. There was not much consolation in again knowing that they were probably the second best team in football to the Steelers who earned the right to go to the Super Bowl for the fourth time in six years. Earl discussed the American hostage situation in Iran with firefighter Red Adair and clothier Harold Wiesenthal. "Tell you what," said Earl, "you give me five hand grenades and three brothers from deep Third Ward and I'll go over to Iran and get those hostages."

Back in Houston, another crowd began gathering at the Dome as soon as the game was over. By 7:30 p.m., the doors were shut and police were on the radio pleading for fans in their cars to turn back. A crowd of over 60,000 was already inside while another 10,000 were shut outside in the parking lot. Then the parking lot gates were closed and street barricades turned away thousands more.

Inside, the mob was treated to cheerleaders, a Columbia blue Santa Claus, a cement truck painted as a giant football, noisy firetrucks, lots of rolls of toilet paper and an unbelievable number of repetitions of the Oiler fight song. It was a sea of blue pompons and "Love Ya Blue" T-shirts. Mayor Jim McConn proclaimed it the "year of the blue."

The roof blew off around 10:30 when Pastorini, Campbell and Brazile burst onto the scene on the backs of police motorcycles. Several players spoke, but it was hard to hear over the screaming. There were tears and laughter. Mauck said they had been "robbed," and the others promised a Super Bowl the next year. Phillips had the most memorable line, saying, "One year ago we knocked on the door. [dramatic pause] This year we beat on the door. [pause] Next year [pause] we're going to kick the son-of-a-bitch in." The place exploded.

Afterwards, Phillips, who initially played down the call on the Renfro catch, produced film he said conclusively showed it was a TD. Plus, the interference was blatant. "If coaches have to live with what they do," said the coach, "then the officials should, too. When I was a kid and I came home after doing something wrong, I knew to go cut a switch for my daddy. If they were raised as I was, there should have been a whole lot of switch-cutting Sunday."

THE FALLOUT

Bob Verdi of the Chicago Tribune had this take: "As soon as the officials, like hens in heat, called time out to discuss what they hadn't seen, you sort of knew that injustice would be done ... They took the easy way out, and now only Rosemary Woods can save them. Because it is right there on tape, the touchdown-that-never-was, the touchdown that the second best team in football desperately needed to entertain any hope of beating the best ... It was no call at all, but rather a surreptitious limp, an almost frightened gesture by side judge Donald Orr that precipitated the malfeasance at Three Rivers Stadium. A guy petting his poodle or flipping the ashes from his cigarette is more emphatic."

The play caused a national discussion about replays. At Super Bowl week in Los Angeles, Pete Rozelle and Art McNally, director of officials, replayed the film for 200 reporters in an attempt to defend the call. The vast majority of the reporters were not convinced, and became combative the more the play was rerun. When shown in stop frame, Renfro could be clearly seen cradling the ball with both feet in bounds. At that point

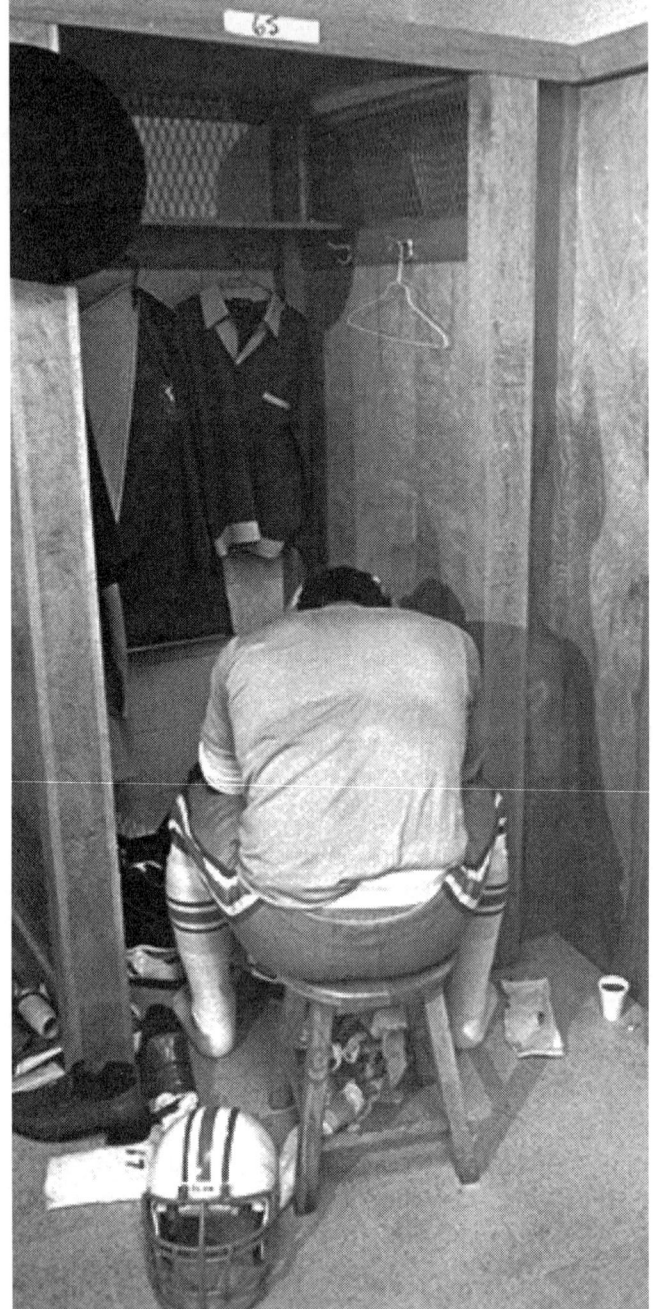

Above, a grim-faced Pastorini faces the music. He told them, "I saw it. It was in." In what would turn out to be his last game as a Houston Oiler, Dan was terrific, going 19-of-28 (68%) for 203 yards, 0 TDs (officially) and 0 interceptions.

Left, at a locker not too far away, 12-year veteran Elvin Bethea sat alone and cried. "I just can't describe the frustration," he managed. "Last year was a nightmare, but this time we came to win. I knew we were going to win. I can't believe it ... We were 60 minutes away from the Super Bowl. Then 30 minutes away. I thought we were in good shape at the half, that we could catch them. But I guess we weren't strong enough. Now we have to go back home and work like hell all over again. I hate it."

even Rozelle admitted, "When you see it frame-by-frame, he might have had full possession."

OVERVIEW

Earl led the NFL again in rushing with 1,697 yards on an NFL-record 368 carries. He also led the NFL in rushing TDs with 19. He was the unanimous NFL player-of-the-year. He continued to put his mark on the record books. His two-year total, 3,147 yards, were the most ever. Jim Brown was the only other back in history to have rushed for 1,000 yards in each of his first two seasons. He had a record eleven 100-yard games in one season and tied OJ for most 100-yard games in a row (seven). He also had 19 rushing TDs equaling Jim Taylor's 1962 record. Brown, Simpson and Taylor: not bad company. "I wouldn't say Earl is in a class by himself," said his head coach, "but I'll tell you one damn thing: It don't take them long to call the roll."

Gray, Brazile, Fritsch and Mike Reinfeldt joined Earl as a first team All-Pro. Reinfeldt was picked up as a free agent in 1976 after being cut by the Raiders. He switched from strong to free safety in 1978 on Phillips' advice and led the league with 12 interceptions in 1979. Teamed with SS Vernon Perry in 1979, they formed one of the best safety tandems in the league.

Bethea made Pro Bowl just like he did in 1970. He was the only Oiler to span all three decades. Baker, who led the team with 15½ sacks, was named defensive rookie of the year by one publication. He and Perry made the all-rookie team. The AFC, which won 36 of 52 interconference games, placed 17 players on the All-Pro first team to the NFC's 8.

Once again not receiving any post season honors was Houston's model of consistency, MLB Bingham (6'1, 230). The championship game was his 108th consecutive start. In each of his first 7 seasons, he led the team in tackles and assists. Throughout this period, however, he was overshadowed by such names as Bounicotti, Lanier and Lambert. For the 1979 regular season, he made 100 unassisted tackles, forced a fumble, recovered 3 fumbles, had 3 interceptions and made 7 touchdown-saving plays, including an interception of Bob Griese at the Houston 15 to preserve a 9-6 victory. "I'm just part of the woodwork," he said.

Pastorini threw for 2,090 yards on 163-of-324 passing (50%), had 14 TDs and 18 interceptions. Burrough led WRs with 40 receptions for 752 yards and 6 TDs. Barber had 27 for 377, Renfro 16 for 323 and Caster 18 for 239.

The defense held together despite the aging front pair of Culp and Bethea, and first-year starters Perry, JC Wilson, Andy Dorris and rookie Daryl Hunt. They ended up leading the NFL in interceptions with 34 and finished third in sacks with 51. They ranked No. 7 in the AFC in scoring, No. 9 against the rush and No. 6 as a pass defense.

1980: IT SHOULD HAVE BEEN THEIR YEAR

As the new decade approached, the Oilers appeared to be in good hands. Their popularity and image were at an all-time high. The future looked bright. It was plenty to make a veteran Oiler-follower nervous.

OBSESSION BY OAIL

Although the Rams gave the Steelers a good game in the Super Bowl, Houston still felt it was the second-best team again. Although it was hard not to blame them, the entire Oiler organization became obsessed with Pittsburgh. They were blind to the fact that the Steelers had made their run. They were getting older and would be harder to motivate.

In March, Bum traded Dan Pastorini for Ken Stabler. It was a rare one-for-one swap. Dan cried. Bum cried. It came down to this — besides being the most accurate passer in the history of the game, Stabler also did one other thing particularly well: beat the Steelers. He had beaten them the last three times he faced them before the trade.

Dan spent 9 years in Houston leading the team in passing every year. He finished his Oiler career with 16,864 yards, 96 TDs and 139 interceptions. His highest QB rating was 72.4 in 1974, but his best year was 1978 when he hit 54% of his passes for 2,473 yards, 16 TDs and 17 picks. In 12 pro seasons, he never had more TDs than interceptions. Although Dan's off-field activities were reminiscent of another strong-armed QB, Joe Namath, he did not have Joe's touch or ability to read defenses. It must be noted, though, that through much of his career, he was cursed with below-average (and sometimes awful) WRs and OLs.

Phillips also swapped draft picks and Kenny King

for controversial safety Jack "the Hitman" Tatum. The one-time All-Pro made himself famous by admitting in his book *They Call Me Assassin* that he kept score with another Raider player on how many opposing players they had put out of the game. That reputation also led to a defamation suit against Chuck Noll after the Pittsburgh coach referred to him as one of the league's "criminal element." And, oh yeah, he liked to punish Steeler receivers.

Draft pick Craig Bradshaw, little brother of Terry Bradshaw, also made the team. Many thought it was a psychological ploy but Terry had plenty of other problems to deal with such as his marriage to skater Jo Jo Starbuck which was on the rocks.

Bum and the gang also devised new plays and revamped the offense just for Pittsburgh. It was bit much.

1980 TRAINING CAMP

Houston embraced Stabler. His timing was good. The city was flourishing. The employment Mecca had become the nation's fourth largest city. Urban cowboys in pickup trucks prowled the streets and places like the ever-popular Gilley's.

The Snake's easygoing manner and love of honky tonk made him a good fit. Pretty soon he could be seen in commercials pushing everything from air travel to furniture. There was even a song written about him, "Snake Bite." He quickly became a fixture at Gilley's.

Out in West Texas, Phillips was a model of consistency — same boots, hat and haircut. Camp was still laid back. He did not get in people's faces or yell at them and did not allow much hitting at practice.

However, in Houston, there was quite a bit of discussion whether he was changing. Besides Stabler and Tatum, he acquired veteran Sammy Green and tried to acquire troubled LB Thomas "Hollywood" Henderson. People worried about the character of the new players. Herskowitz asked whether Houston was replacing Oakland as the "port for troubled players."

Phillips did not see it that way. He was busy trying to seize history for himself, his team and his town. He had built a strong team and thought the time was right. After two straight seasons that each ended just 60 minutes away from the Super Bowl, Bum figured all he needed to do was tweak his team a little to reach the promised land. In any event, he had been doing this for years, pointing to the trades for LeVias, Wright, Taylor and Taylor.

But there was evidence of change — most notably, the departure of younger players. This was the reversal of a key theme. LeVias, Wright and the Taylors did not oust youngsters. With Stabler, Phillips gave up four years at QB. The arrival of Tatum caused the release of Bill Currier ('77, 9th round), a starter in '77 and '78. Adding Green led to the subtraction of LB Mike Murphy ('79, 6th). Moving 32-year-old Caster from flanker to TE

In March 1980, Bum traded Dan Pastorini, who he described as a son, for 34-year-old Ken Stabler — the NFL's all-time passing accuracy leader.

meant good-bye to hard-working Conrad Rucker ('78, 6th). It continued with the acquisition of 37-year-old OG Bob Young, and later Thomas Henderson and Dave Casper. It signaled a sense of desperation.

Of 11 new players, only five were drafted. The top pick was second-rounder OT Angelo Fields (6'5¾, 347) of Michigan State (New England wasted Houston's pick on RB Vagas Ferguson). It was a questionable choice that could have been used on Keena Turner, Dave Waymer, Rulon Jones, Matt Millen or Dwight Stephenson. Ed Biles compared him to Art Shell. Scout Joe Wooley said, "He's got real quick feet. He can waltz like a ballet dancer." No one asked if that was a compliment. *Pro Football Weekly* called him "lazy, sloppy, fat, *huge*, yet an extremely athletic and mobile youngster ... not an overly aggressive run blocker but seems to engulf the defender." Fields was surprised but happy, saying, "I didn't think I'd go before the fifth or sixth round."

Also in the second, they took the equally unheralded DT Daryle Skaugstad, who was coming off major knee surgery. One rating service had him ranked twenty-fifth among tackles in a lean year. Like Fields, his weight was a concern, but the problem with Skaugstad was that he was too light (237) to be a tackle. They left DT Steve McMichael of Texas on the board.

Many thought Bum was losing his touch. Jack Gallagher was in rare form: "The only thing harder to believe than Fields' selection was No. 2 choice Daryle Skaugstad ... There were more unanswered questions than Chappaquiddick ... Fields and Skaugstad. Sounds like a vaudeville act ... but will (they) leave audiences laughing or crying? ... Selection of a couple of unknowns suggests another economical Oiler draft, shades of Mo Towns ... Phillips said he was going to take the best player regardless of position and instead took the most player (Fields)."

Other picks were WR Tim Smith of Nebraska (3rd round), LB John Corker (5th) and QB Craig Bradshaw (7th), while rounding things out with the customary cache of WRs were Ed Preston of Western Kentucky and Wiley Pitts.

With offseason knee surgery to Merkins, Carl Roaches was signed as the new kick return man. They signed another kicker — Gerd Zimmerman. Gerd was a 30-year-old soccer player who earned the nickname "Thunderfoot" because he could kick a ball 80 mph. One reason he was brought in was that Toni Fritsch was involved in an automobile accident in Dallas in which a woman riding with him was killed. He pled guilty to manslaughter and received an eight-year probated sentence. The family sued for wrongful death.

The DL had Bethea, Culp and Dorris rotating with Baker, Stensrud and Kennard in obvious passing situations. Kennard would replace Culp during the season.

The safeties were set with Reinfeldt and Perry, but Tatum came to camp overweight and out of shape. Stemrick and Wilson were the CBs. The LBs were Bingham, Brazile, Washington and Hunt.

Gray and Mauck anchored the OL. The OGs were Fisher and David Carter ('77, 6th) with Conway Hayman as the right OT. Mo Towns, Bob Young and Fields were the backups. Reihner was still recovering from injury. Billy Johnson returned from a serious knee injury to replace the injured Burrough. Renfro was the flanker.

One major offensive change was a greater reliance on their "Ace" formation. Developed in 1978 by Ken Shipp when injuries depleted the running back corps, the Ace employed two TEs on the line. The FB was sacrificed. The change in 1980 came because Stabler worked well with TEs. Barber and Caster were happy as they looked forward to more than the 45 passes they caught between them in 1979. Tim Wilson, the starting FB for the last 3 seasons, was not. He moved to TE. Carpenter went in as a wingback on some passing downs while Coleman just had to wait for his chances.

Another new idea was the get-Earl-more-involved-in-the-passing offense play. Earl had just 28 catches over two seasons. In Oakland, where Pastorini and King were starting in the backfield together, Dan noted, "I'm taking nothing away from [Earl], but he can't catch a cold."

Robertson told readers to look for Stabler to spread the ball around. "The bottom line is this: The Oilers now have a possession-type passing game to go with a ball-control running game. Given continued strong [blocking]...Houston may have the most potent all-around offense in football." He added to the Steelerphobia by saying the Oilers were "the only AFC team with a better than average shot at derailing them."

Gallagher's words would come back to bite him: "After years of turmoil, the Oilers (are) now solid at the top." Forecasting prosperity, he added, "The revolving door (at Fanin Street) has long since stopped operating....Stability is the word for the Bum Phillips' administration. It appears settled for a long and happy run."

Adams was lurking around. After promising the team a new practice facility in Missouri County where most of the players and coaches lived, he later backed out. That left the team with the decrepit old facility on Fanin, widely recognized as the worst in football.

Their schedule was difficult. They opened with the four-time world champion Steelers at Three Rivers where they had won 16 straight. Four of the first six were on the road, including a Monday game in Cleveland. On the other hand, road games against their chief rivals Pittsburgh, Cleveland and Cincinnati came early, avoiding any late season Ice Bowls.

Earl, Bum and Willie were living symbols of the good times in Texas as the decade turned. Everything seemed so right. But soon enough, Bud Adams would disrupt this picture. Photo © Joel Durate.

THE 1980 REGULAR SEASON — THOSE DARN RAIDERS

In Pittsburgh, they had "One for the Thumb in '81" T-shirts which bore a likeness of Joe Greene sticking his hand out showing a bare thumb but with a Super Bowl ring on each finger. The Oilers did not need such reminders of the difference between the fortunes of the two franchises.

The Oilers fell behind early. Although they came out in the second half and scored 17 quick points, they still lost 31-17. The Steelers continued to strangle Earl, holding him to 57 yards on 15 carries, which kept him tied with Simpson at 7 straight 100-yard games. Stabler threw 45 passes. Of those, 11 were dropped and 5 were intercepted, although 3 were off deflections. They were 3-10 overall in Pittsburgh.

Next, they were at Cleveland. After those early embarrassing losses, the Oilers had become *MNF* darlings, winning 4 in a row (Pittsburgh twice and Miami twice). Campbell averaged 129 yards in those games. They made it five in a row by winning 16-7. Snake was 23-of-28 and Campbell had 108 yards as the Oilers established a grinding, ball-control offense.

They beat the Colts next 21-16 as Carpenter and Wilson combined on 201 yards. However, the right side suffered as Hayman went down. The following week, Bum signed Hollywood Henderson, saying, "You don't know a ladder's got splinters until you slide down it."

With Earl on the bench, they won in Cincinnati 13-10 in the game that saw one-time undrafted free agent Ken Kennard replace the legendary Curley Culp as a starter. The 13-year pro "wrote the book" on playing NT in a 3-4 defense. As a kid on a ranch in Arizona, Culp got strong lifting 55-gallon drums. In college, he was the NCAA heavyweight wrestling champ. His acquisition in 1974 did more to turn the Oiler defense around than any other single event.

That brought up Seattle for Steve Largent's first appearance in the Dome since 1976 when they traded him. "I remember going 0-6 in that preseason," he replied when asked of his memories. "It really gave the boo birds something to shout about."

They were at it again after underdog Seattle embarrassed Houston 26-7. The Seahawks led 23-0 at the half.

It was the repeat of a tired theme — lose the games they were supposed to win. The story in 1980 was that in spite of having the best RB in football, one of the greatest passers in history and two Pro Bowl OLs, they were last in scoring in the AFC. In 6 years, Bum's teams had been shut out 34 times in the first quarter while scoring over 10 points just 3 times.

Despite 178 yards from Earl, they lost to KC 21-10 to fall to 3-3. Fans were tired of watching the Oilers dig holes for themselves. Phillips told his team they had learned how to be successful, but had not yet learned how to handle that success.

Then he made a career-on-the-line move. He acquired Dave Casper for 1981 first and second picks and a 1982 second-round choice. It was a high price for a TE, especially for a team in need of new blood. Casper came in saying the Texas heat might kill him and recommending they paint the Astrodome gold to match Notre Dame's. Predictably, Barber was unhappy. "I'm upset about the way it was done. The way it happened. It hurts to swallow ... I think Bum owed it to [the receivers] to talk to us, to let us know what was going on."

Bum thought it would improve his new two TE offense. Casper could not only catch, but he blocked like a tackle. Unlike their other TEs, he liked blocking.

It worked as they won 5 straight. The additional blocker put Earl in a groove, as he had consecutive games of 203 yards against Tampa, 202 against Cincinnati, 157 against Denver, 130 against New England and 206 against Chicago. In the Pats game, the Oilers fell behind 24-6, only to come back and win 38-34 to extend their *Monday Night* streak to 6 wins. Tragedy struck, however, as a HB pass from Campbell to Burrough ended in a broken wrist for double zero.

Against Chicago, Earl showed them why he was the man. The Bears took cheap shots at him the whole game. He broke one late, but slowed to allow a safety to catch him. Acting as if he was going out of bounds, he waited for the safety to go for the out-of-bounds hit, and then suddenly stuck a stiff arm in his face, knocking him on his can.

At 8-3, the Oilers had passed 7-4 Pittsburgh and were alone on top of the division while tying Buffalo and Oakland for the best record in the AFC.

Then they blew two golden chances to sew up the division and a piece of history. On November 23, they came out flat and even hung over as the Oilers made the 2-9 Jets look like world-beaters. After a night of hard partying in Manhattan by Stabler, Caster and others until 4 a.m., they trailed 21-0 on 6 turnovers. Stabler woke up in the fourth quarter to tie it at 21 and again at 28. He finished with 388 yards and 4 TDs, but the Jets won the coin toss and then the game in OT. Earl was lost to a knee injury after 60 yards.

It was such a shocker that the *New York Times* later printed a story that purported to link Stabler to a known gambling figure. The paper suggested he might have *thrown* the game. Apparently, in New York, the Jets were seen as so bad that the only way they could beat Houston was if the Oilers threw the game. Al Davis was reported to be the source of the rumors.

The next week, they blew a game to the less-talented Browns in the Dome 17-14. Earl's 109 yards could not overcome 5 turnovers. A hurting Fritsch uncharacteristically missed a 38-yarder in the fourth quarter. "I miss, my fault, I'm sorry," he said with red, swollen eyes afterwards. Brian Sipe completed 13 passes for just 92 yards, but the Browns had slipped by for the crown, home field and first round bye.

The Oilers suddenly found themselves in a second-place tie with 8-5 Pittsburgh and 3 games remaining. With everything to lose, they punched

out the defending Super Bowl champs 6-0 to knock them out of the playoffs for the first time in 9 years. During the game, Fritsch was in traction with a bad back. Worst of all, they lost Gray to a torn Achilles tendon. Rookie Angelo Fields, who had trimmed down to 315-pounds, replaced him. The Browns and Bills were 10-4, while the Oilers, Chargers and Raiders were 9-5 with two to go.

They easily dispatched the Packers and Lynn Dickey on the frozen tundra 22-3. Earl's 181 yards did not impress Green Bay fans as they doused him with frozen beer after a TD.

With the playoffs still up in the air, the Oilers took on the Vikings in the last game at home. After 15¾ games, the season was still on the line as Houston clung to a 20-16 lead with time running out and Tommy Kramer on the Oiler 10. But the defense held as the Oilers tied Cleveland at 11-5. Earl had his fourth 200-yard game of the season with 203.

All 5 AFC playoff teams were 11-5. The Browns won the division on the tie-breaker — conference record. The Oilers would be on the road as a wildcard team again.

The site, however, had to wait on the Monday game between the Steelers and Chargers. A win by Pittsburgh would mean Houston opened in the Dome against New England, but a San Diego victory meant they opened at Oakland. The outcome had far-reaching implications for Houston as the Chargers prevailed 26-17.

The losses to the Seahawks and Jets, who were a combined 8-24, burned deep. That those teams were in the AFC also ruined the Oilers' chances in the tie-breaker. Just one more victory and Houston would have possessed the best record in the AFC, gained a first-round bye in the playoffs and owned home field throughout.

The team programmed to conquer Pittsburgh from day one did not have to deal with them. The Steelers were out of the playoffs for the first time since 1971.

"I'm as confident as I've ever been," said the coach, "maybe even a little more confident. We're stronger both running and passing this year and I'm also not sure that we're not a better clutch team than in the past."

Statistics largely bore him out. The Oilers led the AFC in rushing and were a close second to San Diego in total offense. The defense ranked second overall and first as a scoring defense.

Earl was virtually unstoppable, finishing with 1,934 yards, the second highest single season mark in history to just miss Simpson's record (2,003). His closest competitor, Walter Payton, was 500 yards off the pace. He tied another Jim Brown record, leading the NFL in rushing for his first three seasons while averaging a career and league high 5.2 yards per carry. He also set records with four 200-yard games and for most carries in a season. Obviously, this was the best rushing Oiler team ever as they outgained opponents by 64 yards a game and ran over 100 more plays.

Despite missing Burrough most of the season, Stabler passed for 3,202 yards, just missing George Blanda's 1961 team record. The pass offense averaged 46 yards a game more than the 1979 club. His completion ratio of 64% far surpassed Pastorini's team record. Eight different receivers caught 27 passes or more. Cleveland coach Sam Rutigliano called them the "biggest challenge" in the playoffs.

Still, considering that they were the lowest scoring of 10 playoff teams, there were some perplexing problems. Of 11 victories, only three were by more than a touchdown. The defense saved the season by allowing just 295 points (18 per game), second least among playoff teams.

The Oilers' number one pick in the 1980 draft was Michigan State offensive tackle Angelo Fields. The player he is standing beside, All-Pro tackle Leon Gray, was listed at 6'3, 260. Of Angelo, Bum said, "He's not overweight, he's over-big."

OILER BLUES

Campbell, Gray and Brazile made first team All-Pro. Casper, Stemrick, Reinfeldt and Perry were added to the Pro Bowl.

THE 1980 PLAYOFFS

And so the Oilers returned to the scene of some bad memories. In 1967, they missed the Super Bowl by losing 40-7 in Oakland. In 1969, they were blown out 56-7 in the first round of the last AFL playoffs. Since 1962, they had only won one game there.

Despite Houston losing Gray and Burrough, the betting line was pick-em. The at-home Steelers gave Houston the edge. "They run the ball better," said Bradshaw, "and play better defense." Joe Greene added, "Oakland will have its hands full trying to stop Earl."

The Oilers seemed cautious. "We've got Snake, Dave and Jack," said Brazile, "but the thing we have to remember is that they've replaced them with some quality people." Biles sounded a similar note: "Despite the changes, it's the same Oakland offense. Put Plunkett in for Stabler, Bob Chandler for Fred Billetnikoff and Ray Chester for Casper. Cliff Branch is still their big play guy.... Up front? They've still got Dalby, Upshaw and Shell. And van Eeghen's their fullback. Those names never change."

Pastorini had gone down to a broken leg on October 5. Oakland was 2-3 at the time. He was replaced by Jim Plunkett and they won 9-of-11 the rest of the way (in the end, it was 13-of-15). Dante watched from the sidelines. But his life was still eventful. In November, Santa Clara sheriffs took him into custody on possession charges. Then, the night before the Oiler game, he had another confrontation with Dale Robertson.

They ran into each other at the Edgewater Hyatt where the Oilers were staying. After a few words, Robertson made a hasty retreat. Dante Antonio chased him outside and then back into the lobby where he pulled him around by the back of the coat. Pastorini had to be restrained. About thirty minutes later, Dan totaled his car after losing control in Alameda City. It was not exactly the omen the Oilers needed.

On the first play from scrimmage, Campbell was downed and laid the ball out. But the refs ruled it a fumble, and the Raiders quickly took a 3-0 lead. Late in the first quarter, Houston took a 7-3 lead on a 1-yard Campbell TD. It was their only lead.

In the second quarter, Fritsch bounced a 45-yard FG attempt off a post. Midway in the same quarter, Plunkett found Todd Christensen for a 1-yard TD. A 32-yard Fritsch FG to tie was called back on a motion penalty. John Matuszak blocked the second attempt. Oakland led 10-7 at the half.

The third quarter was a draw. Halfway though, Houston made it to the Raider 11, only to watch the drive die when

Bum Phillips induced peak performance out of others' castoffs. In 1978, he acquired ex-Jet Rich Caster (right) who responded with 5 TDs and a 15.8 yards per catch average. In 1980, the versatile Caster (6'5, 228) moved from TE to WR to fill the void left by Burrough and collected 27 receptions. Likewise, undrafted Greg Stemrick (below talking to his friend Pat McInally of the Bengals) signed in 1975, was starting by 1977 and in the Pro Bowl in 1980 with 4 interceptions.

With the playoffs on the line in the last game of the 1980 season, Earl rushed for 203 yards as the Oilers beat Minnesota 20-16. It was his fourth 200-yard game of the season. His season total was 1,943 yards, the second best single-season mark ever. He also led the league in TDs (13), yards per carry (a career high 5.2) and carries (373).

Billy Johnson deflected a pass into the arms of Lester Hayes. On the first play of the fourth quarter, Plunkett hit FB Arthur Whittington with a bomb to make to make it 17-7. At that point, the Oilers abandoned Campbell. Earl, who had 67 yards in the first half, finished with 91. In response, the Raiders doubled their blitzes and buried their old teammate. One key was the loss of Angelo Fields. His replacement was Conway Hayman, who was grossly out of shape. The Raiders ended up with 7 sacks for 65 yards worth of losses.

With 5:29 left, Hayes intercepted another and ran it back all the way to stick a fork in the Oilers. The final was 27-7.

The statistics did not justify the score. Plunkett had a Plunkett-like performance, completing 8-of-23 passes. Oakland converted 3-of-15 third downs and managed 12 first downs. Stabler was 15-of-26 for 243 yards.

Houston's play calling took quite a bit of heat. "I'll tell you what I will remember — all the things we could do, but didn't," said Coleman. "We just don't have enough imagination when we try and score points ... You just can't depend on one or two formations to win ballgames against good defenses."

Bingham agreed. "We've got one of the best quarterbacks in football over the last 7 or 8 years," said the linebacker, "yet all of a sudden, he can't get it into the end zone. That just doesn't happen. You got to start looking at some things. We have 7 All-Pros in our offense (Campbell, Stabler, Johnson, Young, Casper, Fritsch played while Gray and Burrough were out). It's not the players ... We have got to make some changes ... We have the best talent in the league and we will all be sitting at home during Super Bowl week."

For the second year in a row, an opponent questioned the Oiler coaches' strategy. Former Houston Wheatley Wildcat Hayes, who had 2 sacks to go with his 2 interceptions, described the offense as "high school." He added, "It's more brawn football than anything else. They don't trap. They don't pull. We never blitzed like that before, but it was free."

HAPPY NEW YEAR HOUSTON

In Houston, fans and those who told them the Super Bowl was there for the taking were stunned and embarrassed. Still maintaining that the Oakland team was "inferior," Robertson wrote that the problem was not with the players or Bum's slack atmosphere, but with his lack of an offensive coordinator. The Oilers had never hired anyone to replace Ken Shipp. Robertson suggested offensive assistants Joe Bugel, King Hill and Andy Burgeois be replaced because "their best isn't good enough."

On Monday morning, Bum was back in his office defending his coaches. "I'm not gonna change anybody," he said. "We've got three guys who were good enough to get us into the playoffs three years in a row. Then we lose a game and this stuff starts.

"Obviously, when you don't win, you didn't get the job done. If I could explain what was wrong, I would have corrected it before it was too late. Maybe I didn't do a good enough job of coaching. I didn't see things until they were thrown back in my face." His thoughts had already turned to the next season. "The first thing we're gonna do now is make a thorough study of all aspects of our team ... to see if we have a design problem, an execution problem or a lack of effort ... Maybe we've asked people to do some things they can't. If that's the case, we have to face the facts and move on."

Phillips was not about to admit he needed a coordinator on the Monday after a loss. That would look as if he was giving into pressure and blaming the loss on the offensive coaches. He was too loyal and stubborn to do that.

Everyone seemed to have an opinion on what went wrong, but on Wednesday morning the one person whose opinion mattered the most weighed in. Bud Adams called Phillips over to his office and within 15 minutes it was over.

"This is the most difficult decision I have had to make in my 21 years as owner of the Oilers," began Bud's statement. "At the end of each season I always sit down and evaluate the job that has been done and determine if we've made the degree of progress we were looking for prior to the beginning of training camp. In recent years I've felt we've taken significant steps forward, but after this season I feel we've taken a large step backward. I don't feel that the drop-off in our level of performance was justified in light of the considerable investment of time and energy by all the people connected with the Oiler organization."

He was at least right about the significant steps forward. In the 10-year period prior to Phillips, the Oilers had just one winning season — Wally Lemm's 1967 Divisional Champions. From 1964-73, they won 42 games for an average of barely 4 wins per season. In his last 3 seasons, Bum's teams won more games than any other teams except Pittsburgh and Dallas. He was the most successful coach in team history.

Adams said it came down to his unwillingness to hire an OC. "Around midseason I met with Bum and expressed concerns over the lack of scoring and recommended he either consider elevating one of the three existing offensive coaches to the post of offensive coordinator or go outside and bring in the best available man to work in that capacity ... I was very disappointed to learn through the newspaper, instead of first hand, that he had totally rejected the idea of hiring an offensive coordinator for the 1981 season."

Phillips' reply was that his team "had beaten a lot of teams with offensive coordinators. Denver didn't have one the last couple of years and they made the playoffs. They got one this year and didn't make the playoffs. The three years we had an offensive coordinator, we didn't make the playoffs. Then, without one, we made it three years in a row. A lot of teams with offensive coordinators didn't make the playoffs once, much less three straight years. It just goes to show you it's the players and not an offensive coordinator."

Attempting to make his case, Adams stated: "When Bum came to me and asked for permission to make a trade or acquire a player I was always supportive by providing him with what he thought he needed to be a winner on the field. I was willing to spend the necessary money to bring in a solid offensive innovator to work with our existing coaches, but according to press accounts, he rejected that idea totally. Everyone is aware of the widespread criticism of our play Sunday. I'm a firm believer you can't make decisions affecting the football team to simply silence the criticism of the media, fans or opposing teams.

"However, there's also the old adage that where there's smoke there's fire, and Bum's adamant refusal to even consider the possibility the offense needed some fresh blood and input weighed heavily on my decision. It also became obvious to me that the confidence of members of our own football team was being shaken by concerns about the performance of the offense."

The Oilers playoff hopes in 1980 were effectively carted away with Leon Gray in Game 14 against the Steelers.

KIND OF LIKE A DEATH IN THE FAMILY

Upon learning his fate, Phillips returned to his offense and fought back tears. "I'm surprised, really surprised," said Phillips, "but life goes on." He added: "The last time I talked to Bud about this was concerning extending my contract, then they fire me. I went to the phone to let my wife know. My 13-year-old had already heard it on television and went to bawling. I'm a little disappointed about that. At least they could have given me 24 hours to let my family know and to notify my assistants."

That was the extent of his commentary. He was sad but not bitter. "I guess they expected more than I could produce," he said.

Bum's then wife Helen said, "Bum told me everything would be all right. He wasn't upset. I don't think he would show those feelings to his wife and children anyway. I've seen him cry after a game. It takes a big man to do that. I think we'll cry a whole lot tonight."

It caught players off guard. Brazile, the first player drafted by Phillips in 1975, said: "It's got to be a joke ... As much as Coach Phillips has done for this team, I never thought it could happen. Maybe some players or someone else could get fired but never him. He taught me many things. He was a father, not only a coach, to most players."

Stensrud called it "impulsive" and suggested that if the new coach is a hard liner "some people will walk out on him." Daryl Hunt added, "It's like I've got a big lump in my throat. I don't see where our loss was Bum's fault ... They fired a helluva coach and helluva person. Bum turned this team around. He built it. Hearing this is kind of like a death in the family."

Mauck called it "ridiculous. I'm a Bum Phillips man. I found him easy to play for. His mark is on our team. We were always aggressive. We ran the ball hard and played defense hard." Even mild-mannered Giff Nielsen questioned the move. "It seems odd to me when the team has been extremely successful and everybody talks about the 1-13 years before Bum came ... When people think of the Houston Oilers, they think of Bum. Things got rockier this year but we went to the AFC championship game the last two years. I have a great deal of respect for Bum and all our coaches. I guess when you lose, it's easy to point fingers." He suggested, "There might be something we don't know about."

Only Bingham sounded an upbeat note. One of the couple of players who openly criticized the offense after the Raider game, the LB said, "I'll be honest, I was afraid to go to camp next year and waste another year. I'm not here to make money. I'm here to win. A coach can do his job for 40 years but a player has only X number of years in him and I'm running out of mine ... Almost everybody else felt the same way I did ... Our big mistake this year was our offense. I was right in my estimation but I didn't think it would come to this. What's happened could be our loss, or it could be our gain."

THE PUNDITS' REACTION

Local pundits quickly weighed in. Jack Gallagher called it "a colossal blunder." He said the team was "predictable because of its unpredictability" and surmised that Adams' ego caused the dismissal of "the most popular and successful coach Houston ever had." He wrote: "Now we're back to the days of square one, back to Bud Adams glorifying in the daily headlines ... Bum represented the recognition Adams craved — a popular figure with the media, in demand for commercials and speaking engagements, a man respected and loved throughout the city. Adams' image was the opposite."

The *Chronicle's* John Wilson wrote: "Because of the way the team has been run from the top, the Oiler organization has been volatile and marked by strife, turmoil, dissension, infighting and controversy the 21 years of its existence. Phillips had a personality — or at least a persona — and specific attributes that made it possible for him to produce a winning team under these encumbered circumstances. That is why I believe [the firing] was the most shortsighted action by a management that I have seen in 25 years of sportswriting.

"From Adams' perspective, the Oilers' history no doubt does not even resemble the way we see it. We see the Oilers as a franchise failure, a sometimes downright embarrassment ... But [to Adams] the Oilers are a smashing success because it is under all probability the best business deal of the scores of ventures he has undertaken ... I don't think Adams even considers that he is competing with [other teams] ... the financial scoreboard is the only one he watches."

Chronicle staffer Ed Fowler wrote: "Don't buy that claptrap about Bum Phillips being handed his crewcut because he refused to hire an offensive coordinator ... Phillips was fired because Bud Adams didn't want a personality cult on his payroll ... Since it had been the offense which malfunctioned, with a resulting riptide of criticism in the press, much of it from the players, Adams made it the general issue and Phillips' stubborn stand on the coordinator matter the specific point. It's known as a smokescreen ... Phillips was fired, in fact, because Adams couldn't stand the sight of him anymore."

Fowler quoted a "source close to the situation" who purportedly said, "Bum was making money for him hand over fist but he still couldn't live with a guy upstairs in a cowboy hat." The source said Bum's popularity, his demand as a speaker, his commercial endorsements, his book and even the fact that Dick Emberg quoted "Bummisms" was too much. "Adams cannot tolerate that kind of popularity on someone else's part. The offensive coordinator thing is an excuse."

Back at the *Post*, Dale Robertson wrote, "Only Bud Adams could fire a man on New Year's Eve." He maintained that "Adams tolerated the hoopla but never liked it. He went so far as to accuse Phillips last summer of using the Oilers' good name for his personal gain. Heaven forbid. 'I wouldn't have to take any endorsements,' Phillips told me at the time, 'if Bud would pay me fair.'"

Among the locals, only Mickey Herskowitz avoided directly criticizing Adams. He called Bum "the victim of his own success. The Oilers had grown so prosperous that 11 wins was not good enough to save his job. What one feels now is sadness and more of what old Oiler fans felt the moment they heard the news. Fear. Even a little terror. Oilers fans are like people who lived through the depression and still keep their savings in sock under the mattress ... They can't help but wonder if this move will mark a return to the days when the Oilers were the NFL's answer to the French Revolution."

The firing got a reaction around the nation. Sid Gillman called it "typical", adding, "if anybody can screw up a franchise, it's Bud Adams." NBC commentator Bob Trumphy, who worked the Oakland game, said, "They overreacted. Okay, they lost a football game. When they lost Angelo Fields, the game was lost ... The Houston Oilers don't need an offensive coordinator; they already have the greatest weapon in the game ... it's going too far to throw it in now. I hate to see Houston panic. They're simply too good of a team to do that."

Long-time opponent Joe Greene of the Steelers offered, "I think they have made one helluva mistake because now they have to take another step backward before they can take a step forward ... I think they would have won this year if they had had Pastorini. That's not saying anything against Stabler. But there's a transition involved with a new quarterback. It takes time when a person of that magnitude and a position of that magnitude are involved ... A football team is a very fickle machine. It's very temperamental. You have to stroke it just right or it will crack up ... derail." Greene also pointed to the loss of Gray. "They didn't have any wide receivers," he said, "then Leon Gray went down ... There are very few Leon Grays in the league. I *know* there aren't any on that football team .... It's going to seem a little strange playing Houston and there ain't no Bum."

"I think Bum Phillips is one of the most capable coaches in football today," said Merlin Olsen. "Remember, when Bum came to the Oilers, he came into a pretty pathetic situation — no depth and not many building blocks. I think he's done a helluva job. Look at the roster. It still looks like the Foreign Legion ... It's difficult to find quality coaches, especially one who can take a team without great talent and make winners out of them ... He won't be out of a job very long."

PHILLIPS' LEGACY

It was the fans who were the beasts of burden. They had just seen a similar thing happen with their baseball team. In 1980, the Astros had won their first title of any kind and came within 6 outs of the World Series. The architect was Tal Smith, who turned around a team that once finished 43½ games out of first. He was named baseball executive of the year, but a week after the Astros lost to the Phillies, he was fired.

Now came Phillips. That was their man whose sad mug appeared on the front page of both local newspapers just below the *Happy New Year* headlines. This one shocked everyone. There was a protest at the APC Building. Signs read, "Houston got rid of the wrong Bum," and "Fire Bud, Keep Bum."

But most just sat in stunned silence. Some still are. No doubt they had seen a lot from Pop Ivy, Sammy Baugh and Bones Taylor to Ed Hughes and Bill Peterson. After the merger, they became the worst team in football. Every good player except Bethea was sent packing. It was during this period that, for the first time in sports history, one city's fans adopted a rival city's team — the Cowboys.

It took an old enemy, Sid Gillman, to get Bud's ship righted again. Sid bridged the gap and gave them Phillips.

Phillips' six-year reign was the longest in the team's 21 years. From Gillman's foundation, he transformed the biggest joke in the NFL into a respected and even feared unit. It brought all of Houston together for the first time.

In 1975, he took a team that went 1-13 in 1973 to a 10-4 record and just barely out of the playoffs. It was their best record since 1962 as they set attendance records.

The 1976 team finished a disappointing 5-9 because of injuries and a lack of depth. Many believed they were just reverting to form, but Phillips was building a good team. The 1977 team rebounded to finish 8-6 and barely out of the playoffs again after losing some games to bogus umpiring. Phillips' popularity began to spread beyond Houston and Texas to the rest of the country. There was just something about the homespun coach in the crewcut.

In those first three years, Phillips as GM built through both the draft and trades. He made a name collecting free agents and players shunned by other teams.

The Oilers were the Bermuda Triangle of pro football.

They broke out in 1978 after Phillips pulled off a trade for the rights to Earl Campbell, who would turn out to be the best RB in the NFL. That team won Houston's first ever *Monday Night Football* game (against Pittsburgh), came back from 23-0 to beat a very good New England team and beat Miami 35-30 in arguably the greatest *MNF* game of all time. Making the playoffs for the first time since 1969, the Oilers beat the Dolphins and Patriots again on the road to earn a berth in the AFC Championship Game. Their dream ended 34-5 in dreary Pittsburgh, but they returned home to an unheard of 50,000-person pep rally in the Astrodome.

The 1979 team overcame devastating injuries, including the loss of the entire left side of the OL to finish 11-5 and back in the playoffs. The Love Ya Blue era blossomed and the city went wacko. They beat the Orange Crush in the first playoff game in Houston since 1962, and overcame impossible odds to beat a great

Charger team on the road. They lost the AFC Championship to Pittsburgh in a game marred by a call so controversial that the NFL would soon employ instant replay. Despite the loss, the Oilers returned to another throbbing mass in the Astrodome that had grown to 70,000. That night, Bum gave his "kick in the door" speech.

For the 1980 season, Phillips traded away prodigal son Pastorini for grizzled veteran Stabler. He also picked up Casper and Tatum, but the team finished with the same 11-5 record and in the playoffs as a wildcard team for the third year in a row. During the season, the offense was unimaginative and predictable. It moved the ball but did not score. Phillips was criticized. After losing to Oakland in the first round, two or three players joined the media in calling for an overhaul of the offense, but none dreamed their complaints would be used as an excuse to fire the most popular man in Houston.

Phillips took a team that had a 15-52-2 after the merger, turned it around and won 59 over the next 6. He stopped the bleeding caused by Cincinnati, Cleveland and Pittsburgh and set up some fine rivalries with those clubs. His was the only AFC team to make the playoffs the last 3 years. His playoff record was 4-3. Twice he was 4 quarters or less from landing Houston in the Super Bowl. Each of the 3 teams they lost to won the Super Bowl.

And it was as much about how he did it as it was what he did. He had guys like Thomas Henderson who was on his way to prison, Ken Stabler who was not paying his child support or student loans, Toni Fritsch who had a drinking problem and a secondary with several cocaine users. They tried Jack Tatum, Duane Thomas and Tim Rossovich. Elvin Bethea said, "We had outlaws and pirates, but on Sunday afternoons everyone worked as a machine. The characters had character."

And so on Wednesday, December 31, 1981, Bud fired another coach. This one just happened to be coming off consecutive 12- and 13-win seasons.

Adams pinned his decision on two factors, the loss, and Phillips' refusal to hire an OC. It did not wash. His '79 and '80 offenses were the team's best since the wild, early years of the AFL. He had no discussions with Phillips after the game except to fire him. If he really wanted to know if Bum would hire an OC, he could have asked him directly. Instead, he relied upon newspaper accounts. With some more time to recover, Bum may have come around.

By all appearances, Adams was just looking for a reason to fire Bum. Many say he was envious. He wanted some recognition for approving the trades and forking out for the salaries. Yet Phillips got all the credit. He heard about it at the River Oaks Country Club.

It did not make much sense. Bud's team was the most popular it had ever been. And it was because of Phillips. He filled the stadium. Houston was in love with the man with the funny sayings. He liked his players. They liked him, as well as the other coaches and their teammates. The mutual affection spread through the city. They were *the* talk of the town. Merchandise selling became so hot that Pete Rozelle made them give up the Love Ya Blue image. There were songs, signs, and lots and lots of partying.

In this regard, this firing was like that of Klosterman, and to a lesser extent, of Gillman. Each event revealed the paradox that is Bud Adams. He formed the Oilers to make money. The team made him the most when the stadium was full. Attendance was highest when the team was popular. With Phillips, Adams was making more money off the Oilers than ever.

But his ego could not handle someone else becoming popular off *his* team. So he overreacted, the result always being another crash to the bottom accompanied by an attendance decline, which of course meant he made less money.

As Phillips said on his way out, "If Bud Adams wants to pay me *not* to coach, that's his privilege. An owner

Perhaps the most unfair twist to this saga is that Bum Phillips was, at least in part, a victim of the success he created. Of his famous speech on the night of January 6, 1980, he later said, "They wanted to hear something. It didn't seem like such a big deal at the time."

has the right to do whatever he wants with his property, and the Houston Oilers are Bud Adams' property."

THE DECADE IN REVIEW

The 1970s debunked the theory of NFL superiority. In its first 10 years, the AFC held a 214-180-6 edge over NFC teams. The best the NFC could do was in 1973 when it forced a 19-19-2 tie. The AFC won 9-of-11 Super Bowls and 12-of-16 when combined with AFL teams' victories.

The Pittsburgh Steelers were the team of the decade, beginning in 1969 when Art Rooney named AFL assistant Chuck Noll as the head coach. Rooney gave him some time. By 1972, they had won their first AFC Central crown and first playoff game on the immaculate reception.

They won the division again in 1974 and continued to do so through the end of the decade. In total, they won 7 of the first 10 Central titles, appeared in 6 AFC Title Games and won 4 Super Bowls (1974-75, 1978-79) with a roster full of Hall of Famers. Some 20 players played on all four Super Bowl teams, including Bradshaw, Harris, Bleier, Blount, Greene, Greenwood, Furness, Ham, Grossman, Lambert, Shell, Stallworth, Swann, Webster and White.

From the merger through 1980, the Oilers and Steelers played 24 times. The Steelers won 17. On the other hand, Houston was the only team to beat them in each of their four Super seasons. The Steelers' best seasons were 1978 (14-2) and 1979 (12-4) when the Oilers also had their best teams. "I would like to think we were the second-best team in the league during those two AFC Championship Games," said Coach Phillips later. "Unfortunately, the best team that ever played was in our division."

"The Steelers of the 1970s were the greatest team of all time," says Gregg Bingham. "But the entire division was great back then. In 1975, we were 10-4 and didn't make the playoffs. Pittsburgh was 12-2 and Cincinnati was 11-3."

When asked years later to compare the team of the '70s — Pittsburgh, with the team of the '80s — the 49ers, Phillips said, "San Francisco is a great team now, but they don't have the defense Pittsburgh had then. That was the most dominating defense that ever played. I don't know if there will ever be another defense like that one."

CHAPTER 7

THE THIRD DARK AGES
1981-85

The Oilers went into another serious funk after Bud Adams fired the popular Bum Phillips. The transition was rough, as the team would have a hard time playing up to the standard set during that era. Many of the players left behind were older, and without Bum there to humor and coax them, unmotivated. A dearth of draft picks prevented an infusion of new blood. Most of the picks they did have, they wasted.

Beginning with the 1982 draft, the Oilers started the slow climb out of their deep hole. It was a torturous process. During this period, a new figure emerged who would have more influence on the club than anyone. Though neither a coach nor a player, former accountant Ladd Herzeg would be the primary force behind the Oilers of the '80s.

1981: SOME BIG BOOTS TO FILL

Bud Adams named his new GM the same day he fired Phillips. At 36, Cleveland-native Ladd Herzeg (formerly Herczeg) became one of the youngest GMs in football.

The round-faced Herzeg left Arthur Andersen in 1976 to become financial VP of KSA Industries, the parent company of Bud's various entities. Later, he became senior VP of KSA and was instrumental in keeping several of Bud's businesses afloat in troubled economic waters. In May of 1978, he became chief administrative officer of the Oilers. In the John Collins mold, he had no pro experience apart from his bookkeeper's role.

Herzeg tried to distance himself from the backlash by reminding everyone that he was not the GM when Phillips was fired. However, the public would always associate his ascension with Bum's demise.

It did not help when he took a few swipes at Phillips' management style. He said, "My personal opinion is that the trade for Casper was not in the best long-range interest of the Oilers ... We feel that the duties of a head coach and general manager are really too much for one person to handle." Incredulously to some, he said the most crucial factor to success would be "continuity of the program." Phillips had given the club more continuity than it had ever known.

Herzeg was in charge of the new coach hire. He said he would make a list of 12 to 15 candidates, quickly reduce it to 3 or 4 and make recommendations to Adams. Rumored candidates included Dan Reeves, Ted Marchibroda, Jack Pardee, George Allen, Hank Stram, Dan Devine, John Madden and Ed Biles.

This "search" lasted less than 48 hours. On January 2, 1981, Ed Biles became the eleventh head coach of the Houston Oilers. When pressed, Herzeg admitted his interview process consisted of speaking to three candidates by phone. The swiftness left the impression that Biles was anointed heir before Phillips was fired.

So began Ladd Herzeg's controversial reign as Oiler GM. He would prove to be a tough contract negotiator in a time when player salaries were expanding exponen-

Ladd Herzeg

tially. He also turned into an excellent horse trader, making the best string of trades in team history. There would be no more giveaways of Willie Browns, Charlie Joiners, Ken Houstons or Steve Largents under Herzeg, and no more trades like those involving Vic Washington or Dave Casper.

On the other hand, Herzeg could be arrogant, combative and sometimes an embarrassment, which eventually would lead to his departure. He also got on the bad side of a couple of Houston sportswriters. In the tradition of *Gallagher/Perkins vs. Blanda, Gallagher vs. Adams* and *Robertson vs. Pastorini*, Herzeg's battles with local press would become personal and, at times, overshadow the games and the team.

WELCOME ED BILES

Everyone said nice things about the new coach. Hired in 1973 by Sid Gillman, he was one of the top DCs in the league. His 1979 defense led the AFC in interceptions and was second in sacks. In 1980, they were first in points allowed and second overall.

ILB Bingham said, "Ed's an extremely competent person. He knows the system. He's always thinking. He knows what the defense should be doing 24-hours a day."

The 5'6, 49-year-old Biles was personable, but also quiet, disciplined and analytical. He had his quirks. For example, a frequent dieter, he often played racquetball over lunch wearing an Oiler jacket to promote maximum sweating. Most opinions of him ended with "but he ain't no Bum," which would have been a compliment anywhere else.

"I'm not a rookie," he said. "I've been coaching for 28 years and I think I've paid my dues." With a straight face, the man who used to ride to work with Phillips in his pickup truck said, "I feel I owe this opportunity to Bum." He added, "Our main objective is to win the division."

AS THE OILER COACHING WORLD TURNS

The most immediate concern was the coaches, most of whom had another year left on their contracts. It was odd that a team that had just fired its head coach would want to keep all of his assistants, but Herzeg said he wanted continuity.

Phillips was not out of work long. Houstonian John Mecom hired him "in about 20 minutes" to coach his Saints. Things quickly got testy between the two organizations. Initially, the first six assistants (Wade Phillips, King Hill, John Paul Young, Bob Gambold, Joe Bugel, Andy Bourgeois) all said they wanted to leave. Biles fired two (Young and Hill), only to have Herzeg bring them back. When Phillips called them to see what was going on, Herzeg complained to Pete Rozelle about "tampering." Herzeg then agreed to let Wade go but not the others. He also agreed to let the remaining group "resign" (to get Bud out from under the last years of their contracts), but only if they did not go to New Orleans. For that, he demanded "compensation."

Once the dust settled, Biles had retained only Gambold and Burgeois. Wade Phillips, Hill and Young ended up with Bum. Mr. Bugel went to Washington.

Biles hired Dick Nolan as the DC and almost landed Ted Marchibroda as the OC, but a deal snagged over money. Jim Shofner ended up with the position.

1981 TRAINING CAMP

The two big issues in the off season were Earl's contract and QB. Campbell's situation was not the customary greedy player speaking through a ruthless agent. Earl's first contract had all the appearances of an Adams' scam. The original front money was less than $150,000 and then deferred over 40 years. At each Pro Bowl, he heard he was underpaid. He renegotiated a six-year deal in 1980 which paid him around $300,000 a year and spread the deferrals over 20 years. That deal caused quite a stir at the time because the Oilers always said they did not renegotiate contracts and Mike Barber and Robert Brazile were attempting to get better deals. This time Herzeg said no new deals. Earl's agent asked for a trade.

Although another Ken Stabler Diamondback Saloon opened in February, he was not happy. Not long after taking over, Biles pronounced that Nielsen would be giv-

Eddie Biles (left) did not see eye-to-eye with the Snake.

en an even chance to compete. Stabler, the NFL's all-time passing accuracy leader, led the AFC in 1980 hitting 64% of his passes for 3,202 yards (he also had 28 picks). Biles also announced he was putting the Snake on a weight training program. This news did not play well on the *Redneck Riviera*.

There was no relief with the April draft. Newly hired personnel man Mike Holovak had little to do because of the Casper trade. The first pick was WR Michael Holston in the third. Other clubs had him rated as only a seventh- or eighth-round prospect, and he would be another in a long line of busts at that position. The only additions to help would be DB Bill Kay (6th round), WR Willie Tullis (8th) and LB Avon Riley (9th).

Camp began without Stabler, who "retired." He and Biles were not a good match. The coach said that if he wanted to play he had to prove he still wanted to win rather than just collect a paycheck. Biles' weight program comments embarrassed him. Biles said, "We have not closed the door on Kenny, but we are not going to actively pursue getting him to change his mind."

It made for some nervous WRs. Double zero Ken Burrough said, "All these years I watched Snake and I used to think, 'Oh my God, what would it be like to work with a quarterback like that?' So he becomes my teammate and I get hurt ('80). Then I get well and he retires. When I look back on my career someday, that would be my biggest regret — not getting to play a full season with Snake."

That left it to Giff and free agent John Reaves, who they found working in a real estate office in Florida. The non-drinking, non-swearing Nielsen had quietly waited three years for his chance. Then, after looking good in the new offense, he hurt a shoulder. Before you could say "beer gut," Ken was back with a nice tan and new $800,000 deal. Mauck said he was getting sick of the "milkshake breath in the huddle" anyway.

Stabler claimed it was not the money. It was the talent and fact that Shofner promised to open up the offense. After a few days, he said, "This is much better than drinking beer and lying on the beach. Running plays and dying, that's much more fun."

Mike Renfro was glad to see him. "Snake can help us," he said. "He's a masterful quarterback. And he's fun to go out with because there's always a lot of women around him, and I need all the help I can get."

The other big news was discipline, or at least the Biles' version. Phillips' lack of it was one of the major complaints following any Oiler loss. The 1981 Oilers had curfews and fines. They fined a rookie $2,000 for taking a girl back to his room. Another rule was mandatory attendance at all meals. One morning, a sleepy Dave Casper showed up for breakfast with his blanket and pillow. He promptly passed out in his plate. Told to wear his helmet "at all times," he started wearing it to meetings. Unlike the rookie, however, the 4-time All-Pro was not fined.

On the road, Biles posted a guard by the hotel elevator to see that no players slipped out after curfew. He even had the players wear blue bathrobes in response to the issue of women reporters in the locker room.

Fans were still giving it all up for their team in 1981.

Biles released several of Bum's favorites, including 8-year veterans Caster, Young (bad back), Hayman, Clark and Tatum. They had released Culp the previous November. Injuries forced Reihner to retire. Merkins, Groth and Caster ended up with the Saints.

Shofner added a spread formation and multiple sets even though the "I" resulted in Earl gaining nearly 2,000 yards in 1980. Carpenter was in at HB and Wilson out at FB. The only change on the OL was John Schumacher ('78, 12th round) in for Young at OG. Casper, first team Pro Bowl in '80, was the starting TE, while Barber, second team Pro Bowl and a subject of trade rumors, was the backup. Burrough was back at WR, but Smith broke a finger in the preseason. The other WRs were Renfro, Holston and Carl Roaches.

The DLs were Kennard, Bethea and Dorris, with Baker and Stensrud as backups. The LBs were Bingham, Brazile, Hunt and Washington with rookie Riley pushing for PT. Stringer was injured again. One corner had backup All-Pro Stemrick, which made JC Wilson the target for many a QB. Reinfeldt and Perry returned as the safeties.

Biles promised things would not be the same, but they went the usual 1-3 in the preseason. If there was a noticeable change it was that the defense was giving up more points. "I'm pleased with what we accomplished," said the coach. "We obviously had some distractions and disruptions that didn't help but we're on the right track. We're all anxious to get started."

With the Steel Curtain rusting, 1980 should have been the year Houston established itself as the beast of the AFC Central. Instead, they let Cleveland backdoor the division at the end of the season. With a good defense and the best RB in football, the foundation was there in 1981. But firing Phillips caused too much turmoil.

THE 1981 REGULAR SEASON —
WHAT WAS WRONG WITH 11-5?

The Oilers opened with road wins at LA (27-20 on a 96-yard Willie Tullis kick return with 57 seconds left) and Cleveland (9-3 behind two blocked FGs by 35-year-old Bethea). That would be the last road win for awhile.

Things were not well. Campbell and KR Carl Roaches were carrying the team. They lost in New York with the media there flaming the Stabler-gambling rumors. Then they lost to Miami. The breakdown in pass protection almost killed Stabler. In 1978, the Oilers led the league by only surrendering 17 sacks. In 1981, they gave up 16 to the Dolphins and Jets alone. At 2-2, the front office started getting nervous.

The coaches blamed Carpenter. After calling him "selfish," they traded him to the Giants. They abandoned the new schemes and went back to the I.

The deeper start for Earl worked as he had 182 yards on 37 carries to beat the Bengals 17-10. But Stabler was just 1-for-6 as they had more yards rushing (191) than total yards (187). After beating Seattle 35-17 behind Earl's 186 yards to move to 4-2 and into first place, fans thought it was the same old team they loved so much.

However, the wheels were about to come off the wagon. The wake-up call came when New England, the worst team in football, pasted them 38-10. Biles called it a "team effort." They lost six of the next seven, including a loss to Bum's 4-12 Saints. A banner in the Dome for that game fairly summed up the collective conscience of an entire community. It read: "Hey Bud, what was wrong with 11-5?"

Kenny wrote in *Snake*, "We hadn't given our line and backs time to adjust to the new blocking combinations. But in the I, defenses were stacking their fronts against Earl, and in that formation you can't get your backs out to catch the ball. It was frustrating. The whole season was frustrating. While other teams were using modern, multiformation offenses that spread defenses and gave them room to run or pass, we were stuck in an antique system that had defenses standing on our toes before every snap of the ball."

With Stabler out injured or pouting, the only victory during that stretch came on a miracle play by backup QB John Reaves. Then, after Reaves got into a public dispute with the coaches over who called the winning play, Biles cut the born-again Christian.

After beating Cleveland again 17-13, another Kodak moment came with the finale. Despite being out of the playoffs for weeks, a boisterous crowd showed up for Pittsburgh. In a testament to the lasting afterglow of Love Ya Blue, fans carried on as if they had won the Super Bowl after the 21-20 victory. They had a reputation to uphold. A 1980 national poll of pro athletes rated Houston's football crowd third most enthusiastic.

The Oilers finished 7-9. The Bengals, who Houston beat during the year in a game in which they completed one pass, finished with the best record in the AFC at 12-4. The wildcard teams were the Jets (10-5-1) and the Bills (10-6).

In the NFC, the Giants made the playoffs for the first time since 1963 behind ex-Oilers Bill Currier (cut in '80) and Rob Carpenter, who was personally credited with turning their offense around. The playoffs were exciting. San Diego beat Miami 41-38 in OT in one of the best playoff games ever, while in the NFC, San Francisco beat Dallas 27-26 on "the catch" from Joe Montana to Dwight Clark.

The Super Bowl featured two teams that were 6-10 in 1980, the Bengals and 49ers. Frisco, with 3 rookies starting in the secondary, won a close game 26-21 for only the NFC's third victory in the previous 14 championships. No one appreciated it at the time, but that game signaled the beginning of a dramatic power switch from the AFC to NFC. It was also the beginning of a dynasty in the Bay area.

OVERVIEW

It was an interesting sports year in Houston starting with the firings of Phillips, after an 11-5 season, and Tal Smith by the Astros, after he had overseen their first divisional championship. The Raiders, who Bud thought were an inferior team, became the first wildcard team in history to win the Super Bowl.

In the Spring, the Rockets, who squeaked into the playoffs after finishing 2 games under .500, beat the Lakers, Spurs and Kings to make the NBA finals for the first time. They lost in six to the Celtics. That summer, baseball players went on strike and the Astros ended up in a 5-game split-season playoff with the hated Dodgers. After winning the first two at home, they had 12 hits and 2 runs in 3 games in LA, losing them all. LA went on to win the World Series.

The Oilers' 1981 season started off ugly when Stabler retired. Then Nielsen hurt a shoulder and Stabler returned, but had few practices with the radically new offense. After disasters in Miami and New York, Biles dumped Carpenter and went back to the I. After 6 games, they were 4-2 and in first. Then the defense collapsed and they lost 7-of-10 to finish out of the playoffs for the first time since 1977.

Overall, the defense fell from 5th best in the NFL to 25th for its worst season since 1973 (the last pre-Phillips defense). The scoring defense, second in 1980, gave up

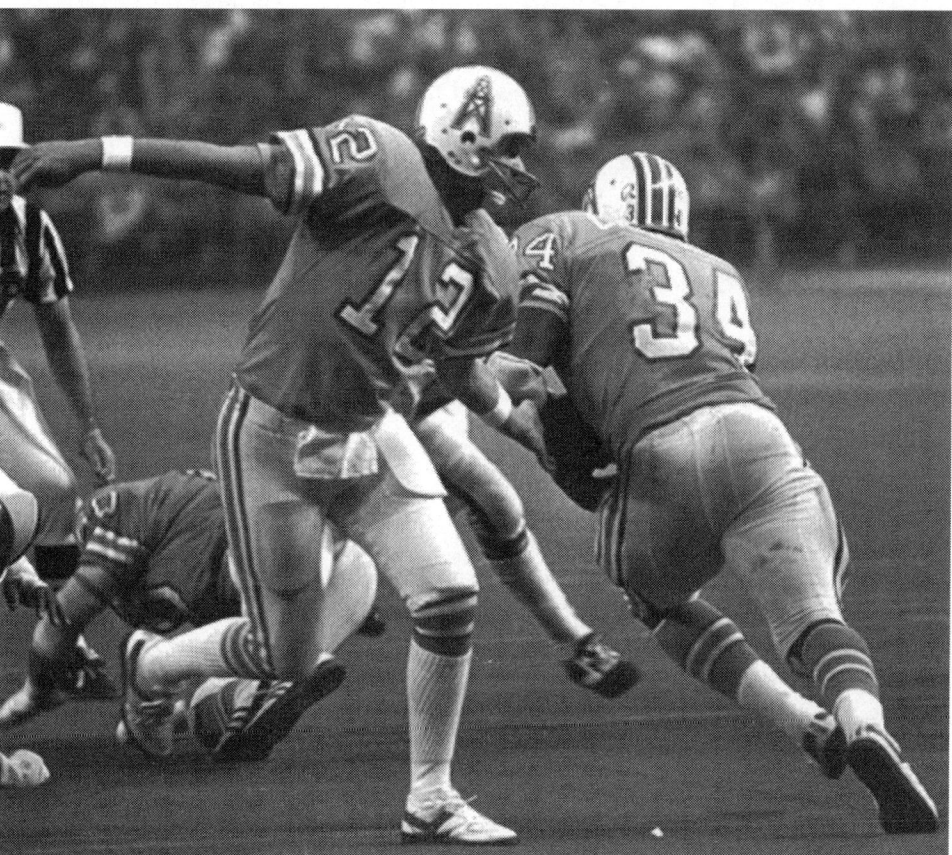

The Oiler rush offense fell all the way from No. 1 in the AFC in 1980 to next to last in 1981. Their average rush per carry fell from an NFL high 4.6 to 3.7. Earl led the AFC again in rushing with 1,376 yards (3.8 per carry) but trailed four rushers in the NFC.

104 more points without any significant changes in personnel. The line play was poor with an old Elvin Bethea while Jesse Baker and Mike Stensrud were unable to take up the slack.

That kind of defense did not go well with a ball-control offense. While great at sitting on leads, it was not a good catch-up scheme. Despite Jim Shofner, who they hired away from the Browns specifically to jazz up things, the offense averaged 75 fewer yards per game to rank last in the AFC.

Campbell's numbers dropped as he had to take on entire teams. He had 1,376 yards to lead the AFC, but for the first time in his career, failed to lead the NFL. That honor went to Bum's new buddy, George Rogers, who had 1,674 yards. Casper and Barber were almost forgotten. Stabler's numbers fell to 58% and 1,988 yards. "When you run the I," he said, "you scrap the pass."

Considering the lack of injuries, a large part of the blame had to fall to effort and commitment. The coaches were prepared, but when things started going bad, players started looking around for Bum. Biles was not the people-person that Phillips was, and morale suffered accordingly.

In *Snake*, Stabler wrote, "The Oilers after Bum left didn't have much going for them. Ed Biles didn't have Bum's charisma, and I don't think guys put out for Biles like they had for Bum." He also suggested there was a credibility issue, accusing Biles of talking "out of both sides of his mouth. He's come over to me and said, 'Boy, our defense is struggling. I don't know what's wrong with Robert Brazile,' and then he'd tick off a couple of other names. Then a defensive player would say to me, 'Do you know what Biles said about you and the offense?'"

Bingham led the team in tackles again, but received no post-season honors. Named to the Pro Bowl were Campbell, Brazile, Gray and Roaches (who led the AFC in kick returns). Joining Gray on the OL were ex-Oilers Doug Wilkerson and Jimmy Giles.

The word "rebuilding" came up, but Biles denied it, saying they would not make wholesale changes. He said all they needed was "a little restructuring."

1982: FOR WHOM THE BELL TOLLS?

The offseason contained many questions. Foremost was how long Adams would stick with Biles, even though he had two years left. After the collapse and his run-ins with Stabler and Reaves, he appeared neither overly secure nor inspiring.

An equally pressing question was whether they could win with the players they had or needed to start rebuilding. Herzeg would address this issue during the upcoming strike. There was a stewing problem at QB where local writers told fans Nielsen was ready. At WR, the *Post* kept wrongly telling readers Holston had "All-Pro potential."

Trade rumors swirled regarding the TEs, Brazile and Campbell. With the Oilers falling behind so often, Earl averaged only 68 yards a game the last half of the season. Houston, which was 27-4 in games in which he gained at least 100 yards, was 3-7 in the 10 games in 1980 he did not reach 100. About the rumors, he said he was "expecting the worst. Because pro football is a business and players don't have a lot of say about what goes on ... I love Houston. I don't want to leave. I've lived in Texas all my life, and like a lot of players, I want to finish my career here. I don't think there's another place in America where I could have achieved what I did here because of my teammates and because of the people."

In with the new: The slow climb back began in 1982 with top pick Mike Munchak, an offensive guard from Penn State. Mike would give meaning to the phrase "perennial Pro Bowler," making it 9 times in 12 seasons

Herzeg, meanwhile, was busy. Before the draft, he traded Barber to LA for a second-round pick and to move up in the third. He also signed CFL linebacker Tom Cousineau to an offer sheet, comparing him to Lawrence Taylor. But when Herzeg refused to meet Buffalo's terms for its former No. 1 choice, he ended up in Cleveland.

1982 TRAINING CAMP

Camp opened with more labor unrest on the horizon. The holdout du jour was 30-year-old Pro Bowler Leon Gray, the best left tackle in team history. Herzeg did not budge in negotiations with infamous agent Howard "Hold-em-out" Slusher. Further weakening the OL were the release of Carl Mauck and trade of Angelo Fields. Biles maintained they could not win with Angelo starting. The outspoken Mauck, of course, was a living symbol of the Phillips years.

Ken Stabler was released. He wrote in *Snake*, "I couldn't have been happier when Ed Biles put me on waivers in July 1982. I knew I couldn't play for the man some of the Oilers referred to as 'The Shaky Corporal.' I liked offensive coordinator Jim Shofner, who had tried to open up the offense, but Biles had been too scared to stick with it. He had kept the team in disarray all season, and I wanted no part of that again."

Other camp cuts were Toni Fritsch and Ronnie Coleman. Fritsch, the second leading scorer in team history, lost out to Florian Kempf.

The draft produced one great player — OG Mike Munchak of Penn State, although Biles almost blew the choice on Ohio State QB Art Schlichter. Fortunately, the Colts took him first. They also took Rhodes Scholar candidate QB Oliver Luck (Barber trade), RB Stanley Edwards (Carpenter), LB Robert Abraham (Barber), WR Steve Bryant (4th round), Tennessee State DE Malcolm Taylor (5th), RB Gary Allen (6th) and Louisville RB Donnie Craft (12th).

Biles tried to solve the DL woes by moving Ken Kennard, who had a good 1981, outside and Mongo Stensrud inside. Jesse Baker, who led the team in sacks each of his first three seasons while playing only in passing situations, moved ahead of Elvin Bethea at right DE. The play of the two '79 second-round choices had been erratic. Baker had 15½ sacks in 1979, but tailed off with 6½ in '80 and 10 in '81. Stensrud was a wash in '79, but came back with a strong year in '80. In 1981, however, he found Christ and his production fell off again.

Avon Riley ('81, 9th) passed Washington at OLB. Bingham went into the season on the IR with a fractured hip, snapping his consecutive game streak at 134. In the backfield, Reinfeldt was back at FS, but Perry was out with a broken collarbone. Stemrick and Wilson were the CBs. Before a year would pass, three of four starting DBs would be in trouble with the law. Substance abuse was by now a recurring theme in the NFL.

The offense looked shaky with Nielsen and Luck. Campbell's new backfield mates were rookies Gary Allen and Donnie Craft. At WR, Burrough broke his ankle leaving the job to Holston, Renfro and Smith. Wilson moved to TE as Casper's backup.

Whoever started at QB was going to be in deep do-do with Koncar and Towns at tackle, David Carter at center and Fisher and Schumacher at OG (although Munchak would immediately press for PT at guard).

This was a team and coaching staff in trouble. There were holes on both sides of the ball. Biles had unloaded 16 of 45 roster players from the Oilers' last payoff team. On offense, only four starters remained from that team. Most predictions had them in last place.

And out with the ... 1981 was Ken Burrough's last season (421 receptions and a career 16.9 yards per catch average). Giff Nielsen played through 1983.

THE 1982 REGULAR SEASON — BETTER HOPE FOR A STRIKE

The Oilers opened in Cincinnati without Gray or Bingham. Although only the sixth start of his career, Nielsen gave no reason to believe he was the answer. Needing an 11-yard drop to set up as opposed to the standard 6- or 7-yards, Giff gave rushers too much time to fight off blocks. They batted down his pass attempts at the line. Most of the ones he completed were to the RBs. His arm was weaker than Stabler's. The unimaginative offense put the burden on Campbell, who did not have Wilson as lead blocker. Tim saw the field for one play at TE. Houston lost 27-6. As the Houston players were leaving the field, a Bengal fan yelled, "You bums better hope for a strike."

Somehow, they beat Seattle 23-21 the next week. Nielsen was 11-of-37 for 131 yards, and did not complete a pass to a WR until the final two minutes. He had five attempts blocked or tipped at the line. "Gifford is trying so hard to please everybody — his coaches, his teammates, the fans and the press — that I think he's pressing a little," said a defensive Biles. "He's been a little tentative. But you've got to expect him to have some games in which his inexperience becomes a factor."

Herzeg had seen enough. He traded Gray to New Orleans for QB Archie Manning. In the preseason, the Oilers had knocked the Saints' backup QB out for the year. Bum picked up Stabler to replace him. Snake's presence, in turn, made Manning available.

Then the strike started. The main complaint this time was football pay was lower than it was baseball or basketball. "The owners can still be millionaires and maybe let us catch up with the rest of the sporting world," said Renfro.

It was the third one since 1970. Union leader Ed Garvey was the villain for fans, owners and some players. Garvey did have an interesting solution — a sliding wage scale paid by position and years in service, somewhat like the agreements real unions obtain. It would have controlled rookie salaries while paying the vets better. But no one paid any attention.

In Houston, this one seemed particularly appalling in light of the failing local economy. With oil dropping, many average people (otherwise known as football fans in some circles) had lost their jobs and some were in the process of losing their homes. They had trouble with the idea that a group of highly compensated underachievers like the Oilers had much to complain about. Yet there was Archie Manning, who made $600,000 a season, walking a picket line. Fans knew all too well where that money ultimately came from.

Meanwhile, an Oiler minidrama unfolded. With Bethea on the NFLPA executive committee, Houston was considered a strong union team. As things dragged on, however, a few players (Bingham, Fisher, Hartwig, Reihner, Brooks) started a grass roots movement to oppose the union hierarchy and accept the owners' offer. It embarrassed Elvin, but the little Oiler countermovement spread and hastened the strike's end. When it did, the strikebreakers received credit, which made Elvin even more resentful.

The strike lasted 57 days and seven games. Purportedly to appease fans, the NFL expanded the playoffs to include eight teams from each conference. For the Oilers, the remainder of the schedule began with the Steelers. A victory would leave them tied for first.

They lost 24-10. Manning, who used to run for his life in New Orleans, could now be seen running for his life for Houston. Former trainer Bobby Brown compared the OL to "Kleenex Tissue." The new offense, next to last in 1981, was dead last in 1982.

The next week they had the chance to pull their record to .500 against a rotten New England team but lost 29-21. Half of the Patsies' four victories over the past two seasons came against Houston. Frustrated but unsure where to turn, Biles cut punter Cliff Parsley. Eternal

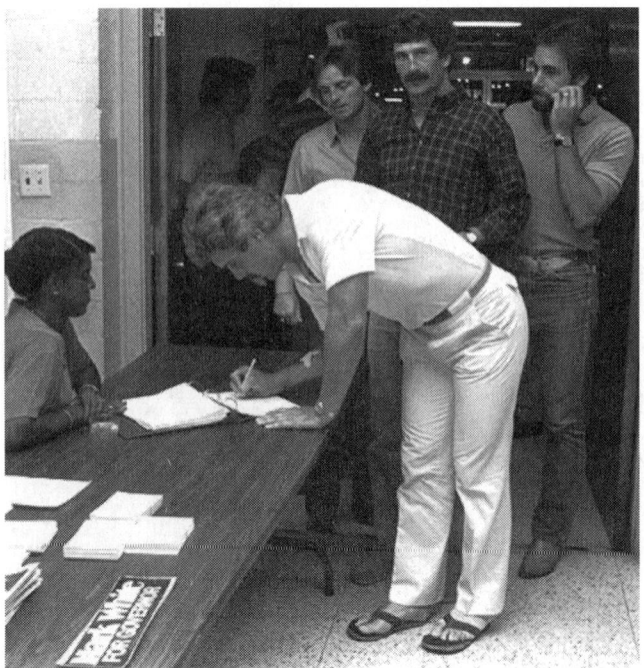

Strike central complete with Mark White for Governor bumper stickers. Many felt it was the best thing that could happen to the 1982 Oilers.

The only victory in 1982 came in Game 2 against the Seahawks. While Earl Campbell had a substandard year (3.4 yards per carry and no Pro Bowl for the first time), he was still a force to be reckoned with as Seattle's All-Pro safety Kenny Easley finds out.

optimist Bingham said, "All we need is a win to turn this thing around, to get everybody believing in themselves again and knowing they can get something accomplished out there. A break here, a break there and everything might be different."

They got no breaks against Dallas, losing 37-7 on *Monday Night Football* to fall to 1-5. Biles said, "Nobody goes through a transition without struggling." Coaching rumors again swirled as "Ed Biles" became a synonym for Oiler failure reminiscent of "Ed Hughes."

In December, a desperate Biles replaced Dick Noles as DC with himself. OC Jim Shofner was also taking heat. Meanwhile, Bum was winning games in New Orleans with a group of ex-Oilers. That story was so compelling that the CBS affiliate in Houston began carrying Saints games for the first time. Oiler focus turned to the possibility of backing into the number-one choice already identified as John Elway.

The day after Christmas, they fell to Cleveland 20-14 on two Campbell fumbles at the goal line. Dale Robertson called Earl a "ghost of his former self." That was harsh, but it was certainly difficult to watch the punishment Campbell was taking every week with the rotten line play and predictable offense.

There were 22,611 no shows for the final game, which the Oilers dropped to the Bengals 35-27. A sign hanging in the Dome read: "Warning: If Earl goes, we go." The atmosphere was a dramatic contrast to the big pompon waving crowd for last game of 1981. The 1982 version of the Oilers finished 1-8 and in last place.

It seemed as if every other team was still playing, and in fact, every other team in the Central was. The Browns, Bengals and Steelers made the playoffs, but each prompt-ly lost in the first round. The Saints finished 4-5 and just out of the playoffs.

The Redskins won the Super Bowl 27-17 on two fourth-quarter touchdowns. It was an asterisk victory, however, as they might not have even made the playoffs

Dave Casper (No. 87) had the best season among the Oilers with 36 receptions and 8 TDs in the 9-game season. But neither he nor any Oiler made the Pro Bowl.

but for the strike. No one could deny that the Skins had a great staff that included three former Oiler assistants: Joe Bugel, Richie Pettibon and Larry Peccatielo. Pettibon left in a pay dispute over a couple of thousand dollars. Bugel left with Bum. Another tie was Dave Butz, who the Oilers passed up for John Matuszak in the '73 draft. Butz was not only still playing in 1983 but was an All-Pro and the anchor of the champs' DL.

OVERVIEW

The decline was hard for fans to swallow. Just a few years before, everything seemed so perfect. The Texas economy was in overdrive and Houston was one of the happening places to be. The movie *Urban Cowboy* was a hit, the Astros and Rockets were winning, and the Bum and Earl were prime time.

Then the economy headed south, the Astros fired Tal Smith and the Rockets lost John Lucas, Mitchell Wiggins and Louis Lloyd to drug suspensions. In the cruelest blow of all, Adams fired Phillips and the football team went to hell. Then the players struck because they were not making as much as the baseball players who had struck the previous summer.

The Oilers were not a Super Bowl quality team, but did play below their talent level. "It all goes back to attitude," said one player. "The attitude on this team is lousy. Our problems go way beyond X's and O's." The strike breakers took part of the blame. Although applauded by management and most fans, their position created a rift.

While Biles may have been a better tactician than Bum, his teams lacked the same togetherness and drive to succeed. Mike Reinfeldt said, "We used to take pride in ourselves. But we're not stopping anybody anymore. The whole game is like a two-minute drill against us."

The defense fell to last, allowing 382 yards a game. For the season, they had 3 interceptions. The backfield was arguably the worst in football. Reinfeldt, who had 12 picks in 1979, said, "We didn't have the same camaraderie that we've had in the past. Obviously the whole year has been a disaster but I still think we're a lot better than 1-8."

The offense was just as bad, starting with the OL, which lost Mauck, Gray and Munchak (to an early injury). Archie had 877 yards (66-of-125), 6 TDs and 6 picks. Casper had the best year on offense with 6 TDs. Earl had 538 yards and just 2 TDs. For the first time in his career, he did not lead the AFC in rushing or make the Pro Bowl. Brazile was the only one to make Pro Bowl.

Bethea said he was postponing retirement rather than going out a loser. "It's very tough to take when you look back on those playoff years," said the Hall-of-Famer-to-be. "I would never have believed we would be in this position in just two years. The intensity definitely dropped."

"I guarantee we'll be better next year," said Bingham, who failed to lead the team in tackles for the first time in his 10-year career. Missing the first two games, the only ones Gregg had ever missed, gave the tackling title to fellow ILB Daryl Hunt.

1983: THE BELL TOLLS FOR THEE

Adams decided to retain Biles for at least the final year of his contract. Sportswriter John Hollis told Houston fans, "The retention of Eddie Biles is a hopeful sign of the restoration of sanity to an organization that could use a little credulity." (sic)

But former trainer Bobby Brown, fired by Adams over his association with a health club, cautioned that a contract with Adams was no reason to feel secure. "Bud changes coaches like musical chairs," he said. "Working for Bud is like having a contract with a kamikaze pilot.

"I had a helmet displayed over my taping bench. It said 'Wear This With Pride.' That is what the Oilers have lost over the years — pride, to make the Columbia blue stand for something. We damned sure did in the early years. They were people who wanted to play without a strike. They were underpaid but loved the game." Bobby passed away in 1984.

THE 1983 DRAFT

The 1983 draft would prove to be the most pivotal of the decade, as there was a flood of talent due to a special redshirt rule that put an extra 100 players in the system. Players available in the third round were of first-round quality.

It started for Houston with the Colts saving them from a sticky situation by earning the top choice by half a game. John Elway, called the best QB prospect since Joe Namath, said he would only play on the West Coast. The Colts took him anyway. John said he would "never play for Baltimore" and went to pitch for the Yankees. The national press called him a "crybaby."

Houston breathed a sigh of relief. Though they were desperate for a QB, not being able to draft Elway was spun into a positive. That is how bad things were in 1983.

Next in popularity were RBs Eric Dickerson (SMU) and Curt Warner. That forced them to decide whether to keep Earl or trade him and take one of the youngsters.

Predraft rumors had Campbell going almost anywhere. It was a tough time for the big man and his family. He said could not go to the store without someone asking where he would be living next season. PR-sensitive management was afraid to pull the trigger. It was a difficult decision, no doubt, but with the beating he was taking, a trade was probably best for both parties.

Dickerson helped them decide. He said his parents, who lived outside Houston in Sealy, did not want him to play for the home team. "They tell me the Oilers aren't going anywhere," he said. "They don't want to see me come here and get all beat up." Sadly, the Oilers' reputation had come full-cycle and returned to that of the mid-1960s when players like Donnie Anderson, Tommy Nobis and even Jerry Rhome worked to avoid ending up with the Oilers.

Herzeg had something else in mind anyway. During the strike, he made a detailed analysis of the team's prospects and concluded this group could not get it done. He stayed quiet about it because of ticket sales, but the Oilers were officially rebuilding.

Thus the No. 2 choice was for sale. The Rams had the No. 3 pick and wanted Dickerson but were worried the Oilers would trade the pick to another team. So they gave up their first- and two fourth-rounders ('83 and '84) to remove the uncertainty. Seattle also wanted a back. They offered their first- (No. 9), second- and third-round choices to move into the No. 3 spot.

Hindsight shows those picks were worth more. By the end of the season, Dickerson had broken a number of rushing records. Warner was also very good. Both would have more yards than Earl in '83, causing Herzeg to be criticized. But in the long run, Eric would prove to be a headache who complained his way out of LA while Warner would be injury-prone

Mike Reinfeldt

In any event, the Oilers were in great shape. For giving up six spots, Herzeg acquired an extra second-, third- and two fourth-round choices. They had 10 picks in the first 5 rounds in one of the deepest drafts in NFL history. Making it pay off was Holovak's job.

Elway, Dickerson and Warner went 1-2-3. After watching players they liked (OG Chris Hinton, LB Billy Ray Smith, OT Jimbo Covert) go early, they breathed easier when KC blew the No. 7 choice on QB Todd Blackledge and Philly did the same with RB Michael Haddix. That left them USC guard Bruce Matthews (6'5, 275). Like Munchak in '82, he was a solid pick.

The '83 draft would be best known for the QBs. After Elway and Blackledge, Buffalo took Jim Kelly, followed by Tony Eason to the Pats, Ken O'Brien to the Jets and Dan Marino to Miami with the next-to-last choice in the first round. Marino, who some consider to be the most talented QB of all-time, was the sixth QB taken. The Chiefs, Jets and Pats are still kicking themselves.

Houston kept the focus on its Kleenex Tissue line and police blotter defensive backfield. In the second, they took OT Harvey Salem (6'7, 270) of Cal, passing on WR Henry Ellard, DT Leonard Marshall and LB Daryl Talley. Late in the second, they took safety Keith Bostic (6'1, 205) from Michigan, passing on Baylor DB Cedric Mack, RB Roger Craig and DE Bill Pickel.

The true test of this draft came later as they had three picks in the third, two in the fourth, two in the fifth and one each from the sixth through ninth.

They continued to load up on DBs with CB Steve Brown (3rd round), CB Greg Hill (4th), S Steve Hayworth (6th) and S Kevin Potter (9th). These picks were aimed at Wilson (DUI), Stemrick (cocaine possession), and Perry (drug charge at home in Mississippi). "Shape up or ship out," was Biles' message to them after the draft.

Their craziest pick was LB Tim Joiner in the third. After multiple knee surgeries, he rated much lower with other teams. They raised more eyebrows drafting TEs back-to-back in the third and fourth with Chris Dressel and Mike McCloskey. Other choices were 25-year-old body-building FB Larry Moriarty (5th), 258-pound NG Jerome Foster (5th), Texas' 5'8 WR Herkie Walls (7th) and LB Robert Thompson (8th).

Bruce Matthews

With so many picks, some had to stick. Matthews would for a long time. Bostic also reached the all-star level. Salem had talent but was immature. Brown started a few years, Moriarty was a good fifth-rounder and Walls was worth a shot in the seventh.

However, Hill, Hayworth and Potter were wastes. Ditto for Joiner. Neither TE would pay big dividends. Foster was undersized and Thompson lost. It was a shame.

Houston whined that the good teams could take a chance on a USFL player, while the poorer teams had no choice but to draft a player they could sign. It was true that some good players, like Jim Kelly and Anthony Carter, signed with the other league. However, with the great depth and all their picks, the Oilers had a rare chance to reverse the decline of the program in just one season, especially the defense. Here is how:

Rd.	Was (Overall Number)	Could Have Been	All-Star By
1	OT Bruce Matthews (9)	OT Bruce Matthews (9)	1988
2	OT Harvey Salem (30)	DT Leonard Marshall (37)	1985
2	S Keith Bostic (42)	RB Roger Craig (49)	1985
3	LB Tim Joiner (58)	S Albert Lewis (61)	1988
3	TE Chris Dressel (69)	DE Charles Mann (84)	1987
3	CB Steve Brown (83)	S Vince Newsome (97)	1986
4	CB Greg Hill (86)	LB Johnny Rembert (101)	1988
4	TE Mike McCloskey (88)	DE Greg Townsend (122)	1988
5	FB Larry Moriarty (114)	CB Carl Lee (186)	1988
5	DT Jerome Foster (139)	DE Richard Dent (203)	1984
6	CB Steve Hayworth (142)	CB Ronnie Lippett (214)	1986
7	WR Herkie Walls (170)	WR Mark Clayton (223)	1984
8	LB Robert Thompson (198)	LB Karl Mecklenberg (310)	1985
9	S Kevin Potter (226)	WR Anthony Carter (334)	1987

Had they opted to bite the bullet and trade Earl, Jim Kelly or Dan Marino could have been added to this list. Fans would have gobbled up tickets to watch former USFL Gambler Kelly (or Marino), protected by Munchak and Matthews, throw passes to Clayton and Carter. The defense could have had a to-die-for line (Marshall, Dent, Mann, Townsend), a complete set of all-star DBs (Lewis, Newsome, Lee, Lippett) and two new hard-working LBs (Rembert, Mecklenberg).

In the late '80s and early '90s, Houston sports reporters swooned about the talent Mike Holovak built through the draft. It is true that the Oiler teams of that era were talented, but also true they failed to reach the promised land. Figuring out how and why requires a look at the wasted opportunities the 1983 draft presented.

1983 TRAINING CAMP

The new OC was Kay Dalton and new OL coach Bill Walsh (not that one). By the second game, there would be an 80% turnover on the line. Matthews was to be the left OT, but when he held out they picked up Doug France from the Rams. Schumacher was out for now. Munchak was the left OG. Carter returned at center. Once Matthews showed, he replaced Fisher at right OG. Salem replaced Mo Towns (who always belonged in Detroit) at right OT. While talented, they were young.

The rest of the offense was static. Manning, Nielsen and Luck were the QBs while Earl was the featured back. Ken Burrough, holder of many team records and its best deep threat, was released. Double zero finished his career with 7,102 yards and 50 TDs. That left a sad group of Bryant, Holston, Smith, Roaches and rookie Walls. Renfro was out with hepatitis. Rookies Dressel and McCloskey backed up Casper at TE.

The new DC was Chuck Studley. Ralph Staub was the new DL coach, while Ken Houston replaced Bob Gambold as DB coach. Perry and Stemrick, All-Pros in 1980, were cut. That left Reinfeldt, Hartwig, Tullis, Wilson, Kay and rookies Brown, Bostic and Hill.

The LBs remained Bingham, Brazile, Hunt and Riley. On the DL, Baker was a holdout and Kennard hurt a knee. Malcolm Taylor ('82, 5th round) came to camp 300 pounds of blubber. By the opening game, the starters were Stensrud, Baker and Bethea (13th season). Skaugstad, Bum's No. 2 in 1980, was cut.

They continued to be plagued by off-field problems. Casper and JC Wilson were hit with driving under the influence charges. Wilson, already on probation, got his on his birthday for the second time. Tullis was arrested for purportedly breaking into a woman's apartment in San Angelo.

The Oilers lost to the Saints (20-13) and Cowboys (34-31) in the preseason. Expectations were not high. They did not disappoint.

THE 1983 REGULAR SEASON — TAPS FOR THE SHAKY CORPORAL

The Oilers dropped the opener to Green Bay 41-38 in OT. The lone bright spot was Tim Smith, a special teamer for three years, who arrived with 8 receptions for 197 yards in his first start. The game would have been considered a moral victory except that Campbell, Casper and Smith were all injured. Missing the main cogs of their offense, they fell 20-6 to Oakland the next week, followed by a 40-28 thrashing at the hands of the Steelers.

They were terrible. Many of the players looked like they had been eating leftover strike donuts all summer. About the only interesting question was whether they would be the first team to finish 0-16. Herzeg traded Manning and Casper to Minnesota for second- and fourth-round picks. The Vikings had lost their starting QB and were somewhat desperate, but not that desperate, as the Oilers still had to pay a large chunk of their high salaries to get the draft choices Herzeg wanted.

The trade gave closure to two of Phillips' bigger deals. In 1979, he obtained Gray for a first and a fourth. In 1982, Leon was traded for Manning. In 1980, Casper cost a first and two second-rounders. The net of it all was that for two first-rounders and one second-rounder, they got almost 3 seasons from Gray, just over 2 from Casper, and part of one out of Manning.

So inspired by these events were they, that the Oilers lost to Buffalo 30-13 to complete September without a victory. They lost Reinfeldt to injury. And so it went.

On October 10, 1983, Ed Biles resigned to join the already bloated ranks of the ex-Oiler coaching fraternity. He compiled an overall 8-23 record. His replacement was Chuck Studley.

Studley took over a team that had lost all six games in 1983, four games in the preseason and its last seven in 1982. It was his first head coaching job after 13 years

He came on a pale horse. JC Wilson might have lasted longer in pro football had he stuck with this mode of transportation, at least on his birthdays.

as an assistant in Cincinnati and San Francisco. He said the first thing he did was "literally [sit] around with the other coaches wondering how [to] win a game."

Studley went 2-6. They beat Detroit in November (27-17) and Cleveland in December (34-27), which kept them from the number one pick in the draft.

They finished 2-14. Studley resigned, saying he saw the handwriting on the wall. His career lasted 69 days. Honest and bright, Studley was fairly popular. He fought back tears at the news conference, recognizing that at 53, this was his only shot. The picture that appeared in the morning papers of Studley, his disappointed wife and his dog Eric made for a melancholy scene.

"I knew I was stepping into a difficult situation," he said, "but it was a chance that I had already convinced myself would never come along. So I'd do it again knowing everything. The fact is, I wasn't a successful head coach, for whatever reason. Therefore, my career as a head coach has been a short one ... We've been here less than 10 months. Nobody comes out ahead on this deal except the movers."

Much of Houston was following the Saints. Going into the last game, Bum had his team at 8-7 and needing a win to make the playoffs for the first time in franchise history. They lost a squeaker to the Rams 26-24, denying New Orleans its first winning season.

Joe Bugel and the Skins made the Super Bowl again as Joe's line paved the way for Joe Theismann to win, and his teammate John Riggins to place second, in league MVP voting. The Raiders crushed them in the Super Bowl 38-9.

The game would mark the last AFC Super Bowl victory for a long time. After winning 11 of the first 16 Super Bowls, AFC teams were destined to lose the next 13, although it would have been hard to convince anyone of that in 1984. It was also the last hurrah for the once-dominant Raiders.

OVERVIEW

The players with the best seasons were Campbell, Smith, Munchak, Bingham, Riley, Salem, Tullis and Brazile. Earl's 1,301 yards were second in the AFC to Curt Warner. His 4-yard average was the best since 1980, and he was the only Oiler to make the Pro Bowl.

The long season full of turmoil had changed his attitude. He said, "I'm tired of hearing every week how I'm too dumb, washed up, too dumb to read holes, can't block, can't catch the football." He asked for a trade, saying, "I'm just one individual in America who wants to get a new address."

Fourth-year WR Tim Smith had a great season with 83 catches for over 1,000 yards. He and Campbell made history by becoming the first RB/WR tandem to both gain over 1,000 yards. His reception total was the second most by an Oiler behind Charley Hennigan's 101 in 1961.

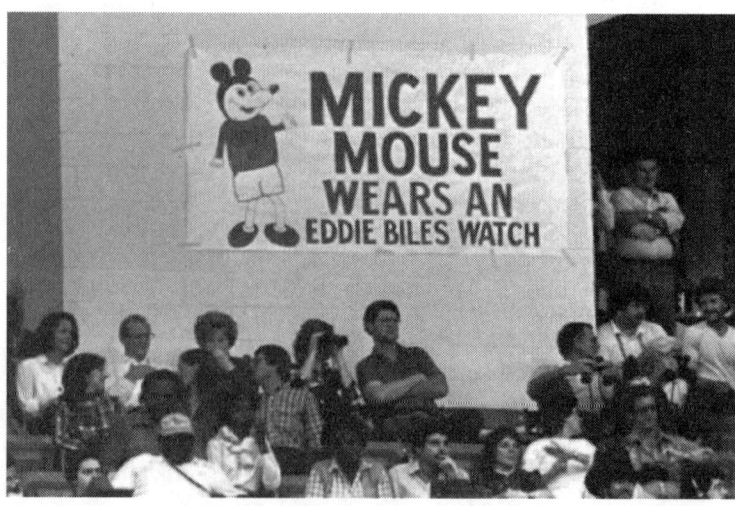

Following a legend is never easy. Ed Biles knew he had to win. But after going 7-9 in 1981, the bottom fell out and he stumbled to 1-8 in 1982 and 0-6 in 1983.

Chuck Studley

The offense was otherwise sorry. It fell behind early and often, trailing at the half in 12 of 14 losses. The leading passer was Luck, who did not take the starting job from Nielsen until the tenth week. The second-round draft pick from '82 was 124-of-217 (57%) for 1,375 yards. He had 8 TDs and 13 interceptions and led them to both wins. In his last season, Giff went 90-of-175 (51.4%) for 1,125 yards, 5 TDs and 8 interceptions.

Interestingly, old friend Lynn Dickey blew away the QB competition with an NFL-high 4,458 yards and 32 TDs in Green Bay.

The defense gave up more points than any other Oiler team ever, and the most in the AFC. They were dead last against the run, giving up an almost shocking 4.8 yards per rush. They were also tied for last in sacks.

There were varying opinions on the nature of the problem. Some players complained of a harsh atmosphere. For example, Stabler wrote: "Biles ran the team like a Marine sergeant, and very few players applauded that." Others said there was a lack of discipline. In camp, Biles said he would crack down, yet many players were out of shape throughout the year.

Studley said, "I'll be very honest. Most of our players played too heavy this season. I'm a great believer in movement, and particularly as a defense, we suffered this season because we lacked quickness. How can you tackle a target if you can't get to it? Jesse Baker, Malcolm Taylor, Jerome Foster, even Robert Brazile and Earl Campbell — all of them carried too many pounds. So did a lot of others. And it wasn't necessarily their fault. I think we set their weight limits too high from the start.

"I noticed back in training camp there was a lack of seriousness about most things. It was a lot looser than other teams I'd been with, especially for one coming off a season like they had last year. Nobody seemed to care if players walked into meetings four or five minutes late." He also pilloried the planning. "The game plan, it seemed, was the same for every team they played," said Studley. "No effort was made to find a better way. They took the easy way out, and you don't win that way."

As 1984 approached, the Oilers turned the corner on the past and headed into a new future and a new cast of characters.

Fear knows no man like that of a defensive back upon seeing Earl Campbell break free into the secondary. Earl returned to form in 1983 with 1,301 yards in 14 games. He also had 12 TDs, raised his per carry average to 4.0 and made the Pro Bowl.

The Oilers were rudderless in 1982-83, trying a succession of QBs that included Gifford Nielsen (above), Archie Manning (below) and Oliver Luck (right). Neither Giff or Archie would be on the roster in '84, while Luck lasted through 1986.

1984: TRADING HEROES

Once again, the Oilers were down looking up. They had won three games over two seasons and had lost all road games going back to the second game of 1981. The team was at another crossroads where some big decisions were going to affect the future for a long time. Obviously, they needed a coach.

Their first choice was Nebraska coach Tom Osborne. But after interviewing with Herzeg and Holovak in Dallas, he turned them down. Holovak wanted to shift focus to his friend Lou Holtz.

But the Oilers were also after a new QB. One decision influenced the other. The third big decision was what to do about Earl.

WELCOME HUGH CAMPBELL

The Oilers did not waste much time naming Hugh Campbell. He became the third person in 86 days to be Houston's head man, causing old jokes about the coach-of-the-year to give way to ones about a coach-of-the-month plan. He was their thirteenth head coach.

At 42, Campbell was the youngest head coach in team history. He came from a one-year stint with the LA Express of the USFL and 6 years as head coach of the Edmonton Eskimos of the CFL. In Canada, his teams won five straight Grey Cup championships. It was no coincidence that Warren Moon, who quarterbacked those championship teams, was shopping his talents to the NFL at the same time, or that Leigh Steinberg represented both men.

He got a three-year contract reported at $160,000 per year. He said, "The idea wasn't particularly appealing when it first came up ... Based on their record, which is all I had to go on, I thought the organization must be a real mess and I didn't want to be the one to have to straighten it all out. But, after I investigated further, it didn't look so bad."

Herzeg had all the customary comments, starting with, "He was our number one choice" and, "The allure with Hugh, No. 1, is his proven track record as a coach ... No. 2, I feel his philosophy about being aggressive both offensively and defensively fits into our thinking, and No. 3, for a man who has achieved all the success he has, Hugh is very low key and humble."

Dale Robertson called him, "dedicated, knowledgeable and self-effacing ... an over-achiever."

Campbell said, "I pride myself in getting the most out of everybody, assistant coaches and players alike, and I try to be flexible. I'm not programmed any one specific way." Maybe the Oilers should have gotten a clue when he said he wanted to be "unpredictable" and "consistent" in the same sentence, or when Cowboy personnel guy Gil Brandt spoke glowingly of him. No doubt, at the time, the Oilers had their collective eye on another prize.

THE SIX-MILLION-DOLLAR MAN

While the Oilers were choosing a new coach, Warren Moon was making his tour of cities seeking his services. He had come a long way. The LA native played college football at Washington, but went undrafted and had to go to Canada to prove himself. He did that winning five CFL championships, passing for 5,000 yards twice and even once leading his team in rushing.

Ladd Herzeg first noticed him in a hotel room in Minneapolis in 1983 before Chuck Studley's head coaching debut. Watching a televised CFL game, he said, "Look at this guy throw the football ... Watch how well he moves to get away from the rush ... This guy's going to throw for 5,000 yards." He had 5,648. Herzeg said, "Bud doesn't know it yet, but we're going after this guy, and he's going to cost us a lot of money. He's going to be worth it, though, I'm telling you."

Moon's list of suitors included the Oilers, Seahawks, Raiders, Giants, Bucs and Eagles. He said, "After winning and winning, it just wasn't the same challenge anymore. I needed something new." In the pre-free agency days of the NFL, it was not easy to acquire a starting QB with proven passing skills. Any trade for such a hot commodity would ordinarily cost high draft picks and/or starting players, but not Moon. All one needed for his services was the ability to show him the money.

It came down to the Seahawks and Oilers. Seattle was thought to have the edge because Moon had lived there since his college days and the Seahawks had just been to the AFC Championship game, whereas the Oilers were in disarray. Others thought Moon might not want to be a black quarterback in the southern half of the United States.

The Oilers had two aces, however. First, they had Moon's friend, Hugh Campbell, who knew how to utilize Moon's multiple skills. Seattle had Chuck Knox, who was devoted to the ground game. Second, they had Herzeg in relentless pursuit.

On February 3, 1984, Warren Moon officially began his relationship with the Houston Oilers. His contract called for $6 million over five years, which edged out John Elway's $5 million, 5-year deal and made Moon the highest-paid player in football.

Adams, who, since he had fired Phillips, had been seen about as frequently as Jimmy Hoffa, came out for

Post sports reporter Dale Robertson wrote that new head coach Hugh Campbell looked like "a surf shop owner, an aging Sixties' flower child clinging to his lost youth."

Warren Moon signed in 1984 after winning everything there was to win in the CFL. He said he wanted to be the "first black quarterback in the Super Bowl."

the party. He happily agreed to let Moon have No. 1 as his jersey number. Herzeg commented, "I will say this. If we put Warren in the right system and if we can get some talented receivers for him to throw to, he might just break every NFL record."

Moon, 27, said leaving friends behind was a tough decision but that the "security of the contract" tipped him over. A large portion of the Oilers' offer was up front and more or less guaranteed. Seattle could not match the up-front amounts. Leigh Steinberg said the amount of letters they got from Houston fans encouraging him to sign played a role.

The coach said he would have to compete for the job. "It's my opinion that Warren will earn the starting job," said Coach Campbell, "but he will not be given the starting job." His competition was Nielsen ($175,000 in '83) and Luck ($90,000).

THE $350,000-DOLLAR MAN

Earl Campbell was among the many observing the Moon sweepstakes with interest. No doubt he made some comparisons. Earl wanted a pay raise before they gave all that up-front money to Warren. Herzeg said no deals. The contract they reworked in 1980 had a no-renegotiation clause.

Herzeg did not baby or coddle athletes. He simply stated, "We have lived up to our contractual obligations to Earl. We expect him to live up to his." He felt Earl was fairly paid.

Earl was scheduled to make $350,000 plus a deferred payment. His base salary was close to Tony Dorsett's $400,000, and better than Marcus Allen's $175,000 and Pete Johnson's $125,000. On the other hand, John Riggins made $890,000. Rookie rushing champ Eric Dickerson had a base of $150,000 but a signing bonus of $900,000, while Curt Warner had a base of $150,000 with a $825,000 signing bonus.

Thus, while Earl's salary was arguably in the ballpark, it was also a good example of how the team frequently missed the big picture. Earl was the best thing that had ever happened to the Oilers. He brought countless accolades to a team worth few before he arrived. In a day characterized by pro athletes' greed, misdeeds and immaturity, Earl brought a refreshing personality. That winning character and his unusual talent single-handedly changed the image of the entire organization. If anyone ever deserved to be treated a little differently, it was Earl Campbell. He deserved the best they had.

Instead, trade rumors persisted. One had him in Buffalo. Closer to the draft, the Chargers offered a deal they almost took — the No. 6 pick, RB James Brooks, and a future pick. According to Herzeg, he and Holovak favored a deal, but Coach Campbell did not and they deferred. Campbell later denied knowledge of any deal.

THE 1984 DRAFT

The Oilers were again in great shape for the draft. They had the No. 2 pick overall for the second consecutive year, plus two second-round choices, three fourth-rounders and two sixth-round choices. It could have been a killer with such A-list players as Steve Young, Mike Rozier, Reggie White, Herschel Walker and Gary Zimmerman.

But this was the year of the great USFL raid. Those players all signed with the new league. Up to 90 NFL prospects signed before the draft.

So instead of mulling over Young or White, the Oilers got to choose between Wilber Marshall and Dean Steinkuhler. After New England inked Irving Fryar, Houston spent weeks trying to reach a deal with Marshall, but failed. They opted for the massive Steinkuhler and had him signed before the draft. Without the USFL, Steinkuhler would have gone No. 7 or 8. Marshall ended up falling to No. 11 because other teams were afraid of his salary demands. He would make an impact in Chicago.

After Steinkuhler (6'3, 275), the Oilers' next 7 selections and 12 of 14 overall were defense, including NT Doug Smith (2nd round), safety Bo Eason (2nd), LB Johnny Meads (3rd), Tennessee DE Mark Studaway (4th), DB Patrick Allen (4th), LB Robert Lyles (5th), LB John Grimsley (6th) and DB Jeff Donaldson (9th). Holovak's goal was to find tough guys that fit the new DC's philosophy. "You only have to spend three minutes with Jerry Glanville," said the assistant GM, "and you know that's all he believes in — hitting."

Under the circumstances, it was a terrific draft as they gathered 8 starters (Steinkuhler, Smith, Eason, Meads, Allen, Lyles, Grimsley, Donaldson). Then again, it did not take much to be better than their last few (five starters out of fourteen picks in '83; one regular out of eleven in '82; one out of ten in '81). Holovak looks at the '84 draft as his finest work with these players acting out significant roles in turning Houston into a contender.

Steinkuhler, like Fryar and Rozier, was off the mighty Nebraska squad. The best collegiate lineman in the country as a guard, Houston projected him at tackle. His 4-year, $2.6 million contract made him the highest paid Oiler OL. It turns out that steroids helped him achieve his dominance in school. In the pros, he was a solid player but frequently injured. Smith (6'4, 305) was be lost to the USFL but would later sign and start.

Still, no review is complete without considering what might have been. Absent the USFL, the Oilers' first three picks could have been Reggie White, Keith Millard and Boomer Esiason or Steve Young, John Alt and Sean Jones. Then again, they might have chosen Billy Cannon, Jr., Victor Scott and Fred Cornwell, which is what Dallas did.

CLOSE TO THE GREAT WHITE

In June, before training camp, the NFL held a supplemental draft of first-year players under contract with the USFL or "any other league." Officially, the players could not sign until their existing contracts expired or the USFL folded. The Oilers had the second choice in each of three rounds.

When the Bucs took Steve Young first, Reggie White fell into Houston's lap. There was just one problem: they did not take him. Obsessed with the thought of replacing the legendary Campbell someday soon, they took Heisman Trophy winner Mike Rozier of Nebraska. It was a questionable choice. At 5'9, 205, Rozier was short but strong. In the USFL, he was frequently injured. Herzeg at least gave some thought to Tennessee's White. It was another one of those pivotal future-of-the-team-on-the-line decisions. He did say he would have taken Young if available.

Rozier's contract was due to expire in 1986. Herzeg said, "We're building an offensive line that could be a running back's dream. It's an offensive line that should begin reaching its peak just about the time Rozier's contract expires." They took OT Don Maggs.

1984 TRAINING CAMP

Hugh Campbell met Jerry Glanville at the Senior Bowl in Mobile in January. He hired Glanville shortly afterwards. During 1983, he was the backfield coach for the Bills. From 1977-82, Jerry coached Atlanta's defense and made the playoffs three times. In 1977, the Falcon defense set an NFL record by allowing only 129 points all season. Hugh and Jerry promised an aggressive defense.

Campbell retained Ken Houston as the secondary coach. Bob Padilla was hired as the DL coach, Bruce Devlin for the LBs and Gene Gaines for special teams.

In a surprise, Kay Dalton was retained as OC. Hugh and Kay promised an aggressive offense. He retained Bill Walsh on the OL while naming Bruce Lemmerman the WR coach and Al Roberts RB coach. It was a fairly young staff led by two 42-year-olds, Campbell and Glanville. The youngest were Lemmerman (38) and Houston (39). Walsh (56) was oldest. Campbell brought Lemmerman, Roberts and Gaines with him from the USFL. The only assistant Herzeg pushed to retain was Walsh.

Several players were coming off surgery. Campbell, Munchak, Bob Hamm and rookie Tim Joiner all had knee surgeries. Doug France had rotator cuff surgery and was through in Houston. Besides Moon, 12 rookies made the team. Mike Renfro and a fifth-round pick were sent to Dallas for WR Butch Johnson. Giff Nielsen, Mo Towns, JC Wilson and Mike Reinfeldt were also gone. They added TE Jamie Williams. And the only Oiler to span all three decades, Elvin Bethea, finally hung them up before heading to Canton. He was with them for 210 games from 1-13 to 2-14, but had a few good years in between.

The biggest change was obviously the 27-year-old rookie QB who was supposed to be protected by an OL that had three first-round picks (Munchak, Matthews, Steinkuhler) and a high second (Salem). However, because of injuries, the opening day lineup had Matthews at C and Schumacher and Pat Howell at OG with Salem and Steinkuhler at OT. Ed Fisher was released in 1983.

What they lacked most was skills players to pair with Moon. In a mistake, they traded Butch Johnson, keeping rookie WR Eric Mullin. The starting WRs for the opener were the dynamic duo of Mike Holston and Steve Bryant, with Tim Smith lurking in the background. Dressel and McCloskey would lose out at TE to Williams. The papers said that despite a knee scope in May, Campbell looked good at HB, but it was not true. In reality, his recovery was slow going.

On defense, Stensrud and Brian Sochia were both tried at NG. A slimmed down Jesse Baker was on the right side with Jerome Foster on the left. Projected starter Bob Hamm was out until midseason. Taylor was off to the USFL. Second-round choice Doug Smith came to the minicamp fat and immature, then left for the USFL. At LB, Riley and Abraham ('82, 3rd round) joined golden oldies Bingham and Brazile. The DBs were Keith Bostic, Carter Hartwig, Steve Brown and Willie Tullis.

The new DC said years later it was obvious that they were "in a whole lot of trouble." Statistics told the tale. In 1983, the Oilers gave up a frightening 28.6 points per game. They were the worst team in football against the rush and had an anemic 31 sacks. In his 1990 book co-written with J. David Miller, *Elvis Don't Like Football*, Glanville compared improving the Oiler defense to "eating an elephant (you know, one bite at a time)."

He asked for a new attitude. He repeatedly drilled it in that they were to "hit to the whistle. If there's seven helmets on the ball, let's get eight. If there's nine helmets on the ball, let's get ten. If there's eleven helmets on the ball, and you're near the sideline, what the hell, let's get twenty." It meant putting out to pasture the prevalent Tom Landry-style "read and react" defense.

However, the necessary aggressive players were scarce. "The Oilers had some guys who were really good boys with the nicest mommies and daddies you ever met," wrote Glanville. "But they wouldn't hit anybody if you gave them a stick and leaked on their boots." They were also a little long in the tooth. "We had a lot of older guys who were at the end of their careers," he wrote. "They still looked mean, like an old huntin' dog, but their huntin' days were over." What he wanted was "some trained killers." He got a few in the draft with Eason, Meads and Lyles. Allen and Grimsley would also prove to be of starter quality.

Many were excited when the Oilers rolled up 534 yards in the final preseason game against the Cowboys, which they somehow they managed to lose 31-24. Ray Buck told readers to look for the team to finish 8-8 and in third place behind Cincinnati and Pittsburgh. He wrote, "This isn't the same Oiler team anymore."

In with the new: Nebraska All-America OL Dean Steinkuhler joined the Oilers in 1984 as their number 1 pick (No. 2 overall). Although widely regarded as the top offensive lineman in the draft, the advent of the USFL cost Houston a shot at either Reggie White or Steve Young.

THE 1984 REGULAR SEASON — SO LONG BIG FELLA

The Oilers opened at home against the world champion Raiders. Running a single-back formation, they played ball control to lead at the half 7-0. They stuck with it even after falling behind and lost 24-14. Dalton refused to let Moon have a go at the Raider secondary. Of 22 first downs, the $6 million QB threw five times.

Fans had heard a lot about a new aggressive philosophy, but it was more of the same. Give it to Earl. Coming off knee surgery, he was not running with the same authority. The head man's explanation was characteristically amorphous. "I wanted to be more aggressive," said Hugh, "but there was a situation, something I don't want to discuss, that dictated the approach we took. I'd rather set a bad example than risk disaster. But that's defensive offensive football and I don't like to play that way. That's not me." That is what the man said.

They kept losing, averaging just 78 yards rushing over the next three. Moon threw only in obvious passing situations and was getting nailed (21 sacks) behind his *Gucci* line. In their defense, Matthews moved from OT to OG to center. Steinkuhler was playing OT for the first time and Salem moved from right OT to the more demanding left OT position. Munchak, with one full season under his belt, was the veteran.

They then had to suffer the indignity of facing a smug Bum Phillips in his return to the Dome. Things had gone to hell since he left. Some thought he put a Louisiana voodoo curse on the team. It was a tough weekend. Not only did the Oilers lose, but so did UH, Rice, TSU and the Astros. The Rockets even lost an intrasquad game.

Before you could blink they were 0-6 again with the trade deadline fast approaching. Herzeg was back on the phones.

One of the most heavily-rumored deals, Brazile for pass rusher Greg Townsend, did not happen, but they did acquire Raider center Jim Romano for third- and sixth-round picks in 1985. Romano ('82, 2nd round) had been the center on Munchak's Penn State team and was a good pickup. Then came the big one, Earl Campbell to New Orleans.

Even though he already had George Rogers, Bum surrendered a No. 1 to be reunited with his old friend.

Most people thought Houston got away with one since Earl was 29 and had a bum knee. Through 6 games in 1984, he had 278 yards and a 2.9 yard average, the lowest of his career. Phillips was sanguine. "Earl will play this weekend and play just like he's been here all year," he said.

Herzeg was properly deferential. "It was an extremely difficult decision to make because Earl has meant so much to this franchise over the past 6½ years," said the GM. "However, when New Orleans offered a No. 1 in next year's draft, it was very difficult for us to turn down. I believe this trade is in the best interest of both the Oilers and Earl, because it gives us the opportunity to select an outstanding young player next year and it gives Earl a chance at this stage of his career to hopefully be bound for the playoffs in 1984." Herzeg said there would have been no deal without a first-round pick "due to Earl's popularity in the community."

The NFL may never again see the same combination of power, speed, determination and stiff arms. As a rookie, his accomplishments were incomparable — the rushing title, All-Pro, rookie of the year and league MVP as he carried his team to the AFC championship.

He did it all again in 1979, and then had a career year in 1980 with 1,934 yards, the second-most all-time. He and his tree-trunk sized thighs led the AFC in rushing his first four seasons as he made the Pro Bowl five of his first six seasons. He set the NFL record for most 200-

And out with the Big E, Elvin Bethea, who called it quits after 16 seasons, 210 games and 8 Pro Bowls. He was the only Oiler to span all three decades.

yard games in a season (4), and tied OJ Simpson for consecutive 200-yard rushing games (2), 100-yard games in a season (11) and consecutive 100-yard games (7).

Most of his records came behind a line that never had more than one Pro Bowl quality starter. There is no telling what he might have accomplished behind a great line like the Cowboys of the early to mid '90s. In spite of the constant pounding, he only missed 6 of 115 games due to injury.

But the Tyler Rose was more than records. Never liking the comparisons to Jim Brown and OJ, he always said, "I just want to be Earl." In an era of obnoxious athletes like Eric Dickerson and Brian Bosworth, Earl was a breath of fresh air. He was always a superb representative of Houston, and by virtue of his Heisman Trophy in college, the entire state.

Meanwhile, there was a season to complete. Hugh Campbell admitted "the team had become predictable on offense." He said they were "more apt to run when Earl was in there and more apt to pass when he wasn't in there. We may be a little better disguised now."

Speculation immediately turned to Mike Rozier. The idea of being able to replace one Heisman running back with another was comforting. But Herzeg said the negotiations were over for the 1984 season.

Larry Moriarty ('83, 5th round) and rookie Willie Joyner moved into the backfield. Jeff Donaldson ('84, 9th) moved to FS and Joe Cooper replaced Florian Kempf as the PK. With Romano at center, Matthews was back at right OG. Together with Munchak, they formed a good, if inexperienced, front three. Romano was fiery and was the kick in the butt the others needed.

They came together to win three of four. Moriarty had several 100-yard games. Spiderman Jamie Williams was a nice surprise at TE, and Tim Smith was having another productive season as the possession receiver. During this period, they were able to win at KC to end the NFL's longest road losing streak at 23 games.

The offense was still plain vanilla. With Steinkuhler lost to a knee injury, defenses came with a hard rush. Play selection was conservative. When Moon did try to stand in the pocket, he got "happy feet." Holston, Bryant and Mullin were not the answer at WR. Against Cleveland, the coaches benched Smith, their best WR, because they did not think he could handle the Browns' secondary. They played three TEs. Moon never went deep, had 38 yards passing and they lost 27-10.

While the defense was showing spunk, it lacked talent at key positions. Eason moved in at SS and became a crowd favorite because of his big hits. The rush defense was hopeless. In December, Dickerson laughed his way to a career-high 215 yards, which allowed him to break OJ's all-time single season record against the team he made fun of before the 1983 draft.

At the end of the season, with the 2-11 Oilers going nowhere, they finally turned Moon loose. Against Pittsburgh who was gunning for the playoffs, Moon went 27-of-45 for 303 yards to win 23-20 in OT. He completed 6 straight in OT to set up the winning FG.

In the finale against Cleveland, Moon had 306 yards. Smith, allowed to play this time, caught 7 for 167 yards. Houston lost 27-20, but they at least put up a good fight.

The Oilers finished 3-13. Mike Munchak was the only Oiler to make a post-season team for the third straight year. He was Houston's first Pro Bowl guard since Bob Talamini.

Pittsburgh won the division at 9-7. It would be their last of the decade. They lost the AFC Championship to Miami where Dan Marino had a record 5,084 yards passing on the season. Chuck Studley coached the Dolphin defense. The 49ers won the Super Bowl 38-16.

OVERVIEW

Despite the lack of a legitimate deep threat and some serious happy feet, the new guy went 259-of-450 (57.5%) for a team record 3,338 yards (a record he would break 5 more times). He started slowly, completing just 47% for 1,203 yards in his first six games and losing them all. In the final 10, he hit 64% for 2,135 yards. He had just 12 TDs to go with 14 interceptions. Marino, passed over by Houston in the draft, had 48 TDs.

Smith had over 1,000 yards for the second straight year. His two-year total of 152 receptions was tops in the league. TE Williams chipped in 41 catches while

Dressel had 40 from the H-back position. Moriarty became the first back not named Earl to lead the team in rushing since '77. He had 785 yards and a 4.2-yard average.

Nonetheless, the offense was fourth from the bottom. The defense was worse (last in rush defense and worst overall in AFC), but did not have the same talent.

Herzeg was not happy. "The one thing I'm disappointed in with Coach Campbell is that when I interviewed him for the job, he assured me he would play aggressively offensively and defensively," the GM complained. "I thought we had an aggressive defense, although we lacked talent. But I don't think we were aggressive on the offense at all.

"The offense this year was a carbon copy of last year's offense. If Hugh Campbell had told Mike and I before we hired him that he would run the same one-back offense we had in '83, he never would have been a candidate for the job ... I don't care if people rap me for being open and honest. We lived up to our commitment to Hugh Campbell; I don't think Hugh Campbell has lived up to his. It's as if you hired somebody after they told you they had a college degree, then you find out later they don't have a college degree at all."

GOOD-TIME CHARLIE AND OTHER OILER GOOFS

During the 1984 season, one-time Oiler Charlie Joiner broke Charley Taylor's all-time NFL reception record. Interestingly, not only were Joiner and Taylor Oiler draft picks, but so was the man hot on the heals of Joiner, Steve Largent.

Joiner, who played 18 seasons, was a class act. He gave the ball with which he broke the record to one-time Oiler assistant Fran Polsfoot, who was battling cancer. It was Polsfoot who, back in 1969, fought off the defensive coaches to keep him at WR. Otherwise, the greatest receiver in NFL history would have been a DB. In 1972, he was traded for Fred Willis and Paul Robinson.

Ironically, it was Polsfoot who later took the blame for Largent. Bum cut the fourth-round draft choice in 1976 in favor of over-the-hill Otis Taylor and the enigmatic Melvin Booker. They cut Taylor before the season, while Booker dropped more passes than he caught (3) and was dumped at midseason. Largent was an immediate success in Seattle, causing Polsfoot to be fired. The rumor was that he said Steve was "too slow." Fran

Earl Campbell may have been the greatest running back of all-time. He is definitely the best to ever put on an Oiler uniform and probably the city's best athlete ever. He is without a doubt its most loved. As Bum Phillips said, "I wouldn't say Earl is in a class by himself, but I'll tell you one damn thing: It don't take them long to call the roll."

always maintained that all he ever told Bum was he could not start right away.

FAN SUPPORT AND THE BOTTOM LINE

Not surprisingly, home attendance dropped from its heyday. In 1980, the last playoff year, the Oilers averaged 52,712, well above the Dome's average capacity of 47,600 (the average could vary depending on the amount of home games during baseball season). In 1984, average attendance fell to 40,441, the lowest level in 10 years, which made the decision to fire Phillips appear to be the work of a madman. In reality, fans took it much harder than Bud.

Fans saw 35 losses in the last 41 games and an NFL-record 23 consecutive road losses. But fans reacted differently this time than they did during the last disaster, the early- to mid-1970s. Back then, fans gave up totally including refusing to buy tickets. When the team became good again, many were left without any tickets. This time, even though they stopped going to games again, they held onto their season tickets, just in case. Indeed, there was a long waiting list for the better seats. Herzeg called it "unbelievable, when you consider what we've gone through."

The drop in season ticket sales from 1980 through 1984 was only about 2,500. Thus, while the no-shows increased to an all-time high of 9,528 in '84 in response to the dreadful on-the-field product, Adams continued to make a profit. Season ticket sales were the key and, thanks to Bum, Bud still had that going for him. For the time being, this cash flow would keep him satisfied.

1985: CUZ' WHEN YOU'RE TALKIN' HOUSTON, YOU'RE TALKIN' SUPER BOWL

As usual, rumors of a coaching change swirled. About the possibility that Bud might be scheduling another press conference, Herzeg said, "Bud really has nothing to do with the situation. Bud wasn't the one who hired Hugh Campbell. I hired him and it was on the basis of what he told Mike Holovak and me separately when we interviewed him for the job."

Campbell, who took the job with some trepidation, recoiled at the lack of support. He blamed the media for blowing their differences out of proportion and complained about the lack of a "big play" guy. Herzeg responded, "I thought the big play guy was Warren Moon." Asked about a solution, Herzeg replied, "Run the type of offense he promised."

After a clear-the-air love-in, Campbell stayed put. Herzeg said he never really considered firing him, that he just wanted some action, but added that he would be "disappointed" if they didn't finish at least 8-8. Campbell would not commit to a number, but said he, too, would be "disappointed if we don't improve."

The fall guy this time was OC Kay Dalton. CFL "offensive wizard," Joe Faragalli, replaced him.

THE 1985 DRAFT

The Oilers had two first-round choices and extra fifth- and sixth-rounders. With Rozier unsigned and Moriarty threatening a holdout, Herzeg traded a third-round choice for RB Butch Woolfolk. In New York, the former first-rounder could not unseat Rob Carpenter. They also traded down in the third for another pick.

The late season wins cost them Bruce Smith. Next best was QB Bernie Kosar. Bernie graduated early and announced he would go pro. Several teams, including the Browns and Vikings, desperately wanted him. Cleveland was Bernie's preference, but Houston cut a deal with Minnesota for their first- (the No. 3 overall) and second-round choices. It was a good deal for Houston until Kosar, like Elway, thumbed his nose at the NFL.

Unwilling to play for the frugal Vikings, he found a technical loophole and never sent the NFL his formal notification. Apparently acting in concert with the Browns, he waited until after the draft to make his declaration, thereby forcing the NFL to hold a special supplemental draft for him later. Buffalo, who also had the No. 1 pick in the supplemental, traded it to Cleveland for their 1986 No. 1. The NFL had supplemental drafts before, but for legitimate grounds. This one was just to let Bernie avoid Minnesota.

Pete Rozelle not only let them get away with it, but tripled-screwed Houston in the process. First, Kozar would be a thorn in their division for several years. Second, Buffalo was allowed to reap a windfall by gaining an extra No. 1 choice for the rights to a player for whom Houston had the rights. The Bills, who would be the Oilers chief competition in years to come, would put the extra pick to good use. Finally, Rozelle, who had never grown to like Bud Adams, made Houston forfeit Minnesota's second pick effectively making them move down from the No. 2 overall pick to No. 3 for no compensation.

The Oilers threatened to sue to enjoin the entire draft. But a suit might have called the legality of the entire NFL draft into question. Adams, who enjoyed socializing with the other owners, was vary of dropping into that quagmire. Furthermore, Minnesota, who left Adams and Hunt standing at the altar back in 1960, left Adams to go it alone. Bud pulled the plug on any legal action at the last moment.

It was mud on Herzeg's face. Cleveland had offered Tom Cousineau or Chip Banks and the No. 7 choice, but he went with the Vikes because he was afraid if he dropped any lower, he would lose DE Ray Childress. He came away with nothing, actually less than nothing. However, considering all the other Oiler screwups over the years, this one was minor. In the end, they got the players they targeted. Moreover, Kosar never led the Browns to a Super Bowl or played at a Pro Bowl level.

The Oilers had 11 picks, including 3 of the first 31 and 5 of the first 87. While the draft was not particularly strong in terms of first-rounders, it was deep in the middle rounds where Houston lacked picks (Woolfolk, Butch Johnson, Romano trades).

For the predraft party at the Astro-Village Hotel, the Oilers had a special treat — the 1984 Oiler highlights video: *New Frontiers*. It was a short film. They took Texas A&M's Childress first and CB Richard Johnson with the Earl Campbell choice. In the second, they took Southern Miss DE Richard Byrd. The Oilers said that Childress and Byrd were two of the top three DEs and that Johnson was the top rated CB.

Childress (6'6, 270) was the first great DL ever drafted by the Oilers in the first round (Bethea was a third-rounder) and first defensive player taken in the first round in 10 years (since Brazile in '75). He would start immediately. To get him, they passed on one of the best pass rushers of all-time, Chris Doleman. Nonetheless, Ray was a good choice and would anchor the line for the next decade.

The Johnson pick (No. 11) was dubious. The Oilers had been loading up on DBs. They took five in '83 (Bostic, Brown, Hill, Hayworth, Potter) and three more in '84 (Eason, Allen, Donaldson). Of those, Allen and Brown were ready to start at CB. There was also a question whether Johnson, who played zone in college, could handle the man-to-man coverage of the NFL. If they had to have a CB, UT's Jerry Gray was a better choice.

Moon was dismayed with the Johnson pick. He asked, "Where was Eddie Brown?" As of the No. 11 pick, there were still two good WRs on the board. Brown went to Cincinnati at No. 13. Then SF took Jerry Rice at No. 16. Johnson over Rice sums up Oiler fate pretty well. In fact, had they taken the Cleveland offer, they could have had Banks, Rice and Gray. On the other hand, given their history and the amount of balls Rice dropped his first year, they probably would have cut him.

The remaining Oiler picks were OG Mike Kelley (3rd round), LB Tom Briehl (4th), LB Frank Bush (5th), punter Lee Johnson (5th), WR Mike Aikiu (7th), WR/KR Steve Tasker (9th) and WR/KR Willie Drewrey (11th).

1985 TRAINING CAMP

Herzeg kept moving after the draft. In one of his better moves, he picked up WR Drew Hill from the Rams for two mid-round selections. He also picked up PK Tony Zendejas from Washington. Zendejas was the best kicker in the USFL and was the Skins' first pick in the June '84 supplemental draft. Cooper was cut.

Mike Rozier signed. With him, Woolfolk and Hill aboard, the offense suddenly looked dangerous. Moon said, "I feel I can increase my touchdown throws by being more aggressive-minded. I personally want to get the ball in the endzone via the air more than I did last year." Possession-receiver Tim Smith started opposite Hill. Holston and Bryant, the 1984 opening-day starters, were waived.

Most of the top draft picks, including Childress and Johnson, held out and missed a big part of camp which was split between San Angelo and Greeley, Colorado. Moriarty also held out and missed camp. Although he only started nine games, Larry led the team in rushing, was a fan favorite and decided he was worth more. He was also represented by Howard Slusher, who really got under Herzeg's skin. His absence created problems.

Once the season started, Woolfolk and Moriarty were the starters with Rozier, who had already played a full USFL season, coming off the bench. Jamie Williams was the TE.

Injuries to Steinkuhler and Salem dampened any excitement over the offense. Steinkuhler's knee was particularly troubling. He would not play a down all season. The year started with a line of Romano, Munchak, Schumacher, Matthews and Eric Moran.

The defense had several changes. Missing were two long-time cogs in the wheel. Gregg Bingham finished his career as the team's all-time leading tackler. He was second only to Bethea in both regular season games played (173) and seasons (12). He was third to Bethea and Robert Brazile in consecutive starts. Brazile played 10 seasons and held the team record for most consecutive starts (147). Like former Oiler George Webster before him, he was one of the best OLBs to have ever played and should be in the Hall of Fame.

Without the vets, the influence of the DC increased. In 1985, the defense became Jerry Glanville's. The safeties were Keith Bostic ('83, 2nd round) and Bo Eason ('84, 2nd) who went by "Batman and Robin." The corners were Allen ('84, 4th) and Brown ('83, 3rd). Stensrud and Baker were joined by Childress ('85, 1st). Byrd was injured early and never a factor. The new OLBs were Johnny Meads ('84, 3rd) and Robert Lyles ('84, 5th), but Frank Bush pushed them hard. Avon Riley ('81, 9th) and Robert Abraham ('82, 3rd) returned at ILB. Childress was the only first-rounder starting on defense and the only rookie starter on the team. Missing camp sank rookie CB Richard Johnson's chances.

Despite a 1-4 preseason, Coach Campbell said he was "quite excited ... On defense, we're not only getting to the ball, but we're making big hits. We completely shut Dallas' offense down in the first half ... Our special teams showed so much improvement, and our offense is displaying so many more weapons than in the past. I'm very enthusiastic about our progress."

"I know this team can be good — and it can be good this year," said Moon. "Because of the big weapons we've added, I'm hoping we can come up with some big plays to overcome some of the boo boos we're going to make early."

The schedule was tough, including the now brutal NFC East. Four of the first five games were against payoff teams. The young defense would have its hands full with Miami (Dan Marino), Washington (Joe Theismann), St. Louis (Neil Lomax), Denver (John Elway), San Diego (Dan Fouts), the Giants (Phil Simms) and Cleveland twice (Bernie Kosar).

The Astrodome got a $44 million facelift that was reportedly financed by a hotel-motel tax. However, the improvement failed to address two issues that would crop up again later—seating capacity and the AstroTurf.

THE 1985 REGULAR SEASON — THESE LOSERS SMELL OF BOOS

The season started off great except for bookies. The Oilers opened against the defending AFC champion Dolphins. Trailing 23-19 with five minutes left, Moon hit Hill for 48 yards and then Smith for 10 more on a fourth-and-three play. Rozier ran in the clincher as they won 26-23 before a capacity crowd at home. Moon finished 12-of-17 for 270 yards. The defense held the Fish and Marino, who would finish 12-4, to 16 points. It was the high point of the season.

The next week saw a signature example of the frustrating theme that would characterize the Oilers of this era. On September 15, the Oilers played the Redskins at RFK Stadium. Houston had lost 24 of its last 25 road games going in and was a 10-point underdog. The game started out predictably as Washington scored on its first three possessions to take a 16-0 lead. They outgained Houston 167 yards to two in the first quarter with each score coming out of a three-TE formation. "If you're a seasoned vet," explained Glanville, "you've seen that formation ... You know what to do. But these guys had never seen that at Vanderbilt — or wherever."

Five of the starters on defense had three NFL starts or fewer, including Childress, who was going on just three weeks of practice. In any event, Glanville made some adjustments and Washington did not score again. The Oilers cut it to 16-13 before it became really frustrating. Zendejas, playing against the team that traded him, missed FGs from 42 and 33 yards, the latter one hitting an upright with 4 minutes left. Even worse, the refs not only flagged them for 111 yards in penalties, but called back *four* Oiler TDs on questionable calls. They lost 16-13. In a refrain as applicable in 1985 as it was in 1987 or 1989 or 1992, Hill said, "We beat those guys." Welcome to Houston, Drew.

Another signature moment came at Pittsburgh. On a play blown dead by a penalty, a Steeler grabbed Moon and piledrove him like Andy Kauffman in his wrestling match. Not a single Houston player reacted. Pittsburgh won 20-0.

Then they had Dallas in the Dome. With Tex Schramm conceding before the game that Houston already held an advantage in raw talent, Houston fell on its face. The Pokes sacked Moon a record 12 times. Glanville's defense kept it close by limiting Dallas to one third down conversion the entire game. They lost it in the last two minutes 17-10.

Despite all the money sunk into the offense, it was the defense that was playing better. Over the previous four games, the defense surrendered an average of 17.3 per game, or almost twice as good as 1984 over the same period (31.2 points). They ranked fifth in the AFC. Glanville said, "It's hard to say how good this defense can be because we're still defining who we are. We're still trying to climb right now. But I think we're going to be fun to watch in the future."

They would have been a lot more fun to watch without penalties. In the next game, they received 15 flags, losing to Denver 31-20. Despite the penalties, the defense hustled. Not so of the offense, which was the worst in the NFL.

Mike "Mongo" Stensrud (6'5, 280) was Bum's top draft pick in 1979 out of Iowa State. Many felt he never played up to his potential, giving legs to the well-worn complaint that being a dedicated Christian athlete is antithetical to success on the field.

After losing to Cleveland 21-6 in Kosar's first start, a *Post* headline read: "These losers smell of boos." With Steinkuhler on the sidelines, the rest of Houston's high draft picks stank. It was hard to believe players with that much talent could look so bad. Moon was susceptible to and rattled by the blitzes which were coming from everywhere. Their response was perplexing. Even though traps, draws and screens can often beat blitzes, the Oilers kept sending their backs in motion away from the QB. It did not make much sense. Moon fumbled snaps, made terrible passes and danced the happy feet. Making matters worse, the boo birds came out to roost. Dale Robertson even referred to him as a "turkey."

Rumors flew about Hugh Campbell. Herzeg suggested that Bud was not getting his money's worth out of Hill, Woolfolk and Rozier. Campbell did not help his cause. He regularly said they were "improved." After the Browns game, he said he was "happy" with the first half "like everyone else." He said his team "did what we wanted to. We'd move the ball 20 yards or so before we had to give it up." Joe Faragalli's CFL tricks were not working in the NFL. Glanville later wrote, "Hugh Campbell had been quite a coach in the CFL, where the playing fields are about the size of Texas."

The players did make a brief rally for their embattled coach, crushing Cincinnati 44-27 and winning the next two to climb to 4-5. That got them close enough to smell the top of a weak division. But it was a short-lived as they dropped two of the next three.

The owner and GM had both said they expected a 8-8 season which did not leave much room for error. They went to Cincinnati talking playoffs but returned with a 45-27 loss as the Bengals rolled up 555 yards of offense. On December 8, they lost to the Giants 35-14 to fall to 5-9. On December 9, Herzeg fired Campbell.

Glanville became the interim coach and was told he would have to win the last two, both on the road, to keep the job. It was asking a lot. Houston had won just five road games in four years.

He pleaded for a new attitude. He wanted them to dish out punishment instead of being passive. He told them to stop worrying about playing "smart. If they hit you, I want the entire team hitting back .... If you want respect, you have to start standing up to people."

They played better but lost to the Browns 28-21 in a game that included the now customary barking snowball bombardment as the Oilers tried to make a goal line stand. They lost the last one to the Colts 34-16. Cleveland won the Central at 8-8, the worst record to ever win an NFL division.

Chicago had all the fun that year. The Bears dominated the NFC and blew out New England in the Super Bowl 46-10 to finish 17-1. The MVP of the game was Richard Dent, an eighth-round pick in 1983 who blossomed under DC Buddy Ryan. Ed Hughes was also a coordinator for the Bears.

OVERVIEW

Even though their five victories were the most since 1981, the season was horrifying. Eight of the 11 teams that beat them had losing records, including the terminally ill Bills (2-14) and Colts (5-11). They came in fourth place in a four-team division that was the worst in football. The hard part was that they were doing it with a load of talent. Robertson wrote, "The only thing the Oilers do well is collect draft choices."

Munchak made the Pro Bowl for the second straight season and for the first time as a starter. Matthews made it as an alternate, which means he came in fourth in

After watching their team twice come within 4 quarters or less of the Super Bowl and arguably field the second best team in football from 1978 through 1980, Oiler fans had to endure consecutive seasons starting in 1981 of 7-9, 1-8, 2-14, 3-13, 5-11 and 5-11.

balloting. Baker led the team in sacks for the sixth year in a row, but did not make it (he never did).

Woolfolk caught 80 passes, third best in the AFC. That a runner led the team in receptions did not speak well of the team's downfield game. Moon threw for 2,209 yards on 200-of-377 passing. He had 15 TDs and 19 interceptions. His measly QB rating of 68.9 stood in stark contrast to $1.1 million he made for the season. Mitigating factors included misuse by the coaches, who seemed afraid to turn Moon loose.

After his disruptive holdout and an uncharacteristic cave-in by Herzeg, Moriarty (called "the quintessential average white back") came back to romp for 381 yards (24 per game). Rozier started the final 5 games and led the team with 462 yards, the lowest total for any team rushing leader. Woolfolk added 392.

The plight of the offense was heavy with irony. After averaging 353 yards a game with his "high school" offense, Bum Phillips was fired for not having an OC. From 1981 through 1984, OCs Jim Shofner and Kay Dalton put together offenses that ranked next-to-last, last, fourth-from-the-bottom, and fifth-from-the-bottom. In 1985, it was Faragalli's turn. His team averaged 12.7 points and 240 yards per game, both well below the NFL mean. Going back to the merger, the only Oiler offense that consistently moved the ball was Bum's. The best post-merger Oiler offenses were 1979 (eighth in scoring) and 1980 (fourth in total offense).

In another reversal from the Phillips' years, the Oilers could not win on the road. Bum's road record from 1978-80 was 18-12. Since '81, the Oilers were the worst road team in football.

PK Zendejas started off terribly, missing pressure kicks against both Washington and Dallas. He improved over the course of the season, beating KC 23-20 with 14 seconds left and San Diego 37-35 with kicks from 46, 52 and 51 yards, the last one coming with 2 seconds left.

Glanville's defense collapsed over the last five despite picking up Doug Smith from the USFL in October. Losing Meads, Riley and Eason hurt over that final stretch. By the end of the year, they were again next-to-last in the league and last against the run. Jerry was unimpressed, saying, "I have a circular file for statistics. It's called a trash can."

CHAPTER 8

THE GLANVILLE YEARS 1986-89

The one absolute for Oiler fans was frustration. Whenever one level subsided, another always rose to replace it. It was a perpetual process. By the middle '80s, a new kind of frustration arrived. The team was remade. There was a bounty of high draft picks produced by the 18-55 post-Phillips record. They had a multi-million dollar QB, another Heisman RB, an OL full of high picks, a WR on one side who caught 200 passes over a three-year span, one on the other side who could get open and catch the deep pass, and finally, a swarming, tough defense.

It was a very good team *on paper*. However, not only did they keep losing, but also they embarrassed themselves in the process. At least, they should have been embarrassed. Everyone else around them was. The players looked as if they had no idea what they were doing. They stumbled, bumbled and fumbled. They drew more penalties than anyone had ever seen. They looked like a pick-up team. They were the most talented underachievers in the history of sports.

His two-year experiment with CFL coaches lying in ruin at his feet, Ladd Herzeg had to find another coach. The new one would last longer than the average and would carry the team to the end of the decade. He got them winning again, but it came at a price. It was frustrating.

1986: THE RULE OF FIVE

The final two losses of 1985 seemed to seal Jerry Glanville's fate as Herzeg set off on another "exhaustive search" for a new coach. It was a bad omen. In 1970, another of Adams' corporate officers named John Collins promised the same thing after Wally Lemm quit. That led to "Hughes he?" and "Ed Who?" and back-to-back 1-13 seasons.

The Oilers had developed an unusual pattern. They employed five coaches for the first half of each decade of their existence. In the '60s, it was Rymkus, Lemm, Ivy, Baugh and Taylor. In the '70s, it was Lemm, Hughes, Peterson, Gillman and Phillips. The '80s had already seen Phillips, Biles, Studley, Campbell and Glanville.

Adams' proclivity to hire and fire was staggering in comparison to other teams. The Packers, Giants and Bears, each founded in the 1920s, had hired fewer coaches than Houston, which did not begin play until 1960.

Comparisons to that other Texas team were inevitable. Tom Landry was Adams' original first choice, but he declined. In his first season, Landry's boys did not win a game and looked bad for several years thereafter. But the owner left him alone, and by 1966, Landry had them in the playoffs. Through 1985, Dallas had won 13 divisional championships. The Oilers, meanwhile, won the very first AFL title, but Adams fired his coach a few games into the next season, and it has been off to the races ever since.

NONE OF THE ABOVE
(*aka* WALKING WITH KINGS)

Replacement names bantered about included Ron Erhardt, Terry Donahue, Jim Mora, Sam Rutigliano, Mike White, Jack Pardee, Jerry Rhome, Paul Hackett,

Lindy Infante, Howard Schnellenberger, Tom Osborne, Don Coryell and Glanville. While this was going on, Herzeg took more swipes at Campbell, calling him the "worst mistake of my professional career." Invoking Al Davis, he asked, "Does he ever say, 'Just Improve Baby?'"

The Houston press, in turn, began to take more and more swipes at Herzeg. Explaining why George Allen, Hank Stram and Dick Vermeil were not viable candidates, it was suggested that their strong personalities were too much for Herzeg. Some thought Herzeg should join Campbell. Robertson called him "Bud, Jr.," and wrote, "For reasons we can only speculate upon, Herzeg's flanks are impenetrable."

Mickey Herskowitz disagreed. He suggested Adams had grown impatient with Ladd and this would be his last shot. Adams purportedly told him in private, "If we don't get the right coach in there this time with the talent we have, well, knowing the kind of person Ladd is, I think he would come to me and say, 'I've given you my best. This is the third time I've struck out, and I feel I ought to go back to the corporate books.'"

Mickey implored the team to either "attract one of the proven winners — Landry, Shula, Knox, Noll, Walsh, or Allen, or look to their staffs ... There is nothing wrong with hiring an assistant coach but check his pedigree ... As Vince Lombardi said, 'Winning breeds winning. All anyone learns from losing is how to lose.' At losing, the Oilers are *magna cum laude*. This time they ought to go where the winners are. They ought to surprise us."

Robertson thought Adams was "certain to seek an accomplished offensive mastermind to maximize the Oilers' super young talent."

They interviewed 5-10 candidates with Herzeg refusing to say exactly how many. In mid-January, the Oilers revealed the three names on their short-list. They were Glanville, Paul Hackett and Dick Coury. Herskowitz complained there was "not a winner among the bunch."

Hackett had no record as the OC for the 49ers. Coury was 28-26 in the USFL. Dick Vermeil, recruited to say something nice about him, offered, "He's a great guy whose teams were blown out by weaker USFL teams." Glanville was 0-2.

The local writers split on Jerry. Robertson called him "qualified." Ray Buck thought he was "a bona fide head coaching candidate, if not in Houston then surely some other NFL port." Herskowitz wrote that he had "not exactly walked with kings ... Under Jerry Glanville, Warren Moon threw for 300 yards and the Oilers were praised for getting creamed." He said his best quality is that he "makes no excuses for losing." Mickey was dead set against hiring any Oiler assistant, warning, "You don't promote assistant coaches from losing staffs." With Bones Taylor, Ed Hughes and Ed Biles as exhibit A, he wrote, "This practice hasn't worked for the Oilers and there is no record of it working anywhere else."

Herzeg said the three men on his list all had "charisma." However, the winner of a *Post* poll was *none of the above* with 38% of the vote to Hackett's 29% and Glanville's 18%.

WELCOME JERRY GLANVILLE

The announcement was suspenseful. Coury holed up in a Houston hotel room with the expectation of a favorable phone call. But it was Glanville, interviewed five times, who got the call. On January 20, 1986, he became the Houston Oilers' fourteenth head coach.

Herzeg said it came down to three factors. First, Glanville had the type of personality to motivate the young players. Second, he already was familiar with the personnel. Finally, drawing on his 12 years in the NFL, he promised a good staff.

He received an unusually long five-year deal. The only other coach to ever get one that long was Bill Peterson. He was Herzeg's and Holovak's choice, but Bud endorsed it. Adams came out of hiding to join the announcement party, cigar in hand.

Jerry is the "man to take the Houston Oilers to the Super Bowl," said a shorter and plumper Bud. Looking at the expressions around the room, he quickly added, "I don't want y'all to laugh about that ... Jerry is going to be a motivator ... that's what the team needs right now — someone to kick 'em in the butt."

He described the search with the now familiar phrase — "probably the most exhaustive" in history. He said he would be "very surprised" if they did not make the playoffs. "We wasted two years," said Adams about Campbell. "We've spent over $10 million the last three years on players. We're just looking for the right man with the right assistants to take these guys to the playoffs."

He promised "more togetherness ... a loyalty from the janitor to the owner." To underscore that point, the papers ran a photo of Glanville and the team custodian in a big embrace. In another shot at Hugh Campbell, Glanville said, "We're going to be family. If you get into an argument with your wife, you don't run next door and tell your neighbor. The strength of the Houston Oilers will now be its organization."

Herzeg predicted the Oilers would become a model organization. "Other teams will look at us to see how we do it," he said, "because we will win. And because we feel we've selected the right person to get us winning, we wanted to give him as long a contract as possible."

Holovak added it would be his fault if the new coach did not succeed. "Jerry is a man and a football man. We have the coach ... if it doesn't work out now, then it's the personnel."

Fan reaction was almost immeasurable. Most had returned to the self-protective apathy of the mid-'60s and the early '70s. Glanville was the winner of the consolation bracket. Even Adams conceded there were "not a lot of highly qualified candidates available."

Glanville's only promise was, "We'll be better my first year. And we'll be in the playoffs every year after that."

Chronicle columnist Ed Fowler fired his first shot before Jerry called a play. "Glanville means more of the same," he wrote. "To lead the Oilers in their rise from their ashes, Herzeg is giving you one of the people responsible for starting the fire."

NINE GOOD MEN

A key to the Glanville hire was his assurance of a good staff. It seemed like a breakthrough. The Oilers had long been one of the stingiest organizations when it came to coaching salaries. It was a sore point for team followers. Now they were at least giving lip service to teaching, game plans and game-day coaching. Adams said, "We want Jerry to go get the best people he can get. We'll pay 'em what it takes."

In the interview process, Glanville submitted a three-deep list of names of assistants that he indicated he could land, including current assistants on both Super Bowl teams. This made quite the impression on Herzeg. Glanville said, "We're like the Marines. We're looking for nine good men." Glanville's success or failure would turn, to a large degree, on his ability to follow through with this claim.

They released seven of the remaining eight Campbell assistants. Only Bill Walsh survived. A favorite of Herzeg's, Walsh oversaw the highly paid, frequently penalized OL.

Fired DB coach Ken Houston shortly made the Hall of Fame on the first ballot. While largely remembered for his days with the Redskins, all 9 of his record-setting interceptions for TDs were while playing for the Oilers. Wally Lemm presented him at the ceremonies.

Glanville went after his old roommate, Joe Bugel, but he was still having too much fun in Washington. He ended up with Doug Shively, Floyd Reese and Tom Bettis, all of whom had been DCs. On offense, he hired Dick Jamieson, Gary Huff and Milt Jackson. Steve Waterston was the conditioning coach.

There were no OCs or DCs. Jerry said, "Nobody is. Everybody is. That's the beauty of it." He considered it a question of loyalty. If things went bad, he thought he should be the one to bear the brunt of criticism, not the assistants.

THE 1986 DRAFT

Focus soon turned to the May draft, which draftniks could now watch in all its glory on cable television. Again, the Oilers had a high draft choice. It was the

third year in a row they had a top-three pick and fifth straight year for a top-10 pick.

The *Post* questioned the talent level, calling it "the weakest draft defensively in 20 years." Houston had the No. 3 pick overall. After Bo Jackson and Tony Casillas went 1-2, Houston got to pick between DEs John Hand and Leslie O'Neal, QB Jim Everett, OT Jim Dombrowski and LB Anthony Bell.

Herzeg said Everett was the "only logical choice," but his scouts disagreed. He took much heat in the press for even thinking of using a 5-11 club's first pick on a backup QB. The idea did seem to contradict the organization's promise that they were through building and the future was now. But there was quite a bit of interest in Everett around the league, and Herzeg attempted make deals before and after the draft.

Ed Fowler liked the choice, if only because it let him economize barbs. With Everett, he wrote, "Herzeg made a tacit admission that he blundered in acquiring Warren Moon," adding Everett was "confident and aggressive ... exactly the qualities Moon failed to exhibit."

Houston's new coach was undaunted. He was on record as saying it did not matter who they drafted, they already had a good team. That was a good attitude, especially since his new Oiler family did not consult him much on the draft.

The Oilers made good use of their second pick with Louisville WR Ernest Givins, passing on Webster Slaughter, Tom Newberry, Pepper Johnson, Rueben Mayes and Pat Swilling. In the third, they took RB Allen Pinkett (5'8½, 190), who was Notre Dame's all-time leading rusher. Some of the other Oiler selections were TE Jeff Parks (5th round), FB Ray Wallace (6th), CB Larry Griffin (8th), LB Bob Sebring (9th), OG Don Sommer (10th) and RB Chuck Banks (12th).

The Oilers' heavy emphasis on offense was questionable strategy, considering the defense's No. 27 overall rank (28th against the run and 23rd vs. the pass). With their first five choices, they took a QB, WR, TB, TE and FB. They took no defensive player until the eighth round, and none made the team. Holovak said, "You have some fellows here who can break up ball games in a hurry ... with just a single play. I think we have the right formula, I really do. I'm extremely pleased with the players we have drafted." Glanville said, "We would like to draft defensively but you can't force the draft."

That view was faulty. Were they better talent evaluators, they could have turned the defense around in one draft with rush ends Leslie O'Neal (1st round) and Clyde Simmons (9th), LBs Pat Swilling (2nd), Charles Haley (4th) and Seth Joyner (8th) and run-stuffing tackle Joe Phillips (3rd).

All things considered, the best draft would have been OT Will Wolford (2nd), OG Tom Newberry (2nd), LB Swilling (3rd), LB Haley (4th), TE Brent Jones (5th), WR Mark Jackson (6th), LB Joyner (7th), DE Simmons (8th) and LB Jesse Soloman (9th).

Lest one think that no one team could be so good and lucky in one draft, the 49ers made five trades and came away with Larry Roberts, Tim McKyer, Tom Rathman, John Taylor, Charles Haley, Steve Wallace, Kevin Fagan and Don Griffin. To top it off, by trading down, they picked up extra first- (Washington's) and third- (Philly's) round choices in '87.

Then again, it could have been worse. No. 1 pick Tony Casillas was overrated while No. 2 choice Bo Jackson played baseball. The Giants traded away Mike Haynes and Gary Zimmerman to be able to move up to draft Eric Dorsey. Likewise, the Redskins, who had not had first-round picks in 15 of the last 18 years, traded away their 1987 No. 1 to move up to take some guy named Walter Murray in the second round.

1986 TRAINING CAMP

Come July, the Oilers were back in the San Angelo heat. Like most camps, there was good news and bad. In the big picture, the USFL ceased to exist, except as a plaintiff in a lawsuit. The USFL won the suit in July, but won damages of only $1 (automatically trebled). The players thought the lack of competition would hold down salaries. Houston got seasoning for players like Mike Rozier and Doug Smith. They also gained OT Don Maggs, C Jay Pennison and DE Malcolm Taylor. Smith was second team all-USFL.

The bad news was Jim Everett. While unproven, he was the second highest QB taken in the previous 10 years. He wanted a "Jim Kelly-like" contract ($8 million/ 5 years). His agent was Marvin Demoff. In an era of headline-grabbing agents, Demoff led the pack. He found his match in Herzeg, and Everett never came to terms. It was the second year in a row Herzeg failed to get the first pick into camp. Everett was the only first-round pick unsigned. His holdout and the other big one of the day covered '86 camp like a dark cloud.

The other one was OT Harvey Salem ('83, 2nd). He was under contract but wanted to play "on the West Coast," citing "irreconcilable differences" with Herzeg. Maybe after watching years of pointless protests at Berkeley, he felt it was just something he had to do. His coach called him "big and lazy." Even his teammates grew tired. Breaking the usual player-solidarity line (the thin Columbia blue line?), they stuck his locker nameplate over one of the toilet stalls.

Salem's absence messed up the OL. Otherwise, Herzeg had surrounded Moon with the type of offense he mentioned back in that early 1984 press conference.

Jerry Glanville claims he enjoyed summer training camp in San Angelo which he compared to "playing football in hell." He wrote in his book: "The conditions were so bad, so nasty, that we didn't have to cut the wimps. The wimps went home on their own." Photo © Joel Durate.

Moon had a talented line, Hill and Givins (who beat out Smith), a good TE and solid backfield.

On the other side, Glanville asked for a "stand-up defense," that is, when many defenders crush the ball carrier, "the crowd stands up." He claimed, "Defenses get beat by mental mistakes. Your players have to know what they're doing. They have to react, not think. So, we set out to simplify things." He would find difficulty converting that from theory to practice.

The DL consisted of Childress, Smith and Byrd. Baker and Stensrud were cut. Along with Schumacher, they were the last players from the '70s, although Baker was brought back. The LBs were Lyles, Meads and Bush on the outside with Abraham, Riley and Grimsley on the inside. The secondary consisted of Allen, Brown, Bostic and Eason as starters.

The safeties and OLBs were the strength. They expected improvement out of the young ends and better run support from the CBs. The primary concern was up the gut where Smith and the ILBs caused worried expressions.

Glanville said, "I believe in setting the pace and then seeing if the other team can keep up. I told our coaches that our football team would go 100 miles an hour for four quarters- wide-open, smash-face football.... We're gonna knock people down. We're not going to trick or finesse you. But every player wears a cage, a face mask, on his helmet. We're gonna show people why. We will be living on the edge."

He made Chuck Noll the common enemy, saying, "No team mistreated another team the way Pittsburgh mistreated us ... We'd be down by 40, and they're still blitzing, still killing our running backs, still punching our guys in the mouth, still jumping offsides and crushing our quarterback for no reason ... I vowed they would never treat us like that again." One of his pet sayings was, "Somebody's going to pay for these hangings."

Practices were generally shorter and more focused, but there was more hitting. Discipline was supposedly back and there were fines handed out for such things as showing up late for a meeting. But when the owner of a San Angelo bar called at 3 a.m. to say four of Jerry's kids were there sleeping over a pitcher of beer, the coach said, "That's okay, let them sleep. They're probably tired."

The players bought it. Matthews said, "We seem to have a purpose now." Lyles called it "attitude." Moon said, "We're in better condition. That was a problem in the past." Moriarty added, "We've had talent all four years I've been here. Jerry has just found a way to channel us all into one. He's added the discipline that — being a young team — maybe we lacked ... He's extremely organized and detailed. He works your butt but also makes the game fun."

Dale Robertson wrote: "They have the talent and favorable schedule to win 10 games, which should be enough to win their first" AFC Central title. Pointing to the Pats' surprise in '85, he figured they had a shot at the Super Bowl. "They are tough, eager and just naïve enough to believe they deserve to be taken seriously."

Ray Buck added, "Mashmouth football, hands-on coaching and a full-bloom Moon are only a few of the noticeable differences between the 5-11 Oilers of '85 and the honest-to-gosh, playoff hopeful Oilers of '86." He pointed to the coaching staff ("one of the strongest defensive staffs in the league"), the discipline ("Hill was fined $3,500 for reporting late" to camp), the offensive talent (Givins and Pinkett added to Moon, Rozier, Hill, Smith, Moriarty, Woolfolk), the cohesiveness of the front office and coaching staff ("Glanville and Herzeg actually like each other") and an easier schedule ("11 of 16 games against non-playoff teams").

Mickey Herskowitz seemed won over, too, predicting up to 10 wins. "This is a sound football team," Mickey told readers, "well-coached, young but street smart, able to strike quickly, with an offensive line and secondary on the brink of stardom."

This was also a team coming off five losing seasons. It had a fragile psyche. To build confidence, Glanville had them playing to win preseason games. They won them all for the first time since 1965. Against Dallas, Munchak set the tone with a blow-out clearing block on Randy White that freed Moriarty for the winning TD. After the game, Glanville met the legendary Tom Landry for the customary handshake. Glanville's account is that Landry, who was not good with names, glanced down at his palm where he had the name of Houston's latest coach written and said, "Great game, Gary."

This was when Jerry started wearing black on the sidelines. He said that besides being his favorite color, "It helped players spot me from the field." It played to Herzeg's worship of Al Davis and the Raiders, but set Glanville up for criticism. Ed Fowler, for one, started calling him "bobo in black." Looking back years later, Glanville said he thought the calamity about his clothing took the focus away from the game and the players.

Salem showed up just before the season liable for a huge fine ($56,500). Glanville was unimpressed. "Harvey isn't very high on my priority list at this time," said the coach, "but he was gracious enough to say that if I drop the fine, he wouldn't tell the team." He added later that Salem, "looks like Tarzan but plays like Jane."

THE 1986 REGULAR SEASON — STATISTICS ARE FOR SUCKERS

For once, Houston's other teams put on the pressure. Over the summer, the Rockets made it back to the NBA Finals. As football season opened, the Astros were heading for another divisional title and fateful showdown with the Mets. The Oilers at least started off well.

They opened at Green Bay with a roster that averaged 25 years and two seasons of experience. Glanville was determined to ram Rozier down their throats. He came out in a power formation with Matthews and Steinkuhler at tackle. They blew out the Pack 31-3 for their biggest victory margin on the road in 11 years and fifth road win in five seasons.

Then came the proverbial fork in the road. To the extent a season can turn on a single play, it happened the next week in the Dome. Despite losing Romano to a knee injury, they dominated the Browns most of the game and seemed to have it put away, leading 13-9 with 2½ minutes left. But after Drewrey fumbled a kick, they got caught blitzing from their nickel defense. The Browns had the perfect counter, sending 3 WRs and keeping everyone else back to block. Looking for the home run, Kosar somehow got one of his wounded ducks to Reggie Langhorne who beat Eason for a 23-20 Cleveland victory.

That TD was a gutshot. Houston had 405 yards to Cleveland's 243, twenty first downs to their nine and 6-of-9 third-down conversions to Cleveland's 3-of-14. But (there always is one) they also had 5 turnovers and 9 penalties. Houston's confidence wilted. On that single play, they lost it. Cleveland, meanwhile, used the game as a springboard to the playoffs.

Behind the scenes, Herzeg was hard at work. On September 18, he pulled off one of the bigger trades in team history, sending the rights to Everett, who wanted more than the Falcons paid the No. 2 pick ($2.35 million for 4 years), to the Rams for Kent Hill, William Fuller, 1987 first- and fifth-rounders and a 1988 first-round pick. It was a 5-for-1 swap. Hill was a 5-time Pro Bowl OG. Fuller was an All-American DE at UNC who was projected as a first-rounder but went to the USFL. It was a blockbuster, and for once, Houston came out ahead.

A few reporters had to eat their words as Herzeg regained stature in dealing with LA (many felt he was outmaneuvered on Dickerson). Robertson called it "highway robbery." Fowler was unrelenting, saying it was "converting instant help into faraway dreams."

Herzeg did it by playing off division rivals LA and San Francisco. The 49ers, worried about Joe Montana's back, agreed to give up two No. 1s in 1987, a No. 2 and NG Manu Tuiasosopo. The Oilers held out for the younger Michael Carter. Otherwise, it would have been Everett and not Steve Young following Joe there.

Everett would go on to quickly become a starter for the Rams, who made the playoffs in 1986. However, he never turned into the star they hoped for. Eventually, some LA fans started referring to him as "Chris" because of a perceived lack of toughness.

The Oilers immediately put Hill at RG where they had already tried Schumacher, Kelley, Moran, Williams and Salem. Harvey, who claimed he was being "treated like an ax murderer," was then immediately traded to Detroit and "the west coast" of Lake St. Clair. Glanville said he hoped Salem enjoyed "the lovely breeze blowing off the Detroit River." Herzeg hoped it sent a message.

Next up was KC. Only Houston could hold a team to 34 yards and no pass completions in the second half, and lose 27-13. It was the same old story — penalties, turnovers, dropped passes and sacks. The Chiefs got to Moon seven times. They also lost promising OLB Frank Bush to an injury that would force him to retire.

It was the same thing against Pittsburgh as they played well but lost 22-16 in OT behind 6 more sacks of Moon. After four games, they had 59 first downs to 30 for their opponents. They led the other guys in yards per game (354 to 230), completion percentage (58% to 37%) and touchdowns (8 to 5). Yet they sat at 1-3. It seemed mathematically impossible.

They kept it up against Detroit with 454 yards to the Lions' 234, but lost 24-13. Moon, who had 400 yards passing, said, "When I get good protection, I can be a bitch." After losing Munchak for the year and the next game to the Bears (a 20-7 loss), they were 1-5.

Incredibly, the defense was No. 1 in the AFC and making a name for itself with some hard hits. They knocked so many QBs out that most of their opponents lost the week after playing them. But they hurt themselves with penalties, especially late hits and roughing the passer calls. Moreover, they were not getting any help from the refs. They complained that the Bears did the same thing to no flags. They were, once more, on their way to being the most penalized team in the league.

In a surprise, Herzeg dealt Larry Moriarty to the Chiefs for a draft pick. He was considered a hard worker and leader. But his 1985 holdout hurt the team and Herzeg never forgave him. In his view, with Ray Wallace coming off the IR and Butch Woolfolk also available as a FB, Moriarty was expendable.

On October 19, the Oilers discovered another new way to lose. With 1:30 left, they took their first lead against Cincinnati on a 93-yard fumble return by Lyles. With the offensive players dancing on the sideline, Boomer Esiason calmly drove the field against a prevent defense. With 43 seconds left, James Brooks outran Bo Eason for a 21-yard TD and 31-28 victory. "I guess maybe we celebrated too early," offered Moon. Williams said, "I've never been on a team with such bad luck. It's like the wrong thing always happens at the wrong time." It hurt Houstonians who had just seen the Mets eliminate the Astros in the baseball playoffs.

The media, full of hype before the season, turned vicious. Robertson called them the "masters of disasters." McClain wrote that "a 2-year-old could predict" the plays. Blinebury called them "a half-baked franchise that is lucky to show up for games on time, let alone win them." He added, "The only thing duller than the head coach's wardrobe is his offense ... their GM, who could not see the .500 mark without a telescope, likes to brag about his job security."

It reached a fevered pitch after two more losses. After 9 games, Hugh Campbell was 4-5. Glanville was 1-8 (and 1-10 overall). Fowler wrote that their only hope was "amassing enough talent to overcome the coaching. With 22 All-Pros on the roster, the Oilers *might* have a shot at a wildcard playoff spot ... no coach, no matter his talent, can create this kind of shambles without help, and Herzeg has given his little black-clad bobo Glanville loads of it." Blinebury wrote, "Eight is enough, so now's the time to fire Glanville."

This time the tribal drumming expanded beyond the papers. The Monday following the eighth straight loss, the sports directors for each of the three major TV stations went on the air with harsh commentaries. It was an unusual event in that it was not coordinated, but seemed that way. NBC's normally reserved Ron Franklin addressed Adams. "No more accountants, no more

GM Ladd Herzeg stole five-year veteran Drew Hill (5'9, 170) from the Rams in 1985 for a couple of low draft picks. Hill immediately connected with Moon, posting career highs in 1985 in receptions (64), yardage (1,169) and TDs (9). He remained Moon's top target for the next 6 seasons. In 7 years in Houston, he never had less than (nonstrike years) 64 catches or 938 yards. He led the AFC in receiving yards in 1987 and 1988, and placed in the top 5 in every other season with Houston. He tied for the AFC lead in total receptions in 1990 and placed second in 1991.

yes men," he said. ABC's Bob Allen (who Glanville described as, "that little, short, fuzzy-head guy") called on Herzeg to step down. "The failure of the Oilers rests squarely on your shoulders. The Houston fans deserve better. Enough is enough," he said.

Milk-shake breath agreed. "It's time for the Oiler hierarchy to step forward and look into a mirror," said Giff Nielsen, now the main man at the CBS affiliate. He accused Herzeg of "manipulating the system to get Bum Phillips fired. Ladd, please step aside." Glanville, he said, "can't recognize the limitations of his players and put together game plans to maximize their talents. Jerry, please step aside." To Bud, he said, "Take a look [your team] is going down the tubes. Do something about the mess you helped create!" Giff, who also doubled as the team's radio analyst, said later, "I've sat up there and done games for two years. I've seen how the team has talent but doesn't use it properly. It's very frustrating."

Moon was also unhappy. He pointed at the play calling. Against the Dolphins, 18 of their first 20 plays were runs. Asked if he had confidence in Glanville, he replied, "Little as an offensive coach." The game plan made sense on paper. Moon had thrown 18 interceptions in nine games and the Dolphins had the worst rush defense in the league. However, in the end, all they proved was that they could not run on anyone. In fact, the Oilers did not have a 100-yard rusher all season. Miami won 28-7 with Moon in self-described "handcuffs."

So the coach and QB had a touchy-feely session and agreed Hill and Givins were the biggest offensive threats on the team. They pronounced, "We understand each other better now." The next game, the offense came out aggressive and gambling. Moon was 25-of-44 for 310 yards as they beat Cincinnati 32-28.

After losing to Pittsburgh on penalties that called back a TD and a FG, Williams said, "It's a nightmare that just won't end." The following week, the Oilers bought a former NFL ref to practice to grade them. He threw no flags.

That brought up the terrible Colts and a small watershed. As usual, Houston dominated the first half, but led only 10-3. In the lockerroom, Glanville pleaded for more. This time, he got it. "We were hitting them the first half," said LB Grimsley, who replaced Riley in Week 7, "but we had to turn it up a couple of notches and make them say, 'Jeez, these guys are trying to kill us.' Hitting like that makes a team give up." They won 31-17 before 31,792, the smallest crowd since the strike season.

They played tough against the Browns in Cleveland the next week, taking them into OT. Kosar was just 16-of-41, but Houston lost 13-10. Rozier joined Woolfolk on the sideline for the rest of the year. Glanville sensed his defense had turned the corner. "Some players on defense," he said, "like Meads, I think their voices changed ... I think we're on our way."

After losing to San Diego without Moon, they clocked playoff-hopeful Minnesota 23-10. Moon was 22-of-37 for 280 yards in only his second game without an interception. "We've knocked two teams out of the playoffs," said Matthews, "the Vikings and the Oilers."

Herzeg and Glanville were both taking serious fire from the media in 1986. It was during this period that Jerry started wearing black clothing on the sidelines, and both men made a point of displaying open affection after games.

In the finale, they beat the Bills 16-7, sacking former Houston Gambler Jim Kelly 6 times in his old home. One player called the game "our Super Bowl." It was their first two-game win streak since 1980 and first 4-game home win streak since 1979.

They finished 5-11 again. While cleaning out his locker, Steve Brown summed up the feelings of many as he said, "I hate the media, but Merry Christmas anyway."

The Cowboys, who had not won a playoff game since '82, went 7-9 and out of the playoffs. It was their first losing season since '64. The best AFC teams were Cleveland (12-4), who twice beat Houston by 3 points, and Denver. Those two played a memorable AFC Championship Game with John Elway, stealing it in OT for the Broncos. He was no match for the latest NFC bully, though, the Giants. Trailing 10-9 at the half, Bill Parcel's team erupted in the third quarter and ran away with a convincing 39-20 victory.

OVERVIEW

There were two turning points to the '86 Oilers' season, one good and one bad. The first came on September 14 against the Browns on the Langhorne TD. After the undefeated preseason and accompanying hype, it let the air out of them. "I don't know what I was thinking," said Eason, who was beaten in single coverage. "We were looking at a playoff season. One play ... and everything went bad." Glanville echoed that sentiment. "If it wasn't for that game," said the head coach later, "I believe we would have had more confidence in ourselves. And who knows how far it would have taken us?"

They lapsed into a familiar rut. Mike Stensrud, who ended up in Minnesota, had this take: "At certain key positions, they've got some people who are satisfied with mediocrity. And that hurts them ... A few are satisfied with losing and they know it."

The second turning point came in early November after the Miami game. In that one, the Oilers were determined to run. Moon was a decoy. Despite all the money in the OL, they faltered against the worst DL in football. Local media went ballistic, as did Moon. The QB came away with a more wide-open offense as Givins and Hill gave teams fits down the stretch. Moon went 4-2 over his last six starts. "It sort of makes you wonder," said Givins, "what would have happened if we'd done this early in the season too."

Although he had a club record 3,489 yards, Moon was the lowest rated QB in football. The bugaboo was his league-high 26 interceptions compared to just 13 TDs. That was the primary cause of the team's poor give-away/take-away ratio of minus-11. Moon's response was, "Statistics are for suckers."

The importance of being Ernest: The Oilers added another undersized but gifted receiver in 1986 with second-round pick Ernest Givins (5'9, 172) of Louisville. Like Hill, he would immediately become one of Moon's favorite targets, which helped him put up some eye-popping numbers for a rookie with 1,062 yards (career high) on 61 receptions. He and Hill were the top receiving duo in the NFL that year and the next. Ernest was also consistent. Through 1993, he did not have a (nonstrike) season with under 55 receptions or 787 yards.

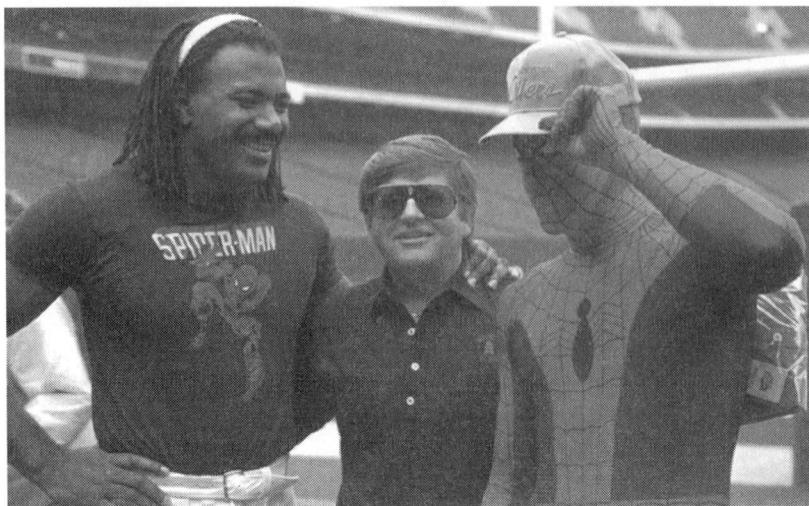

TE Jamie "Spiderman" Williams was a solid addition in 1984 when he had 41 catches for 545 yards. Those turned out to be career highs. With a woeful line and expensive QB, he was required to do more blocking and less receiving with each season. His production fell to 39 receptions in 1985, 22 in 1986, 13 in 1987 and, finally, 6 in 1989.

On the bright side, Hill and Givins each had over 1,000 yards receiving. Drew caught 65 for 1,122 yards, while Ernest had a great first year with 61 and 1,062. Rozier started the first 13 games before tearing an MCL. He led the team with 662 yards. His high game was only 85 yards (Bears) and he had a poor 3.3 yards per carry average. The Oilers had gone 23 games, longer than any other team, without a 100-yard rusher (Earl Campbell had 41). The offense was third from the bottom in scoring and tenth overall in the AFC (out of 14).

Heading into the late '80s, they were supposed to have an all-star O-line of LT Matthews ('83, 1st), LG Munchak ('82, 1st), C Romano ('82, 2nd), RG Steinkuhler ('84, 1st) and RT Salem ('83, 2nd round). This group played together in these positions once — part of one game in 1984. The Salem trade ensured it would not happen again. Steinkuhler missed part of '84 and all of '85 with a knee injury. He played '86 at RT. Romano played hurt in 9 games in '86 and needed more surgery after the season. Munchak played in 6 games in '86. Only Matthews finished '86 at his designated spot.

The defense, playing with the same scheme for three years, completed a remarkable turnaround to rank first in the AFC (7th in the NFL). While the rush defense was still in the lower half, opponents' yards per carry declined from an NFL high 4.8 in 1985 to 3.8 in 1986 (6th in the AFC). The pass defense was No. 1 in the AFC.

No Oiler finished in the top 11 in sacks. Childress led the team with just five, which brought up the defensive coaches' unwillingness to play William Fuller. While young, he was the best pass rusher on the team, yet played behind Byrd. With Byrd injured at the end of the year, Fuller finally got to play and played well.

A bright spot was the impact of the 1984 class at LB. Johnny Meads, back from knee surgery, and Robert Lyles were playing well at OLB, while John Grimsley took over at ILB to lead the team in tackles. Their QB pressures resulted in opponents having the lowest completion percentage in the league. Grimsley said, "I think it might have something to do with the way we fly around the ball, the way we hit, the way we dish out punishment."

Glanville's enthusiasm also aided the good finish. He kept his young team energized and eager to play despite their record. In previous seasons, they would not have recovered. Although he did complain during the season about some of the calls, he generally did not make excuses. Glanville said, "If you're not in the playoffs in the NFL, you didn't get the job done."

There was an inhumane string of penalty calls. They also lost, at various points for the season, 11 starters, including Munchak, Romano, Rozier, Woolfolk, Smith, Bush, Wallace, Eason and Kelly. Bush was the Oilers' most promising LB since Brazile, but his playing career was over. He and Childress made the all-rookie team.

GLANVILLE'S TAKE

Years later, Glanville indicated the problem with the team he inherited was simple — "personnel." While this notion was counter to the opinions of the locals, the rest of the NFL and the national sportswriters agreed, as no Oiler made either the Pro Bowl or All-Pro.

Glanville wrote in *Elvis*, "We had the slowest receivers in the NFL. Our whole division had turned into a bump-and-run, man-to-man conference, and here we were with the slowest receivers in the league." He said he had a TE "who told me he would prefer not to do much blocking. 'I don't mind blocking, as long as I'm not running right at the guy,' he explained. 'I'm a better blocker when I can sneak up on somebody.' I'd never seen a 250-pound tight end sneak up on *anybody*. I wasn't smart enough to design an offense to help this guy."

He continued, "We had running backs who would run out of bounds rather than bang it up inside for an extra yard. When they did run inside, they ran with their eyes closed. Our offensive line hated our backs worse than our opponents' defense. Our backs would just close their eyes and go, run right up the backs of the offensive linemen. Our linemen had cleat marks all over their backs. 'Jeez, Coach,' Mike Munchak said one day, after he'd been smeared again by the same back. 'Can't we just ask him to run *through* the holes?'"

Although he did not name names, the roster WRs in 1985-86 were Mike Aikiu, Steve Bryant, Willie Drewrey, Ernest Givins, Drew Hill, Mike Holston, Tim Smith, Steve Tasker and Herkie Walls. By 1988, only Drewrey, Givins and Hill remained (Buffalo snagged Tasker off waivers). The TEs in '85-86 were Chris Dressel, Mike McCloskey, Jeff Parks and Jamie Williams. In '88, only Williams remained. Among RBs, the 1985-86 teams had Chuck Banks, Stan Edwards, Larry Moriarty, Hubie Oliver, Allen Pinkett, Mike Rozier, Ray Wallace and Butch Woolfolk. By 1988, only Pinkett and Rozier remained.

The coach wrote that he felt he had a good nucleus in Rozier, Hill, Matthews, Munchak, Steinkuhler, Pennison, Lyles and Meads. He also singled out rookies Givins and Pinkett. Noticeably absent was Moon, whose name does not appear anywhere in the book.

Glanville believed they were about to arrive. Of the 11 losses in '86, four were by a total of 15 points and two more were in OT. He said he did not worry about criticism. "I grew up in the projects (in Detroit)," he said. "When I was 11, I got shot."

Glanville claims he received an offer to coach another NFL job at the end of '86. He went to Herzeg and Adams and "offered to let them off the hook." They not only reassured him but gave him a raise. "I think some in the media come after me because they want Ladd fired," he said.

Those two made a point of being seen walking off the field arm-in-arm after games. "When Jerry took this team," said the GM, "it was really in chaos, attitude and morale-wise. What he's done is a great job of getting everybody on the same page."

FAN REACTION

Fans were cynical. After being set up again by the undefeated preseason and cheerleading in the newspapers, their beloved turned out to be the same old unorganized and uncommitted group they always were. Since Phillips, they had strung together consecutive records of 7-9, 1-8, 2-14, 3-13, 5-11 and 5-11. The only teams they had not lost to were the Cardinals and Seahawks. They finished in last place five years in a row. From 1981 through 1986, they had a 3-39 road record.

It hurt just to watch. Every game was like bad theatre with a predictable plot and poor actors. They came out fired up and playing tough early. Then something would go wrong and boom — it would snowball. An onset of penalties, dropped passes, missed tackles, interceptions and blown coverages always ensued.

Was it a curse? Most of their players came from the winning college programs of the day, such as Nebraska, Penn State, USC, Oklahoma and Notre Dame. Yet, when they got to Houston, they lost. Even Kent Hill, who was a Pro Bowler for 5 years, started jumping offsides within a few weeks of arriving in Houston.

Two of the first three home games were sellouts (Cleveland, Chicago). But when they tanked, so did attendance. The last four home games — all wins — (Cincinnati, Indianapolis, Minnesota, Buffalo) averaged only 32,000.

The lack of sellouts garnered much media attention. No doubt the Hindenburg nature of the team's fortunes played a major role. There was another factor. Sellouts in Houston are traditionally determined by the walk-up crowd. The day-of-game, Friday paycheck fan is usually what pushed them over the top. In the mid-'80s, this fan was reeling.

Oil fell below $20 per barrel (each $1 dollar drop in the price per barrel cost the state $100 million in revenues). It hit Houston hard. The real estate market began to collapse. Long-time Houston retailer Sakowitz filed bankruptcy, and even Gilley's was in trouble .

Another factor was the Astrodome, which had the fewest "good" seats in the league. Those seats rarely changed hands. The remaining 30,000 seats did. When the team was hot, fans bought the bad seats just to get inside. When the team was crappy, obstructed view seats were hardly worth the price.

Nonetheless, Bud still sold well over 90% of his tickets. Herzeg said that a lot of people were wrongly "wrapped up in the attendance counts. Those really aren't the important economic bottom line. What's important is that we were selling between 95 and 97 percent of our tickets despite the fact that we were putting a poor product on the field. The fans bought the tickets, then chose not to come."

One might reasonably assume that those circumstances, combined with the fact that Bud had one of the lowest payrolls in the league, would have made Adams content. That theory would soon be tested.

1987: SUCKERS SUCH AS YOU

About the only item the team gave its community to rally around was finding someone to blame. Herzeg became the focal point. He was blamed for the Bum ax and destruction of Love Ya Blue, the latest parade of coaches, the draft bobbles (Dickerson led NFL in rushing 3-of-4 years) and the string of losing seasons. He was the lightning rod of lightning rods in Houston.

The press was mean. One writer described Ladd as "a pompous, big-headed, little boy." Fowler wrote that so long as Adams continued to get 1/28th of the television revenues, he had no "financial incentive to move Herzeg out and hire a capable man to run the club." He claimed Herzeg was "not secure enough to bring in a top-notch coach." Fowler encouraged fans to stay home. He claimed that nothing would change so long as "suckers such as you buy tickets."

THE VIEW FROM THE HOT SEAT

Herzeg admitted, "Bud is embarrassed. So am I. Neither of us enjoys this. We don't like the prospect of going out in public."

He was quick to remind anyone who would listen of the whys and hows of Houston's predicament. There was more to it than just the coaching change. He thought most of his transactions were good ones.

In a memorable press conference complete with pie charts and graphs, he said the first thing to remember was that the team that existed when he took over was old. The 1980 Oilers were the oldest team in football.

The future was mortgaged. Sid Gillman and Bum Phillips used veterans to turn the program around. To get them, they gave up their tops picks. From 1974-81, the Oilers traded away over half (55%) of their picks in the first five rounds. Over that eight-year span, they only had 18-of-40 picks in rounds 1-5, and just 26 choices overall. That is a record only George Allen could top. By comparison, the Bengals had 100% of their rounds 1-5 choices and 62 choices overall. The Steelers had all but one of their 1-5 picks and 49 choices total.

Houston wallowed in a vicious cycle. They were grooming no young players. To keep the team playing at a high level, they had to have more veterans, which meant surrendering more draft picks. That style of managing will catch up with a team. An argument can be made that Phillips's ouster saved him from the inevitable big crash, which helped ensure his legendary status in local history.

In 1982, Herzeg committed to rebuilding through the draft. There would be no more picks for veterans. From 1982-85, the Oilers kept almost all of their picks, having 31 overall compared to Cleveland's 21 and Cincinnati's 24.

It was a painful process. As the decade unfolded and the remaining foundation of Phillips' players moved on, Oiler teams became a patchwork of veterans on their last legs, stopgap free agents and rookies. The team became younger each year.

"I'm not going to say every move I've made has been right," Herzeg said, "but I think if you examine my personnel decisions over the last six years, you'll agree I have a high percentage in doing things right."

By 1986, only two players from the '80 squad were still on the team (Baker, Smith) and they were the youngest team in the NFL. The average experience among starters was three years on defense and four on offense. Among 1986 playoff teams, the Raiders had 23 players with 5-12 years of experience, the Broncos had 21 and the 49ers had 22. The '86 Oilers had 8 players with that much experience. By 1987, the two most senior Oilers were from the '82 draft.

Herzeg was upbeat. Except for what he called the "regression" of 1985, he thought they were "on the right track." The number-cruncher had the stats. On offense, they had more net yards and more first downs while surrendering fewer sacks. Overall, the offense improved to No. 16 in the NFL (from No. 24 in '85), the rush offense to No. 19 (vs. No. 25) and the pass offense to No. 13 (vs. No. 19). On defense, they had 28% fewer penalties. Overall, the defense was No. 13 (vs. No. 27), the rush defense No. 20 (vs. No. 28) and the pass defense No. 8 (vs. No. 18). While still losing, they were not losing by as many points. Although 1-5 in the division, two of the losses came in OT, while the other three were by 3, 3 and 11 points.

He said, "We could trade our two first-round picks for a veteran player or two and it would help us get to 8-8 or 9-7 next year. But that's not our goal. We want to win it all, and to do that, you have to continue to draft well and stay with those players."

He had Adams' support. "I have a better than average general manager," Bud said with a smile, "especially in his ability to negotiate with players and agents ... He's the best in world. He'll always have a job here."

While they had high expectations, no one could foresee all that was about to happen. It would turn out to be a wild year with another player strike, replacement teams, a drawn-out threat to move the team, acrimonious holdouts by Matthews and Highsmith, a feud between Glanville and Noll, and an embarrassing incident in Buffalo. Almost overshadowed by everything else, the Oilers would sneak back into the playoffs.

THE 1987 DRAFT

The Oilers invited fans to enjoy the team's draft festivities in the lovely Maple Room on the lobby level of the Quality Royale Inn. The Oilers assumed the position with the No. 8 overall selection. They had 4 picks in the first 2 rounds (4 of the top 36) and 14 choices overall. Their needs were clear. They had to get defensive help, particularly a pass rusher and MLB. They also needed to get Moon better protection. Naturally, they drafted a FB and WR.

The first pick was Vinnie Testaverde by the Bucs, who first made room for him by trading Steve Young to the 49ers. Cornelious Bennett was second by the Colts, but ended up in Buffalo. Houston tried to swing a deal for him with its many choices, but failed. They also looked at ILBs Shane Conlan and Mike Junkin. Instead they traded up with Buffalo at No. 3 to take Miami FB Alonzo Highsmith.

At 6'1, 235-pounds, Highsmith was a load who could run a 4.5 and catch the ball. He was the best back available and highly coveted. To make the move, Houston gave up a second-round pick (Salem trade). Buffalo took Conlan with Houston's first pick and Nate Odomes with the other. Cleveland took Junkin at No. 5.

With their other first-round choice, Houston took NC State WR Haywood Jeffires (Everett trade). Jeffires (6'2, 198) was the top-rated WR and would give Moon a bigger target. Hill and Givins were not amused in light of their 1,000-yard seasons but Glanville said, "For the quarterback's sake, we wanted to get one receiver who doesn't qualify as a jockey."

The rest of the first round included Reggie Rogers (No. 7), who was on the Oilers' list, Jerome Brown (No. 9), Rod Woodson (No. 10), Harris Barton (No. 22) and Bruce Armstrong (No. 23).

Glanville said, "It's interesting that we got the best fullback and Cleveland got the best inside linebacker (Junkin). You can look for those two players banging on each other for 10 or 11 years." Actually, the two that would go at it for years would be Woodson and Jeffires.

The vision Jerry Glanville had for his offense was made clear when the Oilers traded high draft picks to move up to select a fullback — Alonzo Highsmith of Miami. Highsmith was a unique combination of size (6'1, 235) and speed (4.5 forty) who could be both a devastating blocker and serious threat with the ball. After a tumultuous first season, he put together solid back-to-back years in 1988 (466 yards and 5.0 yards per carry) and 1989 (531 yards, 4.1 per carry and 6 TDs). However, bad knees, a tendency to drop the ball (7 fumbles in '88 and 6 in '89) and the Run 'N' Shoot ended his once-promising Houston career.

St. Louis was supposed to take Woodson at No. 6, but selected QB Kelly Stoufer in another of their bad draft moves. This bungle, though, would cost Warren Moon many sleepless nights as the Steelers, who were set to take Jeffires at No. 10, drafted Woodson instead.

Other Oiler picks were Louisiana Tech LB Walter Johnson (2nd), Baylor QB Cody Carlson (3rd), LB Mark Dusbabek (4th), RB Spencer Tillman (5th), LB Al Smith (6th), LB Tony Caston (6th), LB Robert Banks (7th), WR Curtis Duncan (10th) and OT John Davis (11th).

The talent in the draft turned out to be better than advertised. Other selections included Tim McDonald (2nd), Christian Okoye (2nd), Baylor's Ron Francis (2nd), Dave Wyman (2nd), Eric Thomas (2nd), Winston Moss (2nd), Tennessee's Bruce Wilkerson (2nd), Mark Carrier (3rd), SMU's Jerry Ball (3rd), Henry Thomas (3rd), Michael Brooks (3rd), Baylor's Thomas Everett (4th), Steve Beuerlein (4th), Hardy Nickerson (5th), Greg Lloyd (6th), Ed Simmons (6th), Bo Jackson (6th), Dan Saleaumua (7th), Gene Atkins (7th), Harry Swayne (7th), Dennis Gibson (8th), David Grayson (8th), Kevin Gogan (8th), John Gesek (10th), Howard Ballard (11th) and Fred Stokes (12th).

In hindsight, the Oilers should have either traded up for Bennett or stayed put. At No. 8, they could have had their choice among three great players: DT Brown (to replace Smith), LB Conlan (to replace Abraham) or DB Woodson (to replace anyone). There would have still been a great FB available in the second — FB Christian Okoye ("the Nigerian Nightmare"). Highsmith held out well into the season and then sued the club. He played several seasons, but was cursed by bad knees and a tendency to fumble. Okoye played six years and once led the NFL in rushing. But at least Highsmith played. Four other backs taken in the first round flopped: DJ Dozier, Roger Vick, Brent Fullwood and Terrance Flagler.

The real miss was at LB where they used five of 14 picks. They should have taken Hardy Nickerson, who went 17 picks after Dusbabek (5th) and Greg Lloyd, who went three picks after Smith (6th). The opportunity costs tripled when those two joined Woodson in Pittsburgh's class of '87. They also hurt themselves in the trade with Buffalo by allowing the Bills to add Conlan and Odomes to Bennett, which transformed their entire defense. The Steelers and Bills would be two of the bigger thorns in the Oiler saddle over the next decade.

As it turned out, the Oilers would begin a long playoff run in 1987. Some of the '87 draftees played valuable roles on those teams. Despite the great run, the Oilers always fell short of their goals to the great dissatisfaction of everyone involved. Stated simply, the most direct reason for this failure was that the other teams had better players. Houston was always a couple of good ones short.

It did not have to be that way. With multiple picks in a surprisingly deep draft, the Oilers occupied a once-in-a-blue-moon position in 1987 to add the players who could push them over the top. Here is how the draft could have gone:

Rd.	Was (Overall Number)		Could Have Been		Made All-Star
1	FB	Alonzo Highsmith (3)	CB	Rod Woodson (10)	1988
1	WR	Haywood Jeffires (20)	S	Tim McDonald (34)	1989
2	FB	Highsmith (36, traded pick)	CB	Eric Thomas (49)	1988
2	LB	Walter Johnson (46)	DT	Jerry Ball (63)	1989
3	QB	Cody Carlson (64)	DE	Henry Thomas (72)	1992
4	LB	Mark Dusbabek (105)	LB	Hardy Nickerson (122)	1993
5	RB	Spencer Tillman (133)	LB	Al Smith (147)	1991
6	RB	Al Smith (147)	LB	Greg Lloyd (150)	1993
6	LB	Toby Caston (159)	DT	Dan Saleaumua (175)	1990
7	LB	Robert Banks (176)	S	Gene Atkins (179)	—

That list of 10 players includes two Pro Bowl CBs, two Pro Bowl ILBs, three Pro Bowl DTs, one Pro Bowl OLB and one Pro Bowl safety, plus another safety who played 10 years. Had Houston not been so obsessed with Highsmith, they could have ended up with a secondary for the ages of Woodson, Thomas, McDonald and Atkins. The Oilers could have had a LB crew of Al Smith in the middle with Nickerson and Lloyd terrorizing the outside. Ball, Thomas and Saleaumua could have rotated at the tackles with Smith, freeing Childress and Fuller to attack from DE. That would have been one heckuva good young defense.

Nor did it have to stop there. They still would have had enough late picks to stack the OL with Pro Bowlers Kevin Gogan, John Gesek and Howard "House" Ballard (all taken after Round 7). An Oiler O-line of Matthews, Ballard or Steinkuhler at tackle, Munchak, Gogan or Matthews at guard and Gesek or Gogan at center probably would have caused Chuck Noll to spontaneously combust.

JUST A GAME

The USFL was still affecting salaries even though it was out of business. This was especially true of rookie contracts. Tony Casillas had the biggest contract in 1986 at $4.2 million. In 1987, Vinnie Testaverde's was worth $8.2 million. Average salaries since 1970 looked like this:

    1970 $23,200
    1975   39,600
    1980   78,700
    1985   193,300

By 1990, the average would be $355,887.

Meanwhile, television revenues were decreasing. The latest package was worth $15.6 million per team over three years, representing a 3.3% decrease ($650,000 per team) over the 1986 amount.

On the other hand, the Super Bowl had become a cash cow. Each 60-second commercial (26 total) was worth $1.1 million. There were 18 minutes of pregame blurbs at $300,000 each and six minutes of postgame commercials at $700,000 per minute. NBC had 150 technicians and 24 cameras at work. The 1986 game was seen in 31 foreign countries and over the Armed Forces Radio and TV Service

Surprisingly, the Oilers were a popular TV draw. Going into the 1987 season, 18 NBC affiliate stations carried them, second most in the AFC behind Miami and Denver (with about 25 each). They had a good part of Texas, including Houston and San Antonio, plus part of Louisiana (Lake Charles and Shreveport). Opting out were Dallas, Ft. Worth, Lubbock, El Paso and Amarillo.

1987 TRAINING CAMP

The draft caused the usual temporary optimism, but reality soon arrived. It was still the Oilers and they were coming off another losing season. Houston's pride had managed a cumulative five-year record of 16-57, worse than the Bills (20-53), Colts (19-53-1) and even Tampa Bay (17-56).

There was the customary holdout by the No. 1 choice. Highsmith wanted more than Everett got from the Rams. Bruce Matthews compounded the tension by holding out again. Matthews, who had a disk removed from his spine in the off season, was one of eight offensive players coming off surgery. The others, Moon, Rozier, Munchak, Steinkuhler, Romano, Kent Hill and Wallace, all had knee surgery.

There were some changes on the coaching staff. Glanville fired 59-year old OL coach Bill Walsh who had 26 years as an NFL assistant. It was an open question whether, considering all the injuries, he was responsible for the line's poor play. On one hand, Munchak made the Pro Bowl; on the other, the rest never fired off the ball, resulting in a rotten running game. They also gave up too many sacks. Moon was sacked 47, 46 and 41 times over the last three seasons for 1,069 yards of losses. Perhaps worst of all, they drew constant flags. "False start" seemed to be their motto. Kim Helton replaced him.

June Jones replaced Gary Huff to become Moon's fourth OC in 5 years. Jones, 34, played QB at Atlanta when Glanville coached the defense. They became friends. Glanville said he wanted an offense that was aggressive and unpredictable. Jones, who once worked with Mouse Davis using the Run 'N' Shoot offense with the Gamblers, installed the "Red" offense which employed four WRs. The "Red Gun" was the four-receiver set with Moon from the shotgun.

Personnel moves included Tim Smith traded to San Diego. The team's third all-time leading WR earned $300,000 to catch four passes in '86. He had become a liability against the man-to-man defenses played by all Central teams. They added additional picks for Dressel, who caught no passes in '86, and Romano.

The waived included RB Butch Woolfolk (last RB to gain 100 yards), WR Mike Aikiu ('85, 7th round), Chuck Banks ('86, 12th), DE Jesse Baker (although he would come back again) and OL Mike Kelley ('85, 3rd) who never really wanted to play anyway. That left Munchak and Abraham as team elders.

Glanville's relationship with local media personalities continued to decline through camp. He tried to have Giff Nielsen replaced on the radio team and refused to grant him any interviews. It seemed fair to Glanville since Nielsen tried to get him fired the previous November.

The media, in return, continued to flame rumors about Glanville's status. Their favorite candidate was Jackie Sherrill, head coach at Texas A&M University. They reported Adams had been going to Aggie games and had become close friends with Sherrill. In August, Adams' helicopter made a dramatic landing in the middle of the practice field and out popped Sherrill, to the delight of several reporters. They poured it on the rest of the year. Glanville's response was that airplanes dispose of their waste over College Station (sight of A&M campus).

The Oilers went 2-2 in the preseason, including an 18-13 win over Dallas. In the process, they found the missing Governor's Cup, last seen in '73, stashed away in a closet.

In another nobody-but-the-Oilers story, George Bush telephoned the coaches' office one practice looking for Glanville. Legendary equipment guy Bill "Mojo" Lackey took the call, saying, "I'm sorry, Mr. Vice-President, but Coach Glanville doesn't come off the field for nobody but Mr. Bud Adams." Mojo stood and saluted the entire call.

There were not many changes on the field. On offense, free agent Doug Williams replaced Matthews at LT, Pennison was at center and Wallace the FB. On defense, rookie Al Smith (6th round) replaced Abraham at one of the ILB spots. With Eason injured, Donaldson ('84, 9th) was the starting FS. Otherwise, the lineups were the same. Matthews and Highsmith held out well into the season. As the season opened, the players, coaches and fans were forced to endure another eruption from the owner.

THE JACKSONVILLE SAGA

In January, Bud Adams said, "I want to be more visible for the overall togetherness and pride of the club." His intentions became clear in June.

That is when stories began to hit that the Oilers were in preliminary discussions with officials from Jacksonville, Florida, about relocating there. It was another crazy Oiler tale that started slowly but gathered momentum as it went along, eventually becoming a daily news item.

Jacksonville had long been in the market for a team to fill its empty 80,000-aluminum-bench-seat stadium, the Gator Bowl, on which they were losing over $500,000 a year on maintenance costs alone. Previous discussions with the Falcons, Saints and Colts had failed. At the winter meetings, they issued an open offer to all 28 teams, guaranteeing 10 years of sellouts.

Jacksonville claimed they had a football-crazy town, boasting the 1984-85 USFL Bulls averaged crowds of 46,000. Because they were small (ranked 61 as a TV market), they figured they had to steal an existing team rather than take their luck with expansion. They rationalized that it was not stealing if the team was already looking for a place to move.

The Oilers had been negotiating with the HSA for 18 months over the lease, due to expire in 1987. They complained about seating and the rug. The Dome seated just 47,695 during baseball season, increasing to 50,495 in October. That was lowest in the NFL and 18,000 fewer than the NFL median. The nine-year-old faded turf had exposed seams, and the cushion underneath no longer gave any protection from the concrete below. It was voted worst in the NFL three straight years by the NFLPA. Jerry Glanville said the turf "had seams so wide that small guys, like Ernest Givins, would fall in and be lost for days." Players called it "the green driveway."

Nonetheless, considering their history, an attack on the Astrodome by the Oilers was not exactly a good PR move. While inadequate, the Dome was still a part of the Houston identity and character. After Harris County Commissioners dragged their feet for one-and-a-half years, the Oilers looked East.

Jacksonville offered to rent the Gator Bowl for $25,000 per game ($200,000 per season). The Oilers would get the rights to 10,000 parking spaces for a dollar, 60% of concessions, 26 luxury boxes at $5,000 each and a promise to add 40 more. They could resell those items at a profit (the parking alone was worth $20,000 per game). In Houston, the Oilers paid 11.2% of their gross ticket sales for each game as rent ($750,000 to 1 million), received no revenue from concessions or the 55 luxury boxes, and almost nothing from parking.

Bud scheduled a trip to Florida in late June to discuss the matter with city officials, but canceled it due to the sudden death of his son (ruled a suicide). The canceled trip allowed Houston to catch its breath and make some decisions.

The most immediate question was whether they were worth any effort. In an article headlined "A new meaning for Go Oilers," *Post* columnist Charles Reinken wrote, "It's not that we wouldn't look kind of silly without a professional football team. The question is whether we have one now."

Given Bud's image, not many public officials were willing to stick their necks out for him. City Councilman John Goodner said, "I just wish they'd get their act together, get a winning attitude, look like they're trying …. If they'll do their part, I think Houston will get behind them like it did before. The street runs both ways, you know." The Chamber of Commerce trotted out statistics to show the devastating economic and psychological effects wrought on Baltimore and Oakland when they lost teams.

Many questioned Adams' sincerity. They saw a charade to get the Commissioners off their duffs. Jacksonville had been a pawn before. Others recognized the Gator Bowl had 30,000 more seats and guaranteed ticket sales.

Mickey Herskowitz offered early on that "Jacksonville's chances of enticing the Oilers" were "tepid at best," but added, with words that would ring just as prophetically 10 years later, when "you look at the deals struck by the Giants, the Chiefs, the Cowboys, the Patriots, the Lions — the list is endless — in obtaining their new digs ... you conclude that it is far cheaper to keep a team happy than it is to go out and attract a new one." Later, he grew somewhat testy, offering, "We would merely suggest anyone who believes the city can afford to lose this franchise and replace it with an expansion team should grow up."

Rice University tried to fill the void, offering its 70,000-seat football stadium which had better seats (for viewing, not sitting). Plus, it had the history, character and tradition arguably lacking in the "stale" Astrodome.

It needed work, but the design was so good that once improved, it would have been a great stadium. Except for the humidity which kept the Oilers from taking them seriously. The Oilers were convinced that fans pampered by the Dome would mutiny over Rice's great outdoors. In addition, there was a real question of who would fund those repairs. The Oilers would not.

Harris County Judge Jon Lindsay got the ball moving. He somewhat short-sightedly stated the county would "want a long-term lease from the Oilers — a 10- to 15-year lease, preferably 15. We don't want to do this and have them leave in 5 years." On July 15, the *Post* reported that the Oilers' Dome deal was "nearly done." Lindsay also indicated that he had been in contact with "the No. 2 guy in the NFL" about hosting a Super Bowl and was told "that if we get close to 70,000 seats in the Dome that they would like to come back here."

After nothing happened, there were trips back and forth to Jacksonville for Herzeg and Tommy Smith, Bud's son-in-law and executive VP. Their mayor flew to Houston with a delegation. Meanwhile, they continued to negotiate with the county.

At camp in July, Bud said, "Maybe we've outstayed our welcome in Houston. Maybe we should move along and start over. Let somebody else come in." The NFL estimated the J'Ville deal would be worth roughly $70 million more than if the Oilers stayed under the terms of the existing lease. Bud said if it came together, he "would be crazy" not to take it.

Harris County eventually agreed to most of the improvements. That shifted the focus of negotiations onto the landlord, HSA. The Oilers said the HSA only paid the county $750,000 per year for the Dome, thereby netting $2 million annually off them alone, not to mention what they made off the 200-plus events there each year. Herzeg said, "We're treated like a stepchild while they're (the Astros) a favorite son."

It was *almost* enough to draw sympathy for Adams. In the words of Jerry Glanville, "Every time he goes to a game this year in the Dome, it's gonna cost him about $700,000 to sit in his seat and watch the Oilers. You sit there awhile and think about that."

Making matters worse, a guy from New Jersey, John McMullen, controlled the HSA and Astros. That really drove the natives wild. Bud said that he hoped people would understand if they had to move because they "were unable to work out an arrangement with the South Jersey people." He demanded the same terms as the Astros. At a Rotary Club luncheon, he bellowed that his cause was "Equal Rights!" The HSA countered that the Oilers paid only $765,000 in rent in 1986. Somebody was not telling the truth.

With the *Jacksonville Times-Union* reporting a "done deal" and Oilers calling HSA's latest proposal a "slap in the face," stories started to surface that the Gator Bowl was structurally unsafe. The upper deck was crumbling and cracks dumped small waterfalls into the luxury suites. Prospects for the credit line also ran into problems.

Meanwhile, Adams stopped speaking to the Houston press, but told a San Antonio reporter he was considering moving there. "It would be a way for us to stay in Texas," said Bud. "I've been a Texan for 41 years and as the saying goes, once a Texan, always a Texan." Never mind that San Antonio did not have a stadium. A Jacksonville official called the report "humorous."

Pete Rozelle, still licking his wounds from losing to Al Davis in court over the Raiders' move, nervously stated, "I don't like the idea of the Oilers moving, because I think Houston is very important to the NFL. It's one of the two teams we have in the southwest, an area I think is very important." He refused to answer a question about whether Houston would get an expansion club if the Oilers moved. Houston was the AFC's and NBC's third largest TV market.

Adams next told a Florida reporter that if the Jacksonville deal fell through Phoenix was a likely option. This shocked officials there, who stated they were "leery" of people who "may not be serious." Asked about San Antonio, Bud said that was just "good conversation."

Adams then turned back to Florida. "I think of that first game, of those 80,000 people," he told a Florida paper. "I would look into the sky and say you've given me the Super Bowl in the first game of the season ... The Jacksonville Oilers. It doesn't sound bad." He then laughed and said, "We'll skim a little oil off the St. John's River to make it credible." Around that time, he circulated a secret memo to his employees to see who was willing to move to Jacksonville.

Jacksonville started preparing to sell tickets for the 1988 season. Their mayor said they were "in the drivers' seat," and he was "98% sure we" will get the Oilers. But as they met Bud's demands, he came up with new ones.

At the same time, McMullen announced the HSA had "done all we can do." Negotiations in Houston were stalled. Next, Pasadena (Texas) entered the sweepstakes by offering to build the Oilers a new 80,000-seat dome just for football. Bud toured the proposed locations by helicopter. On October 8, the Jacksonville mayor alleged his town was "only a signature away."

After admitting he never dreamed Jacksonville would comply with his wants, Bud announced he would make a personal visit, since he had never been there. J'Ville was thrilled. They planned a pep rally and local businesses printed a full-page ad with a large picture of Adams' face with lipstick marks drawn across his cheek.

The caption read, "We Love You Bud!" in large letters. Then Adams canceled the trip.

He finally visited on October 14, wearing a cowboy hat and silvered-toed boots, and toting a big cigar. He got the royal treatment and a key to the city. A five-car, police-escorted motorcade took the Adams family around to see the sights. But Bud did not sign.

When he finally did make up his mind, he chose not Jacksonville, San Antonio, Phoenix or Pasadena, but Houston. The announcement came on October 26, after the Atlanta game. The new deal was for 10 years, which would have some significance about 10 years later. The HSA wanted 20. The Oilers got a rent reduction to 9.5% of gross ticket sales, a graduated per customer concession fee, $3 each from 6,500 prime parking spaces and $2 net from the next 5,000 spaces, and a "high percentage" of in-stadium advertising revenues. The added value of the package depended on attendance, but was estimated at $750,000 annually.

The county agreed to not the new field and 10,000 new seats but also new luxury suites. Jon Lindsay received credit for getting it done. He said the $50 million in bonds would be paid back mostly with the hotel-motel tax, although some property tax money would also be used.

Adams said he was leaving on the table $60 to 80 million over a 10-year period. He denied "using" Jacksonville, and promised to "do everything I can to help them get an NFL team."

Jacksonville seemed to take it in stride, although one reporter started calling the Oiler patriarch "Mud Adams" and suggested he be nominated for an Academy Award for "his acting job while negotiating a possible move."

The deal did not magically make things right in Houston. Herzeg said the '87 crowds to date upset Bud "since we had a pretty good season last year." At the Falcon game, the first full-squad game (30,000), Bud said, "It's kind of hard for me to figure the city out. When you're winning, you'd think the people would come out to watch us. Maybe Houston's not a pro football town. Maybe they just don't want the Oilers. I don't know what it is."

Post columnist Lynn Ashby offered to explain. He wrote:

> The team draws poorly because it has one of the worst public relations images in professional sports. The reasons for such an unseemly situation are so well known as to require only the briefest of mention: the owner and general manager for years have had a unique way of saying and doing the wrong things. Firing Bum Phillips. Trading good players. Losing constantly ...

Bud Adams upon his return from touring Jacksonville, Florida (and presumably San Antonio, Phoenix and Pasadena).

Signs of the times. Amazingly, this scene would repeat itself in just seven years.

Put it on a referendum: *Would you mind the Oilers moving to Jacksonville if Houston could get another NFL franchise within three years?* Even the Oiler management would know the overwhelming outcome of such a vote...

[W]hat bedevils the Oiler owner and operators is a deep-seated apathy on the part of people who in other cities would be season ticket holders. This, in turn, gives the front office a justifiable bunker mentality. Then one feeds off the other.

What has happened has happened. We can't change the past, but now is an excellent time for the front office to step back and take a long honest look at the problem ... Blaming the press, the economy or a small stadium is foolish and won't solve anything.

In the end, Jacksonville got an expansion team, the Jaguars, who began play in 1995. Adams played a role in the franchise award. Phoenix got the Cardinals. Pasadena got nothing. San Antonio built a huge stadium, but has never been seriously considered for an NFL team.

THE 1987 REGULAR SEASON — HOUSTON'S TWO MOONS

Yes, there was a season. The opener came September 13 against Dickerson, Everett and the Rams. Before the game, Eric said he "still wouldn't want to play for Houston." Trailing 16-3, they staged a furious rally, scoring 17 points in the final 7½ minutes to win 20-16. Moon was 21-of-43 for 310 yards and two fourth quarter TDs. Everett was awful.

Then came a memorable game in Buffalo. With Rozier rumbling for 150 yards, the Oilers took leads of 17-6, 20-13 and 30-20. But Jim Kelly led the Bills to two penalty-aided TDs to win in the final five minutes 34-30. "We played dumb," came the familiar refrain from Jamie Williams.

Blinebury wrote, "And they wonder why half the population doesn't care if they pack up and move ... This isn't a football team, it's a disaster waiting to happen. It's a traveling comedy, managed by sad-faced clowns who ought to be wearing fright wigs and rubber noses instead of titles as executives."

That last line was a reference to what occurred the night before at the Oilers' hotel. Ladd Herzeg reportedly went downstairs to a wedding reception in gray sweats and no shoes to complain that the music was too loud for his sleeping team. This did not go over well and someone in the band soon made a remark about the Oilers. Fists flew. Herzeg ended up on top while

But for the play of the replacements, the 1987 playoffs were probably out of reach. Although none of the regular players appreciated this fact, at least a handful of fans did.

the groom's brother ended up with a black eye and swollen lip.

Ladd was handcuffed and arrested on misdemeanor assault charges. "I couldn't believe that it was the general manager of the Houston Oilers," said the bride. "He came in and mooned the reception twice." Others in attendance said Herzeg "appeared drunk." For his part, Herzeg "categorically denied" that he bared his better side to anyone. He even threatened to sue the matrimoonial couple for "smearing and dragging his reputation through the mud across the entire nation." A judge later agreed to drop the charges if he could manage to stay out of trouble for six months.

Fortunately for Ladd, a larger disruption was on the way. After the game, the players voted to go on strike again. The 100% salary rise since the last one was not enough (average of $102,300 in '82 vs. $205,000 in '86). The players liked to say, "Nobody is putting a gun to their heads, forcing them to pay these salaries." Yet whenever owners tried to bring their costs under control, the players would either strike or take them to court.

To the basic blue-collar football fan already sickened by shocking salaries and pampered lifestyles, million-dollar babies on picket lines seemed obscene, even worse when both sides said they did not want a strike. Football had come a long way. By 1987, it had obtained a grotesquely twisted importance in American society, one nobody wanted to tackle.

It was worse in Houston. How could players from a team with a five-year winning percentage of .274 argue they were underpaid? In the real world, such underperformers would be fired. But there was Warren Moon, who averaged over $1 million per year, smiling and holding a sign. Some regulars even threw rocks at the replacements at the practice facility.

This time, the players said it was for free agency. Unlike the last time, the owners fielded replacement teams. They were playing by the second weekend.

Houston went 2-1, winning at Denver and Cleveland. Before the Browns game, a pro union stadium guard refused to let the replacement Oilers in to practice. As the coaches turned their backs, their collection of wrestlers, corrections officers, truck drivers and a karate instructor *finessed* their way inside. During the game, a replacement player for whom there was no replacement separated his shoulder. "Tape me up," he said. Glanville wrote, "So we taped his arm to his chest, and he played the second half with one arm. He couldn't tackle, but he put his head down and butted the hell out of some people."

Although the games generally did not draw well, the networks carried them. That, combined with breaks in the ranks (like Joe Montana), doomed this strike. It lost steam around the time the Jacksonville saga was coming to a close. The union lost the battle but not the war.

The real players played their first game back on October 25 as Houston beat Atlanta 37-33 to move to 4-2. However, there was no joy as unsigned No. 1 pick Highsmith filed suit against Houston and the rest of the NFL in Miami. He was able to get a Florida state court judge to issue a dubious injunction temporarily making him a free agent. Herzeg had offered a four-year, $1.8 million deal. Highsmith wanted $3.2 million.

The Herzeg-bashers, who were sure Jim Everett and Bernie Kosar were on their way to the Hall of Fame, loved it. Robertson wrote, "No NFL GM has more difficulty signing his top picks. None." He put the Highsmith situation "on a par with fumbling away the rights to Kosar in 1985 and receiving zilch in return, a goof that made Herzeg an NFL laughingstock. Should he also lose Highsmith? Let's just say his reputation would then be beyond any possible repair."

Highsmith signed for $2.5 million and then ominously fumbled his second carry. With that situation quieted down, Matthews erupted. He wanted more than Munchak. Since Mike was a two-time Pro Bowler and Bruce was not, Herzeg refused. Matthews filed a $10 million lawsuit to bring down the entire NFL system while hanging out in LA. Desperate for an OT, the Oilers acquired Bruce Davis from Oakland. That caused Matthews to quickly end his one-man, 99-day strike ($1.55 million, 4-years) while complaining he was still very "unhappy."

Meanwhile, the 5-3 Oilers headed to Pittsburgh where they not won since 1978. The Steelers were using Mark Malone at QB, who Glanville described as a "used-up landmark." This was when the great Glanville-Noll feud began. At one time, Chuck liked Jerry enough to interview him for a position. That was about to change.

Glanville said it took no special effort to get his team fired up. The Steelers had beaten Houston more than any other team. He wrote:

> We lined up in the tunnel. Guys were bouncing on their toes, smacking their fists and breathing fire. You should have seen the looks in their eyes. It looked like somebody had given 45 guys at a mental institution a weekend pass ... The boos were deafening. 'Ladies and gentlemen,' the announcer said, 'let's welcome Gary Grandview and the rest of the Houston Oilers.' Every tackle we made in that game sounded like a car wreck. Pads were popping, helmets were cracking ... On the sidelines, I was smiling. We had

preached toughness. We had drafted toughness. And it was finally becoming reality on the field ...
Pittsburgh wasn't happy. They started getting angry. Five years earlier, if the Pittsburgh players had started roughing it up, our guys would've gone into a shell. Not anymore. Pittsburgh threw a few punches. Surprise! We punched them back. That really confused them.

Houston whipped them 23-3 on their home field. One-time great coach Chuck Noll ran around the field screaming. His face was red and his hair out of place. He had become a sad caricature of his former self. He accused the Oilers of late hits and of spearing "with the intention of ending people's careers." He said Glanville was behind it all and filed a complaint with the NFL. It was quite a turn of events for Oiler fans who could still remember Steelers safety Mike Wagner spearing Oiler TE Mike Barber in the 1978 AFC Championship Game, taking away Pastorini's main pass threat.

That brought up Cleveland in a battle for first. It was the biggest game in the Dome in a long time and the first time in 7 years they had been in playoff contention this late in the season. The sellout crowd was juiced. The Oilers talked a bunch of noise beforehand, but when game time came they were tight. They choked, trailing 26-0 at the half and losing 40-7. It was the third worst home loss in history. Fans were disgusted. They would remember this one. Moon was 5-of-23 to move to 0–7 lifetime against the Browns.

They had to try to pick it up against Dickerson again, now with the Colts. Indy blew them out 51-27 with Ron Meyer running up the score at the end. In the two-game collapse, they had surrendered 91 points. While

Jerry Glanville catches an earful from Chuck Noll as they exit Three Rivers Stadium on November 15, 1987, after a 23-3 Houston victory. Going back to 1978, the Oilers had lost nine straight there by scores of 34-5, 38-7, 27-13, 31-17, 26-13, 17-10, 35-7, 20-0 and 21-10. This meeting was a precursor of more to come.

While his offenses ranked higher in most statistical categories, it was defense —tough, swarming team defense—that Glanville's teams were known for. On December 20, after half the team hit him on a run up the middle in a close game, Steeler RB Frank Pollard reacted by throwing the ball at Richard Byrd. After the brouhaha subsided, the Oilers took the momentum and won 24-16 for their first sweep of Pittsburgh in 18 seasons.

the offense had 454 yards and Rozier 122, they lost Brown, Moon, Duncan, Steinkuhler, Munchak, Smith and Grimsley to injuries.

The press, which once called the offense "too basic," now said it was "too fancy." The Detroit rumors resurfaced. Robertson called their playoff chances "dead" and said to look for Sherrill. "You know what I told Bud?" responded Glanville. "I told him this is going to be the best coaching job in America and a lot of people are going to want it. Let Jackie get in line."

The Chargers came to town December 6. At the coin toss, Robert Lyles said, "Welcome to the House of Pain." It was pretty nervy considering their most recent home game was a 33-point loss. The Chargers were not impressed. Co-captain Steinkuhler also winced. But the Oilers creamed them 33-18 to kick off a long home win streak. Lyles said he took the idea from his martial arts "dojo," a place where pain was administered.

In a three-way tie for first at 7-5, the Oilers faced a stretch-run of New Orleans, Pittsburgh and Cincinnati. Win out and the AFC Central was theirs.

They lost 24-10 to a good Saints team headed for its first winning season (they finished 12-3). Ray Buck wrote that the Oilers were a team that "did not know whether to print playoff tickets or go and hide." They had to win the last two just to make the playoffs.

All of this made a fine backdrop for Noll vs. Glanville, Round II. Noll promised to personally settle the score if the league refused. He had a point. For example, they were hitting kickers. Glanville said, "Kickers wear a lot of lipstick and try not to get their skirts dirty." Patrick Allen was fined $5,000 for clocking the Colts' Dean Biasucci. Against New Orleans, Walter Johnson put a tough lick on Morten Anderson and he started spraying the ball around. It was legal but drew much criticism.

The Steelers tried to shove and trash talk Houston into fights the entire game. Things came to a head in the third quarter when RB Frank Pollard threw the ball at Byrd after being snuffed on a run. A large rumble ensued. Houston drew the momentum before a raucous crowd and won 24-16. At the gun, Noll ran after Glanville. He was hyperventilating. Clamping onto Glanville's hand, he wagged a finger in his face and yelled, "Your f—g guys coming over, jumping on people like that, are going to get your ass in trouble. Just know that." He filed another complaint and held more press conferences. It was the first time the Oilers swept the Steelers (18 years).

Jerry called Chuck "childish." He put together the video he had won of 8-10 cheap shots by Steelers players in the game, showed it to the press and sent it to the league office. He wrote later, "Here's a guy who coached Jack Lambert, Mean Joe Greene, LC Greenwood and he's telling me *my* guys are violent? ... Chuck's biggest problem wasn't the hitting. He just couldn't believe Houston had beaten him twice. I'm sure it made him want to slit his wrists."

Glanville credited the feud with establishing "Houston's identity. Thanks to Chuck Noll, the Oilers now had a reputation around the NFL as a team that wouldn't quit, wouldn't walk away from a fight. Chuck had given Houston the identity it had been looking for."

Houston was one of four teams tied at 8-6 going into the final weekend. Only Cleveland (9-5), Denver (9-4-1) and Seattle (9-5) had better records. Beat the erratic but dangerous Bengals and they were in the playoffs. Nonetheless, the media abused them. "Without the clutch of a 'replacement' season,'" they wrote, "the Oilers wouldn't be in serious contention for a playoff spot ... they would presumably be under .500 and going nowhere fast." Robertson blamed the strike for "the poor quality of play" in the NFL and resultant Oiler victories.

After building a 21-7 halftime lead, they held on to win 21-17 before a capacity crowd. Glanville got the Gatorade dump while Cincinnati finished 4-12 amongst rumors Sam Wyche might be fired.

The Oilers won 3-of-4 down the stretch to make the playoffs for the first time since 1980. But there was no joy in Mudville. The papers whined. A few players complained over the no-shows at the sold-out Bengals game (52,655 sold with 49,275 attendance). "People around here say, 'We'll wait until they win some games,'" said Pennison. "What kind of an attitude is that?"

Others were not excited with the idea that the replacement players might get a share of the playoff money even though they would not have made the playoffs without them. Millionaire Warren Moon said they should have something only "as long as we get our full share."

THE 1987 PLAYOFFS

The Oilers hosted their first playoff game in a long time with NBC announcer Paul Maguire proclaiming Pappasito's fajitas "the best in the country."

The Seahawks had to play without Curt Warner and Houston dominated with 437 net yards to Seattle's 250, including a 178 to 29 yards rushing advantage. Naturally, Houston almost lost as Steve Largent kept them in the game with 7 catches for 132 yards, including the game-tying TD with 26 seconds left. Seattle won the toss in OT, but the defense forced them to go 1-2-3 punt and the Oilers won it 23-20 on a 42-yard Zendejas field goal. It was the second home playoff victory in Houston since the merger and only the third in 28-years of existence.

A happy Glanville said his team was "on its way to San Diego," site of the Super Bowl. This set off a furor in Denver where the defending AFC champions had not lost a non-strike game. It drew criticism in Houston, too, but Jerry had reason to feel good. With Matthews and Davis in the lineup, Rozier running outside and Highsmith pounding the inside, the Oilers had developed one of the better running games while Denver had one of the poorer run defenses.

Fowler agreed, but he was just trying to set Glanville up. Ignoring the oddsmakers who made them 10-point underdogs, he wrote, "The Oilers should win ... Denver can claim a decisive advantage in just one (category) quarterback. That determination is no knock on Warren Moon ... (the Oilers hold) imposing advantages in the offensive line, running backs and secondary, and lesser edges in the wide receivers and defensive line." He credited Holovak.

The outcome was unalterably determined on Houston's first possession. After the defense held, Denver's punt went out at the Houston 5. The Oilers had extracted themselves from this very situation multiple times throughout the season on 15-to-20-yard comeback patterns to Hill or Givins. This time, they sent Highsmith up the gut on first for minus-1. On the play, however, Denver lost its fine SS, Mike Hardin, to a broken arm. A third stringer replaced him They thought it might just be their day if they could get out of this hole. That is when Glanville chose a gutsy but risky play that made him a laughingstock around the country and helped seal his fate as Oiler coach. He called on *Stagger Lee*.

Named after a blues song, the wacky play was designed to take advantage of confusion and mismatches. Rozier lined up 15 yards wide left behind OTs Davis and Steinkuhler and TE Williams. Moon set up in the middle of the field behind the center and OGs while the WRs went wide right. It had three options: a long lateral to Rozier, Highsmith up the middle, or a quick pass.

The Broncos had just one player on the line across from Rozier and a safety about 15 yards off the line. Going with no huddle, Moon took a quick snap, retreated one step and fired a bullet to Rozier, who was standing behind the goal line. It was a perfect throw. Glanville said, "When I saw how they were lined up, I was thinking a 20-yard gain. When I watched it on film, it could have gone for 30 yards."

There was just one problem: Rozier dropped it. He took his eyes off the ball for a split second. Since it was a lateral, it was a live ball. Somehow, the lone Bronco beat four Oilers to it. Two plays later, Denver took a 7-0 lead. On the ensuing possession, Moon threw an interception and Denver took a 14-0 lead. At that point, the Oilers abandoned their running game.

NBC replayed *Stagger Lee* over and over. It sucked the emotion out of the Oilers. Living up to their reputation, they lost their composure and finished with 10 penalties, many of which were for jumping early when Elway waved his arms in the shotgun. They also threw two interceptions in the end zone. Once, they even snapped the ball into the leg of the man in motion.

The offense moved the ball up and down the field the entire game. It just could not put it in the end zone. Houston had more first downs, more rushing yards, more passing yards and a better time of possession. They also trailed 24-3 at the half and lost 34-10.

A dejected Moon walks off the Mile High field after Stagger Lee.

Stagger Lee got most of the blame. They ran it only once before and it was not included in the film exchange. However, the one game was against the Steelers, and a vindictive Chuck Noll telephoned the Broncos' staff to forewarn them of it. In the end, however, it was Rozier's drop, not the defense, that ruined the play. Moreover, the 7-point deficit should have been no big hill for this offense. If Moon had not come right back with the interception, they might have been able to get the running game going, and have made a game of it.

Moon and Pennison questioned the call and even Bronco NG Greg Kragen said, "It seemed really stupid ... but that's Glanville for you." Fowler wrote, "Not content to restrict his comedy routine to Houston, Jerry Glanville went national ... Adding a stunning blue sweater to his customary dashing black, Glanville trotted out a play that put the country in stitches ... It capped a season of slapstick unrivaled since Laurel and Hardy."

Al Carter tried to put it in historic perspective. "What Glanville contributed to Houston sports tradition Sunday," he wrote, "was the most widely panned coaching travesty since Guy Lewis gave the 1983 NCAA basketball title to North Carolina State. 'At least Guy V. could roll out the basketballs,' a Colorado columnist noted. 'I don't think this guy could do that.' The national media laughed like hyenas when Lewis put the brakes on his high octane Houston Cougars and blew the game under the restraints of an offense called the 'Locomotion' ... Enter 'Stagger Lee,' destined to be a most requested oldie on Denver radio this week."

About the team, Carter wrote, "All the Broncos had to do was wait for the Oilers to go collapse under the weight of false grandeur. It was an ugly fall, reminiscent of so many of the Oilers' other past playoff blowouts. Remember Oakland 40-7 in 1967? Or Oakland 56-7 in 1969? How about Pittsburgh 34-5 in 1978? Chuck Noll smiled that day too."

Blinebury and Fowler reveled. Fran wrote, "If optimism were gold, Glanville would be a walking Fort Knox. But if brains were made of that precious commodity, he couldn't fill a tooth." While admitting the "Oilers have finally arrived," Ed complained "they should have obtained (this) level two years ago. By now, they should be serious Super Bowl contenders." He claimed Denver "had men in the starting lineup who couldn't have made the Houston roster." (The Broncos went to the Super Bowl). He called Glanville a "mean-spirited little man," and urged Bud to "give Herzeg and his bobo the hook."

Nor was Bud spared. A *New York Daily News* piece described "the Bud man" as all "full of Texas bluster" when he "leaned out over the edge of the window of the visiting owners box (first quarter), peered down on all the Bronco fans and whipped (his Oiler) towel in a frenzy over his head ... Looking so much like the football fat cat he is — his plump body stuffed in a blue custom-made suit, dark shades, gold cufflinks shaped like little footballs and a humongous watch with enough gold on it to wipe out the national debt of most third-world nations."

Finally, *Dallas Times Herald* writer Skip Bayless wrote, "Oh, them poor Oilers."

OVERVIEW

What a year. The momentum gained by winning 4 of their last 7 in 1986 continued into the draft where the Oilers had 2 first-round picks. They made what appeared to be good choices, but things soon started getting weird. They could not sign their No. 1 for the third year in a row. Then the Jacksonville caper arose. The season started off well until the GM disrupted a wedding in Buffalo the night before a game and was arrested. Then the players struck and Houston's replacements did something the regulars could not, win at Denver and Cleveland. The vets showed their appreciation by refusing to share any of their playoff money with the "scabs."

Houston fans, unsympathetic to whining millionaires, got behind the replacements. Eugene Seale and Brent Pease became crowd favorites ("Give Pease A Chance"). The only replacement game in Houston drew about the same. As soon as the veterans returned, Highsmith filed his lawsuit. He finally signed but made no significant contribution until the last game. In the meantime, "Mr. Oiler" Bruce Matthews sued the team and the league for $10 million.

All the while, the media abused Herzeg and Glanville. Then Chuck Noll jumped on the bandwagon and threatened to kick Jerry's butt. That feud became a national spectacle. So far as the season went, they could not beat a good team, losing to the 49ers and Saints and getting blown out by the Browns, Colts and Broncos.

Yet they did something no Houston team had done in a long time — win. Glanville said, "Up until 1987, the Oilers had been an automatic win on the schedule." They did more than win by making the playoffs, coming from last place to do it. They even took it a step further by winning a playoff game, something no Houston team had done since 1979.

Neither Glanville nor Herzeg got much credit locally. Not only did they quickly field replacement teams, Coach Jerry and staff did a very good job of molding them into a fighting unit, winning 2-of-3. The game they lost was to a Pats team of regulars. Once Houston's regulars came back, they managed to diffuse a potentially divisive situation and win 6-of-10.

The offense improved to eighth best in the NFL (5th overall in the AFC and 5th in scoring). The catalyst was the high-priced OL that finally came together justifying the replacement of Bill Walsh. Adding Matthews and Davis helped a lot. The rush offense ranked sixth in the conference. Rozier enjoyed his best year with 957 yards in 11 starts and a 4.2 yard average. He finished fourth in the NFL, and had five 100-yard games. He also had 27 receptions (3rd on the club) and made the Pro Bowl. Munch was the only offensive player named a starter.

Moon had 2,806 yards on 184-of-368 passing (50%). For the first time, he had more TDs (21) than interceptions (18). Those were the most TDs since Blanda's 24 in 1963. June Jones proved a good choice at QB coach as Moon established himself as the team leader. His three fourth-quarter rallies to victory helped quiet critics, but he still displayed the maddening tendency to make the bad pass at the worst time. Givins caught 53 for 933 yards while Hill had 49 for 989. Duncan was a nice surprise with 5 TDs, but No. 1 pick Jeffires had only 7 receptions. WR coach Milt Jackson did a good job as the passing game ranked sixth in the AFC.

The regulars averaged the most points since 1968 (23.0 per game). The turnaround could be charted directly back to the November 2, 1986, Miami game after which a humiliated Moon complained to the coach. Glanville pretended to ignore his QB, but rumor was that orders came from Adams to open it up. According to Herzeg, setting the offense free was something they discussed on the plane home. Whatever the reason, from that point forward, the Oilers played with a more wide-open offense, becoming one of the most exciting in the NFL for many years to come.

The defense collapsed from the AFC's best in 1986 to No. 11 (8th vs. the run, 9th vs. the pass). The pass rush was still a weakness as Childress led with just 6 sacks. Bostic (6 interceptions) made the Pro Bowl as a first teamer. Rookie ILB Al Smith led the team in tackles.

The Oilers were Dome monsters. Counting the Seattle game, they had won 11 of their last 13 home games. What gave them the playoffs was their 5-1 divisional record. That was something they had never done, even under Phillips. In 1986, they were 1-5.

WAS BUD BLUFFING?

"Whoever said they were leaving?," asked old No. 65 Elvin Bethea. "It was just a ploy to get things rolling here." Ed Fowler agreed and for years referred to the event as "the Jacksonville scam." He wrote, "We let (Adams and Herzeg) sucker us into believing that the team was on the brink of moving to this minor league city that seeks to be big-time." Ed called it "an ingenious negotiating strategy" and claimed the "media took the bait."

Could Bud and Ladd hatch such an "ingenious" plan? Not likely. The Oiler organization has never been sufficiently organized, committed and unified to execute any plan that flawlessly, let alone think of it.

What happened is that Adams was dissatisfied with the Astrodome. He always had been. In addition, the HSA was screwing him on the lease. After one-and-a-half years of negotiating, he came away with no concessions or firm commitments to make repairs or add seats.

So he sent Herzeg to speak with the Jacksonville people. Initially it was a tactic. Then the GM came back with better news than expected. It was enough to make Bud give it some attention. It became more serious when the Oilers asked Jacksonville to guarantee the money and they said they would. Adams admitted that he originally set his terms so high that he never thought Jacksonville had a realistic shot at meeting them. But they did, or most of them.

Thus, it was touch-and-go. He took his family to visit (they were not thrilled) and circulated a memo to see who would move there. But he really did not want to go. Glanville said, "Bud is a man who loves Texas and the Oilers are a Texas team. If he loved money, he'd be in Jacksonville right now. Bud belongs in Texas, and so does the team. I just can't picture him on a sailboat wearing Topsiders."

So what started off as good gamesmanship turned serious. It had to be painful for the Bottom Line guy to leave so much money on the table (estimates were anywhere from $5-12 million per year). Moreover, in the end, he still had a bad stadium that even with the added seats (all 10,000 were end-zone seats) would still be the second smallest in the NFL.

Bud said, "It would have been tough, really tough. Jacksonville made a great financial offer. But you don't easily uproot from the place you've called home since 1946." About the repairs, he added, "When everything is finished ... it will be one of the greatest domed stadiums in the country. The only thing that will keep the Astrodome from being No. 1 will be its size, and that's a limitation with which we have to live."

1988: THE HOUSE OF PAIN

The excitement was back leading up to the 1988 season. Bud said, "We've been rebuilding for the past five years through the draft and it's been a long, tough process, but I think last year was the turning point. We've got the talent now. It's a matter of the staff putting it all together ... I think we're geared up to go for the big one."

Sounding as lucid as he ever had, he said, "You can't be a winner all the time. Given the way the draft and our league are presently set up. You're going to have teams winning over a period of time, then you're going to have your down years, then you'll be back up near the top again. I would hope we're now back up for a series of anywhere from five to seven years before we become an old team again. You don't have many years in there to get to the Super Bowl, so the next three seasons are going to be key for us to go all the way."

About his goals for his team, he said he had just one main objective: "To give the community a team of which they can be proud. That's reward enough for me."

There were plenty of issues starting with the cheap shot — dirty player image. The main concern was the old adage of what goes around comes around. Besides Pittsburgh, other teams complained in '87, including the Saints, Colts and 49ers. One guy who never walked away from a fight, Lou Rymkus, said "It's going to catch up with them. It is getting around the league that this team hits late, tries to spear you, tries to hurt you." Jamie Williams said, "We still have to cut down on penalties. I think we've got the respect of other teams, so we don't need to beat guys up after the play."

Glanville said, "I was here under a different regime when if someone punched you in the mouth, you were ordered to turn around and walk away. We will not order our team to do that. That's not the way we're going to play." Childress added, "Nobody was crying when we were 1-8 and losing to them. I guess losing to the Houston Oilers is hard for some people to swallow."

Another issue was contract negotiations and holdouts. Herzeg employed a salary structure. Excluding QB, the scale began with Munchak. The others had a tough time, arguing they deserved more than Houston's only three-time Pro Bowler. Nor did Herzeg like to give in to holdouts. He thought any perception that they were being rewarded for holding out sent the wrong signal to the ones who signed and reported on time.

Some players viewed him as a little fascist. The word was he took care of the ones he liked behind the scenes but tried to publicly embarrass the others. Two examples often cited were Givins and Brian Sochia. Told they had one deal over the telephone, they were offered something less once they arrived. Things like that made it around, affected team pride and bred disloyalty. Players tended to want to play for themselves and maybe their teammates but not the organization. Players and management alike needed to address the situation.

Coaching was a third issue the press constantly revisited. Al Carter wrote, "To Bud Adams, (Houston) is both home and fiefdome. But the Middle Ages, rumor has it, are over. Super Bowls aren't won with jousting sticks and hard spearing. Neither are they won with the kind of low-grade management skills that have kept both Adams and Houston football on the bottom line for nearly three decades." He added, "The watershed has arrived. At the core of Oilers' disharmony is perhaps the most curious development of all: through no one's fault but their own, the Oilers have evolved into a group of superior football athletes. The talent gap between the players and their handlers, irrelevantly small in the past, now represents a discrepancy in commitment that neither patrons nor players can ignore."

Whether the coaching staff that had molded a last-place club into a playoff team in one season was now holding them back was hard to answer. Bud showed what he thought by giving Glanville a raise. "Mr. Adams said it was because of the two guys in the media who are always calling for me to be fired," offered Glanville. "He said he didn't pay me enough to put up with those two guys. He said, 'Every time they come at you, I'm gonna give you another raise.' Then he laughed and said, 'Those guys are gonna make you a rich man.'"

THE 1988 DRAFT

The Oilers had two first-round choices (Nos. 9 and 21) but no second (Davis trade). They needed DLs, and the '86 and '87 drafts notwithstanding, LBs. They also needed a safety, a breakaway RB, a punter, KR and OLs to groom. Local writer John McClain said, "If they take an offensive player (in the first), everyone associated with the draft should be fired."

They liked Neil Smith and tried to trade up, but KC beat them. In response, just before the draft, they traded their first No. 1 and a fourth-round choice to the Raiders for DE Sean Jones, a second-round choice, plus a swap of third-round positions. Jones, 25, led the AFC with 15½ in sacks in 1986 but tailed off in 1987. As the Raiders' player representative during the strike, he was expendable. The deal concluded the last segment of the Everett trade.

Atlanta blew the No. 1 on Aundray Bruce. The next five were Smith, Bennie Blades, Paul Gruber, Tim Brown and Sterling Sharpe. LA used the Oiler pick on DB Terry McDaniel. Available at the time were Michael Irvin (No. 11), Ken Harvey (No. 12) and Randall McDaniel (No. 19).

When the Oilers' choice rolled around, they were busy on the phones trying to trade down. There were so busy that they let their time expire, which allowed the hated Browns to jump ahead of them and take LB Clifford Charlton. Herzeg said, "We were talking to five different teams about a trade. We considered trading down for extra picks in the second round."

Art Modell blathered on about another Houston faux pas. An unnamed Oiler source responded that they did not want Charlton because his NFL IQ test score was so low. They quickly selected Michigan State RB Lorenzo White. At 5'11, 213-pounds, he was something of a Rozier clone. On the surface, it seemed as if they were drafting to strength. But the Oilers were privately concerned with Rozier's frequent tardiness and alcohol consumption, and Highsmith's knees. White was a tough, sturdy hard worker. He was also a good citizen. He made it in the NFL while Charlton did not.

Nonetheless, with Lorenzo, the Oilers passed up a load of great players, including Chris Spielman, Eric Allen, Thurman Thomas, Ken Norton, Jr., Dermontti Dawson and Gerald Perry. Had they been able to trade down, they might have come away with two off that list. Houston-area product Thomas, who would play longer and better than White, always juiced up his performances against Houston as payback for the slight.

They took S Quinton Jones in the second (LA trade). He did not sign until after the season, then flopped. With that choice, they passed Brian Blades, Michael Dean Perry, Dante Jones and Kevin Porter, any of whom would have been a much better choice.

They followed Jones with punter Greg Montgomery in the third, passing on Erik McMillan, James Hasty, Bill Romanowski, Tim Goad and Houston Hoover.

Sean Jones, White and Montgomery would each make the Pro Bowl at some point. However, had management assessed team weaknesses differently or altered player grades, they might have come away with Michael Irvin, Chris Spielman, Dermontti Dawson *and* Michael Dean Perry.

The rest of their choices included CB Cris Dishman and TE Chris Verhulst in the fifth, DB Tracy Eaton in the seventh and OL David Viaene in the eighth. They also took 3 more LBs: Kurt Crain (6th), Danny Spradlin (9th) and John Brantley (12th).

After the draft, Herzeg announced Holovak would be reassigned. "A big part of Mike's duties in his previous position was extensive travels," said Herzeg. "He will be 69 years old this season and we were concerned about that travel." Holovak said he felt fine. The press complained "the wrong man was being slowed down," and "through almost a decade of turmoil, controversy and revolving-door changes within the Oilers' gulag, Holovak has stood above it all, a beacon of class, stability and quiet dignity." Fowler complained that, "Immediately upon becoming head coach, Glanville went to work wrestling control of the draft from Mike Holovak, the shrewd veteran personnel man. By the 1987 flesh lottery, Glanville pretty much had things his way." Dick Corrick was named scouting director.

BUD ON LADD AND JERRY

Herzeg later announced that '88 would be his last year of negotiating contracts. "I'm not talking about quitting as far as the Oiler organization, but I think that next year there will be a new contract negotiator because I've had all the fun I can stand with this."

Bud said he "would beg" him to keep at it. "I back Ladd 100%," he said. "I'm pleased with the way he's handled himself everywhere but Buffalo, but we won't go into that one."

The Sherrill rumors intensified as his activities at A&M were under the NCAA microscope. Adams denied ever discussing the job with him. Besides, he liked his coach. "What I like most about Jerry is that he is a straightforward, no-nonsense guy, and he has demonstrated to the general public that he's not a yes man," said Bud. "He's going to say it the way he sees it. He tells the players the way it is. And he's that way with everyone, including the media.

"When the players go out on that field, he wants them to knock your you-know-what off. It's a tough game, and he wants players who are tough. He doesn't want dirty players, but he's not going to put up with a player who doesn't give 100%." About the feud, he added, "That had to be a tremendous blow to Chuck Noll's ego to have Jerry Glanville really wax him twice last year."

THE ROAD TO FREE AGENCY GOES THROUGH MINNEAPOLIS

The players went through the '87 season with no collective bargaining agreement. Somehow Gene Upshaw held onto his position as Executive Director of the union despite salaries and benefits that trailed those in basketball and baseball. Things were about to change. After years of backbiting and mismanagement, the union was on the verge of stumbling onto a victory.

After the strike ended, it filed an antitrust lawsuit in Minnesota. Forum choice would be a key. Although he denied their request for an injunction that would have made free agents of 300 player/plaintiffs, Judge David Doty did determine that "the players were likely to prevail at trial." That finding was buried on page 15 of his 16-page opinion. The owners should have taken a clue and immediately cut a deal. Instead they chose to take their chances at trial in a place Karl Marx would feel at home. It was not a bright move.

1988 TRAINING CAMP

The Oilers moved camp again, trading in the heat of West Texas and San Angelo for the heat of Central Texas and San Marcos. Just as constant as the heat were the holdouts. Leading the list were starting corners Steve Brown and Patrick Allen. They wanted more than safety Keith Bostic made, even though he was Pro Bowl and they were not. Herzeg offered either one to the 49ers for Tim McKyer who was in a contract dispute, but San Francisco refused.

Second-round pick Quinton Jones also held out. He eventually got permission to seek a trade from Herzeg, who said he had missed too much camp to help. On the positive side, Lorenzo White was signed by the end of July, and Sean Jones agreed to a new deal at the time of the trade.

The Oilers were beginning to look like a powerhouse. The offense was stacked. Moon and Carlson were the QBs with Rozier, Highsmith, Pinkett, White and Tillman at RB. Hill and Givins were backed up by Duncan, Jeffires (injured), Drewrey and ex-USFL star Leonard Harris. At TE, four-year starter Williams was back, although his reception totals had dropped from 41 in '85 to 15 in '88. The line was fairly set with Steinkuhler, Matthews, Pennison, Munchak and Davis, although Steinkuhler's knee was always a concern and Davis was on the down side of his career. Maggs was a capable backup.

The DL appeared ready to jell with Childress, Smith, Fuller, Jones and Byrd. LB was finally settled with Lyles, Meads, Grimsley and Smith, but only after countless wasted draft picks. The scouts got one good LB for every four they drafted. From '87, there was Walter Johnson (stuck on special teams), Caston (overweight), Dusbabek (IR) and Banks (third team DL). At least that class had Al Smith. None from '88 (Crain, Spradlin, Brantley) made the regular roster.

Brown and Allen's holdouts caused problems in the secondary. Rookie CB Dishman (5th round) would see early PT, but Johnson ('85, 1st) was chained to the doghouse. Another problem was safety Keith "Norman Bates" Bostic's low blood-iron condition. He toughed it out, but was never at full strength.

The rookies who made it were White, Montgomery, Dishman, Verhulst and Eaton. The year started with Jeffires, McMillian, Wallace, Dusbabek and Doug Williams on the IR. Unlike some teams, Oilers on the IR really were injured, as there was pressure to play through pain. Guys who could not play were referred to as "Lassies," after the TV collie that always came home limping and whimpering.

In a disturbing development, Doug Smith left camp after refusing to give Glanville a spot urinalysis. He came back later and passed, but there would be more trouble down the road.

The biggest area of improvement was special teams. To his credit, Glanville was one of the few Oiler coaches to devote the necessary time and manpower to it.

In 1988, he added 33-year-old Richard Smith from the University of Arizona. Glanville described him as, "whacked. Crazy. And he had that boola-boola enthusiasm that you get in college." They wanted the special teams to set the pace for the entire team. "We [didn't] want kickoffs and punts to be something you do between offense and defense," wrote Glanville later. "We want to score points, crush people on kickoffs."

Smith devised a kick coverage play called "over the top," where one player would run down the field screaming and jump over the top of the other teams' return wedge. Opponents did not much care for that one. He also came up with an Army helmet with skull and crossbones on the front, which went to the player with the best hit on special teams. Eugene "the One-Man Gang" Seale won the first. He was embarrassed to wear it on the field but when the crowd saw it and applauded, he turned and saluted them. Soon, everyone wanted the helmet. Even the veterans started volunteering for special teams duty. Smith started calling them, "Hit the Beach."

The special teams' group had a lot of spirit. It eventually rubbed off on the defense and, in turn, even the offense. Team meetings turned into pep rallies. Replays of big hits were shown over and over to shouts, cheers and banging chairs.

They went undefeated in the preseason for the second time under Glanville. This was the year he started leaving tickets at will call for dead people. It began in Memphis when he left one for the King. Elvis did not show (thus the name of Jerry's book), but he did show up at practice about a month later. Glanville claims he left some for DB Cooper and the FBI staked out the ticket office. He left a pair in Cincinnati for Loni Anderson "for two good reasons." While the Houston media ignored it, the national media loved the story.

In the final exhibition game, they destroyed Dallas 54-10 before 48,400 in Texas Stadium. In one more bit of good news for Glanville, Giff Nielsen was dropped from the radio team.

THE 1988 REGULAR SEASON — SON OF STAGGER LEE

The opener came at Indianapolis, a playoff team in 1987. With the previous year's bad blood game as motivation, there were many fights and ejections. After 60 minutes, it was 14-14. In OT, old nemesis Eric Dickerson coughed up the ball, allowing Houston to escape with a 17-14 victory. Moon suffered a serious shoulder injury that would cost him five weeks. Going into the season, he missed only three games because of injury.

Blinebury and Fowler championed Carlson as the new savior. He complied with a comeback win over the Raiders in the Dome opener, with Dishman and Pinkett in for Brown and Rozier. It was their first 2-0 start since 1981. They held LA to 74 yards rushing and had 5 sacks. Childress and Fuller were coming on, but Jones was unhappily (and inexplicably) stuck behind Byrd.

Then, some local writers thought they were in hog heaven when Herzeg's personal life exploded on the front page. An ex-lover filed a suit against him for child support and other relief. The married Herzeg admitted the child was his. The plaintiff, an ex-flight attendant, claimed he promised to marry but later reneged. She wanted compensation.

The newspapers happily aired her claims. Fowler appealed to Bud to fire him blaming the lack of sellouts in such a "football crazed area" on their bad image for which Herzeg was responsible. "Herzeg's high jinks," he wrote, "have everything to do with the way the Oilers are perceived in the community and outside it." Citing Buffalo, the Jacksonville scam, a conspiracy with Ed Biles "to depose" Bum Phillips, and "bitter and protracted battles with holdout players," he contended Herzeg had "never been an asset to the Oilers in terms of community relations."

Herzeg offered to resign but Adams refused, calling it a "personal matter." Fowler suggested Herzeg's offer was only a ruse to hold down the child support payments. He continued to run with the story for years after Herzeg disappeared.

Meanwhile, those following the on-the-field high jinks began the hype. The Oilers had never started 3-0. Kenny Hand thought they should be favored to win the division even with a backup QB. He wrote, "The Oilers have built a team so deep in talent that not even the

Glanville's imagery and attempts to regenerate the fun and excitement of "Love Ya Blue" caught on with many fans. Among them was Bud Adams, who enjoyed seeing the Dome full again. Bud also empathized with Jerry over the beating he took in the local papers.

The idea that Elvis liked football, just not the Oilers, was put to rest with this appearance in 1988 (although he may have revised his opinion after the 1997 season). Not everyone was thrilled with Jerry Glanville's still-developing off-field persona which caused a division among supporters. This split helped lead to his eventual outster.

Oilers can self-destruct." Naturally, they self-destructed in New Jersey with 10 penalties, including 4 personal fouls. Dishman alone had 52 yards in penalties three plays into the game. They lost 45-3.

The inconsistency continued. After pounding the Pats 31-6 at home, they then blew a 16-0 lead in Philly to lose 32-23 to the 1-3 Eagles. As Glanville and Helton walked off the field, a hoagie buzzed their heads. With Carlson joining Moon injured on the sidelines, they beat KC behind scab hero Brent Pease. Overwhelmed, he hit only 3-of-14 with three interceptions and no touchdowns, but did run one in which was good enough for a 7-6 victory. Moon returned in Week 7 to win at Pittsburgh 34-14. His line zealously protected him as the Steelers got no sacks and touched him only twice. The Oilers were 5-2.

That set up a huge game at the 6-1 Bengals. It was the biggest game since the 40-7 debacle with the Browns in '87. The players said they were more "seasoned" this time, vowing it would not happen again. They trailed 14-0 before Moon touched the ball and 28-0 in the first quarter. To their credit, they did rally. Early in the fourth quarter, Hill dropped a wide-open TD pass that would have cut it to 35-28. Boomer said, "I thought you guys were going to come back and win it." They ran out of time, losing 44-21.

The home/away thing had become extreme. In Houston, they were 13-1 in nonstrike games since mid-1986. But since their 1979 Thanksgiving victory in Irving, they had beaten just one team with a winning record on the road in a nonstrike game (a total of 64 road games).

That brought up an important Sunday Night game against the defending Super Bowl champion Redskins. In their best game since the Phillips' era, they destroyed Washington 41-17 as the crowd went postal. It was their first appearance on national television since 1982.

They were putting fannies back in the cushioned seats. Lyles' House of Pain imagery stuck. "That's when I knew our message had sunk in with the players," wrote Glanville. "The local press still didn't have anything to do with us, but we were all over the national media. Soon there were 'House of Pain' hats, T-shirts, logos, you name it. And with the crowd behind us, we were unbeatable in the House of Pain. The players were proud of their reputation."

The Browns, winners of the last three AFC Central crowns, were next. With another sellout and their first *Monday Night Football* appearance in 6 years, the stage was set for disaster. It looked bleak when Hill left with a concussion in the first quarter. But 5'8 Leonard Harris, who had one catch on the season, came off the bench to snare four as Houston won 24-17. They moved to 7-3 and into first place. It was their first non-strike win over Cleveland since '83.

However, all was not well. Doug Smith, who was having a good year, was suspended 30 days for substance abuse. Then, despite 237 rushing yards, they flopped in Seattle 27-24. The Oilers did not trail the entire game until the last three seconds, blowing leads of 7-0, 10-7, 17-10 and 24-17. The Glanville-to-Detroit rumors reflexively reappeared.

The NFC East-leading Cardinals then came in, calling the House of Pain the House of Pancakes. They left flattened 38-20. Moon threw three TDs and ran for a fourth. That brought up the Cowboys on Thanksgiving. Things had become so bad for them that the Oilers were now the television team of choice in Texas. Herschel Walker was their offense. All day long, he kept getting free with only Jeff "Lethal Weapon" Donaldson to beat, and all day long, JD kept stopping him. Dallas played over their heads, leading 17-10 in the third quarter before Houston rallied to win 25-17 in Irving. It was the ninth straight loss for Dallas, who was on the road to Troy Aikman. "I almost feel sorry for them," said J. Williams. "Well, then again, no I don't."

Glanville wrote in *Elvis Don't Like Football*, "One day we woke up and the Houston Oilers were a real football team again. We had done most everything we had set out to accomplish. We were playing more bump-and-run than any team in football. We were blitzing more than any team in the NFL. We could throw deep whenever we wanted. We were gang tackling. We were standing up for ourselves and fighting when necessary." He felt that "the Oilers were finally a team, not a group of individuals. They had an attitude and a purpose."

At 9-4, they were gaining a following. People started mentioning them in Super Bowl talk. Comedian Bill Murray predicted the Bears-Oilers in the big game.

The defense was third in the AFC. Using 3- and 4-man fronts on running downs, they improved to second against the rush. They were also getting a pass rush and were fourth in sacks. Obvious passing downs saw Childress move to DT beside either Smith or Byrd, with Fuller and Jones at end. They were a big play defense that looked to cause turnovers.

The remaining games were all divisional (Steelers, Bengals, Browns). The math was simple. Win out and they had their first division title since the AFL.

They started with Pittsburgh on a sold-out *ESPN Sunday Night* game. The 3-10 Steelers played tough and angry, leading 17-13 at half. At the end of 3, Houston had pulled in front 27-24 and, with 1:30 left, they took their third and final lead 34-31. That should have done it. But the defense let a third-rate QB named Bubby Brister drive 80 yards in 1 minute for a 37-34 Steeler victory. It was the only loss all season in the House of Pain and ended a 10-game home win streak. It was more than just a big blown opportunity. Tied with the Browns at 9-5 and trailing Cincinnati at 11-3, the whole season was suddenly on the line.

They pounded the Bengals 41-6, but it did not take the sting out of the Steeler loss. In a dumb move, they threw deep on Cincinnati with a 24-point cushion. Sam Wyche would remember. They still had an outside shot at the AFC crown, but on the other hand, a loss in Cleveland and they were either out of the playoffs or, at best, would have to return there for the first round. The pressure was great and things got a little crazy.

Fowler replaced "Bobo in Black" with "Motor City Bobo" in deference to the Detroit rumors. The rest of the media obsessed with an arctic storm blowing through Cleveland, basically conceding the Oilers could not win.

The Oilers were 7-1 in the House of Pain in 1988, winning by an average score of 31-15. From 1987 through 1989, they were 19-7 at home (including playoff games). Pictured at right are DE Richard Byrd (71) and LBs John Grimsley (59), Robert Lyles (93) and Al Smith (54). It was martial arts practitioner Lyles who came up with the House of Pain nickname for the Dome. He got the idea from his dojo.

Mike Rozier joined the team in 1985 as the Oilers third Heisman Trophy winning running back. He took over as a starter in 1986 until a late season knee injury. In 11 games in 1987 (strike year), he had 957 yards (third in the AFC), a 4.2 yards per carry average, 27 receptions and made the Pro Bowl. He returned to the Pro Bowl in 1988 as the team's first 1,000-yard rusher (1,002) since Earl Campbell.

Then Glanville started a small war. "You know what you do for fun in Cleveland?" he asked during a telephone press conference. "You take a walk across Lake Erie." When asked about the weather, he replied, "We're not coming up there to live. I've talked to everybody I know in Houston, and nobody wants to go up there and retire." He also hit the facilities, saying he had to bring a hammer and nail just to have a place to hang his coat. He added, "They don't have real grass there, just painted dirt," and "The good thing about playing for the Oilers is that when the game is over, you get to leave Cleveland." Reporter Bob Kravitz came to his city's defense. He called Houston "nothing more than a rancid, impoverished cow town everyone left when the oil wells went dry." He added, "In Cleveland, 80,000 people show up to cheer their team — in cold, in snow, during plagues of locusts ... In your beloved Houston, you can't even find 51,000 fans to fill your temperature-controlled pleasure dome."

Cleveland, with its dilapidated downtown and skyline filled with smokestacks, shared something with Houston — sports misery. The Indians had not won a pennant in a very long time, and the basketball team was so bad they were called the Cleveland "Cadavers." Likewise, they had a bad football stadium. They called theirs the "Mistake by the Lake."

While their football tradition included Jim Brown, the Browns had never been to a Super Bowl. They put together a decent team in the middle '80s at a time when the AFC Central was at its worst. Consequently, their record in those years was bloated. Still, they had been to the '86 and '87 AFC Title games, and beating Houston meant a fourth straight playoff appearance.

Their fans made a name for themselves with the "Dog Pound," which began in 1984 when DBs Hanford Dixon and Frank Minnifield (who killed the Oilers) started barking at WRs. It caught on and fans started wearing dog masks to games. They barked when the other team had the ball. It was perhaps the most persistently sustained loud noise in the NFL. They also threw dog biscuits. Glanville saved the ones Minnifield did not eat for "Bo", his Labrador.

While the television jockeys glamorized the Dog Pound, the situation was out of control. Besides biscuits, they threw bottles, batteries, rocks, you name it. Police and security were too afraid to make arrests. Denver owner Pat Bowlen compared them to English soccer hooligans. Probably only Modell's long-standing friendship with Rozelle kept the league from coming down hard on the Browns.

By game time, not only were the Oilers psyched out by the deep freeze, but also they were being bombarded by snowballs. Despite complaints, Cleveland officials did nothing, saying, "Your coach didn't help the situation." The barrage was so ferocious that Harris ran a pregame warm-up route into Glanville, injuring his knee. Another toss knocked the ball off the tee just before Zendejas kicked off to start the game.

In spite of the distractions, the Oilers took a 16-point (23-7) lead midway through the third quarter. With Kosar out, it appeared Cleveland was out of luck and the Colts would be coming to the House of Pain for the first round. All they had to do was hold the lead. With the defense shifted into a zone, ancient Don Strock sustained drives of 63, 78 and 89 yards to win it 28-23. In the snowstorm, Allen lost coverage on Webster Slaughter a couple of times late. Going in, no WR had beaten him for more than 2 catches in any game. Slaughter had 4. As the clock wound down, Cleveland fans chanted "Jer-ry, Jer-ry."

The Oilers won three of the last five to finish 10-6 and in the playoffs again. They also dropped two of the final three to lose the division and home field. The big dogs in the playoffs were Buffalo (12-4) and Cincinnati (12-4).

THE 1988 PLAYOFFS

Glanville called it a "new season. It's our opener. We always do well in our openers." He also wore a bulletproof vest and had a police escort on and off the field in response to death threats.

The Oilers outplayed them again, but the Browns stayed close on Moon's three interceptions. With Rozier out, they rode Pinkett's 82 yards on a muddy (but not icy) field to take a 14-3 lead. With under 2 minutes left, they thought they had it after a 49-yard Zendejas FG gave them an 8-point lead. But again, the defense could not hold, making another washed-up QB look like an All-Pro. This time it was Mike Pagel who took them 71 yards in about one minute to cut the lead to 24-23 with 31 seconds left. Needing only a FG, Matt Bahr began a string of onsides kicks that gave yet another Oiler game a bizarre finish.

There was much groaning back in Houston. With crowd noise at a peak, Donaldson knocked the first kick out of bounds, costing Houston 10 yards and shortening the field for the Browns. By the second kick, many fans in Houston could not watch. It flew out of bounds. The Browns got another shot 5 yards back. By this time, a majority of Houston was outside getting some air. Cleveland recovered the third kick. But it was touched by a Brown before it traveled the requisite 10 yards. Houston ball. Game over.

Modell quickly fired coach Marty Schottenheimer. It was a page right out of Adams' book. Like Bum, Marty had taken his team to back-to-back AFC championship games and then crashed in the first round. Losing to Houston twice in one year was too much for Art.

The Oilers, meanwhile, headed to the next garden spot — Buffalo. Glanville left game tickets for ex-Bill and NBC analyst Paul Maguire's liver, saying, "It's been dead for years."

Just two years before, the Oilers beat the Bills 16-7 to finish 5-11 and leave Buffalo 4-12. Armed with many high draft picks, both teams were now among the AFC's final four. While Jim Kelly, Andre Reed and rookie Thurman Thomas propelled their of-

Not much matches the frustration of watching another team simply run over your team, but that is what happened to Houston most of this decade. In 1981, the defense gave up 4.4 yards per carry (second worst in the NFL). They surrendered 4.1 in 1982 (sixth worst), 4.8 in 1983 (worst in the NFL and team's worst since 1965), 4.7 in 1984 (worst in NFL) and 4.8 in 1985 (worst). Herzeg's rebuilding (Childress, Smith and Byrd via the draft, Fuller and Jones via trade) and Glanville's philosophy began to bear fruit in 1986 as opponents' per carry average dropped to 3.8 (sixth best in the AFC). After a slip in 1987 (4.1), it all came together in 1988 as they ranked first in the AFC, allowing 3.7 per carry (team's best since 1978). At left, Fuller and Childress make a stop behind the line.

fense, the real turnaround came with the acquisition of Cornelius Bennett. While they were ranked No. 24 in defense in the league in 1986, they improved to No. 12 in '87 and No. 4 in '88 (No. 1 in the AFC).

Fowler again tried to set Glanville up. He wrote, "The Oilers have the best talent in the AFC," meaning that if they lost, there could be but one explanation. His evidence was the "ease with which they thrashed the Bengals in the Astrodome." Actually, Buffalo and Cincinnati were the ones who were 12-4 and the Bengals had pounded the Oilers in Cincinnati. The Bills, meanwhile, had Kelly, Reed, Thomas, Bennett, Bruce Smith, Shane Conlan, Will Wolford, Leonard Smith, Kent Hull, Art Still, Nate Odomes, Howard Ballard and Fred Smerlas. They even had Steve Tasker.

At game time, it was 33 degrees with no snow and little wind. It was a close game. The Bills reached the Oiler 18 on their first possession, but missed a FG. On their second possession, they went for it on fourth down from the Houston 3, but Donaldson batted down the pass (JD was later knocked out of the game). The Oilers then reached the Bills' 34, but Smith sacked Moon for a big loss and Montgomery's punt was blocked. It was 0-0 at the end of the first quarter.

Buffalo got a TD in the second off the blocked punt. Houston reached the Bills' 18 on its next possession, but had to settle for a FG. When Houston got it back, they drove from their 13 to the Buffalo 25. On first, Hill dropped a TD pass over the middle, crashing headlong into a goal post. Gone was Houston's leading WR, who was having a great game (4 catches for 62 yards). On third-and-1, they took a delay of game penalty. Then Hill's replacement, Harris, dropped Moon's third down pass. The Bills blocked Zendejas' FG attempt.

That is how it went. It was 7-3 Bills at the half. On their first possession of the second half, the Oilers were poised to take the lead after reaching the Bills 2. On third down, Moon ran a college-style option and muffed the pitch to Rozier, resulting in an 11-yard loss. Zendejas then missed a 31-yard FG. Late in the third, the Bills went up 14-3 and, after a Moon interception, 17-3 early in the fourth. On their next series, the Oilers were again moving until Buffalo stripped Jeffires (5 catches for 78 yards) of the ball. The defense held, and on their next possession, the Oilers went 80 yards for a TD. The defense then forced another punt with 1:45 left to give them a final shot until Tasker knocked the punt away from Duncan. Houston lost 17-10.

Houston had 351 yards to the Bills' 372. The Oilers had 20 first downs to their 18, and held the ball for 31:02 to 28:53. Kelly was 19-of-33 for 244 yards, no TDs and 1 interception, while Moon was 17-of-33 for 240 yards, no TDs and 1 interception. Moon was hit in the elbow in the first quarter, rupturing a bursa, which affected his passing the rest of the day.

An inspiration all season, the special teams broke down, suffering their first blocked punt and FG of the season. Montgomery's other punts were so deep he outkicked the coverage. The Bills' average start was their 46, while only once did Houston take possession beyond its 21. There was also the missed 31-yard FG and fumbled punt at the end of the game.

It was their first loss since late '86 when they held the opponent under 20 points. They were 19-0 over that streak. "They created some turnovers," said Grimsley. "That was the key." Houston had three turnovers in the fourth quarter.

"This is a much better team than a year ago when we lost in Denver," said Moon. "I don't want to say we quit then. But we got out of that game in the first half and could

Hard-hitting safety Keith Bostic (6'1, 216) (at left stopping 6'6, 240-pound TE Russ Francis) made his only Pro Bowl in 1987 with 6 interceptions in 12 games. Although he would play in all 16 games in 1988, he did so with a strength-zapping blood condition. He was replaced in 1989 by Bubba McDowell.

never come back. Today, we kept coming back and coming back. But the thing is, we can't keep trying to do it like this. We're doing it the hard way by playing in everybody else's park.

"I can go back and say the Seattle game was one we'd like to have back. There was the game in Philly. But Pittsburgh, yeah. Pittsburgh is where we blew it. We had that game won and let them come back. We win that and we're playing Cincinnati the next week for the divisional title. Of course, we beat Cincinnati. So we'd have had that week off."

Glanville said, "They played hard. They're a fine team. Rather than us doing something wrong, give them credit for doing something well."

The fumbled option on the Buffalo 2 drew much criticism. Some writers called it the "Son of Stagger Lee." The same play generated 8 TDs on the season.

Fowler contended "they ... went as far as Herzeg's bobo is capable of taking them. As long as he's around, the Super Bowl will be a mirage shimmering on the horizon." The record under Glanville had gone from 5-11 to 10-7 to 11-7.

Ed said, "Glanville incited various foes to heights of passion they had never before known with his criminally stupid shtick of cheap shots and insults .... Just to think a coach as talented as Marty Schottenheimer is on the job market and the Oilers continue to employ a comedian."

His pal Blinebury added, "It will simply go down in the records as one more time 'The Little Dynasty That Couldn't' failed to get over the hump." He asked, "How many more times are we going to sit around and console ourselves with the fact that the Oilers have the best offensive talent in pro football, while four other teams go on to play for a birth in the Super Bowl?"

OVERVIEW

The Oilers won 11 games and made the second round of the playoffs again. They did it in the best division. For the first time since the merger, three teams from a 4-team division made the playoffs. Those three split their season series, but had a 28-10 record against all others.

Post-season honors fell in line. Five offensive players made the Pro Bowl, although Matthews was the only starter. Munchak, Moon, Rozier and Hill were backups. Matthews made first team All-Pro while Munchak was second team.

Despite losing Moon for all or most of 6 games, they finished second in scoring. Hill had his third 1,000-yard receiving year, while Givins caught 60 for 976 yards. They were the most proficient pair of receivers in the league for the second year in a row. Hill's 4-year yardage total of 4,411 was second only to Jerry Rice. Jeffires also started catching some balls in the playoffs.

Moon had his best season, finishing 160-of-294 (54.4%) for 2,327 yards, 17 TDs and 8 interceptions. His QB rating was fifth in the NFL. Rozier finally had a 1,000-yard season, gaining 1,002 with 10 TDs. Pinkett added 513 yards to Highsmith's 466, as Houston had the fifth best rushing attack in football. Besides the two Pro Bowlers, Davis had a good season, and for the most part, shut Bruce Smith down in the playoffs. Steinkuhler also played well at RT, especially on running plays. They gave up the fourth fewest sacks.

The Buffalo game notwithstanding, Coach Smith worked out very well on the special teams. In 1987, the Oilers were last in the AFC in punt and kickoff coverage. In 1988, they were in the top five in the NFL in both. They also blocked 5 punts, tying an NFL record. However, as a result of always going for the block, the returns were short and the returners frequently injured.

The defense was a no-name outfit with just one Pro Bowl player, Childress, who made it as a backup. Grimsley made it later as a replacement. As a team, they were No. 5 in the AFC (1st vs. run but 11th vs. pass). The line was the biggest improvement, as they held 12 of 18 opponents to fewer than 100 yards rushing. They also generated 28½ sacks led by Childress and Fuller with 8½ and Jones' with 7½. The team total was 42. The line coach was Doug Shively.

Before the Dallas game, Tom Landry noted they did not play well on the road and said toughness on the road was the mark of a mature team. It became bulletin board material for their win in Irving, but his words lingered. Houston finished 7-1 in the House of Pain and 4-6 on the road (including playoffs). Although it was a group effort, the defensive performance on the road was hard to ignore. The killers were blowing late leads to Seattle, Pittsburgh and twice to Cleveland. They surrendered 45 points at New York, 32 at Philadelphia, 44 at Cincinnati, 27 at Seattle and 23 at Cleveland to Don Strock.

THE ANTICS

Glanville later wrote, "We made up our minds that in 1988 we would teeter on the edge. We wanted to hang on the edge by our fingernails. We didn't care if people didn't like us. They're not supposed to. The media hated us. But we kept on winning and kept on smiling."

But Bud cared, and he spoke to Jerry before the season. Some of the tactics toned down. For instance, they stopped taking out kickers. Accordingly, there were not as many "dirty team" accusations in 1988. Many were still concerned about the aggressive style. The school of thought was that while Glanville was an excellent motivator, for some reason, he did not appreciate that antagonizing opponents motivated them, too. It was one thing when the press wrote something negative about an opponent, but something else when players and coaches took the pot shots. The Jets and Steelers games were good examples of what could happen.

Glanville thought it was much ado about nothing. To him, the game came down to the players. The outcome had nothing to do with what someone wore or said the week before. That stuff was just fodder for the newspapers.

But even his most necessary supporter, Ohio native Herzeg, had grown weary. About the Cleveland-baiting, the GM told an Ohio newspaper, "I'm convinced there's a better way to do it." Nor was he a fan of the House of Pain imagery saying, "Once ... things temper down, we're going to have a long discussion about a lot of things. I'm not happy with the 'House of Pain'...You talk about firing teams up on the road, we're firing teams up that come into our place."

It never happened. Soon after the season, Herzeg confided to Glanville that he was leaving, and told Jerry, "The guy who's going to replace me is going to make it a bad job for you." Jerry asked for and received written permission to shop around.

At the Super Bowl, Glanville reportedly approached three teams about their vacancies. He told Chiefs GM Carl Peterson, Browns owner Art Modell and 49er owner Eddie DeBartolo, Jr. he had permission to interview. None showed interest.

1989: EXIT STAGE LEFT

The Oilers were finally contenders. Just a few years before, the talk was of their "losers' mentality." Now they spoke of a Super Bowl.

Coming just short of the AFC title game in consecutive years combined with watching Cincinnati give the 49ers a run for their money in the Super Bowl was both comforting and painful. There were the Bengals, a team the Oilers destroyed 41-6, one play away from the whole enchilada. Players, fans, coaches and management all believed that of all AFC teams, theirs was the only one with enough firepower to beat an NFC champion. They just needed a chance.

They approached 1989 confidently. The statistics and Pro Bowl selections added weight. Besides knocking the AFC champ silly, they proved they could win at Cleveland, sweep Pittsburgh and play Buffalo even on their home field under January skies.

The national experts agreed. Pro Preview had the Oilers in the Super Bowl. Sport had them winning the division. The cover of Athlon's Pro Football had a picture of Moon with the caption, "Oilers Chasing Super Dream."

Expectations were high. The bar was raised. Naturally, the year would proceed anything but smoothly. It started before the draft.

PLAN "A" MUST HAVE BEEN A REAL DOOSY

With the reality of the Minnesota lawsuit coming to bear on them and unable to strike a deal with the players, NFL owners unilaterally trotted out the solution they hoped would pacify Judge Doty. They called it Plan B, which provided for limited free agency.

In light of the return of winning and playoff appearances, management, fans and even the media might have been able to look past Glanville's off-field activities had the team stopped killing itself with penalties and other self-destructive behavior. While the fights, shoves in the back and late hits began to subside in 1988, it would not happen fast enough to save Jerry's job. At left, LB John Grimsley comes to the defense of a teammate.

Each club got to protect 37 players. The rest became unrestricted free agents until April 15 whether they were under contract or not. A total of 617 players became free agents. It was a boon for some clubs, but torture for others.

Houston was in the latter group. The timing could not have been worse. After years of suffering, they had stockpiled an impressive stable of players who were just reaching their prime. With 58 players on the roster at the end of the season, they stood to lose up to 21.

They lost two 5-year starters, Keith Bostic and Jamie Williams, depth and a large chunk of their special teams including W. Johnson ('87, 2nd), McMillian (Pats '85, 3rd), Tillman ('87, 5th), Drewrey ('85, 11th round), John Davis ('87, 11th), R. Wallace ('86, 6th), D. Williams (Jets '86, 2nd), Pease (free agent), Banks ('87, 7th), Caston ('87, 6th), Crain ('88, 6th), Dusbabek ('87, 4th) and Viaene (free agent).

The Oilers lost a league-high 15 while gaining no player of significance. Glanville said, "We were gutted like a deer." They would feel the loss of depth for years.

NOT KEEPING UP WITH JONES

The Oilers would lose more than players. It comes with the turf that once you start winning, others come after your assistants. In 1989, Houston lost June Jones to Detroit. His old Run 'N' Shoot mentor, Mouse Davis, was hired as their QB coach to install that offense. Jones wanted to help prove that offense could work in the NFL. The Oiler offense and Moon flourished under his direction. He would be missed. Kevin Gilbride replaced Jones, becoming Moon's fifth different QB coach in six years.

In addition, Frank Novack was hired as RBs coach and Ray Sherman replaced Milt Jackson as WRs coach. On defense, Richard Smith was assigned TEs in addition to special teams. On the line, Doug Shively suffered heart irregularities in camp and had to lighten his workload. Jim Stanley was hired off the unemployment rolls as a substitute.

GOOD-BYE LADD

GM Herzeg faced the media immediately after the Buffalo loss. Somewhat reminiscent of Don Klosterman in 1969, he asked for patience, pointing out that the Oilers were the youngest team in the playoffs. In a long interview with the *Chronicle* on January 4, 1989, he promised better days ahead. "The best is yet to come," he said. "We haven't peaked yet."

Once reviled because the team was so lousy, he was now criticized because it did not play up to its "Super Bowl talent," talent he received little credit for procuring.

He said he was "proudest of the fact that we were so far behind and we've been able to catch up and even surpass organizations led by people like Al Davis with the Raiders, Art Modell with the Browns, Tex Schramm with the Cowboys and Dan Rooney with the Steelers."

He also acknowledged naiveté with PR. "I came from a background where I was more comfortable in the boardroom ... than at a press conference," he said. "I did a horrible job of trying to explain the franchise's problems to the media and fans."

He promised a better effort. "I'm making a conscious effort to be more mindful of public relations," he said. He had become more accessible over the past season; for example, answering fans' questions on a sports talk radio show. He wanted to show he had a sense of humor and prove he was not as "hard-line" as "the press has projected."

It was along those lines that he met radio host Barry Warner and newspaper critic Fran Blinebury at Tony's Restaurant about a week after the *Chronicle* interview. It did not go well. After Warner left, some not-so-latent hostilities surfaced and another classic brouhaha between Oiler personnel and a member of the Houston press ensued. Following the tradition established by Jack Gallagher and Dale Robertson before him, Blinebury did not put up much of a fight. Witnesses said this one lasted two "slaps."

Rather than trying to win this impossible battle with the media, Herzeg issued a public apology and said the fight was "unprovoked." Adams blamed the champagne and took a "boys will be boys" attitude. It shocked no one, considering the history. If there was anything surprising at all, it was that Glanville did not get to one of them first.

On February 1, Herzeg resigned. "I feel like I've accomplished my goals in Houston," he said. "I can walk away with my head held high .... It's been a tremendous challenge to rebuild the Oilers into one of the elite teams in the NFL ... At this point in my life, I'm ready for a new challenge. I wanted to go out a winner. I'm not a loser. I've succeeded at everything I've ever done." He denied that any of the well-publicized personal problems had anything to do with it.

"The fact that we've gone to the playoffs the last two years and won proves that the team has arrived. This team is a definite Super Bowl contender," he said. "The fact that the so-called experts said that we could not do it makes it especially gratifying ... There are 18 players on our roster who came through trades. A lot of people didn't think those trades would work."

He said he was going skiing in Europe with his wife, whom he had remarried. "I want to thank Bud for hav-

Moon and Glanville were never best friends, but Moon got along well with QB coach June Jones (at right). For the two seasons he worked with Jones, Moon lowered his interceptions (from 26 in '86 to 18 in '87 and 8 in '88) and raised his TD totals (from 13 in '86 to 21 in '87 and 17 in '88) (noting '87 was the strike year and he missed 5 games in '88). Overall, the Oiler offense rose from next to last in scoring in 1986 to fifth in 1987 and second in 1988.

ing the confidence in me and for supplying me with sufficient time to get the job done," he said.

It shocked the players. "I can't believe it," said Lyles. "Even after everything that happened to him off the field, it seemed like he had been forgiven by Bud and that he had a strong hold on his office ... You know, Ladd was in a position a lot of people would love to be in. He had power and authority. He was able to do just about anything he wanted. Since I've been with the Oilers, Ladd's done a lot of good and bad things. A lot of players are probably happy he resigned because there isn't a tougher negotiator than Ladd Herzeg. He was very good at his job. I'm sure some players are relieved ... I guess it just goes to show that he was very unhappy."

Although Herzeg and Glanville's relationship was not the same it once was, Jerry knew he had lost a key ally. "I enjoyed working with Ladd," he said. "He was my biggest supporter when I was 1-8 in 1986. I'll always remember that."

Ditto for Ed Biles, even though Herzeg fired him. "I think he got to the point he realized he had maybe put together the talent there, but he has no control over what happens when they hit the field," said Biles. "It got to the point he realized there were so many 'X' factors involved. The chances of winning the Super Bowl depend on so many factors that are uncontrollable — the injury factor, the way the game has changed in the 1980s, the drug factor that's involved now. There are just so many factors that are uncontrollable."

The vast majority of the Houston media was happy. For example, television sports reporter Bob Allen said, "With Herzeg gone, the public image of the Oilers is raised immeasurably ... The Oilers are a better organization with him gone."

One of his few supporters, radio personality Anita Martini, said, "You can't do some of the things he did and not be criticized. But I think some got on the horse and rode it too hard. The original wrap against him was he's not a football man. Others won't forgive him because of the Bum Phillips situation. And he didn't try to get along with the media, which they resented."

With Blinebury covering other sports, Fowler had plenty of parting shots for the "Gadhafi of general managers." He wrote, "Through the years, Herzeg steadfastly tried to reorder reality by insisting the world accept his version of it. Generating a stream of charts and graphs born of his own contorted thinking, he endeavored to convince us that the team we watched falling short of expectations year after year was a product of genius ... Others believe naively that success in the NFL is measured in terms of Super Bowl victories, or at least appearances, but Herzeg stuck adamantly to his own definition. He had assembled talent, he declared, and thus he had succeeded."

It came down, in part, to a contract dispute between Adams and Herzeg. Herzeg purportedly wanted a new five-year contract that would have given him even greater control over the team. Adams was willing to give in on some but not all of his demands. Both Herzeg and Adams denied that was why he quit.

About a year later, Adams said he thought Ladd "self-destructed." Sounding a bit too empathetic, Bud added, "Even when we started to win, Ladd was still getting flak. I think he felt he wasn't getting the accolades that he deserved ... He was getting a complex [feeling of] ... *what do I have to do*?"

Adams summed up his bottom line as follows: "When he got to the point of getting into trouble outside his job, I don't think he thought that was going to faze me. He didn't think it was that important, I guess. But I have to wonder what direction Ladd was going. I knew I was going to have to make a change because he and

Jerry weren't seeing eye-to-eye. But I'll say this about Ladd, he worked hard."

HERZEG'S RECORD

Ladd Herzeg replaced Bum Phillips as GM on December 31, 1980. At the same time, he was named executive VP. As GM, he had multiple duties. Although Adams retained a few responsibilities such as final authority on player personnel decisions and front office salaries, Herzeg ran the show. This left Adams to deal with his other interests.

Adams liked Herzeg because he made him money. Herzeg understood the business side of football. He kept the payroll low and ticket sales high enough. Recognizing his deficiencies, he surrounded himself on the football side with Mike Holovak and scouts C.O. Brocato and Glen Cumbee. In 1987, the Oilers had one of only four scouting departments ranked "excellent" in a poll of GM's and front offices by *Pro Football Weekly*.

He hired Biles, Campbell and Glanville as head coaches and Studley as an interim. Biles went 8-23, Studley 2-8, Campbell 8-22 and Glanville 26-27 (through '88).

One area of controversy was contract negotiations. Herzeg took the difficult ones, leaving the lower rounds to Holovak. It was not an easy job. On the one hand, fans thought players made way too much money and despised them for the strikes. On the other, they complained about the team's cheapness during holdouts. The Oilers were not alone having trouble signing their top picks; it just seemed that way.

Herzeg unnerved some agents. Craig French, agent for Patrick Allen, called the change "addition by subtraction." He added that Herzeg "would try to intimidate you and then be thin-skinned when you responded to that." French said "a poison affected the Oilers for a long time. There was constant player unrest. You never went into a season without trauma from the front office as a result of contract negotiations."

Mike Sullivan, who represented Salem and Eason, said, "There was a prejudice against Ladd being an ex-accountant by some people, but I never felt that way. Ladd's style was complicated. I think that was intimidating to agents and people. I think Ladd had a hard time dealing with people who weren't very smart. And I think that he felt there were quite a few agents who weren't very smart."

Herzeg said the draft and trades were his favorite part of the job. In this realm, Herzeg was the best Oiler GM next to Don Klosterman. No doubt Ladd would have benefited from some PR lessons from the Duke.

The first Herzeg-Holovak draft in 1981 was a bust. In 1982, they narrowly dodged a bullet as Ed Biles' favorite, QB Art Schlister, was gone, forcing them to take Mike Munchak, the team's best and one of the NFL's best guards.

During the 1982 strike, Herzeg analyzed the rosters of all teams, determined the Oilers were behind and concluded they had to rebuild. Many disagreed with this assessment in light of the 1980 club's performance. But the case was compelling. He slowly starting dumping the vets with value for draft picks.

Their theme, as stated by Holovak, was: "Normally your offensive linemen last longer than most people in pro football. When you make a first-round pick, it's a big investment, and the longer you're getting a return on that investment, the better off you are."

In 1983, Herzeg unloaded Casper and Manning, and put Houston in great position with 10 picks in the first 5 rounds of the most talent-laden draft in NFL history. They added Matthews, Salem, Bostic, Brown and Moriarty.

The '84 draft was affected dramatically by the USFL. The Oilers used the No. 2 pick on Steinkuhler, the best lineman in college. It was a watershed year as they also signed D. Smith, Meads, Allen, Lyles, Grimsley and Donaldson in the regular draft, Rozier and Maggs in the supplemental, and Moon as a free agent. Houston got 10 starters, which propelled them on a long playoff run starting in 1987. During the '84 season, Herzeg traded Earl Campbell for more picks.

In 1985, they finally shifted to the defense, taking Childress, Johnson, Byrd and Bush. In addition, for the first time, Herzeg gave up high picks for veterans, trading a third-round pick for Woolfolk and another for Romano. At the time, filling those positions was crucial. In two of Houston's better moves ever, he dealt low picks for Zendejas and Drew Hill.

In 1986, Herzeg took Jim Everett, Givins and Pinkett while signing Pennison as a free agent. Early that season, Herzeg manipulated the 49ers and Rams in a bidding war for Everett. He ended up with Fuller, Kent Hill and three more picks, including two first-rounders.

He acquired still more picks in '87 by dumping Salem and Moriarty, and trading down. They ended up with Highsmith, Jeffires, Carlson, Al Smith and Duncan from the draft, Seale from free agency and Bruce Davis for a fourth-round pick.

In 1988, Herzeg traded for Sean Jones and drafted Lo White, Greg Montgomery and Dishman. It was the first time in 8 years that he traded a first- or second-round pick for a veteran player.

In summary, he signed the best QB in team history without giving up another player or draft pick. He pulled off the best trade in team history, unloading Everett for what turned into 7 players, including 5 Pro Bowlers (S. Jones, Fuller, Jeffires, Dishman, K. Hill). His first-round picks were Munchak, Matthews, Steinkuhler, Rozier, Childress, R. Johnson, Highsmith, Jeffires, White and Sean Jones (the equivalent of a No. 1). While one can argue with this pick or that one, none were complete busts, which is something prior (and subsequent) incarnations of this team, or others (see Cards, Giants), may not boast. He also acquired a great WR (Hill) and PK (Zendejas) for middle-round picks, and a good RB (Rozier) and LT (Maggs) in a supplemental draft.

He took criticism for most moves, including Moon. The Everett draft caused such a big stir that some of those critics have never admitted the deal turned out as good as it did. The Dickerson and Warner deals in 1983 also generated plenty of controversy, but each player had his drawbacks. The screwup was not that they made those trades, but rather what they did with the draft choices. For example, of 16 picks in the deep '83 draft, only 3 remained as of 1987 (Matthews, Bostic, Brown). Blind luck should have produced more. That 1983 draft was the most pivotal of the decade, and Houston's failure in it did as much damage to their Super Bowl aspirations as anything.

Indeed, even some of their better choices came at a price. For example, to get Matthews they passed on Jim Kelly and Dan Marino. Taking Rozier cost them Reggie White. Ditto for Richard Johnson (Jerry Rice), Alonzo Highsmith (Rod Woodson), Haywood Jeffires (Bruce Armstrong) and Lorenzo White (Dermontti Dawson).

The second round was worse — Luck (Vann McElroy), Salem (Leonard Marshall), Bostic (Roger Craig), Bo Eason (Michael Carter), Walter Johnson (Bruce Wilkerson), Quinton Jones (Michael Dean Perry). Ditto the third — Tim Joiner (Albert Lewis), Chris Dressel (Charles Mann), Mike Kelley (Kevin Greene), Allen Pinkett (Joe Phillips), Cody Carlson (Henry Thomas). The list goes on and on.

Herzeg was not a scout or personnel man. He made the deals, but relied on the expertise of others to make the personnel selections. In terms of giving them a chance, he was outstanding.

Perhaps his best result was ending the maddening impulse to trade away picks (V. Washington, Casper) or give up good players (Joiner, K. Houston, Largent). For this was a cancer that had eaten the Oilers.

He was always active and never content to sit idly on draft day hoping something would fall in his lap. He aggressively pursued all options. He put them in as good a position as any team to take advantage of the draft. If he had Jimmy Johnson or Bill Walsh making the personnel decisions, the Oilers would probably have rolled through a couple of Super Bowls.

But Herzeg hired the scouts and coaches and was responsible in that sense. In terms of grading him, he deserves a "B+" for trading and draft maneuvering. His hiring decisions are more difficult, with a "D" or "C" likely on most votes, but maybe up to a "B" for the Glanville or Holovak fans. In PR, he gets an "F."

THE FALLOUT

Adams promised improved relations with the media. He had 10,000 new seats to sell. "A large part of the public's perception of a sports franchise is based on what they observe through the media's eyes," he said. "To a large degree, the public forms their opinions while using the media as their eyes and ears." Acknowledging things had "deteriorated over the last three or four years," he promised they would "come out of the fog."

He quickly named Holovak the new GM. It was an easy choice. Holovak was popular with the press and worked for little. Fowler called him "a good and decent man with an outstanding reputation as an appraiser of personnel. Holovak promised fairness and honesty in his dealings with everyone and he'll make good on that pledge, by his very presence scrubbing away the film of scum that has accumulated on the club's name over the years." Mike said, "I try to be honest ... fair and pleasant. I'd like everybody in our organization to be friendly and pleasant."

Bud also said the club would hire a designated contract negotiator. The press was still fixated on Jackie Sherrill and speculated that he would soon be working for Adams, but it never happened.

Adams did, however, hire former Texas A&M Sports Information Director John Keith, who ran interference for Coach Sherrill during the NCAA investigation. Bud also hired Caldwell & Hurst Attorney Steve Underwood as chief contract negotiator. Underwood had worked with Herzeg on many of the more challenging holdouts. He also brought back Lewis Magnum as an executive administrator.

Marketing soon took a different direction. For starters, they hired a marketing director — Mike McClure. McClure held the same position during Love Ya Blue, but left with Phillips. They soon hired an advertising agency and took out radio and TV ads. They brought back cheerleaders (albeit high schoolers and tap dancers) and thankfully changed the outrageously bad music inside the Dome.

1989 TRAINING CAMP

It became clear early that Holovak was not much of a deal maker. He had several opportunities to trade, but was afraid to pull the trigger. The Dolphins offered their first (No. 9) for Houston's (No. 23) and FB Highsmith. That pick could have been Andy Heck, Eric Metcalf or Steve Atwater. Holovak also turned down Washington's offer for holdout RB Rozier, as well as the 49ers' offer of Tim McKyer (Pro Bowl in '88) straight up for Steve Brown before the draft. McKyer went back to the Pro Bowl in '90 while CB weakness would continue to plague the Oiler.

In the draft, he took David Williams, the third- or fourth-rated OT in a poor year for linemen. He would eventually start, but they blew it by not taking OG Steve Wisniewski (who has not missed a Pro Bowl in the 1990s) or center Mark Stepnoski. Both went a few picks after Williams. SS Bubba McDowell (3rd round), NG Glenn Montgomery of UH (5th) and FS Bo Orlando (6th) salvaged the draft.

The major holdouts this time were Hill and Rozier. Hill was under contract, but wanted more than the scheduled $400,000. He missed most of camp. Rozier just hated practices. In the offseason, Moon signed a new deal ($10 million/5 years). Childress received an offer sheet from the Bears ($4.75 million/5 years) that the Oilers matched.

Injuries were also a major theme as Houston went through most of the preseason without 8 to 9 starters. NT was a major concern with Doug Smith out with a knee injury and Byrd coming off foot surgery. Bruce Davis was also hurt, as were Al Smith, Jeffires and Givins.

Rosters were at 47, including a 6-man developmental squad for the first time. The rookies who made it were Williams, McDowell, Montgomery, Eason, LB Scott Kozak (2nd round), TE Bob Mrosko (9th) and FB Tracy Johnson (10th).

The only line-up change was McDowell in at SS. With Bostic lost to Plan B, Quinton Jones was the heir apparent. But Bubba seized the opportunity, including three knockdowns of Aikman in the Dallas preseason game. They cut Jones, conceding another second-round defeat.

They went 2-2 in the preseason. They lost to Dallas, for the first time under Glanville, with Jerry Jones cheering on the sidelines.

Despite the problems, the Oilers were optimistic. Rozier and Hill reported just before the opener. Their offense was varied and talented, and put a lot of pressure on defenses. The running game was solid with Rozier, Pinkett and White running behind a veteran line and Highsmith. In the Red package, they spread the defenses with 4 WRs, removing a back and the TE. That scheme was complicated based on reads by the QB and WRs. It took awhile for all concerned to master it. "I think at this point, we've got it down pretty well," said Moon. "I think if we ran it exclusively, we'd be even better at it, but we do so many other things." One by-product was that the LBs tended to be spread out, which opened up some large rushing lanes for the backs.

The defense had veterans everywhere except safety. They had improved in most categories over the past few years but needed to learn how to hold a lead, especially on the road. The whole team knew that to get to the Super Bowl, they first needed to win the division, which meant they had to win some road games against playoff-caliber teams.

The consensus was Glanville had to get past the second round to keep his job. He said, "You know, some people in Houston hate to say it, but things have turned around here. We've been a good football team. We're going to be a good football team."

Ed Fowler advised: "Before we get too caught up in the euphoria ... it's prudent to consider that the Oilers primary impediment to success on the field remains in the person of Coach Jerry Glanville .... No longer Ladd Herzeg's bobo, will Glanville be Mike Holovak's albatross? .... This is a guy whose IQ could soar to average this season — and with the talent the Oilers have, that would be enough."

THE 1989 REGULAR SEASON — FADE TO BLACK

About twice a week, Houston sports page readers saw that the Oilers' offensive line was "one of the top three in football." They did not look like it at Minnesota in the opener. Moon was sacked seven times as the Viking defense led by Keith Millard, Henry Thomas and Chris Doleman held the Oilers to 104 total yards. Minnesota won 38-7.

Oiler penalties drew the most commentary. The most memorable was Dishman standing over and taunting Carl Hilton, who was flat on his back with a neck injury. Dish's response was, "It's my role to talk to my teammates and the opposing players. Because of it, I feel my teammates get up. We hit until the whistle blows. If players and fans don't like it, they don't have to watch." That attitude was causing some problems. Brown said, "We've got to grow up. We can't help them, we can't do stupid things, personal fouls and hacking guys." Viking Tim Irvin said of the score, "Couldn't have happened to a nicer bunch of a—holes."

They snapped back to win in San Diego 34-27, but Dishman was the biggest story again with untimely penalties that kept the game closer than it needed to be. Trying to assume the leadership role, Moon chewed out Cris on the sidelines during the game. Glanville wanted to keep the matter in-house. He said, "I'm not going to talk about it. Dishman's one of the family. He's going to be a big-time football player. If we have a problem, we keep it among ourselves."

The Dome opener came September 24 against the Bills in the refurbished and expanded Dome. Critics who whined that they would never sell the extra seats had to be surprised at the record turnout of 57,278. They saw a wild one. It started with Dishman getting another unsportsmanlike conduct penalty on the opening kickoff that cost them 3 points. On one TD, Givins did a spectacular head-over-heels flip from the 3, landing on his feet in the end zone. Trailing 27-10 in the third quarter, the Oilers rallied to take a fourth-quarter lead of 38-34. But he defense could not hold as Buffalo went up 41-38. Zendejas' 52-yarder tied it with 3 seconds left, but he later missed a 32-yarder in OT. Kelly's fifth TD pass won it 47-41. The Oilers led in most other categories, including first downs (33 to 23), time of possession (43:11 to 25:31), third-down efficiency (10 of 15 vs. 6 of 10) and return yards (175 to 100).

They crushed the Dolphins 39-7 the next week, holding Marino to 103 yards passing. That is the way the whole season went. They lost to the Pats and Doug Flutie 23-13 on 4 turnovers. Then they beat 4-1 Chicago 33-28 after trailing by 9 with 4:55 left at Soldier Field with Mike Ditka exploding on the sidelines.

In late October, they faced the Steelers for the first time. Before the game, a water moccasin bit Glanville on the foot near a construction site behind his house. With Jerry vomiting on the sidelines, they crushed Pittsburgh 27-0. Glanville said his foot "looked a lot like Dan Dierdorf's nose." Noll speculated it "was a family dispute."

Next, they fell to the Browns 28-17 after leading 10-0 at the half. Then they turned around and blasted Detroit 35-31.

While the team was just 5-4, Moon was having a great season. Against the Lions, he was 30-of-38 for 345 yards with 2 TDs and ran for another. Trailing 24-14 early in the third quarter, Moon took them on scoring drives of 57 and 77 yards to take a 28-24 lead. During that span, he hit 12-of-13 passes for 132 yards and two TDs. His QB rating for the season was 94.7 with a 63% completion percentage, both career highs. Holovak said, "He's the team leader. He's throwing with so much accuracy and such a nice touch. He runs well when he has to. He's done these things before but he's just doing them even better now." Givins added, "When we're in the huddle and he starts to talk, the only thing you can hear is silence. Nobody makes a noise when Warren's talking. Everybody has so much confidence in him."

The first big game of the year came on November 13 against Cincinnati on *Monday Night Football*. The defending AFC champs were also 5-4, and the loser would be in bad shape. Before the game, the teams traded taunts through the papers. Cincinnati OC Bruce Coslet called the Oilers "a bunch of loud mouth jerks," adding, "Ironically, most of these guys are the weak links of their defense. It's always the marginal players who are shooting their mouths off." In the first half, a fight broke out after almost every play. Trailing 24-23, Moon took them from the 20 to the Cincinnati 10, calmly calling time out with 2 seconds left. Zendejas nailed the kick and Houston won 26-24 as the new record crowd of 60,694 raised the roof.

After mashing the Raiders, Art Shell and Bo Jackson 23-7 before a crowd of 59,198 (61,824 tickets sold), the Oilers stood at 7-4 and alone in first. They had remaining games against the Chiefs, Steelers, Bucs, Bengals and Browns. "The main thing is we're playing well in the second half of the season," said Brown. "A lot of teams are frontrunners, but then they fade."

They imploded in KC without Pennison, Hill, Givins and defensive captain Lyles. Moon even picked up one of the 16 penalties as he lost an early shoving match with Derrick Thomas. It was the first personal foul of his career; he was shot for the rest of the game. They lost 34-0.

The Oilers were the most penalized team in the league. It was a problem that just would not go away. Everyone in Houston thought it was the one thing holding the team back. Fowler wrote, "The team is an extension of (Glanville's) ego, his instrument for showing the world how tough he is. He has never really wanted to be smart. In four years, he hasn't changed in that regard, and there's no reason to believe he will now. He encourages hooliganism among his players at the cost of composure and efficiency, and sets the tone himself with sideline eruptions that divert his concentration from the business at hand."

Reached in San Francisco, former TE Jamie Williams said going from the Oilers to 49ers was like "driving a Horizon for 4 or 5 years and then all of a sudden you jump into a Mercedes-Benz, and everything's working like a fine-tuned machine." He said San Fran played better with less talent than Houston's because the ownership and management were superior, and the players had more discipline. He refused, despite encouragement, to criticize Glanville, saying he "has done better than most people expected him to. I think if he had more control, he might be able to do a few more things. Here, the management, players and coaches work together. It's not as good as it should be in Houston."

Williams, who would later earn his masters and Ph.D., did agree that the aggressiveness created problems. "I think the defensive guys like the philosophy of all-out, reckless abandon," he said. "It's fun for them to play like that. But I don't think the offensive guys necessarily appreciate it. They don't like the penalties, and they don't like the fact that the other teams are out to prove something, and they take it out on the Oilers' offense."

Spencer Tillman, who also went to the 49ers by way of Plan B, was more direct. "You can be an unchained idiot and play for Houston," he said. "Here, it's a more cerebral approach."

Despite the KC blowout, they went 3-1 in November and again put themselves in a position to win the Central. All they had to do was win the last four. Failing down the stretch in 1988 forced them into the wildcard scenario with no home games in the playoffs. They said they were wiser. They said it would not happen again. Snowy Pittsburgh was next.

Fowler wrote, "Don't blink on Sunday. The rest of Jerry Glanville's professional life begins at noon ... this one could determine, more than any other, whether Glanville is allowed to grace our city with his dark presence for another year or he trundles off to the Laugh Stop."

With Steeler fans dangling rubber snakes from poles, they came up with a huge 23-16 victory on the road and in the cold. They did it on two goal-line stands, a safety, a spectacular sideline grab by Jeffires to keep the winning drive alive late in the game and Lorenzo White's snowshoe-sized feet. Meads was also huge with 3 sacks for 30 yards of losses. It was their third win in a row at Three Rivers and only the second time Houston swept the Steelers.

They beat Tampa to move to 9-5 with their sixth straight home victory and Ed Fowler howling about conservative play calls. It was crunch time. Heading into Cincinnati with 2 games to play, they needed just one victory to win the division. They would have to do it without Childress (broken leg), Lyles or Byrd.

With about 99% of Houston tuned in hoping to see them overcome the past and take their first divisional title, they choked. Moon fumbled the first snap and the Bengals scored 3 plays later. It was downhill from there. They trailed 30-0 at the half. In the second half, Sam Wyche called for an onsides kick leading 45-0. Cinci led 52-0 heading into the fourth quarter, but kept going for TDs. With 22 seconds to go, Wyche called time out to try a FG that made the final 61-7. It was the worst loss in franchise history.

As if out to prove who could be the bigger jerk, Coach Sam smiled and made childlike bye-bye waves at Glanville as he ran for the locker room. He wanted Glanville fired. "The Oilers just got embarrassed and humiliated," he said from his clubhouse, "and I would hate to ride that plane back home ... They are a sorry football team ... His teams have no discipline, and when you have no discipline, you have trouble winning. They are the dumbest, most stupid, undisciplined football team we've ever played, and it's hard to believe they can ever win games."

Some thought Wyche was losing it. He was under pressure. Going into the game, Houston had beaten the Bengals 5 of the last 6 and they were in danger of missing the playoffs. The week before, he had grabbed a microphone to chastise the Cinci crowd for throwing snowballs, yelling, "This isn't Cleveland!" After they lost that game, he shut off his locker room to reporters, which assured he got slammed in the papers.

Sam kept it up later. "He's probably the biggest phony in professional football," he said later, "and I don't like phonies. He's a liar. He tells me he didn't say things when I saw him say them on TV. And then, he comes and puts his arm around me. They've got the best talent in the AFC, possibly the league, but he brings them down. They play stupid football."

The Oilers, meanwhile, had to lift themselves off the floor for another game. The division came down to a winner-take-all match between the 9-6 Oilers and the 8-5-1 Browns. Houston fans were in for another emotional roller coaster.

A conservative offense and penalties left Houston trailing 17-3 at the half. The Browns scored, as usual, on ugly plays. A lazy flip to Metcalf turned into a 68-yard TD. It came after Lyles' interception was called back because Jones lined up in the neutral zone. Later, one of Kozar's wounded ducks found Slaughter for 40 yards and their second TD. It came after a holding call on Smith wiped out a fourth-down incompletion by Bernie.

The offense finally went to the Red formation late in the first half and quickly moved for a FG. They kept it up in the second half on their way to a season-high 483 yards. Moon was 32-of-51 for a career high 414 yards. Hill had 10 catches for 141 yards. The defense also did its part, limiting Cleveland to 53 yards in the half until the last drive.

Trailing 17-13 with under 5 minutes to go, Moon drove them to the Cleveland 15. On first down, Moon attempted an audible from the shotgun. With the crowd noise, Pennison thought he called for the snap, and the ball squirted around before Clay Matthews picked it up. It was a typical turn of events, but then something atypical happened. Matthews (Bruce's brother) inexplicably attempted a crazy lateral. Givins recovered. With hearts pounding, Moon calmly hit Hill on the next play for a 27-yard TD and 20-17 lead. It seemed they had dodged the bullet and would be the last man standing.

On the ensuing possession, the defense held. Houston got the ball back on their own 40 with about 4 minutes left. All they had to do was grind down the clock. On first down, Pinkett scampered 23 yards to the Cleveland 37, but another penalty killed the play. This time it was a hold on Davis. Two plays later on third-and-11, the Browns sacked Moon on a CB blitz and they had to punt. Still, they had a good chance to win if the defense could hold.

A low snap from Bruce Matthews resulted in a bad punt from the AFC's best punter, giving the Browns the ball at their own 42. With 2 time-outs left, Cleveland aimed for the tie. Kozar, playing with extreme pain in his right arm, predictably came out with short passes. He hit one for 10, then 9, then 8 yards. On third-and-1 from the Houston 39, Bernie ran for 4. On third-and-2 from the Houston 15, Kevin Mack ran for 11. On the next play, Mack bowled over from the 4 with 39 seconds left. Cleveland won 24-20.

The usual suspects had the usual comments. Moon said, "We've got to let go of our offense to succeed. We were let go tonight, but maybe we were let go too late." Glanville said, "I thought we had it won." Hill added, "I feel so bad for a lot of guys who have been here for a long time. This was their first real chance to win the AFC Central, and we didn't take advantage of it. It really hurts to be so close and not win the division."

The last Kosar drive eerily resembled the one by Bubby Brister a year earlier that also dashed divisional hopes. Backing into the playoffs thanks to a Vikings' win over the Bengals (which knocked Sam Wyche out of the playoffs), they drew Pittsburgh again. At least they did not have to play in Cincinnati in the first round. The Browns (9-6-1) got the week off, as did the Bills (9-7) and Broncos (11-5). Dallas (1-15) took the season off.

The talk all week in Houston was of Glanville's future, not of the Steelers, who they had already beaten twice. Although Houston won 3-of-4 in November and 2-of-4 in December, the perception was they collapsed "down the stretch." It was their fifth loss at home to the Browns in the last 6. It was also the first time they had lost two in a row since early 1987.

Fowler was the only happy person in Houston. He wrote, "Now, Bud — are you listening, Bud? — here's a marketing strategy for you next year if Jerry's back: Move to Jacksonville. You're going to need a new crowd of suckers, a big one, to sell this dundering herd."

Sean Jones had heard enough, saying, "To go to the playoffs three years in a row is a feat in itself. I've never seen a place like this before where they condemn you when you win. It's ludicrous. After the season's over, you guys can witch hunt all you want. You can get Jerry fired after the season ... What we've done has no relevancy right now. It's what we're going to do that I'm concerned about."

Adams was smoked out by an NBC pregame comment by Bobby Beathard that the only way Glanville would be back was if Houston won the Super Bowl. Trying to quash the rumors, he said, "There's no way Jerry's on the griddle. He's got another year left on his contract ... Jerry's built a winner here. We lost some games we should have won this season, but we won some games we were supposed to lose. I think Jerry's done a good job."

The national media liked him, too. In a *Houston Post* poll of writers assigned to the 28 NFL teams, Glanville was voted "best interview." In fact, those on the outside did not share many of the views about Glanville and the organization that the local media accepted. It was Buddy Ryan who was "least respected." The worst organizations for "direction and planning" were the Cards, Bucs and Jets. The "cheapest" team was Minnesota, followed by Cincinnati and Phoenix. Jimmy Johnson was not only voted (a distant) second to Ryan as least respected, but also won the "least capable to draw up a game plan for the Super Bowl" award. Joe Walton (Jets) and Jerry Burns (Vikings) followed.

THE 1989 PLAYOFFS

The Oilers came out conservative again, running on every first down. They moved the ball, and at the half led overwhelmingly in all stats including net yards: 215 to 138; first downs: 14 to 5; and time of possession: 21:21 to 8:39. All stats, that is, except the most important — the score. They trailed 10-6.

The offense was not "set free" until late in the third quarter and did not score a TD until the fourth, tying the game at 16. When they went ahead 23-16 on a dramatic Givins TD, his second, the swarming sea of blue almost blew the top off the Dome. The sound was deafening. But the defense cracked and let the worst offense in the AFC, led by Bubby Brister and Merril Hoge, drive 82 yards in 11 plays to tie the game at 23, taking 5:16 off the clock to do it.

With 46 seconds left, Houston got the ball back at its 20 with 3 time-outs left. The ran twice, tried a short pass and then a Hail Mary. The sellout crowd booed.

The OT was theirs after Pittsburgh won the toss, but was forced to punt. Taking over at the Steeler 45, White ran wide on first down and got smacked hard by Rod Woodson right in front of the Houston coaches. The ball popped out. Four plays later, Gary Anderson nailed a 50-yarder to drive another stake into Oilers fans' hearts.

It was one of the tougher losses in team history. Houston took them lightly to move to 0-3 all-time against Pittsburgh in the playoffs. Since 1963 (27 seasons), they had made the playoffs just 8 times. The Steelers or Raiders knocked them out in 6 of those.

Houston led in most stats. Moon was 29-of-48 for 315 yards, 2 TDs, 0 interceptions and 0 sacks. Brister was 15-of-33 for 127 yards and no touchdowns. The one weak link was rush defense which, playing without Childress, surrendered 177 yards. The defense did, however, limit Pittsburgh to 1 TD on 4 possessions it took inside Houston territory.

Ultimately, the offense let the team down. They went in knowing the defense was beat up and had trouble stopping anyone the last few games. The burden was on them to step it up and carry the team. They waited too late against a team Adams said "didn't have five or six players who could make our team."

Holovak said, "Nobody had a better team. That's what makes this so disappointing to me. I believe we had the players to do it."

In the dressing room, young Justin Glanville sat bawling in his daddy's lap. Givins said, "I'm shocked that we lost today, but we just didn't play like we are capable of playing." Munchak added, "This is definitely the lowest feeling I've ever had. We should have won the division. They came down here and we didn't take care of things. We just didn't get it done. I'd rather not ever make the Pro Bowl to play in the Super Bowl."

The head coach's postgame comments evidenced the strange dichotomy that was Glanville. Trying to be philosophical, he said, "There is no man in the world who can put out the light that's in my heart." He also felt for White. "There are few players in the NFL as competitive as he is," he wrote. "He would've given every penny he's earned in the league to have that fumble back." But he also uttered this line, "I still consider the season a success."

OVERVIEW

Just one more victory and the Oilers would have won the division, been off the first week of the playoffs and then opened the second round at the Dome. Those two weeks would have given Childress' broken fibula time to recover. The opponent would have been the 9-7 Bills who lost at Cleveland instead. The games that made the difference were losses to the Bills (late lead squandered; missed 37-yard FG in OT), the Pats (gave away game to 5-11 team) and the Browns (late lead squandered).

Those losses left them disappointed and flat heading into the first round. They could not motivate against the lesser talented Steelers led by Bubby Brister.

Until the last three games of 1989, the Oilers had not lost back-to-back games since mid-1987, and had not lost three in a row since early 1986.

The reasons were multiple, starting with the loss of depth caused by Plan B. Often overlooked was that the front office signed almost no one.

The defense ranked eighth overall (2nd vs. the rush and 11th vs. the pass). No defensive player made the Pro Bowl. The line suffered so many injuries that by the end of the year, Jones and Fuller played DT with Meads and Fairs at end in four-man fronts. Childress was a difference-maker, and his absence from the last 3 games proved devastating. Lyles, a leader on the defense, was also missed down the stretch. Those injuries plus ones to Smith, Byrd and McDowell caused many problems.

Johnny Meads was never a Pro Bowler, but he was the best and most versatile Oiler linebacker during the Glanville era. A third-round pick out of Nicholls State in 1984, he played in 117 games in Houston through the 1992 season. One of his best games came on December 3, 1989, with the Oilers' playoff chances hanging in the balance. On a cold and snowy day in Pittsburgh, he came up with three huge sacks for 30 yards of losses to help seal a 23-16 victory. It was only the second time in team history they swept the season series with the Steelers.

Before the rash of injuries, the rush defense had a streak of 19 straight games where only one runner gained over 100 yards.

The secondary was a weakness. Talented but raw Dishman replaced the once-dependable Allen. Even though Johnson was senior, he was moody and always ticking off the coaches. He was deactivated for the playoff game after arguing with secondary coach Nick Saban. As Holovak's No. 1 pick in '85, his benching did not sit well with the GM. Donaldson also had a bad season while Brown and McDowell played well.

The primary reason for the defensive problems lay with the draft. They had not retooled. Their first two picks in '89 were a backup OT and another third-string LB for the special teams. The one good pick, McDowell, was a Glanville choice, and they almost missed him by waiting until the third round. The '88 draft produced a HB on a team overloaded with them when LBs Chris Spielman and Ken Norton, Jr., were available. They also took Quinton Jones when they could have had DT Michael Dean Perry or DB Kevin Porter. In 1987, they moved up to take Highsmith when they could have had CB Rod Woodson or LB Shane Conlan. By taking a WR with the other first-round choice, they passed on safeties Nate Odomes and Tim McDonald. With the Johnson (2nd) and Carlson (3rd) selections, they could have had DT Henry Thomas and LB Hardy Nickerson.

The other major culprit was penalties. The Oilers again led the entire NFL with a club-record of 148 penalties for 1,138 yards. It was something Glanville teams never rose above.

Considering Plan B, the special teams played remarkably well, especially on kick coverage. Montgomery led the AFC in punting and Zendejas tied Blanda's team record of 115 points. However, he missed 12 field goals. The return game suffered with White and Kenny Johnson returning kicks. They had needed a true return man for years, but never developed one.

Gilbride directed the offense, but did not have the authority of June Jones as Glanville seized more control. Moon had another great year, finishing as the AFC's No. 2 passer behind Boomer. He went 280-of-444 (60%) for a club-record 3,631 yards, 23 TDs and 14 picks. He spread it around. Hill was sixth in the AFC with 66 receptions and 8 TDs, although he missed most or all of 6 games. Givins had 55 for 794 yards, while Jeffires caught 47 for 619 and Duncan had 42 for 613. The rushing game suffered as the FB led the team in yardage with 531. Rozier had only 301 yards. The OL did not allow a sack in 6 games. Matthews, Munchak and Moon made the Pro Bowl as starters. Munchak was the only Oiler to make the all-decade team.

THE FALLOUT

Fowler shrieked for Glanville's scalp. Although the offense was fourth in the AFC (3rd in scoring), he blamed the failure to name an OC as the reason they did not get beyond the first round. That theme helped get Phillips fired. Blinebury called Glanville the "clown prince of self-promotion" who let "a promising season go down the drain."

Jerry's one consistent supporter in the print media, *Post* writer Kenny Hand, called for Holovak to be fired. For about a week, the whole thing turned into another Oiler melodrama.

There were meetings going back and forth, and plenty of debates. While Glanville had another year, public opinion had turned against him, helped in no small part by the press.

His other problem was the GM. He hated taking a back seat in the draft. Then there was the issue of support. Glanville made his only statement on matters on Anita Martini's Jerry-friendly radio show. "It wears on your family," he said. "It wears on your coaching staff. You wonder what you have to do for the local people ... or your general manager ... to brag on your team or coaches for one game. I think Mike Holovak rewrote the book. I don't think in 20 games he ever once said, 'Boy, the Oilers' coaches did a good job.' That was like a forbidden statement."

It was true. The GM did not care for the Coach. During the year, Holovak was publicly neutral, not making criticisms, but not offering any encouragement either. Privately, he let his true feelings be heard. Fowler was one of his confidants.

While Glanville stayed otherwise silent, his wife Brenda spoke. "You can quote me on this," she said. "I call this cruel and unusual punishment and it's getting worse by the day. I'm tired of it. There are other jobs. The only reason I'd hate to see him leave is that it would look like he is giving up. But I think he is real worried about Justin and me. We've given just about everything to the city and to the football team. Almost nobody appreciates it ... It makes you wonder why anyone would want to come here and coach."

Moon said, "It's really got me kind of mind boggled ... this is all becoming like a soap opera, like *As the Coaches Turn*. We need leadership. I don't know if a coaching change is the answer, but I do know the coaching side and the management side don't see eye-to-eye right now. Those things have to be brought together before this team can get on the right track."

Adams was in a pickle. Both men wanted more control. He liked Glanville, but also thought he should name a DC and OC. Bud went so far as to procure a list showing Houston was one of only two NFL teams without either, which he presented to Glanville at their last meeting on January 6 and asked, "What do you know that the other 26 teams don't know?"

Glanville asked for and received permission to talk to other clubs, even though he had a year left on his contract. Atlanta jumped. Reporters chased him around airports. There were daily and even hourly updates. In Atlanta, Glanville uttered another poorly conceived line, "If you're not sleeping in Atlanta, you're just camping out." It was supposed to be a historical reference understood in Georgia, but it received a cool response in Houston.

Seven days after the loss to Pittsburgh, there was a press conference at the APC to announce Glanville was leaving by "mutual agreement." Adams said, "He wasn't pushed out the door. I never asked Jerry to leave. I think it comes to Jerry and Brenda felt they didn't want to stay in Houston any longer ... Brenda was more forceful than Jerry. They wanted to look someplace else for a different situation."

The scene was very unOiler-like. There was real emotion. Twice Adams choked up and had to pass the microphone. A composed Jerry gave Bud a reassuring pat on the back and even a hug. Herskowitz called it the Oilers' "finest hour ... You might even describe it as their finest two-and-a-half hours." To his chagrin, Adams later told an employee he got something in his eye and "just decided to run with it."

Glanville wrote in his book, "The tension in the front office at Houston after our third playoff loss was obvious. In my heart, I felt it was time to move on."

Adams said later, "You can't take away the fact that Jerry put us in the playoffs each of the last three years. Only three other teams (did) that. But I think Jerry tried to do too much. As we progressed, he was still too involved with the offense. That's a case of not delegating authority. I think that hurt him." Bud believed that Glanville, like Herzeg, "self-destructed." He felt neither's association with the team had to end the way it did.

THE REACTION

"Before the Cincinnati game, I'd have been surprised if this had happened," said Matthews. "Events of the last month, especially the last few days, seemed to point to its inevitability. Even if he'd stayed, people always seemed to be waiting for him to misstep. So much friction had built up that something had to give."

Ray Buck wrote, "Apparently, Glanville felt that he no longer could be himself in Houston because of the way he was perceived by the media and fans."

"He leaves as possibly the most misunderstood sports figure in the history of Houston," wrote Kenny Hand.

NC State's Haywood Jeffires came with some high expectations as a No. 1 pick and the top ranked receiver in the 1987 draft. His first two seasons, however, were anything but stellar. For 1987 and 1988 combined, he caught 9 passes. The team's patience began to pay off in 1989 when he came up with 47 receptions and 619 yards. After that, he put up numbers with the league's best receivers. From 1990 through 1995, he made the Pro Bowl three times and never had fewer than 61 catches or 684 yards.

"The Oilers never had a coach who was more serious about winning and more serious about having a fun time doing it. Something was lost in the translation, though. Because he was quick with a biting quote and alienated other coaches with his brash, iconoclastic style, he came off as a selfish, self-promoting clown."

Assistant Richard Smith felt it went "to the first game at Minnesota. Everything started when we lost that game. I've seen this kind of thing happen before when everybody builds up your team to be something spectacular. If the team doesn't live up to those expectations, then they look at the coach as a failure. The one thing that bothered me was that we didn't get much support from Mr. Adams during the season. If he would have come out in the middle of the year and said, 'Jerry is my man and he's going to be here,' that would have shut up a lot of people .... All I know is I worked as hard as I could the last two years I've been here and know everyone else did, also. If it wasn't enough for the fans, then I'm sorry. But I know in my heart we did everything we could to win."

Fowler wrote, "One immediate benefit is an end to the divisiveness in the city over an issue that had generated more friction than any sports matter ever had. Hordes of longtime fans admitted to rooting against the Oilers in the hope that losses leading to Glanville's departure would prove a long-term benefit to the team. A sport that can unify Houston like no other and lift the spirits of a town pulling out of a serious economic slump had become instead a wedge, with the focus diverted from the players to a cartoon character."

Robertson may have said it best with: "The bottom line here is the credibility thing. While Glanville may be a good coach, the Oilers don't perform as though they are well coached. They are prone to extreme lows, make too many fundamental mistakes, and with the season on the line against Cleveland and Pittsburgh, fell flat in the clutch, in their home, against inferior opponents. Somebody has to be held accountable."

GLANVILLE'S RECORD

Jerry Glanville's regular season record as Oiler coach was 33-32 (35-35 including the playoffs) over four season and two games. His 28-19 record from 1987-89 compared favorably to the top AFC coaches of the day — Dan Reeves (29-17-1 with Denver), Marty Schottenheimer (28-18-1 with Cleveland and KC) and Marv Levy (29-18 with Buffalo).

Glanville's teams were toughest at home. After finishing 4-4 in '86, they went 5-2 in '87, 7-1 in '88 and 6-2 in '89 in the regular season. Starting with the '87 season, they went 23-6 over their last 29 in the Dome, including the playoffs.

His teams did better within their division than most Oiler teams. In 1987, the Oilers went 5-1 in the AFC Central while finishing 3-3 in 1988 and 1989. He swept Pittsburgh twice ('87 and '89), won in Pittsburgh 3 years in succession, won in Cleveland and Pittsburgh in cold weather and went 5-2 against Cincinnati their last seven meetings.

Glanville took pride in having his team ready for the "stretch drive" of November and December. In 1986, they went 4-4 down the stretch, 5-4 in 1987, 4-3 in 1988 and 4-3 in 1989, for a four-year total of 17-14.

Statistically, most aspects of the team improved once Glanville took over, as the following table showing their ranking among the 14 AFC teams indicates:

	Offensive Rank			
	Points	Overall	Rush	Pass
1985	13th	13	8	13
1986	13	9	6	8
1987	5	5	6	5
1988	2	6	2	10
1989	3	4	6	6

	Defensive Rank			
	Points	Overall	Rush	Pass
1985	13th	12	14	8
1986	5	1	11	1
1987	11	11	8	9
1988	11	5	1	11
1989	14	8	2	11

Despite his defensive background, Glanville's offenses played a bigger role in turning the team around and took them to the playoffs. Except for 1988 when Moon missed six games, they were balanced and put points on the board. On defense, the line play improved each season until collapsing to injury at the end of 1989. Pass defense was the weak sister — part was risky schemes, part the players. Glanville's blitzing schemes required great cover corners. He later called the ones he had "cardboard cornerbacks."

His teams were criticized for not being able to win on the road. The Oilers were 1-8 away from home in '86, 4-4 in '87, 3-5 in '88 and 3-5 in '89. Those records were better than most. In general, a team that wins at home plus 3 or 4 on the road makes the playoffs. However, when they did lose on the road, they did so spectacularly. In 1987, they surrendered an average of 34 points per game in the road losses, 35 in '88 and 37 in '89.

On the other hand, they snapped back well, not losing consecutive games from mid-'87 until the end of '89. Three times in '89 the Oilers avoided consecutive losses by winning a road game the week after a road loss (Chargers, Bears, Steelers).

Glanville was also criticized for not being able to win the big game, beat teams with winning records, or just beat any team when it mattered. In 1987, there was the crushing 40-7 loss to Cleveland in the Dome followed by a 51-27 blowout in Indy and loss at New Orleans. In 1988, they started out 7-3 but lost games at Seattle (27-24), to the Steelers (37-34) and at Cleveland (28-23) in the last game of the season to lose the division by half a game. In 1989, again with the division on the line, they closed with losses at Cincinnati (61-7) and to the Browns (24-20). Kosar was a nemesis, winning 3-of-4 in the Astrodome under Glanville's reign. In 1989, Pittsburgh was the only playoff team and only team with a winning record that Houston beat.

They also won their share of significant games. In 1987, they opened with a win against the Rams (playoff team in '86), beat Pittsburgh and Cincinnati twice and Seattle in the playoffs. In 1988, they opened by beating the Colts (playoff team in '87) followed by the Raiders, Pats ('85 AFC Champs), Skins ('87 Super Bowl champs), Cards (NFC East first-place team at the time), Browns on *MNF*, Cowboys in Irving on Thanksgiving, Bengals ('88 AFC champs) and Browns in Cleveland in the playoffs on Christmas Eve. In 1989, they came from behind to beat the Bears in the waning moments at Soldier Field, and beat the Dolphins, Bengals on *MNF*, Raiders and Steelers twice.

Glanville did learn from mistakes, if slowly. *Stagger Lee* went into storage. He changed from a run-it-up-the-gut offensive coach to one of a multiple, varied offense. The late hit count declined over time, as did the corollary "cheap shot" accusations. By his last season, the rhetoric had smoothed. He also came to recognize the importance of special teams and directed attention there, a lesson subsequent coaching staffs had to relearn the hard way.

Throughout his tenure, Glanville received more attention than the players both locally and nationally. There were two views on this. According to Glanville, he wanted to shield his players and assistants from criticism by making himself the focal point. When something went wrong, he shouldered the responsibility. That was fine when things were bad, but some of the players became jealous when things turned good.

His modus operandi wore thin with many. Sean Jones, who was originally supportive, later called it "an act." The black clothes and muscle cars, the hanging out with bad boy musicians, the tickets for the dead, the coaching feuds and so forth were all designed to further his career, a career, according to Jones, far beyond the Oilers.

A related theory saw a calculating Glanville trying to replace Bum Phillips, the homespun coach who enjoyed saint-like status. He wanted the same adulation. He developed his persona accordingly.

If this view is true, he miscalculated. Phillips was not a show. Well, maybe it was a show, but it was not an act. Bum was who he was. Fans responded to his genuineness. Houstonians have always responded to those kinds of people, the kind who admit mistakes and let their warts show. While the boots, big buckle and funny sayings were inherently believable for a guy hailing from the "Golden Triangle," it was a stretch for a guy from Detroit. Perhaps Glanville never figured that out. Perhaps he lacked the capacity to understand it. Maybe it never was an act.

In any event, the problem between Glanville and fans went deeper than just personalities. It was more complex than just Fowler's attempts to become as talked about as the coach. It had to do with the teams and the players, only so much of which he could control.

Phillips' teams were characterized by overachievers. They were not the most talented but they left it all on the field, frequently overcoming long odds to steal a victory. There was Pastorini with his knee brace and flak jacket, Carpenter crawling back to the huddle and the magnificent but ever humble Campbell. The players of that era got the job done without crying about it.

As Bum says, his guys "loved each other. That's what it takes when it comes down to getting that little extra you have to have to make the tough plays. Wanting to do it for yourself only goes so far. You have to want to do it for the guy next to you to reach the next level. Those guys just didn't want to let their buddies down."

Fair or not, Glanville's teams were seen as underachievers. They played below their potential. Instead of snatching victory from the jaws of defeat, they manufactured losses though self-mutilation. Instead of honorably taking defeat, they gave excuses, whined and complained. They did that even when successful. Jerry's kids gave a fan every reason to believe that they cared more about their contracts than winning a Super Bowl. There were constant holdouts and lawsuits. Crawling back to a huddle gave way to not showing until the end of camp, then doing so in a big Mercedes, covered in gold necklaces, bitching about a lack of respect. Throw in the strikes, Herzeg's missteps, the Jacksonville ploy, constant sniping by the media, and the economy, and Glanville had a tough sell on his hands.

After he left, news surfaced of a side of Glanville that rarely got any publicity. He spent much of what spare time he had with underprivileged groups, especially terminally ill children. He made weekly visits to Texas Children's Hospital; hosted over 100 pizza or ice-cream socials at the Ronald McDonald House; assisted efforts to open youth recreation centers in poor neighborhoods; gave anti-drug talks at area schools; and he, his wife and son even personally handed out blankets on cold nights to the homeless living beneath Houston's underpasses.

Even here, Fowler did not cut him any slack. Sometime later he wrote that Glanville could relate to "sick children in hospitals" because he was "the little man in the big man's game."

In the final analysis, Glanville, the coach, accomplished a lot. When he took the job, he said they would be in the playoffs every year after the first. They were. He promised to play better within the division. They did, going 12-8 against Central foes over his last 3 seasons (including playoffs). He promised to change their league-wide perception as NFL's wimps. By 1987, the Oilers' reputation was that of a tough team that you had better show up ready to play against or they would bust your chops.

He wrote in *Elvis Don't Like Football* that it really hit him when he saw some of his players crying after the Pittsburgh loss. "When I arrived in Houston, it didn't bother the players to lose," he wrote. "But now, the Oilers had tasted winning, and anything short of victory no longer satisfied them."

Still, like every other Oiler coach before or after him, he did not get the Oilers to the Super Bowl. Like all other Oiler coaches except one, he could not win the AFC Central.

When you make it to the top or at least get close, it is often easy to forget from where you came. Before Glanville, the Oilers were *the* biggest losers in the game. They were reportedly talented, but it was hard to tell as they rarely did anything right. They needed someone get them organized, focussed and playing like a team. Even Glanville's critics had to admit that he did that much.

THE DECADE IN REVIEW

The Oilers' decade closed as it began, with a loss in the playoffs. A lot happened in between. The 1980s started out marvelously with another appearance in the AFC championship and Bum's famous "kick in the door speech." He said, "They wanted to hear something. It didn't seem like such a big deal at the time."

Focused on the Steelers, he picked up Ken Stabler, Jack Tatum and Dave Casper. That year, Earl Campbell had the second highest rushing total in NFL history and Stabler set a single season club passing record. But they were unceremoniously bounced in the first round while the Steelers were not even in the playoffs. Adams fired Phillips within 48 hours.

That was probably the single most unpopular move in Texas sports history. "Life goes on," said Bum. As the news spread, there was shock and outrage, but it was a done deal. Ladd Herzeg was quickly named GM and it was up to him to find a new coach.

He went through several: Biles, Studley, Campbell and Glanville, not exactly the roll call for the coaching hall of fame. The Love Ya Blue era died a sadistic death as Adams kept blaring the once popular fight song through dwindling crowds and a substandard team. "That's what we'd always heard about Houston — 'Love Ya Blue,'" said Penn State grad Mike Munchak who arrived in '82. "By the time I got here, things were a little different."

Indeed. After going 7-9 in 1981, they bottomed out with consecutive records of 1-8, 2-14, 3-13, 5-11 and 5-11. "We were losing when I got here," said Matthews, who arrived in 1983 from USC. "And the worst part was no one seemed really bothered by that. It was totally foreign to what I was used to." The turn began in 1984. Holovak said, "When we got Warren, things began to fall into place. He was the guy who could get you from here to there."

Moon's hazing was rude. In 1984, he had 3,338 yards but 14 interceptions. The next year, he had 19 more picks, which helped get his friend Campbell fired. "That was a little unsettling," Moon said. "All of a sudden, the guy you came in with was gone." In 1986, he had a league high 26 picks. "When Warren came in he was supposed to be a franchise player," said John Grimsley. "But we were young. Coaches got fired. Every time he turned around, he was being asked to learn a new system." Fans, still angry over Phillips, were disgusted at their ineptitude. Attendance swooned to 37,973 per game in 1986.

"My first couple of years here," said Munch, "you'd see a lot of empty seats, but it was always loud. You could tell there were good fans here. You always wondered what it would be like if the place was full." He found out in 1987 when they started playing like a team again. That season, they went into the second round of the playoffs for the third time ever, only to lose a frustrating game in Denver.

In 1988, they finished 10-6, their second best record since the merger, and again went two rounds into the playoffs. They followed that with a 9-7 season and another playoff appearance. Attendance in 1989 set a club record at 54,882 in the expanded facility. But with the successes came some casualties, as first Herzeg and then Glanville quit to escape their hostile environs.

Moon was the acquisition of the decade. By the end of the '80s, he was the starting QB in the Pro Bowl. There was just one thing left for him to accomplish. Asked if Moon was the right man, Holovak responded with an

The perception during the Glanville years was that the Oilers were always battling themselves. That they were their own worst enemies. Players visible in this shot include on offense — Dean Steinkuhler (70), Bruce Matthews (74, at center) and Mike Munchak (63, standing). On defense are William Fuller (95, left DE) and Sean Jones (96, standing at right).

enthusiastic, "Absolutely. There is no doubt in my mind that Warren Moon is the guy who can get us there. None whatsoever."

On a broader scale, it was an era marked by controversy. The most far-reaching effects were the franchise moves (Raiders, Colts, Cards and almost the Oilers). Pete Rozelle foresaw the danger. Explaining why the league opposed the Raiders' move from Oakland in the early '80s, he said, "What the Davis case created was, in effect, franchise-free agency. Frankly, I'm worried about just what may happen next. When one person can get away with violating the prime rule of the league, it sets the stage for others to follow."

There were other issues like instant replay, situation substitutions, parity, smurf receivers and the length of games caused by an explosion of commercials. There were plenty of fights over money, including strikes, lawsuits, expansion, holdouts and pay-per-view. There were all sorts of peripheral problems like drug abuse, the USFL, Rozelle's retirement and division among the "new" and "old" NFL owners.

Then again, there was Joe Montana, Dan Marino, Walter Payton, Bo Jackson, Jerry Rice, Marcus Allen and Mike Singletary. There were some great teams like the Bears with William "Refrigerator" Perry, the Redskins with Doug ("How long have you been a black quarterback?") Williams and the Raiders who won titles for two cities.

The team of the decade was the 49ers. It started with "the catch," the Montana-to-Clark pass in the 1981 NFC Championship Game that signaled a passing of the torch. The Cowboys were dead. By the end of the decade, Tom Landry and Tex Schramm would be booted out in Dallas while San Francisco had won four titles. The performance of that team, its players, management and owner made for an easy contrast with Bud Adams and his team.

San Francisco owner Eddie DeBartolo got those results by sparing no expense to get the best management and coaching personnel. Once he had them, he treated them very well. For example, he flew the players and other employees to Hawaii to present them their Super Bowl rings. He ignored the NFL's $3,500 limit on the rings and put 40 diamonds in each. The players ate prime rib on team flights prepared by his private chef, and every player got at least two seats. He sent roses to players' wives or girlfriends, and gave them gift certificates to Neiman Marcus for Christmas. Maybe it was race track money, but such actions inspired loyalty and the players responded with many winning seasons. Accordingly, the 49ers became popular outside their area. They sold out all their road games, drew the biggest TV ratings and moved a lot of merchandise.

Bud has never seen the point of incurring such expenses. Once, he promised his AFL championship team diamond rings as a reward. He fulfilled the promise two decades later. When he did, it was nowhere near Kauai.

CHAPTER 9

THE PARDEE YEARS 1990-94

The Oilers of the 1990s were really something. There were characters everywhere. It was a colorful bunch. There was the fearless 5'9 Ernest Givins whose personalized license plates read "Pure Elegance" and who was friends with MC Hammer. There was Warren Moon, the hardest-working QB on the charity circuit. His Crescent Moon Foundation, which benefited the underprivileged, had become a full-time job. He was all over the country accepting awards, making appearances and hanging with the likes of Jesse Jackson.

They also had the articulate giant, Sean Jones, and wild men Cris Dishman and Lamar Lathon. There were the strong silent types in Al Smith and Ray Childress, and the hard-working pair of Mike Munchak and Bruce Matthews. The once immature Doug Smith had converted into a family man in front of everyone. Later there would be chatterbox Michael Barrow and shadow boxer Buddy Ryan. They had Mojo, too.

Local interest approached meltdown. Several of the coaches, Moon, Childress, Givins, Pinkett and even Bum Phillips had or would soon have local radio and/or television segments. There were no less than seven separate television shows and five on the radio devoted to the Oilers. There were shows hosted by local experts John McClain, Dan Patrick, Anita Martini, and Ralph Cooper, as well as national experts Mel Kiper, Jr., and Joel Buchsbaum. Pinkett, Childress, Givins and Jeffires even started 1-900 services to let their fans know of any and all important Oiler developments, for a small fee. The Oilers, the biggest show in town, were bigger than ever. Fans could not get enough.

Coming out of the 1980s, they oozed talent. Pro Bowlers were everywhere. More talent arrived with every new season. Expectations were high. But despite the departure of Jerry Glanville and Ladd Herzeg, they continued to misstep. With each disappointment came more pressure. Everyone felt it. Something had to give.

This time, unlike the time before that and the time before that, the crushed dreams and unfulfilled promise would prove to be too much. Not only would the team return to the dregs of the football world, but also it would leave for greener pastures without many tears shed.

It is a heck of a story.

1990: ENTER THE RUN 'N' SHOOT

The Houston Oilers' last decade began like all others, with the search for a new leader. It also began with a strong belief among fans, players, coaches, management and pundits that the team was good enough to win a Super Bowl, if only they could find the right coach.

The one they hired, like Phillips and Glanville had done in their own ways, would bring them up a notch. He would remake the team in his image. In the end, while the journey at times was spectacular, the results were the same.

WELCOME JACK PARDEE

The list of potential candidates in this go-round included Joe Bugel, Wade Phillips, Jackie Sherrill, June Jones, Jack Pardee, Bruce Coslet, George Perles, Lou Holtz, Mike Holmgren, Dick Coury, Floyd Peters and Fritz Shurmur. This time, there were no search committees. Holovak wanted Holtz, but Adams focused on the man who turned the UH program around (22-11-

1 over three seasons). On January 9, 1990, Jack Pardee became the Oilers' fifteenth head coach.

Adams felt good. "We've never had all the parts together like this — *ever*," he said. "Jack Pardee comes in with all the credentials ... [and] the player personnel in place. It isn't necessarily *the* answer, but we do have a good thing going."

Holovak concurred. "Let's go forward," he said in reference to incessant questions about Glanville. "That's what excites me."

Bud Adams is the most prolific introducer of new coaches in NFL history. At the time he introduced Jack Pardee, his average was a new one every two seasons. Photo © Corbis/Bettman-UPI.

Pardee, a linebacker at A&M, finished his pro career with Washington in 1972. He played under Bear Bryant, Sid Gillman and George Allen. He was one of the few Oiler hires with previous NFL head coaching experience. He coached the Bears, winning Coach of the Year honors in 1976, and the Redskins, winning the same honor again in 1979. He also coached the USFL Gamblers and WFL Florida Blazers.

Pardee did not say that much. "Texas has been good to me, and so has the city of Houston," was one of his offerings. Jack was being a little coy. Like Phillips, there was a little more there than met the eye. Despite the jeans and baseball cap, this was a man who read the stock page every day.

As to discipline, he said, "Your image is the way you play. The best way to lose is to beat yourself. I don't know any team strong enough to overcome *stupid* penalties. There are four or five plays that make the difference in every game ... and you just can't win with excessive penalties. No team's that good."

As to playing favorites, he promised to put the best players on the field. No more dog houses. "A player might not have the best work ethic," he said, "but if he can help us win without hurting the team, well I'm sure not going to cut off my nose to spite my face."

The Houston media went ga-ga. Ray Buck wrote, "In 30 years [Adams had] never done so much, so quickly, to win over so many people as he did by hiring Jack Pardee." Robertson called it a "day for celebration. Without a reach, you can make a case for it being the single best day in Oiler history ... for the first time *ever*, Adams finds himself in a no-lose coaching situation. Should Pardee fail, none of us in the media business can dare raise a stink. He fails, we failed."

The choice was also a hit with fans who had never read a negative word about Jack. Adams was suddenly in the odd position of being popular. "People stop me on the street," he said, glossing over that it was now safe for him to be seen on the streets, "and tell me they like my coach. Jack Pardee is one popular man. If he ran for office in this town, he'd get elected, no matter what office."

Many of the accolades regarded how much he would not be like Jerry. For example, Herskowitz wrote, "If anything is certain about the 1990 season, it is that Pardee will not overshadow his players. His one-liners will not wind up on the bulletin boards in rival locker rooms. He will not divide the city, the press, the talk shows." Robertson chipped in that Pardee was "strong on fundamentals and long on discipline, meaning he has zero tolerance for mistakes of execution. He favors a quiet toughness. In Jack's book, revenge is extracted on the next play or the play after, not after the whistle blows."

But more thought could have been put into what Jack would do as opposed to what he would not. The rush to dump Glanville clouded the thinking. It was almost as if the Oilers' collective braintrust thought they were going to get to keep all the good parts of Jerry's teams, severing only the bad parts and replacing those with Jack. But a new coach not only brings a new philosophy and system, but also his own limitations. Once Pardee Time came to a close, many felt they had been sold a bill of goods.

LEAGUE MATTERS

In a showdown between the old guard and new guard owners in the NFL, Paul Tagliabue became the commissioner replacing Pete Rozelle. Saints' GM Jim Finks had been the odds-on favorite, but was opposed by the new rich kids on the block. Adams voted for Tags.

In another development, television revenues jumped gigantically. Per team shares increased to $32 million from $17 million in 1989.

JUST A SCHEMING

The conversion to the Run 'N' Shoot came without much discussion. Pardee felt the team's experience with the Red Gun made it a natural progression. "These guys had success in throwing the football in a four wide receiver offense," said the coach, "so Warren Moon doesn't have to learn a whole new system. The biggest difference will be in the protection schemes."

He also paid lip service to some well-worn coachspeak. "Formulations don't move the ball," he cautioned. "*Players* move the ball. When I coached the Chicago Bears, fans thought I was the stupidest guy in the world. All we did was run 'Payton left' and 'Payton right' and never threw it. Then with the Houston Gamblers, we had Jim Kelly and threw it all the time. I look at personnel. How can we use our players to be winners?"

The sincerity of that claim was dubious. The existing personnel fit well enough to rank fifth, second and third in AFC scoring from 1987-89. While Pardee was right that the Oilers had a great QB and good WRs, they also had a good rushing attack, including 3 HBs good enough to start for half the teams in the NFL. They also had a very talented FB. They used three first-round picks building that foursome. It was that rushing threat that helped open up the passing lanes. Furthermore, they were the epitome of balance. In 1989, they ran exactly 50% running and 50% passing plays and finished sixth in the AFC in rushing and sixth in passing. The stats hardly supported the idea that the personnel dictated an end to FBs and TEs.

Furthermore, every Super Bowl champion had a good running game. Installing the Run 'N' Shoot meant running plays would drop to about 25% of the calls.

A more likely explanation for the Run 'N' Shoot lay in the national beating Pardee took at UH for his NCAA record-setting "gimmick" offense. It was the Rodney Dangerfield of offenses. He came back into the big leagues with a chip on his shoulder. He wanted to prove the scheme was more than just a college offense. What the existing Oiler offensive personnel did provide was the best opportunity to make such a case.

Before you knew it, there were smurf receivers everywhere, the TEs were gone and the FB and surplus HBs were on the bench. Journalists, so vocal in their opposition to Glanville and support of Pardee, did not ask many questions. Everyone was still busy feeling good. Had they attacked employment of the Run 'N' Shoot with anything close to the vigor they pursued Glanville's clothing or taste in music, it would have implied their assessment of the coaching situation was wrong. That was not likely to happen. Without ever having seen them run a play, Robertson told fans "It should be practically nuclear in its effectiveness by year's end."

Focus belonged on the defense. From 1987-89, Houston's scoring defense ranked a sad 11th, 11th and 14th in the AFC. It ranked 26th overall in the NFL in 1989.

Pardee and his DC Jim Eddy canned the 3-4 originally introduced by Bum Phillips in favor of the 4-3 they employed at UH. They wanted an NFC-type defense with a bigger front seven. The idea was to get better pressure on the QB which would allow a different scheme in the secondary, one that took fewer chances and gave up fewer big plays. This change set the tone for the defense for the next four years, as Jones, Fuller and Childress would be on the field at the same time. Ray was not happy moving to DT because he knew his sack total would decline along with the accompanying recognition and riches.

1990 TRAINING CAMP

For the second year, Holovak failed to make any deals. This came despite knowing before the draft they were going with a single back. With the stable of backs they had (Highsmith, Rozier, Pinkett, White), one or two should have been converted into draft picks. He said not to worry, "There's so much talent out there this year you almost can't miss. We'll get some people who can step in and help us now, I promise you that."

That prediction did not come true. Out of 12 picks, they got Pardee and Eddy's ex-Cougar LB Lamar Lathon (No. 15 in the 1st round), DT Jeff Alm (2nd), DE Willis Peguese (3rd), Texas WR Tony Jones (6th), Mississippi WR/KR Pat Coleman (9th) and S Dee Thomas (10th). None would help in 1990. The worst crime was ignoring the beleaguered secondary (passing on LeRoy Butler and Eric Davis for Alm).

The press said Lathon (6'3, 240) was "capable of becoming the finest defensive player ever to throw on a Columbia blue jersey. Period." Scout CO Brocato said that if Lathon had not injured his knee in a car wreck prior to his final season, he would have been the No. 1 selection overall ahead of Cortez Kennedy, Junior Seau and Emmitt Smith.

Notre Dame's Alm (6'6, 275) came in with a sort of Dave Casper flair, saying, "I can't see myself saying 'y'all' real quick but I guess I can learn." The coaches were eager to get him up to 300 pounds and put him beside Childress so QBs would have to throw over a pair of 6'6 DTs. They were also worried about Smith, who was shot in the leg during the off season.

Besides Eddy at DC, Bob Young was the new OL coach and Pat Thomas on the DBs. Pardee tried to hire June

Doug Smith (6'4, 300) was a great run-stuffing tackle. The trick was keeping him on the field. In eight years in Houston, he never made it through the entire season without missing time. Going into 1990, he was trying to recover from a gunshot wound to the leg.

Jones as OC but failed, and so he moved Kevin Gilbride to that position.

There was more position competition in camp than there had been in years. On defense, the contests were at LCB between Brown and Dishman, at RCB between Allen and Johnson, at OLB between Lyles and Lathon, and at MLB between Smith, Grimsley and Seale. Donaldson was let go through Plan B and replaced with Terry Kinnard. On offense, there was serious competition for the one RB spot. Maggs became the starting LT, replacing Davis, who was released. Maggs was the quickest OT on the team, a premium for the Run 'N' Shoot, and he was cheaper.

The holdouts included Jones, Carlson, Grimsley, Davis, Allen, Harris and Pinkett. Carlson, Rozier and White asked for a trade. Cody said, "My contract's up. I definitely don't want to be here." Givins also complained. Byrd was cut. Jones' holdout required the acquisition of 34-year-old Ezra Johnson. They also signed OG Doug Dawson.

The Oilers beat Dallas 27-6 in their only win of the preseason. The most memorable moment of the exhibition season came at Minnesota after a Dishman interception when he waived the ball in the Vikings' faces on his way to a TD. Just before he crossed the goal line, he was blindsided and lost the ball. It made CNN's play of the day and brought harsh criticism on the third-year player. Like Glanville, Pardee defended him. "I hate the perception people have of him," said Jack. "Cris is playing good football for us. He's really a team player. He's highly emotional. He's a tough guy. I wish everybody perceived him that way ... (and) I wish he'd quit doing things to get that wrong perception."

By the time the season rolled around, there were plenty of other problems. Brown, Allen, Grimsley and Rozier lost their jobs and were not happy. Pennison, Lyles, Highsmith and Hill's grips on theirs were tenuous. While Brown and Allen were particularly vocal, all of this group would be heard from at one time or another. Moreover, most of the veterans, in general, complained about the 5 a.m. practices and Friday and Saturday practices during the season.

"That stuff doesn't bother me," said Pardee. "I worry more about being prepared. I was with George Allen long enough to know the importance of being prepared when you step on the field. Players are going to complain anyway. I used to be one. The biggest thing is making sure they're prepared."

Holovak sent Highsmith to Dallas before the opener. After passing up Miami's No. 1 in 1989 (Metcalf or Atwater), he was lucky to get a second-rounder. The former No. 3 overall selection who the Oilers traded up to draft said, "I finally go to a team where I'm wanted ... I've regressed since I went to Houston mainly because of the system."

As happened in the past when the Oilers put together a good team, so too did the other AFC Central squads. It was the best division from top to bottom with three star QBs in Esiason, Kosar and Moon, plus Eric Metcalf, Webster Slaughter, Eddie Brown, Barry Foster, Louis Lipps, Michael Dean Perry, Eric Green, Rodney Holman, Rod Woodson, Anthony Munoz, Greg Lloyd, Clay Matthews, Max Montoya, James Francis, David Fulcher, James Brooks, Frank Minnifield, Dermontti Dawson, Raymond Clayborn, Carnell Lake and the Oilers.

Asked to compare the Oiler teams of the late 1970s with this team, new radio voice Bum Phillips said, "The team the Oilers have now probably has more talent. But we'll have to see if they have as much heart."

THE 1990 REGULAR SEASON — ALL THUMBS

The schedule-maker must have grinned when he put Houston in Atlanta for the opener. Despite assurances of a minimal transition, the Oilers were not ready.

A 3-13 team the year before, Glanville had the Falcons breathing fire. He said it was nothing special, but this was a guy who sent Floyd Reese a black rose after Reese refused to join him in Atlanta. The rose was supposed to signal that Reese's career was dead. The Falcons focused all of their training camp on the opener.

After winning the backfield derby, White promptly fumbled twice in the first quarter as Atlanta built a 21-0 lead. Moon brought them back late, getting within 37-27, but that was it. The final was 47-27.

The defense allowed one drive over 50 yards and just two offensive TDs. The difference was six turnovers (4 in the 1st quarter), Atlanta's blitz and three bad calls that cost them 21 points.

Houston reporters tried hard to get Oiler players to trash Glanville, but not many bit. Jones said, "They played hard and above their heads. I wouldn't be surprised if they went 1-15." (They finished 5-11)

While the outcome made Glanville's point (that it was not all his fault), he threw a few gratuitous barbs. He sent the game ball to SMU coach Forrest Gregg, whose team lost to Pardee's Cougars 95-21 in 1989. He said, "I'm giving the ball to SMU because they played a total jerk last year who tried to run up 100 points on a bunch of freshmen." He added, "Texas can kiss my butt."

Goaded by the press, Pardee's best comeback was, "He ought to know what a jerk is." Eventually the Commissioner had to order a cease-fire. It was the sort of story that would have consumed the national press if one of the combatants coached for New York (see Bill Parcels) but, since it was just Houston and Atlanta, it blew over.

What did consume them was the offense. The naysayers had the upper hand after Week 2. Even though Pittsburgh converted just 1-of-13 third downs and produced an anemic 123 total yards, they won 20-9. Back when the Oilers were producing those kind of offensive numbers, they were compiling 1-13 records. It was the Steelers' first win at home over Houston since 1986.

The Oiler defense did not give up a point. Pittsburgh did it by playing six DBs deep to prevent any long passes and pounding the WRs whenever they touched the ball. In a game referred to as the "drop and flop," Jeffires, Hill and Givins together dropped 10 passes. Rod Woodson claimed they were "hearing footsteps."

The rest of the league was watching. In two games, they had been exposed to heavy blitzing and hard hits on the smurfs. Buddy Ryan called the offense the "chuck and duck." He said the "quarterback is going to get hit on every play when they play the Eagles." Chris Collinsworth said on HBO's *Inside the NFL*, "By the end of the season, the Run 'N' Shoot will be dead in the NFL." NBC's Will McDonough said, "If the coaches don't back off from the Run 'N' Shoot, we're going to see some quarterbacks get killed."

Winning the next two quieted things somewhat. After Rozier refused to play special teams, he was released outright. In 1989, he was worth a second-round pick. Not so in 1990.

Then came a big game, one of those rare opportunities to prove to the world that the Oilers could play with the big boys. San Francisco had won four Super Bowls, including the last two. They came in 3-0, having tied an NFL-record with 11 straight road games. They were first in the NFL in offense. Houston was second.

It was another in a long line of "almosts." Houston led 14-0 after one quarter, 21-14 in the third and 21-17 in the fourth. But the defense could not hold and they lost 24-21. The turning point came with about 7 minutes left and San Francisco trailing by 4. On second down from the Houston 46, Ezra Johnson nailed Joe Montana, knocking him out of the game. Steve Young came in for the third-and-four situation and fumbled the snap. Childress recovered. But McDowell called time-out. Montana came back for the do-over and hit John Taylor with a 6-yard completion that he turned into a TD after Dishman went for and missed the strip. "We just blew a golden opportunity," said Jones.

That brought up the Bengals for the first time since the 61-7 game. Houston crushed them 48-17 to move to 3-3. Afterwards, Holovak waived Robert Lyles, the man who coined "House of Pain." He ended up in Atlanta where he beat out No. 1 pick Aundray Bruce. Rozier was there, too, but not doing as well. In Dallas, Highsmith was benched for fumbling and dropping passes.

Then came an unscheduled break. They beat the Saints, but lost Tony Zendejas to a broken fibula. Management's poor reaction to this situation would cost them. The next week, they lost to the Jets 17-12 as the new kicker, Teddy Garcia, missed 3 FGs and an extra point. This would be a problem that would not go away.

The more immediate concern at the time was how they lost to New York. Houston led convincingly in every conceivable category, including yards (425 to 229), first downs (28 to 13), time of possession (37:30 to 22:30) and passing yards (381 to 142). Houston converted 9 of 14 third downs. But ... Hill dropped a wide-open sure TD. Moon was hit from behind in his own end zone. Moon and White fumbled a hand-off at the Jets' 1. Moon was sacked 5 times. Munchak jumped offsides on a crucial third-and-2 in the fourth quarter. It added up.

The Run "N" Shoot generated controversy both in Houston and around the league. The first couple of games in 1990, ugly losses to Atlanta and Pittsburgh, brought criticism to a fevered pitch. But by the end of the year, the Oilers had the No. 1 pass offense in the NFL (by a long shot) and the No. 2 scoring offense. Naturally, the WRs had big years as their top 5 all put up career highs in receptions. Drew Hill (at right scoring in Pittsburgh) caught 74 for 1,019 yards, Haywood Jeffires had 74 for 1,048, Ernest Givins 72 for 979, Curtis Duncan 66 for 785 and 5'7 rookie Tony Jones caught 30 for 409 yards and 6 TDs.

That game and the season to that point were a good snapshot of things to come. The offense was flying up and down the field. On the year, they enjoined a huge edge on total yards (3,029 to 2,157), first downs (192 to 127) and time of possession (4 minutes a game). The defense was not letting the other teams score many points. Yet they were 4-4.

The right medicine appeared to be in LA as the Rams had the worst pass defense in football and the Oilers had the best pass offense. Houston lost 17-13. "This is as bad as I've felt since I've been playing football," said Meads. "This just seems to happen to us every year. We had another golden opportunity in front of us, and we screwed it up."

In trouble at 4-5, they got hot again. For the second time in the season, they won 4 of 5. They creamed the Browns in Cleveland 35-23, beat 9-1 Buffalo in the Dome 27-24 before 60,130 on *Monday Night Football*, lost at Seattle 13-10 in OT, smeared Cleveland again 58-14 and beat the Chiefs 27-10.

The Kansas City game was a solid win against a playoff team on the road. Moon was unconscious, going 27-of-45 for 527 yards against a secondary recognized as one of the NFL's best. With Norm Van Brocklin's all-time record of 554 yards in his grasp with under two minutes to go, Moon handed off 7 straight times and then took a knee on the final play. The veteran Moon said, "You don't ever want to give a team a motivating factor when you don't have to."

With two games left, the Run 'N' Shoot had quieted critics. Moon (337-of-536 for 4,401 yards) was within reach of Dan Marino's single season records (378-of-623 for 5,084). More importantly, the team was 8-6 and two wins away from their first AFC Central crown. Their last two opponents were the Bengals and Steelers.

They went to Cincinnati confidently, having won 6 of the last 8 against them, including a 31-point victory in the last one. They were the NFL's top offense while the Bengal defense was ranked No. 27. Then again it was another late season game in the home of a fictional geographic rival. Originally scheduled for October, the game was switched because the Reds were in the World Series. Game time temperature was below freezing.

They lost 40-20 despite leading 20-13 in the third quarter. "It's the same old crap," said Meads, "screwing up our chances again. I've been tired of it since we started this crap two years ago." Worse yet, with under 2 minutes left and the Oilers out of it, Moon dislocated his thumb on a helmet. A bone stuck through the skin. He would be out at least 3 weeks.

They had to start Carlson in the finale against Pittsburgh. With the playoffs on the line for both teams, it brought back memories of some great battles, most won by the Steelers. There was the 13-10 win in 1974 under Sid Gillman that helped turn the team around; the 1975 "hold the rope" *Monday Night* game when Houston was blown out 32-9; the 1978 game when Campbell had 3 TDs to lead Houston to a 24-17 upset; the 1978 AFC Championship mugging; the 1979 championship game marred by the bad call on the Renfro TD; the 6-0 shutout in 1980 that ended the Steelers' playoff run; the Glanville-Noll feud in 1987; the snow storm in 1989 when White rushed for 115 yards; the 1989 playoff loss in the Dome on New Year's; and the earlier 1990 game when the Steeler secondary embarrassed Houston's WRs. Overall, Pittsburgh owned a 29-14 edge.

The '90s Steelers did not deserve to be in first. They had beaten only one team all year with a winning record (Oilers). They had a good defense (No. 1 pass defense), but their offense stank. They were third from the bottom in scoring. It was amazing they were 9-6.

The Commander came through hitting 22-of-29 for 247 yards. They won 34-14. Though the division ended in a 3-way tie, Pittsburgh was out and Houston in.

The top AFC teams were Buffalo (13-3), the Raiders (12-4), Miami (12-4) and Kansas City (11-5). Houston, Cincinnati, Pittsburgh and Seattle were all 9-7, but the wildcard game was Houston at Cincinnati. No fewer than six Oilers "guaranteed" a win.

THE 1990 PLAYOFFS

Any attempts to invoke the memory of Giff Nielsen's heroic performance against the Chargers quickly faded. Carlson was a different man. In the first half, he was 4-of-10 for 35 yards and one interception. His longest pass play of the game was 15 yards.

Jim Eddy's beaten up defense got pushed around. It was 20-0 at the half. After falling behind 34-0, they lost 41-14. It was the most points Cincinnati had ever scored in a playoff game. Fuller said, "The Bengals did a good job but we helped them. I don't think we were in the right scheme. We didn't seem to be putting ourselves in the best position to stop them. That's a coaching decision."

Among the postgame locker room queries of the players came this question, "Do you see now why Houston fans are the way they are?"

The responses were boilerplate. "I feel like we have the talent," said Meads, "but I can't put my finger on it." Jones added, "It's a big surprise. I've felt all year we were a better team than the Bengals." Moon said, "We're close, we're very close. It's just a matter of us doing the little things that help you win and cutting out the mistakes — the needless penalties and turnovers — that keep you from winning." Pinkett noted, "The guys were saying to each other that the only way we're ever going to get over this hump is to win the division. We realize that's the only way we're ever going to get to where we want to be."

Munchak promised more "changes. I thought we made some pretty good ones last year with the new staff, the draft and Plan B, but here we are again in the same situation. It's getting old." His buddy Matthews went so far as to utter that ugly 9-letter word. He said, "I don't think this game is indicative of this team's — well, I hate to say it, but — this team's *potential*. Looking at this season, with a few breaks we could have won the division and played at home this week, or even had a

Despite having the top offense in the NFL (over 405 yards and 25 points per game) and the No. 7 defense in the AFC, the Oilers were only 8-7 and scratching for a playoff spot going into the final weekend. With Moon on the sidelines, the stage was set for another heartbreak. But backup Cody Carlson came through with the game of his career as they clocked the overrated Steelers 34-14 to squeak into a wildcard spot. At right, ILB John Grimsley celebrates afterwards with his No. 1 fan and the festive sellout crowd.

When he dislocated his thumb against the Bengals in Game 15, Warren Moon was not only working on a career year, but also was on his way to breaking Dan Marino's all-time NFL marks. He ended up leading the league with 4,689 yards (395 yards short of the record) on 362-of-584 passing (23 completions short of the record) and 33 touchdowns (3 short of George Blanda's 1961 team record). His QB rating of 96.8 was the best of his career. He was named AFC offensive player of the year, first team Pro Bowl and second team All-Pro. One of the weaknesses of the Run 'N' Shoot, however, was exposed in his fumble count. Having no tight end and only a single back for protection from a hard rush, he led NFL in fumbles with 18.

bye. Eliminate the mistakes in Atlanta and Pittsburgh, when the offense was totally new to us, and we're division champions."

Hill had other thoughts on his mind, namely Hill. The 34-year-old did not enjoy splitting playing time in the playoffs with Harris. "Here we are playing in a playoff game," he stated, "and I'm wondering if they want me to be a part of the team." He caught 1 for 5 yards and dropped another on a third-down play in the first quarter. Harris had 4 for 37 yards.

The Bengals fell to the Raiders while Buffalo beat Miami. Then the Bills creamed LA 51-3 to earn the first of several berths in the Super Bowl. The Giants won the NFC championship, squeaking by the 49ers 15-13. The Bills, a team the Oilers beat during the season, lost the Super Bowl 20-19 after missing a 47-yard field goal in the waning seconds. It was the seventh straight championship for the NFC.

OVERVIEW

The Oilers improved in some respects. They led the NFL in total offense (vs. 5th in 1989), passing offense, third-down conversions and first downs. Had he not suffered the broken thumb, Moon may have had the best single season in history. He had 4,689 yards (5th all-time) on 362-of-584 passing (62%), and led the league with 33 TDs against 13 interceptions. Twice during the season, he threw 5 TDs in one game (Bengals, Browns). His rating of 96.8 was second to Jim Kelly's 101.2 (Kelly had 2,829 yards and 24 TDs). Moon was the AFC offensive player of the year and came in third to Joe Montana as league MVP.

He was also very good at spreading the ball around which kept his WRs happy. Jeffires and Hill led the AFC with 74 receptions each. Jeffires led in yardage with 1,048 while Hill had 1,019. Givins caught 72 for 979 yards while Duncan had 66 (5th in the AFC) for 785 and rookie Tony Jones caught 30 for 409 and 6 TDs. White led rushers with 702 yards. Both he and Givins also had 1,000-yard seasons in combined yardage.

Five offensive players made the Pro Bowl. Moon, Munchak and Matthews were starters, while Hill and Givins made it as backups. In a slap, Jeffires did not.

The defense was converted from an attacking, risk-taking mob to a reactionary, bend-but-don't-break mode. Not everyone was pleased with the passive style. They finished No. 7 overall in the AFC (11th in the NFL), No. 2 against the run (8th in NFL) and No. 8 against the pass (15th in NFL). Jones led the team with 10½ sacks while Fuller and Childress each had 8 (Derrick Thomas led the NFL with 20). Johnson led the AFC with 8 interceptions while Kinnard and Dish each had 4. Smith led the team in tackles. Only Childress made the Pro Bowl. Montgomery led the NFL in punting, but did not have enough kicks to qualify.

POOR FANS

For the fourth straight year, the Oilers fell one victory short of claiming their first outright AFC Central title and avoiding the wildcard game. Fans were bewildered. It was not supposed to happen this way. Everyone knew teams go through cycles: up for awhile and then rebuild. The Oilers had done more than their fair share of down time. It was their turn now. All teams eventually get to play in at least one Super Bowl eventually, don't they?

They knew this was the best Oiler team ever. The offense was more productive than the 49ers, Bills, Bengals or Dolphins. They scored more points than any other team except one. The defense gave up 18 fewer TDs than it did in 1989. They beat the Bills, Bengals, Chiefs and Steelers. They traded Glanville, who was supposed to be what was holding them back, for the popular Pardee. But they finished with the same record.

The analysis started with penalties. Despite the promises, the '90 team finished with only 13 fewer than the '89 club and still led the NFL (135 for 1,009 yards). The worst offenders were the team leaders, the QBs, who produced 13 flags in delay of game penalties alone. Jones had 11 (9 offsides), Johnson had 11 (5 interference calls), Dish had 7, Munchak 7 and Matthews 6. Three times they were flagged for too many men on the field.

A superficial review would also finger the defense. But the stats were somewhat misleading. The offense and punt teams together gave up 7 TDs. That was over 3 points per game. Take those away and the defense surrendered only 15.9 points per game. With this offense, that should have at least been worth 12 or 13 wins.

Three times during the season, the defense held teams to 17 points or fewer, but they lost (Jets 17-12, Rams 17-13, Seahawks 13-10). Then there was Pittsburgh, who had 123 total yards but somehow won 20-9. Against Atlanta, the defense gave up only two TDs, yet they lost 47-27. The Oilers were reverse miracle workers.

One key was opponents' ability to keep the offense from scoring TDs. Tony Woods of the Seahawks, who held Houston to 10 points, explained, "We knew they would take the ball down the field. You really can't stop them between the 20s but we didn't want to let them in the end zone. We wanted to make them use 10 and 15 plays on every drive. That gave us a better chance to force turnovers, and that's what happened."

That strategy led to turnovers. Besides interceptions (16), the WRs and QBs fumbled a lot. Moon had 17. It explained why Montgomery did not have enough kicks to qualify for the punting title. Through the first 11 games, the Oilers did not punt on their first drive. They had four TDs, a FG and six turnovers.

It also got tough for the Run 'N' Shoot in the Red Zone. On 60 trips inside the 20, the Oilers scored 32 TDs and 14 FGs (.766). Good teams average at least .850. Oiler opponents scored at an .888 clip.

Often overlooked was the performance of the GM. Several of the defensive players and coaches complained loudly when just one defender made the Pro Bowl. A look at the selections showed that ahead of Fuller and Jones were Bruce Smith, Greg Townsend and Jeff Cross. Ahead of Johnson and Dishman were Rod Woodson, Albert Lewis and Kevin Ross. In front of Al Smith were John Offerdahl, Shane Conlan and David Little. Childress was the backup to Michael Dean Perry. Except for Smith, the Oilers had the chance to draft each one of those players, but passed. Ultimately, it always comes down to the players.

Houston's sports authorities were still gentle with the coach. "Expecting Pardee and his lieutenants to remake the team into a champion in one season might have been totally unrealistic," wrote Ed Fowler. Dale Robertson, having defected from the *Post* to the *Chronicle*, wrote, "Jack's consummately professional no-nonsense approach and carriage weren't enough to bring overnight change to the bad work habits and mental flabbiness instilled by his pure-nonsense predecessor, Jerry Glanville. Twelve months after Glanville's good-bye and good riddance, the Oilers are no closer to being the team they can and *should* be."

McClain blamed the players and advised getting rid of "some players who have talent but are not the type with whom Jack Pardee believes he can win with." He also called for changes on the coaching staff. June Jones, now out of his contract with Detroit, was at the top of their list but ended up in Atlanta.

A WACKY YEAR

It was also an interesting year apart from the Oilers. The biggest controversy occurred early in the season in the New England dressing room. After the game, Pats' TE Zeke Mowatt introduced his manhood to Lisa Olson, a reporter for the Boston Herald. A few choice words accompanied the presentation. It was bound to happen sooner or later. Pro athletes frequently give interviews and parade through locker rooms nude. Mix into that testosterone-laden scene a reporter who Patriot owner Victor Kiam (the electric razor guy) described as a "classic bitch," and you had a story waiting to happen.

The national media could not get enough of the story. It overshadowed the games for weeks. Despite the controversial nature of the issue, the media was unanimous in its support of Olson. There was no dissension.

There was only one man crazy enough to challenge the establishment on this issue. He lived in Cincinnati. Wacky Sam Wyche thought allowing female reporters in while the men were trying to shower and dress was "unfair" to them and their wives. So he barred all women from Bengal dressing rooms. He was quickly and unanimously condemned as a Neanderthal. Smelling some free publicity, *USA Today* dispatched a woman reporter to challenge Sam's ban. He not only refused to let her in, but also accused her employer of "planting" her there just to make a story. The media was in a tizzy. Commissioner Tagliabue eventually made Sam back down and fined him a hefty $30,000. Sam's response was to give his players wraparound towels.

On another front, Jimmy Johnson had managed to bring the University of Miami spirit to the pro ranks. Both Kelvin Martin and Nate Newton were arrested in what was to become a long running police blotter show in Dallas.

In Los Angeles, Al Davis was still playing musical stadiums. At one point, he had Oakland, Sacramento, Irwindale and LA strung out on where the Raiders might play. Opponents had to schedule travel plans to both Oakland and LA because nobody knew where they would end up. He shrewdly pocketed $10 million to stay in Los Angeles — for the time being.

1991: FINALLY

Despite another quick exit from the playoffs, the team was wildly popular. It even got to Bum Phillips, who joined the radio broadcast team. The GM was not beating up writers and the coach was well-liked. For the '90 season, the Oilers averaged a record 60,194 tickets sold.

Bud agreed they "made some headway." He said Pardee would eventually "do what I thought he would when I hired him, and that's get us to the Super Bowl." Bud's keys to improvement were: (1) "Do away with some of the penalties. I don't think you're going to the Super Bowl if you lead the league in penalties;" and (2) "We've got to learn how to win on the road. I'm confident Jack will find a way to do it."

Ironically, he called for more toughness, something for which Glanville was criticized. In fact, Adams sounded as if he had just read Jerry's book that was for sale at the time. "I think we need a certain meanness injected into our guys," he said. "We have a lot of guys who are big, nice and good athletes who don't want to really hurt someone. We've got to get a little more killer instinct in our players." Kenny Hand agreed. He wrote, "This club needs more hit and less quit."

THE FRONT OFFICE

The Oiler front office was not coming off its best year. The 1990 draft was unproductive. The only pick to contribute was 5'7 WR Tony Jones. After showing up with "Sudden Impact" license plates, Lamar "the next Lawrence Taylor" Lathon hardly played. This was despite being handed team captain Robert Lyles' spot in camp without earning it. The linebacker who lacked discipline and maturity in college gained neither by retaining his college coaches in the pros.

Nor did the transition go well. New coaches and schemes left several players unhappy or obsolete. Instead of having the foresight to deal them, they bumbled around, eventually obtaining just one draft pick for Rozier, Lyles and Highsmith.

Nor did they do much in Plan B, although 35-year-old Ezra Johnson played a valuable role out of position at DT. Even that had a dark liner as valuable playing time was denied Alm and Glenn Montgomery.

In 1991, Plan B claimed Steve Brown. The year before, Holovak turned down an offer of Tim McKyer for Brown. Tony Zendejas was also allowed to leave in one of the dumber moves of the decade. They added LB Rick Graf and FS John Hagy while trading starting LB John Grimsley to Miami for a third-round choice. Just before the draft, they traded their first-round pick (No. 17) to New England for their second- (first choice in Round 2) and fourth-round picks.

THE 1991 DRAFT

The 1991 draft was another one of those mighta, coulda, shoulda ones. The Oilers had 8 picks in rounds 2-5 with three in the second and two in the third and fourth rounds. They took S Mike Dumas (New England), CB Daryll Lewis (Highsmith), C John Flannery, former Houston Klein Forrest CB Steve Jackson, OL Kevin Donnalley (Grimsley), DT David Rocker (New England), S Marcus Robertson, WR Gary Wellman, RB Gary Brown and WR Shawn Jefferson.

Reporters were happy, as were Holovak and scouts CO Brocato, Glen Cumbee, Dub Fesperman and Frank Bush. They got two safeties, two CBs, two OLs, three WRs, a RB and a DT. The *Chronicle* called it "draft gold." DBs coach Pat Thomas said, "We wanted defensive backs with savvy." He said not to worry about the size of the *Young Guns* (Dumas 5'11, Lewis 5'9, Jackson 5'8, Robertson 5'11½). "There are guys who play football for a living and then there are football players," said Thomas. "These are football players." Jim Eddy said of Dumas:

"You're going to love watching this guy play. He's bringing the correct attitude and personality to our football team." Dale Robertson mentioned him for the Hall of Fame.

It was a good draft as 9 of 14 choices made the team. Two would become Pro Bowl quality (Lewis, Robertson), five others at least part-time starters (Jackson, Donnalley, Flannery, Brown, Wellman) while one more started for other teams (Jefferson).

However, it could have been a lot better starting with the second round where they burned a pick for the fifth straight year. Holovak liked to say, "Anybody can make picks in the top rounds." But those high picks made the difference between contender and pretender. Dumas would never rise above glorified special teams status, which was consistent with fellow second-rounders Jeff Alm ('90), Scott Kozak ('89), Quinton Jones ('88) and Walter Johnson ('87).

Flannery would become a starter, but by selecting him, they passed on perhaps the ideal RB for this offense — Ricky Waters (as well as LB Mo Lewis, WR Jake Reed and QB Brett Farve). If they wanted an OL, one of the best OTs of the '90s, Erik Williams, was available in the middle of the third round. With the Jackson, Donnalley and Rocker choices, they passed on William Thomas, Yancy Thigpen, Brian Cox, Merton Hanks and Ben Coates. Jimmy Johnson did not take DE Leon Lett until the seventh round, 44 picks after Houston selected Gary Wellman.

Focusing on the defense, here is how the draft could have gone:

Rd.	Was	(Overall Number)	Could have been	Made All-Star
2	SS	Mike Dumas (28)	CB D. Lewis (38)	1995
2	CB	Darryll Lewis (38)	CB Aeneas Williams (59)	1994
2	OL	John Flannery (44)	FS M. Robertson (102)	1993
3	CB	Steve Jackson (71)	OLB William Thomas (104)	1995
3	OL	Kevin Donnalley (79)	ILB Brian Cox (113)	1992
4	DT	David Rocker (101)	SS Merton Hanks (122)	1994
4	FS	Marcus Robertson (102)	DT Andy Harmon (156)	1995
5	WR	Gary Wellman (129)	DE Leon Lett (173)	1994

Combining these standouts with Childress, Fuller, Jones, Lathon, Al Smith, Dishman and McDowell would have propelled them through the decade (not to mention given them a defense that could hold a lead).

A more balanced draft would have been Brett Farve (No. 33 overall), Aeneas Williams, Erik Williams (No. 70), Marcus Robertson, Yancy Thigpen (No. 90), Cox, Hanks, Harmon, Lett, Gary Brown (No. 214), Shawn Jefferson (No. 240) and Keenan McCardell (No. 326).

THE RUN-AND-SHOOT

The Giants won the Super Bowl with a ball control offense and strong defense, putting Houston's offense back in the cross-hairs. Pardee said, "I know football. I'm a mentally sound football coach. I don't play high-risk football. I don't think the run-and-shoot is a high risk offense when it's carried out the way it's supposed to be .... Hey, the game has changed a lot since the Woody Hayes' era."

He said the "key is not how much you throw but how successful you are when you throw." Gilbride said, "For us, the bottom line on our system is that it best fits our players. We want to maximize what our guys do best, and we believe the run-and-shoot allows us to do that. Besides, when you've got a quarterback like Warren Moon, you've got to do everything you can to take advantage of him."

Moon pointed out the 49ers won four Super Bowls as a passing team. He also noted their strong defenses. "I don't care how good your offense is or how well you throw, you've got to have a good defense to get to the Super Bowl," he said. "I still believe defense is what actually gets you there." That was as close as Moon ever came to directly criticizing teammates.

1991 TRAINING CAMP

The Oilers were the top choice on TV in Texas again like they were in the late '70s. The Cowboys, however, were not only about to close the gap, but pass them. For the first time since 1985, Bud was heavily involved in training camp and contract negotiations. He moved camp to San Antonio where he was popular, at least with local dignitaries. He championed hard for their WLAF team. Camp began with a water parade down the Riverwalk in front of about 1,000 folks.

There was a sense that the window of opportunity would soon close. Moon said, "This season could be our best opportunity, but if we don't make it, that doesn't mean it'll never happen. I'll say this year or next." Pardee added, "We lost five games last year where one more big play on offense or defense could have changed the outcome. Just think, five more big plays last season, and we would have been one of the elite teams!"

When asked what they needed to get over the hump, he said, "Great teams have some real strong veterans, guys who just won't be denied."

Moon wanted to be one of those guys. "I think there was too much complaining last year," he said. "It started in camp when some guys didn't like getting up so early for practice. It continued in the season with complaints about the Friday and Saturday practices. Even before the playoff games, I heard some guys talking about their contracts. That kind of thing just doesn't do us any good."

He continued: "A lot of players just don't seem to realize or understand the situation they're in as a professional athlete, all the good things that can happen to them. When you get close to a championship, you have to do whatever's necessary to take advantage of it. If a championship is important to them — and it might not be important to some guys — they should never take it for granted when they have that opportunity. To be in the position we're in, to have a realistic shot of winning a championship, you should throw everything else out the window, at least for those six months when we're together ... if your contract isn't done, wait until the offseason. Don't keep complaining about it."

It all sounded great, but this was the Oilers. As of the opening of camp, 7 vets (Jones, Meads, White, Dishman, Gr. Montgomery, Carlson, Harris) plus 5 draft picks (Dumas, Lewis, Flannery, Rocker, Robertson) were holding out. For the many who thought the Oilers played with no "heart," this camp made their case. Mickey Herskowitz wrote, "I remember a time when players just wanted to get an opportunity to play."

Jones ($795,000, 12½ sacks in '90) wanted money comparable to the top ends such as Chris Doleman ($1.75 million, 21 sacks in '89), Reggie White ($1.4 million, 15 sacks in '90) and Bruce Smith (19 sacks in '90). For the second straight year, he signed on the eve of the opener.

Childress ($820,000) had a slightly better case at DT compared to Keith Millard ($1.7 million) and Michael Dean Perry ($2 million). Greg Montgomery wanted to be the top paid punter in the game since he had the highest average. The Oiler said he only punted twice a game. Loyal and hardworking Johnny Meads probably had the best argument for a raise from his $350,000. He was the only LB to play on all downs.

They really blew the kicker situation. Before camp opened, Pardee said, "Our kicking game has to improve." It was lip service. He had a blind spot when it came to special teams. So did Holovak. The trouble began in 1990 when Tony Zendejas broke his leg trying to make a tackle. Teddy Garcia replaced him.

The decision of who to protect on the Plan B list came down to money. Garcia made $200,000 while Zendejas got $400,000, no matter that Tony held many team kicking records. Holovak brought in Raul Allegre and Ian Howfield for competition. To the surprise of no one, Garcia bombed. Howfield, who had never kicked in a regular season NFL game and who last kicked professionally for the Oklahoma City Twisters, won the job.

It made for some temporarily good PR. Howfield, whose dad kicked for the Jets, was watching the Oilers play a preseason game in a bar in Oklahoma City. He thought he could kick better than what he saw on TV. He called them up, came in and won the job. But it turned out to be another one of those mind-numbingly stupid decisions for which the Oilers were infamous. Zendejas, meanwhile, took a pay cut to sign with the Rams.

The other big move of camp was a questionable trade. With Jones holding out again, they were sweating the pass rush. In August, they acquired one-time Pro Bowl DE Lee Williams (6'6, 270) who was involved in a contract squabble. The Oilers paid a high price for the 29-year-old, surrendering their 1992 No. 1 and rookie Shawn Jefferson, who was looking good at WR. At one time, Holovak maintained trading for a veteran was too risky because there was usually some reason his old club wanted to move him. Rumors had Jones being traded.

On the whole, the Oilers were suddenly younger. The Young Guns replaced DBs Brown, Allen, Kinnard and Knight. Gary Brown replaced Rozier, Flannery replaced Pennison, Howfield replaced Zendejas and Graf replaced Lyles. In total, 13 new players, including 8 rookies, made the roster.

Starters at new positions included Orlando at FS, Lathon at OLB, Williams at RDE (Jones hold out), Matthews at C, Flannery at RG, Pinkett for White (hold out), Kent Sullivan for Greg Montgomery (hold out) and Howfield.

The Oilers went 2-2 in the preseason, beating the Cowboys and Rams (in Memphis). With the holdouts and other turmoil, expectations were subdued.

They had a tough seeding. Seven payoff teams were on the schedule. They had the mean NFC East, including the defending Super Bowl champion Giants. They had late-season road games in Pittsburgh, Cleveland and New Jersey. The first three games were against playoff teams, starting with the Raiders, who were followed by the Bengals and Chiefs. They played two *Monday Night* games (Chiefs, Eagles) and two Sunday Night games (Bengals, Browns).

THE 1991 REGULAR SEASON — THIS TOWN WOULD HAVE BEEN ON FIRE

First up were the Raiders, who had played for the AFC championship the previous January. The Oilers came out like gangbusters before a record home crowd of 61,367 and knocked LA silly 41-17. Moon was 18-

of-33 for 250 yards and 2 TDs. He ran for a third. Pinkett rush for a career-high 144 yards, which caused White to quickly end his holdout. Former Twister Howfield missed his first extra point attempt. "We played like a diamond today," said Fuller. "But we can go on the road and turn out to be cubic zirconia."

He was referring to the next game at Riverfront Stadium where Houston was 1-10 since 1980. The average score over that span was 37-17. The thing about the Bengals that got to Houston players was, unlike the Steelers or Browns, they never played straight up. Wyche always used cute plays and tricks. That stuff riled the defensive types. "We don't dislike the Bengals," said Childress, "We hate them." The game started just like all the others with the Bengals marching 80 yards on the opening drive. But this one took a radical turn. Just before Rodney Holman crossed the goal line, Dish stripped the ball from him and it flew out of the end zone. Cincinnati never recovered and Houston won 30-7. Big Ray called it "the biggest win on the road we've had since I've been here."

The Chiefs were next in the Dome for a *Monday Night* game. With Moon hitting on 29-of-38 passes, they won 17-7 in a tough game before 61,058. As unbelievable as it may seem, it was the first time the Oilers had ever started a season 3-0.

They had beaten three playoff teams in three games, and in a surprising development, each opponent had more penalties than Houston. They had the second highest scoring team and had given up the second fewest points. All was beautiful, right?

So long as you love *The Oprah Winfrey Show*. Instead of focusing on something boring like performing their jobs, the Oilers were very busy getting in touch with their feminine side. They were into sharing their feelings. Jeffires shared that he was unhappy alternating with Tony Jones. Childress confessed he really did not want to play tackle. What Jones really wanted for Christmas was a trade. Hill confided he disliked rotating with Leonard Harris. White became an activist for free agency. Lee Williams, who was moaning before he ever got to town, told anyone who would listen he should be the starting *left* end. Even Moon, who held team meetings in the preseason to persuade his mates to concentrate on football, stormed out of a dressing room unhappy with the details of his $10 million contract. In protest, he refused to accept his paychecks.

It caught up with them. After sleeping through 3 quarters at New England, Moon woke up long enough to direct two 69-yard scoring drives and take a 20-17 lead with 1:52 left. But somehow the Patsies got to the Houston 32 for a final shot. With time running out, Greg McMurtry took a Hugh Millen pass looking for a miracle. He found one when Dale-Robertson-Hall-of-Fame member Mike Dumas not only whiffed the tackle but also crashed into Darryll Lewis, letting McMurtry score the game winner. "Well, it was pretty sickening," offered the coach. New England finished 6-10.

Lee Williams broke an arm early in the game on a helmet. He blamed it on playing out of position, something about the way he swung his left arm on the first step of his rush move. After never before missing a game due to injury, he was looking at 4-6 weeks. They also lost Munchak to a knee scope, Harris to a leg fracture and Ezra Johnson to a shoulder injury.

After an off-week, the hot Broncos came to the Dome for what was supposed to be a shootout. It was not. Houston led 35-0 at half and cruised to an easy 42-14 victory. Elway was harassed all day as Fuller had 3 sacks and Jones 2. Givins caught 5 for 151 yards. The new Cris Dishman continued his string of big plays with an interception and fumble return for a TD. The two teams would see each other again later in a different forum.

A 4-1 record and impressive wins over good teams were still not enough to keep the turmoil at bay. Moon's contract situation was spinning out of control. Journalists were angry that he refused to discuss it with them. Blinebury responded by calling him the "Teflon QB," and accused him and Leigh Steinburg of attempting to manipulate the press. He wrote, "The timing is perfect to point out that Adams' miserly ways could derail an express ride to the Super Bowl."

From out of this smoldering controversy, the team that could not win road games won two in a row. They beat a good Jets team 23-20 before 70,758 by overcoming a 10-0 first quarter deficit. Moon was 35-of-50 for 423 yards and 2 TDs. Jeffires caught 13 for 186 but Howfield missed an extra point for the second straight week, and for the fourth straight week, they fumbled a punt return. The next week, they escaped Miami with a 17-13 win on the strength of 5 takeaways by the defense. The most dramatic occurred when the improving Lathon met Sammie Smith in midair on a dive from the Oiler 1-yard line.

Those wins were followed by a 35-3 pasting of the Bengals at home. Because they did not affect the outcome, management seemed oblivious to Howfield's 3 missed extra points and a FG. Besides, that game sold a record 62,584 tickets.

At the halfway point, the Oilers were 7-1 for the first time. They had the No. 1 defense and No. 2 offense in the AFC. Adams called them the best team in franchise history. The next 8 games were all tough — four in their own division and four with the beasts of the NFC East. Only one team had a better record, the 8-0 Redskins. They were next.

In a great stadium on real grass before Dan Quayle and Bill Cosby, the Oilers dealt with their past by not choking. The Redskins played slightly better, but the Oiler defense made up for it with huge hits all over the field. At the end of the third quarter, it was 6-6 despite Houston's defense spending 13 of 15 minutes of that quarter on the field. A White fumble to open the fourth ended up a 13-6 Skins' lead. But late in the fourth, White redeemed himself by scoring to knot it at 13 with two starting OLs on the sidelines. They were thinking OT until Washington fumbled the ensuing kickoff and White got them to the 15 with 4 seconds left. It seemed the Oilers' ship had finally come in. Almost according to some grand Oiler script, however, Howfield's 33-yarder was wide left. It was a crusher. In the OT, Darrell Green intercepted Moon, which led to a 41-yard FG and 16-13 Skins victory.

For those who believe in moral victories, this was one of those. After so many past road disasters, they finally kept their composure against a tough foe. Pardee called it a "classic battle." Jones said, "You won't hear any excuses from me." Fowler wrote that the "loss did more than some of their victories to catalyze the growth process."

Howfield was cut on Monday. Holovak said, "It was tough to cut him because he's a real fine person, but you have to make those kicks." Ian was hurting. He broke down several times in his farewell press conference. It was all very sad.

Even more so considering that Tony Zendejas was on his way to a 17-of-17 season as the first kicker in NFL history not to miss a FG in the regular season. The press let the GM off light. Over the summer, he passed up veterans Norm Johnson and Mike Lansford. Al Del Greco, who was about to move to Alabama to become a corrugated-cardboard box salesman, won the four-way derby to be the next PK.

Despite having 4 games left against Pittsburgh and Cleveland, the 7-2 Oilers thought they had already run away with the division. They eyed Buffalo (8-1) and Denver (7-2). They also knew the Super Bowl would be played in a domed stadium in Minnesota. The Cowboys were next.

The Oiler offense almost blew the resurgent Cowboys off the planet, rolling up a team record 583 total yards. There was just one problem: on the strength of their special teams, including two blocked punts in the first quarter, the Pokes held the score close. In the fourth quarter, they tied it at 23 after recovering a punt that glazed Steve Jackson's shoulder pad. Jones said, "The Cowboys are like a bunch of little maggots. Right when you think you got them off you, they kept coming back." After Del Greco missed a 41-yard field goal with 35 seconds left, the game went to OT.

It almost lasted the full OT period. When Dallas drove to the Houston 24 late, all that offense seemed wasted. Instead of trying a long FG, they gave it to Emmitt Smith, who ripped off 9 yards before being violently sandwiched between Orlando and Lathon. The

With the coaching changeover in 1990, Sean Jones (6'7, 270) was able to get out from under the thumb of Doug Shively. As the weakside or rush end in the new 4-3 alignment, he became one of the better pass rushers in the AFC. In 1990, he had 12½ sacks, his highest total since 1986 when he was with the Raiders. He followed with 10 in 1991, 8½ in 1992 and 13 in 1993. At left, Jones prepares to lower the boom on Boomer Esiason. In 1991, the Oiler defense surrendered an average of just 15.7 points per game, second best in the AFC and tying the 1979 team for the club record since the merger.

ball popped loose and the Oilers took over at their own 15. Eight straight Moon completions later, they were at the Cowboy 3. Instead of kicking, they tried to run it in, only to watch Moon and White botch the hand-off as White's head was nearly ripped off. Del Greco then kicked the game winner. Pardee later admitted he was afraid to turn it over to a kicker. Moon was almost perfect, hitting 41-of-56 for 432 yards. Yet they almost lost.

They beat the Browns next 28-24 to move to 9-2 for the first time, but it took more late Moon heroics. After completing his last 13 passes against the Cowboys, he hit 8 of his last 9 against the Browns in the fourth quarter, including two TDs. The game is best remembered, however, for the spine-rattling hit McDowell put on WR Danny Peebles that caused him to retire.

Then, with a chance to stay ahead of the Bills for home field, they blew it in Pittsburgh 26-14. Playing without Eric Green and Rod Woodson, the 5-7 Steelers intercepted Moon 5 times in a light snow and swirling winds. The defense gave up just one drive over 40 yards.

The next opponent, the Eagles, had the best defense in football. They held Houston to a season-low 283 yards as the Philly DBs embarrassed Oiler WRs on a nationally televised Monday game. It was the return of the drop-and-flop as they were more concerned with ducking than catching. Moon was nervous, too, and starting fumbling snaps. Despite having to play with castoff QB Jeff Kemp, Philadelphia won 13-6 on the strength of five turnovers.

The Oilers had quickly gone from competing for the top seed to being in danger of blowing one of the largest division leads in football history. Nobody would put it past them. Their last 3 were with the Steelers at home and then on the road to Ohio and New Jersey.

They responded by crushing Pittsburgh 31-6 as Jack Pardee accomplished what no other Houston coach ever had, winning an undisputed AFC Central crown. The championship banner (in storage for 21 years) was unfurled. Bud had tears in his eyes greeting players in the dressing room. "It's great to win the division against the Steelers," he said. "We returned the favor today." Meads added, "After struggling through all the bad years, today is the most satisfying moment of my career. This was the end of a long, long struggle."

That brought up the Browns in Cleveland. It was cold and wet with the usual dirty gray skyline. The field was frozen dirt. The crowd cheered when it started to snow. The Oilers trailed until late in the fourth quarter, when Moon took them on a 13-play, 82-yard TD march into the teeth of a driving snowstorm. They led 17-14 lead with 2:19 to play. But the defense could not hold. With no time left, Matt Stover missed a chip shot 19-yard FG to seal the win.

Fan favorite Ernest Givins had the best end zone routine since Billy Johnson. And he had plenty to celebrate in 1991 as he was again part of the top passing offense in the NFL (over 300 yards and 24 points per game). Ernest put up the second highest reception (70) and yardage (996) totals of his career. Haywood Jeffires led the NFL in receptions (100) as he became only the fourth man in history to top the century mark. Drew Hill had 90 (second in AFC behind Jeffires) for 1,109 yards. Curtis Duncan caught 55. Only Jeffires, however, made the Pro Bowl.

The Oilers had won 11 games for only the fourth time in team history. No Houston team had ever won 12. Tied with Denver at 11-4 with no chance to catch Buffalo, one more win would give the Oilers a week off and let them open the second round of the playoffs at home, which meant everything to this team. All they had to do was beat the 7-8 Giants. The defending Super Bowl champions had fallen on hard times. They were out of the playoffs and just another team going through the motions.

With so much at stake, it was and still is hard to believe the weak Oiler effort. The game was there for the taking all day and the Giants were ready to fold their tents at any moment. But the Oilers could not be bothered. The defense collapsed and the offense acted like they wanted to hurry and get in out of the cold. New York won 24-20. The papers called them heartless. It was one more late season letdown. The repercussions would weigh heavy as Houston had to first beat the Jets just to have the opportunity to go to Denver.

THE 1991 PLAYOFFS

Fans felt shafted once again. The frustration was palpable. They did not understand what happened in East Rutherford, New Jersey. What was it with these guys? Did they not realize and appreciate what was at stake? How could they come out flat and unmotivated in a game with so much riding on it? Who was responsible? Was it Moon, Adams, Pardee, Holovak, Glanville, the curse of Ian Howfield? Was it drugs, racial disharmony, low morale, lazy practice habits, bad coaching? Perhaps the players were not really that good? Did they only cared about their paychecks? Why was Houston damned when it came to sports?

It was an ignominious ending to a season that started out with so much promise. At one point, they were 7-1 and on top of the league. By season's end they had to play the 8-8 Jets in the first round. Ticket sales got off to a slow start. Instead of trying to understand fan angst, Jones and Givins complained about support. Things got tense, but by game time all seemed forgiven. The sellout crowd (61,486) was jacked. Yes they were underachievers, but they were *their* underachievers. Signs hanging in the Dome read "Look Out Denver."

The Oilers played down to the competition. After missing a 46-yarder at the end of the half, Del Greco connected on a career-long 53-yarder in the third quarter to put them up 17-10. The burden then shifted to the defense for the rest of the game. They responded

Another popular player was Allen Pinkett. Fans appreciated the friendly, articulate ex-Golden Domer because he worked hard and did not complain. They also liked to see a smaller player succeed in the big man's game. The Oilers drafted the 5'9, 190-pound Pinkett in the third round in 1986 and effectively used him as a third down or change-of-pace back. In 1991, after the departures of Rozier and Highsmith, and holdout of White, he got his chance as a starter and had a career-high 720 yards (4.2 per carry). However, he was replaced in the playoffs by the 222-pound White, who was a better blocker, and then traded in the offseason.

by turning away the Jets with no score on 3 possessions inside Houston territory in the fourth quarter, including one dramatic goal line stand. The defense had finally done it, they held a late lead in an important game.

Moon was 28-of-40 for 271 yards and 2 touchdowns to Givins. Fans were back in love with them. Maybe they had some heart after all.

That brought up Denver, who Houston creamed early in the season in the Dome. But everyone knew the Broncos were a different team at home. It looked like a good matchup: the classic battle between hard-driving overachievers and more talented underachievers.

The good news was that the game-time temperature was above freezing (36 degrees), the sun was out and there was no wind. The bad news was injuries. Doug Smith was out. Childress tried to play on a bad back, but came out in the second quarter and did not return. It was the second time in three years Ray was on the sidelines in the playoffs. Lee Williams and Jeff Alm took up the slack, but neither the rush defense nor the pass rush were the same as the first game.

The offense rocked from the coin toss. Denver opened with one DL, four LBs and six DBs, but did not play their safeties back in a deep zone like most teams. Moon made them pay. He only used 4 plays to score first on a 15-yard TD to Jeffires. Their next possession ended in a 9-yard scoring pass to Hill. The Broncos got going at that point, but only because of penalties: a facemask call on Childress, a 15-yard personal foul on Johnson for throwing a WR around and a deadly offsides by Lathon on a third down that would have forced a FG try. Denver got the TD but missed the kick. Penalties accounted for 25 yards on the 65-yard drive. Fuller said after the game, "We were relatively penalty-free all year and then this happens. We gave them some momentum. Here it was 14-0 and all of a sudden it's 14-6 and they had some confidence. It wasn't what they were doing. We gave it to them with stupid penalties."

Moon took the ensuing possession for a six-yard TD to Duncan. Three possessions, three TDs and the Oilers were up by 15. Moon made it look easy. Their fourth possession was stopped at the Bronco 12 by an interception, one of Moon's few mistakes. Elway then took his team 88 yards to cut it to 21-13 just before the half.

With the Oilers passing their way up and down the field, the Broncos changed defenses in the second half, dropping the safeties back. Houston responded by riding White down the field. It looked like they would score another TD until Jeffires dropped a third-down pass that would have given them a first down at the Denver 5. Del Greco then missed the 33-yarder. It was a big miss. Late in the third, David Treadwell kicked a 49-yarder to cut the lead to 21-16.

No one left the stadium or turned off their TV for the fourth quarter. On the next Oiler possession, the Broncos brought a safety closer to the line so Moon went back to the air. He marched them 67 yards to the Denver 7 where Jeffires dropped another pass, this one in the end zone on a third-and-two that would have iced the game. It went right through his arms. This time, Del Greco connected on a 25-yarder to push the lead back to eight. The Broncos' missed extra point was looming large. Elway then used up 6½ minutes on a 12-play, 80-yard drive to cut the lead to 24-23, twice converting on third down and once on fourth.

The Oilers got the ball back at their 27 with 6:46 left. They understood their mission. Eat up the clock and they were in the AFC Championship. They could not give the ball back to John Elway with time for one of his late comebacks. The Broncos had not stopped them all day. What followed was perhaps the most memorable drive in Oiler history.

On first down, Moon hit White with a short pass for 9. On second, White gained 5 and a first down. On the ensuing first down, Houston's 7-time Pro Bowl OG Mike Munchak committed a motion penalty to stop the clock and push them back 5 yards. But White gained 8 on a draw and then 11 up the middle to gain another first down at the Denver 45. They were moving, but because of the penalty and White running out of bounds, they had used up only 2 minutes. Moon then hit Jeffires for 6 yards and then another 5. That was good enough for another first down at the Denver 34 with about 3 minutes remaining. Three running plays and a field goal would ice it. Four straight running plays alone might do it. It was time to make some history.

White's first-down run was stuffed for a 1-yard loss. On second down, White forgot the play, ran up to Moon to check it and could not get reset in time. The delay of game penalty pushed them back to a second-and-16, again killing the clock. Next, Munchak was flagged for illegal use of hands. Just like that, the Oilers had gone from first-and-10 on the Bronco 34 to third-and-26 at the 50 with a still clock. To top it off as only the Oilers can, Moon misread Gilbride's hand signal from the sideline and ran a draw. It went for 4 yards. Gilbride's actual call was a corner pattern to gain enough back to give Del Greco a shot. Instead, they punted. The collective groan that came out of Houston at that moment registered a reading on a Richter Scale in California.

But optimism peaked anew as Montgomery unloaded the punt of his life, putting the ball out of bounds at the Denver 2. True blue believers knew this was it. This was where the Oilers would make that long-awaited stand. This was when they would show the world they had heart. This was when they would grab destiny by the tail. For once, they would be heroes.

The odds were stacked against Elway. He had no time-outs and was taking the snap in his own end zone. But Denver fans had seen it before. So had Houston.

Eddy switched the coverage from man-to-man to a two-deep zone. On first down, Elway hit Michael Young for 22 yards. It was a huge play, but the gritty Oilers held for the next 3 downs. On fourth-and-six from the 28 with 1:28 left, Elway scrambled for 7 yards, just beating Lee Williams to the marker. They had worked all week on containment for situations like that, but on this play, Sean Jones lost it. Three more incompletions brought up a fourth-and-ten from the Denver 35 with 59 seconds left. Elway went on an impromptu scramble. The Oilers, exhausted in the mountain air, chased him all over the field. When Richard Johnson broke off coverage thinking he was running, Elway calmly hit Johnson's man for 44 yards to the Oiler 21. He was 3-of-3 on fourth downs. A couple of plays later, Treadwell lined up to kick for the game from the 16. Despite another bobble by holder Kubiak, Treadwell sent the Oilers home losers 26-24.

Every Oiler possession except their last of each half resulted in points or a FG try. Moon's second-quarter interception was their only turnover. Montgomery punted once. Moon was brilliant, hitting 27-of-36 for 325 yards and 3 TDs. White rushed for 79 yards and had another 35 off receptions. Givins caught 6 for 111, Jeffires 7 for 99 and Duncan 6 for 40.

The main Denver defensive weapon was keeping the Run 'N' Shoot off the field. They did it by rushing for 151 yards. It was just enough to sustain some drives and burn time. Houston's ends were unable to get the same pressure on Elway. Actually, they got pressure until Childress went out. It is hard to believe one player could make that much difference. One other difference maker was penalties. Houston had 13 for 85 yards while Denver had just six.

Any one of several plays could have changed the outcome. The missed FG would have won it, as would the dropped TD pass. There was Jeffires' other drop on third down. There were the two late penalties on Munchak (he had 4 in the game and 6 in the 2 playoff games); White stopping the clock by running out of bounds and drawing a penalty; Johnson's 15-yard penalty and broken coverage; and Jones' lost containment. Change any one and it was a different outcome. Jones complained loudly after the game on Denver's holding tactics, especially on the last fourth-down play when Bronco OT Harvey Salem used a wrestling move to drag him to the ground. Houston had no sacks and Denver suffered not a single holding call.

To call it gut-wrenching is to understate the emotional impact of the loss. It was like having the stock market crash on the same day you learned you had to have both cancerous testicles removed. All over Texas, wives, girlfriends and sisters looked at their dazed and despondent husbands, boyfriends and brothers and said some variation of, "I told you not to watch. They do it to you every time. When will you ever learn?"

By now, even Jack Pardee had to be wondering if there really was a curse. Officially, he said, "We had opportunities, but we couldn't make the big plays." He also offered some classic Jack, saying, "There's no gratification in self-pity."

The stats were even (422 yards to 418; time of possession within one minute), but most Houston players thought they gave it away. Hill said, "We knew coming into the game that we matched up with them. They were a team we should have beat. We had them beat for 59 minutes ... the season's been a big disappointment. We're better than Denver. We dominated them offensively." Dish added, "I have to say that I honestly believe that they are not the better team ... we did things that put the game on a silver platter for them."

Al Smith, who led them in tackles, said, "It hurts. It just hurts so bad. We had them. We should have won this game but let them off the hook." Givins said, "When you're beating up on someone, you've got to keep them down. You don't let them get back up ... My father always said, 'When you're grown up son, don't let your talent go to waste. Not many people have what you have.' We had the talent. But it got away from us once again." Jeffires added, "We can come back, but I'm tired of using that phrase, too."

Elway said, "We were really out of the football game from the first play. We were chasing them the whole day .... I really think no one thought we had a chance to win it until (the 44-yard pass completion)." Asked what made the difference, Elway replied, "I guess it's just determination and heart. I'm not saying we have more, but in that situation, we were able to get it done. They got tired, which also helped us."

Dale Robertson declared a moral victory: "Although prone to their usual prime-time errors — the Oilers didn't make utter fools of themselves. There would be no disgrace, no Bengals-style facial administered by the Broncos .... Mercifully, with the whole country watching, there would be no Stagger Lee II." He rationalized they would have lost at Buffalo anyway.

Fowler wrote: "The Oilers did what they have learned to do so well, just enough to lose ... This is Team Almost, a bunch that is big enough, strong enough, fast enough, but never quite good enough."

Upon their return, thousands lined the aisles of the airport to greet them. "There was a lot of heartfelt emotion when we saw those people," said Pinkett. "It let us know that we do represent something. But just think if we had won. This town would have been on fire."

OVERVIEW

It took over two decades, but the Oilers finally won an undisputed AFC Central crown (they tied in '80 and '90 but lost the tiebreakers). It was their first division title since 1967. They had a 5-1 record in the Central for only the second time, sweeping both Cinci and Bernie and the Browns. They beat five playoff teams (Raiders, Chiefs, Jets, Broncos, Cowboys) and tied Buffalo for the best AFC record at 10-2.

It started out as the greatest season in Oiler history. Then they faded. After going 7-1 against AFC teams, they stumbled home 4-4 with losses to Washington, Philadelphia and the Giants. Mounting injuries played a major role as each defeat was close. Defenses also seemed to play the run-and-shoot better later.

One more win might have put Houston in the Super Bowl. They would have had a week off and then a home game. As it was, the Broncos lost in Buffalo by three points (10-7). Many in Houston thought Denver must have picked up the yips from the Oilers and passed it on to the Bills who lost the Super Bowl.

There was plenty to contemplate: the Howfield miss at RFK, the weak effort in New England, the swirling winds inside Three Rivers Stadium, the 7-point loss to Philly and Jeff Kemp at home and the quit against the Giants. Of 6 losses, only one was by more than 7 points.

They also had three big breaks: the fumble by Miami's Sammie Smith on the goal line, the fumble by Emmitt Smith late in OT and Matt Stover's shanked field goal at the end of the Browns' game. Take those away and the season looked much different.

The offense was 'da bomb. They were first in the NFL in passing, second overall and third in scoring. Moon set NFL records for attempts and completions which still stand. He was 404-of-655 (61.7%) for 4,690 yards, becoming only the second QB in NFL history to have consecutive 4,000-yard seasons. The one blemish was that his TD total was down from 33 to 23 and he had 21 interceptions which prevented him from finishing among the top three QBs (which meant his escalator clause did not kick in).

Hill caught a career-high 90 passes for 1,109 yards. He was the first WR in NFL history to gain 1,000 yards in 4 straight seasons after reaching 30. He also extended his consecutive game reception streak to 76. Jeffries led the NFL with 100 catches, becoming the fourth WR to reach that plateau. He made the Pro Bowl. Givins had 996 yards as the Oilers fell 4 yards short of becoming only the third team in history to have three 1,000-yard receivers

With White holding out, Pinkett started most of the year gaining 720 yards rushing plus 508 off receptions. White came on at the end of the year and finished with 465 yards. He started the playoff games because he was a better blocker. Munchak made the Pro Bowl on a bad knee. Matthews made second team All-Pro.

The defense played well most of the year, but fell back late after some key injuries. The scoring defense improved under Eddy. The Oilers gave up 412 points in '89, improving to 307 in '90 and 251 in '91. That was second in the AFC (6th in NFL). The problem was they gave up too many long drives which kept the offense off the field, this despite ranking second in the AFC against the run and sixth against the pass.

Fuller made the Pro Bowl after leading the AFC with 15 sacks, most since Jesse Baker's 15½ in 1979. Lathon recovered from his bad rookie season to have a good second year. He made the Pro Bowl, as did Al Smith who again led the team in tackles. Dishman made first team All-Pro and the Pro Bowl while McDowell made second team All-Pro. A total of 8 Oilers (35% of the starters) made one of the various all-star teams.

They set an all-time attendance record with an average of 60,341 in the enlarged capacity, breaking the 1988 record of 56,378. The playoff game was their number 12 consecutive sellout.

THE TEAM THAT COULD NOT LEARN

The Oilers never seemed to learn. Every year for the past five they managed to lose winnable games, which would come back to haunt them at playoff time. And every year, it was the same two problems. They could not hold a lead to save a life, and they blew games against crummy teams. These two themes stretched through the years, and the various coaches and players.

In 1987, they won 3 of their last 4 to make the playoffs for the first time since 1980. But one more win would have meant the division crown. They finished 9-6 (strike season) behind Denver 10-4-1 and Cleveland 10-5. The loss that hurt most was the early Bills game where they led 30-20 with 5 minutes left. Win it and they opened at home in the second round against the Colts while Cleveland would have had to play at Denver. Instead, the Oilers got Stagger Lee.

The next year was full of disheartening losses. They were in first with a 7-3 record that would have been 8-2 had they not blown a 16-0 lead in Philadelphia. Then they fell to Seattle because the defense could not hold late leads of 17-10 and 24-17. At 9-4, they choked against 5-11 Pittsburgh at home, unable to hold leads of 27-24 and 34-31 against Bubby Brister. In the season finale in Cleveland, they continued to achieve the impossible by blowing a commanding 23-7 third-quarter lead to journeyman Don Strock. Buffalo and Cinci ended up tied at 12-4 while Houston and Cleveland were both 10-6. One more win would have allowed them to open at home, while two more would have resulted in a first-round bye and second-round home game.

In 1989, they again zoomed out to a 7-4 record and first place, but were haunted by blown games to Buffalo (defense could not hold a 38-34 fourth-quarter lead) and Cleveland (led 10-0 at half but lost 28-17). At 9-5, with a chance for the third year in a row to win their division by winning out, they fell apart at Cincinnati (61-17) and at home to Cleveland (24-20). In the Browns game, the defense could not hold a 20-17 lead with 2 minutes left. They finished 9-7, just a half a game behind Cleveland. Buffalo got the bye at 9-7. One more win would have given them the first week off, which would have allowed Childress time to recover from an injury. A second-round game would have been in the Dome. Instead, they collapsed at home in the first round. Sitting on a 23-16 lead with about 5 minutes left, the defense again let Brister beat them with a 5-minute, 80-yard drive for the tie followed by a FG in OT.

By 1990, they were inventing ever-novel ways of losing. They opened by getting the crap beaten out of them 47-27 by a 5-11 Atlanta team. The next game, they held the offensively-challenged Steelers to 123 yards, but somehow lost 20-9. Against San Francisco (14-2), they blew leads of 14-0 in the first quarter and 21-17 in the fourth at home to lose 24-21. The top offense in football then managed to lose 17-12 to the Jets (who finished 6-10), 17-13 to the Rams (5-11) and 13-10 at Seattle (9-7). Stumbling to 8-6, they could still have their first division title by winning their last two. But after leading Cincinnati 20-13 in the third, they lost 40-20. They ended up in a 3-way tie with Cinci and Pittsburgh at 9-7. One more win and they would have won the division and opened with the Bengals in Houston where the Oilers usually

Warren Moon followed up his superlative first year in the Run 'N' Shoot with a terrific 1991. He again led the NFL in passing yards by a wide margin with a new career and all-time team high 4,690 yards. His 404 completions are still the NFL record. Although he made the Pro Bowl as a replacement, he was not named All-Pro. The primary reasons were his decreased TD total (from 33 in 1990 to 23) and his increased interception total (from 13 in 1990 to 21). He also had 11 fumbles. However, in the playoffs, he held up his end. Against New York, he was 28-of-40 for 271 yards and 2 TDs. At Denver, he was 27-of-36 for 325 yards and 3 TDs.

killed them. Instead, they opened at Cincinnati and were obliterated.

In 1991, two plays — a missed tackle caused by a collision between rookies and a missed FG by a wannabe kicker — kept them from an 11-0 start. At 9-2 and looking Super, they wilted under the pressure. In the last 5, three hard-hitting defenses turned the yard-hogging Oiler offense into a mass of quivering Jell-O. They lost to the Steelers (26-14), Eagles (13-6) and Giants (24-20). At 11-5, they were once again one victory shy of a first-round bye and a second-round home game. In the playoffs, they could not hold a 15-point second-quarter lead or an 8-point fourth-quarter lead. The defense fell apart when it mattered most, allowing drives of 80 and 87 yards in the fourth quarter, including three fourth-down conversions.

Denver made it five straight premature ejections. McClain wrote, "No matter how many big games they blow, Saturday's (loss) will rank among the most exciting, disappointing and frustrating the Oilers will ever experience."

The Oilers had the No. 2 offense in the NFL and No. 2 defense in the AFC plus 8 All-Pros/Pro Bowlers. Yet they could not get past the second round. Fans thought it could not get any worse. They were in for a shock.

1992: PEOPLE WILL TAKE THIS GAME TO THE GRAVE

The days of Herzeg and Glanville providing cover for were over. With press favorites at GM ("Holovak had done an exceptional job of assembling players"), and coach ("We can find no serious fault with the coaching"), the players were now under the microscope.

Ed Fowler complained of the "hot dogs, showboats and today's 'me generation' of athletes," who dwell on "narrow, personal goals such as achieving a milestone for receptions or yards or sacks, and gluing the cameras to themselves with juvenile antics after scoring, the consequences be damned." About Denver, he wrote, "In the biggest game of their lives, they committed 13 fouls, many of them arising from either the inability to control their emotions or failure to cope with the tension of a do-or-die situation on the road."

The players blamed everyone else. Some (with the help of their agents) developed a theory that Oiler management, not the players or coaches, kept them from realizing their potential. That premise was that they were talented enough. The local media agreed, a view supported by gaudy number of Pro Bowl berths.

They said that, after years of bad faith, they did not trust management. The Oiler front office did not deal fairly. Adams was cheap and they were underpaid. Accordingly, there was no sense of loyalty to the organization. Individuals played for themselves because they had to. It was the only way to get a decent contract.

However, Oiler pay was both competitive and rising. The players' own lawsuit showed as much. Adams' payroll was twelfth highest in the NFL, and the team played like it was about twelfth best. Each year, the top 12 NFL teams made the playoffs. Each of the previous 5 years, the Oilers just barely made it into that group, and then bowed out early. Furthermore, the Oiler payroll was about the same as the Bills and Broncos, two teams whose players did not have the same trouble motivating or playing as a unit.

Coach Pardee stood by his men. "It's hard for me to get mad at the players," he said, "when they play so hard and give every ounce of energy they can give. We're a good team that's getting a whole lot better. We're better than we were a year ago. We improved by 30% this season from 9 wins to 12. That next 30% is the toughest. You have to be a super team to win 12, 13 or 14 games. We haven't showed we're a super team yet but we have the potential to be. The encouraging part is that we're a team heading in the right direction."

But Jack's free ride was also nearing the end. Those upsets at the hands of Pittsburgh hurt. Fans remembered Glanville swept the Steelers in 1987 and 1989.

LEAGUE MATTERS

At the league level, instant replay was voted out while Adams voted to keep it. In a story that Oiler fans would find more interesting as time went by, the NFL assumed ownership of the troubled Patriots from Victor Kiam. One of Paul Tagliabue's first pronouncements was that he would not allow the club to be moved. League President Neil Austrian said, "I think it's very important to the league that we have a team in the New England area. It's the sixth-largest television area, and it's clearly a market that is critical to NBC as well as to the fans."

Meanwhile, in a Minneapolis courtroom the players' labor lawyers were beating the owners. The antitrust trial lifted the curtain somewhat on many of the long-held secrets regarding league finances. For example, the NFL in 1991 grossed roughly $1.4 billion. Of that, twice as much came from television and radio ($850 million) as ticket sales ($402 million).

For 1990, the seven most profitable teams averaged $46.5 million in income and $6.8 million in net profits, while the seven least profitable teams had average revenue of $44 million and average losses of $5.2 million. The most profitable teams had an average player payroll of $20.9 million, while the seven net money-losers paid an average of $26 million.

The Oilers' figures for 1989 showed revenues of $31.3 million, expenses of $9.9 million and player payroll of $21.1 million for a net profit of just $44,000. But Adams' salary draw was $409,000, while family members who served on the board of directors each made $78,000.

Bud made up some bottom line with below-average coaching expenses. Pardee's '90 salary was $390,000. By comparison, Don Shula took down $1 million, Dan Reeves $800,000 and Chuck Noll about $500,000.

Among assistants, Eddy made $126,000, Gilbride $125,000, Chris Palmer $100,000, Richard Smith $90,000, Jim Stanley $87,000, Pat Thomas $77,000, Bob Young $77,000 and Frank Novak $68,000.

Holovak was paid $158,000 versus Bobby Beathard's $1 million. Bud saved even more on scouts. He had always had one of the smallest operations in the league (the staff was at three for '92). Furthermore, with Floyd Reese's help, workaholic Holovak oversaw the scouts. Since most teams had another individual in charge of that area, Bud saved that salary, too.

WHINING AND DINING

The offseason was eventful, including almost losing Kevin Gilbride to Pittsburgh. After cutting Chuck Noll loose, Dan Rooney asked Adams for permission to interview his offensive coordinator. Under Gilbride, Houston had the top offense in '91. Ironically, two years before, the teams' coaches were holding Wrestle Mania at midfield. In a decision that would affect both teams for a long time, Bill Cowher got the job.

Allen Pinkett was traded to New Orleans, leaving the starting RB job to Lorenzo White for the first time. Although Pinkett provided a nice change of pace, it came down to blocking. Pinkett weighed 195, while White was close to 230 and Gary Brown around 224. Holovak turned down slightly higher offers to give Pinkett a better chance of starting.

It was the usual with Plan B. In the first three years, Houston lost 15, 7 and 4 players while signing no one memorable. In 1992, they lost four more, including Drew Hill and Tony Jones. They signed Spencer Tillman, WR Jeff Query and CB Jerry Gray.

Because Hill was due to be paid $1.05 million for '92 and they had other younger players to protect, Houston took a "calculated risk" and exposed Hill. It made sense, but he was insulted. Instead of sucking it up in the name of team unity, Hill complained publicly.

No team picked him up. But Hill was so angry, he signed with Atlanta for $800,000. Adams said, "I have never known a player to voluntarily take a $250,000 pay cut. I have never publicly issued a personal plea for a player to stay with the Oilers, but I did for Drew." Moon said it made him "sick to [his] stomach." Pardee said, "Drew caught a lot of passes, but we wanted to get more yards after the catch from that position." That was an oblique reference to Hill's propensity to roll to the ground after a catch.

On the field, Hill was the Oilers' all-time leading WR and Moon's main go-to guy since arriving in 1985. He had a career year in 1991. He was another story off the field. McClain asked, "Who's going to burp and change Drew? ... We only hope he doesn't let the door hit him in his Pampers on the way out of town. For a guy who was supposed to be a steadying influence on younger colleagues, he has acted recently very much like one who never got over the terrible 2s."

Leonard Harris was anointed the new starter, but they hoped for big things from Jeff Query who was said to run a 4.4 forty. The Oilers gave him a two-year deal for $1.1 million, including a $130,000 signing bonus.

But the Query deal caused Duncan to hold out. Dishman held out because he was jealous of Jerry Gray's contract. Fuller held out because of what he heard other NFL ends made. Munchak held out too.

Childress did not like it that Lee Williams made more ($1 million). Williams, meanwhile, had an on-going feud with Jim Eddy over Lee's optimum position. Eddy told him he was going to be labeled a "crybaby" if he continued to complain.

Moon was quiet, but the contract situation that caused a distraction in '91 was still out there. Eventually, Bud capitulated, making him the second-highest paid player in the NFL with a $14 million, 4-year deal. It included a buyout of the controversial escalator clause.

Sean Jones spent most of camp working as a stockbroker in Beverly Hills after "retiring." He also sued the NFL. He was unhappy with the $800,000 he was due. Like Matthews in '87, he did not think he could get a Houston jury to stop laughing, so he filed in LA.

1992 TRAINING CAMP

Fans were left only with their dreams of how good their team might be if it spent just one summer concentrating on football. Camp was back at Trinity University for the second season. Among the coaching changes was Frank Bush moving from scouting to LB coach. Richard Smith remained special teams coach and assumed assistant line coach duties behind Bob Young. Floyd Reese was named assistant general manager.

Among their assignments was to figure out how to score more TDs. The Run 'N' Shoot moved the ball (4th in the NFL in number of trips inside the 20), but did not take full advantage (11th in the number of TDs once there). Defenses gave Moon the short game, forcing them into long drives that gave the other side multiple shots at forcing a turnover. Once within sniffing distance of the goal, it also became more crowded and the WRs had less area to work. "As a defensive player," noted William Fuller, "you feel like the odds are in your favor if you make a team drive 14 or 15 plays. The more plays, the more chances for them to make a mistake. And, if they use seven or eight minutes, that time is off the clock for good. They can't get it back."

Although the coaches were opposed to the idea, one solution was bigger, stronger WRs who could take a lick and hold on. In addition, a more serious commitment to the running game would have forced opposing safeties closer to the line, opening some deep routes to single coverage. But Houston rarely focused on the run.

The draft finally produced some immediate help in Alabama State LB Eddie Robinson (6'1, 241), who had the coverage skills Meads lacked. Others included Vanderbilt WR/KR Corey Harris (3rd round), LB Joe Bowden (5th), 6'6, 309-pound DT Tim Roberts (5th) and A&M QB Bucky Richardson (8th).

Many in Oilerland wanted the Lee Williams pick back. He had only 3 sacks and 17 tackles. They would have been better off with Shawn Jefferson and the No. 1, which could have been Tennessee's Carl Pickens (or Levon Kirkland). Pickens (6'2, 206) was the package they needed at WR and would have let them go into '92 with a scary group of Pickens, Jefferson, Hill, Jeffires, Givins, Duncan, Harris and Jones. But instead of Pickens, Jefferson and Hill, Moon would have to look to Corey Harris, Gary Wellman and Jeff Query.

In the meantime, the coaches tried to get who was there ready for the season. This was hampered by the Republican National Convention which George Bush wanted in Houston. The Oilers played all 5 preseason games on the road, including one in Tokyo against Dallas. The powerful combination of sake and nouveau riche Southwesterners probably did not convey the message the NFL hoped to send. But Bud had fun. At one point, he climbed on stage to join a drum ceremony. The crowd of 500 was thrilled when he twice tossed his drumstick in the air, catching it both times. Later, he jumped back on stage to join some Japanese dancers. He also charged players' wives pay for their seats on his chartered plane. In the game, his kamikazes beat Jerry Jones' 34-20.

The Oilers liked their schedule. Their opponents' combined record in '91 was 115-141, and 11 of 16 games would be in domed stadiums. Three of the first four games and three of the final four were in the Astrodome, while they had only one late road game in the American Gulag — December 20 at Cleveland. The weak NFC Central replaced the rough NFC East.

That schedule, combined with some of the weakest divisional competition in memory, put the Oilers on the spot. The core of veterans (Moon, Givins, Munchak, Matthews, Childress, Fuller) had been together a long time. They were getting older in football years. If they were ever going to do it, this was the year. It was time to put up or shut up.

THE 1992 REGULAR SEASON — RENDEZVOUS WITH DESTINY

John McClain told readers, "The AFC Central has one team and one team only — the Oilers ... If they don't repeat, there should be an investigation ... The Oilers are so much better than their opponents in this division that they could beat an all-star team comprised of Browns, Steelers and Bengals."

Fans bought it, as well as a record 64,934 tickets for the opener against Pittsburgh (breaking the record of 63,971 set in '91 against Pittsburgh).

But the defense was in trouble with Dishman, Fuller and Jones still holding out. After Houston sprinted out to a 14-0 first quarter lead, rookie coach Bill Cowher fooled them on trick play that changed the course of the game. On fourth-and-16 at the Houston 45, their punter threw a pass over the middle that went to the 1. Before it was over, Moon needed 5 interceptions to overcome the offense's 434 total yards. The last was deadly. With under 3 minutes left, he overthrew Givins poorly from the Steeler 14 on second-and-one. They lost 29-24.

Pittsburgh had Moon's number. "It felt like we knew everything that was coming," said Rod Woodson, who had two interceptions, including one after Houston drove the ball to the Pittsburgh 3 in the third quarter. "As soon as we saw one receiver do one thing, we knew what all the rest were going to do. It came real easy." The Oilers were left to repeat some well-memorized lines. "We had too many blown opportunities," said Bruce Matthews. "I don't think it was the Steelers. They didn't stop us. We lost the game."

The Oilers quickly signed Dishman. Jones and Fuller also reported. More high-draft picks fell by the wayside to make room as Richard Johnson ('85, 1st round), Willis Peguese ('90, 3rd) and Mike Mooney ('92, 4th) were released. The Dishman deal ($1.55 million, 2 years) caused McDowell ($1.2 million, 2 years) to walk out. His agent said the team promised he would be paid "in the same ballpark" as Cris. In addition, starting FS Bo Orlando was lost for the year with a bad knee, while in Minneapolis, a federal court jury struck down Plan B.

The Oilers snapped back to beat Indy (20-10), KC (23-20 OT) and San Diego (27-0). At 3-1, they were tied with Pittsburgh for first heading into the bye.

Dwight Andre Sean-O'Neil Jones came to the Oilers via Jamaica, New Jersey, Northeastern University and the LA Raiders. While often a great player, he could also create problems. Despite agreeing to a new contract as a part of the trade in 1988, he held out in 1990, 1991 and 1992. Each time, he reported around the start of the season so that he missed all or most of training camp but few, if any, game checks. He also sued the NFL in 1992 and threatened to do so again in 1993.

After "retiring" in the summer of 1992, he told a sympathetic Roy Firestone on ESPN's Up Close, "If I'm going back to football, that's the only place I can go, I know nobody will deal with the Oilers. No team wants to deal with them. They're too underhanded." Asked what he thought of Bud Adams, Jones said, "I question my respect for him a lot of times. I think he's careless with the truth." Several years later, he told radio host Jim Rome that he never understood how he got the "clubhouse lawyer" tag in Houston.

The off week gave them time to make some more awkward personnel moves. They released nine-year veteran Johnny Meads, the most senior player on the defense. He started the Steeler and Colt games, but Rick Graf replaced him for the big backs of the Chargers and Chiefs. It was Eddie Robinson's job after that. In more of a surprise, they waived rookie third-round pick Corey Harris, the best KR since Billy White Shoes. He led the team with a 20.6 yard average and had a 98-yard TD called back against the Colts. Holovak said he missed too much practice after his holdout. "Corey was a running back at Vanderbilt, and a rookie needs time to become a receiver in this system," said the GM.

Then, in a rare, bold move, Adams forked out $2 million-plus for WR Webster Slaughter. He and a few other players had jumped into the suit in Minnesota and were granted "temporary" unrestricted free agency status by Judge Doty. Bud's quick move let him stick it to Art Modell and played to rave reviews. Slaughter was seen as the replacement for Hill they missed in the draft. He cost about the same but was younger (27) and bigger (6'1). He was also tough and not afraid to go over the middle. It was Bud's first good free agent signing since Plan B began. But there was a downside. Slaughter suddenly was the highest paid WR on a team full of emotional receivers. In fact, he became second highest paid player on a team that had 18 players whose contracts expired at the end of the season.

Once back, they ripped the now docile Bengals 38-24 with Moon throwing five TDs and White rushing for a career-high 149 yards. It was the second straight year they embarrassed the Bengals at Riverfront and the first time since '81 they won their first two road games. The Oilers were sitting pretty at 4-1 and looking forward to their rematch in Denver.

The Bronco game generated a lot of interest around the state. But with the Cowboys' return to the playoffs, battle lines were being drawn. A good litmus test was Austin where KXAN Television was forced to chose between the Houston-Denver and Dallas-KC games. They aired the Houston game after the Oilers won a week-long telephone survey by 30,000 votes. Irate Cowboy fans telephoned death threats to the station. In addition, the sports director's home was egged and a "derogatory" sign placed on his lawn.

Houston played like the sign. The refs agreed, flagging them 16 times. Included were 4 rarely seen illegal formation calls. McDowell was even flagged for an illegal formation on special teams, while Pro Bowler Matthews drew three penalties by himself. Mild-mannered

Curtis Duncan, who never argued, was called for an unsportsmanlike conduct penalty when an official did not allow a catch. Duncan slammed the ball at the ref's feet. "Some weird things happened," said Pardee. "I think we lost a little poise by worrying about the officiating too much ... We had some penalties called that we hadn't had called on us before."

Still, the Oilers seemed to take control after a 72-yard Moon to Duncan bomb, followed by a 7-yard TD to Jeffires. They led 21-20 with 1:56 remaining. But there was still the matter of John Elway, Mile High Stadium and the Oiler defense. Rookie Eddie Robinson told Elway, "Not this time." This time, it took him 3 plays and 22 seconds to go 80 yards and take a 27-21 lead. Moon (23-of-39 for 321 yards) could not get past the 50 in the final 1:30.

Dale Robertson wrote, "What the Oilers have done by coming up short for so long is take the fun out of the game-by-game process ... A supreme effort one weekend serves simply to create worry about the next ... They have programmed you to expect a flat tire around every curve ... There's really no football precedent for what the Oilers have put Houston through with their long legacy of false starts. No team has ever been gifted enough to make the playoffs five seasons running, yet fail to reach a conference championship game once — much less the Super Bowl .... What have the Oilers done for you lately? Nothing except cause heartburn and facial tics. What will they do for you in the future? In light of the Pittsburgh 'faux pas' and now, certainly after the Denver trip, I expect the usual; i.e., the worst."

After pounding the Bengals again (26-10), they went to windy Pittsburgh where Woodson knocked Moon on his head on a blitz causing a mild concussion. Enter the Commander.

Cody calmly took them to their only offensive TD and a 20-7 lead. But in the fourth, the defense allowed TD passes to 280-pound Eric Green and 268-pound Adrian Cooper. As Pittsburgh clung to a 21-20 lead, the offense got the ball back once more. Taking over at his 14, Carlson passed the Oilers down to the Pittsburgh 22. But with a light rain starting to fall, they went conservative. With 34 seconds and 2 time-outs, White ran twice. Then Carlson let 13 more seconds tick off before using a time-out with 6 seconds remaining. Enter Del Greco. See the missed 39-yard field-goal. Watch the Oilers return home 5-3.

This one caused division in the ranks. "On that last drive," said McDowell, "I thought we should have gotten closer instead of just trying to get by. I'm not the coach, and we have to live with it, but we played for the field goal ... we have to play to win." Dishman said, "We were moving the ball and we should have been playing for a touchdown, not a field goal." They also lamented the decision to kick a FG in the first quarter on fourth-and-goal at the Pittsburgh 1, leading 3-0.

With Moon still groggy, they were upset by the Browns 24-14 in the Dome. The game turned in the third quarter with Houston trailing 10-0, but driving. On fourth down, Moon hit Givins at the Cleveland 22. "We had them on the ropes," Moon said later. But Givins fumbled and Stevon Moore ran it back for a score. Moon hurt his neck while missing the tackle. Trailing 17-7 in the fourth, the defense let the Browns use up 7 minutes to score a TD. It was the eighth TD they had allowed in the fourth quarter in 9 games. Man-of-few-words Childress went off after the game saying some players acted like prima-donnas and lacked discipline.

Big Ray had a factual basis for his claims. Jeffires and Givins whined about game statistics and whether their bonuses would kick in. Lathon stormed out of film sessions or meetings upon criticism. Jones did not always show for meetings. During one practice, Dishman became so upset after getting beat that he started coming out of his pads feigning injury. GM Holovak told him to get back to practice. Dish screamed, cussed and gave him the finger. It is hard to imagine Vince Lombardi, Tom Landry or Bill Parcels putting up with it. Jimmy Johnson once kicked a player off his team for falling asleep during a film session.

Things did not look good. After a 4-1 start, they had fallen to 5-4, and the next three were all on the road within a 12 day period. In Minnesota, the defense came alive to hold the 7-3 Vikings to one penetration inside Houston territory. The Oilers won 17-14, but Moon was lost for the next 4 weeks. In Miami, they held Dan Marino to 19-of-40 passing, but lost 19-16 on a dropped Carlson-to-Harris TD pass that was followed seconds later by Del Greco's missed 41-yarder. In Detroit, Carlson hit Jeffires for a TD with under 2 minutes remaining to slip by the Lions 24-21 on Thanksgiving. They were two missed FGs away from 9-3.

After blasting Chicago 24-7, they choked at home to Green Bay. With OC Kevin Gilbride watching from a hospital bed, the Commander hit 25-of-36 for 330 yards and 2 TDs. White had 132 combined yards. The Pack managed 215 total yards and 1 TD. They also won 16-14. It was a microcosm for the season. The defense played well enough for them to be 11-3. While the offense moved the ball, it did not score. In fact, the offense had not scored more than two TDs in any game since Cincinnati on October 25.

The difference was turnovers. They had four against Green Bay. Since the game at Pittsburgh, they had 15 turnovers to just 12 TDs. Many occurred in opponents' territory after long drives.

At 8-6, the Oilers seemed to have wasted another season. In need of a big team effort, practices were anything but harmonious. Prior to the Browns game, Tillman walked out of practice after getting into a fight with some defensive players. He said he did not know if he would come back. Instead of disciplinary action, the coaches just shrugged.

Carlson was 2-2 as a starter, but it was more of the team carrying him than the other way around. In those four games, he had scored one first half TD. In Cleveland, he threw an interception with his first pass as the offense piled up 84 total yards to trail 7-3 at the half. In the second half, Cody fumbled and was intercepted as the Browns took a 14-3 lead. Playoff hopes appeared dead. In the fourth, they turned it over on downs at the Cleveland 1. A television pan of a dazed Commander standing on the sidelines epitomized a lifetime of Oiler frustration. With his helmet pushed partially back on his head, he tried to spit. The wad hit his facemask. It seemed to dangle there for an eternity. The team that had always shot itself in the foot now could not even spit straight. Television sets all over Texas went off.

Back on the field, the defense forced a punt, but Carlson threw another interception at midfield. "The fat lady wasn't singing," said Jones later, "but in the background, I could hear her practicing her scales." Then Cleveland pulled a Houston. On fourth-and-one at the Houston 28, Kozar went back to pass but was foiled by a false start. They decided to punt from the 33 instead of trying a 50-yard field goal. Taking over at the 15, Carlson found Duncan for the TD four minutes later to cut the deficit to 14-10.

On the ensuing possession, Childress, Williams, Smith and Robinson stopped the Browns on three straight running plays and the offense took over at the 26 with 1:51 left. Naturally, they first went backwards on a Donnalley penalty and a sack. With the stage set just right with a second-and-23 from the 23, White took a screen pass on the right side, and led by a convoy of Matthews, Williams and Norgard, zigged and zagged his way down the field, avoided Frank Minnifield, and did not stop until pushed out at the Cleveland 12. After hitting

The Run 'N' Shoot was, in part, a response to the blitzing defenses that were prevalent since the mid-1980s. The base set was two WRs on each side with one going in motion. The QB frequently rolled out of the pocket. The idea was to spread the defense and create a weakness by flooding one side with receivers. The WR's job was to read the defense and adjust his route; for example, go to the spot vacated by a blitzing LB. He not only had to recognize what was happening, but he had to hurry. Thus the premium on quickness and advent of the smurf receiver. The flipside of quickness, however, is size, with its corollary danger, as seen below.

The other danger of this offense was exposing the QB. In November, Minnesota's talented DL of Chris Doleman, John Randle and Henry Thomas pounded Moon so hard that he missed the next five games. After churning up 317 yards per game in 1990 and 300 per game in 1991, the pass offense slowed to 264 per game in 1992. That was still No. 1 in the NFL, but not good enough to win the division. One consistent producer in '92 was Curtis Duncan (at right). The 5'11, 184-pound Duncan had his best season with 82 receptions (second best in the AFC behind Jeffires' 90) and 954 yards. It earned him a Pro Bowl berth.

Givins for 9 more, Carlson then found him again alone in the right corner of the end zone for the game winner with 34 seconds left.

They were usually on the other end of these types of dramatic finishes. "This is the best comeback I've ever been associated with," said Lee Williams. "I'm sure in the future, it will be listed on 'Fantastic Finishes.'" Jeffires, who was trying to become the offense's vocal leader, said "I told the receivers I'd buy each of them a Gucci watch if we won the game. When we didn't score from their 1 in the fourth quarter, I figured I wouldn't have to come up with the money. Now, I'm going to keep up my end of the deal."

Their playoff hopes shot, Browns fans shuffled out. "This place is Heartbreak Hotel," screamed one of the Dog Pound's gentle souls. Another yelled at the passing coach, "Hey Belichoke. Way to sit on a lead."

Having clinched a wildcard spot, they had one game left, the Bills in the Dome. With Buffalo trying to win its division, Houston blew them out 27-3 behind 7 sacks and 3 interceptions. Most significantly, Jim Kelly suffered a strained MCL on a Childress sack. The game also saw the return of Moon for two series.

The Oilers finished 10-6. The Bills were 11-5, as were Miami, Pittsburgh and San Diego. The Chiefs were the other wildcard team at 10-6. The winner of the Oiler-Bills game would play the overrated Steelers who had dropped 2 of their last 3.

1992 PLAYOFFS

The last two games had people believing again. The view in Houston was that the Oilers and Bills were the two best teams in the conference. Buffalo was first in scoring, Houston second. Each placed 9 players on the Pro Bowl team. The next closest team had 4. The winner had a clear path to the Super Bowl.

The Oiler offense was No. 2 in the AFC while the defense was No. 1. The defense, unlike recent AFC Super Bowl representatives Buffalo, Denver and Cincinnati, was styled after the NFC. In addition, they had a 5-3 record on the road and were becoming healthy with the return of Moon and Doug Smith while Buffalo was going the other way, losing Kelly, LB Cornelius Bennett, CB Kirby Jackson and safety Matt Darby. Buffalo had stumbled down the stretch going 5-5 over its final 10 games. Of particular note to Moon, Buffalo ranked next to last in pass defense. They were vulnerable.

John McClain got sucked in. A couple of days before the game, he wrote, "If you are the true-Columbia blue fan, sometimes you close your eyes so hard wishing for the Oilers to win you get a headache. (But) the Oilers have broken more hearts than Casanova. (They) play mind games. They mess with your head and tug at your heart. Every time you give in unconditionally, they jilt you again by failing to live up to expectations ... If they do it again, you swear you are going to tear up the season tickets and never attend another game ... You hope almost beyond hope that this year will be different, that they are not setting you up for another big emotional letdown ... You really believe they are going to beat the Bills .... This time, you just know they are going to reward your dedication." He foretold it would be different this time because they "have talent, confidence and momentum." This was to be the Oilers' "*rendezvous with destiny.*" This time, they were "positioned to make a fan's dream come true."

Some in Buffalo agreed, as the game did not sell out (over 5,000 short). Still, this was the two-time defending AFC champs who were 5-0 in Rich Stadium in the playoffs over the preceding four years. Game time weather was typically Buffalo — damp, gray, cold and windy.

Not that it bothered Warren Moon. Any thoughts that he would be rusty or tentative after missing the last third of the season were quickly put to rest as he exhibited the greatest first half passing performance in NFL playoff history. Touching the ball four times, he passed for four TDs: 3 yards to Jeffires, 7 to Slaughter, 26 to Duncan and 27 to Jeffires. Duncan's was a showstopper as he leapt high between two defenders to make the catch. The last one came after Houston got the ball back with 1:15 left. They quickly gobbled up the 67 yards culminating with Jeffires beating Nate Odomes down the left sideline with 14 seconds left. It was a mismatch of Gothic proportions as Houston lead 28-3 and the Bills were booed off the field.

Moon was as close to perfect as a QB can get. He had 218 yards on 19-of-22 passing. One of the 3 incompletions was caught by Jeffires but ruled out of bounds. The halftime network television pundits, some of whom did not like the Run 'N' Shoot, were speechless. "I've never seen us be so effective, so efficient," Givins said after the game.

Buffalo coach Marv Levy admitted afterwards that he did not hold out much hope. "I was just thinking this was a humiliating day," said the professor, who also lost Thurman Thomas to injury. "Did I think we still had a chance? Well, there was a lot of time left, so there was a glimmer of hope. But it was about the same chance as you have of winning the New York Lottery." It got worse for him before it got better.

Moon tried to keep them focused and not looking ahead. "The first thing I said was, 'Remember Denver last year? Don't let it happen again,'" Moon said.

In a fateful choice, the Oilers elected to kick into the wind so they could have the wind at their backs in the fourth quarter. It seemed a wise choice after McDowell returned an interception 58 yards for a TD to push the lead to 35-3. According to the laws of time and space, the game was over. The crowd started streaming out of Rich Stadium and fans in Houston headed to golf courses and shopping malls, raked leaves and did laundry. They missed the greatest collapse in the history of football. It could not have happened to anyone else.

Over the next 7 minutes, Buffalo went on an improbable splurge, scoring 28 unanswered points against the top defense in the AFC. They scored almost as many TDs (4) as the Oilers had offensive plays (5).

After the McDowell TD, Del Greco tried to squib his kickoff. He did it because of the strong wind. But in the first of many Keystone Cop-like errors, it hit a Bill at the 50 and was recovered there. It amounted to a 15-yard kickoff. It turned out to be a huge break. The

Below, Warren Moon and the Oilers get a big send-off as they head for Buffalo. The return of Moon and 27-3 thumping of the Bills in the last game of the regular season led to hopes that this Oiler team would finally live up to its potential. In his column just before the game, the Houston Chronicle's John McClain told fans it would be different this time because the Oilers "have talent, confidence and momentum." He wrote that this was to be the Oilers' "rendezvous with destiny." This time, they were "positioned to make a fan's dream come true."

Bills took 10 plays to score, including a 16-yard pass to Andre Reed on third-and-15 and 5-yard run by Kenneth Davis on fourth-and-two. Davis scored on a 1-yard run to make it 35-10 with 8:52 remaining in the third.

Then came another major blunder. For whatever reason, the Oiler coaching staff did not expect the desperate Bills, who had just gone for it on fourth down, to attempt an onsides kick. They put their blockers in instead of their good hands people. They were in full retreat when the ball hit near Rick Graf. The LB made a stab at it, but the ball squirted away and the kicker recovered it. The special teams returned to the bench looking for the bus back to the hotel.

The Bills took over at their 48. Four plays later, Reich hit an uncovered Don Bebee down the left side for a 38-yard TD. The reason he was alone is that he first ran out of bounds and then back in to make the catch. Technically, he was an ineligible receiver. The replay was clear. But defensive players can never rely on a foul being called, even a flagrant one. They are taught since childhood to play until the whistle. There was no flag and no whistle as the score tightened to 35-17 with 7:56 remaining in the third.

Most teams would still feel confident about an 18-point lead in the second half of any game, especially one with a highly ranked defense full of all-star players with names like Childress, Fuller, Jones, Smith, Lathon, Dishman and McDowell. But this was the Oilers. More than a few shoulders began to slump from the weight of history.

When the offense finally got the ball, they understood the magnitude of the matter at hand. They needed to move the chains and eat up some clock. Scoring was not even paramount just so long as they took some time off the clock and got to the fourth quarter when they would have the wind. Maybe it was the seed of doubt, but they came out cold and stiff making like a chorus line: 1-2-3-kick. After Montgomery uncorked a 25-yard punt, the Bills took over at their 41.

Reich immediately hit Davis for 19 yards, then Reed for a 26-yard TD. Steve Jackson was toast. How the Oilers let any Buffalo WR, especially Reed, get deep in single coverage at any time in the second half of this game is something the FBI should have looked into. Suddenly, it was 35-24 with 4:21 remaining in third.

The handful of Oilers who were not smart enough before to realize what was happening now knew, and their collars were tightening. The Bills had scored 3 unanswered TDs in the blink of an eye. Houston had run 3 offensive plays. What seemed impossible just a short while before now seemed more than plausible. Still, they had an 11-point lead. All eyes turned to Moon to lead them out of this mess.

Moon did not exactly have an air of confidence about him as he trotted back onto the field. Rather, he looked like a man deeply constipated. He promptly overthrew Slaughter. Henry Jones intercepted at the 23. The defense held for 3 downs, but on fourth-and-five from the Oiler 18, Reich hit Reed again for the TD with the Oilers in zone coverage. It was 35-31 with 2 minutes left in the third quarter. The Bills had thrown for 4 TDs against the No. 2 ranked pass defense in the league. Buffalo's drives covered just 50, 52, 59 and 23 yards

Even the most jaded Oiler fan had to be a little surprised by the turn of events. Despite their long tradition, nobody believed, or wanted to, that they could actually blow a 32-point second half lead. Such things just did not happen in pro football. In fact, it had *never* happened — maybe in college once every 30 years, but not in the pros.

With the wind at their backs, the Oiler offense began to warm up. After the teams swapped possessions, Houston finally put together a drive moving from their 10 to the Buffalo 14. A TD here would have been huge but they stalled. Even so, a FG would at least give them some confidence and stretch the lead back to 7 points. But Del Greco did not even get the chance to miss as Montgomery, the holder, bobbled the snap. Del Greco picked the ball up and was mashed like an ant. Montgomery said, "The wind was gusting, and it blew the ball. I tried to grab it, but I couldn't catch it." Del Greco was still woozy after the game.

Buffalo, seemingly oblivious to the strong wind, responded with another drive, this one for the lead. The highlights were a 35-yard run by Davis and 17-yard Reich-to-Reed TD. It took 7 plays as Buffalo took a 38-35 lead with 3:08 remaining. Andre Reed, who had just one TD in the previous six games, beat Houston for three in one-and-a-half quarters.

It was hard for the Oilers to hide their dismay. It showed in their faces. They knew their names were about to be etched in time associated with the biggest choke in the history of sports. They could not swallow. Pardee paced the sidelines in a catatonic state, habitually raking his hand across the patch of hair on top of his head. Occasionally, he offered a light hand clapping.

Moon finally responded. Starting at his 28, he worked the ball down the field using the sidelines. With 1:42 left, he hit Slaughter for 18 yards to the Buffalo 16. The paranoia that had enveloped them then caused the Oilers to let 59 seconds run off the clock without calling a time-out. They had three left. Having lost faith in the defense, they wanted to use all the time so Buffalo would have no time to come back. On first down, Moon overthrew Duncan in the end zone. Then they played for the FG. White gained 5. On third down, Moon ran for

2. But there was still the matter of the wobbly Del Greco. No one would have been surprised if he missed, but he hit the 26-yarder to tie it with 12 seconds left.

The Oilers knew that no matter how it ended there was going to be a lot of emotional damage and fallout. But they had to put it all out of their minds for the OT. On the third play, Moon forced a pass into the wind at Givins, who LB Darryl Talley had tightly covered. The coverage was actually closer than tight, as Talley held Givins. But there was no call, and Odomes picked off Moon's 50th pass of the game. After Jeffires' 15-yard face mask penalty was tacked on, the Bills got the ball at the Oiler 20. Three plays later, Steve Christie kicked a 32-yard field goal to eliminate Houston from the playoffs.

It was a tale of two halves. In the first half, the Oilers outgained Buffalo 284 yards to 79 and outscored them 28-3. After halftime, the Bills outgained Houston 287 yards to 145 and outscored them 38-10. It marked the third playoff game in the last two years that the offense failed to score a TD in the second half.

The 32-point collapse was the largest in the 73-year history of the NFL (roughly 9,500 games) and happened on Adams' 70th birthday. The regular season record was 28 points by New Orleans, who fell to San Francisco in 1980. The playoff record was by the 49ers who lost to Detroit in 1957 after leading by 20.

"It's like somebody, somewhere has a voodoo doll, and when the Houston Oilers go on the road to play a playoff game, they start sticking pins in the voodoo doll until there's nothing left of the Houston Oilers," said Givins. "I've never seen anything like it," offered Fuller. "I thought it would never end," admitted Jones.

Pardee said, "We let the crowd get back into the game, and their noise created a lot of problems."

Dishman was somewhat more direct. "It was the biggest choke in history," he said in the dressing room. "Everyone on the team — everyone in the organization — choked today. We were outplayed and outcoached in the second half."

The Bills used the momentum to win in Pittsburgh (24-3) and Miami (29-10), but lost the Super Bowl to the Cowboys. Dallas finished the season 13-3 just three years past a 1-15 season.

OVERVIEW

The season got off to a bad start when three top defenders held out. They lost at home to an inferior Steeler team, who dogged Moon for 5 interceptions. But four wins set up the game circled on the calendar in Denver. Characteristically, they blew a 21-20 lead with under 2 minutes left. The loss left them in a serious funk.

They lost 3 of the next 4. The lowlight was losing in Pittsburgh again after leading 20-7 in the fourth. Del Greco missed the game winner in the final seconds. Childress lashed out about poor attitudes and lackadaisical effort. The team was falling apart. Some of the players ignored the coaches and did what they wanted. There was no discipline. Sitting at 5-4, they faced an impossible stretch of three road games in 12 days. With backs against the wall, they dominated a good Viking team on the road but lost Moon. They played well enough to beat playoff-bound Miami, but Del Greco and the defense gave up the game in the fourth quarter.

Early in the third quarter of the wildcard playoff game in Buffalo, strong safety Bubba McDowell intercepted Frank Reich and returned it 58 yards for a touchdown. The Oilers led 35-3.

After clawing to an 8-5 record, they had a chance to win the division, but fell to a marginal Packer team at home. They closed fast to finish 10-6 and get hopes up, but then crashed and burned in Buffalo.

One more win, and either the Oilers were off or the Bills would have had to travel to Houston for the first round. Two more wins and Houston would have been off the first week and played all playoff games at home. In five of their seven losses, the defense gave up fourth-quarter leads. Six losses were by less than a touchdown. Missed kicks alone altered the outcome of the entire season just as they had the previous season.

The team did make several statistical strides. For starters, their winning road record of 5-3 was the team's first since 1980. The kickoff-coverage team ended the season No. 1 in the league. Montgomery led the NFL in punting with an amazing 46.9 average.

The defense was No. 3 overall in the NFL (1st in AFC), No. 9 in points allowed (3rd in AFC) and No. 2 in pass defense (1st in AFC). New schemes increased the sack total to 50 (4th in NFL), one short of the 1979 team record. Childress led the way with 13 sacks, becoming the first DT to lead the team since Curly Culp in 1975. He was followed by Williams' 11, Jones' 8½ and Fuller's 8. Al Smith led the team in tackles and was named first team Pro Bowl and All-Pro. Childress made first team All-Pro and the Pro Bowl as a reserve. Williams was named as an alternate.

The offense ranked No. 3 overall in the NFL (2nd in AFC) and No. 6 in scoring (2nd in AFC). Amazingly, with Moon missing 6 starts and parts of two other games, the Oilers were still the No. 1 passing attack in football. The rushing game improved to sixth best in the AFC. They tied for third in the AFC in average time of possession.

Moon was 224-of-346 for 2,521 yards, 18 TDs and 12 interceptions. His 89.3 rating was tops in the AFC. Carlson was 149-of-227 for 1,710 yards, 9 TDs and 11 interceptions. Interestingly, he led the AFC in completion percentage (65.6%). Jeffires led the AFC in receptions with 90 for 913 yards and 9 TDs, becoming only the second player since the merger to lead his conference in catches three consecutive years. Duncan was second in the AFC with a career-high 82 receptions. He also had a career-high 954 yards. Givins added 67 catches for 787 yards and a team-high 10 TDs. Slaughter and Harris combined produced some Drew Hill-like numbers. Slaughter caught 39 for 486 while Harris had 35 for a career-high 435.

White had his best season and was team MVP. At times, he carried them. He had 1,226 yards (5th in NFL) plus 57 receptions for another 641, all career-highs. He also had 8 TDs.

The team improved red zone scoring. They had 33 TDs and 14 FGs on 54 trips inside the 20, ranking second in the NFL in red zone points and TDs, and tying for fourth in red zone penetrations. The 49ers led the league with 308 points on 62 trips in the red zone for 39 TDs and 14 FGs.

The Run 'N' Shoot impressed opponents as Houston placed seven offensive players in the Pro Bowl. Munchak (8th time), Matthews (5th) and Jeffires (2nd) were named starters. Moon (5th), White (1st), Givins (2nd) and Duncan (1st) were picked as reserves. David Williams and Greg Montgomery were named as alternates. Munchak tied Elvin Bethea's team record of 8 appearances. Givins and Duncan were the first players to ever tie for a spot. The 9 total to make the Pro Bowl were one short of the 1969 team record.

The statistical rankings were all the more remarkable in light of the multitude of injuries. Besides Moon, Smith missed 10 starts, Lathon 5 and Orlando 15. Munchak, Maggs, Flannery and Dawson also missed games with injuries. Their ability to make the playoffs rested on their depth, which had been slowly rebuilt after being ravished by Plan B. The subs stepping up were Carlson, Graf, Alm, Robertson, Donnalley and Eric Norgard. Plan B signee Gray led the team with 6 interceptions. Rookie LB Eddie Robinson started the final 12 games.

THE ANALYSIS

Trying to come to grips with what happened in 1992 and more specifically in Buffalo on January 3, 1993, like trying to decipher the whole Oiler story, is a bit like peeling an onion. It is not easy and there are many layers. It might even make you cry.

The regular season was another paradigm. With an easy schedule and abundance of indoor games, the Oilers had the top defense and second-best offense in the AFC, plus nine Pro Bowlers. Yet they barely made the playoffs. It did not add up.

The Moon injury jumps out as a cause until Carlson's 4-2 record as a starter is considered. Cody also threw the game-winning screen pass to White at the end of the Viking game.

A better place to start is the rush defense. The Oilers were No. 10 in the AFC (slipping from 7th in '91). Perhaps more telling, they gave up an average of 4.0 yards per carry, the league average. Their best run-stopper, Smith, could not be counted on. As a result, they frequently had DEs playing DT (Childress, Williams). None of the DL starters was particularly good at stopping the run. Those guys all wanted sacks. Sacks got them their contract incentives, on ESPN and in the Pro Bowl. Stopping the run did not. What it did do, though, was get teams to the Big Dance. It was no coincidence that the two best rush defenses in the league, Dallas and Buffalo, met in the Super Bowl.

With a better rush defense, opponents would not have been able to eat up the clock and keep the Oiler offense off the field. For the most part, the coaches did what they could with what they had. Failing to address this weakness through the draft or Plan B fell on management. Had they gone out and gotten the players to shore it up (and they had plenty of chances), the turnovers and missed kicks would not have been so devastating.

As it was, the turnovers killed them. As a team, they threw 23 interceptions, the sixth highest total in the NFL. In addition, Moon, Carlson, Slaughter, Givins, White and Jeffires combined for an incredible 31 fumbles (Givins alone had 10). That is 54 turnovers (3.4 per game), which is way too many. It went a long way towards explaining why the No. 3 defense in the NFL was No. 9 in points allowed. Opponents frequently did not have to go far to score.

The kicking game was another area of frustration. Despite complete disaster in 1991, they basically stuck with what they had. Del Greco, who would later turn into a steady kicker, cost them some important games in 1992. In addition, the coaches inexplicably cut third-round draft pick Corey Harris, a good return man. He was waived because the coaches did not think he would make it as a Run 'N' Shoot receiver. He ended up returning kicks and playing in the secondary for 7 years in Green Bay and Seattle.

The kicking woes provide a nice segue to the Buffalo game. While Greg Montgomery was the best punter in the NFL, he was not exactly a prime-time player. Besides releasing two of the worst punts of his life (25 and 28 yards in the second half), he bobbled the snap that cost the Oilers a field goal in the third quarter. Del Greco contributed as well with the poorly executed "squib" kick that jump-started the Bill's comeback.

The list goes on and on. Moon's two interceptions were crucial, and his failure to get the offense moving on their first possession in the third quarter may have been the crime of the day. Much like Denver the year before, the DL failed to generate anything near the effort it had in the prior game. The lack of pressure let career backup Reich build confidence in the second half. In light of the fact that they knew he had to throw, the weak pass rush was unforgivable.

Moon thought the offense spent too much time on the bench, and suggested the McDowell interception was what beat them. "It seemed like it took forever just to get the ball," said Moon, who was 36-for-50 for 371 yards, 4 TDs and 2 interceptions. "I'd warm up and warm up, then sit down, then warm up again. It's a shame, too, because I was in such a good rhythm the first half. I was seeing the whole field. Our audibles were working. Everything was clicking. But your rhythm can break down when you stay off the field so long."

Several players blamed the coaching. Dishman said, "We knew they were going to feature Reed in the second half, but we stayed in the same zones. When you play the same things all the time, teams are going to beat you. It was the same old coverage. We didn't make the adjustments we should have in the second half." He also thought he should have covered the Bills' best WR instead of Jackson, who history would make one of the main goats. Dish said, "I'm one of the best cornerbacks in the league. If the ball is going to a certain guy, then I want to be the one on him. I think I should have been."

Sean Jones later called it "brain lock." Coaches were so shocked by the turn of events, their brains hemorrhaged. They went blank. They could not think. They came up with no adjustments. They just stood there in a daze and watched it happen.

Eddy's response was, "We played the Bills for six quarters as well as any defense in the history of the game."

THE FALLOUT

A Houston sport team finally made the big times. The national news and sports organizations could not get enough. They even made the David Letterman Show. The category was the Top 10 Oilers Excuses:

10. Shouldn't have skipped breakfast — it's the most important meal of the day.
9. Started giving 109 percent instead of 110 percent.
8. Even though fans loved it, shouldn't have replaced Warren Moon with folk singer Suzanne Vega.
7. Busy making mental tally of football players with girls' names: Fran Tarkenton ... Rosie Grier ...
6. You try tackling those guys — some of them are huge.
5. Bills QB kept looking one way, then throwing the other.
4. Wanted to honor another Houstonian who let a big lead in the polls slip away.
3. "I'm telling you — maybe you didn't see the Dobermans on the field, but there were Dobermans on the field!"
2. Preoccupied about getting home in time to see all the Amy Fisher movies.
1. Didn't want to go to Disney World.

They also made Rush Limbaugh's radio show. On the following Monday, he played the Oiler fight song, but kept switching the speeds up and down to simulate the Oilers' ups and downs. Jay Leno and Arsenio Hall got their licks in, too. Houston's dirty little secret, their football team, was out of the closet. The whole country now knew about them. They were a national joke.

And, of course, other NFL players saw the game. One-time Oiler Jamie Williams said that the consensus among the 14-win 49ers was that the Oilers would be in the Super Bowl. "When Houston beat Buffalo in the last regular-season game," he said, "it was like, 'Wow, they're the ones'... it looked like Houston got it together at the right time." After the game, there was a new battle cry among NFL teams. "It's not 'Remember the Alamo!' anymore," said Williams. "After that Buffalo game, it's 'Remember Houston. Remember the Oilers!'"

Fans were devastated. Even the ones who suffered through all 33 years were shocked by this one. The Oilers had really outdone themselves. Stagger Lee did not hold a candle to losing a 32-point lead to a backup QB from Maryland. There was at least one suicide and more than a few busted televisions. Other than that, they could write letters, which they did, or call local radio shows, which they also did.

Charlie Pallilo, host of a sports talk show on KTRH radio, called the reaction "unprecedented." The volume of calls was overwhelming. Callers were harsh, mean, critical and even threatening. Some, of course, suspected a conspiracy. They were ready to fire everybody. Pallilo said, "No one will forget about this, ever. People will take this game to their grave."

Indeed, there was a theory that the Oilers were the main reason Houston's population was so large. It said many people were hanging around cheating death just to see the Oilers win something. Funeral directors were their biggest cheering section. A Super Bowl might have left Houston the size of Rhode Island.

Bruce Matthews bravely appeared on one of the radio spots and could not believe what he heard. "Some people were totally out of control with their anger and frustration," he said. "I have never seen anything like this." His "Hey, it's just another game," attitude did not sit well with natives and dramatized the depth of the disconnection between the modern professional athlete and fan. If a player as thoughtful and seasoned as Matthews did not understand by now the emotional link between the Oilers and their fans, none of them did.

DANGLING ELEMENTS

Jack Pardee had a habit of making a slight rocking motion and stroking the top of his head whenever he had to answer questions he did not want to answer. There was a lot of that going on after Buffalo.

When asked how they were fooled by the onsides kick, he answered, "We talked to everybody about it. We did everything we could to prepare for that. We were crowding the 10-yard restraining line. Otherwise, we would have lined up two, three or four yards deeper."

Asked about his decision to kick into the wind in the third quarter, he stated, "Looking back, if I could do anything different I wouldn't have chosen to do that because field position in the second half was the biggest difference in the game. Obviously, I didn't think they'd get four touchdowns in one quarter. I wanted to get them in the fourth quarter where they wouldn't have a fourth-quarter flurry. One of the best ways to keep that from happening is to have your offense control the ball. In the first quarter, we were going against the wind, and we had the ball for over nine minutes. I was hoping that would have been the case in the third quarter."

Asked why he did not do more, he borrowed one from Hugh Campbell, saying, "I got more involved because so many decisions had to be made. We knew the possibilities, starting with the kickoff."

THE SCAPEGOATS

The birthday boy was hurting. Of the original AFL teams, only Houston and San Diego had never been to a Super Bowl. It must have been tough on old Bud going to league meetings and being forced to nod in agreement to the stories about how great the Cowboys were.

No one would have been surprised if he fired everyone on the spot. He had done it before and certainly considered it. Heavies like Bill Parcells, Dan Reeves, Mike Ditka and Buddy Ryan were available. Instead, Pardee saved his job by agreeing to fire Jim Eddy and DB coach Pat Thomas. It was pretty distasteful. Eddy and Thomas coached under Pardee with the Gamblers 1984-85, Cougars 1987-89 and Oilers 1990-92.

Eddy was caught off guard. That morning, he was at team facilities talking about next year. "This is the best defense to play for the Houston Oilers," he said. "There's been an overall improvement since 1989 defensively. I'm really proud of our improvement in all areas, and I know we're headed in the right direction." A few hours later, he was fired by an old friend.

He had a point. The '89 team gave up 25.8 points per game vs. 16.1 in '92. They were No. 1 in the AFC. Pat Thomas saw the pass defense improve from No. 20

in '89 to No. 2 in '92. He helped Dish become a Pro Bowler and developed Robertson, Lewis and Jackson.

Still, the question remained how a backup QB playing without the team's best RB was able to do that to his statistical juggernaut of a defense. Maybe Sean Jones was right— it was brain lock.

Holovak made the announcement. "He was in charge of the defense and I wasn't happy with what I saw yesterday," he said. "There were a lot of receivers running loose in the second half." When asked about the wisdom of firing the coordinator of the top defense, he replied, "Stats might mean something somewhere, but I'm not sure they're all that valid in this case. There must have been four or five games when we played second- or third-team quarterbacks, and that helps the statistics. I just have to go by what I see." Adams refused interviews.

Eddy landed on his feet, hired as an assistant by the Super Bowl champion Cowboys. Apparently, Coach Johnson was not worried that his team would catch whatever it was that Houston had.

THE PUNDITS

The local experts were unsure who to blame. Surprisingly, Fowler laid off Bud, "We know that when the season for Houston's favorite sport ends in crushing disappointment, it's only natural to turn to Houston's second-favorite sport, but I'd still like to declare a moratorium on Bud-bashing. Over the years, Bud Adams has been a pretty decent owner ... his payroll is among the top 25 percent ... Making mistakes is one thing. Refusing to try to field a champion is another. Bud has tried."

Ed's culprits were "clowns," "jokers" and a lack of "discipline." He blamed an "organizational flaw ... The Oilers' attitude problem festers because there is no broad-based organizational response to it. Holovak deals with it on a piecemeal basis [and] dresses down players on a regular basis, but, perhaps because the role shouldn't be his, the effect of his lectures appears minimal."

John McClain wrote, "A lot of fans want Jack Pardee fired, but his job is not in jeopardy for another season. Pardee is an honest man, but being a good guy and a competent coach is no longer enough. He is going to have to put down his foot or lose his job next season. He has been forced to make changes in his staff, and now he has to make some changes in personnel."

Fran Blinebury's take was, "The Oilers did not just blow a historic 32-point lead to the Bills. They kissed off the best chance at a championship in the history of the franchise, and that window of opportunity, at least for this bunch, soon will close ... If the head coach won't do more than sit on his weekly television show and shrug his shoulders at concerns about a defense that went over Niagara Falls in a barrel and special-teams play that was mindless, then perhaps what the Oilers need is someone with a sharp needle for a tongue who won't be afraid to hit a nerve."

A few weeks later, after Pardee had weathered the storm, Fowler wrote: "In three seasons, the Oilers haven't improved a lick under Pardee. In their last game ... Pardee stood paralyzed on the sideline and watched a 32-point lead float away like a puff of breath on the frigid Buffalo air ... Pardee didn't instruct defensive coordinator Jim Eddy or special-teams coach Richard Smith to change their schemes. He didn't lift a finger to take control and arrest the carnage.

He called 'The Choke' a "grander element of Oilers lore than Earl Campbell. As long as that statue of Pardee adorns the sideline each autumn Sunday, The Choke lives."

1993: THE EFFECTIVE END OF THE HOUSTON OILERS

There was only one way to overcome the humiliation of Buffalo. Everyone connected with the Oilers knew what it was. The pressure to win or at least make a Super Bowl was suffocating. They knew if they failed in 1993, the taint from that game would follow them all around like a dark cloud the rest of their careers.

There was no shortage of issues, including a new DC and free agency. It would be a wild year both on and off the field, probably the craziest in team history and that is saying a lot. While the way the '92 season ended had a powerful effect on the relationships among the team, its owner and the city, the '93 season would push them all over the brink of no return.

THE DEFENSIVE COORDINATOR ISSUE

The rumored candidates for the man who would teach them how to hold a 32-point lead included Floyd Reese, Wade Phillips, Vince Tobin and Buddy Ryan. On January 29, 1993, Bud Adams once again raised a few eyebrows by hiring the 59-year-old Ryan.

Ryan made a name as the Bears' DC from 1978-85. He is perhaps best remembered for being carried off the field by his players when Chicago won the Super Bowl. He became head coach of the Eagles in 1987 and led them to three playoff berths from 1988-90.

It was a desperate move. There was no doubt of Ryan's pedigree. But controversy surrounded him wherever he went. He did not get along with Mike Ditka or

Eagle ownership. On the other hand, his players always seemed to love him.

Speculation began immediately that he was after Pardee's job. It was no secret he wanted to be a head coach. The only reason the Oilers got him is that Bill Parcels beat him to the Patriot job. He said, "I told Jack that my goal is to help him win the Super Bowl, and everything is great. I do want to be a head coach again, but the Eagles retired me a little early." Pardee, who played little part in the hiring, said, "I want good coaches," Pardee said. "I want coaches who want to be head coaches but aren't planning on being the head coach here. I want the best staff possible, and Buddy's a proven coach."

Buddy said he "turned this job down twice." He added, "Most teams that wanted me to be defensive coordinator didn't have the talent the Oilers have [who had] the best defensive personnel in the AFC." All they needed to get "to the Super Bowl" was Buddy.

He said, "Their attitude's going to change as soon as I get there. They should start out by having respect for a guy with my track record. I'll give them an identity. Usually, they don't start out appreciating me, but they do down the line. We're the ones who made coaches start sleeping in their offices. We'll play 13 different fronts and about 20 coverages, so it's going to challenge them mentally.

"What I bring to a defense is toughness. With Buddy Ryan, the other team will know it's going to get its head knocked off. I know I can win, and I know how to do it. I don't anticipate any problems. There's my way or Trailways."

About the "chuck-and-duck," he said, "I've seen the Run 'N' Shoot all my life. It's a third-down offense played on every down. When I coached defense, we worked two downs trying to get them in that formation, and now they come out in it automatically. The Oilers run it better than anybody else because of the personnel they have."

About Buffalo, he offered, "Bud asked me that, and I told him I don't ever remember defensing a 32-point lead. I don't think I ever had one that big, but I'll tell you what: I've protected a lot of three-point leads in my time."

Warren Moon, reached for comment in Hawaii, said, "Nobody really understands the Buddy Ryan move completely. A lot of players are aware that Jack didn't have a whole lot to do with that hiring. That makes the players wonder, 'What are they doing over there?' Players ask me, 'Are they trying to squeeze Jack out? Are they trying to make Jack quit?' That's an uneasiness we don't need."

THE FREE AGENCY ISSUE

The biggest issue facing the Oilers was free agency. The Minnesota case came down for the players. A new collective bargaining agreement was reached in January, the first since 1986. Fuller said it was about "fairness and equality. It means more freedom and allows us to be treated like athletes in other professional sports."

The owners fought it as long as they could, but the result was inevitable. They thought it would ruin the game as it had other sports. Many saw their stance as hypocritical since owners had the freedom to move to the city that made the best offer. Adams got a better lease by threatening to move to Florida while Al Davis and Robert Irsay moved. Judge Doty effectively put the players in a similar position.

For 1993, teams had the option to protect up to three "transitional players" and/or one "franchise player." A transitional player could sign an offer sheet with another team, but the original team could keep him by matching the offer. The salary cap did not kick in until the '94 season.

It was going to be a brave new world, one that immediately put more pressure on front offices. They suddenly had to become experts in the "cap." A premium would be placed on scouting other teams.

Houston's list of unrestricted free agents included Carlson, Al Smith, Givins, White, Gray, Doug Smith, Maggs, Graf and Del Greco. The transitional player designations came down to Carlson, White, Smith and Givins. Out of the blue, Adams inked Carlson to a whopping three-year, $8.85 million contract that made him the highest-paid backup in the history of football. It let them protect Smith, White and Givins, and kept Seattle, KC and New England off Cody. And the coaches did not have to teach another QB the Run 'N' Shoot.

But it was a lot for a career backup (whom they twice offered in trade for Andre Ware) and meant they already had $6.25 million committed (almost 20% of the coming cap) to two players — Moon and Carlson — with over half the starters with contracts expiring at the end of 1993.

Jerry Jones, who let Steve Beurlein go in a similar situation, recognized the danger. He said, "I'm surprised at some of the teams that are spending a lot of money at this time. They're going to have to make some drastic reductions in the future. It's like a credit card where your bills don't come due for a year. Based on what I'm seeing, there are a lot of clubs who are going to have a nice little hangover."

To make it worse, they failed to renegotiate with any others. They thought player costs were coming down. Bud said, "It's going to be a different game. I don't know if the players can adjust to the changes." As a result, they offered only one-year contracts to their unrestricted free agents.

Bud was getting bad advice. As a direct result, the Oilers would tumble from first to last within another season. In the end, they would blame it on the fans and city, and leave town.

It did not have to be that way. Other teams faced the same hardships. The successful ones signed the players they wanted to keep, restructured contracts, massaged the cap and appealed to players' sense of loyalty.

Dallas kept a solid core together (Aikman, Smith, Haley, Novacek, Irvin), then filled in around them. The 49ers let go of aging stars (Lott, Craig, Montana) and used their winning tradition to attract experienced free agents at bargain prices. The Bills lost Cornelius Bennett, House Ballard and Jeff Wright but kept winning the division. The Steelers were slain in free agency (Nickerson, Searcy, Seals, Woodson, Green, Hastings, O'Donnell), but made the playoffs every season under Bill Cowher with a budget smaller than Houston's. While these teams each had different approaches, they were all determined to survive and did. In fact, they thrived. And each did it without a new stadium.

The bean counter who emerged during this period in Houston was Mike McClure, the team vice-president. McClure had Adams' ear and convinced him of the coming Armageddon.

An example of his marketing genius could be seen in the "Oiler Dancers" he debuted in 1992. The original Derrick Dolls were disbanded in the early '80s amid lawsuits and allegations of too much attention from the front office. For awhile, the Oilers had no cheerleaders. Later, they brought in high schoolers and finally the Dancers. The problem was that they really were dancers. They staged halftime routines based on shows like "Cats" and "Phantom of the Opera," not exactly what Joe-football-fan was looking for in his pro cheerleader. "We tried to go beyond the traditional drill-team concept of cheerleading and provide Houston with something different," said McClure. "But it didn't go over. A concept designed for the stage just wasn't going to work on the vast expanse of a football field. The response was lukewarm."

The guy who came up with that idea was the same one who would be charting the path through free agency. Instead of increasing the scouts and front office to handle the additional workload, he and Bud fretted over how to squeeze out more revenues. It was McClure who convinced Adams he would perish without a new stadium right away. It was under McClure that the team quickly disintegrated and the Oilers left Houston for greener pastures.

THE 1993 DRAFT

Despite Buffalo, the team was still incredibly popular, so much so that the annual draft festival, Oilerfest '93, had to move to the Astrodome. For the first time since 1990, they had a first round pick — No. 19.

Unfortunately, they were not in a position to immediately shore up the rush defense. That is because OT Don Maggs left for Denver. Maggs was the first unrestricted free agent. He did not give the Oilers a chance to match. The size of the contract (almost $4 million over 3 years) for a lineman surprised some, but the market was determining value. Next to QBs, the most valuable players were the ones who chased them, the DEs. Logically, the value of the ones who protected the QBs was about to rise. Maggs was a left tackle, a right-handed QB's best friend.

The Oilers hoped for Willie Roaf or Lincoln Kennedy, both tackles. Roaf was best, but management said the price was too high to trade up. When he and Kennedy went quickly, they panicked traded up with the Eagles. To move from No. 19 to No. 13, they gave up their third-round choice. They took Brad Hopkins (6'3, 306). Although short for an OT, they said he had "quick feet" and was "as good an athlete at his position as anyone in the draft."

The second-round pick was a battle between Gilbride and Ryan. Gilbride wanted a speedy WR. Buddy won and took MLB Michael Barrow (6'1, 236). He said, "He's a little taller than Mike Singletary." Barrow was good, but MLB Al Smith was coming off an All-Pro year.

They also added smurf WR Travis Hannah (4th round), TE John Henry Mills (5th), Tennessee State WR/KR Patrick Robinson (7th) and DB Blaine Bishop (8th).

Mills (6'0, 220) was the most talked-about, but the coaches were just blowing smoke. They had no intention of incorporating changes suggested by an owner into the No. 1 ranked passing offense in the NFL for the past three seasons. Their best pick was the player from whom the least was expected. Blaine Bishop, their last selection, would turn into a fine safety.

What they should have done was move up for Roaf (Lee Williams and Nos. 1 and 4?). He was worth it, plus it was a weak draft. Houston's line and beleaguered QBs needed the help. They also could have added OG Will Shields or OT Earl Dotson in the third.

In Dallas, Jimmy Johnson was showing the difference a great talent scout could make. Since '89, JJ's drafts produced Troy Aikman, Daryl Johnston, Mark Stepnoski, Tony Tolbert, Emmitt Smith, Alexander Wright, Russell Maryland, Alvin Harper, Dixon Edwards, Erik Williams, Leon Lett, Kevin Smith, Robert Jones, Darren Woodson, Kevin Williams and Darrin Smith. With those same picks over the same period, his Houston counterparts drafted David Williams, Scott Kozak, Rod Harris, Lamar Lathon, Jeff Alm, Willis Peguese, Eric Still, Richard Newbill, Mike Dumas, John Flannery, Steve Jackson, Corey Harris, Mike Mooney, Brad Hopkins and Travis Hannah.

ANOTHER NEW MARSHALL IN TOWN

After the draft, the Oilers were involved in another crazy tale involving former Pro Bowl LB Wilber Marshall. Buddy said Wilber would lead them to the Super Bowl. The Oilers unwisely offered Washington their first- and fifth-round choices contingent upon being able to negotiate a new contract.

When they could not reach a deal, Adams withdrew the offer. Unbeknownst to him, Redskin GM Charley Casserley and Marshall's attorney, Robert Bennett, secretly cut a deal calling for Washington to pay the salary differential (showing how badly they wanted to be rid of him).

It turned into another PR nightmare for Houston, with Casserley getting national airplay at Adams' expense. Bennett, a high-priced DC attorney political types look to when they get in trouble (see Bill Clinton), peppered the media with a bunch of specious contract law arguments.

When it went to the Commissioner for decision, most assumed the Oilers would get hosed since Tags had a long-standing friendship with Skins' owner Jack Kent Cooke. Houston fans were used to getting the short end of the stick. But Tagliabue not only let the trade stand, but also allowed Washington only third- and fifth-round picks. He even chastised Casserley (one of the worst GMs in football), for what amounted to a tortious interference with contract.

It seemed liked a great moment in Oiler history until Adams issued a gag order, which was typical of Oiler PR. In any event, the sports gods soon got even. A couple of weeks into camp, Marshall injured a knee, requiring surgery. He never fully recovered.

1993 TRAINING CAMP

Summer meant the arrival of the plaintive wail coming from Oiler training camp. The Carlson contract sent players into a jealous tizzy. The holdouts were legion.

Hopkins and Barrow were unsigned when camp opened. Hopkins showed he was an Oiler at heart when,

The 1993 season would be the last together for Houston's all-star duo of OG Mike Munchak (No. 63) and C-OG-OT Bruce Matthews (74). Together they logged 327 games. Matthews, who was still an all-star through the 1998 season at age 37, would later top Munchak's team record of 9 Pro Bowl appearances.

after signing ($3.2 million, 4 years), he angrily stomped out of the practice facility over a holdup regarding a technicality in his contract.

Givins and Duncan were also peeved. Because they tied for the last WR spot on the Pro Bowl team, the Oilers paid each only half of their Pro Bowl bonus. Right or wrong, the team looked bad by putting the bottom line ahead of recognizing their players' great seasons.

Duncan sued. He said he wanted to be declared a free agent. Givins held out even though he was named a transitional player, which meant the team had to pay him $1.79 million for 1993 (100% over his '92 salary of $800,000). It turned into another mini-opera. He wanted $2 million, saying, "I'm very frustrated." It was so tense, Bud issued a personal plea for him to return.

Fellow transitional player Lorenzo White also held out, his second in 3 years. This one a real tragedy. The designation meant he would receive $1.5 million, a three-fold increase over 1992. He said, "I have the stats to prove I'm up there with the best running backs. Emmitt, Thurman and Barry are outstanding backs, but I think Lorenzo belongs up there, too." To him, that meant a multi-year deal at $2 million per year. The Oilers declined. So he did the couch potato. It was a bad career move. Once he returned, someone had stolen his job and he did not get it back. He should have sued whoever convinced him to hold out.

The third transitional player, Al Smith, made noise about doing the same thing, but reported so he would not lose his job to Barrow. It was ridiculous for any of them to hold out, considering what the Oilers had to pay them. There was not much upside. Besides, White was not Barry Sanders or Emmitt Smith, nor was Givins Jerry Rice or Sterling Sharpe.

Backup RB back Gary Brown, who had 172 yards on his career, also held out and then wisely reported ahead of White. Leonard Harris held out and then signed a deal with a $530,000 base saying, "I'm not happy, but I'm going to make the best of it. You get used to the way they treat you sometimes.... I've given the Oilers a lot of good years of my life." He was later cut.

Another was RT David Williams, who finally signed at $3.5 million over 2 years. The last item in a short newspaper report on the signing would be of some significance later. It read, "Williams and his wife, Debi, are expecting their first child in October."

DT Jeff Alm did his part. Although he had only started 7 games, he turned down an offer of $2.35 million over 3 years. The most they had to offer the restricted free agent was $319,000.

Ironically, Sean Jones could not come up with a good enough excuse this time. He must have felt left out. For good measure, he threatened to sue. "If I couldn't be treated fairly at the bargaining table, my only recourse was to take them to court," Jones said. "I would expect to become a free agent, and I'll cite the Reggie White precedent."

Some of the biggest whining came from an unlikely source, Ray Childress. The Big Aggie cultivated an image as the quiet, strong, blue-collar type. That was unless someone else made more money than him. "I'm totally disgusted with the situation," said Ray. "If some-

If anyone deserved to feel secure about his position in 1993, it was Al Smith, who was the first team All-Pro middle linebacker and who was coming off back-to-back Pro Bowl appearances. But when Buddy Ryan arrived, Smith was suddenly too heavy and draft pick Michael Barrow was the next Mike Singletary.

thing's not done, I won't play for the Houston Oilers." He wanted a new deal now (while Bud was throwing it around), not next year (when there might not be as much to go around). "They added $2.5 million to Warren's contract, and then they told me they wouldn't do mine. I don't think it's right, and I don't think it's fair."

The players' views of their values came mostly from their agents. Childress had Leigh Steinburg, who was practiced at manipulating the media. He publicly requested a trade. It might have passed the smell test had Ray sacked Frank Reich at least once.

As a group, these were the same guys who had just blown the biggest lead in the history of the world. Here they were a few months later demanding huge raises. They had no shame. The greed was thick. Funny how none of them were ever willing to discuss a pay cut after a bad season.

Interjecting himself into this situation was Adams, who appeared at camp with the rookies for the first time since 1960. Underground since Buffalo, he not only showed up early but came with a megaphone which he used to cheer on the players from the sidelines.

The medieval cheerleader routine, Buddy Ryan, Wilber Marshall and a TE, were all designed to win back fans. Then he outdid himself. He ordered head coach Jack Pardee to wear headphones on the sidelines. In his own words, Adams said, "I told him just in a casual way there are some coaches who don't wear headsets, and you're one of them, but I think it looks better with a headset, whether it's turned on or turned off."

He called the playoff loss "probably the most disappointing, devastating day of my whole career in football." Despite firing Eddy and Thomas, he said he did not blame the defense because "the offense stunk in the second half." About the fans, he said, "I can't see our fans being disillusioned about a team that's winning every year." About the criticism, he said, "To hear some of the talk, it almost makes you feel that if we had gone to the Super Bowl, and if we won, we'd get criticized for not looking good winning."

He was also the messenger of doom, warning that with the cap, he saw no way to keep them together. "It's ironic that we're taking in more money (from TV) this year than we ever have, but we're going to lose money for the first time since the AFL days," said the boss.

The largest variable in that equation was the television contract which was expiring. NBC and especially CBS were expected to make lower bids. Bud said, "It gets back to the television money. We averaged $32 million a year on this last contract (4-year deal), and I'd be real happy if we can get $32 million next year."

Asked about Bud's activities, Moon responded, "I don't know if that shows commitment or if it shows panic." About the holdouts, he said, "Bud hasn't been a tightwad or anything like that, but I wish it didn't have to always come down to these situations before you get a player signed. You have to wonder what psychological effect it will have on that player when he gets in."

About the owner's suggestions for the offense, he said, "We don't need a tight end in our offense. Don't let the fans and media intimidate you about what we need. A tight end isn't going to get us to the Super Bowl."

About himself, he said, "I have mixed emotions for the first time going into camp. Usually, I'm real excited." The 5-time Pro Bowler said, "I might not be wearing an Oilers uniform after this season, and that's something I'm really concerned about. I want to finish my career in Houston. Houston's my home. I've made a lot of friends and built a lot of great relationships. This is where I want this phase of my life to end and the next one to begin .... What I'd really like to do is to win the Super Bowl this year and then play one more season. I want to wean myself away from football. It would give me a chance to say my good-byes around the league and bow out gracefully."

Regarding the playoffs, he said, "The thing that frustrates me is that I feel that I played two of my better games in the playoff games we lost the last two years, but we had nothing to show for it. It makes me question myself and wonder what I can do to make sure we get further in the playoffs." Moon was 63-of-86 (73%) for 696 yards, 7 TDs and 3 interceptions against Denver and Buffalo. All 7 TDs came in the first half.

Underlying everything else in camp was the Ryan factor. Much was made of how Pardee would handle it. His job was on the line, while Buddy was featured in team advertising and even had his own television and radio shows. But Jack was cool. He knew he was going to collect his nearly $1 million salary for '93 and '94 no matter what.

He stayed out of it by delegating. The feud that developed was between the two stubborn and independent coordinators. After directing the NFL's top passing offense the last three years and losing several ribs in a battle with a tumorous kidney, Kevin Gilbride thought he was due a little deference. Ryan had been to Super Bowls with three different teams, and was thought of as one of the great defensive minds in football. He did not care for Gilbride's offense.

Gilbride also wanted to be a head coach. He had deftly positioned himself into heir apparent status in Houston. Then came Ryan to shake up those plans.

They clashed at practices and meetings. They shouted. They had to be separated. They could not agree on how to practice or how long. Gilbride and some of his players did not care for the hard licks they were taking. There were many fights. Ryan encouraged the rough play, saying, "Practice like you play, and play like you practice — that's the way you win." But Gilbride was tough, too. He was determined not to give in or appear weak. Pardee was frequently called on to mediate. The conflict pushed the Oilers from the local papers to the national scene. They would follow this story closely.

Ryan also created a situation among a few defensive players. He praised some of the young guys like Lewis and Robertson, but moved Lathon to third team behind not just Marshall but Bowden as well. Lamar and Joe had fistfights all summer. Ryan called Al Smith overweight (played at 255 in '92; Ryan wanted 235) and constantly touted Barrow. "Barrow's got the quickness, toughness and brains," said Ryan. "He'll be a hell of a football player in this league before long."

Smith and Lathon bore down instead of crying. All the defense did. It was that way wherever Buddy coached. Whether it was his reputation or the way he handled them, the players responded. They got on board the Von Ryan Express.

Ryan brought in Ronnie Jones for the LBs (replacing Bush) and Tom Bettis for the DBs (replacing Thomas). Charlie Baggett replaced Palmer. The holdovers were Bob Young (OL), Frank Novak (RBs), Jim Stanley (DL) and Steve Watterson (strength and conditioning). In a mistake, they let special teams coach Richard Smith go to Denver. Richard Williams replaced him. Frank Bush moved to quality control.

Five rookies made the team: Hopkins, Barrow, Hannah, Bishop and Mills. New starters on defense included Glen Montgomery at DT, Robertson at FS and Lewis at CB. Bowden was in at OLB, as both Marshall and Lathon were injured. Lamar worked hard only to break an arm. Lee Williams also went into the season hurt, and an Achilles tendon injury put Dumas out for the season. They later signed former No. 1 Keith McCants off waivers.

On offense, Hopkins worried Bob Young. "I like the kid, thought he was smart right from the start," he said. "But I think you'd call him intellectually smart, not smart in football. He's got a lot to learn about the game. And there's another thing. He's weak. They beat him up every time." Williams' holdout and Flannery's injury caused Matthews to shift to LT. But while solving one problem, it created others. Just before the season started, Young moved everyone back with Matthews at C, Donnalley at LT and Dawson at RG. They were not ready when the season started. Desperate, they signed former No. 1 Stan Thomas off waivers.

Among the final cuts was rookie KR Patrick Robinson. He averaged 23.3 yards on kickoffs and 10.4 yards on punts in the preseason. When Cincinnati claimed him, it set off another open conflict among the coaches.

Richard Williams, whose job it was to breathe some life into a rancid return game, said, "I'm not very happy about it. He's the best returner we've had around here for years. I guess it's obvious I'm the only one who puts a priority on that."

Gilbride played a hand in the decision, which meant Ryan was not far away. As had happened with Cory Harris, Gilbride insisted on keeping nine WRs (most in the NFL). It would have been smarter to expose one of the five backups (Pat Coleman, Damon Mays, Gary Wellman, Travis Hannah, Reggie Brown). It was unlikely another team would want Houston's ninth best smurf receiver. Once cleared, he could have been added back to the expanded roster.

Ryan called it a "mistake." "You don't easily find people like (Robinson) running around the country," he said. "We didn't give him a chance.... Now, Cincinnati gets to play him twice against us." The idea to draft Robinson came from Ryan's son, who coached him in an all-star game. Pardee said he could be "replaced."

The Oilers beat the Cowboys in the annual exhibition game to make it eight of the last nine. However, the crowd in the Alamodome was decidedly pro-Cowboy even though San Antonio was supposed to be Adams' biggest hotbed of support outside Houston.

Dale Robertson did the honors. "What I'm saying here is the '93 Oilers should be heading for their third consecutive Super Bowl, not their first," he wrote. "Nevertheless, given Houston's cruel sporting history, a first Super Bowl is infinitely better than none at all .... Mohammed reached his mountaintop. Moses crossed the Red Sea to the promised land. Indiana Jones found the Holy Grail. The Oilers will claim the AFC championship. Finally, vindication."

No one would have blamed fans if they had stayed away, but the Oilers were hard to ignore. They were in the news every day with injuries, holdouts, an amusing owner and dueling coaches. Season ticket sales were off only 5%. It goes without saying that they were in for another long season.

THE 1993 REGULAR SEASON — THEY SHOULD TURN THAT THING INTO A SOAP OPERA DOWN THERE

Ryan's brash talk led to some great expectations for his "46" defense. But it was a thick playbook and not everyone picked it up quickly. Plus, it was hard to concentrate when you were preoccupied imagining the ways you could spend Carlson's salary. Marshall, Lee Williams, Lathon and Alm were out for the opener with New Orleans, but fans expected a win.

They fell flat on their faces — on national television. It was the same old story: turnovers (5), penalties (13 for 84 yards) and a defense that let the opponent control the clock. After jumping to a 7-0 lead, Houston trailed 19-7 going into the fourth quarter and lost 33-21. Houston's offense rolled up 405 yards while Wade Wilson completed 16 passes for 206 yards and no TDs.

Givins fumed, "Coach Pardee makes the decisions, not Buddy Ryan. Everybody wants to be a chief and call the shots, but there's only one man who should call the shots, and that's Jack Pardee." He was upset over comments Ryan made about the offense.

Ryan responded, "I don't even know who he (Givins) is, but I'll tell you one thing: I haven't said anything about our offense. We're all on the same page and, hopefully, trying to win the Super Bowl. If somebody's a little tender, he ought to get out of the kitchen." He added, "People ask me how come I call it the chuck-and-duck — well, that's what I called it when Jerry Glanville put it in here. That's the first time I'd seen it. I'm not going to be a hypocrite and change what I call something. What's the difference if you call it the throw-and-duck or Run 'N' Shoot or the shoot-and-duck?"

Moon said, "Everybody just needs to shut up and start playing."

The Chiefs were next for the only glamorous home game of the year. However, Marty Schottenheimer held Joe Montana out to not expose him to Ryan's blitzes. Houston won 30-0 in a game much closer than the score showed. It was the Oilers' fourth straight win over KC, but their defense was catching up to the Run 'N' Shoot, this time holding it to only 247 yards.

They fell in San Diego 18-17 on 6 John Carney field goals, 4 Moon interceptions and a terrible call on a fourth-quarter Carlson-to-Jeffires TD catch. The NFL's director of officials later admitted it was a blown call, but the Oilers were still 1-2. Carlson was in because Moon was yanked for the first time in his NFL career.

After they fell to a crummy Rams team, people started calling for Pardee's head. "As for Jack Pardee, better call the undertaker," wrote Robertson. "Fair or not, he's dead in this town." Speculation centered on Bum Phillips, which was enough to flush out Adams, who issued a statement of support for Pardee.

In Buffalo, a sign read, "OK, we'll spot you 33." The Oilers were blown out 35-7 on seven turnovers, multiple penalties and an inability to protect Moon. Childress said, "This is the lowest point I've ever seen here." But he added, "I think Buddy is the best defensive coordinator I've ever played under. For me to say that after the way we played Monday night and being 1-4, you probably think I'm crazy. But I'm not."

Team Turmoil, the latest pet phrase for the Oilers, had reached a new low. Five games into a year filled with promise, they were out of the division and playoff races. It was remarkable, considering their offseason whining and the huge salaries. Robertson wrote that it was time to throw in the towel, "Me, I'd start rebuilding today. They've still got a week before the trading deadline." Moon was No. 1 on his list.

He was benched for the upcoming Pats game. "It's a difficult day for me," he said. "This is something I've never been through before. My pride is a little hurt, and my ego is a little hurt. I think a lot of people finally got what they wanted .... I hope everybody is happy." At the same time, opponents accused him and Jones of putting silicone on their jerseys to make them slippery.

There were other problems. Starting CB Lewis, who was having a great year, was lost to a torn ACL. Marshall's knee kept him on the bench for the first time in his career. Alm was still holding out. White came back tubby and slow. Tempers began to flare on all those radio and television shows. Adams, who would soon deny Gilbride permission to interview for the head-coaching position at the University of South Carolina, weighed in with his usual analytical acumen. He said the problem was charity — too much of it. "They have to get their off-field commitments off their backs so we can start playing football," said the boss.

Meanwhile, Houston had not won in New England since the '78 playoffs. Neither Marshall nor David Williams made the trip. Gilbride and Jeffires got in a shouting match on the sidelines. Carlson went down with a groin pull. Houston won anyway, 28-14. Matthews could see the light. "We had a lot of built-in excuses for losing," he said, "but I see this game as being the turning point. This win could be the start of something big."

The big story, however, was David Williams, who missed the game to be with his expectant wife.

Bob Young said, "When you get paid $120,000 a week, you have to give away some things a normal person does. You've got to be here in this situation. This is like World War II when guys were going to war and something would come up but they had to go ... Shoot, I had a baby when I was playing. Ninety percent of the guys have babies when they're playing, but you never miss games. My wife told me she was having a baby, and I said, 'Honey, I've got to go play a football game' ... He called me [and] I said, 'Look. Go to the hospital and make your own arrangement to be here. If you can't get a flight, charter a plane. It will be $10,000 or $20,000 and save you a lot of money."

Gilbride added, "Actually, to say we're disappointed would probably be the grossest understatement of the year. I don't think I could put into words how disappointed I am ... To me, his place had to be with us, considering the way we've been struggling and the fact that we had our backs against the wall."

Williams' response was simple. "They were calling me in the delivery room," he said. "But my family comes first. That's the way I've always been, and that's the way I always will be. Debi lost a baby a year or so ago, and I wanted to be there for the birth of my first child. I don't regret what I did." Holovak quickly docked him one game check: $111,000.

With national reporters already in Houston scribbling down Buddy's every word, "Babygate" was off to the races. The spotlight brought out the bandwagon pundits and politicians, sparking something of a national forum on parenting issues.

The team took the brunt. The harsh statements made by angry coaches left the Oilers appearing insensitive and politically incorrect. The problem for Williams, who made about $1.75 million a year, was that the baby was born 17½ hours before kickoff. With flying time to Boston roughly 4 hours, he easily could have made it.

Vice President Al Gore tried to spin it into an issue of family leave. "We're with David Williams," he said. "They're [Republicans] with management of the Houston Oilers." When the VP left a message for Coach Young, he did not get a return call.

Williams' agent, who had him hold out through part of camp, recommended the Oilers donate the paycheck to Kid Care. Oiler general counsel Steve Underwood responded: "I don't think we need Leigh Steinberg's advice as to what charities we should be associated with .... However, we do have a suggestion: It is obvious that Kid Care is a worthwhile organization and one that is very close to Mr. Steinberg's heart. What a wonderful gesture it would be for Mr. Steinberg to donate to Kid Care his fee for the negotiation of David Williams' recent contract ($3.5 million/2 years). I'm sure that such a gesture would be widely applauded."

Interview offers came pouring in. Williams entertained 72 requests from the likes of *Prime Time Live*, *Inside Edition*, *Hard Copy*, *Jerry Springer*, *Phil Donahue*, *The Today Show*, *Good Morning America* and *Connie Chung*.

"I didn't realize it was going to be this crazy," he said. Asked if he would do more interviews, he responded, "I don't know. I'm not a media-oriented person ... I'm going to let my wife decide everything."

Debi picked *Eye-to-Eye* with Connie Chung. It was nothing special. The funny thing was how fast the Democrats dropped their new poster boy when he said he did not vote for Bill Clinton. There were some unfunny parts, too, as when local radio personality Dan Patrick referred to the Chung show as "Slanted Eye-to-Eye."

The organization was up to its old tricks. There was no forethought, no contingency planning and no loyalty. Communication between the parties was poor. In its fourth decade, the Oilers were still employing Fred Flintstone-era management techniques.

The players still had games to play. Behind Gary Brown's 194 yards, they beat the winless Bengals 28-12. Next, Moon stopped pouting long enough to go 36-of-55 for 369 yards and beat the Seahawks 24-14. They lost White, however, to two blown hamstrings when he tried to carry Cortez Kennedy on his back. The scheduling fairy then gave them another break and they pounded Cincinnati again 38-3. In his first start, 3-year pro Brown had 166 yards.

With everything else going on, the 4-game win streak almost slipped by unnoticed. It came at the expense of the worst teams in the league. Nonetheless, they were back in the race just in time for a 4-in-5 stretch with the Browns and Steelers. The defense had caught up to Ryan's system. Over the win streak, they allowed just over 10 points per game. They were causing turnovers by flying all over the field. It was fun to be a fan again.

They got another break when Browns coach Bill Belichick put Bernie Kosar on waivers just before Houston came to town. It upset the team. Houston won 27-20 behind Gary Brown's 194 yards and 3 interceptions by Marcus Robertson. It set up a showdown with Pittsburgh in the Dome for first place, something that seemed improbable just a few weeks before.

Bud sold over 64,000 tickets (3,000 over capacity). The game had a carnival-like atmosphere. There were fights and penalties. Houston dominated and won 23-3. The defense had 6 sacks, 4 takeaways and held Pittsburgh to 65 yards rushing. Ryan said, "I had flashbacks to the 1985 Bears." On offense, Moon went 21-of-34 for 295 yards. Brown had 79 against the No. 1 run defense. Givins caught 5 for 86 yards to become the Oilers' all-time leading receiver.

That game made people feel good. It was one of their best performances ever, and probably was their best defensive effort against Pittsburgh. They did it with basically the same talent they had had for years, which pointed a pretty big finger at the prior coaches.

Lathon said, "We kicked their butt on ESPN. We showed that the Houston Oilers are not going to be pushovers for anyone." Adams concurred, "The Steelers got their butts whipped ... That may be the greatest defensive performance I've seen." It was their first 6-game win streak since 1962.

Once 1-4, they were now 7-4 and in first. The Falcons and Jerry Glanville were next. Time had softened Glanville's edge a little, but many of the Oilers remembered being embarrassed 47-27 the first game in '90 and 36-7 in the preseason in '92. They settled the score. Trailing 14-13 late in the third quarter, the defense went on the attack. Dome officials contributed by repeatedly flashing Jerry's picture on the big screen to a shower of boos. They came away with 6 interceptions, 1 fumble recovery (3 forced) and a 33-17 victory. At one point, they intercepted Bobby Herbert on 4 consecutive possessions. Sean Jones, who kept a low profile under Ryan, said, "I told Doug Shively he could kiss my butt. He's a puppet for Jerry." Moon also got his licks in on the field by connecting on 24-of-42 passes for 342 yards.

The Oilers had developed a distinctive personality. Give them a lead and the defenders pinned their ears back and came after people. They had produced 16 turnovers in 3 games against the Steelers, Browns and Falcons. Most teams could not handle the pressure Houston was bringing. Against Atlanta, there were 19 penalties overall, including 7 personal fouls and 14 fights or shoving matches. In the end, the Falcons came unglued.

Marshall said, "I really think this defense can be better than the 1985 Bears. This locomotive's going downhill and picking up speed." When asked what was making the difference, he replied, "We have better safeties. Marcus and Bubba are great athletes. They are two of the best safeties in the league." Buddy echoed the sentiment. "I've been around a lot of excellent safeties, and Marcus is by far the best free safety I've ever had," he said. "He's a hitter. He's got great range. He's smart."

All of this made losing him for the season on the last play of the first half of the second Cleveland game hard to swallow. The Oilers won 19-17 behind 4 Del Greco FGs and 3 more turnovers, but the mood was dark. Ryan called losing Robertson, who led the AFC with 7 interceptions, "the worst (loss) we could suffer on the whole team, except for Warren Moon."

But news about DT Jeff Alm quickly surpassed Ryan's brooding. After starting 7 games in 1992, Alm was in line to take over the starting role from Doug Smith. On the questionable advice of his agent, he turned down a $2.35 million/3-year offer and held out. Signed late into the season, he did not take the field until the Seattle game, by which time Montgomery was entrenched as the starter. On early Tuesday morning after the Browns game, Alm wrecked his car into a Houston freeway overpass guardrail. Sean Lynch, Alm's best friend who was visiting from out of town, was thrown from the car and fell to his death on the freeway below. Overcome by the moment, Alm committed suicide on the side of the road with a shotgun from his trunk.

It was a gut-wrenching story to which the organization responded with some class. They quickly organized a team-only memorial service and got the Steelers to allow them a moment of silence at the upcoming game at Three Rivers Stadium. They also had a counselor available to help players deal with the loss.

Despite their talent level, the Oiler defense had a tough time adjusting to Ryan's system. By the time they started to come around, they were already in a 1-4 hole. By the end of the season, however, they were the top scoring defense in the AFC, as well as the No. 1 rush defense in the NFL. Even though he was overlooked in All-Pro and Pro Bowl voting in 1993, DE William Fuller (left) had his best season and was one of the best players in the league.

The voice of calm was Pardee. He said, "To me, it's a pretty stiff sentence he put on himself for the death of a friend. Jeff's always been pretty much the same. He's an emotional guy. Evidently, he convicted himself for doing something wrong. He tried and convicted himself." Pardee later shared his own battle with cancer.

After the moment of silence, the Oilers took it to the Steelers, jumping out to leads of 14-0 in the first 6 minutes, 20-0 in the second quarter and 26-10 in the fourth before winning 26-17 to clinch the AFC Central and extend their winning streak to 9 games. "They could talk the talk, but they couldn't walk the walk," said Ryan, regarding comments during the week by Steeler players. His defense had 6 sacks, forced 3 turnovers and held them to 38 yards rushing. Brown contributed 100 yards rushing and another 80 receiving.

Childress said, "To go from 1-4 to 10-4 and the division title, that's no joke. That's some serious business. Think about it." It was Pardee's first win in Pittsburgh as the Oilers became the first team since the 1975 Super Bowl champion Steelers to sweep through the Central.

Unfortunately, the bad news kept coming in bunches. Houston lost its other starting safety, Bubba McDowell, in circumstances similar to those that felled Robertson. "Two weeks in a row now, we've had safeties get hurt at the end of halves when they (the offense) should have been out there," said the coach.

Another crushing injury came when Webster Slaughter was lost for the year. He was having a brilliant season and led the AFC in receptions. He was the fifth lost starter (joining Lewis, Robertson, McDowell and White), and third having a career-year to fall to a bad knee.

Meanwhile, having sewn up the division, the Oilers were fighting for playoff position. The remaining games were at San Francisco and the Jets at home.

Some were calling the game at Candlestick Park a Super Bowl preview. The Oilers saw the nationally televised Christmas Day game as a chance to prove something. Both teams were 10-4 and shooting for home field. San Francisco was No. 1 in scoring and total yards, and second in rushing.

Houston was banged up. Munchak joined the other missing starters on the sideline. Moon had deeply bruised ribs. This was the type of game they usually lost. It turned into one of their finest moments.

The first half was hard hits and turnovers. In the first quarter, they were saved first by Jackson, who intercepted Steve Young in the end zone, and then by Mike Cofer, who missed a 47-yard FG attempt. With Houston up 3-0 and the 49ers facing third-and-10 at their 26, rookie SS Blaine Bishop leveled Young on a blitz, forcing a fumble. He recovered at the 18. Three plays later, Moon hit Givins with a 7-yard TD pass to make it 10-0 with 10:20 remaining in the half.

Then came the play of Cris Dishman's career. With the 49ers threatening again in the second quarter, Young lofted a perfect pass into the end zone for Jerry Rice,

Jeff Alm

just like they had done 100 times together before that. This time, he was defended man-for-man by Dishman, who made a beautifully timed leap to take the ball away from Rice as both men were at the height of their jumps. It was probably the best individual defensive play by an Oiler since Ken Houston's back-to-back TDs off John Hadl. Houston led 10-0 at the half.

In the third quarter, Houston threatened again after Moon read a blitz and hit Duncan with a perfectly thrown deep sideline pass for 33 yards to the 36. Instead of going with Brown (75 yards in the first half), Moon threw two incompletions and then, with a blitz coming on third down, he threw off his heels for an interception. San Francisco drove to the Houston 6 but Cofer's FG attempt was blocked by Eddie Robinson. After that, Young was replaced. The league MVP had a fit on the sidelines yelling at George Seifert.

Backup QB Steve Bono cut the lead to 10-7 with 12:11 left. "When they scored the touchdown," said Lathon, "I could hear some fans start to chant, 'Buffalo, Buffalo.' I told them it was the wrong time and a different team." Needing to eat up some clock, Houston threw five straight passes which resulted in one first down and a sack. The 49ers got the ball back at their 31 with 9:54 remaining, but the defense held again.

So there they were once again needing a late clock-killing drive to seal a win. To make it more dicey, Moon had to come out because his cracked ribs were reinjured on the previous sack. That left it up to Cody. With 6:41 left and the crowd making its most noise of the day, Babygate Williams was flagged 5 yards for a false start. On the next play, he was tagged for holding. It had a familiar look to it as the Oilers were suddenly looking at a second-and-21 from their 9-yard line. But the Commander came up with a miracle, hitting Gary Wellman for 24 yards and a first down. Remembering the running game, they rode Brown the length of the field, eating up the remainder of the clock to win 10-7.

Brown had 114 yards and the defense held the 49ers, who averaged 31 points and 402 yards per game, to one TD and 90 yards rushing. Even more remarkable, they did it with substitutes everywhere, including Bo Orlando (Robertson), Steve Jackson (Lewis), Blaine Bishop (McDowell), Brown (White), Wellman (Slaughter) and Eric Norgard (Munchak). In addition, both Glenn Montgomery and Brad Hopkins were rookie starters.

Brent Jones said, "That's the best defense we've played all year. They're a great, attacking defense." Rice added, "I wanted to win this game because the whole world was watching. You try to make a statement in a game like this."

In Houston, even the hardened cynics had trouble ignoring this one. It may have taken Buddy Ryan, but they finally won a crucial road game against a great team (actually the best over the previous 14 years). They belonged among the elite.

But the Christmas Day win had a price. Long-time followers could hear the danger in the voices of the team's "emotional leaders" after the game. Moon said, "Something special is going on with this team. It's all coming together." Givins added, "What we're doing is damn good." Jeffires chipped in with, "This team has a chance to go all the way."

They failed to grasp what the 4-time Super Bowl champs knew well. The season was not over. The really important stuff was yet to begin. It was not the time to rest on their laurels.

Furthermore, there were some dark clouds gathering. After the game, Ryan grumbled, "As far as I'm concerned, that's (the final game-winning drive) the most exciting thing I saw all day. We finally proved we can run out the clock for a change."

They had one left, a rare regular-season game in January. After overcoming an array of obstacles and disruptions to reach the top that no Hollywood screenwriter could dream up, the stage was set for a sensational spectacle.

They won by holding a good Jets team to nine first downs and 164 yards total offense. They stopped New York on 10 of 13 third-down attempts and held Boomer Esiason to 11-of-26 passing. The crowd was psyched. These were the days of "Whoop, There It Is," and Houston fans pumped up the volume. "That song gets all of us kind of pumped up," said Montgomery. "I think every time they play that song, we make big plays."

Jets' coach Bruce Coslet admitted, "This is the first time we've had our butts handed to us this year. We've been beaten before, but not like this. This is by far the best defensive team we've played." Boomer added, "I think the only thing that might hold this team back is if the coaches kill each other."

Indeed, the Oilers had managed to accomplish another seemingly impossible task. They made fools of themselves on national television despite winning 24-0. The big event came in the final 37 seconds of the first half with the Oilers leading 14-0. Getting the ball back on their own 34, the Oilers had Carlson throwing instead of running out the clock. On second down, he was hit from behind and fumbled, forcing the defense back on the field. Ryan believed such play calling had cost him both Robertson and McDowell.

Jack Pardee

Yelling, he moved toward Gilbride. Gilbride moved toward Buddy and barked back. Ryan closed and threw a punch that glazed the side of Gilbride's head. Before Gilbride could launch a response, Curtis Duncan and Keith McCants separated them.

Meanwhile, two other Oiler coaches were going at it up in the booth. Assistants Charlie Baggett and Frank Bush got into a shoving match at about the same time. They claimed no punches were thrown.

Naturally, it was a nationally televised Sunday Night game. The rest of the otherwise unsuspenseful game was dominated by slow-motion replays of Buddy's powder puff punch to the head of the former cancer patient. Gilbride left the Astrodome with a police escort before the locker room was opened to the media. Ryan said the incident was caused by "a difference in coaching philosophies in the heat of battle."

The players tried to play it down. "What happened is irrelevant," said Jones. "We just won a game; why can't we talk about that? We started the season 1-4, and look where we are now. Let's talk about that." Dish said, "I don't care if they kick each other's butts. I'm only concerned with covering receivers." Duncan said, "Things happen. Fights happen. Let's just keep it as that. We're still a family. Families have arguments." Barrow added, "(Ryan) just wants to win. He's a competitor, and he doesn't tolerate stupid mistakes. He's aggressive. That's his nature, but we all love him." From Fuller's perspective it was, "All part of being a Houston Oiler, I guess."

This latest embarrassment came one day to the year of the humiliation in Buffalo. For his seventy-first birthday the next day, Adams found himself having to issue a public statement that he "was very concerned and disappointed," and that "this type of situation will not be tolerated within our organization." He ordered silence.

Pardee tried to lead. "We can't let anything detract from our preparation for the playoff game," he said. "We've got 65 people around here, and everybody's not going to agree on everything, but the key is to make sure we have a good working atmosphere. Coaches don't have to be best buddies, but we have to make sure everybody's on the same page and the opponent is wearing a different-colored jersey."

By Monday, every football fan in America had seen "the punch" at least 10 times. Fowler called it "the most senseless and classless act on a football field since Ohio State coach Woody Hayes slugged a Clemson player in the 1978 Gator Bowl." NBC analyst Mike Ditka supported his old coordinator, saying, "Houston's defense never had any toughness until Buddy got there. All Buddy wants is for his defense to dominate the game, and that's not wrong." Jimmy Johnson added, "They should turn that thing into a soap opera down there. It would rate high in the Nielsen ratings."

It all overshadowed the fact that the Oilers had become only the third team in NFL history to win its last 11 games. They also ended up with 12 wins for the first time in team history. But the incident would not die.

On Tuesday, ignoring Adams' gag order, Ryan spoke to a reporter from the *Philadelphia Inquirer*. His remarks were printed a few days later. He accused Gilbride of provocation. "See, here's the thing I don't understand," Ryan said. "Everybody thinks that's all my fault, and they keep showing that on TV. I've seen it about five times, but they didn't get the whole thing, see. He is the one who made the move." Admitting he may have "called him a high school coach, something like that," he maintained it was Gilbride who was "cussing me and coming at me."

He continued, "He's not going to run over me the way he runs over some people. He's a wimp. He's got no business coaching in the pros. Making calls like that, he's hurting the team. I'm not the only one he's had trouble with. They had to pull a coach off him a couple of years ago. Right in there. Had him on the floor." He said Gilbride "should be selling insurance."

Moon tried to respond with, "Coaches are in a fraternity, and they shouldn't attack each other. Kevin's proven himself as an outstanding offensive coach, and for Buddy to attack him like this just doesn't seem necessary, especially at this time of the season. I don't understand it, and I wish it would stop."

It forced Adams to resurface. He chewed out the head coach and GM. Ryan claimed he thought his remarks were being made in confi-

Cris Dishman overcame a troubling first few years to turn into one of the better cover corners in the NFL. His game against Jerry Rice on Christmas Day, 1993, may have been his best performance. His game against the Chiefs in the playoffs was not.

dence to a reporter he had "known for years ... He came here, spent the day with me. That was just he two of us talking. I didn't know it was going to end up in the paper." He issued an apology, one obviously drafted by an attorney. It read in part: "I regret my comments.... I am sincerely sorry that it was made public, and I regret any embarrassment it has caused the Houston Oilers ... We have a monumental task confronting us this Sunday."

The incident also buried one very troubling matter on the field. LT Brad Hopkins got his butt beat by Marvin Washington as the Oilers gave up six sacks. Against the Chiefs, he would be up against a much better pass rusher, Derrick Thomas.

THE 1993 PLAYOFFS

One strongly held belief in Houston was that the only thing keeping the Oilers out of the Super Bowl was the lack of home field advantage in the playoffs. Now they had it, at least through the second round. It was time for them to stand up and be counted.

The bandwagon was full again and the atmosphere charged. The 18,000 available tickets sold out in 15 minutes. A win at home over the Chiefs, who knocked off the Steelers in OT in the first round, was expected.

It seemed reasonable. KC had not won in Houston since 1983, and had lost their last 4 against the Oilers, including earlier that season (30-0). Moreover, the Oiler defense had not allowed more than 2 TDs in a game during the streak. Only twice all season did they allow more than 2 TDs (Rams and Bills). In the final 7 games (and in 12 of 16), they limited opponents to under 4 yards per carry while allowing a third-down conversion ratio of just 28% (41 of 145).

On the other hand, the secondary had been decimated by injury. Three-of-four starters were out. This caused Ryan to modify schemes to help the subs, which cut back on their aggression.

Nor was all well on the other side of the ball. Over the last five games, the offense had not scored more than two TDs and had only one in each of the last three. In fact, only four times on the season did the Run 'N' Shoot score more than two TDs. The loss of Slaughter was large. Moreover, the line was in bad shape. Munchak was barely able to play and Dawson had a hurt back. Neither OT (Hopkins and Williams) was playing well. Line coach Young said, "We're probably the weakest we've been in four years with the injuries and the way people are playing ... Our subs are average NFL linemen. That's not to get ugly, but they're average."

Nonetheless, most fans, team officials and apparently many of the players were looking ahead. City officials were planning for a massive Super Bowl rally. There was more talk of an all-Texas Super Bowl. Bud knew that a Super Bowl appearance would sway the public to support his plans for a new stadium, news of which had already been leaked to the media. More than anyone appreciated at the time, the game proved to be something of a referendum on the Oilers' future in Houston.

But it was a mistake to overlook the Chiefs, who were blessed with an able coach, a solid defense and the calming presence of veterans Joe Montana and Marcus Allen.

The record crowd of 64,184 loved the start when Fuller hit Montana on the Chiefs' first possession. Jackson intercepted. But in a sign of things to come, the drive went backwards and Al Del Greco had to salvage a 3-0 lead on a 49-yard field goal. The partying began when, on their next series, the Oilers went 80 yards in 11 plays for a 10-0 lead. Brown scored on a two-yard run with 1:59 left in the first quarter.

Houston got lucky in the second quarter, as Montana was twice foiled on what looked like sure TDs. The first came from the Oiler 42 when he had Willie Davis behind Dishman, only to watch his perfect strike at the goal knocked away at the last moment by a diving Dishman. On the Chiefs' next possession, Montana went deep again with Davis well behind Jackson. But Davis let the well-thrown ball slip through his fingers.

The Oilers then put together a nice drive from their 9 to KC's 9 on four straight completions by Moon and a 17-yard scramble. With a great chance to put the game away, Gary Wellman was flagged 15 yards for an illegal chop block that moved the ball back to the 24. On the next play, Albert Lewis blitzed Moon and knocked the ball loose. Jamie Fields recovered as Houston came away with no points.

As the half closed, Neil Smith sacked Moon, causing another fumble. Ryan slammed a cup of water to the turf, pulled off his headset and glared in Gilbride's direction. But the Oilers recovered the fumble and took a 10-0 lead into the locker room.

Both sides were kicking themselves. The Oiler defense had hit Montana six times but had no sacks. Although Joe was just 9-of-20 for 87 yards, he came very close to hitting for two long scores. And he was still in the game. Moon was also getting slaughtered on the other side as both Munchak and Williams left the game with injuries. Still, they could have easily been up 17-0.

KC scored a TD on its first series of the third quarter as Montana found UT-ex Keith Cash wide open for a 7-yard score. At the end of the quarter, Moon killed another drive by throwing an interception into triple coverage at the Kansas City 2. But the Oilers liked their chances. They were 11-1 on the season when leading at the end of 3 quarters.

They got another break early in the fourth quarter as Terry Hoage intercepted Montana at the Chief 25-

yard line. They were so close they could almost taste the victory. But the offense could not get the TD, settling for a 43-yard Del Greco FG and a 13-7 lead with 9:37 left. Then, just like the year before, the defense collapsed. This time, they gave up three TDs in the final nine minutes to squander their final golden opportunity to get to an AFC Championship Game.

Montana hit Cash for 22. Then Dishman was called for a 38-yard interference penalty after he was beaten deep by Davis again. On the next play, JJ Birden fooled Jackson on a slant route for an 11-yard TD to give the Chiefs their first lead at 14-13 with 8:38 left.

On the first play of the Oilers' next possession, Thomas sacked Moon and Dan Salcaumua recovered. Montana quickly found Davis in front of Dishman for an 18-yard TD. Just like that it was 21-13 with 7:44 left.

The Houston offense finally got going for the first time in the second half. With Moon hitting 8 consecutive passes, they went 80 yards, culminating in a 7-yard Moon-to-Givins touchdown. The Chiefs' lead was 21-20 with 3:35 left.

Houston's playoff life was on Ryan's defense. It came down to a third-and-one from the KC 30. As Montana dropped back on a pattern called "Y-Banana," Fuller hit his arm and caused the pass to wobble. Robinson had TE Cash covered stride-for-stride. But the knuckler floated just enough to cause Robinson to mis-time his leap and the 6'4 Cash pulled it in with one hand. Bouncing away, he rumbled 41 yards. Montana's fists lifted above his head in one of those famous poses. Three plays later, Marcus Allen scored on a 21-yard run to secure the 28-20 victory.

"I got to Montana right as he cocked it, and I hit him hard right on the arm," Fuller said. "I just knew the ball was going to flutter away. And I turned and looked around, and he (Cash) was running free down the field .... Thirty minutes ago, we were playing like it would go on forever, but now it's over. This team may never be together again. It's a sickening feeling."

The difference was in the trenches. Moon managed to hit 32-of-43 passes for 306 yards despite being sacked nine times as Thomas repeatedly smoked Hopkins. He fumbled five times, losing two, and was intercepted once. Houston had seven total fumbles. Furthermore, the Chiefs held Brown, who had five 100-yard games in eight starts, to 17 yards on 11 carries. Brown also repeatedly failed to pick up the corner blitz. Most telling perhaps were the possessions they took at the KC 23 and 25 after interceptions that for both produced only field goals.

The opposite was true for the Chiefs. Their offensive line (John Alt, Ricky Siglar, Dave Szott, Will Shields, Tim Grunhard) allowed only two sacks to the ferocious Oiler rush and generally allowed Montana just enough time to pass. Lathon said, "Buddy told us that if we put the leather on Montana, he would fold like anybody else. We put the leather on him early, but he sure didn't fold." Joe, who had 212 yards and 3 TDs in the second half, said, "It feels as good as ever."

Other players offered the usual array of post-playoff game comments. "It's so very frustrating knowing this team will never congregate in this form again," said Matthews. "We had so much going for us, and now it's over." Dawson said, "Right now, I feel incredible disappointment." Jeffires, who came up big with nine catches for 88 yards, added, "I just can't believe we lost. Why did Joe Montana have to play this game? How does he continue to do it?"

Gilbride said, "We strung together three big drives but had only two touches to show for it," he said as he also attempted to deflect some heat to the defense. "When we scored late (with 3:35 remaining), I was convinced if we'd gotten the ball back again, we would have won. I'm still convinced."

"I thought we played 3½ quarters of defense that was as good as anybody in the world could play," said Ryan. "But at the end we didn't make any plays, and I didn't help them much. There were some coverages I could have called that I didn't." About losing to Montana, he said, "We had some pretty good licks on him, and he kept getting up. He looked like the same guy to me he has always been." About the TD over Dishman, he said, "Dish had great coverage then. That's how things went today. We had one blown coverage, one interference call and one touchdown where the guy was covered like a blanket. It was just one of those plays when you wonder what the good Lord is thinking."

He added, "It's really disappointing because I thought we were going to win the game. I thought we were going to Buffalo and then catch the Cowboys in the big one." Asked if he would be back next season, Ryan said, "Yeah, I'll be here. I hope the future here is bright. We have some good football players. Hopefully, free agency won't hurt us."

Adams said, "It was a great season. We had a hell of a comeback from 1-4 to win 11 in a row. I'm not complaining. It's something I can live with. I just thought we could get through this and go to Buffalo next week." He added, "We've got a great defensive staff and a great offensive staff. They need a little more harmony, but that will come about. This isn't the first time there has been disharmony among coaches, and it won't be the last."

Buffalo blew out KC in the AFC title game 30-13. Barrow said later: "We got a 10-point lead in that game, and we were getting to Montana. We got a lot of pressure on him, but we couldn't take him down. It's like we were the tenderizer, and we softened him up, but it was Buffalo that cooked him a week later." The Cowboys beat the Bills again in the Super Bowl 30-13.

OVERVIEW

Somewhat like 1987, the tumultuous 1993 Oiler season was akin to alien sightings. Unless you saw it for yourself, you probably would not believe it.

The year began with the humiliation in Buffalo. Parts of millions of human beings died that day. Then Bud fired coaches, hired Buddy Ryan, acquired Wilber Marshall and gave Cody Carlson a pie-in-the-sky contract.

The Carlson deal increased the usual clamoring about money before, during and after camp. It was obscene in the shadow of the Buffalo fiasco. More interesting was the intrigue brought on by Ryan. He talked big, promised a Super Bowl and generally hogged the limelight. But while the wags speculated about Pardee's job security, it was Ryan and Gilbride who feuded.

By the time the regular season began, the Oilers were in full anarchy, more closely resembling a traveling circus than a football club. After falling to 1-4, there was open animosity between the offense and defense, Moon was benched, his OL had was falling apart, White was running in slow motion and the defense failed to grasp the "46."

Then came New England, Babygate and a bye week. Catching their breath, the Oilers ran off an improbable win streak highlighted by a series of wins as pleasing to fans as any since the days of Big Earl. They annihilated Pittsburgh twice, creamed Glanville and Atlanta, and won in San Francisco before the nation on Christmas.

The defense was superb, led by the DL which finally played as a unit and lived up to the big salaries. With a lead, they attacked to such a degree that the whites of opposing QBs' eyes were literally visible on TV screens. The turnovers piled up. The streak came despite losing 3/4s of the starting secondary.

They swept their final 11 to finish 12-4, the best record in team history. They had a conference-best 10-2 record against AFC opponents. They won the Central title for only the second time, went 6-0 against Central opponents for the first time and finally earned that long-sought-after first-round playoff bye.

Pardee was the darling of the coaching world. He said, "Winning makes you look a whole lot smarter."

But no matter how much they overcame, it was never enough. An unimaginable suicide was followed by the inconceivable punch.

Then, after earning the bye and home field, they came out overconfident and lost to a team with a gimpy QB and bad WRs. Trying to rank that loss in terms of Oiler heartbreaks is difficult, because deep down, most people thought that somehow they would screw it up. Nonetheless, it was a huge letdown.

Fuller said some 10 months later, "I think it all starts with Mr. Adams and filters down. The right hand doesn't know what the left hand is doing. No one knows who is really in charge. There are guys who think they have a lot of say, but they're really just figureheads. The system is set up for divisiveness. (Ryan) came in and had complete autonomy over the defense, and Kevin Gilbride had complete autonomy over the offense. Under that arrangement, you're going to have a stressful situation, and that's definitely what we had all last year. It was chaos.

"Sometimes it was like Jack wasn't even there. Jack had been stripped of all his power, so he couldn't do anything about it ... He was caught in the middle. As players, you need a visibly defined leader. You want to be able to look at that leader for inspiration, but we couldn't look to Jack. He really wasn't in control, and it was very apparent to all the players ... I have no problems with Jack Pardee. He's a great person. But as far as being a head coach is concerned, people have different feelings on that. To put it simply: Would I hire Jack if I were an NFL owner? I don't think so."

Despite operating in what Gilbride described as "a difficult atmosphere to function in," the offense finished No. 3 in the NFL (3rd passing, 12th rushing, 4th scoring). It was not as good in the Red Zone. On 61 possessions inside opponents' 20, the Oilers scored 28 touchdowns (46%), which was below the league average.

Their performance turned on the health of the line. In the eight games with all the starters, Oiler QBs were sacked 16 times. In the eight with backups, they were sacked 27 times. In the first six games, the Oilers averaged 3.8 yards per carry. In the next eight, with all the starters, they averaged 4.6. They finished the season averaging 4.4 yards per carry, tied for third in the NFL.

Gary Brown came out of nowhere to place fourth in the AFC in rushing (1,002 yards on 8 starts) and first in per carry average (5.1 yards). While he had problems with Moon's audibles and frequently failed to pick up CB blitzes, he generally was a good blocker and could catch the ball out of the backfield. RB coach Frank Novak did a great job of having him ready to play.

Moon had 3,485 yards on 303-of-520 passing (58.3%) with 21 TDs and 21 interceptions. He did not rank among the AFC's top five. No WR finished in the top five, either. Jeffires caught 66, Givins 68 and Duncan 41. Slaughter's great season stopped at 77. His replacement, Gary Wellman, had 31 receptions for 430 yards as a one-season phenom.

The defense was probably the best in team history. With Ryan's system and confidence combined with Marshall's leadership, they played most of the year as a group.

Consequently, they were the AFC's top scoring defense (14.9 points per game) and led the NFL in rush defense (79.5 yards per game), sacks, third-down conversions and TDs scored. They were second in forcing turnovers (43 versus 31 in '92). Their 52 sacks broke the '79 team record. Jones' contract year proved his best with 13 sacks and better run support. The line coach was Jim Stanley. Greg Montgomery was the top punter.

Eight Oilers made the Pro Bowl led by Munchak (team record 9th time), Moon, Matthews, Slaughter, Greg Montgomery and Childress. Jones and Jeffires made it as injury replacements. Ryan decried the exclusion of Robertson ("the best free safety I've ever coached"). Marcus did make first team All-Pro along with Montgomery, while the writers named Matthews, Munchak and Childress to the second team. Lathon also had a great season after returning from injury, as Ryan's psychological ploys turned him into a team player for the first time in his career.

A survey of personnel directors and scouts by *Inside Sports* seemed to confirm the talent level. Asked to chose the "best of the best" in the NFL, they named Matthews best center, Robertson second best FS (behind Eugene Robinson), McDowell second best SS (behind Henry Jones), Smith second best ILB in a 4-3 (behind Junior Seau) and Montgomery second best punter. Fuller was chosen a top 5 strongside end while Jones was named a top 5 weakside end.

1994: TURN OUT THE LIGHTS, THE PARDEE'S OVER

If the melodrama of the 1993 season was a natural follow to the humiliation of 1992, then 1994 would provide the last leg of this three-act Greek tragedy. After making the playoffs for 7 straight seasons (3-7 record), age, the salary cap and mismanagement were about to catch up with them. And in the grandest of Oiler traditions, the collapse could not have come at a worse time.

It did not have to happen the way it did. With more television money than originally contemplated, Adams had a fair opportunity to keep the team together and even make it better. But the team's performance in free agency was terrible, sealing their fate. Then, in the battle to win over politicians and voters for a new stadium, they stumbled and never recovered.

RAN 'N' SHOT

The first order of business was to find someone or something to blame. Despite the fact that the defense surrendered the lead and three TDs in the fourth quarter of the playoff game, most fingers pointed at the offense. If they had scored TDs with the two possessions inside the KC 30, the defense would not have been on the spot. After seven years of some form of a 4-WR set, including four years exclusively in the Run 'N' Shoot, the lack of an AFC championship was proof enough.

Even the man who brought it in wavered. "I've never been married to any offense," said Pardee. "That's something we're going to have to look at and study ... Our personnel has a lot to do with that. Our players have fit into a run-and-shoot more than anything else, but there's no magic in any system."

Gilbride was always in sort of in an odd spot. It was not his offense, as he had worked for the Oilers before Pardee took over, but he was the one identified with it and the one who regularly defended it. Jeffires said, "It's been a great offense. You shouldn't change it just for the sake of change." Moon, too, opposed a change. "I don't agree with it," he said. "I think they're doing it because of the public outcry for a change. Last year it was the defense. This year it's the offense. I understand it, but it doesn't mean I have to agree with it."

The Run 'N' Shoot was reported dead as of January 27, 1994. The messages were a little mixed. First, they announced it would no longer be the offense of choice. Then they said they were not abandoning it. According to Floyd Reese, they just wanted to diversify to add better blocking and pass protection. This meant the addition of a FB or second back and a TE while retaining the four WR formations for certain situations.

Most Oilers took a nonchalant attitude. "The game is still football," came the comments. The biggest reaction came from those who had to defend it.

All-Pro cornerback and Oiler nemesis Rod Woodson said, "Tell the owner thank you, and tell the front office thank you. The Run 'N' Shoot got the Oilers where they are, and I think defenses all over the league are going to be very relieved when they hear about it. It's hard to match up with four receivers running all over the field. You have to put four cornerbacks on them, and it's hard for a team to get three and four good corners."

LB Derrick Thomas said, "They're very effective in the Run 'N' Shoot, and you need to utilize your resources. They've won a lot of games with that offense. I think it's a bad rap that the Run 'N' Shoot can't win the big one. I've seen them beat everybody on the schedule. Look at the numbers they've posted. With the Run 'N' Shoot, they've won more games than a lot more conventional offenses. I just don't see how you can change something that works."

LB Cornelius Bennett added, "For them to get out of the Run 'N' Shoot is definitely to the defense's advantage because you have to play the entire game with your nickel or dime package, and that leaves you with a limited number of big men on the field. They're going to have to change a lot of personnel ... I hear they might get rid of Warren. If they do that, they might not have as good a season as this past one."

IN THIS CORNER

Ryan's response to the change was, "All you have to do is look at history. Look at who's there (Super Bowl) this year, who's been there in past years. They all have two tight ends or a tight end and a couple of backs. That's what you need to win it all."

Two days after making that statement, Phoenix Cardinal owner Bill Bidwill hired the 59-year-old Ryan to replace Joe Bugel, another former Oiler coach. The contract was estimated at $2 million over four years.

GM Mike Holovak was next. He stepped down to become a semi-retired vice president of player personnel and scouting. "It was a difficult decision," said the 74-year-old Holovak. "I had a fine meeting with Bud, and I have to give him a lot of credit because everything's just worked out beautifully."

Ed Fowler wrote that Holovak's career "must certainly be described as distinguished. His keen eye for talent, more than any other factor, was responsible for the Oilers' seven consecutive trips to the playoffs ... He can match draft selections that have turned into Pro Bowlers with any personnel man in the game." Even Ed admitted Holovak left with "the job left unfinished" but blamed it on "two mistakes in selecting coaches."

Adams quickly promoted Assistant General Manager Floyd Reese to general manager/executive vice president. Reese was lucky. He had almost gone to Atlanta with Glanville after the 1990 season and Glanville had just been fired as Falcon's coach.

Ryan hired away Ronnie Jones to be his DC. That left the Oilers scrambling because they wanted to continue to employ Ryan's system. They settled on 49er assistant Jeff Fisher who played for Ryan for four years in Chicago and coached under him four more in Philadelphia. He became the Oilers' new defensive coordinator on February 9.

Gilbride was bumped up to the newly created position of assistant head coach and Dick Coury was named offensive coordinator. Coury had finished second to Glanville in the '86 head coach derby. They said Coury would work under Gilbride to switch from a pure Run 'N' Shoot offense to a multiple system, but that Gilbride would continue to run the offense and call the plays.

THE PROMISE KEEPER

A big item on the NFL's agenda was expansion. Team owners have never loved this idea, but it has always been a good way to keep Congress off their backs and bring in truckloads of money. They decided to expand by two teams beginning with the 1995 season. The bidding came down to five areas: St. Louis, Baltimore, Carolina, Jacksonville and Memphis.

A group from Charlotte was awarded the first franchise while Jacksonville won the second a month later. The Jacksonville decision was surprising, considering the much larger communities in the running. It instantly became yet another small television market for NBC at 56th (second-smallest) and one of the smallest cities in the country to have a pro team. The ownership group, which included Jeb Bush (son of George), had dropped out of the bidding for a month, but came back at Tagliabue's request. They promised a $121 million renovation to the Gator Bowl, including 10,000 club seats and 68 luxury boxes that would reduce capacity to 73,000.

Tagliabue said, "It became clear to the committee that the southeast has become a tremendous area for expansion." The NFL was already in Miami, Tampa Bay and Atlanta.

Adams was on the committee. Bud actively supported Jacksonville, as he had promised back in 1987. Among the reasons the Memphis bid was rejected was because a team would have to play in the Liberty Bowl, which they felt needed a lot of help. Memphis would not forget.

TELEVISION DEAL

The most important issue on the NFL agenda was a new TV contract. The outlook was not so rosy. The two big players, CBS and NBC, cried about losses. The old deal generated $3.65 billion from CBS, NBC, ABC, TNT and ESPN. Predictions were that the new agreement would be worth about 75%.

That was until Rupert Murdoch entered the bidding. Murdoch started Fox Television Network in 1987 with a nucleus of 7 stations. By 1993, that total was up to 139 independent stations and cable systems. Nonetheless, its reputation at that time was only as the network that gave us *The Simpsons* and *Married With Children*. Murdoch thought the high profile of America's most popular TV sport would get them over the hump. He originally sought the AFC, but once he got into it realized he could have the more valuable NFC. He was willing to pay almost anything.

His bid was $1.58 billion over four years or about $100 million higher than CBS's. Even the NFL people were shocked. A stunned CBS made a last-minute unsuccessful attempt to get the AFC. NBC ended up paying $880 million for the AFC, some $88 million more than it paid in the last deal. The CBS bid for the AFC was $1 billion (the same it paid for the NFC in the last contract), but the NFL owners chose to honor their previous oral acceptance of NBC's offer.

ABC kept the *MNF* $950 million while ESPN and TNT continued to split Sunday nights for $475 million each. The new 4-year contracts totaled $4.36 billion, about 20% over the old deal, which was a reported $300 million loss for CBS and NBC. It left CBS out of professional football for the first time in 38 years.

Fox's willingness to bear a huge loss ushered in a new era of bidding on sports packages, one not based on the direct value of the product but upon its overall programming value. In the increasingly diversified world of television, not much else could consistently deliver such a large male (and growing female) audience. Of course, not everyone fully appreciated what was happening.

HOW TO BUNGLE THE SALARY CAP

The Oilers guessed wrong on the direction of the television earnings. Upon this faulty premise rested their entire salary cap and free agent strategy.

Even after the playoff loss, Bud was still cavalier. He said, "We'll lose some, but not many. If we get guys who say they'll play for less money, we'd like to keep all of them." Poor planning in 1993 meant they had an unusually high number of free agents to deal with in 1994. They quickly became so overwhelmed that they never pursued those from other teams. Trying to maintain the team close to the same form became the obsession. They hunkered down.

But if the last 7 years had shown anything, it was that even with 100% of their players back, they were not good enough to get past the second round. To become a championship club, they needed to add some and let a few go. This was the great opportunity free agency provided. But this was not the Houston mindset. They were more afraid of what the cap would do to them than what it could do for them.

The adjusted cap figure was $34.6 million. The Oilers were already obligated for about $26 million in 1994, leaving about $8½ million for their 28 remaining free agents (restricted and unrestricted). Many of the 15 unrestricted free agents were big names such as Jones, Fuller, Smith, Jeffires, White, Munchak, Marshall and Glenn Montgomery.

Given a window of opportunity at the end of '93 to sign players to front-loaded contracts whose bonuses would not count against the cap, they signed only Givins and McDowell.

Kevin Gilbride later described Buddy Ryan as a cancer that ate at the Oilers. After he was fired by Bud Adams in 1994, Gilbride became the Jacksonville Jaguar's offensive coordinator. Success there led to his first head coaching position with the San Diego Chargers. In 1998, he was unceremoniously dumped by GM Bobby Beathard early in the season.
Photo © F. Carter Smith.

In 1994, the three big tasks were: (1) re-sign Fuller; (2) deal with Moon; and (3) re-sign Jones. These were the litmus tests for the off season. The direction of the franchise, at least on the field, hinged on retaining them. The Oilers failed not just on one or two, but on all three.

They indicated they would lock in either Jones or Fuller as a transition player. The other transition slot was Dishman's. Their plan was to keep one DE and let Lee Williams (due to make $1.125 million) step in at the other spot.

In a surprise, they named DT Glenn Montgomery as a transitional player. They said he had improved to the point of being one of the best in the league and other clubs coveted him. However, his minimum transition salary was $1.9 million compared to the $2.9 million it would have cost to protect Fuller or Jones.

It cost them both Jones and Fuller. Before starting on his "tour," Jones said, "There's not going to be any loyalty, because there hasn't been any loyalty to the players. They've created an atmosphere where there isn't any loyalty. That's what's missing in this organization: There's no loyalty whatsoever."

Fuller also took it personally. "I'm mad," he said. "If they had protected me, I would have felt like I was wanted and respected. I would have felt like I was a valuable part of the team and worthy of keeping around next year ... At this point, I just don't feel much loyalty to the Oilers ... They created this monster. Now they have to deal with it."

Meanwhile, Moon was in a holding pattern. He and Carlson were under contract for $6.25 million in '94 (18% of the cap). Bud's options were simple: cut or trade one of them, or renegotiate with one or both. In January, he decided they could not keep both.

The idea of Warren Moon leaving Houston caused some mixed feelings. He was very popular. Many took pride in him as a thoughtful and articulate representative of the city. Dale Robertson summed up the other view: "It's not like the Oilers can't possibly win without him, because they haven't won a thing with him." Pointing to the $15 million in salary Moon had earned "since signing with the Oilers as the NFL's first true, unfettered free agent in 1984," he appealed to the QB take a pay cut to bring the city a championship.

The Oilers said they wanted to keep him. Moon said he wanted to stay, but apparently not if it meant taking a pay cut. Speaking through Leigh Steinburg, he contended the $4 million he was due in '94 was below the average of QBs he was "comparable with." In '93, he threw 21 interceptions, the second-worst total of his career. His 75.2 QB rating was his lowest since 1987.

Adams announced that he was going to personally tend to the matter. Moon was "too valuable a commodity" for anyone else to handle, he said.

But Bud just shuffled his feet. While he did, Carlson left for an African safari without ever being approached about a renegotiation. In the interim, the market became flooded with free agent QBs (Bobby Hebert, Jim Harbaugh, Wade Wilson, John Friesz) and Carlson's trade value plummeted. Adams also let an offer from the Rams wither on the vine. The LA people said they called Houston "four or five times" about trading for Moon (offering two second-round choices) but gave up, saying Bud would not return their calls.

The uncertainty hurt their ability to deal with Fuller and Jones since they did not know how much money they had to bid. As Bud fiddled around, Fuller and Jones toured. Even as of this late date, Adams was still in the dark. Asked if he was worried, Adams replied, "No, not really. There isn't that kind of money out there ... Last year, there were about 200 free agents and they had $320 million spent on them. Now, there's only about $117 million to spend on 426. The dollars aren't there ...

Buddy Ryan always said Kevin Gilbride would end up selling insurance. After one season in Houston, he left to become head coach of the Cardinals. In Arizona, he went 12-20 in two seasons and was then dumped by Bill Bidwill. Back at his stables, he named a race horse "No Chuck and Duck." Photo © F. Carter Smith.

We're in no big hurry ... We have to see as we go along where we have to fill in the holes."

That attitude cost them as the whole mess was about to come to a sorry conclusion in a series of rapid moves. At the end of March, Fuller agreed to a 3-year, $8.4 million contract with Philadelphia ($2.7 million average). He made $1.2 million in '93.

On April 14, 1994, the *Chronicle's* John McClain wrote: "Quarterback Warren Moon, a superstar in the National Football League and a pillar in the Houston community, is going to the Minnesota Vikings in the Oilers' most talked-about trade since Earl Campbell was dealt to New Orleans ... the six-time Pro Bowl quarterback ... guided Houston to seven consecutive trips to the playoffs, the longest current streak in the NFL." They received a fourth-round pick in '94 and conditional pick in '95.

The next day Jones signed with Green Bay for $7.8 million over three years ($2.6 per year). Houston offered $2.3. Jones said, "A lot of teams in this league are on the information superhighway, and the Oilers have always chosen to be on the feeder road. You can't get where you want to go that way. I wanted to go to a team that can win games and has a chance within the next couple of years to win the whole thing." Jones retired in 1997 after winning the Super Bowl with the Packers.

Once Carlson came out of Africa, he agreed to restructure his deal, shaving approximately $1 million off the cap. But the damage was done. For surrendering their starting quarterback and two starting ends, all they got back was a single mid-round draft choice. With them went Houston's last shot at a championship.

The loss of Moon was the most controversial. The man Butch Johnson called "a receiver's dream" was the first player to pass for more than 20,000 yards in both the CFL and NFL. In Houston, he had 33,685 yards, averaging 3,368, 19.6 TDs and 16.6 interceptions over 10 seasons. *Chronicle* writer Terry Blount told fans, "Moon's place in Houston sports history is secure. He sits at an honored table with men like Nolan Ryan, Earl Campbell and Hakeem Olajuwon as one of the finest professional athletes to represent our city."

Fowler wrote that having Adams handle the negotiations was "like sending a chimp into space and telling him to fly the rocket." He also told fans, "They kept the right guy in Carlson." Robertson wrote, "You can't cut Cody, who's seven years Warren's junior. That would be stupid, no matter how relatively unproven he is."

THE 1994 DRAFT

The Oilers again had their draft strategy dictated to them. They had to have a DE. They took Arkansas' Henry Ford (6'3, 284) first. They said he was fast (4.8 in the 40), and had 14 sacks and 23 tackles for losses in 1993. "We were awfully pleased to get Ford," said Pardee. Reese said he "seriously considered" trading up to get him.

Others and the comments about them were Alabama DE Jeremy Nunley (6-5, 278)("same recklessness and attitude of Ray Childress"); WR Malcolm Seabron ("a sprinter who can beat defenders deep"); CB Michael Davis ("Dishman clone"); FB Sean Jackson ("can catch and block"); TE Roderick Lewis ("best tight end in the draft" per Mel Kiper); OT Jim Reid ("four arthroscopic surgeries on his right knee"); WR Lee Gissendaner ("no one expected him to be drafted"); UTEP LB Barron Wortham (5-10, 230)("WAC Defensive Player of the Year"); and Alabama LB Lemanski Hall ("tough and aggressive" but "undersized").

None would contribute in 1994 and only Ford, Wortham and Lewis got any playing time. Ford, who was supposed to take over for Jones, would eventually move to DT after a subpar performance at end. Nunley made it a staggering six years in a row of bad second-rounders (could have been Gabe Wilkins or Keith Lyle).

WHAT THEY SHOULD HAVE DONE

The Oilers were in worse shape than they knew. The three big losses plus the upcoming retirement of Munchak had set them up for a tumble of historical magnitude. It did not have to go down that way.

Despite how they sought to portray it, dealing with the cap did not require a Ph.D. in nuclear engineering. It was not that difficult. Here is how the whole episode mighta, coulda, shoulda gone.

In general, the Oilers needed to learn how to play the salary cap game instead of approaching it like scared bunnies. A good starting point would have been recognizing where TV revenues were heading. The Fox deal was not a one-time windfall. It was the trend. The next one would be larger. Jerry Jones, a member of the NFL broadcasting committee, knew this and accordingly postponed balloon payments until 1998 when the cap would expand again.

The Oilers said the money was not there. But with a payroll of about $43 million in 1993, Adams cleared around $3 million. In 1994, the payroll would be capped at $34.6.

They said they were $10 million over the cap. However, most of that (about $8.8 million) went to 5 players who were not necessarily counted on for '94: Marshall ($2.75 million), Al Smith ($2.17 M), White ($1.5 M), Lee Williams ($1.12 M) and Munchak ($1.1 M). Except for Munch, each could be replaced by a good player already on the roster.

Early in 1993, they should have gone on the attack by re-signing the players they planned to keep to long-

While he would maintain his home and still make various public appearances in Houston, the loss to Kansas City was Warren Moon's last as an Oiler. In 10 seasons, he threw for 33,685 yards and 196 touchdowns while making the Pro Bowl 6 times.

term deals. Those that refused could have been trade bait. But they signed only McDowell (chronic knee problems and a good-looking rookie behind him) and Givins (29-years-old with a body racked by years of his courageous high-wire act).

The focus of that free period (through December '93) should have been Dishman and Fuller. If unable to sign either, then they should have locked in Glenn Montgomery. By taking care of at least one of those three, they could have used the transitional tag on the others.

On the DL, they knew they could not afford Fuller, Jones, Williams and Montgomery. Strongside end Fuller should have been first priority. Although Jones had more sacks, Fuller had more responsibilities in the "46" and was more valuable. He was the better player overall. Williams should have been traded long before. Somehow, the front office overlooked that Montgomery's performance was due in part to the Pro Bowlers around him. They also already had a substitute for him in DT Tim Roberts (6-6, 320). Any combination involving two of those four players would have been better than what happened as they kept Williams and Montgomery over Fuller and Jones.

The decisions at LB were even easier. Letting go of Marshall and Smith saved $5 million and would have left a solid group with Lathon and Robinson at OLB, Barrow at MLB, and Bowden as the backup.

From there, the next move should have been locking in the nucleus of young players who were the future of the defense, including those four linebackers plus Lewis, Robertson and Bishop.

They also needed to make a quicker decision about the offense. If they were going to can the Run 'N' Shoot, they did not need to pay four starting WRs and nine total. They should have cut the best deal they could between Slaughter and Jeffires, then let the others go. This would have saved millions. Instead, they just mumbled about their plans.

At RB, they could not afford Brown and White. Considering their offseason workout habits, they could not afford either. They should have quickly released or traded at least one.

The QB choice would explode in their faces. They went with Cody because of age and some decent relief appearances. While the team's record was respectable with him as a starter, his performances were nothing spectacular. Furthermore, he got hurt a lot for a guy who did not play that much. He was simply too much of a risk on which to bet the ranch. Conversely, Moon was a proven commodity. He was a great athlete who kept himself in terrific shape. Normal rules on declining skills did not apply to him. It did not require genius to recognize that his stats dropped in '93 due to a porous line. As of the 1998 season, Moon was still starting (MVP of the '97 Pro Bowl), while Carlson was long gone. Had they made the right decision earlier, Cody would have been worth some good draft picks.

The string of bad moves was completed before the draft when they turned down a good offer for Kevin Donnalley. The desperate Rams offered their first-round pick (No. 5 overall) in one of several proposals. They had already signed the restricted free agent to an offer sheet ($4.1 million/4 years). There was nothing to discuss. The No. 5 for Donnalley was a miracle. But Reese turned it down as they ate a fat contract on an average OG and got no draft choices.

In terms of '94 cap figures, they kept 11 players at about $15 million: Carlson ($3.1 million), Montgomery ($1.93 M), Slaughter ($1.7 M with incentives), Givins ($1.47 M), McDowell ($1.46 M), L. Williams ($1.125 M), Donnalley ($1.025 M), Al Smith ($1 M), Jeffires ($900,000), McCants ($550,000) and White ($475,000).

With that same $15 million, they could have retained Moon ($4 M), Fuller ($2.7 M from Eagles), Jones ($2.6 M from Packers), Montgomery and Jeffires, and still had another $2.87 million left over. This would have avoided taking chances on the health of Slaughter, McDowell and Givins, and brought extra draft picks for Donnalley, Carlson and Williams.

A more draconian solution might have been best. By keeping only Moon, Fuller and Jeffires (for $7.8 million), they could have performed some long-neglected house cleaning. This would have meant saying goodbye to Jones (litigious holdout), Carlson (injury prone), Slaughter (bad knee), Givins (36 catches in '94), McDowell (played 3 games in '94), Donnalley (overpaid), Lee Williams (retired before '94 season), Smith (Barrow ready), McCants (never lived up to hype), White (motivational issues) and Glenn Montgomery (or sign for less). Not only would they have unloaded many of the malcontents who ate at the Oilers from the inside, but also they would have had over $7 million to repair the OL and find a DE and backup QB.

With extra picks in the '94 draft, they could have added the missing pieces: DT Bryant Young (top DT in the '90s), OT Todd Steussie (to replace Hopkins or Williams), OG Larry Allen (to replace Munchak), WR Isaac Bruce, DB Keith Lyle (Lewis had knee surgery; Jackson was shaky), DE Gabe Wilkins (to replace Jones), RB Dorsey Levins or RB Jamaal Anderson (either could start), QB Glenn Foley (backup QB), and C Tom Nalen (moving Matthews to OG).

Had the followed the foregoing simplistic plan, they would have had the defense to carry them until the offense caught up again. The secondary would have had Lewis, Robertson, Bishop and Dishman (transitional player) with Jackson the chief backup. The LBs would have been Lathon, Robinson and Barrow with Bowden the backup. The would have still had Childress and Fuller (the other transitional player) and possibly Montgomery. In addition, Lathon would prove he could play rush end minimizing the loss of Jones. Finally, more help was available in the draft (Young, Wilkens).

The offense was in worse, but not impossible, shape. They had no choice but to turn to the draft to repair the OL, which dictated the need of a new scheme. Put simply, run-and-shoot blocking was too sophisticated for rookies. The average collegiate OL, however, does come into the league knowing how to run block. Thus, the Oilers should have decided early to convert to a structured running game, and devoted the entire spring and summer to it.

There were good linemen available in the draft (Steussie, Allen, Nalen) who they could have mixed with veterans Matthews, Hopkins, Williams and Flannery to forge a functional rush offense. Moreover, retaining Moon and either Jeffires or Slaughter would have presented a sufficient deep threat to keep defenses honest and give the new offense a chance. The main thing, however, is they would have had the leadership of Moon to help them through the transition.

While this team would not have set the world on fire, it could have reasonably been expected to make it to .500, or possibly slip into a wildcard spot.

The biggest tragedy of this entire process was that, going in, the Oilers were strong on the DL but weak on the OL. They came away weak in both.

It all came down to the ability to evaluate talent and team needs. This went to the heart of why the 49ers, Cowboys and Steelers kept winning while the Oilers did not. The bottom line when it comes to winning is that judging players is more important than paying them. "The judgment factor is a very important one," says Dan Rooney of the Steelers. "I don't think it should change. I think you have to have good people in your organization ... good coaches, good front office people, scouts, personnel people."

Agent Leigh Steinburg agrees. He says, "The key to winning in football has always been the quality of ownership, management and coaching."

DELIVERANCE

Meanwhile, during the summer of 1994, the Houston Rockets were trying to get back to the NBA finals. After winning the division and first round, the Rockets received a gift from the Nuggets who upset Seattle, leaving Houston with home field advantage for the rest of the playoffs, including the finals. Hopes were high that the city could ride the broad shoulders of Hakeem Olajuwon to its first-ever national title.

But they had to first get by Charles Barkley and the Suns. In game one, they blew an 18-point lead on Mother's Day to lose 91-87. In game two, they blew a 20-point lead with 10 minutes left in the fourth quarter to lose 124-117 in OT at the Summit. That represented the biggest fourth-quarter collapse in a playoff game in NBA history.

Naturally, it brought up memories of the Oilers' 41-38 loss in Buffalo 16 months before, which was the biggest playoff collapse in NFL history. In a remarkable twist, both Houston newspapers blared the same capitalized heading the next morning: "CHOKE CITY!"

In his book *Living the Dream*, Hakeem wrote, "That was the headline: 'Choke City.' It wasn't any fun to see that in the papers. We couldn't ignore the media. We had no choice, we had to pay attention, they were on our case. Houston takes its professional teams to heart and it had happened to the Oilers, it had happened to the Astros, now it was happening to us. When it came time to deliver, we choked. Choke City. We understood how people were feeling. We ourselves were devastated. Blowing 18- and 20-point leads in back-to-back games and losing both? At home? That was terrible."

Indeed, the Rockets' collapses were just the latest in a long line of blown expectations and shattered dreams. No Houston team had ever won a major championship.

The Rockets had come closest. Founded in San Diego in the late 1960s, they moved to Houston in 1971 thinking former UH star Elvin Hayes could sell tickets. But they soon traded the Big E and did not have a winning season until 1976. In 1981, they rode Moses Malone to the finals, giving Houston its first such appearance ever. But they lost to the Celtics in 6 games as they would again in 1986. Until the 1993-94 season, it appeared that they would waste one of the greatest talents in the history of basketball (Olajuwon) without ever winning a title.

Of course, there were the Oilers. Buffalo was just the tip of the iceberg. Although they had the first two AFL championships, those wins got no credit because of the NFL. Since 1962 (35 seasons), they had almost twice as many non-winning seasons as winning ones (22 to 13) and just 3 division titles. By this time, they were the only original AFL team to never appear in a Super Bowl

Astros history may be more bleak. They were a joke from the start in 1962 when Roy Hofheinz made them wear blue cowboy suits on the road, with matching boots and hats. They were so bad that a pitcher named Ken Johnson threw a no-hitter against the Reds in 1964 and lost. It took them 10 years just to have a winning season. They did not win a division until their third decade (1980). That was the year of their first big choke.

For starters, they blew a big lead in the final days of the season to allow the hated Dodgers to force a one-game playoff. They survived, but used up their best pitcher (Joe Niekro) in the process. The National League Championship Series against the Phillies came down to a decisive fifth game on October 12, 1980. The Astros had it in the bag with a 5-2 lead in the eighth inning and Nolan Ryan on the mound. But Philadelphia scored five times that inning and went to the World Series after an 8-7, 10-inning win. The Astros followed that up by blowing a short playoff series to the Dodgers in a strike-divided season the next year.

It happened again after the second division title. On October 15, 1986, they lost a 3-0, ninth-inning lead in Game 6 of the championship series with the Mets. New York came back to win the series-clincher 7-6 in 16 innings. Had they gotten to game 7, the Astros would have had the unhittable Mike Scott pitching.

That was all they had to show for 36 years of pro baseball in Houston: two-and-a-half divisional champs and no World Series. The Astros are better known as the team that dealt away an all-star lineup and for the time a player urinated on a reporter's notebook.

Well into their fourth decade of pro sports without any titles, Houston fans were the most cynical in captivity. Yes, they were one of the few American cities with teams in all three major league sports, but those teams played like minor leaguers. Sadly, it got even worse.

It extended to the colleges. Of all the suffering, the worst was that inflicted by Guy V. Lewis and the University of Houston basketball team in 1983. Going into the NCAA tournament that year, Phi Slama Jama was ranked No. 1 and a prohibitive favorite to win it all with Akeem Olajuwon, Clyde Drexler, Larry Michaux and Michael Young. On April 4, 1983, feeling the pressure of the championship game, Lewis had the high-flying Cougars, perhaps the greatest fast-breaking, slam-dunking team in college history, go into a puzzling stall. In that set, UH blew a late five-point lead and watched Lorenzo Charles slam home an airball at the buzzer to give Jim Valvano and North Carolina State a 54-52 win in Albuquerque.

That game is still recognized by many as the greatest upset in college hoops history, or in Houston terms, the biggest choke. Valvano's untimely death has insured that UH fans must regularly relive the moment as various sports programs replay Jimmy V's frantic post-buzzer dash across the floor to hug his players.

This was the history the Rockets were battling in 1994 and the source of the Choke City label. It took an African to break the curse. Olajuwon and the rest of the Rockets turned the series around in Phoenix by winning the next two and won back the heart of the city in the process.

He wrote, "Meanwhile Houston, which had been dead when we left, now became alive! 'Choke City'? It was 'Comeback City'! When the team flew back in its own chartered plane, the crowd who came to welcome us home at Hobby Airport was so huge it took the players an hour just to get out of the parking lot." After finishing off the Suns and Jazz, they set their sights on the finals. Rudy Tomjanovich wrote in *A Rocket At Heart*, "We were ready for the final, definitive step that could forever change the psyche of long-suffering Houston sports fans."

They beat the Knicks in seven games. At the trophy presentation in the exploding Summit, Coach T said, "Houston ... you wanted it so long. I'm proud to be a part of the team that got it for us. And when I say team, I mean it in the truest sense of the word." In his book, he wrote that those words were "straight from the heart. I knew there had been a lot of frustration in Houston because none of its major sports teams had ever won a championship beforehand. This was for our franchise, our fans, and our city."

The Rockets did affect Houston's collective sports psyche. Until that summer, the hierarchy of wants of the typical Houston sports fans was first, the Oilers win the Super Bowl. Second, UT or A&M football win a national championship. Third, the Astros win the World Series. And finally, fourth, the Rockets win the NBA championship. That changed in 1994.

Cody Carlson had his own band of loyal supporters, including many of the local writers. They were not quite prepared for what would happen in 1994.

Although it did not get much coverage by the networks or ESPN, the outpouring of love and support for the Rockets was off the charts. A half million people lined the roads on a scorching July day just to wave at the players and coaches as they went by in the parade.

Rudy T, a career Rocket who did not start coaching until 1992, wrote in *A Rocket At Heart*: "When you grow up in an era of dynasties and you see the Boston Celtics, you think, These are the guys who win championships. The Yankees win. The Packers win. For those who don't win, I think you start to believe it's always somebody else who gets the ring. We learned that the impossible dream can come true. It's not only for someone else. It takes hours of hard work; it takes sharing and sacrifice. There will be many tests along the way, and it takes the strength of character to face adversity and overcome it. It takes believing in yourself and the men who stand with you. But it can happen. It *did* happen. The 1993-94 Houston Rockets shared this impossible dream. This championship wasn't for the Knicks or the Suns or the Bulls or some other team. This was Houston's time. Why not us?"

1994 TRAINING CAMP

"Change was inevitable during this offseason," said GM Floyd Reese. "In an ordinary year, a team that made as many changes as we have would be worried, but other teams were forced to do the same thing ... We knew it was going to be hard, but we've actually had few changes compared to a lot of teams. San Diego lost 18 players."

Reese was mistaking quantity for quality. Those few changes included Moon, Jones, Fuller, Marshall, Munchak and Greg Montgomery. The poor Chargers, meanwhile, would end up AFC champs.

Montgomery stopped long enough to strike a Pastorini pose and say, "As long as Bud Adams owns the Oilers, they're not going to the Super Bowl. The players have to take responsibility when the team loses, but it's Bud's fault. I really don't think it's the money to Bud. I think he just wants to see what he can get away with."

Camp opened with all players and rookies signed for the first time in memory. They kept Robertson ($6.1 million/4 years), Brown ($5.24 million/3 years), Slaughter ($5.5 million/3 years), Smith, White, Norgard, Jackson, Lewis, Bowden, Roberts, Flannery and Wellman. Duncan was released. They added free agents RB Todd McNair and DE Kenny Davidson, who was supposed to replace Jones.

One of the more amusing stories involved Haywood Jeffires, who went on a Sean Jones-like tour. Turning down a $3.9 million offer from the Rams, he said, "When you're as free as a bird, you're free to do what you want. I'm not saying what I'm going to do, but a million dollars a year is easy to come by. I can get that from a lot of teams." He later re-signed for less.

Another sideshow involved the backup QBs. Free agent Sean Salisbury ($1.1 million) was the first option off the bench while Bucky Richardson was third string. When the Oilers drafted the "running quarterback" from Texas A&M at Bud's urging in 1992, he was seen as a kid with heart who might make a good special teams player. When Moon left, he moved up the depth chart. His fans, who had seen Richardson work miracles in college, were very happy.

Later in the preseason, the coaches moved Bucky to No. 2 while management tried to get Salisbury to agree to a pay cut. Sean told them to take a hike and took his large signing bonus back to Minnesota where he backed up Moon. The Richardson fan club was ecstatic. They had faith. But it meant the Oilers would start the season with no experienced backup to Carlson. They should have known better, considering Carlson's injury tendency. It would cost them.

The OL was also in sad shape. After trying to nickel and dime starter Doug Dawson, he signed with Cleveland for $300,000. It is astonishing the Oilers did not meet this minimal demand. The biggest blow was the retirement of Munchak, forced out after multiple knee operations. The 12-year veteran and 9-time Pro Bowler was one of the best guards to ever play. "My biggest disappointment," said No. 63, whose jersey would be retired, "was not going to the Super Bowl. The game that stands out in my mind was our overtime wildcard win against Seattle in the Astrodome. It was 1987 and the Dome was full, and when we won that game, all our hard work from those losing years had finally paid off." Munch took a job in the front office. The heat was on replacements John Flannery and Kevin Donnalley.

There were other problems. Offensive sensation Brown came back looking like the Michelin tire man. Ditto for rookie Henry Ford. The most ominous no-show was Lee Williams, who they were counting on to be "an integral part" of replacing Fuller and Jones. He soon retired unable to overcome prior injuries. To compensate, OLB Lathon was moved to rush end.

The rearranged staff included Kevin Gilbride as assistant head coach/offense, Dick Coury as OC, Jeff Fisher as DC, Jim Stanley on the DL, Bob Young on the OL, Gregg Williams on the LBs, Charlie Baggett on the WRs, Tom Bettis on the DBs, Frank Novak on special teams/RBs, Steve Watterson as strength/rehabilitation coach and Frank Bush as quality control assistant.

Fans knew the drill. Diminished expectations were routine. But just like every other Oiler season since 1962, the disappointment of the previous year faded by the time the new season arrived. They looked forward with hope and promise even though failure was anticipated.

Ed Fowler waived his pompon. Having argued for years that they needed to clean house, he got his wish. "Count us among the minority," he wrote, "and it may be a minority of one — but we don't see the precipitous drop in the Oilers' fortunes foretold by so many ... These Oilers feature a much more diversified attack. Defenses won't be able to lay back in a deep zone and descend play after play on receivers like the wrath of god ... The D? It could be awesome ... At the tackles, linebackers, cornerbacks and safeties, each spot is held down by a guy who could qualify for the Pro Bowl ... After this season, the Oilers will be crowing that they've made the playoffs eight straight years."

THE 1994 REGULAR SEASON — HAS ANY TEAM EVER GONE 0-16?

The lowly Colts squished those unrealistic expectations in the first game. They had 13 penalties and gave up 4 sacks as rookie Marshall Faulk ran over them. Carlson's career as Houston's No. 1 QB did not last long. His last play came in the third quarter when OT David Williams went to bench to repair a broken face mask. His replacement, Stan Thomas, played matador to Tony McCoy, who destroyed Carlson, separating his shoulder. Houston lost 45-21.

"It was a hurricane," said Dishman. "They swarmed in there and the next thing I knew, it was 35-0 at the half and I was like, 'Man, where'd they get all those touchdowns?' Obviously, we've got to respond quickly. If not, I mean ... has any team ever gone 0-16?"

A vocal minority saw a silver lining. Bucky Richardson came off the bench to lead them to three fourth-quarter TDs. They were happy to ignore the fact that the Colts were already up by 42 and playing their scrubs. Delirious supporters peed in there pants at the thought of their Buckster getting the start the next week against the Cowboys.

He did, and it was surprisingly close. The defense pounded Emmitt Smith on every carry, held Michael Irvin to 3 catches and pressured Troy Aikman the entire game. When Dishman intercepted a pass while laying flat on his back, things looked good. But they lost 20-17 because they had no offense.

Against Buffalo in the Dome opener, the defense allowed no TDs but lost 15-7 on five field goals. As the reality of Richardson being the No. 1 QB began to sink in, Bucky heard his first home boos from the crowd of 54,424. The offense reached Buffalo's 38-, 32-, 39-, 27- and 8-yard lines without scoring. Those possessions ended with an incompletion on third down, a fumble on fourth-and-one, a flag for intentional grounding, a sack and an interception in the end zone.

Signs of dissent began to show. Dish said, "I feel like we're playing two offenses — ours and the opponent's." Lewis added, "It was a terrible performance by the offense. I think it's time to point fingers and name names." Robertson was direct. "Our offense is a joke," he said.

Adams had to issue a vote of confidence for Pardee. He did, however, complain about his high-priced rookies. "Some of these No. 1 draft choices ought to be further along than they are right now. Who do I blame for that? I blame the guys who are coaching them. They ought to be teaching them more."

He was talking about Brad Hopkins, benched for the Buffalo game, and Henry Ford. The coaches were so worried about Bruce Smith that they moved Matthews to tackle and added a TE to help him. Smith still had four sacks. The two position coaches referenced by Bud were Jim Stanley (Ford) and Bob Young (Hopkins).

Carlson limped back on the field as they squeaked by the lowly Bengals 20-13 to save them from a possible 0-16 season. He was 12-of-33 with 2 interceptions (Cincinnati dropped 3 more) and 2 fumbles. His immobil-

The Commander — Cody Carlson.

ity combined with the poor line play was leaving him a sitting duck as he suffered a broken nose and sprained knee to go along with the shoulder separation. With Carlson unable physically and Richardson simply unable, they turned to free agent Billy Joe Tolliver of Texas Tech. The fact that the Oilers had three former Southwest Conference QBs named Cody, Bucky and Billy Joe led to a few jokes, but the outcome was the same.

At the halfway point, they were a miserable 1-7. The sixth-ranked defense played well enough to be 5-3 or 6-2 with just an average QB (perhaps Salisbury). Meanwhile, Moon was having a great season in Minneapolis.

So was William Fuller, who was second in the NFL in sacks with the Eagles. He said, "Losing me and Sean Jones was a big loss, no doubt about it. But a huge loss was losing Warren Moon. I think they underestimated his presence, what he meant to the organization, how he ran that Run 'n' Shoot. Not any quarterback can just come in and do it. They thought Cody was ready. Obviously, he's not. He's been injured, yes, but still, I don't think he's the quarterback that Warren Moon is. And surely Bucky Richardson [isn't]."

Adams blamed the modified Run 'N' Shoot they were still using. "Last year, I tried to get them to (add a tight end)," he said. "We don't have Warren Moon and Mike Munchak and the guys who made that thing run right. If you don't have the horses, you'd better adjust to what you've got ... Teams are able to defense [it] now ... There's no secret to what we are doing. You put four guys out there and try to find one open. That usually doesn't work now."

When asked if they could have won a Super Bowl with a different scheme, Bud replied, "Yes, I think we could have with the personnel we had those years. We had the talent, but you can see the production on the Run 'n' Shoot has gone down every year in the five years Jack has been here." Buddy Ryan agreed. "Last year was the best talent I've ever been around," said the Card's coach. "If they had run an intelligent offense, they would have won it last season."

Despite taking three possessions in OT, they lost to Pittsburgh 12-9. It was the third time they lost a game to a team that did not score a TD. Things were starting to get ugly. Dish, Barrow and Robertson threw their helmets in disgust while Childress and Smith got into a fight in the dressing room. After getting yelled at for not making a better effort on an overthrown ball, Jeffires gave Fisher the finger. Fisher had to be restrained.

There was also a public tussle over the decision to start the injured Carlson, who was 22-of-48 for 205 yards, no TDs and 6 sacks. Gilbride said he was ordered to, while Pardee and Reese denied it. Carlson underwent knee surgery a couple of weeks later, ending his season and career.

After losing to Cincinnati 34-31, they were alone at the bottom of the NFL with a 1-9 record. The ax fell on November 14 as Adams replaced Pardee and Gilbride with Fisher.

The local media, which had overwhelmingly supported Pardee's hire back in 1990, had little to say. McClain wrote, "No matter how many coaches owner Bud Adams employs before he goes to that big oil derrick in the sky, he will never hire anyone with more class and dignity than Jack Pardee. In almost five seasons, Pardee brought integrity to an organization that often looked as if it was managed by Don King. Before Pardee ... the Oilers had been coached by a black-clad thug and run by a general manager whose picture is nailed on the post office wall."

Pardee finished 43-31 (.581), the fourth-best winning percentage in team history behind Phillips (.608), Rymkus (.600) and Ivy (.586). Jack probably had the most talented teams.

Gilbride said, "All through the time I was here, certain things were done that weren't exactly the way you would have liked. But the key is how you handle the situation. I did the best I could with what was asked of me." Asked about his Buddy, he said, "I had a cancer each of the last two years, but unfortunately, only one was operable. In his time here, Buddy did everything he could to undermine the cohesiveness between the offense and the defense so he could promote his own personal agenda ... He is greatly responsible for some of the things that happened this year ... He was an ignorant jerk long before he came to Houston."

Ryan replied, "I said he would be selling insurance in two years, and he's a year ahead of schedule."

Gilbride got support from Mike Ditka this time. "Buddy is an ass," said Iron Mike. "I'm surprised Kevin Gilbride waited this long to fire back at Buddy. Kevin is right. The Oilers may have brought Buddy there with good intentions, but he destroyed the team. That's what happened. He ruined the ingredient of cohesiveness that a team needs."

Meanwhile, many in Houston wondered why Adams did not pursue Jimmy Johnson. Even though Bud reportedly coveted him, the truth was he never spoke to him. He said, "Jimmy is happy doing what he's doing. I'm not so sure he wants to get back into coaching." More likely Johnson knew enough about Adams to avoid him.

Fisher's first act was to formally kill the Run 'N' Shoot. His second was to lose his opener, a 13-10 snoozer on *MNF* before a sellout. The only entertaining moment came in the third quarter when cameras caught Adams dancing a jig after the Oilers took a lead. It would be the last home sellout ever of an Oiler game in Houston.

In Cleveland, Slaughter threw a tantrum and criticized the coach. He was trying to manipulate his release. It was a test for Jeff. "We're fining him one game check and providing him with a letter explaining how he should conduct himself publicly," said Fisher. "If he violates anything in the letter, he will be suspended for the season for conduct detrimental to the club. I'm not going to waive him, because that would be doing him a favor. My desire is to discipline him. We have 44 guys here who are working to win, and he's not going to bring down this team."

A crowd of only 39,821 showed up for the return of Buddy Ryan. They saw the Oilers blow a 9-point lead and lose 30-12 for their ninth straight defeat. It was the smallest crowd since 1988. "For seven years it was heaven, but now it's hell," said Jeffires. "I never knew what hell was like until now."

In the finale, they beat New York 24-10 before 31,176. The unmotivated Jets saved them from becoming only the fifth team to ever go 1-15.

OVERVIEW

The Oilers finished 2-14. In another in their long series of firsts, they were the first team in the 75-year history of the NFL to go from first place to last in one season.

Management kept saying they were not that bad. Seven of the losses were by a TD or less. At midseason, they lost three straight by a FG. With a QB and another lineman or two, they could have been competitive.

After finishing third in scoring in 1993, the offense fell to last (from 23 points per game to 14). Total offense fell from No. 3 to No. 23 (354 yards per game to 280). The OL was troubled all year, allowing a league-high 65 sacks, although many were the fault of the QBs. The trifecta's cumulative totals were 274-of-553 (49.5%) for 3,216 yards, 13 TDs, 17 interceptions and 20 fumbles. One of the inventors of the Run 'N' Shoot, Mouse Davis, asked, "Would you rather watch the Houston Oilers of the past two years or the Houston Oilers of this year?"

Warren Moon led the Vikings into the playoffs with 4,264 yards, tops in the NFC, while completing 62% of his passes. Dishman said, "Management and everyone else underestimated what (Moon's) loss would mean." A defensive Adams responded that he "wanted to keep Warren. I didn't want to trade him. That's why we waited so long to trade him. I thought we might be able to keep him. We had no choice, though. We're barely staying within the cap right now." He blamed Moon and Leigh Steinburg for refusing to renegotiate noting they did so with Minnesota. However, had Moon stayed, he would not have had Chris Carter and Jake Reed or a good line. Adams admitted, "Warren probably would have gotten killed if he had stayed here. He probably wouldn't have been playing by the end of the season, but our record would have been better."

The WRs' numbers were down for good. Slaughter had 846 yards on 68 catches but just 2 TDs. Jeffires also had 68 receptions to go with 6 TDs. Givins had his worst season with 36 receptions for 521 yards. Much ballyhooed TE, Pat Carter, caught 11. White came back with 757 yards (4.0 yards per carry average) and 4 TDs, while Brown had 648 yards (3.8 average) and 4 TDs.

The defense played very well early, but eventually collapsed. As a scoring defense, they fell from No. 1 in the AFC (14.9 points per game) to No. 21 in the NFL (22.0 points per game). The rush defense, first in 1993 (79.5 yards per game), fell to dead last (132.5 yards per game). The pass defense was a deceptive No. 1. While they had a good secondary, opponents never had to throw since they could run all over them.

Childress and Montgomery did not have the same years without Fuller and Jones. Lathon led the team with 8½ sacks. MLB Smith played well, as did punter Rich Camarillo. Bishop continued to come on as McDowell's replacement. Lewis led the team in interceptions with 5. In addition, the Oilers led the NFL in kickoff coverage and ranked third in punt coverage under Frank Novak.

Perhaps most noticeable was the drop-off in intensity and aggressiveness. Without many leads, they were less willing to blitz and saw their sack total fall from a team record 52 (No. 1 in NFL) to 31. Takeaways dropped from 43 to 26.

Center Bruce Matthews made the Pro Bowl for the seventh consecutive year. Childress was named first alternate and John Henry Mills second alternate as the special-teams player. It was the fewest number of players to make the team since 1987.

BUD'S TAKE

Adams later revealed he wanted to make a change as far back as the '92 playoffs. "When we lost to Buffalo, I knew we were in trouble," he said. "[But] when we won our last 11 to finish 12-4 the next year, I really couldn't change the staff. I knew our defense would be in good shape with Buddy Ryan despite the disruptive things he did. I never thought he'd get another job."

He called the '94 season "more than frustrating ... I don't know a word to describe it exactly, but it sure wasn't any fun. I didn't think there was any way a 12-4 team could fall to 2-14. I could see why we weren't winning. We weren't putting any offense on the field. We lost seven games by three points or less ... When you don't have a quarterback for your offense, you're doomed."

Addressing some of the criticisms, he said, "A lot of people say that I control the team. That's not right. I'm the chief executive officer, and I leave the running of the team to whoever's in charge. I really don't get involved in the day-to-day operations ... I'm not the hands-on guy everyone thinks I am. That's a misconception. I'm not a tough, hard-nosed guy. I've always been mellow. I don't get upset about too many things. I don't think of myself as a taskmaster."

When a reporter pointed to his foot-dragging, Adams replied, "I didn't do any of the negotiating on Warren. Floyd (Reese) and Steve (Underwood) did the negotiating. I was hoping to keep both of them (Moon and Carlson). Warren went up there (Vikings) for less money than we offered him. If Warren and Leigh Steinberg had agreed to redo his contract, Warren would still have been here ... It takes a hell of an arm to run that offense, and Warren was ideal for it."

He also passed the buck on the trouble at DE. "We wouldn't have lost both ends (Jones and Fuller) if we had known Lee Williams wasn't going to be here," Bud said. "He had a $1.2 million contract. Had we known we had those funds to play with, we wouldn't have lost Fuller. But we probably couldn't have kept Sean."

Adams indicated the '94 Oilers lost money, but this claim did not meet the smell test. After clearing $3 million in '93, he sold 45,000 season tickets in '94, not far off the high of 48,000 set in '92. In terms of stadium revenues, the Dome generated $4.5 million, which was slightly below the league average of $5.4 million, but still good enough to rank in the middle of the NFL at No. 14. Gate revenues were fourth from the bottom at $12.5 million (the Dome was the second smallest stadium), while the league average was $14.9. Only the Colts, Bucs and Rams (who were about to move) took in less on their gates.

However, Bud made up for the shortfalls with lower expenses. The Oilers' operating costs of $55.2 million were below the NFL average of $58.6 million. No doubt Houston's low cost of living helped.

The bottom line was that despite a 2-14 record and some of the worst PR in the history of pro sports, total operating income (revenues less most expenses except debt payments and depreciation) for 1994 was $2.8 million. That placed them slightly below the NFL average of $3.1 million but ahead of 15 other teams.

CHAPTER 10

WAITING TO EXHALE
1995-96

Stadium talk was a topic in Houston in 1993 and 1994. The discussions subsided without any direct threat of a move. At the close of the 1994 season, no one in Houston, not even Bud Adams or Mike McClure, knew the Oilers' days in Houston were about to end. Likewise, no one in Tennessee knew a team was on the way. But that is the way it would play out. All in the matter of a few months, Houstonians would lose the team they had supported since 1960 without ever having the stadium issue put before them for a vote. Tennesseans, who had been negotiating for a hockey team, suddenly had an NFL franchise.

It would take some time for the consequences to sink in. For Houston, it meant not just a battle to acquire another NFL team, but bigger ones to keep its other professional teams. For Adams, it would prove a long journey just to get to Nashville. For Nashville and Tennessee, it meant getting to know Bud Adams.

THE LIFE AND DEATH OF THE BUD DOME

The events in Houston over the one-year period from the disaster in Buffalo to the exodus of Ryan, Moon, Fuller and Jones were a lifetime of turmoil for teams like the Vikings and Packers. Even by Oiler standards, a lot had happened. For fans, it seemed like the chaos would never end. Actually, the end was at hand.

It started in June 1993, when Oiler management approached Mayor Bob Lanier for support for a new stadium. It was not a new idea. The Oilers had long been unhappy in the Astrodome.

The Dome was no longer the shining star it was in 1965 when it was the Eighth Wonder of the World. Gone was the exploding scoreboard, the waitresses dressed like flight attendants and the grounds crews in orange spacemen suits. By the 1990s, it had lost its charisma. A 1994 Street & Smith's Pro Football magazine poll voted it the "shabbiest."

It had always been a baseball stadium first. The immobile walls and floors made squeezing a football field into the same space bad for viewing. Fans were pushed far from the action. There were only 17,000 seats between the 20-yard lines, worst in the NFL. Roughly four of every five football seats were bad ones. The 60,500 capacity (including the 10,000-seat expansion) was second from the bottom, although they had the option of cramming another 3,000 into seats with obstructed views and standing room only. The non-retractable roof denied them the ability to take advantage of the mild fall Texas weather, and the stadium was not in a great location. In general, multiuse stadiums had fallen out of favor. Of the five or so left, the Dome was the worst with the possible exception of the Kingdome. The trend was toward football-only facilities.

That last point was most relevant to Adams. The financial landscape had changed. Team owners used to be content just to have teams as extensions of their egos. Now they wanted to make money off them. Selling or acquiring a new cashcow stadium was about the only way to realize a return. Adams' $25,000 investment in 1960 was worth about $150 million in 1993. But while the asset itself had appreciated tremendously, the cash flow had not.

The primary cause of that was the effect of free agency on salaries. Prior to free agency, teams with inexpensive players made the most money. The reason was that about 90% of all revenues were split evenly. The 49ers would win a Super Bowl but lose $20 million, while a team like Tampa Bay or Houston would go 3-13 and make a bundle.

But by 1993, all teams were paying roughly the same every year in salaries. Introducing a capitalist idea into the socialistic world of pro football, the winning teams were now going to be the ones that made the most. Suddenly, the key to making more money was having a better team. The players took advantage of the situation by demanding huge signing bonuses. This put a premium on sweet stadium deals. The owners who got ahead were the ones with who received big revenue streams off luxury boxes, parking and concessions. The better the team, the more it could demand. The rich were getting richer.

Tweaking this scenario was a frightening breed of new owner led by Jerry Jones, a champion self-promoter. Jones was playing off the Cowboys' well-earned identity to cut side deals with corporations like Nike and Pepsi. Those deals allowed him more money for more free agents. The old guard thought such actions vitiated the spirit, if not the explicit terms of the salary cap and CBA. Lawsuits and countersuits were filed, but in the meantime, Jones's team developed into the league's strongest.

Bud's team also had a carefully crafted image. Unfortunately, it was not one that would attract any sponsors. So he tried to do what everyone else was doing, turn to the public trough. Indianapolis, Minneapolis, Detroit and Atlanta had done the same. Baltimore, St. Louis, Carolina and Jacksonville were doing it. Cleveland was supposed to. Philadelphia, Chicago, Cincinnati, Boston, Washington and San Francisco wanted to. The trend was unquestionably towards public-financed downtown stadiums. Of the eight most recent stadiums, six had been or were being built in downtown areas and only one was financed without public help.

Ironically, it was the Astrodome that started the whole thing. With its corporate skyboxes and gift shops, the Dome was the first to treat a stadium as a profit center. Now it was obsolete.

Another factor weighing against the Dome was the lease. Although Harris County owned the Astrodome complex, the master tenant baseball club subleased to the Oilers. Their payments to the Astros were about $3 million a year. Over 30 years, they had paid enough to pay off the original debt on the Dome. Over that time frame, they received only a fraction of the parking and concession moneys they generated, if they got any at all. The football team was, in effect, subsidizing the baseball team, a situation that existed nowhere else.

With Mike McClure laying out a bleak future, Adams made up his mind in the summer of 1993 not to return to the Astrodome when the lease expired after the '97 season. The timing seemed right. The Oilers were winning and selling out all their games. The 1993 team was going to be the strongest in team history.

Aware that he was the least popular man in town, Bud knew he could not run the point on such a project. Thus, he went to see the well-liked first term mayor. He claimed a new stadium could be the centerpiece of what then were Bob Lanier's plans for sprucing up the CBD with a casino, a convention center hotel and more than $100 million in street improvements. The stadium would cost $235 million and could not only house the Oilers, but also the Rockets, a hockey team and more. He argued that money already requested to renovate the Dome ($130 million) and the Summit ($35 million) would be better used on a new stadium with the balance coming from private sources. Bud pledged $50 million but in a fact not widely debated, the source of that pledge would be "future revenues."

Lanier was initially intrigued. He recommended Adams hire some local attorneys who were members of his inner circle. He also recommended he hire consulting firm Coopers & Lybrand, which had just completed a study for the city on a downtown hotel. And he wanted Bud to talk to Astros Owner Drayton McLane and Rockets Owner Les Alexander.

At this point, Adams made a strategic error. He assumed Lanier was on board. Never a political player, he left it in Lanier's hands. Lanier floated a trial balloon in November of 1993 on a local sports show. It came as the Oilers were in the midst of their long winning streak and as the Rockets were enjoying a 15-0 run to start the '93-94 season.

Things started to go bad right away. The public gave an underwhelming response. Those with the most immediate financial interest opposed quickly. The controllers of the Astrodome and Summit (home of the Rockets) knew what losing their anchor tenants meant. They hired lobbyists to help shape public opinion in their favor.

McLane, who wanted $95 to $135 million to upgrade the Dome, said, "It doesn't make sense for Houston to build another domed athletic stadium." He also argued that the Dome already had 30,000 parking spaces while downtown and limited parking.

Greenway Plaza developer Kenneth Schnitzer wanted $30 million for improvements to the city-owned Summit (now the Compaq Center) that he managed. He used a scare tactic. "If the Rockets left (in 2003 upon lease expiration), it could very easily cause The Summit to shut down," he said. "At this point it would be the

city's problem. It would become a burden to the city and the taxpayers."

Most of the media was neutral or negative. The exception was the *Chronicle's* John McClain who wrote in November, 1993, "It is foolish, if not downright stupid, to arbitrarily dismiss the idea of a downtown domed stadium without learning the facts ... At some point, we will have to expand and renovate the Astrodome and The Summit or build a facility. Houstonians should carefully consider all three proposals, and remember one thing: The longer we wait, the more expensive it becomes."

The Oilers made the formal announcement in January with Houston at a high pitch before the playoff game. The proposal was for a 70,000- to 75,000-seat stadium that might attract a Super Bowl, NCAA Final Four, NHL franchise and even the Olympics. McClure said, "A new stadium would centralize the city's football, basketball and entertainment facilities in downtown in close proximity to residents throughout the metropolitan area."

Public sentiment would rest on the '93 Oilers finally getting to a Super Bowl. The popular wisdom was that Houstonians were so starved for a sports title that they would respond by rewarding the Oilers. As the playoff game approached, the project was given a 50-50 chance of succeeding if they had at least some playoff success.

The loss only made potential voters more cynical. Rather than being prompted to look to the future, they were forced to recall the humiliation in Buffalo and every other painful moment incidental to being an Oiler fan. And now Bud was trying to get them to pay for another domed stadium

At the Super Bowl, Paul Tagliabue said Houston's chances for hosting a Super Bowl would improve with a downtown domed stadium. Comparing the situation to the Georgia Dome, he said, "Houston is a city that has the hotels and other things that we need. I think a new stadium would really be a plus ... The Oilers get great crowds in the Astrodome, but in this day and age, it's a little small for the Super Bowl." The NFL made virtually the same comments in '87.

The team presented a design model at a news conference on March 1, 1994. The plans called for a "one-of-a-kind" domed stadium built next to the George R. Brown Convention Center downtown. Employing new technology, the stadium would seat 74,838 for football, shrink to 24,454 for basketball or hockey and 17,000 for concerts, but could expand to 83,900 for large conventions. They promised that, unlike other multipurpose stadiums, the stadium would not lose the intimacy for smaller events caused by the spaciousness of a large dome. This would be accomplished by lowering the roof and moving sections of the stadium to create the feel of a small, self-contained arena. Public costs were estimated at $145 million while the Oilers and Rockets combined would contribute about $75 million, again from "future revenues." McClure said, "There isn't anything like this in the world. It would be the most cost-efficient stadium anyone could imagine."

But the playoff flop brought more opponents out of the woodwork. The project acquired derogatory nicknames such as the Bud Dome and Budbubble. Former Mayor Fred Hofheinz (son of Roy) added another perspective: "People in Houston are conservative by nature, they don't want to spend money just because someone wants them to. They don't want to spend their own money because deep in their hearts, they believe that the Astrodome and the Summit are good places to play baseball, football and basketball."

And, as often happens in emotionally charged debates, the truth became a casualty. For example, Harris County Judge Jon Lindsay reminded the public that the county still owed more than $100 million on Astrodome improvement bonds that came out of the Adams-to-Jacksonville incident (a deal he negotiated).

This claim was thrown around with ease. It was also misleading. The $85 million improvement project (the $100 million figure included interest) not only included 10,000 new end-zone seats for the Oilers, but also renovation of the Astrohall and Astroarena, remodeling of the Astros' clubhouse and offices, replacement of the theater seats, repainting the stadium inside and out, landscaping, and adding or improving women's restrooms. The Oilers' share of the improvements was $17 million. Furthermore, that figure included removal of the Dome's famous exploding scoreboard, which the Oilers opposed. They preferred adding seats through elimination of every third aisle, which would have created new yard-line seats.

City Councilman John Kelley typified another misconception when he said, "We don't have enough people going to the games now."

This erroneous opinion was based upon the Oilers' failures to meet the NFL blackout deadline. In reality, the Oilers averaged 61,000 tickets sold for the 40 regular-season games from 1989 through 1993 (102.2% of capacity). For the 16 seasons 1978-93, they oversold the Astrodome's capacity nine years.

"There's been too much nonsense about our ticket sales," said Don MacLachlan, Oiler senior VP for marketing and broadcasting. "We don't consider success on the basis of whether we sell out by the 72-hour blackout deadline. What's important is how many tickets we have sold by kickoff. By that yardstick, the indisputable fact is that the Oilers have been very successful. When the Astrodome expansion was proposed, critics charged that we weren't selling out. The fact was that we had oversold the stadium in five of the previous 10 seasons. Ten thousand additional seats were installed, and we have oversold the expanded Astrodome four consecutive seasons. When people ask me what we'll do with 75,000 seats in the proposed new downtown dome, I tell them, 'We'll do the same thing we've always done — sell them.' We've got a very loyal core of longtime fans."

Then there was the special case of Drayton McLane. The Bible Belt grocery magnate had become something of a local hero, rescuing the Astros from the clutches of a New Jersey carpetbagger. He made a good effort at restoring the team and improving Dome ambiance, but was hit almost immediately with some rough situations, such as the astronomical free-agent contracts to washed-up native Texans Doug Drabek, Greg Swindell and Mitch Williams, and the collapse of the network TV contract and players' strike. His investment was hurting.

He was in no mood to forfeit Adams' $3 million a year (through 1997), even if it meant Houston would lose the Oilers. Publicly, he championed the Dome as a "world-class facility." Privately, he had been to Baltimore and seen the greatness of Camden Yards. He knew that this was the future and that multiuse stadiums were dead. But he was determined to fight Adams, saying, "There is only one Astrodome, the original and everyone in the country knows what and where it is." He bragged about a purported architect's report, stating, "This thing is going to be here 100 years from now." He called Adams' idea "the height of arrogance." Adams responded with his typical flair, saying McLane could not understand because he was "from North Texas, where they play football without a roof."

Among the strangest opponents was the *Chronicle*. Its position was somewhat suicidal. A large block of its circulation was sports page readers. Many never made it to the other sections. Among that group were a large percentage of Oiler followers. Closely keeping an eye on the daily dealings of the Oilers was an addiction that afflicted a good part Houston. It was part sports, part entertainment and part celebrity worship. It was a living soap opera that crossed gender and age lines. The bottom line for the *Chronicle* was take away the Oilers and you remove a big reason many subscribed.

In a March, 1994, *Chronicle* piece entitled: "There's no place like tax-free dome," Jim Barlow asked, "Isn't that a dandy stadium idea Bud Adams and Leslie Alexander have come up with? ... I'd love to pay for a ticket to attend an event at such a spiffy stadium, but Bud and Leslie, keep your hands off my tax dollars. You want the stadium? Pay for it yourselves ... There are upfront solutions, like raising the city's hotel-motel room tax. It is, after all, paid by visitors, not voters. But that's why Houston already has the second-highest room tax in the United States — behind only New York City."

Thom Marshall wrote, "Bud and some buddies ... apparently are willing to pay in advance some $75 million worth of rent to help fund the project. Bud said his secret partner plans to buy a National Hockey League franchise IF this new dome gets approved. You know hockey, right? Skaters hitting each other with sticks and getting involved in huge arguments. Like Olympics figure skating, but with a puck. So let's see now, that was $235 million total, minus $75 million ... Aren't you excited? We'll be the first city in the world with TWO of these eighth wonders of the world."

Ed Fowler added, "This bubble won't fly with Adams in the lead. Too many citizens remember the Jacksonville Scam, and Bud's PR skills in general never have been on the cutting edge." He later added, "Bud is still Owner. If he chooses to be the loose cannon in the organization, that's exactly what he will be ... He called a news conference recently and amazed and stupefied everyone, including his people who helped put together his presentation. He left out some of the salient points he was supposed to hit upon and rambled on. It must give other proponents of the Bud Dome pause when they consider that Adams is going up against Drayton McLane Jr. and Sidney Schlenker, either of whom could outwit him while in a coma."

The fight for public support polarized the camps. Adams restated his pledge not to play in the Dome after the lease expired. "We would not be able to survive in the Astrodome," he said. "We could not be a viable team. If I sold it to somebody else, you know what would be the first thing they would say?— 'I want a new stadium here.'"

If the loss to the Chiefs was the first shoe, then the second dropped in mid-March when a poll of 1,000 registered Harris County voters showed that 56% opposed a new dome.

Even though McLane and Schnitzer paid for the poll, it was all Mayor Lanier needed. After that, he started saying bad things about pro team owners. "I'm going to be very, very reluctant to put taxpayer money into an athletic stadium that is not amortized by the owners," he stated almost concurrently with the poll's release. "I am going to be very, very slow to support the idea of Joe Six-pack paying the bills for the more affluent owners and athletes. And I am a great sports fan, I love athletics. But I have a hard time with that."

He later expanded on what he meant by "amortized by the owners." He said, "I see my job as protecting the taxpayer as best I can, and telling the teams that there's plenty of profit out there to build stadiums. Sports is profitable enough that they ought to be able to pay for their own stadium. That's not a criticism of individual owners, that's just the way things are today. I think it's gone too far." With Houston still crawling out of a long economic recession, he did not believe the public would go for sales or property tax increases.

Les Alexander likewise got off the fence. "At first, I thought it was what the public wanted," he said. "But it's become obvious that the fans don't want it. So I'm looking now for a basketball arena, which I think can be built for around $85 million instead of $235 million. That would save the citizens $150 million."

But that was not the full story on Alexander. What he really wanted was for Lanier's casino idea to float with him running it. New to sports, he apparently did not appreciate how strongly the league would oppose such an agreement. As to the Oilers, he initially committed to a percentage of costs. Later, buoyed by the Rockets' success, he tried to take over the entire project. Bud did not appreciate that gesture, and their discussions died.

Adams said, "This process began with the Oilers and Rockets both determining the Astrodome and Summit were not long-term solutions to their needs. The operators of the Astrodome and Summit led the fight to halt the downtown dome and bankrolled the PR and lobbying campaign. Management of these facilities haven't accomplished anything except to increase the resolve of the Oilers and Rockets to vacate their existing facilities at the earliest possible opportunity. Due to the actions of the dome stadium's opponents, the ultimate cost will likely be much greater and the potential benefits far less."

He added, "I still believe the downtown dome is the best plan to meet Houston's sports facility needs into the twenty-first century. However, we will now explore other options that will include the possibility of a 65- to 70,000-seat, open-air football stadium in Houston or one of the rapidly growing adjacent communities ... There must be a new football stadium if Houston is going to continue to enjoy NFL football."

The deal was dead. It had taken barely four months. In that short period, the debate over a new stadium in Houston had deteriorated to the point of the Oilers making vague threats of leaving. It seemed inevitable. There was no coordination of the varying parties, and at the first sign of trouble, the would-be leaders ran for the hills. It became a Bud Adams popularity contest.

The Oilers kept up the lonely fight throughout the summer. McClure stumped for support before every group willing to have him. "If you have to build two facilities, it'll cost more money, and neither will provide what a downtown dome would," he said. "They won't provide for the mega-events that are important to a city because we're no longer focusing on what's in the best interest of downtown Houston." Overall, however, their PR effort was extremely weak.

In early July, they offered a funding proposal that did not create an added burden on the average taxpayer (5 cents per $100 valuation tax on downtown property plus a $5 downtown parking fee on the nights of events). "We have maintained all along that Joe Six-pack does not have to pay for this," said McClure. They also released a Coopers & Lybrand study (that cost them $1 million) showing a new stadium for football, basketball and hockey would attract 3.7 million visitors to the downtown area who would spend an additional $151 million there. They predicted the stadium would be used up to 200 times a year. A Super Bowl was again promised.

But Mayor Bob said, "I enjoy the Dome. I know the Oilers don't and they have their reasons for not liking it, one of which relates to luxury boxes and new income you get from selling those. But I go to ball games and athletic events all over the world, and to me, I love the Dome, I think it's a wonderful place ... I'm sure you could have bigger ones and so forth. But I'll tell you this, it beats Jeppesen Stadium."

In mid-July, they started making threats. "We're not making any threats," said McClure. "But we've been talking with the city for more than a year and we haven't gotten past the cursory stages. It's critical that in the six to eight weeks that we see some kind of progress if we want to move into a new stadium by 1998."

A *Chronicle* staff editorial the next day read, "The Houston Oilers' campaign for a new domed stadium may be some of the worst public relations that come to mind. The Oilers have now managed to infuriate the public with a pretty clear implied threat that if city officials don't decide by mid-September they [will begin negotiations to move] ... Part of the problem is that the Oilers have never really made it clear — in the public's mind, at least — exactly what they really want ... It has had the effect of constantly managing to confuse and upset the community, which just went through an episode a few years ago where the Oilers explicitly threatened to move to Jacksonville, Fla., unless the Astrodome was renovated."

At training camp in August, Adams said, "People are saying this is a stadium for Bud Adams. This isn't a stadium for Bud Adams. We're looking at this as a stadium for Houston ... The people of Houston will see the football team, the basketball team, a hockey team, possibly a soccer team and concerts to give a tremendous influx in the downtown area ... It's going to cost me a ton of money to put this thing in. The city is going to own it, I'm not going to own it."

Later, he sent his jet to pick up Lanier (vacationing in Martha's Vineyard), for a tour of Cleveland and Indianapolis to see the changes brought on by downtown stadiums. Bud said, "When he sees what has gone on there, he will know this is the way of the future. I think it will be something he can't turn down. The mayor is a very practical man." The result was typical.

High over Pennsylvania, the passengers heard a large noise and then felt a jolt. They looked up to see the cockpit filled with smoke and the pilot using an oxygen mask. After a forced landing, an abbreviated trip was completed aboard a chartered plane. "I think a stadium would make a contribution to downtown," said a calm Lanier afterwards. "The question is the role the taxpayers are called on. [sic] Is it worth whatever money they are called on to make? And how would that compare with using those same dollars for something else?"

The project seemed to gather momentum again as the 1994 season got close. There was word that Alexander might reconsider. The Oilers announced they had, "informally agreed with [Lanier] that for a period of time [they would] not engage in any negotiations or discussions with any other potentially interested parties." This was in reference to surrounding counties. But Lanier knew the surrounding areas could never afford a football stadium.

Then came some more body blows. First, Alexander pulled out permanently. He figured he would make a lot more money if the Rockets had their own stadium to be shared only with the NHL team he hoped to acquire. The other deal breaker was the Oilers' skanky 1994 season.

In late September, Lanier called it "a sick duck" and quietly began looking at the city's legal options. *Chronicle* staffer Jim Barlow gleefully noted, "Ding dong, the Dome is dead."

Adams sent out a press release stating, "In the absence of any strong and positive leadership or support from those interests who would benefit most from the proposed facility, I've determined that further investment of time, effort and money won't be productive. I will now concentrate my efforts on developing a comprehensive plan to meet the long-term interests of the franchise and ensure its continued financial viability."

The *Chronicle*'s John McClain provided a good summary of where most people felt things were left at the end of 1994. He wrote, "At some point, Adams will resurrect the idea ... He believes — and he knows Lanier and other prominent city and business leaders agree — that a downtown dome could be the centerpiece to the Houston of the 21st century. When the climate is right, they will approach it in a different manner ... City leaders are going to realize that something must be done for Houston to attract convention business, which is the lifeblood of so many businesses. Sports can have an economic impact on a city like no other event. If Houstonians could see what downtown stadiums have done for such cities as Cleveland, Indianapolis, Baltimore and Minneapolis, among others, they might look on the idea more objectively."

Then again, McClain pronounced, "Some try to read between the lines to find veiled threats to move, but they are searching for something that does not exist. Adams will not move the Oilers. You can bet the house."

1995: IS BUD A CAPITALIST OR SOCIALIST?

The collapse of the season and stadium negotiations cleared a path for the Rockets to solidify their claim as Houston's new darlings. For the first time, the football team was a second-class citizen. Management had more immediate concerns, such as a new coach, free agency and the draft.

The groupthink was that the team was not as far away as the 1994 record indicated. After all, seven losses were by three points or fewer. And while the defense allowed 17 points or fewer eight times, they still managed to lose six of those games.

Cris Dishman said, "I can see a light at the end of the tunnel. It's a dim light, but if I squint, I can see it. If we make the right moves in free agency and the draft, there's no doubt in my mind that we can turn our team around next season. We have talent on this team."

First, they needed another coach. The next one, if someone other than Jeff Fisher, would be the Oilers' No. 16 for an average of a new one every 2.25 years.

WELCOME JEFF FISHER

The candidates this time were reported to be Fisher, Wade Phillips, Gene Stallings, Forrest Gregg and Rich Brooks. Several players spoke up in favor of the incumbent, especially those on his side of the line of scrimmage. "Losing Jeff would be devastating to this team," said Dish. "We let Buddy Ryan get away, and that was a mistake. If we let Jeff Fisher get away too, that's going to be another mistake." Barrow said, "Jeff's like Frankenstein. He's part Buddy Ryan, part Mike Ditka, part John Robinson, part George Seifert. They've created a monster."

Adams left the search itself up to Reese with the final decision subject to his approval. Despite rumors to the contrary, he never formally interviewed anyone. On January 5, 1995, the Oilers announced Fisher was the one. At the press conference, Adams said, "We looked at other alternatives and who we could bring in. I talked with Floyd almost every day ... We came to the conclusion that Jeff could do the job, and he was our man."

At 36, Fisher would be a very young head coach. His experience was limited to playing DB for four years with Chicago and coaching with the Bears, Eagles, Rams and 49ers.

Reese liked the change he saw after Fisher took over. He said, "No. 1, he had to get people to perform, to do the right things, be on time, practice with the right tempo." The Oilers did reduce their penalties after the change. After getting flagged 19 times in Fisher's first two games, they had only 16 in the final four. They also ran the ball better. Reese added that Fisher should help with free agents. "In the new system," he said, "not only does the head coach have to coach, but he has to be a salesman."

Youth also worked in his favor. Reese was afraid a veteran pro coach might not be able to relate to young players. A college coach might have been intimidated by some NFL veterans and might not have been able to put together a good staff of proven assistants.

Reese said, "If you look at the style of the coaches who have done what we need to have done, there are a lot of similarities." That was a reference to the Steelers and Browns. Bill Cowher and Bill Belichick were both former defensive coordinators who believed in strong running games to set up the pass. They also relied on tough defense and big-play special teams. Ironically, Belichick was about to be fired.

"Running the football is very important," Fisher said. "In our division, there's always the possibility of playing in bad weather, and you

have to be able to run the ball to have success." He promised they would be "aggressive, not passive — on both sides of the ball. You have to set the tone and emphasize what you want to get done. We want an offense that makes a defense react to it." He foretold of a "sophisticated passing game that relies heavily on play-action passes. We'll also utilize the tight ends a lot. We'll use one- and two-back sets." He also assured no more seasons of giving up 65 sacks. "We have to be in position to protect the quarterback," he said. "I'm excited about the direction our club is going."

"I applaud the organization for this decision," said Childress. "I feel good about it, and I'm really happy about it." Dishman added, "Jeff is the right guy for the job. He did things for us in the last six weeks that we never had before. Jeff will be great, just as long as he doesn't have any more of those four-hour practices like we had a couple of times."

MORE TALK

Next came the hiring of assistants about which the Oilers were making grand claims. Money was not supposed to be an object. They said they planned to hire veterans with NFL experience who are proven teachers and developers of young talent. Ed Fowler wrote, "This is how the best organizations are built. For the Oilers, it marks the first time since the Bum Phillips era that Adams has had both the willingness to spend and a head coach who could deliver." The names mentioned were impressive, and included Mike Shanahan as offensive coordinator, Joe Bugel for the offensive line and John Teerlinck as defensive coordinator.

It was more bluster. Teerlinck went to Detroit for less money. Nor were Shanahan or Bugel persuaded.

Houston ended up with Jerry Rhome, 52, at OC and Steve Sidwell, 50, as the DC. Others included Larry Beightol, Johnny Roland, Rod Perry, Les Steckel, Rex Norris and Russ Purnell.

Sidwell had been the DC at New Orleans for nine years (but never ran the "46"). Steckel was once the head coach of the Vikings where he was chided for his militaristic approach to training. The most amusing was Johnny Roland. The Oilers hired him after the Jets announced they had. Then, a few days later, he was released from his commitment so he could take a better offer from the Rams (now in St. Louis). Sherman Smith replaced him.

Rhome drew the most props. He was a hot commodity and they held him out as proof they could attract the top assistants. They said it showed their commitment to the long term. His claim to fame was developing QBs, having previously worked with Troy Aikman, Joe Theismann, Steve Beuerlein, Mark Rypien, Jim Zorn and Dave Krieg.

Fisher said, "Jerry has a tremendous reputation and a lot of experience in the NFL ... Jerry is going to bring to Houston a multiple-style offense that utilizes all types of formations. It is primarily a one-back system but has some two-back sets. We feel the offense he likes to run is the most difficult to defend in the league."

Fans remembered Rhome for another reason. Back in 1965, the Oilers traded away a No. 1 draft pick for the rights to Rhome, the passing wizard from Tulsa University. He signed with Dallas while the Jets used the Oilers' choice on Joe Namath.

THE 1995 DRAFT AND FREE AGENCY

According to Reese and Fisher, the Oilers did not need that many players. Fisher said, "Because of free agency, you can rebuild and get back to a competitive level fast." Considering it fell apart in one year, it seemed plausible. Reese said, "We have enough room (under the cap) to do pretty much what we want."

Reese spoke as though he understood what they needed. He said, "First is the offensive line. We also would like to look at some people on the defensive line, wide receiver, and we plan to go out and find a quality kick returner. That's definitely an area of concern."

But first, they lost more good players. The biggest name was Lamar Lathon, Jack Pardee's first draft pick who Buddy Ryan helped find his potential. He jumped to the free-spending Panthers ($13.5/5 years) while saying, "It really isn't the money. I was hoping God would bring me to a place like this."

Lathon was talented. Cris Dishman said, "I've never seen anybody with Lamar's package. He's strong as a lineman and as fast as a linebacker." But not everyone was sorry to see him go. In five years, Lamar managed to play a full season once — his contract year. He also got in trouble a few times off the field. Ed Fowler wrote, "Getting Lathon out of town constitutes a big plus for Houston, and putting Haywood Jeffires on the road behind him would mean another. Let other GMs learn what should be obvious to anyone who has watched the Oilers over the last few years." In Carolina, the coaches better utilized his talents, resulting in an All-Pro berth.

Jeffires did not follow, but Webster Slaughter and Ernest Givins were released. Givins was coming off his worst season. The two-time Pro Bowler played nine seasons and held 11 team records, including most receptions (542) and most yards (7,935). At 5'9 and 31-years-old as of September, he did not fit the new system. Slaughter fit, but both sides were pretty sick of each other.

They cut McDowell who missed the season after a knee injury in the third game. Third-year DT Tim Roberts left for a $1 million offer from New England. He had two starts to his credit. White signed with Cleveland. Carlson, Richardson and Tolliver were released.

The Oilers finally signed some free agents. The big three were Chris Chandler, Mark Stepnoski and Mel Gray. Chandler ($5.6 million/4 years) was a journeyman QB who had bounced between five teams in eight seasons.

Luring center Stepnoski away from the Cowboys was big news. Slightly undersized (6-2, 260), he nonetheless was a perennial Pro Bowler and integral part of Dallas' line. The fit immediately shored up the middle of the offensive line as Matthews moved to LG (Munch's old position).

When his $9.2 million price tag was combined with those of Matthews, Babygate Williams and Hopkins, they suddenly had over 20% of their cap tied up in the OL. It reminded followers of the '80s when they invested so much in Munchak, Matthews, Steinkuhler and Salem, and then waited five more years for a winner.

Head Cowboy Barry Switzer said of Stepnoski, "We knew we were going to lose him and there was nothing we could do about it ... He's a hell of a player, but that's a lot of money ... That's the kind of money you spend on quarterbacks, running backs and receivers." The Cowboy school of thought was that it was better to use the top picks and big contracts on skills players. They put together a line of Pro Bowlers from outside round one, including Stepnoski, Erik Williams, Larry Allen and Kevin Gogan while using the first-round picks on Aikman, Irvin and Smith.

Another disappointing aspect was that in 1994 the free agent market was flooded with a number of good centers and guards, as well as many older tackles who were signing for less. A better plan, considering the overall state of the team, would have been to sign three older or medium-level OLs with the Stepnoski money, then draft two or three more to learn behind them for a couple of years.

The Mel Gray deal was aimed at PR ($2.4 million/2 years). While he was greatest return man in history, it was too much money for a 33-year-old at that position.

Then came another controversial draft. They picked a bad year to tank. After earning the No. 1 choice the old-fashioned way, they had to draft behind the Panthers and Jaguars. Without expansion, their five picks in the first three rounds would have been Nos. 1, 29, 58, 80 and 86. With it, Houston had Nos. 3, 35, 67, 89 and 95. It made a difference.

After losing Fuller, Jones, Williams, Lathon and Roberts, all within a 14-month period, they needed DLs. Even with Lathon and Roberts, the line played poorly in '94. They liked DE Kevin Carter, but not DT Warren Sapp because of a checkered past. At WR, they liked Michael Westbrook (6-3, 212, 4.4 speed) who the *Chronicle* called the "real deal."

What to do with the No. 3 pick became a burden, although adding Rhome seemed to telegraph the decision. The top QBs were Kerry Collins and Steve McNair. The debate centered on McNair (6-1, 223), the NCAA career passing leader at Alcorn State. McClain called him "the best prospect in the draft." But many, including several scouts, pointed to the level of his competition (Division II) and saw his big numbers coming against inferior talent.

Chris Chandler

His agent Bus Cook said, "Reggie White is one of the greatest defensive linemen in the NFL, but he didn't take Philadelphia to the Super Bowl. White signed one of the biggest contracts in history, but he hasn't taken Green Bay to the Super Bowl. Great quarterbacks win Super Bowls. You can build all the trains you want, but they're not going anywhere without someone to run them. I know I'm prejudiced, but I think Steve McNair's a great quarterback, and he'd be proud and happy to play for the Houston Oilers. We hope they take him."

They did, but not before a little soul searching. After Ki-Jana Carter was taken first and while Jacksonville was on the clock, Jaguar coach Tom Coughlin phoned Reese saying Minnesota was trying to get ahead of the Oilers and advised that he take McNair. He wanted one of the Oilers' third-round choices, and gave Reese a couple minutes to decide.

Reese said later, "I thought about it for a minute and I wasn't really fired up about it because choices were so important to us. So I really hesitated. But Coughlin called me right back and he says, 'I'm going to trade with Minnesota right now.' He said, 'I'm going to do this in 30 seconds.' Bud Adams was in there. I told everybody the deal and I said, 'Boss, what do you think?' He said, 'We can't miss McNair, we might as well do it.' But I lost my mind. I turned back to the phone and said, 'No, Tom, we're not going to do it' and I hung up."

"That was unsettling," said Fisher. "It was just a gut feeling," admitted Reese. "There was like a minute left before the pick, so we waited ... They stayed put and took (Tony) Boselli. And, of course, our room erupted."

McNair said, "I couldn't even eat. I just wanted to hear my name called." Scout Glen Cumbee described him as "magic. In my 14 years of scouting, he's my favorite player ... He's got a Tom Landry face. By that, I mean you can't look at him and tell what he's feeling, but let me tell you, I know that fire burns inside him. He's going to pay some big dividends about four years down the road."

Fowler called it the choice "right for all the right reasons." Bud, who flew him to Houston in his private jet, called McNair "our most exciting draft choice since Earl Campbell. Drafting Earl Campbell turned our franchise around. Signing Moon turned our franchise around. I see Steve McNair doing the same thing. You don't win the Super Bowl without a quarterback ... and I think Steve's the guy to do it." The Oilers said he would be given time to develop. There would be no pressure to start and he would not play until ready.

The others included DT Anthony Cook, WR Chris Sanders, Aggie RB Rodney Thomas ("just short of grand larceny"– *Chronicle*), TE Michael Roan and DE Gary Walker.

Looking at other scenarios, an Oiler return to the playoffs could have been advanced by giving Green Bay the second-round pick it wanted for QB Mark Brunnell, who was ready to start. This would have let them solve part of the DL problems with Warren Sapp, perhaps the draft's best player, in the first round. In fact, they would have even been able to trade down and still get him. Considering the depth in the second and third rounds, trading down made a lot of sense for a team that needed so many players. For example, both Terrell Davis and Curtis Martin were available after Rodney ("third-round steal") Thomas.

1995 TRAINING CAMP

After decades of holdouts, jokers, infighting, circus performers, cry babies and general turmoil, Oiler camp took on an air of professionalism under Fisher. The only holdout was Blaine Bishop, and all the rookies reported on time for the second straight year. What news there was, generally was about football for a change.

Part of it was the absence of extroverted personalities. Joining the 1994 exodus of Fuller, Jones, Moon and Williams were Lathon, Givins, Carlson Richardson, Slaughter, McDowell, White, Flannery, Tillman, Wellman, Tolliver and Orlando. That was quite a turnover.

The main change, however, was Fisher (now 37). Practices were organized and time managed. Players were drilled on the basics including clock management, a continual sore spot under Pardee. They practiced two-minute and four-minute drills. Fisher asked, "How many times has the offense gone on the field needing one or two first downs and the game's over?"

He also got rid of several time-honored traditions such as the hazing ritual requiring rookies to stand up at dinner and sing their college fight songs. Even fights themselves were discouraged by a $100 fine.

Reese said, "Jeff knows football. It's very, very important to him. He's a good blend of coach, teacher, disciplinarian and manager. He's young for the position, and he's only going to get better. I think a mistake he makes today he will never make again."

There were a lot of changes on the field starting with Chris Chandler. They made it clear McNair would not be competing and signed Will Furrer as the backup. McNair did not complain. He had the richest rookie deal in history ($28 million/7 years including a $5.3 M signing bonus) and no pressure. Jeffires nicknamed him "McMillionaire."

The WRs were Jeffires free agent Derek Russell and the rookie Sanders. Brown was the RB with Thomas at backup. Todd McNair, nicknamed "Spare McNair," returned as a third-down specialist and receiver out of the backfield. There was competition at TE and H-back between Rod Lewis, Michael Roan, John Henry Mills, James Thornton and Frank Wycheck, a late pickup.

Matthews' move to left OG contributed to the release of yet another second-round choice, John Flannery ('91). Franchise player David Williams and Brad Hopkins returned at OT. Donnalley was the other guard. The *Chronicle* contended, "The Oilers assembled what might be the best offensive line in football." This was hyperbole, but they might have been the highest paid. One good move that would pay dividends was signing Irv Eatman as a backup tackle.

The secondary and LBs were set. The safeties were Robertson and Bishop with Chuck Cecil at backup. The CBs were Dishman and Lewis backed up by Jackson and Tomur Barnes. Smith returned at MLB with Barron Wortham the backup while Robinson held down the strong side spot. Barrow and Bowden battled it out on the weakside. The line was a conglomeration of the aging Childress plus Montgomery, Davidson, Ford, Cook, Walker, ex-Cougar Craig Veasey and Kanavis McGhee.

Ford's weight prompted line coach Rex Norris to say, "A lot of rookies show up for camp overweight. They think this is a fatstock show. It's hard for a big man to stay in shape during the offseason unless he has a 300-pound wife to go against during the offseason."

The *Chronicle* told fans the team would be better: "They can count eight players who have been to the Pro Bowl, they have tight ends coming out their ears, a feared kick returner in Mel Gray and, in Chris Chandler, a

RB Rodney Thomas of Texas A&M was a good pickup in the third round of the 1995 draft. He would lead the team in rushing with 947 yards (3.8 per carry) and added another 39 receptions. On the other hand, he had eight fumbles and dropped many more passes. With the choice, the Oilers passed on RBs Terrell Davis and Curtis Martin.

quarterback who may not make your pulse race but has been tested as a starter."

But things were not looking so rosy. Ticket sales were slow. Then, two incidents occurred just before the season.

First, there was Stan Thomas' car. In August, he and his $100,000 Mercedes were carjacked. Stan was okay, but the thieves stripped the car of everything valuable and then burned it. The only thing they left were caps and other items bearing the Oiler logo. A cop on the scene said, "Sounds like an editorial statement to me."

Then, on August 19, the preseason game against the Chargers was canceled. It was another Oiler first — the first game in NFL history canceled because of turf problems. They said it was a hazard to the players. The Oilers said it was the NFL's decision but no one bought it.

The reason was that news had just hit that Adams was negotiating with Nashville, Tennessee, about relocating there. Bud said the cancellation was coincidence. But Bud, who habitually attended all home games, never left home even though it was not called off until 45 minutes *after* the scheduled kickoff.

Bud was looking for a way out of the remaining years of his lease with Drayton McLane. An unsafe carpet might give him grounds and the NFL was more than willing to help. Fans were not amused. A sign hanging in the Dome mimicking the popular Budweiser frog commercial at the time read: "Bud — lose — er."

THE NASHVILLE SURPRISE

Talk of the Bud Dome fell largely dormant from October 1994 to August 1995. The only news came the previous spring when the Texas Legislature killed a bill sought by the Oilers, Rockets and other Texas pro teams that would have allowed some tax subsidies for new sports venues. It might have been enough to keep the Oilers in Houston, but lost out under the pressure from Drayton McLane who spent a nice chunk of change lobbying against it.

After that, any stadium deal was on the back burner. With their history and 2-14 season in 1994, the Oilers did not look like an attractive target. McLane figured he had secured a few more years of lease payments. Lanier thought things could be put off until the end of the lease.

Nationally, franchise hopping was a hot topic. Cities offered rent-free stadiums, debt payoff, luxury boxes, club seats, food concessions, parking fees, tax concessions and relocation bonuses. Communities were pitted against each other and bonds of tradition and loyalty between teams and their long-time homes were forsaken.

It was not limited to football. The Nordiques left Quebec for Denver and the North Stars were about to leave Minnesota for that hockey hotbed of Dallas. The New Jersey Devils were playing Newark against Nashville. In baseball, Sacramento wooed the Pirates and Giants, while St. Petersburg, Florida, which built a 43,000-seat baseball stadium in 1989 before it had a team to play there, went after the White Sox and then the Giants. The Twins, Athletics, Mariners, Brewers, Tigers and Astros threatened to move or sell while the Orioles, Rangers, Indians, White Sox and Rockies got or were getting new stadiums.

In the NFL, no fewer than 10 clubs had moved or had spoken of moving over the preceding 5-year period. The Rams and Raiders left Los Angeles for St. Louis and Oakland. The Oilers, Cardinals, Seahawks, Browns, Bengals, Bears, Bucs, Chargers, Steelers, 49ers and Patriots had all publicly cited a need for more revenue from their stadiums. The Falcons got a new one. San Diego agreed to give the Chargers $60 million in improvements.

The cities pulling from the other end included LA, Baltimore, Nashville, Birmingham and Gary, Indiana. Those places made attractive offers. St. Louis gave the Rams over $20 million as a "relocation fee" in addition to paying $350 million for the sports-and-convention complex. In Cincinnati, a tax plan to finance new sta-

diums for the Bengals and Reds was approved at $540 million. Cinci official Bob Bedinghaus said, "It's just dealing with sports franchises in the 1990s. The truth is, there is a gun to our heads. We are being held hostages. Whether we like it or not, it is a sellers' market because Baltimore and Los Angeles and other cities are sure to offer more. If we want to keep our teams, this is what we have to do."

Unlike most years, none of this was lost on Adams. After fading from league activities for over a decade, Bud re-emerged with the ascension of Paul Tagliabue. His early support of Tags blossomed into places on several committees. The most significant was chairmanship of the finance committee where Bud saw every dollar every owner made. That committee also reviewed relocations, which gave Bud a bird's-eye-view of what cities were offering.

In mid-July, he made his last gesture to Mayor Bob Lanier. It came as a personal letter to Lanier's home. He demanded a promise that by August 1, Houston would commit assistance toward a downtown stadium. Otherwise, he would begin serious negotiations to move. Bud said he needed a commitment in order to secure the team's financial future. At the time, he was finalizing Steve McNair's $28 million-dollar contract.

In early August, in a personal letter to Adams' home, Lanier rejected the demand. He repeated that the city did not have the money and recommended Bud speak to the county about gaining concessions at the Dome.

Mike McClure's public response was, "Mr. Adams has consistently said the Oilers will not play in the Astrodome. He has never backed away from that. We will keep all of our options open." What McClure did not disclose was that he had been negotiating with Nashville since mid-July.

Houston's media was not exactly on top of the story, although they recognized the possibility. On August 5, the *Chronicle* asked, "What if Adams is not bluffing? Would the Oilers leave Houston for Baltimore, Los Angeles or Nashville? Then Lanier is faced with being remembered as being the mayor who lost the Houston Oilers. Not a pretty legacy in a city where football is a major part of the culture."

The answer was at hand. On August 11, the *Chronicle* reported, "Oilers owner Bud Adams will fly to Nashville today for day-long meetings with that city's mayor and business leaders about the possibility of moving his team to Tennessee." Lanier barely had time to respond. He implied it was a bluff, saying, "I hate to see us go through this every 10 years." He pointed out Houston had been good to the team and said he thought Bud would "have a hard time finding another city and other fans who will support his team."

The next day, the *Chronicle* reported that Adams and "Nashville Mayor Phil Bredesen said Friday they had agreed to a 70-day exclusive negotiating period to discuss terms for moving the team to this Tennessee city by 1996. The 10-week pledge prevents the Oilers from talking with officials from Houston about efforts to keep the team there, while Nashville officials cannot talk with other National Football League teams considering moving." The announcement came from the Wildhorse Saloon, a local bar owned by Opryland USA. Adams was surrounded by about 250 Tennessee dignitaries wearing buttons that read, "Tennesseans want the Oilers" and "Welcome Bud Adams." The next night, they all went to see the Oilers play the Redskins in a preseason game in Knoxville. That game's scheduling raised a few eyebrows.

Again, Lanier had no immediate comment other than to suggest that a move to the No. 33 ranked television market would ultimately hurt the team.

The Oilers said they wanted a fresh start. As a native Oklahoman, Adams never lost touch with the region. The first Oiler home game was in Tulsa and several preseason games were played in Memphis. Tennessee had the only two cities marginally large enough to support a pro football team, Memphis and Nashville. Memphis was larger, but many felt its stadium could not be brought up to NFL stadiums. Plus, Memphis was a city somewhat trapped in its past.

Nashville, on the other hand, was no longer just the home of *Hee Haw* and the Grand Ole Opry. It was vibrant, progressive and had a better business climate than Memphis. And it had an activist mayor who wanted a pro franchise to put the city on the map. It was sort of where Houston was in the early '60s when the Oilers and Astros began. In the words of Bredesen, "It puts you in a slightly different category. Your peers are San Francisco and Chicago, not Mobile."

The team hoped for the "Carolina effect." Charlotte was not big enough to make the Panthers successful, so they went after the whole region. The only other comparison in football was the Chiefs, who drew support from a wide area. In baseball, the Rockies stood out as a regional franchise having season-ticket holders from seven states. McClure said Nashville "represents a great opportunity and a market that is certainly deserving of NFL football. We believe [in] the concept of a regional franchise that will basically attempt to market and become a team that the entire state of Tennessee can embrace." They also hoped to draw fans from Kentucky, Alabama and Mississippi, and possibly even Arkansas, Georgia or Illinois.

The Oilers asked for a rent-free 76,000-seat stadium; 65,000 tickets guaranteed for home games for 10 years; 150 luxury suites (42 at $75,000 each, and 108 at $60,000); income from 50,000 personal-seat licenses sold on a one-time basis for $2,000 each (not including the ticket); an enclosed club with 6,000 seats at $1,000 each for 10 seasons; an open-air club with 8,000 seats at $750 each for 10 seasons; and an additional one-time charge of up to $1,500 for 14,000 premium seats. They also wanted a $60 million "relocation expense," not to mention 100% of concessions and parking, plus souvenirs, advertisements, signage and corporate sponsorship of the stadium. Nashville, or "Cashville," as Irv Eatman referred to it, did not blink.

Mike McClure

The package meant well over $300 million to Bud over the first 10 years. Financial analysts estimated the team's annual revenues would instantly increase by $10-20 million, making it one of the most profitable in the NFL. According to *Financial World* magazine, the value of the team to Adams would rise from around $150 million to about $220 million, making the Oilers the second-highest valued NFL team behind only the Cowboys. Not a bad return on a $25,000 investment.

The news was met with a big yawn in Houston. University of Houston political science professor Richard Murray indicated in an August '95 interview with the *Chronicle* that there "is an inverse rule here that the larger the city, the harder it is to get these things done. Big cities don't like to be blackmailed." He said the attitude was that there would always be another team to move in to take advantage of the market.

But agent Leigh Steinberg warned in an interview with the *Chronicle*: "The NFL has not granted expansion franchises to cities that have lost teams, the theory being that if the area couldn't support the team enough to keep it in the first place, it ought not get a new franchise. It would be highly unlikely Houston would get one [and] would have to pull an existing team away from its current home. Since that team would only leave for a better economic deal, it means getting an established team will cost more than keeping the Oilers. The only way Houston can hope to get another franchise is to have a new, state-of-the-art stadium.

"The politicians can't be expected to respond unless there's a public outcry to save the team. Unless people seriously focus on the fact that this would be the last NFL team in Houston, probably forever, they're going to lose the Oilers ... Being passive in a situation like this helps it become a self-fulfilling prophecy."

But there was no rally. Greater Houston Partnership President Jim Kollaer said the consensus of Houston's business community was to let Bud go and then try to land another team. "There just isn't any interest in keeping the Oilers," he said. That was also the sentiment of Joe Six-pack. A random poll taken by the *Chronicle* in mid-August showed that 80% of respondents would be glad to see Adams leave town. They wanted football, but not if it meant making Bud wealthier.

Harris County Commissioner Bob Eckels spoke for most local officials when he said, "They are a great asset to our community and I've certainly been a fan for all my life. I'm going to try to accommodate their needs with the Dome we have."

Nor would the state of Texas help. Governor George W. Bush, Jr., said, "This is not a state matter. There will be no state money. We are not going to compete with the state of Tennessee for sports franchises." The part-owner of the Texas Rangers already had a cozy new baseball stadium in Arlington completed with public assistance, not to mention that the Cowboys also played in a stadium constructed with state aid.

Meanwhile, Nashville quietly went to work to complete its end of the deal by the October 20 deadline. The city hired marketing guru Max Muhleman, who was the national expert on raising private support to fund sports venues, having procured $150 million of such funds for Charlotte and $74 million for St. Louis through the personal seat license. They also retained KPMG Peat Marwick hand Ken Mueller, an expert in maximizing revenues from stadiums.

Bob Lanier was backed into a corner. The popular mayor got good marks for improving the management of city government. His approval ratings were high. Yet he was faced with going down in history as the mayor who lost the Oilers. Enter the lawyers.

Lanier's guys, the county's and McLane's all started beating their lawsuit war drums. They discussed suing the Oilers to force them to honor their lease that ran through 1997 and for the balance of $67 million in improvements made to the Dome in 1988; suing Nashville for attempting to interfere with that lease; and suing the NFL for antitrust violations.

"I don't think that the Oilers' effort to renegotiate their lease after they got the money has any more merit than when the Oilers have a player who wants to renegotiate his contract in the middle of it," said Lanier. "They show some moral outrage at that. And I would think that Nashville and Tennessee are in much the same shape as another club would be if they talked to one of our Houston Oiler contract players who had three years to go on the contract — the league would accuse them of tampering."

The threats got a response. Adams promised not to move before the end of the lease. Paul Tagliabue popped up in Houston to say the NFL would play a Super Bowl there for a new stadium. Nashville Mayor Bredesen said, "Anyone with a $20 bill can file a lawsuit. It doesn't bother me that much. We conducted ourselves absolutely aboveboard — they (the Oilers) came to us." Perhaps Houston and Harris County were thinking of the $25 million St. Louis forked over to Los Angeles to not interfere with the Rams' move. It was against this backdrop that the NFL canceled the preseason game with the Chargers on August 19.

Then the Oilers made the legal equivalent of an end run by filing a suit first in federal court. Although the action was of dubious merit, the tactic worked. The county and city preferred to be in state court where they could get Adams, Tagliabue and the NFL in front of a Houston judge and jury. But despite a bunch of big talk (one lawyer said: "It's going to be Nagasaki") and jockeying between courts, the whole thing died with a whimper in less than a month. The parties agreed the Oilers would play in Houston through 1997, but gave Adams the green light to move after that. If no deal was struck with Nashville by December 1, Houston got an exclusive 6-month negotiating period. The Oilers and McLane agreed to arbitration to resolve their dispute over the canceled game. And, finally, the city and county retained their right to file an antitrust action against the NFL, but not until after the Oilers left.

On October 5, Adams signed a letter of agreement with Bredesen to start playing there in 1998 so long as a financing plan was in place by early 1996. The Nashville city council approved it the next day. The deal was finalized in November, subject to certain milestones.

The formal signing was on November 16. The end product was not quite as grand as the one set out in August. The 65,00-seat open-air stadium, due by August '98, would have 120 luxury suites, 10,700 club seats and a 7,500-space parking lot. The Oilers agreed to a 30-year lease (with a 10-year option) with harsh buyout provisions that would make an early exit painful.

Bud's estimated revenue stream rose to $350 million over 10 years. He received $28 million in relocation costs, enough to withstand losses caused by remaining in Houston through 1997, or to pay for a buyout. The rent maximum was $1 million per year but reducible to $200,000 if they helped save stadium construction costs.

The total stadium and relocation package cost was around $293 million and was accomplished without new taxes. It would be situated on the east bank of the Cumberland River, across from downtown, where old factories and warehouses had been deteriorating for years. By February 15, private sources had to put up $71 million in the form of permanent seat licenses and luxury boxes. The remaining $222 million would come from governmental entities. The Metro Council (Nashville) had to approve $143 million by March 6 (consisting of a water/sewer fee, a rededicated 1% hotel tax, a local sales tax generated by the team, and existing bond capacity), and the state legislature had to approve $79 million by March 10 (consisting of returned sales tax revenues generated directly by the team and money for roads and a bridge).

The signing was in a crowded courthouse building alive with pompons. The crowd went wacko when a smiling Bud asked: "Are y'all ready for some football?" He promised a new team name. "The Oilers didn't seem to be the right name for Tennessee, unless someone knows a place around here where some oil might be coming out of the ground," he said to unanimous laughter. "This is going to be Tennessee's team." He added they would hold a statewide contest for a new name and mentioned the Fiddlers or Pioneers as possibilities.

He also said, "My proudest accomplishment is I've kissed the same woman every night for 49 years. I won't say it's a record, but it's quite a while. When Bud Adams tells you we will come if you live up to your end of the bargain, that's binding." Actually, the rumor in Houston was that Mrs. Adams was very angry with Bud.

While the agreement was still subject to the December 1 deadline set out in the consent decree of September, it was a moot issue considering how Nashville kicked into gear. Moreover, nothing had been done in Houston about a financing package for a new stadium.

On November 21, the City Council overwhelmingly voted in support of the plan. On November 27, the city approved Kansas City's HOK Architects as stadium architects and Bredesen appeared on the *Today Show* with Bryant Gumbel. The mayor said landing the Oilers would aid the economic rebuilding of the downtown corridor, as well as provide sports entertainment for all of Tennessee and surrounding states. It would also give national and international exposure to the city and state, adding to Nashville's and Memphis' already sound reputations for music.

Luxury suites went on sale on December 4 at prices from $50,000 to $125,000 (tickets included). Each suite seated 18. Suite owners received the option of buying 2 Super Bowl tickets per season, more if the Oilers were playing. Eight-five were sold within 8 days, exceeding the sales goal.

Shortly afterwards, 57,000 PSL's (including 13,000 club seats) went on sale. These one-time fees entitled the purchaser to the opportunity to buy season tickets for the same seat for as long as the team played in the Nashville stadium. The response was not as overwhelming as the suites. The most expensive PSL, 50-yard-line lower-level, went for $4,500, plus another $560 for the ticket. Thus, for two people to sit on the 50-yard line for the first season, the cost would be in excess of $10,000 (and at least $1,120 for each season thereafter). The cheaper PSLs ($250 for upper-level) went faster. By mid-January 1996, a model of the proposed stadium went on display.

A MUTED RESPONSE

Adams had little to say to Houston. At the November 16 conference, he mumbled that the fans "had been great" and "it didn't turn out the way I wanted it to." He said he had tried for over two years to get a stadium before looking elsewhere, and then Nashville jumped when it got the chance. "The Oilers have been playing in Houston all their 36 years history," Adams said. "We've played in the baseball stadium there for 28 years, and that's one reason we're over here, because we thought it was time we got our own stadium, and we couldn't get that done in Houston." Asked what he thought of Harris County Judge Robert Eckels' standing offer to renegotiate, he replied, "He's never called me. He came by to get some money when he was running [for office] but that's the last time I saw him."

Giff Nielsen said, "It's a hard thing to accept. You have to realize that Bud Adams is a businessman who got a great business deal, but it just shows you the lack of loyalty that is involved in the game today. It's more the process than the individual ... Bum said we'll find out if Bud loves money more or Texas more. Today, the answer to that question becomes reality. Bud may be smiling on the outside, but in the inside he knows what he's giving up."

THE 1995 REGULAR SEASON — NOT ANOTHER CENT

The Oilers opened at Jacksonville where Adams was greeted by a big sign that read: "Hey Bud, thanks for staying in Texas!" Houston scored a TD on the opening drive and the defense held on as they narrowly won 10-3. In a peek of things to come, Chris Chandler got whacked around and suffered a shoulder contusion.

Then came the home opener against the Steelers. Under normal circumstances, it would be SRO. This time, however, the anti-Adams movement was in full swing. This was his second threat to move in 9 years. It infuriated Houston. For 3½ decades, the city's working stiffs had steadily filled Bud's bank accounts without so much as a single trip to the Super Bowl. Now he was relieving himself right in their faces.

While most people did not like to think of Houston without pro football, the consensus was it was better to have none than to have any more with Bud. The backlash was swift. The response was to withdraw. People did not want to put another cent in Bud Adams' pocket.

The players made an appeal. Barrow said, "We're the kids in this divorce, and it's out of our hands. But we still need the love and support of our fans." Only 44,122 showed. It got off to a comical start as a bunch of NFL guys walked around pretending to examine the field. Drayton McLane drew applause as he made a slow strut over the turf. "Buy the Oilers!" came the cries. The Steelers won 34-17. Fisher said, "I'm disappointed we couldn't give the crowd something to be proud of. [But] I'm pleased that people showed up." He was not pleased that Smith (after 65 consecutive starts) and Robertson were lost for the season.

The season would bob and weave with the health of Chandler. With him hurt, they lost to Cleveland 14-7 at home. With a healthy Chandler, they pounded Cincinnati on the road 38-28. He was nearly perfect, going 23-of-26 for 352 yards and 4 TDs.

Against Jacksonville, they could not overcome Rodney Thomas's two fourth-quarter fumbles and lost 17-16 as Del Greco's 52-yard FG attempt went wide right as time expired. Setting another record, they were the earliest victim of an expansion team in history. Jag offensive coordinator Kevin Gilbride called getting their first victory in Houston "unbelievable."

It happened before anyone knew the Jags were good. Dale Robertson called it "probably the Oilers' worst-ever defeat, arguably the most humiliating in franchise history when you factor in the particulars with the comical caliber of the winless, hapless opposition. [Del Greco's miss was] a final nasty bit of torture for Oilers fans whose pain threshold is remarkable, surely the highest in the country, if not the world." Childress said, "I'm not going to commit suicide because I still have a family to feed."

That set up a prove-something game against Warren Moon and the Vikings. They played hard and rallied to send the game into OT. But Chandler went down with a shoulder injury at the end of regulation and Furrer was intercepted as the Vikings won 23-17. Barrow said, "We should replace the oil derrick on our helmet with the Red Cross symbol because we're playing like volunteers giving away victories. The only thing we should be giving away is butt-whippings."

They easily could have been 5-1. The last three losses were by a total of 14 points. The defense held up despite losing Childress for the year. Chandler was connecting well with rookie wide-out Chris Sanders. The problem was the OL. Their rushing game was poor and Chandler was taking too many hits. In six games, he already had three shoulder injuries. The huge investment in the line was not paying off. Tackles Williams and Hopkins were hurting the team.

In Chicago, Thomas led off with a fumble on the first play for the second straight game. Before they could slow the Bears' momentum, it was 25-0. To their credit, they pulled within 28-25 by the end of the third quarter, but still lost 35-32. Barrow said, "We played like the Bad News Bears in the first half and the Cleveland Indians in the second half, but we still struck out."

They beat Tampa Bay 19-7 then Cleveland 37-10 where Art Modell had just announced he was moving the Browns to Baltimore. Art did not attend the game for fear of his safety. Barrow said, "It's about time we played against a team whose owner is hated worse than ours." The players dedicated the game to the memory of Bill "Mojo" Lackey, the popular equipment assistant who died of a stroke the week of the game.

After losing to the Bengals in Houston for the first time in 10 years, they had the 9-1 Chiefs just as news hit that Bud was completing the deal to move. Adams' helicopter made another dramatic appearance that week to take Mayor Bredesen to his private jet. "Of course, we had to stop practice," said Jeffires. "It's hard to practice when you've got a helicopter on the field. Nashville's mayor was here, but I didn't see Houston's mayor. Maybe he should have come over here too, so they could have a debate." Dish added, "It's very disappointing, and it starts at the top. Our mayor hasn't shown us any support in this matter. A lot of cities are fighting to get NFL teams. Houston has one, and our mayor isn't doing anything to try to keep us. At some point — maybe not now or a month from now — I think Houston's going to regret losing the Oilers. After we're gone, I think

The fans and voters of Houston had no voice in the Oilers move.

Mojo with his kicking "tee." Everybody loved Mojo.

(Lanier) will be the one who gets the most blame. I just wish he was as interested in the Oilers as Nashville's mayor is."

The game had a distinctive Glanville flair as Fisher gave it away on a gimmick called the "Swinging Gate." After scoring in the first half, he called for the Gate, which resulted in a missed two-point conversion. Had they stuck with the usual kick, they would have won 14-13. Instead, with a chance to win it in the waning seconds, ex-Chief Todd McNair coughed it up and KC ran it all the way back. They lost 20-13.

Dishman said, "We're the Houston Oilers and we're cursed. Somebody put a hex on us. If we move to Tennessee, I hope the skeletons in our closet stay in Houston. We always find a different way to lose. Strange has become the norm."

Frustrated with the running game, Fisher released starting RT David Williams. The Babygate star never became the next Houston Pro Bowl OL as expected when drafted by Mike Holovak in the first round in 1989. Nor did he live up to the franchise player designation ($2.53 million) in 1995. The move saved $794,000 on the salary cap. Irv Eatman, 34, replaced him.

After beating Denver 42-33, the 5-6 Oilers went to Pittsburgh with a shot at the playoffs. The players were pumped. Chandler battled flu-like symptoms to go 8-of-11 for 111 yards in the first half as Houston trailed by seven. He spent the entire second half in the locker room with an IV. Replacement Furrer could hit only 8-of-22 in the second half as the Oilers lost 21-7.

It gave the Steelers their third AFC Central Division crown in four years. "It's like we hadn't played football before," said Jeffires. Some players questioned whether Chandler quit on them rather than face the intense Steeler rush in the second half. It turned out he was suffering from mononucleosis. Chandler replied, "Until they walk a mile in my shoes, get mono, lose 10 pounds and try to do what I do, they can kiss my ass."

Out of the playoff hunt, they let McNair play in the second half against Detroit. Although they lost 24-17, he had 203 yards passing to stoke a QB controversy. Many felt the $28 million-dollar man should have gotten a chance against Pittsburgh when it still mattered.

It appeared that the last Oiler game ever in Houston would be December 17 against the Jets. It brought out some slightly premature obituaries.

Ed Fowler wrote: "Maybe it's hard to know how to say good-bye to the Oilers because it has always been so difficult to know what to make of them. How could Bum Phillips and Jerry Glanville have worked for the same owner? ... Bud Adams has never been mean-spirited, but he has been, for as long as there have been Oilers, out of focus. If we couldn't grasp what exactly his goals were, other than making money, perhaps it's because he was never certain himself. He spoke of winning a Super Bowl but seemed to believe he could sit back and simply wait until the prize fell into his lap."

Mickey Herskowitz was more senti-

Chris Chandler had a tough time in Pittsburgh. The 21-7 loss in December had a lasting effect on his relationship with his teammates.

When Chandler had time, he often found round rookie Chris Sanders from Ohio State who led the NFL with 23.5 yards per catch.

mental, claiming Bud was the last owner to turn a profit. He wrote: "A lot has (gone wrong), and not all of it was Adams' fault. What he has been guilty of doing, most of the time, was taking a bad situation and making it immediately worse ... Judging from our mail, and what our ears are receiving via talk radio, the fans have decided they would rather lose the Oilers to Tennessee than run the risk of making Bud Adams happy. So be it. Wave good-bye to the Oilers ... the Astros will be the next to go."

They won 23-6 before 35,873. In his first start, Air McNair was 13-of-27 for 198 yards, 1 TD and no interceptions. "Steve was so calm in the huddle that I'm not sure he knows this is the NFL and people are trying to take his head off," said Matthews. "He thinks he's still at Podunk U or wherever he played in college."

That game was informally treated as a sort of fan appreciation day. After a TD, Jeffires went to the end zone and gave high-fives. He, Matthews, Barrow and others took a long time shaking hands before going into the dressing room. "It was an emotional situation," said Barrow. "It felt like we were college seniors and this was our last home game."

Chris Lockridge, aka the "Oiler Freak," told the *Chronicle*, "I can't imagine not having Oiler football on Sundays." The man who converted his garage into an Oiler shrine said, "I won't support another team. I won't ever walk in that Astrodome." His prize possession was a ball autographed by Earl Campbell. "That's going to my grave," he said.

It was similar for the Demarests, proud members of the Oilers Mammas and Pappas, a group of elderly fans who regarded the players as family. They saw the team off at the airport and were there to welcome them home. They had popsicles for the players after practices. Patsy Demarest said, "We will not go to Dallas. As far as we're concerned when the Oilers leave there is no Texas team. I don't want to even talk about it."

Gary Foster, a season ticket holder for more than 25 seasons, remembered that for the 15 years after the last time the Oilers played for the AFL championship, the Oilers had only three seasons over .500. "We've been with them through the bad years when you couldn't get people to go with you," he said.

Millie Kennedy said her most memorable moment was January 6, 1980, when the players returned to the Dome after the loss to Pittsburgh. That was the night of the kick-in-the-door speech. "Back when Bum Phillips was in charge you were 100% behind the team and you didn't mind telling people you were a rabid Oiler fan," she said.

In the season finale, McNair won at Buffalo 28-17, letting the Oilers finish 7-9, which represented the biggest turnaround in the NFL. Pittsburgh won the division at 11-5. The wildcard teams were San Diego, Indy and Miami, all 9-7. Pittsburgh squeaked by the Colts in the AFC Championship, then lost the Super Bowl to Dallas 27-17 on two Neil O'Donnell interceptions.

OVERVIEW

"I think 'remarkable' is not too strong of a word for this year," said Irv Eatman. "We were so much improved as far as where people expected us to be. This is not something we're satisfied with or happy with, but it's a big improvement from last year ... We have a lot to be inspired about as far as next year."

Indeed, the 1995 version of the Oilers came close to making the playoffs in Jeff Fisher's first full year. Seven of 9 losses were by 7 points or less. The only team that handled them was the Steelers, winning 34-17 and 21-7. They played well enough to win the rest.

The ones they wanted back were the 1-point loss to the Jags (Thomas' fumbles), the OT loss to Moon, the unbelievably awful first half in Chicago, the second game with the Bengals (Gray's 2 fumbles on kickoffs) and the game at KC (the infamous "Swinging Gate").

The defense performed well, overcoming season-ending injuries to Smith, Robertson and Childress, plus significant missed time by Montgomery, Walker and Jackson. Wortham ('94, 6th round) stepped up at MLB, as did Chuck Cecil at FS. Five times they held opponents under 200 total yards. The scoring defense was fourth in the AFC (20.3 points per game) while the secondary was second. Bishop led the team in tackles from SS, probably the most mentally demanding position in this defense. The line play was inconsistent as the rush defense ranked fourth, but the pass rush was poor. Ford, Cook and Walker at least showed promise. Ford and Cook led them in sacks with 4½ each. Ex-Oiler William Fuller led the NFC in sacks.

Cynics said the good stats were due to home cooking. Teams came to the Dome focusing on taking the crowd out of the game. Sidwell and Fisher slyly countered with no crowd. Shocked opponents were taken out of their game plans early and never recovered.

The offense was somewhat schizophrenic, with Jerry Rhome handling the passing game and line coach Larry Beightol the running game. As coordinator, Rhome favored a wide-open passing offense that resembled the now discredited Run 'N' Shoot. It was the team's bread and butter early in the season and worked fairly well with a healthy Chandler. They had over 400 yards against Cincinnati, Denver and Detroit. Chris Sanders proved a lethal deep threat. But the single back sets exposed the immobile Chandler, which eventually caught up with them. As the season wore on, Rhome and Fisher developed differences over schemes which resulted in some very boring game plans late in the year.

Chandler went 225-of-356 (63.2%) for 2,460 yards, 17 TDs and 10 interceptions. His QB rating was 87.2, second-highest of his career and fourth best in the AFC. McNair was 41-of-80 for 569 yards, 3 TDs and 1 interception. Jeffires led the team with 61 receptions (his fewest since '89) for 684 yards and 8 TDs. Chris Sanders had 35 receptions and led the team with 823 yards and 9 TDs. He led the NFL in yards per catch (23.5). Todd McNair added 60 catches out of the backfield, while Wycheck emerged with 40 receptions. Free agent Russell, acquired to go over the middle, was hurt a lot and had only 24 receptions and no TDs. The pass offense ranked No. 19 in the league.

Thomas emerged as the leading rusher with 947 yards, the most by a rookie since Campbell. But he also had 8 fumbles and dropped passes. Brown had only 293 yards. Late pickup Marion Butts added 185 yards and 4 TDs in his last season as a pro.

The 18th ranked rush offense had to be considered a big disappointment in light of Fisher's emphasis on it. They averaged only 3.5 yards per carry and a sad 27th in average per carry on first down. The line was a letdown. They did, however, cut sacks allowed from 65 to 32. Overall, they were 14th in the NFL as a scoring offense.

Bishop and Lewis earned trips to the Pro Bowl with their best seasons. Matthews also made it again at guard and Stepnoski was named as a replacement player. None made All-Pro.

1996: ALL MY EX'S LIVE IN TEXAS

Houston fans thought they lost their football team pretty quickly. Adams first went to Nashville on August 11, 1995. Barely 3 months later, he was signing a formal agreement to move the team to there. This was not a situation like San Francisco or Tampa Bay where voters rejected multiple stadium initiatives. There was no vote in Houston.

Adams did not think it was so fast. He worked for over two years on a deal with Houston and got nowhere. From Nashville's perspective, it took a long time to finally land a big league club. After former Astros owner John McMullen shafted them on a deal to bring the Devils, they were left with a nice, new and expensive hockey arena but no team. They thought it might never happen for them. Then, suddenly, it did.

WHAT HAPPENED?

Mike McClure convinced Bud Adams that the organization had to have new sources of revenue or they would be swallowed by the Cowboys and 49ers. Knowing Harris County officials would not build another stadium, they turned to the City and Lanier. Prior to government service, Lanier was a developer. He understood the issues. As mayor, he was a leading proponent of downtown recovery.

McClure conceived the idea of a multipurpose dome that would also house the Rockets and a hockey team. They approached Les Alexander with a proposal that they jointly contribute a combined $75 million. With the Rockets committed, the deal began to make economic sense.

It made great sense to Adams. Lanier, the most powerful man in Houston at the time, could claim the status as the force behind the revival of downtown Houston. Alexander, owner of the most popular team in town, would have an enlarged and properly anointed arena befitting of Houston's first world champions. And Bud, one of the founders of the AFL, would have a fitting tribute. With those two committed, all Bud had to do was get out of the way.

This was a big mistake. In other cities, teams seeking large public expenditures formed political action groups that lobbied for support. They had volunteers who canvassed the community, actively worked to win over business leaders, sought media support and blitzed the airwaves to sway the public. Adams did none of this.

The playoff loss to KC in combined with the savvy political players lined up against the project gave it the double whammy. The press skewered Adams. The project took on the derogatory catch phrase "Bud Dome." It became a forum on Bud Adams. After the fateful poll, Lanier and Alexander bailed out.

Publicly, Lanier tried to take the moral high ground. For example, he stated, "It's very hard for me to go into neighborhoods that need street lights and sidewalks and police and parks, and ask those people for money for a stadium they probably can't afford to buy tickets for. That's not a slogan, but something I feel strongly in." Adams and Lanier began acting like children towards each other. It became a battle of personalities and will.

In the spring of 1995, state legislators shelved a bill that was essentially the last nail in the Houston Oiler coffin. That summer, Adams made his final pitch to Lanier. At the same time, he dispatched McClure to Nashville, a city that had long been dangling a baited hook.

By the time the news hit, it was too late for Lanier or anyone else to make a difference, not that they would have tried. The final details were flushed out by November. Adams said, "When I made the trip to Nashville to sign the papers, they put the last page in front of me and I was still thinking, 'Do I really want to do this? Do I really want to move?' I was holding the fountain pen and my hand was shaking."

LANIER'S RESPONSE

Lanier's gestures towards Adams basically amounted to an offer to help him pack. As the dust settled and the depths of Houston's repressed desire for a pro football team oozed to the surface, he began to vacillate. In something of a *mea culpa*, he said he misread Adams' fervor for a new arena. He put together a committee to study venue needs in Houston.

Then, he went national. He blasted the NFL and pro sports as greedy businesses that pit cities against each other and blackmail taxpayers into funding new arenas. He said it was not right that a local government should have to spend half a billion dollars on sports stadiums so 1/100th of the population could watch in person what everyone else can only see on television. In Washington, DC, he said, "Sure, sports are important to a city's image. But in my judgment, it's more important to have parks, police, water and youth programs."

Appearing in late November 1995 before the Senate Judiciary Subcommittee on Antitrust, Business Rights and Competition, he proposed that the way to end the raging movement of teams was to reign in the NFL's monopoly status by allowing any city that could afford a team to get one. He called on Congress to force the NFL to expand, with the immediate effect being cities would quit offering huge sums to lure a team from another city. "They are a monopoly," he testified, "any monopoly ... can charge monopoly prices. It's a question of whether you want to accept their prices or get out of the game." He also hinted that while Houston had agreed to not contest Adams' move to Nashville, it might sue the NFL if it did not get another team.

NFL Commissioner Paul Tagliabue was at the same hearings seeking just the opposite — an exemption from antitrust laws that, if granted, would protect the league from suits such as the one Al Davis beat them over the head with. Lanier really angered him.

Lanier said it made no sense to give the NFL *more* monopoly power. He argued owners would never prevent a fellow owner from taking a sweet deal from another city because they might seek one themselves one day. He proposed instead that any exemption be tied to a guarantee that any city that lost a team would get an expansion franchise. Mayor Bob said, "It's kind of like the fox guarding the chicken house. They say, 'Yeah, but we're a nice fox.' And I say, 'Yeah, but Mr. Fox, if you're so nice, why are all of those feathers dripping out of your mouth?' I think if you grant that exemption to the foxes, [you should] put a fox in that chicken house for us too."

Tagliabue responded, "Our problem today is that teams are having difficulty meeting their costs. We have to solve the problems of existing franchises before we start adding franchises. I don't know of any way to deal with the next set of problems before you solve the current set. Teams are moving because they have financial problems."

Lanier responded, "De Beers would say the same thing about diamonds. I have never heard of a monopolist that recommended its demise or diminution ... The truth of the situation is that the ripping away of a professional sports team from loyal fans, a lucrative market and a long history of accomplishments is the business of fans and should be the business of Congress."

Lanier then went to Cleveland for a mayors' conference to discuss how to stop the madness. His movement did not catch fire, however, because the other mayors were afraid a militant stance might prevent them from some day acquiring a for their cities.

Lanier then began to sound conciliatory towards Adams. He and the county sent a December letter asking for another chance to negotiate while the Nashville deal still had contingencies. Apparently, it finally dawned on them that even after he left, Adams would still be chairman of the Finance Committee which plays a major role in determining which cities get teams.

He then rolled out his most dubious strategy. He said forcing the Oilers to stay in Houston for the last two years of their lease could help the city attract another franchise. He thought NFL owners would not like having to accept a reduced gate at the Dome. They would also have to wait to get their percentages of NFL Properties sales estimated at $80 million once they opened in Tennessee. Ostensibly, the theory was that owners would want to quickly cut a deal with the city so the Oilers could leave.

HOUSTON'S IMAGE

Attendance suffered in 1994 due to the team's quit on the field. In 1995, there were many more empty seats. Sunday after Sunday, highlights of home games in a half-full Astrodome made the rounds of the national sports shows.

The suggestion was that Adams was leaving because Houston did not support his team. For example, the *New York Times* reported that the move, like that of the Raiders and Rams, was "based on a lack of fan support."

The problem with this perception was that it was wrong. Fan support had noting to do with why Adams was moving. When news of the Bud Dome proposal first hit, support was at an all-time high. Indeed, 1993 was the Oilers' fifth consecutive year of averaging more tickets sold than seats. Since the additional 10,000 were added, they oversold capacity every year. They sold out a majority of seasons going back to 1978, and that included some very lean years.

In terms of the top 10 Oiler games for tickets distributed and actual attendance, every game was from the 1991-93 period, the seasons just before Bud's request for a new taxpayer-assisted stadium. For tickets distributed, the 1992 season opener against Pittsburgh ranked first with 64,934. The record for actual attendance was the 1993 playoff game with Kansas City at 64,011.

Three times in 1993 they sold over 64,000 tickets. Considering that the Dome's post-baseball season capacity of 60,500 could only be pushed to 62,439 with obstructed view and standing room only seats, these figures show fans had the Dome busting out at the seams, all this in a crummy stadium. It is difficult to conceive of what more fan support the team or NFL could have wanted from Houston considering how Adams had operated over the years.

Anyone who has ever been to Houston or witnessed the Love Ya Blue and House of Pain eras knows the football fans of Houston were consumed with *their* team. All other sports were secondary. Radio and television were flooded with non-stop Oiler-related programming. The coverage in the local sports pages dwarfed that of other cities. In short, there was a large base of die-hard fans who were nuts about the Oilers — just not about Bud.

Even in 1994 when his team went 2-14, Bud still made money based upon season ticket sales alone (45,000).

His net was better than half the teams. The attendance decline in 1995 in response to the Nashville situation should have been understandable.

But Houston did not get the benefit of doubt. The national writers and commentators were either too lazy, too uninterested or too biased to figure it out.

And there was something more nefarious at work at the network television level. The more attention Lanier drew to himself with his quixotic crusade, the angrier owners and Commissioner Tagliabue became. They flexed some muscle. Soon, TV analysts lined up to lambaste the poor support the Oilers got in Houston. What was good for the NFL was good for NBC, Fox and ESPN.

This phenomenon was easy to unravel, but not so easy to combat. There was little fans could do to compete with an NFL-backed negative PR campaign other than sell out the games. This they refused to do. The anti-Adams sentiment was too great.

Then there was the pep rally in December 1994. A loose-leaf group of die-hards believed, based upon unrealistic commentaries in the local papers, that there was still a chance to keep the team. The "Save the Oilers" rally was supposed to demonstrate Houstonians' support. Maybe 50 people showed. Pictures of the "rally" made it all over the country. It was both sad and comical. The news outlets left the impression that a strong rally may have had some bearing on the outcome. In reality, Nashville was already marketing luxury suites.

With the Astros and Rockets also threatening to leave, the town that had the vision and drive to build the first domed stadium, Ship Channel, Johnson Space Center and perhaps the world's most renowned medical center was taking a severe beating as a sports town.

Moreover, there was no relief in sight with Lanier, McLane and the county threatening to force the Oilers to play in the Dome another two years.

It made for a dramatic contrast with what was going with Cleveland at the same time.

CLEVELAND HAD A BETTER PR MAN

In early November, Browns Owner Art Modell announced he was moving his team to Baltimore at the start of the '96 season. Baltimore, which had been trying to attract another team ever since the Colts snuck out in the middle of the night in 1984, rejoiced (a new stadium was being funded by a unique sports lottery). Cleveland fell into depression.

Modell said the new economics of football made it impossible for him to stay. His sole income came from the team, which he said lost $21 million over the previous 2 seasons. "I've run out of options," he said. "I've run out of the capacity to borrow. I've run out of the capacity to be competitive. I want to win."

Partly, he blamed the mayor for forcing him to leave. He said Cleveland Mayor Michael White did not deal honestly with him by promising a new stadium and then going back on his word. White actively supported the $455 million Gateway Project, which included new baseball (Jacobs Field) and basketball (Gund Arena) stadiums. Together, they were the centerpieces of the revitalization of downtown Cleveland. Feeling left out, Modell turned to Baltimore.

Cleveland reacted. There was outrage across all fronts, from cab drivers and construction workers to politicians, business leaders and ex-players. They were unified and outspoken about wanting to keep the Browns.

Fans flooded the league with anti-Modell faxes, hanged the 70-year-old owner in effigy, and took their case to Congress and owners' meetings. Modell's vilification, including death threats, forced him into self-exile in Florida.

They disputed Modell's claims, blaming his problems on his own mismanagement. The Browns were fourth in the NFL in attendance in the 1990s and were among the top 10 in stadium revenues. According to *Financial World*, he was due to make $6 million in '95 off the Browns.

Mayor White took the cue and promised to do everything he could to keep the Browns or to get another team. He immediately held a news conference asking voters to approve a tax package already scheduled for a vote the following week. He persuaded the local media to present a united front and help convince the voters. He said it would show NFL owners that Cleveland was serious about refurbishing the old stadium or building a new one.

He held a second news conference the Saturday before the Oiler game in Cleveland in November. That Sunday night, he flew to New York to meet with Tagliabue. Wherever he went, the cameras followed. The next day, he went to the NFL meetings in Dallas to meet with owners and league officials. Joining him there were about 20 vocal Browns' fans carrying signs. "If this can happen in Cleveland," he said, "there is no safe franchise in America."

His populist cause got the owners' attention. Patriot Owner Bob Kraft said in Dallas, "To me, it's very sad to see a team leave that's been established in a market so long ... I think the Cleveland fans don't deserve to be treated like this." Redskins official John Cooke said, "Our position and feeling is we're very upset the people of Cleveland have been betrayed. They are NFL fans as much as they are Cleveland Browns fans. And the fans are the heart of the game, not the players, not the owners."

Even Tagliabue said, "This is more than just a public-relations jolt. It's a deep psychological jolt to fans of the NFL, not just fans of the Cleveland Browns."

Houston fans had to wonder if Tags had ever heard of Bum Phillips, Earl Campbell or Love Ya Blue. There was no such outpouring for them. The only owner who spoke up for Houston, ironically enough, was Al Davis. Al had a lot of fond memories of playing games in Houston, especially in the '60s. But not much was ever made of his comments.

That Tuesday, Cleveland-area voters approved the tax package, raising $175 million. The next day, White led a group of city and county officials (and TV cameras) to hand-deliver a stadium offer based upon the vote to the Browns' training facility. By this point, White had become a national media darling.

Like Lanier, he went to court to hold Modell to a lease that ran until 1998. Like Lanier, he had some tough talk for the NFL ("You can't have a league that has a bunch of rogue owners doing whatever they want to do whenever they want to do it, destabilizing the league and destabilizing the support"). Like Lanier, he went to the Senate hearings where he was joined by about 200 Browns fans wearing team colors. ("What's the impact for the NFL if it allows that team to kick the city in the teeth? It happened to Oakland; nobody said anything. It happened in Los Angeles; nobody said anything. It's happening in Houston; nobody said a word. How many cities are going to be threatened in this way before the NFL recognizes that it's bad for the country and bad for the league?").

But unlike Lanier, White also worked behind the scenes with the NFL. The Browns were the fourth team of the year to either move or announce a move, and the league was running scared. Public sentiment was against franchise moves. The hearings in Washington made them even more nervous. The NFL was willing to deal.

The national media's sympathetic portrayal of White played a part in that willingness. News clips of the angry black mayor marching through the halls of Capital Hill in a cheap suit with his passion in his hat made a powerful impression that harkened back to the '60s. Neither the NFL nor the networks were going to tackle that one. Mayor Lanier did not enjoy a similar fate. His news clips unfairly left the liberal Democrat looking more like an Alabama sheriff from the same period.

Modell also gave Cleveland two advantages. First, he waited until the season was half over to make his announcement. As a result, Cleveland did not have to suffer through an entire season's worth of highlights from a half-empty stadium. Houston knew it had lost the Oilers before the season started, and attendance dropped for the whole season. Second, the Browns would begin play in Baltimore immediately with the '96 season. Thus, there would be no lame duck seasons in Cleveland like Houston had just suffered through and would again in '96.

In the end, Cleveland put up a united front. Mayor White was willing to take chances with his political career when Lanier was not. He a different political vision. He got in front and led the charge. In February 1996, it paid off as the NFL promised to have another team in Cleveland and to give the city up to $48 million in return for allowing Art Modell to move his team to Baltimore. In March 1997, the league approved an expansion club for Cleveland.

In return for dropping its lawsuit against Modell, Cleveland retained the rights to the Browns' name, colors and logos. To get league approval of his move, Modell agreed to pay the other owners $29 million (of Baltimore's money) as a relocation fee and Cleveland $12 million.

BACK IN LANIER'S COURT

"We'd like to at least do as well as Cleveland," Lanier read in a prepared statement. "That's similar to what would be required if the federal legislation passed. Of course, the issue of a new stadium would have to be resolved. Somewhere out there, there is a user-pay program that could be finalized without a lot of tax dollars."

But the NFL quickly said Houston was different. They said Cleveland had a richer pro football tradition and supportive fans who fought hard to retain the Browns. Tagliabue said, "This was an effort to keep the Browns in Cleveland. The mayor, the fans, the business leaders and everyone in Cleveland has worked hard towards that goal." Jerry Jones agreed. "There is no comparison," he said. "This is a great way for Cleveland to have the Browns. That's it."

Lanier's campaign obviously struck a nerve, primarily because he was right. Pro football should pay for its own stadiums. Governments should stick to schools, police, roads and picking up the trash. But there was no groundswell of support. Only a few others echoed his sentiment. Ohio Senator John Glenn said the situation was a "chaos that is eroding the sport," and claimed "Paul Tagliabue doesn't control the league."

NBC sportscaster Bob Costas, who saw his native St. Louis pay off the Rams' debt in Anaheim plus the huge "relocation fee," said, "No matter how they dress it up, it's unseemly at its best, extortion at its worst." However, the mainstream media, perhaps afraid of cooking the golden goose, never sincerely tackled the issue.

Bob Lanier is a bright guy. Eventually he conceded that he alone could not change the world. "It's unfair for taxpayers to have to pay for these athletic stadia," he said. "But I reconcile myself that it's part of the ambiance of life."

With his city left to pursue the expansion route, he had a lot of burned bridges to mend. Tagliabue said publicly in November, "I don't see expansion on the horizon right now. Maybe after the turn of the century." Privately, Lanier had angered NFL owners to the point that many vowed Houston would never get another team.

Indeed, they would hold out Houston as an example to other cities that did not want to fork over tax money for their owners. It started in March 1997 with Broncos Owner Pat Bowlen, who wanted a new stadium in spite of decades of sellouts at Mile High Stadium.

In support of Bowlen, Tags said, "The Oilers are a good example of the problem. The Oilers were a very successful football team. Over the course of a decade, they got into the playoffs more than anyone in the league other than perhaps the 49ers. But there was no prospect of a viable stadium for the future, and they had to make a decision to protect that future. Hopefully, Denver will make a different decision."

In such light, Houston had to hope Lanier's successor Lee Brown could patch things up. Or, they could always sue.

Back in September, 1994, law school dean Gerald Treece presented his theory: "The city could file a lawsuit in federal court saying that the NFL has essentially created a monopoly on where franchises go. Because the city of Houston has invested so much emotionally and financially in the Oilers, unless we are granted a new franchise, then the policies and practices of the NFL are in violation of the antitrust laws." The idea would be to put the NFL in a position that it had no choice but to give Houston another team. The contemplated action has never been attempted, but were the city able to make it to a jury, it would probably slaughter the NFL. As a city official said back in 1994, "I'm not sure the NFL wants to see such a lawsuit, so they might work something out."

HOUSTON'S OTHER TEAMS

Meanwhile, the owners of Houston's other professional teams smelled blood in the water. Les Alexander began to make similar noises (Las Vegas was one rumored destination). Mayor Lanier came out quickly with support for new digs for the defending NBA champs at about the time Bud's deal with Nashville was being finalized.

"The fans are going to be able to look back at this and say it's not Bud, it's Lanier," said Jeffires before the final game in 1995. "Bud is not the liar; Lanier is. I don't know a lot about Lanier. I'm sure he's done some great things, but right now he's doing the worst thing. He's saying, 'Forget the Oilers; let's do the Rockets.' This is really a shot in our backs." Matthews added, "The Oilers always have been the whipping boys of Houston. [The city] didn't take Mr. Adams seriously. It's just hard to understand, especially when a team has an identity that goes hand in hand with the city like the Oilers do ... The Rockets probably would be in our position if they had asked for a new building before we did. I'm sure Alexander loves us for that."

Drayton McLane was also hard at work. It turns out that while he was torpedoing the Oilers' chances of staying in Houston on a platform that the Dome was world-class, he was secretly negotiating to sell the Astros to an East Coast group. Later, after seeing the rebirth of baseball in Baltimore and Cleveland due to smaller baseball-only facilities, he decided that was the way to go.

Using Adams' exit as a hammer, McLane had a deal for a new publicly-funded baseball stadium worked out by early summer 1996 with the support of Mayor Lanier and County Commissioner Bob Eckels. The proposition passed in November, 1996, with 52% of the vote. It called for a $265 million downtown baseball park (and $200 million left over for other projects). Then, with Lanier and McLane out front, pro-stadium forces got a difficult proposition through the state legislature for new taxing authority, clearing the final hurdle.

That deal let Lanier regain some standing. Before his fight with Adams, he was considered one of the best Houston mayors of all-time. He helped reduce crime, restructured the city's debt, reversed suburban flight by repairing infrastructure, and pushed diversity. Nonetheless, his legacy would be as the mayor who lost the Oilers. The baseball stadium let his supporters claim he was the mayor who saved the baseball team.

"It strikes me as funny," said NFL draftnic Joel Buchsbaum, who had a popular weekly Houston radio show "that the city and the county have now given the other teams all the things they wouldn't give the Oilers. Now, it will cost them twice as much to get a new NFL team."

Adams' proposed domed stadium with portable walls and floors to accommodate basketball and hockey would have cost less than the baseball stadium. He also offered to contribute between $50-70 million towards construction costs in addition to rent payments. The offer was rejected without the public ever having had the idea put to a vote.

MOVEMENT TOWARDS TENNESSEE

In early May 1996, NFL owners gave the final go-ahead for the Oilers' move. With that approval, the only remaining obstacle was a Nashville referendum.

There was a limited anti-Stadium movement. The pro-stadium forces were well-financed and spent about $500,000 versus $20,000 for their opponents. Roughly 700 volunteers planted 30,000 "NFL Yes" yard signs around the city in addition to providing 500 trips to the polls for early voters in need of transportation.

The vote was May 7, 1996. With a high turnout (125,000), Nashville voters approved the stadium's construction with nearly 60%. Only two districts voted against the measure.

A local report of the victors' celebration read: "The line for beer was long, and people were drinking lots of it. The decibel level was high. Every time a television report showed a widening lead for the 'yes' votes, the crowd erupted into cheers. The men in the crowd wore blue jeans, T-shirts and hats. A large portion of the crowd was African-American. As for the women, a good number looked as if they were auditioning for spots on the cheerleader squad. There were a lot of short pants, and there were a lot of tight shirts."

Mayor Phil Bredesen said, "The yeses have prevailed, but there are a lot of good people in this community who felt the other way and voted no. Tomorrow there are no more yeses and nos. Tomorrow, we are all Nashvillians."

Bredesen was the driving force from the outset some 10 months before when he and a few other Nashvillians met with Mike McClure in a Chicago airport conference room. At that meeting, McClure told them the Oilers needed a new stadium and Houston was probably not willing to give it to them. He wanted to know if Nashville was interested.

The negotiations, which also involved the business community and media, soon consumed Bredesen. He approached it like a campaign, employing his election team of Dave Cooley (campaign manager), Mike Pigott (communications) and Byron Trauger (right hand).

One of the first items on the agenda was approaching political adversary Governor Don Sundquist. The mayor needed over $50 million of the state's money. He also had to convince Metro Council to approve its own $80 million bonds package. In both instances he was successful, although it was a tough battle in the legislature to get the Memphis officials on board. All the while, Bredesen gave lip service to the importance of other city needs, such as a new library or better schools.

The whole episode played to the mayor's strengths as a businessman and deal-maker rather than a bureaucrat. It showed in his arm-twisting of businessmen. The Chamber of Commerce agreed to accept responsibility for marketing the thousands of private seat licenses. He also mined the business community for hundreds of thousands for luxury suites. And while the PSLs did not sell as well, he talked banks and rich individuals into picking up the slack.

Soon plans were under way to purchase the land and procure a stadium design. A local report read, "Meanwhile, at some point in time, a new name for the team will have to be chosen. Press reports have suggested that that decision will take the form of a statewide competition. Inevitably, there will also be input from closely monitored focus groups. Whatever name the team comes up with must reflect, as team officials have long insisted, not just Nashville but the state of Tennessee as a whole."

The Oilers opened an office in Nashville. On August 26, 1996, Adams released a "public letter to all Tennesseans," that began "Dear Tennesseans: As the 1996 National Football League season approaches, I wanted to take a moment to say thank you for all your efforts in bringing the NFL to your fine state ... A lot of time has passed since that thrilling evening on May 7, but I want you to know that the emotions felt that day are indelibly imprinted in my memory.

"When we began discussions a little over a year ago to bring the Oiler franchise to Tennessee, I have to honestly say that there were some doubts in my mind. You don't create a franchise and spend 36 years in a city without investing quite a bit of emotion. However, from day one, Tennesseans have exhibited a heretofore unseen amount of enthusiasm for our team that reinforces in my mind daily that we made the right decision. From suite sales to the PSL campaign to legislative victories, Tennesseans have answered with a resounding affirmative when asked 'Are you ready for some football?'

"While the victories achieved may have a bittersweet taste as we play out our lease in Houston, do not think for a minute that we are not working daily to prepare for our arrival. We cannot wait to set foot on Tennessee soil and are very proud that soon we will be your neighbors ... As you watch your team charge toward the playoffs this fall and construction begins on the banks of the Cumberland, give yourself a well-deserved pat on the back because you have achieved what very few before you have even dared attempt. Thank you again."

GM Floyd Reese

1996 TRAINING CAMP

Up until the last minute, the Oilers were prepared to bolt for Tennessee for the 1996 season. Adams said, "As a lame-duck team, I would hope we could work something out to play somewhere in Tennessee. Memphis would be my preference. It would be a very excellent place to play." Behind the scenes, he had a training camp in Johnson City set up, as well as a practice site in Nashville and the Liberty Bowl in Memphis. But with Lanier & Co. refusing to let them out of the lease, they returned to San Antonio.

It was a new world in terms of media coverage. For decades, legions of Houston newspapermen, television reporters and radio commentators crawled all over every burp emanating from in or around Oilerville, in or out of the season. It was big business stoked by advertisers who knew there was no single better way to reach that target market. Coverage in the two competing newspapers (until '95 when the *Post* shut down) was nonstop.

Just like that, it fell off the earth. Almost no one showed for the draft or the minicamp. The final Oiler draft from Houston was an especially spartan affair, held in the remnants of an uncarpeted, abandoned gift shop in the empty APC. Fans were not invited.

They missed the slickest draft day maneuvering in team history. Houston had the No. 9 pick and wanted Ohio State RB Eddie George. With RBs Lawrence Phillips and Tim Biakabutuka going at Nos. 6 and 8, they were comfortable he would be available later and traded down for Oakland's first-, second- and fourth-round picks. The Raiders were desperate for TE Rickey Dudley and Reese took advantage. Then, sensing the Vikings might take George at No. 16, they traded veteran DT Glenn Montgomery to Seattle to move back up to No. 14. The net was that for moving down from No. 9 to No. 14, plus Montgomery, they received George plus extra second- and fourth-round choices.

George was the Oilers' fourth Heisman Trophy running back winner and became the NFL's offensive rookie of the year. The other picks were used on large OTs. Reese had clearly learned on the job.

Naturally, they could not get through the second round without a mistake. This year's was DE Bryant Mix. They recovered with Tennessee OT Jason Layman (Raiders). Other draftees included LB Terry Killens, DE

Kendrick Burton, OT Jon Runyan (Raiders), DB Anthony Dorsett (son of Tony) and RB Mike Archie.

They retained Cris Dishman ($3.06 million), but the stream of outgoing veterans continued. Despite leading the team in receptions, fan favorite Haywood Jeffires was released and signed with New Orleans. The nine-year veteran finished his Oiler career second all-time with 515 receptions. But familiarity tends to breed contempt. Ed Fowler noted that "Jeffires ran up glittering stats in the Run 'N' Shoot years, but he'll never be confused with Jerry Rice for making a play with the game on the line."

Ray Childress was released after 11 seasons, 75½ sacks and five Pro Bowls. Also gone were Gary Brown (waived before the draft), Rich Camarillo and Eddie Robinson (to Carolina). Later in the summer, Glenn Montgomery (Seattle trade) was diagnosed with amyotrophic lateral sclerosis, or Lou Gehrig's disease, for which there is no cure.

Those moves almost completed the house cleaning. Only three from the '80s remained. Thirty-five-year-old Bruce Matthews ('83, 1st round) was only three years younger than the head coach. The others were Smith ('87, 6th) and Dishman ('88, 5th).

They added free agents WR Willie Davis and RB Ronnie Harmon. The defense picked up DT/DE Robert Young for a conditional draft choice.

Camp under Fisher continued to be quiet. Some of the only news coming out involved discipline. Twice in one week, he kicked players off the team. First, special teams demon John Henry Mills was fined and booted out of practice for one day for violating curfew. That was followed by the suspension of CB Tomur Barnes, who had a lackadaisical attitude highlighted by habitual lateness. "I had to take some disciplinary action with Tomur because he's been consistently late to team meetings and functions," said Fisher. "I felt it got out of hand and started to affect his teammates." The love-hate relationship between coach and talented but underachieving defensive back would continue for some time.

The players said they were ready. "The last couple of years, it was a lack of talent, and a lack of confidence," said Dishman. "When we got down early, we didn't believe we could come back. Now we're getting the talent back and we're getting the confidence back. We've got new players in here that everybody believes in."

Chandler returned as the No. 1 QB. After the fiasco following the Pittsburgh game and the attention lavished upon McNair, the sensitive Chandler had asked to be traded. But McNair was not ready. Chandler said, "It won't be the end of the world if he has to sit a few years." Self-described "country boy" McNair tried to stay out of the fray, but was now the No. 2 QB.

They were excited about the backfield of George, Thomas and Harmon. With first-round money invested in George, he obviously soon displaced Thomas. To his credit, Rodney was a good sport about the demotion. At WR, they hoped Davis and Sanders would stretch defenses, opening it up for the running game.

"If we do anything," Fisher said, "we're going to run the ball. We're going to line up and run it. That's our objective." Noting a 3.5 yards per carry average in 1995, Fisher said they expected nothing less than 4.0 in 1996. He added, "There are reasons for that average. We were in our first year in the system. It was the first year when the linemen were required to fire off the ball and knock people back after being in the Run 'N' Shoot for so long."

Underappreciated Frank Wycheck returned at H-back. The strength of the OL was up the middle with OGs Matthews and Donnalley and C Stepnoski. The OTs were Hopkins, who was looking at a contract year, and 35-year-old Irv Eatman.

The strength of the defense was the secondary with Lewis, Bishop, Robertson (coming off knee surgery) and Dishman, who said, "I don't think we're one of the best; I think we are the best. I'm not being arrogant about it, just confident." There was more turnover at LB with the departure of Robinson and the return of Smith. The versatile Barrow played ROLB as well as rush end in some situations. Bowden was the LOLB.

The line was young and lacked quality depth. When camp opened, they switched Gary Walker ('95, 5th round) and Anthony Cook ('95, 2nd) around at LE and LT. Robert Young ('91, 5th by the Rams) was inserted at RT and Henry Ford ('94, 1st) was back at RE. By the time camp broke, Cook was back at LE, Walker at LT, Ford at RT and Young at RE. The backups were the undrafted Josh Evans, rookie project Bryant Mix, Kanavis McGhee ('91, 2nd by the Giants), Kendrick Burton ('96, 4th) and World League pickup James Roberson, who would eventually take over from Young as the starter at RE.

The one question regularly thrown at players, coaches and management was how they would react to the expected low turnouts. Predictions were that they would be below the '95 average of 36,107, which was the lowest since '74. Some thought the all-time low of 20,019, set in their inaugural season of 1960, was within reach. Fisher maintained a steady public demeanor, saying that if they won and competed for the playoffs, attendance would increase.

Somebody chased down Bum Phillips for his reaction. Bum had moved further out to Goliad, Texas, which he said was so far out in the sticks that, "We don't get 'Saturday Night Live' until Tuesday." He said, "So I hear it on the news that the *Houston* Oilers are moving to Nashville. That can't be right. The Oilers belong in

Houston. Nobody had fans better'n ours, or more loyal." He added, "People always used to ask me, 'How's the team? Can you beat the Steelers? Is so-and-so ready to play?' Now all they ask me is, 'Do you think it's gonna rain?'"

THE 1996 REGULAR SEASON — SWAN SONG

Attendance at the last two home openers had declined from 55,000 for Buffalo in '94 to 44,000 for Pittsburgh in '95. In 1996, it was about 28,000 for the Chiefs. Those that did show were reminded that penalties, sacks, blown opportunities and other goofs can lead to a loss.

Twice, the Oilers recovered fumbles deep in KC territory, but came away with little. The first gave them the ball at the KC 16. They lost a yard on three carries and settled for a FG. The second time gave them the ball at the KC 12. Three plays later, they had lost 3 yards and settled for another FG. Trailing 20-16 in the fourth quarter, they used 8 minutes to drive from their 23 to the Chiefs 9. Following two 2-yard runs and an incompletion, they again settled for the FG.

They got one last chance with the ball at the KC 34 in the closing minutes. Trailing 20-19, a first down or even five more yards would put them in comfortable Del Greco range. Not losing any yards would give him a shot at a 51-yarder. But on third-and-9, Donnalley was flagged for illegal procedure. On the next play, Russell was wide-open across the middle, but Chandler overthrew him. Del Greco then missed what would have been the game winner. It was vintage Oilers. "The game's over — that's what I was thinking," said Eatman. "All we have to do is go out and execute the basics and win this game."

In another blow, they lost Smith again. After surgery to repair a torn leg tendon, the Oilers had to decide whether to hold a spot for him. They decided he could not come back and put him on the IR. It was a bad call. He was replaced by Barron Wortham ('94, 6th).

Eddie George arrived the next week with 143 yards as they beat the improving Jaguars 34-27. That was followed by a 29-13 mauling of the Ravens which left them with a winning record.

Next up were a bye week and then a tough stretch of five-of-seven on the road starting with Pittsburgh, to whom they had lost four straight. They caught them at a good time with Greg Lloyd, Kevin Greene, Ray Seals, Neil O'Donnell, Leon Searcy and Ernie Mills all out. But that was too much good fortune to overcome.

They started with a fumble, a fumble and a blocked FG attempt. In the second quarter, Robertson got into a fight with QB Mike Tomczak and was ejected. The Pittsburgh crowd, decidedly anti-Tomczak until that moment, chanted his name the rest of the game. Houston lost 30-16. Afterwards, Dishman called Chad Brown and Jerry Olsavsky "bums" and claimed neither could make the Oilers' roster but they might be able to make the practice squad.

They came home 4-2, however, after winning at Cincinnati (30-27 OT) and at Atlanta (23-13). Next up were the last two premiere home games in the Dome: the Steelers and 49ers. Adams hoped for 25,000 for Pittsburgh and 30,000 for San Francisco.

They surprised the Steelers and perhaps themselves, winning 23-13 before 50,337. It was one last magic in the Dome with the emotion, screaming and cheering of a different day. The most dramatic moment came with

Ohio State's Eddie George was the Oilers' fourth Heisman Trophy winner at running back. The 6'3, 238-pound bruiser was the third RB taken in the first round, but had the best season by-far with 1,368 yards (4.1 per carry) and 8 TDs. He was named rookie-of-the-year and made the UP All-Pro Team. Still, he seemed to tire towards the end of the season, which may have kept the Oilers out of the playoffs. Photo © The Associated Press.

five minutes left when Willie Davis beat a hobbled Rod Woodson on a hitch-and-go for a 34-yard TD.

Suddenly, the Oilers were 5-2 and tied for first. Fisher garnered national attention for keeping his team "focused," and also for the swarming sea of blue in the Astrodome. And so it was time to expect the worst. The next two would be masterpieces.

The 49ers drew the largest crowd of the season at 53,664. It started off great. When Barrow knocked Steve Young out of the game with a concussion, he was replaced by third-stringer Jeff Brohm, who had thrown four passes his entire NFL career. Initially, the undrafted free agent looked the part as the mighty 49er offense had just 154 yards midway through the fourth quarter. Unfortunately, the Oilers sputtered, too. Until he left in the third quarter with a re-aggravated groin, Chandler was 7-of-18 for 57 yards, including an 0-for-6 start. That left it up to Air McNair, who came on in the middle of a drive that ended in a field goal and a 9-3 lead.

With about nine minutes left, the Oilers faced third-and-two at the San Francisco 30. Needing a FG to clinch, McNair took a deep drop for a pass, but was flattened by Chris Doleman for a 10-yard loss. Fisher had to either punt or try a 57-yard FG. Although Del Greco kicked a team-record 56-yarder earlier in the game, the decision to punt seemed prudent in light of the way the defense had dominated.

Brohm took over at his 18 with 8:44 left. First, he caught the Oilers in a blitz with a screen that went for 49 yards to the Oiler 33. It was their first big play of the game and seemed to light a fire. With a third-and-seven from the 20, Brohm found rookie Terrell Owens for their only TD. Houston had two more possessions, but McNair could not get it done. Like they had done before with such players as Mike Tomczak, Bubby Brister and Don Strock, they provided the fodder for Brohm's 15-minutes of fame.

Seattle then left them sleepless. With McNair laboring under an extremely restrictive game plan, they managed a 16-16 tie through the fourth quarter. As the closing seconds ticked away, Del Greco lined up for the game, winning a 37-yard chip-shot field goal. But Michael McCrary stepped into a small crease between Stepnoski and Donnalley and blocked it. He then had the presence of mind to flip the ball to Robert Blackmon, who rumbled all the way for the winning TD with no time left.

It was one of the Oilers' most inventive ways yet of manufacturing a loss against all odds. "I think you've seen it all now," said Chandler. Matthews, who had lived through more strange losses than he wanted to remember, said it was even a new one for him. "To go from winning to losing in that amount of time is shocking," said the 14-year guard. "We have the best kicker in the league. You knew he was going to make it. Such a turnaround is just unbelievable." They were 5-4 and a full two games behind Pittsburgh in the Central.

After recovering to beat New Orleans, they hosted Miami and Jimmy Johnson. They made it look easy, scoring TDs on their first two possessions to lead 14-0 before an enthusiastic crowd of 47,358. But they could not hold and lost 23-20 on a FG as time expired.

The string of collapses reminded Houstonians why no one fought to keep them. Only 20,107 showed up to watch them lay down 31-6 to Carolina. It was their worst loss since October, 1993. After the 5-2 start, they had stumbled to 6-6 and looked whipped.

But after beating the Jets 35-10, they still had a shot at the playoffs with back-to-back home games against Jacksonville and Cincinnati followed by the closer at Baltimore. All three teams had losing records. All the Oilers had to do was win 2-of-3 and they were in.

With Chandler pouting on the sidelines and McNair turning the ball over, they fell to the Jags 23-17 in an uninspiring effort before 20,196. At 7-7, the could still make the playoffs if they won out. Under the pressure,

Chris Chandler returned for his second season, but still had the same conservative scheme, and worse yet, the same level of pass protection. With Steve McNair waiting in the wings and some lingering resentment among his teammates, his days were numbered. Nonetheless, Chandler improved as a quarterback in Houston under the tutelage of Jerry Rhome.

The Love Ya Blue magic returned to the Astrodome for one last time on October 20, 1996. The Oilers' 23-13 victory over the Steelers left them at 5-2 and in first place.

Fisher made a somewhat fateful decision to start Chandler against Cincinnati. Near the end of the half, he lost a fumble. In the second half, he threw 3 straight interceptions in his last three passes as an Oiler. They lost 21-13. In one of those perfect moments that money cannot buy, umpire Neil Gereb ralphed all over the AstroTurf after Chandler's last pick and as the Bengals were driving for the clincher. It seemed a fitting commentary on the Oilers' last game in Houston. The 15,131 paid was the smallest home crowd ever for an Oiler game, including Jeppesen Stadium.

With all the pressure off, they slipped by the disorganized Ravens 24-21 to pull to 8-8. Pittsburgh won the division at 10-6 while Jacksonville finished 9-7. The other AFC wildcard teams were Buffalo (10-6) and Indianapolis (9-7).

The 1996 playoffs had an Oiler flair. Jacksonville had OC Kevin Gilbride, as well as Eddie Robinson and Le'Shai Maston. AFC champion New England had former coach Chris Palmer as QB coach. Carolina, who made the NFC Championship, had Lamar Lathon. Green Bay, the eventual Super Bowl champ, had Sean Jones, Chief Financial Officer Mike Reinfeldt, Pro Personnel Director Ted Thompson and Equipment Manager Gordon Batty.

An Oiler fan could not help but think back to 1993 and the conflicts between Buddy Ryan and Gilbride. The Jones, Lathon and Robinson sightings were a quick reminder of just how stacked Ryan's defense was that year.

For Gilbride, it was sweet revenge. With Mark Brunnell at the helm, his offense took the Jags, who finished 4-12 in 1995 with the No. 28 ranked offense, to a 9-7 record and the playoffs. Once in, they shredded former AFC champions, Buffalo and Denver, on the road in the cold. As a result, Gilbride was named head coach of the Chargers in 1997 just two seasons after being fired by the Oilers. Jacksonville then hired his old WR coach Palmer to replace him.

OVERVIEW

The season peaked October 20 with the 23-13 victory over the Steelers before a boisterous home crowd. They stumbled 3-6 the rest of the way and missed the playoffs for the third consecutive season. The most painful losses were the 1-point home loss to KC, the 3-point home loss to Miami in OT and the 6-point home loss to Jacksonville that cost them the playoffs. But clearly the San Francisco and Seattle games took the cake, slapping what little sentimentality may have been left from the remaining group of loyal fans.

On the high side, they did have a winning record away from the Dome, an unusual claim for a Houston

Steve McNair made the most of the playing time he got in 1996 (parts of 9 games) to complete 61.5% of his passes for 1,197 yards. He also ran for 169 more (5.5 per carry). His QB rating was a healthy 90.6. It was enough to convince the coaches that he would be ready to start in 1997 even though most of his performances came in non-pressure situations.

team. They finished 6-2 to tie San Francisco for the best road record.

The talk of the offense was rookie Eddie George, who rushed for 1,368 yards to join Tolar, Granger, Campbell, Rozier, White and Brown on the club's list of 1,000-yard rushers. He finished fifth in the NFL to win offensive rookie-of-the-year laurels. A classy guy, he gave his top eight linemen Rolex watches as a thanks. As great as it was, his performance tailed off late. Only once in the last 10 games did he have over 100 yards, and he did not seem the same after the 5-2 start. With the ground game gasping, the passing attack suffered. After averaging 26 points in the first seven games, they averaged 19 over the final nine.

The offense ranked No. 18 overall (6th rushing and 21st passing) as Chandler seemed to lose his touch. He finished 184-of-320 (57.5%) for 2,099 yards with 16 TDs, 11 interceptions and 8 fumbles. His QB rating was 79.7. Steve McNair, with 4 starts, went 88-of-143 (61.5%) for 1,197 yards, 6 TDs, 4 interceptions and 7 fumbles. His rating was 90.6 and he also had 169 yards rushing (5.5 yard average).

Free agent acquisition Davis had just 39 catches for 464 yards and 6 TDs. Second-year player Sanders improved his catch total to 48 for 882 yards and 13 TDs. While his yards per catch average dropped from 23.5 to 18.4, it was still good enough to again lead the AFC. Derek Russell caught 34 for 421 yards while Ronnie Harmon added 42 for 488 yards. H-back Frank Wycheck's 53 receptions led the team.

The blame for the shortcomings fell to Jerry Rhome, who again battled with Fisher over use of the one-back set. When George did have a lead blocker, it was sometimes Harmon who no one mistook for a FB. The frustration of the season was epitomized by his fourth-quarter call on third-and-two from the 49er 30. With a chance to put the game away with a FG, he had the inexperienced McNair take a 7-step drop. He was sacked, pushing them out of FG range as the 49ers went the other way for the winning points.

The defense finished No. 6 in the league on the heels of their No. 5 place ranking in '95. The rush defense ranked No. 2 in the NFL as the move to DT of former first-rounder Ford, a disappointment at end, paid off. The pass defense was No. 8. They had two Achilles heels. First, they gave up the occasional big play which resulted in their No. 18 place finish as a scoring defense. The other was the pass rush. The linemen accounted for only 22 sacks. Free agent Robert Young, the '96 version of Kenny Davidson, contributed just 4 sacks in his only season with the Oilers.

Mel Gray became the first Oiler to break the 1,000-yard mark in kickoff returns in two separate seasons. John Henry "Skills" Mills made the Pro Bowl as a special-teams player

BUD'S TAKE

Adams claimed he lost $12 million, but such losses were factored into the Nashville deal. "We averaged 31,000 for our home games," he said, "and that's pretty close to what I projected [he predicted of 25,000 to 30,000]. The attendance would have been better if we kept winning, but not much better. I understand how the fans feel. This is no longer their team. The Oilers are leaving town, so they could care less. I accept that.

"From 1987 to 1993 we were the only team in the NFL to make the playoffs seven straight seasons. In the 10 years from '86 to '95, we had the fourth-best record in the league. If we had made it to the Super Bowl one time, people wouldn't keep harping on it. I think the perceptions of our organization would have been different."

About the upcoming move, he said, "I didn't want to leave, but I didn't go to Nashville and try to use that to play off against Houston. This team has been a big part of my life. It's more of a business than it was in the early years. But it's still a fun business."

CHAPTER 11

THE SHORT LIFE OF THE TENNESSEE OILERS 1997-98

The cumulative 37-year record of the Houston Oilers was 251-291-6 (.463). They won the AFL Championship twice (1960-61) and made the playoffs five times in the ten years of that league. From the merger, they were 181-225-2 (.446). In the 27 seasons they were in the AFC Central Division, the Oilers won the divisional title outright two times. They made the playoffs ten times and advanced to the AFC championship twice, but never appeared in a Super Bowl. Their post-merger playoff record was 7-10.

1997: REQUIEM FOR THE MEMPHIS OILERS

The 1997 season would prove to be anticlimactic. The most pressing item for Adams and management was where the team would be playing. Meanwhile, the head coach and general manager had to put that aside to deal with changes to the coaching staff and player personnel. The coach put pressure on himself by predicting they would challenge Pittsburgh for the AFC Central.

COACHING CHANGES

Immediately after the close of the season, Jeff Fisher fired OC Jerry Rhome and replaced him with WRs coach Les Steckel. Fisher sighted "philosophical differences," which were (1) the overall scheme in terms of pass vs. run and who made that call; and (2) who should start at QB.

Fisher clearly wanted to pound the ball, making his stable of RBs the team strength. Rhome, a former QB, preferred a wide-open passing game that often employed four WRs. Moreover, even as he groomed Steve McNair, his confidence in Chris Chandler, who he coached in Phoenix, never wavered. The stalemate resulted in some bad play calling and a struggle to score TDs. Rhome was surprised, but recovered to end up in St. Louis with Dick Vermeil.

Likewise, there was a revolution on the defensive side, although Fisher accomplished this change in a different manner. He promoted Gregg Williams, 38, to DC and Sidwell to assistant head coach. Sidwell then left for New England. Insiders said Williams, who had been with the Oilers longer than any other coach, was already the de facto coordinator. It was Williams who taught the "46" defense to Sidwell when he arrived from New Orleans in 1995.

THE 1997 DRAFT AND FREE AGENCY

"The best thing about free agency this year is that we have fewer unrestricted players than we've ever had," came the comments from GM Floyd Reese. But the reason they had the fewest in the league (Dishman, Barrow, Bishop, Hopkins, Jackson, Mills) was because everyone else had already left. It also understated the significance of the ones they did lose.

Dishman went to Washington ($2 million), Mills to Oakland (for the minimum) and Barrow to Carolina ($18.75 million/5 years). They cut DL Robert Young. Chris Chandler was sent to Atlanta for fourth- and sixth-round picks, officially beginning the Steve McNair era. McNair said, "Chris and I had our differences. He was really into himself. I wish him good luck in Atlanta. It (trade) should benefit both of us."

They kept Bishop (franchise player at $2.42 million) and re-signed Hopkins ($16.8 million/5 years), but failed in the open market. After making a run at LB Chad Brown and WR Michael Jackson, they ended up with only OLB Lonnie Marts ($6.4 million/4 years). They had a chance to sign aged rush end Richard Dent, but passed. Ditto for Rod Woodson and Warren Moon, who was interested. They went with 38-year-old Dave Krieg as McNair's backup.

Considering all the money Adams obtained from Nashville and the raised cap figure of $40.95 million, their performance was abysmal, as it had been going back to Plan B. It was enough for *The Sporting News* to rate them No. 30 (out of 30) in terms of "improvement during the offseason."

Letting Dish go created the most problems. The Oilers intercepted only 12 passes in 16 games in '96. While he was not great at run support, he was their best cover corner. They did not make him an offer. Reese and Fisher both said the defense would be fine. That meant they had to find help in the draft or from Steve Jackson, Tomur Barnes and Anthony Dorsett.

They went into their last draft as the Houston Oilers with the No. 13 pick. The CB they needed was Texas' Bryant Westbrook, a physical player who fit their scheme. However, they would have had to trade up to get him. Since they rarely added free agents, draft picks were too valuable to let go of. Plus, they were convinced it was a deep draft for cornerbacks.

They would come to regret it, because there was a run on CBs that left them with their pants down. It started with Shawn Springs at No. 3 overall and Westbrook at No. 5. Then Arizona took Tom Knight at No. 9 and Atlanta grabbed Michael Booker at No. 11.

The men in the cramped, secretive Oiler war room on the second floor of their Bellevue headquarters were unhappily surprised. They back-pedaled and quickly traded down, sending their first and fourth to KC for their first- (No. 18), third- and sixth-round picks. At least Fisher was honest. He said, "We have obvious needs and we were a little surprised that Knight and Booker both went before our pick. We didn't take a corner in the first two rounds because there was a group of them we figured we could choose from in the third round."

They took DE Kenny Holmes. "After last season, I told you guys our No. 1 priority was to get a pass-rushing end, and we did that today ... Kenny's a first-class guy who already has his degree, and he fits our system because he can do so many things on the right side. We ask our ends to slide down and slug it out against the run, and he can do that." Line coach Rex Norris added, "We look for Holmes to step up and contribute right away." Scout Glenn Cumbee said, "If you're going to rush the passer, you've got to have speed. In a workout for us, he ran in the 4.6's. He weighs 270 now. I think he can eventually get up to 280 and not lose quickness."

Their credibility was called into question in the second round with WR Joey Kent (6'1, 186) from the University of Tennessee where he was Peyton Manning's favorite target. It was the second straight year they used a second-round pick on a Vol. Fisher said, "He's a receiver who fits our offense because he can play all three positions." But poor Joey would suffer from the hex on Oiler second-round picks.

They could have saved the pandering until the third when Kent likely would have still been waiting for a phone call. In the interim, there was another run on DBs in the second and third rounds. A total of 10 DBs went in between Holmes and their third-round choice.

Jeff Fisher

In the third, they took LSU corner Denard Walker (6-1, 186), a JUCO transfer who had good size but also a reputation for not playing up to his potential. Also in the third, they chose Washington State OT Scott Sanderson (6'6, 290). He made it three tackles in rounds 2-4 of the last two drafts, joining Layman and Runyan. He was originally ranked higher, but his stock fell after unimpressive performances at the combine and in an all-star game. Others included WR Derrick Mason, DT Pratt Lyons, Baylor CB George McCullough, LB Dennis Stallings and LB Armon Williams.

OUT OF HOUSTON

The big issue to be addressed in the offseason was venue. Neither Adams nor the NFL nor most Houstonians wanted the Oilers to remain. Nonetheless, the move took several more months.

The first movement came in February when Harris County accepted $5.25 million, including the team's old practice facility (purportedly valued at $1.5 million).

Next was McLane, who wanted $1 million plus dismissal of the $2.5 million lawsuit still pending over the canceled game. He got a reported $350,000 in May.

That left Lanier who wanted $500,000 in legal fees. There was still bad blood on both sides. In 1996, Adams had vowed that he distrusted the mayor so much he would not speak to him as long as he remained in office. He added, "I'm not going to pay people just to throw money away. Cleveland paid $3 million a year to get out of their deal, and the Rams paid $2 million a year. We're already at almost $6 million (for one year)." He then offered $50,000, but only if it was spent on "library books." Lanier responded that he would accept a deal covering the attorney fees and would throw in a free library card. Later in May, Houston got $250,000.

Lanier attempted to exit from the situation gracefully, saying, "If the Astros are satisfied that they've got what's coming to them, I'm satisfied because they're the ones who had the lease with the Oilers and they're the ones who had the dispute over this canceled game." Bud said, "We're not going to discuss the terms right now. It's all been settled. It is a matter of getting the paperwork done now. It's a great sunny day. We're looking forward to getting the show on the road."

A SHORT GOOD-BYE

The last practice of the Houston Oilers in Houston occurred June 12 at the conclusion of mini camp. The Plaza del Oro training facility off El Camino that the county was about to take over was the worst such facility in football and had been for a very long time.

One of the veterans hanging around afterwards was Bruce Matthews. "I've got a lot of fond memories of the years I've spent at this place," said the Pro Bowl guard who had spent his entire 14-year career with Houston. "When some guys would sign with other teams, they'd tell me how nice their facilities were and what a dump this place is. But you know what? I've grown to kind of like this place. It may be a dump, but it's been my dump."

Matthews added, "A lot of the younger players are excited about going to Tennessee, but to tell you the truth, I haven't felt that excitement yet. I'm a Houston Oiler, and no matter how many years I play in Tennessee, I'll always be a Houston Oiler ... When my career's over and I move back to Houston, there'll be an emptiness. I always dreamed of being able to watch the Oilers in the Astrodome after my career ended. As a Houstonian, I always thought I'd be able to follow the team. After a while, nobody here's going to give a rat's you-know-what about the Tennessee Oilers. I want a team in Houston. I don't enjoy hearing about the Cowboys. Unfortunately, I'm afraid that's who we're going to hear about."

Marcus Robertson said, "It's really, really sad. I'm kind of numb. I'm still having a hard time believing it ... When I came here, Houston was on fire for the Oilers. I'm so thankful I got a chance to experience it ... I like to tell the young guys what it was like. Every game was a blast. Football was fun. We expected to win every week. We didn't worry about reaching the playoffs. That was a given. Our goal was to reach the Super Bowl ... When I look back over my career, I think about teammates like Warren Moon, Sean Jones, Cris Dishman, William Fuller and Ray Childress. We were so talented. I just can't believe that a city like Houston, a city that used to go crazy about us, isn't going to have an NFL team. It's insane."

Offensive line assistant and 12-year Oiler veteran Mike Munchak said, "It's sad because the nucleus of this team doesn't know what it was like to play in the Astrodome when things were going well. They didn't see how great a pro-football city Houston was and will be again someday. They got a taste of it last year when we averaged over 50,000 for three straight home games. When we started losing, the crowds dwindled. If we had continued to win, there's no doubt in my mind the fans would have kept coming.

"I'm going to miss the history of being a Houston Oiler," said Munch. "I've always liked it when old Oilers like Elvin Bethea would come by the facility and watch practice awhile ... I was here for the rebuilding after Love Ya Blue, and we had great crowds even when we were struggling. Through the years, guys across the league would say the Astrodome was the place they dreaded playing the most. Offensive linemen told me they couldn't hear the snap count because of the noise. The crowd helped us win a lot of games."

Daryll Lewis said, "It's a shame it came to this. I feel like the leaders of Houston let us down by not doing more to try to keep us. Looking back, it could have been handled so much better. I think a lot of people are hurt by the team leaving. Let me tell you, there was no greater feeling than to play before 60,000 fans in the House of Pain."

Management, of course, had a different spin. "I didn't lose any sleep over it," said Executive Vice President Mike McClure. Floyd Reese said at the groundbreaking in Nashville, "To get anyplace where the people want us will be great."

Fisher was more diplomatic. "That's the side that's sometimes neglected," he said. "The people a franchise location affects the most is the fans. In September, Houston will realize this team is gone, and I feel bad for those fans who were very, very loyal to us."

BIMBO ERUPTIONS

Bud Adams sort of snuck up on Tennessee. Things happened fast. The negotiations between Adams and Nashville were over in about 90 days. Then came the announcement they were out of the last year of their lease and would start play in Tennessee in 1997.

Tennesseans began to get an idea about Bud with his inconsistent comments about the Houston stadium vote. He seemed bitter. Instead of just disappearing from the Houston scene, something he knew how to do, he lowered himself further into the conflict. A month before the baseball stadium referendum, he said he supported it. Then, just before election day, he changed his mind. "Lanier has been working pretty hard on it," he said. "He and Eckels have some problems. They got themselves in hot water. It's a very loosely written referendum. They talk about not using tax money, but I don't believe it. It's such a screwed-up mess. I don't vote for screwed-up messes, I can tell you that. Lanier and Eckels should stay out of it. Let the commissioners handle it. Maybe Elyse (Lanier's wife) could do a better job."

When the proposition passed, he said, "I started the fire and got burned. Now, others are cooking the steaks."

For awhile, he calmed down. In December 1996, during the lease negotiations, he said Lanier asked him if there was anything that could be done to keep the Oilers from leaving. "I told the mayor it was too late," he said. "Our deal is done. But I would try to be helpful in getting a new NFL team for the Dome."

But the thought that McLane and Alexander would get new stadiums with Lanier's assistance was a bit much. At the NFL meetings in January, he went off again. Posturing for the cameras, he snorted, "Hey, Drayton, I've got a deal for you. Hey, Les, I've got a deal for you."

In a telephone interview with a Houston sportscaster, he said, "You know, if they don't want us here, I accept that. We're going to leave and you helped us leave. I'm not criticizing y'all. You have to look after yourself. We have to look after ourselves. We would like to stay here, don't get me wrong. I'd love to stay in Houston. It's not in the cards. You've said, 'Get rid of Bud.' Well, we're going to leave ... Everyone hates Bud, I have heard before on the program. Why does everyone hate Bud? What have I done?"

He added in another interview, "Two years ago, I spoke to Mayor Lanier, and I told him I'd sign a 30-year lease if we got a new stadium, but he didn't want to listen, so we made a deal with Nashville. I offered to keep the team here. He didn't want to hear it. You'll have to ask Lanier about that, and if he doesn't have anything to say about it, ask his wife, Elyse. She usually has a lot to say."

When asked what he would do over, Bud replied, "I'd let Drayton go first. Then he'd be the one moving and I'd be the one getting a new stadium."

While these comments did not play well in Nashville, they were dismissible since the deal was done. But then Bud's erratic behavior and lack of PR savvy began hitting a little closer to home. He put them on notice in March 1997, when he started doing an about-face regarding the promised change of the team name. Waxing nostalgic, Bud said, "That's been a big part of my life, and I don't want to throw it away."

Photo © The Associated Press.

Next, he demanded Nashville cut his annual rent on the new stadium from $1 million to $362,000. The basis for this request was that the city was no longer going to have to build a practice field near the East Bank stadium, as originally contemplated. Instead, the Oilers reached an agreement to put a practice facility in Bellevue, west of Nashville.

Mayor Phil Bredesen supported Adams before the city council which had to approve the change. "This is not giving Bud any more," he said. "'This is simply honoring our contract." Actually, the new terms and tax breaks would save Bud about $19 million over 30 years. In addition, the new rent was only $111,000 more than Tennessee State had to pay to use the same stadium for fewer games.

There was also the matter of the $25 million relocation fee payable to the NFL. This one caught most people by surprise, even though the NFL imposed it in other franchise moves. Byron Trauger, a Nashville lawyer who worked on the deal, offered the excuse: "It was not spelled out on a separate line item as 'NFL relocation fee,' because we didn't want to suggest to the NFL that they impose a relocation fee." Nashville ended up eating about 80% of it.

Then came another classic Oiler amateur hour. In June, the team held a news conference in Nashville to announce their arrival and reveal a new logo. With reporters held out of the room, they put the logo on a wall and then concealed it behind a black curtain. They then let the media in while Adams, management and some players were sequestered in another room. Before they made their dramatic entrance, the curtain dropped to the ground, revealing the logo. A few seconds later, the duct tape holding the logo to the wall began to peel and it soon joined the curtain in a heap on the floor. The big event was over before Bud came out.

The biggest screwup in their first year in Tennessee, however, was the decision on where to play. With the University of Tennessee's 106,000-seat Neyland Stadium at Knoxville an unrealistic option, they could and should have secured Vanderbilt's 41,000-seat stadium in Nashville (expandable to 52,000 with temporary seating). But they blew it.

The Oilers did not like the capacity, lack of luxury suites and artificial surface. McClure bluntly said that if they wanted the Oilers, they not only had to increase capacity but also Vanderbilt would have to pay for it. This stance made few new friends. Vandy AD Todd Turner said, "Mike made it very clear to us if we didn't add the seats our stadium would be inadequate. We weren't going to add the seats ourselves, and we left it at that."

McClure told Bud not to worry. He promised they would get 55,000 at the Liberty Bowl. Adams might have wished he had asked whether he meant average or total for the season.

BUD AND MEMPHIS

The 62,200-seat Liberty Bowl in Memphis was the only other suitable stadium in the state. The Oilers approached the situation with their usual zeal. The controversy began soon after an agreement was reached with the Shelby County Sports Authority.

The first item up was the travel expenses clause. Even though the Oilers were scheduled to play two years in Memphis, they would live and practice in Nashville. That meant they had to travel 200 miles for their "home" games. Memphis agreed to pay the travel costs estimated at about $300,000 annually. The idea was to pay the expenses from a sales tax rebate on game-day revenues to the sports authority. But this plan, as they would soon see, was flawed.

Other terms were equally one-sided. The Oilers got game-day parking, concessions, luxury suite sales and merchandise sales. The commission got $1 per ticket. It cost $30,000 to operate the stadium on game days. Thus, any crowd under 30,000 created a deficit that had to come out of the general fund.

No one was amused when season ticket and luxury suites sales got off to a very slow start. Attendance at preseason games was dismal. In one exhibition game in Memphis and two in Nashville, the Oilers averaged 22,980. They lost all three.

McClure's excuse was timing. "There's no question the late start hurt," he said. "We had hoped to get the green light in February, and when it didn't happen, we had to do in 75 days what would normally take six to eight months. People reacted as quick as they could. It's been the ultimate challenge for everyone."

There were logistical problems. For example, the Oilers gave out their new Memphis telephone numbers for season ticket sales at the June press conference. However, the telephone lines had not even been installed and would not be for several weeks. Calls were routed to the Nashville office where they were handled by a single secretary. Potential buyers got sick of being put on hold long distance and gave up in frustration.

They looked to the players to act as goodwill ambassadors, but even this failed as Anthony Cook and Josh Evans did not make scheduled promotional appearances at a Memphis restaurant and middle school. Rookie-of-the year Eddie George missed a scheduled appearance to accept a key to the city from Mayor Hereton. A team spokesman called it a "personal matter."

Rip Scherer, head coach at the University of Memphis, did not care much for sharing his home field with the Oilers, who had control of the dressing rooms and press box. They also painted the trash cans and handrails Columbia blue. Taking aim at Bud, he said, "It's like you have a cousin staying with you and the cousin is fine, but it's the uncle back home that creates the problem." The school tried to profit from the situation creating the slogan, "Still the home team," which it plastered all over billboards and bus stops.

Even Adams became disgusted at the lack of progress. He went through three ticket managers in 1997. He eventually had to hire Memphis celebrity Pepper Rogers as vice president of his Memphis operations. The one-time head coach had also been the front man for Memphis' attempt to land an NFL expansion team.

Pepper said, "Since we got off to a late start, I don't think we're going to be real successful selling a lot of season tickets, but that doesn't mean we can't have 60,000 in the stands. We can handle a big walk-up crowd." Adams added, "I think things will pick up as we go along. The play of the Oilers will kind of determine how the fans like us. We'll just have to win them over."

That was wishful thinking. Had the Oilers performed any reasonable level of market research, they would have discovered that Memphis feels about Nashville the way Houston does about Dallas — probably worse. Memphis residents did not care for supporting a team from Nashville. Nor did they desire to support a lame-duck franchise for two seasons.

Furthermore, had they looked into it, they also would have learned how much latent resentment there was towards the NFL, which had spurned the city for over two decades. The people of Memphis were well aware Ad-

Blaine Bishop's strong 1994 led to a great 1995 and Pro Bowl berth, which led to a holdout in 1996 that hurt his team.

ams was on the NFL committee that awarded expansion franchises to Carolina and Jacksonville over Memphis. Now Nashville had a team and Memphis did not.

By late August, Bud had had enough. He demoted Mike McClure, architect of the move and something of a hero in Nashville. In a hushed reshuffling Don MacLachlan replaced McClure. The Oiler press release indicated McClure, who was given a marketing position, would "continue to provide input on non-football operations while focusing primarily on development of the club's new Nashville stadium and continuing his active role in community, city and governmental affairs."

BUD AND BIG BROTHER

These problems were not exactly what Adams had in mind when he left Houston. But it got worse. His brethren were also grumbling.

When they agreed to let the Oilers leave Houston, the other NFL owners insisted that Adams subsidize visiting teams so they would not be forced to take financial baths in the face of declining attendance. The agreement went back to games at the Astrodome and had a $5 million cap for Adams. For Memphis games, the Oilers would need about 28,000 to avoid paying anything out. Visitors were guaranteed $542,000 per game. The problem was that Adams had already paid visiting owners about $3.5 million. Thus, unless the games at the Liberty Bowl averaged over 28,000, some NFL teams were going to come up short later in the '97 season.

1997 TRAINING CAMP

Camp opened July 19 at Tennessee State outside downtown Nashville. Coach Fisher (16-22 career record) said, "When that plane left Houston, it was like one door shut and another opened. The hard part's over. We're here, and we know what our situation is. As far as playing in Memphis the next two years, I think we've proved over the last two years that we can deal with distractions pretty well."

With Jerry Rhome out of the way, he set his sights on establishing the Oilers as an aggressive running team featuring Eddie George. To do that, the highly compensated line had to perform. They saw the left side as a strength with Mark Stepnoski, Bruce Matthews and the improving Brad Hopkins at tackle. The right side was suspect with Donnalley and fourth-rounder Jon Runyan (6-7, 315) replacing the retired Irv Eatman.

Although they hoped this strategy would take the pressure off Steve McNair, it would not take advantage of his strengths, for which Adams was paying a lot. There were problems at WR with a moody Chris Sanders, a disappointing Willie Davis and rookie Joey Kent.

The departures of Dishman and Barrow hurt the defense. Of the two, the LB corps were in better shape due to the signing of free agent Lonnie Marts. They tried to move Bowden inside, but ended up sticking with two-year starter Wortham. With no free agent signings, CB was the glaring weakness. Both starters, Steve "Buffalo Bill" Jackson and Lewis were only 5'9 and more quick than fast. Considering the amount of man-to-man coverage the "46" required, combined with the lack of depth, it looked like it might be a long year. The secondary was further weakened through the long holdout of SS Bishop.

On the DL, right end was unsettled for the fourth straight year. Rookie Holmes would be given every chance to step up, but minimum-wage warrior James Roberson (6'3, 244) would get a lot of snaps. The other starters remained Cook (6'3, 293) at LE, Walker (6'2, 285) at LT and Ford (6'3, 284) at RT. The second team was Pratt Lyons (6'5, 295), Josh Evans (6'0, 280) and Bryant Mix (6'3, 301). Kendrick Burton had to sit out the year for violating NFL substance abuse policy.

Cris Dishman, perhaps stinging from not receiving an offer after nine seasons with the Oilers, said, "Some of the guys really want to say that they want to get out, a lot of them do. It's sad that they're stuck in that situation ... I've got a lot of friends on that team. I've got some coaches as friends, but they won't come out and say it." He added, "I'm in a better situation. The owner cares about the coach. The coach cares about his players. The owner cares about his players. And it makes camp exciting."

Also among the unhappy were the wives and families of players who had to rise before sunlight in order to make the 3½ hour bus ride for noon kickoffs. They got back from Sunday home games around midnight, not exactly the optimal situation for the children. The Oilers did provide an air-conditioned bus.

The players had to make the same bus trips but were saved by Steve McNair's mother, Lucile, who along with his wife and her mother, sometimes provided homemade fried chicken and sweet potato pies.

All things considered, the practice facility in Bellevue took the cake. The players and coaches not only assembled in trailers but had to tote their own portable goal posts. As hard as it may be to imagine an NFL facility without cable or satellite television, it was even more difficult to picture millionaires living in the Depression Era public-housing style dorm rooms. Union head Gene Upshaw called it "the worst in the league."

The prize was the practice field. Despite knowing they would be there for at least two seasons, the Oilers chose to save money by not installing a drainage system. When training camp broke, heavy rains turned the field into a muddy mosh pit. It not only made practices difficult, but risked injury to some very expensive players. It threw timing off, and prevented sharp cuts or full-speed drills. Some days, there was so much standing water that the coaches had to move practice next door to the parking lot of a shopping mall just to be able to perform walk-through drills.

HOUSTON: GOOD RIDDANCE

Just before the season started, the *Houston Chronicle* ran a survey to see how readers wanted it to cover the NFL in 1997. The response, via telephone, the Internet and electronic mail, was overwhelming. Over 30,000 people voted. The newspaper's previous best response in similar polls was 4,000.

Over 76% (3-to-1) voted that the Oilers should not be the primary focus of coverage. *Chronicle* writer Mickey Herskowitz wrote, "They made it painfully clear they don't want to be reminded in print of the team that was theirs for 37 years. They want the Oilers out of their lives, not simply out of town."

Dale Robertson wrote, "Financially speaking, Bud's going to get his whether we like it or not. He can't lose. But it's hard to stomach the thought of him being rewarded for his avarice — and complete disregard for a city that made him a huge sum of cash over the previous 37 years ... He never delivered here ... And Tennessee did nothing to deserve them except throw a lot of stupid public money Adams' way. Personally, I refuse to second-guess Houston's decision to say no to Bud. Because, what he wanted, *when* he wanted it, wasn't a swallowable deal. Period."

Fellow *Chronicle* staffer John McClain wrote, "Houston does not have a pro football team for the first time since 1959, and based on the preseason, some in Tennessee say they don't have one, either. Oilers fans who have managed to cut the cord will be spared the kind of anguish that used to cause heartburn and nausea on most Sunday afternoons."

Bum Phillips said, "When they left Texas, I quit thinking about 'em. I'm not interested in Tennessee. I'm interested in what's happening in Texas."

Long-time fan favorite Billy "White Shoes" Johnson was more sentimental. "It marks the end of an era," said the man who brought the Funky Chicken to football. "We were the Oilers of Houston, and a lot of us have fond memories of playing under the Oilers flagship. There's a lot of history there. To think of the team by another name ... "

THE 1997 REGULAR SEASON — MAYBE IT'S TIME FOR A PR FIRM

After two-and-one-third seasons, a pattern emerged. Jeff Fisher's teams would play the run tough while trying to win games by running over opponents. The offenses would be painfully conservative and in trouble if behind. In this regard, they would resemble Buddy Ryan's Eagles (1986-90) except the defense would not blitz or otherwise dominate. What fans they had were most interested in seeing how Air McNair would perform.

The Oilers opened their new lives in Tennessee still wearing their Houston colors and name. They beat the Raiders 24-21 in OT behind Eddie George's 106 yards. The story, however, was, and would continue to be, attendance. The Liberty Bowl was only half-full and many of those were wearing the silver-and-black which brought this one-of-a-kind response from Adams, "Everywhere you go there are Raiders fans. It's California, home of nuts and you know what? They follow them everywhere. That's OK. We'll take whatever we can get."

Meanwhile, in Houston, the sun came up on game day. True to their word, not many watched. The otherwise exciting game garnered a 7.5 Neilsen rating (16%) on KPRC in Houston. In Nashville (WSMV), the Oilers only drew only a 9.0 (20%). The game, naturally, was blacked out in Memphis. For comparison's sake, the Cowboy game drew a 33.6 in Dallas (63%).

The Oilers blew the next game in Miami as Del Greco missed a 43-yard field goal that would have won it with five seconds left. In OT, Tomur Barnes kicked a Miami WR, setting up the Dolphins for the game-winning field goal. Fisher said the next day that Barnes

It was Steve McNair's team as of 1997. Photo © The Associated Press.

would have "an MRI to see what's in his head." It was the fourth straight game in the series decided by four points or fewer, with the Dolphins winning them all.

Returning *home*, they collapsed 36-10 to the artists formally known as the Browns before an announced crowd of 17,737. Actual attendance was less. McNair called being able to hear fans' conversations in the stands "weird." On the same day, some 60,617 attended the Mid-South Fair next door; another 5,531 went to an exhibit showing items recovered from the Titanic; while about 10 miles away, another 3,000 visited the home of Elvis Presley.

Memphis replaced Houston as the butt of jokes with Jay Leno, David Letterman, radio man Don Imus, *Monday Night Football,* and of course ESPN. Kevin Kane, president of the Memphis Convention & Visitors Bureau, said, "This is a black eye for us. People are joking about us nationally. I think there's some long-term damage being done to our image here that people don't realize." More than perceptions were at stake. While the opening-day crowd just met expenses, the Ravens' game and the earlier exhibition match had cost Memphis about $20,000.

After the Steelers pounded them 37-24, they went to Seattle, scene of their biggest crime in 1996. This time they had the game in hand in the first half only to collapse in the second, letting third-string RB Steve Broussard go crazy with TD runs of 77 and 43 yards. Like many opponents, Broussard seemed to find himself against the Oilers. He said, "I haven't run like that since 10 years ago when I played at Washington State."

The 1-4 record was mostly on the defense and McNair. The defense had already given up 36 and 37 points in two losses after surrendering 30 points only twice in '96. The pass defense, without Dishman, fell into last place. McNair was the lowest-rated QB in the NFL. Against Seattle, he threw two interceptions to go with just 101 yards. That game would mark something of a turning point for him personally as he became more of a vocal leader, starting with criticism of his WRs for not going after the ball better on the interceptions.

They returned to beat the Bengals 30-7 before a new low of 17,071. Fisher used one of the unsold tickets as a motivation, saying, "This ticket belongs to somebody who's not going to make this game, and that's too bad. Someone out there is going to be missing a good football game." He also switched the defense to help the corners. Without blitzing, they sacked Jeff Blake six times while McNair came through with three TDs.

Meanwhile, the league started getting on Bud about attendance. He blamed it on the rivalry between Memphis and Nashville, claiming he did not realize "how much bad blood there is between" the two cities. He also admitted something Houstonians never thought they would hear. "I've never hired a PR firm in my 50 years in business, and maybe that was a mistake," he said. "I've never believed in it, or had a reason to do it before, but maybe it's time now."

They won their second in a row, dogging the overrated Redskins 28-14 before 31,042 spilt evenly between the two teams. For the second week, McNair had no interceptions. He had also become a serious threat to run. "I feel more comfortable in the system," he said, "and the more and more I feel comfortable with it, the more I can do."

After trashing the Cardinals 41-14 in Phoenix to ruin the pro debut of Jake "the Snake" Plummer, they were 4-4. But the streak came against some below-average opponents. When tested, they failed, losing to Jacksonville twice in three weeks sandwiched around a 10-6 win over the Giants (for the first time ever). With their playoff hopes sinking, they released veterans Mel Gray and Ronnie Harmon.

They moved back to .500 by clobbering the Bills 31-14. The defense held Buffalo to four yards rushing on the game. McNair ran for two TDs and threw for a third. Staring at a Thanksgiving Day meeting with the Cowboys in Dallas, he said, "From here on out, every game is do or die." Daryll Lewis added, "This is our biggest game since 1993. We really believe that if we can beat the Cowboys, it'll launch us toward the playoffs."

The few who watched loved what they saw as the Oilers jumped off to a 24-7 halftime lead off 3 turnovers. Riding George's 110 yards, they held on to win 27-14. Dallas fans booed as the loss knocked them out of the playoffs for the first time since 1990. "Yeah, I'm embarrassed," said Barry Switzer. "We should be embarrassed."

Suddenly, Oiler players had a strut in their walk and the playoffs were within reach. After starting the season 1-4, they had won six-of-eight to pull to 7-6 and within a game of Miami, New England and the Jets (all 8-5) for a wildcard berth that, with Cincinnati, Baltimore and Pittsburgh left, it seemed realistic. "We know what we have to do," said Lewis. "We have to win out, and Cincinnati's our next stepping stone ... We're not in the position to look ahead."

They not only looked ahead, but also managed to get themselves on the wrong side of another NFL record in the process. The Oilers lost 41-14 to a gimpy Boomer Esiason and the 4-9 Bengals. But the big story was rookie running back Corey Dillon.

Dillon rushed for 246 yards to break Jim Brown's 1957 rookie single game record of 237. He also set a club record with four TDs. Going into the game, the Oilers had the third-ranked defense against the run. By halftime, it was 28-0. They quit. George was held to 11 yards, his lowest total as a pro, by a defense that had allowed 922 yards in its two previous games. It was surprising that a Fisher-coached team could be so unprepared and unmotivated in such an important game.

Still reeling, they lost 21-19 to the Ravens/Browns. As another disappointing season drew to a close, there was more off-field controversy.

This time, it had nothing to do with pro football. The entire state was upset when Michigan defensive back Charles Woodson beat out Tennessee Volunteer QB Peyton Manning for the Heisman Trophy. The Oiler connection was Eddie George.

As a previous Heisman winner, he got to cast a vote. After the Ravens game, a reporter asked how he voted. He responded honestly. "Woodson," he said, unwittingly lowering himself into a firestorm. His vote was legit. Woodson single-handedly beat Ohio State, George's alma mater, and led Michigan to an undefeated season and No. 1 ranking. But some Volunteer fans said the vote was anti-southern or even racist. Governor Don Sundquist signed a petition protesting the vote, saying, "I think it stinks ... I think the Heisman award has been diminished ... It's a regional vote, and if anybody was better than Peyton, I'd like to know who it was. It's not this guy from Michigan." The NAACP, in turn, complained about the governor. For George's part, fans threatened to boycott the Oilers, just what they needed.

They still had one last meaningless game left. They beat the Steelers 16-6 despite Willie Davis dropping two wide-open bombs for sure TDs. The crowd of 50,677 was by far the largest of the season. But anyone there probably thought they were at Three Rivers as the throng of black and gold booed the Oilers mightily.

"How many teams in this league are outnumbered 2 to 1 in their home stadium by the opposing fans?" asked Hopkins. "That's ridiculous. We heard more boos in the Liberty Bowl than we did in Pittsburgh." Donnalley added, "It was chaotic. You try to focus on football solely, and then there's a new thing each week that kind of distracts you — and it's not football. It's not why you can't run the football. It's 'How about the fans?' or 'What's the nickname?' or any number of things you don't usually have to deal with."

The Steelers and Jaguars finished tied at 11-5. The Oilers were a distant second at 8-8 for the second consecutive year and out of the playoffs for the fourth straight. After four embarrassing Super Bowl performances, the Broncos finally won it. It was the first championship by an AFC team since the Raiders in 1983.

OVERVIEW

The season went into a tailspin in Miami during the second week and culminated with a humiliating second-half performance against Seattle. By the time they awoke from the funk, they were 1-4. Then a string of weak opponents helped them get to 4-4, they changed schemes to help the secondary. McNair also took over leadership and cut down on his turnovers.

The McNair changeover began in a quiet corner of the locker room in Seattle where he let off some steam. He did not yell, but got everyone's attention. He addressed dropped passes, poorly run routes, sacks and his own performance. But it was mainly about giving away a 10-point halftime lead. He later said, "Somebody had to step up. I think I did just that. The guys rallied around me." He added, "The veterans we have on this team are very soft-spoken. It was up to me."

They won 4-of-5 to pull back into the playoff hunt highlighted by thrashings of the Bills and Cowboys. The good run ended in a disappointing week 15 performance against Cincinnati.

The coaches said they were happy with McNair's first full year. "Steve is doing things in the huddle and on the line of scrimmage like a six-year veteran," said Fisher. "He understands what we are doing ... He is laid back and quiet. But then he gets in the huddle and he's a different guy. He's not a guy who is going to grab face masks or that kind of thing. But he is a guy who has the respect of the players around him."

The 27-14 Thanksgiving Day win over the Cowboys was the team's biggest in awhile and propelled them to thoughts of the playoffs.

He did exhibit leadership, toughness and running ability. However, his dropback passing skills stagnated or even declined without Rhome. He finished 216-of-415 (52%) for 2,665 yards, 14 TDs and 13 interceptions. He ran for 674 yards (6.7 per carry) and 8 TD, but was sacked 31 times for 190 yards of losses and led the league with 16 fumbles. The pass offense finished No. 29 and his QB rating was a low 70.4. The Oilers were quick to point out that the numbers compared favorably to Steve Young, Troy Aikman, Warren Moon and Drew Bledsoe at the same points in their careers.

No WR had more than 4 TDs. The high point was Wycheck with 63 receptions for 748 yards and 4 TDs. Davis and Sanders combined for only 74 catches for 1,062 yards and 7 TDs. Second-rounder Joey Kent caught only 6 catches. Fourth-rounder Derrick Mason looked much better with 14 while also taking over the kick return duties.

The workhorse was George, who had 357 carries for 1,399 yards (3.9 per carry) and 6 touchdowns (two fewer than McNair). Fisher made a point of saying he also improved on attitude and conditioning. One area that could improve was receiving, as he had just 7 receptions. Thomas had 67 carries for 310 yards.

Fisher took some criticism for overusing George. His response was, "You must be able to run the ball in the NFL to be successful. Seven teams in 1997 ran the ball more times than they threw it. Six of those teams were in the playoffs. We feel we're on the right track with our offense." They averaged 151 yards rushing per game and a healthy 4.5 per carry. But predictability was again a problem. Since they did not try to go down the field much, opponents often stacked eight and even nine men on the line to stop him. Not surprisingly, his longest run of the season was 30 yards.

The defense improved at midseason after Fisher and Gregg Williams disguised coverages. In one 8-game stretch, they held their opponents to 14 points or fewer six times.

Despite the blowout performances by Steve Broussard and Corey Dillon, the rush defense still finished the year surrendering a very respectable 98.3 yards per game (3.8 per carry). That was good enough to rank fifth in the league.

The line again failed to generate a sufficient pass rush. With the blitz de-emphasized to aid the secondary, they generated only 35 sacks. The tackles were talented, but did not play hard on every down. Walker had 7 sacks while Ford had 5. The ends were disappointing. LE Cook could not lift weights during the season because of injury. He lost strength and did not have a sack. Rookie Kenny Holmes showed promise with 7 sacks, but was weak against the run and lost strength as the season wore on.

Eddie George put up similar numbers in 1997 on more carries (1,399 yards vs. 1,368) But his average dropped from 4.1 to 3.9 per carry. Photo © The Associated Press.

The pass defense gave up 229 yards per game while allowing opponents to complete 59% of their passes. Lewis and Robertson each had five interceptions, but Lewis's bum ankle hampered him most of the year. Bishop did not play up to his usual standards. The biggest problem was left CB where Jackson, while often injured, appeared to be suited as a nickel back only. Rookie Denard Walker played better than expected in his place, but was no Dishman.

Overall, the turnover on the coaching staff caused more problems than Fisher publicly admitted. The coaches promoted to replace the more experienced ones who departed were perhaps not up to the task. In some corners, Fisher was accused of practicing the Peter Principle with those promotions. In more than three seasons, Fisher was 24-30 with no playoff appearances. Then again, he was dealing with some unusual circumstances.

Matthews was voted to the Pro Bowl for the tenth consecutive year, becoming the first lineman to make it at tackle, guard and center, virtually guaranteeing his admission into the Hall of Fame. He also had the longest streak of consecutive games played in the league. George also made the team, while Marcus Robertson made the *Sports Illustrated* All-Pro team.

MEMPHIS BLUES

Fisher was asked whether he thought they would have made the playoffs under more normal practice and playing conditions. He responded in his usual fashion, saying, "It's hard to quantify those outside issues. The bottom line is that we didn't win enough games."

Later, however, he did allow himself to say, "The game's designed to play in front of your home fans. We did the best we could to generate interest, and we appreciate the people who came to see us. But it's hard to give a pregame speech to the players and tell them we need to get off to a fast start so we can take the home crowd out of the game." For at least three of the eight home games (Raiders, Redskins, Steelers), their opponents had bigger cheering sections.

But he preferred to look at the glass as half full. "In the last three years," he said, "the Rams, Ravens and Raiders all relocated. Collectively, they've won 17 games, I believe. If you add the Baltimore Colts and St. Louis Cardinals to the group, the year after the move they averaged just better than four wins. We won eight last season, and we are very much looking forward to removing that travel aspect and moving into our own stadium in 1999."

The Oilers reported attendance at 28,027 (20,000-22,0000 was more accurate). Even the reported figure was 3,000 fewer per game than they averaged their last year in Houston, and placed them last in league attendance for the second straight year.

Along with free agency, getting the team out of the mess in Memphis was the main priority looking ahead to 1998.

THE VIEW FROM HOUSTON

The Oilers retained few followers in Houston. Television ratings backed up the preseason *Houston Chronicle* survey, hitting as low as a 6.4 rating (103,955 homes) and an 11 share (11% of households using TVs were watching the Oilers) for the second Jaguar game. Early season ratings were so bad the local NBC affiliate opted not to show most of the games.

The local college football teams enjoyed some benefit as Rice University had its best attendance since 1972. The University of Houston also saw increased attendance.

Charlie Pallilo, radio talk show host at KTRH-AM, the Oilers' former radio flagship station, said interest "started off small" only to become "infinitesimal ... Out of sight, increasingly out of mind." The most dramatic proof came following the Thanksgiving Day massacre of the hated Cowboys. Pallilo said, "The night after that, we had maybe one Oiler-related call."

1998: ON TO NASHVILLE

The Oilers were finding it hard to be wanted. Just as Houston offered to show them the door, Memphis now held it open for them. At least Houston took 37 years to get to know them first.

While the entire organization felt they would be better off in Nashville, both Fisher and Reese knew they were about to lose their cover. With relocation and crowd size no longer dominating discussion, their methods and techniques were about to come under more severe scrutiny. It was time to produce.

LET ME OUTTA HERE (ROUND II)

The tragedy that unfolded in Memphis in 1997 was classic Adams. While the team always had a ready list of excuses and rationales, everyone in Houston knew better. It was standard operating procedure.

One of the more amusing anecdotes came in October when Adams blamed Tennessee Governor Don Sundquist for the problems. Bud said it was Sundquist's idea for them to play in Liberty Bowl so they would have a statewide presence. These remarks came after Sun-

dquist had criticized the Oilers for botching the move. He also said they needed to change nicknames.

Meanwhile, Memphis got the black eye. As he had done with Houston, Commissioner Paul Tagliabue showed up to make sure that the major media outlets portrayed Memphis, not the NFL, as the bad guys. He turned the dagger by saying the league made the right decision when it awarded expansion franchises to Jacksonville and Carolina over Memphis.

But much to Adams and Tagliabue's chagrin, the antagonism was not limited to Memphis. In a mid-November 1997 Vanderbilt University poll, an overwhelming majority of Nashvillians reported they did not care for their football team's nickname. Only about half said were glad the Oilers came at all.

Bud's response was another classic. "Down here in Memphis," he crowed, "they don't mind. They think the Oilers is a pretty good name." These remarks came several days after about 20,000 showed up to watch the Oilers lose to Jacksonville.

Bud called his 1995 promise of a contest to find a new name a mistake. "I wasn't even thinking about that when I made the statement," he said. Slowly, he softened. He told the *Nashville Banner*, "I want to see what the people have to say. I'm open-minded about it. Put yourself in my place. Why you don't see teams change names is that they build up continuity and a tradition. But if this means something to the people of Tennessee, I'll give it my full consideration."

He added that if he did change names, it would not happen until Nashville. "When you're into a new stadium and everything, that would be the time to do it," said Bud. Again, he got cover from Tagliabue. "The logical time," Tags said, "if there is going to be a different way of presenting the team, a different name, different logo, different uniforms, whatever the differences might be, I think that should probably start for the '99 season when they're in the new stadium."

The implication was simple. If they did change nicknames, they were not about to waste it on Memphis. This did nothing for ticket sales.

Soon, the questions came about whether the team would even stay the full two years in Memphis. In November, Adams promised they would be back unless "the bottom falls out." When pressed on whether the record-low of 17,071 for the Bengals was the bottom, he responded, "I think we hit the bottom there."

Adams may have saved his best for his locker room soft-shoe after the win over Pittsburgh in the final game. Trailing reporters dogged him with questions: "Would they be in Memphis in 1998?" His first reply was, "We've got a two-year contract." When pressed, he responded, "That's not my decision to make." Asked again, he said, "I only have one vote out of 30." They kept asking. Next, he said, "We'll look at everything after the season is over." When someone pointed out it was over, his response was, "I'll have to talk to my players and my staff." Then someone else asked if a previously aired ESPN report that they might play at Vanderbilt in '98 was true, Bud said, "ESPN? Who are they? The NCAA?"

It had been quite a year. There were the bus trips to their home games, the news conference when the logo fell on the ground, the time they were outdrawn 3-to-1 by a fair, the jokes about Memphis, the home games where their opponents had more fans, the name change controversy, Memphis' bitterness and Tagliabue's remarks.

An article in the Memphis paper, sounding much like those in Houston for decades, read: "Frankly, the whole thing would have been comical if it weren't so pathetic. Not many will mind if the Oilers go to Nashville. Not many will miss the arrogance, the incompetence, the drumbeat of moronic Memphis jokes by people who know nothing about the situation. But you wonder about the lying, you wonder how the guy can sleep at night. Outside the stadium, a fan named Jimmy Lawson proudly displayed a 24-foot oil derrick he had built and mounted on the back of his truck. Lawson is a true fan, optimistic, enthusiastic and gullible. 'The Oilers are definitely going to be in Memphis next year,' he said. 'Bud Adams said so.' Yeah, he did. But that was the day before yesterday."

After the season, a petition circulated asking the Oilers to leave. The signees included state politicians. In February, the Oilers reached an agreement with Memphis, the County Sports Authority and the Memphis Parks Commission to let them out of the final year of the lease for $1.2 million. And they did not have to refund the $118,904 the team spent improving the Liberty Bowl (the blue paint). At the press conference, Sports Authority chairman Avron Fogelman referred to the situation as a "bad marriage," while twice calling the team the *Houston* Oilers.

In April, the Oilers formally reached an accord with Vanderbilt for use of its 41,448-seat stadium for the 1998 season. Adams, who basically had to go to university officials with his hat in his hand after McClure's heavy-handed tactics the previous summer, said, "It's great to be home again. This is a wonderful day for the Oilers, and I hope for Vanderbilt and the city, too."

Mayor Bredesen added "I think there's real excitement growing about all of this. We'll have college action on Saturdays and the NFL on Sundays. There will be plenty to cheer about this fall."

THE 1998 DRAFT AND FREE AGENCY

The Oilers felt they were a just a few pieces away from being a contender. The most glaring weakness for the second straight year was CB. In order to be effective, the "46" needed at least three quality ones. They had one, Lewis, although they were happy with the progress of Walker, who excelled in bump-and-run coverage. Otherwise, Jackson and Dorsett made opposing quarterbacks happy.

Next was pass catchers. Floyd Reese said, "Steve's confidence in his receivers is very important. He needs to know that when he throws the ball, it's going to be caught. We can't drop passes next season like this season ... Eddie did a great job of running, but I think the reason he didn't have longer runs was because defenses had an extra player or two to stop him." They wanted better size and speed.

Fisher said, "Let's say this, we're looking to add depth to our club — a veteran pass rusher will help." Also desired were a pass catching TE, a legitimate FB and backup QB with Dave Krieg turning 41. Finally, in light of Matthews' age and the loss of Donnalley to the Dolphins, guard was another need spot.

First, they re-signed DT Henry Ford ($10.5M/5 years) and Wortham ($8.4M/4 years). They cut punter Reggie Roby and signed the Packer's Craig Hentrich ($5.5M/

5 yrs). They also signed injury-prone tight end Jackie Harris ($2.1M/2 yrs).

The biggest predraft news was WR Yancy Thigpen, who they snagged off the Steelers. To get him to come to Tennessee, they had to make him the highest-paid WR in NFL history ($21 million/5 years with a $5.25 million signing bonus). Thigpen, 28, had a career-high 1,398 yards in '97 while being named to the Pro Bowl for the second time. He was the first big Oiler free agent signing since Stepnoski.

The draft was from the trailers again. They took Utah WR Kevin Dyson at No. 16. Ranked first by Mel Kiper, Jr., he was the first wide-out taken. Tall with good speed, Dyson worked in a pro style offense in college. With the perceived depth of CBs in the draft, the Oilers could not pass him up. Another consideration, although downplayed at the time, was that Thigpen had a screw inserted in a troublesome left arch after he signed with the Oilers. Although he was expected to participate in mini camp, the lingering injury might have affected the decision.

Dyson will probably always be compared to the WR they left on the table. Randy Moss was considered the most physically gifted in the draft if not the best in years. A consensus top 5 in talent, many teams, including the Oilers, backed away because of his off-field problems.

The Oilers used their next two on CBs Samari Rolle and Dainon Sidney. Rolle had the reputation of a good cover man from a great program. While not strong or physical, he was said to run well with good closing quickness. Sidney was reported to possess a good combination of size and speed, but was thought to be more of a project.

The remaining choices were DT Joe Salave'a, OG Benji Olson (originally projected as a second-rounder), CB Lee Wiggins (6th round), LB Jimmy Sprottle (7th) and center Kevin Long (7th).

TRAINING CAMP 1998

As training camp opened, the players were looking at playing before the third different home crowd in 3 years. The next year would mark their fourth different stadium. But at least the ridiculous travel routine was over and they would once again enjoy a home field advantage.

The heart of the team consisted of a good defensive scheme complemented by adequate players, a fairly solid offensive line, workhorse Eddie George and the talented but not-yet-arrived Steve McNair. They hoped Thigpen and Dyson would get them over the hump and into the playoffs.

McNair said, "Right now, I feel real comfortable. The main thing is that my teammates trust me, and I trust

Photo © The Associated Press.

them. They look at me as a player who has to be in control." As usual, he worked hard in the offseason, giving up his off time to work with the coaches. "So much of the game is mental," he said. "I have to be prepared for every situation."

One such situation Les Steckel re-introducing the shotgun to the Oiler offense. This was a bright move they should have considered earlier. McNair, who used the formation exclusively in college said, "I like the shotgun because I spent four years playing it. Les lets me put my two cents in. How much we use it just depends on the situation." He also looked forward to the promised 2-back set, even though the Oilers again failed to draft a fullback.

Their suddenly deep receiver corps let them field a team of 6' receivers for the first time since the early 1970s. Moreover, they had to keep Frank Wycheck on the field and get free agent Jackie Harris on it.

The big question on the line was replacing Kevin Donnalley at right guard. When veteran Erik Norgard was hurt, Jason Layman (6'5, 310) took over. Scott Sanderson (6'6, 295) also provided good depth and would sub for an injured Hopkins at midseason.

The secondary was set at three positions with Bishop, Robertson and Lewis. Keeping them all healthy was the trick. At left corner, Walker returned as the incumbent to be challenged by Jackson and rookies Rolle and Sidney. The LBs were altered with the addition of ex-Oiler Eddie Robinson, who went back to SSLB. Bowden moved to the middle and Marts returned on the weak side.

The line was long on young talent but short on consistency and due for a shake-up. The DT rotation was Walker, Ford, Evans and rookie Salave'a with Evans moving in as the starter at right tackle. At end, Lyons would start opposite Holmes, who they hoped would benefit from a full year of pro coaching and weight training. Cook and Roberson would start the year on the second team. Mix ('96, 2nd round) and Burton ('96, 4th) were cut.

THE 1998 REGULAR SEASON — LAST DANCE

After finishing 8-8 in Houston in 1996 and 8-8 in Memphis the next year, 8-8 in Nashville seemed reasonable, although some wags said they had *that Super Bowl look.*

That latter view took a beating as the Oilers opened 1-3. They led in the second half of each loss, but the defense could not hold. Against San Diego, George was held to 15 yards on 11 carries as they lost 13-7 to one of the worst offenses in the league. At New England, they led 16-13 in the fourth quarter, but lost 27-16 on a McNair interception thrown to a phantom receiver. He said, "I was throwing to a zone, not to anyone in particular." Against Jacksonville at home (34,656), they led 19-14 late in the third quarter, but lost 27-22.

Seemingly out of it after four games, they caught fire, winning five of the next six. The highlight was the first sweep of Pittsburgh since 1993. But they were haunted by the one loss in the streak — 23-20 to Chicago. Like the San Diego game, it was a loss at home to a bad team. Among the sea of bungles, the last play stood out. As the final seconds ticked away and the Oilers lined up for the tying field goal, Al Del Greco could not be found. He thought they had gained a first down on the previous play. Out of timeouts and with the game and play clocks winding down, punter Craig Hentrich was forced to rush into position to try the kick. As he did, a confused Del Greco ran onto the field as an illegal twelfth man. With penalty flags flying, Hentrich's poor attempt was blocked. The block made moot the penalty as another round of Oiler-generated Keystone Cop highlights made it around the country.

The other highlight making the rounds was attendance. Even a giveaway promotion featuring Beanie Baby "Chocolate the Mouse" could not sell out the game with Cincinnati. With just 33,288 in the stands and Blaine Bishop, Yancy Thigpen, and Brad Hopkins out injured, they won anyway, 44-14.

Having climbed to 6-4 and back into the playoff picture, they faced a tough final six of the Jets, Seahawks, Ravens, Jaguars, Packers and Vikings. They promptly crashed and burned at home to the Jets 24-3 (37,084). The second-half meltdown in that game with the pressure on was reminiscent of the '97 Cincinnati game, the '96 Cincinnati game and the '95 Pittsburgh game.

Still reeling, they dropped to 6-6 by losing to Seattle 20-18. Once again, seemingly out of it, the Oilers rallied to get back in the race and tease their fans. They first beat Baltimore 16-14 (31,124) and then surprised Jacksonville on the road 16-13. Amazingly, they were 7-1 in the AFC Central. For any other team, this would have meant a division crown. But this was not any other team.

Winning the last two would put them in the playoffs at 10-6, while splitting to end up 9-7 might. But whatever delusions existed among fans and within the organization that Reese and Fisher had put together a playoff-caliber team were quickly shattered. First, they were blown out in Green Bay 30-22. Then, in their final game and home game as the Oilers, they blew a 13-8 halftime lead to lose to the Vikings 26-16 and end up 8-8.

Elsewhere, one of the more interesting stories was that of ex-Oiler Chris Chandler, who was finally surrounded by a solid team in Atlanta. He not only led the Falcons to an 14-2 record, but also into the Super Bowl. In addition, WR Randy Moss, who the Oilers passed over for Kevin Dyson, looked not just like the rookie-of-the-year in Minnesota, but rather like the overall player-of-the-year. He led the Vikings to a 15-1 record and the NFC Championship. Dyson was inactive part of the season.

OVERVIEW

In some respects, the Oilers eked out a little progress. Namely, they plowed through their division, sweeping Pittsburgh, Cincinnati and Baltimore for only the second time in team history. They also gained a split with the playoff-tested Jaguars.

But this bit of hard-earned progress was more than offset by their 1-7 record outside the division that left them with no divisional crown and no trip to the playoffs. It had been five long years since the loss to Joe Montana and the Chiefs.

Their offseason goals were stifled by disheartening losses to the Chargers, Pats, Jags, Bears and Seahawks. Worst were the home losses. Against San Diego, they led 7-6 late in the third quarter, but let Ryan Leaf and the rest of the terrible Chargers' offense sneak off with a 13-7 victory. Likewise, they led Jacksonville 22-21 in the third quarter, but choked it away on penalties and turnovers. They outgained the dreadful Bears 356 yards to 286, but again gave the game away with penalties, turnovers and the muffed field goal attempt.

They led at New England 16-13 in the fourth quarter only to lose 27-16. In Seattle, they led 6-3 at the half and took an 18-17 lead with 33 seconds left, but lost 20-18 on a field goal with one second left.

Progress could be seen on offense in several categories. Overall, the offense improved to No. 4 in the AFC and No. 9 in the NFL. This compared to No. 11 and No. 18 in 1997. The big movement was in the pass offense, which moved up to No. 7 in the conference and No. 15 in the league. In 1997, the Oilers had the worst pass offense in the AFC and the second worst in the NFL. With an improved passing game, the scoring also improved slightly from No. 10 in the AFC to No. 7.

In his second season as a starter, Steve McNair was 289-of-492 (58.7%) for 3,228 yards and a QB rating of 80 (No. 5 in the AFC). He rushed for 559 yards (7.3 per carry). Another positive was only 10 interceptions. On the other hand, he had only 15 TD passes which ranked him No. 8 in the conference behind Vinnie Testaverde's 29 and Peyton Manning's 26. Overall, McNair appeared to be an imposing threat that the Oiler coaches kept under wraps. Their scheme was conservative and rarely let him throw deep or look for the quick score. Ever fearful of the turnover, they wanted to grind it out with an occasional high percentage pass. In addition, McNair's ability to read complex NFL defenses remains an open question.

Partially a result of the cautious approach, partially due to injuries and partial-

Al Del Greco set team records for field goals and points in 1998. But he will be remembered for his gaff at the end of the Chicago game.

Jeff Fisher was not happy when Eddie George failed to appear for his voluntary offseason workout program. Nor did management like that he left the area as soon as the season ended. Nonetheless, George went back to the Pro Bowl as the AFC's third leading rusher (1,294 yards). During the season, he had a string of five consecutive 100-yard games; however, his rush average continued to drop, falling to 3.7 yards per carry.

ly due to bad drafting, no wide out had more than Yancy Thigpen's 38 catches, 493 yards and 3 TDs and Thigpen missed 7 games. Willie Davis added 32 while 1998 No. 1 choice Kevin Dyson had just 21. Joey Kent, the team's second-round pick in 1997, had another disappointing year with only 4 receptions. The stars of the receiving corps were the H-back and tight end. Frank Wycheck continued to produce with a team-high 70 receptions for 768 yards. Free agent Jackie Harris was next with 43 catches for 412 yards. But neither had more than 2 TD receptions, while Wycheck's reception total was merely ninth best in the AFC.

The bad news was the decline of the rush offense. In did not bode well that a team that invested its soul in rushing was ranked only ninth best in the NFL. In 1997, they were third best. Opponents keyed on Eddie George. Stop him and you stopped the Oilers. As a result, he was held under 100 yards in six of the eight losses. He had 15 yards against San Diego, 25 against the Jags, 30 against Green Bay and 54 against Minnesota. Overall, he had 1,294 yards (No. 3 in AFC) and added another 310 off 37 receptions. But his average dropped again down to 3.7 yards per carry which was only twelfth best in the AFC. (Terrell Davis led with 5.1 per carry). George's longest run of the season was 37 yards and he only had 5 rushing TDs.

The main problem with the promising offense was that, while improving in terms of total yards, they usually bogged down short of the touchdown. On the season, they had only two plays of 50 yards or more. One was a scramble by McNair and the other was a pass by Dave Krieg.

This meant fans saw a lot of Al Del Greco, who broke team records with 36 field goals (of 39 attempts) and 136 points. Free agent punter Craig Hentrich averaged an amazing 47.2 yards per kick. They both made the Pro Bowl, as did George and Bruce Matthews. It was Matthews' eleventh consecutive selection, letting him tie Anthony Munoz for the most by an OL. The only two players with more appearances are Reggie White (13) and Jerry Rice (12).

The story on defense was the disappointing defensive line. The rush defense fell from No. 4 in the NFL to No. 11. This was the Oilers' bread and butter, and they were getting worse instead of better. And the pass rush stunk. As a team, they had just 30 sacks, led by LB Lonnie Marts' four. That was the lowest team-leading sack total since the NFL started keeping sack stats (1970). The leader among lineman was Josh Evans, who had 3.5 sacks.

This situation was particularly galling considering that, going back to 1994, they had used a multitude of high draft picks there. In 1994, it was Henry Ford (1st round) and Jeremy Nunley (2nd). In 1995, it was Anthony Cook (2nd) and Gary Walker (5th). In 1996, it was Bryant Mix (2nd) and Kendrick Burton (4th). In 1997, it was Kenny Holmes (1st) and Pratt Lyons (4th). In 1998, it was Joe Salave'a (4th). They had also tried free agents Kenny Davidson and Robert Young. In spite of all of that expensive talent, by the end of the '98 season, undrafted free agents held down three of the eight positions on the two-deep DL roster — James Roberson (the starter at RDE), Josh Evans and Mike Sutton.

As a unit, the defense improved slightly from No. 22 in the NFL in 1997 to No. 17. Joe Bowden led the team in tackles. The pass defense, with better DBs, also improved. In 1997, the only worse secondaries in football were the Raiders and Ravens. In 1998, they finished No. 10 in the AFC and No. 20 in the NFL. Darryll Lewis led with four interceptions.

The tale of the Oilers over the past several years could be seen in the scoring offense and defense. In 1995, they finished 7-9 with an offense that averaged 21.7 points per game and a defense that gave up 20.2 per game. In 1996, they were 8-8, while scoring 21.5 and surrendering 19.9 points. In 1997, they were 8-8 again with an offense that generated 20.8 points per game and a defense that gave up 19.4. Finally, in 1998, they were 8-8 again while scoring 20.6 per game but giving up 20.

The 1998 season closed the books on the Oilers. In 39 seasons, they were 267-307-6 for a winning percentage of .465 and average of 6.8 wins per season.

CONCLUSION

In mid-November 1998, Bud Adams announced the new name of the team would be the Titans. He said, "We wanted a new nickname to reflect strength, leadership and other heroic qualities, and to be equal to, if not better, than great NFL nicknames like Vikings, Giants, Buccaneers and Cowboys. A Titan these days is someone who excels and stands out in his work. He or she is recognized for greatness or special achievement. That's what we want for our football team.

"Titans comes from early Greek mythology and the fact that Nashville is known as the 'Athens of the South' makes the Titans name very appropriate. If we continue to play like Titans, we'll be in the playoffs this January."

Beyond a focus group, fans were not consulted nor were their suggestions solicited, although Bud said "dozens" had contacted him directly. "It was difficult to trim the list (of 39)," said Adams. "Titans was always a strong contender in my mind. Pioneers and Tornadoes also were popular." He said he eliminated the Copperheads and Vipers because he did not want any "snakes or reptiles." Most likely it was due to a fear of jokes.

That did it for the Oilers. Bud was reluctant to change names and did so only upon the promise of Paul Tagliabue that the name would be "retired" by the NFL. That meant no other team would be allowed to use the Oiler nickname. Adams said this would "allow the Tennessee franchise to retain the team's winning tradition."

THE TEAM'S FUTURE IN NASHVILLE

The Oilers thought they were pretty smart getting out of Houston. There is little argument that, at least in the short run, the team would be in better financial shape in a new stadium. But the NFL, the television folks and probably even Adams will not consider the move a success unless the stadium is full on a year-in year-out basis. They face some unusual challenges.

What they are attempting to do is bring pro football to a southern city. This is something that has never been fully tested. Houston and Dallas are not real southern cities. Atlanta has grown so big that it has distinguished itself as a metropolitan area. New Orleans defies comparison. The Florida cities are clogged with too many Northerners to be considered truly southern any more.

Nashville is southern. This is not to say that it does not have a lot going for it. It does. It is progressive and fairly sophisticated. It has an energetic mayor who is trying to push it into the big leagues by acquiring pro sports teams. It is also pretty and has friendly people. But at its heart, it is still a real southern city. The only NFL comparable is the Panthers. Carolina is exactly what Mike McClure had in mind.

Charlotte is also a progressive southern town, but one not large enough to support an NFL franchise by itself. Thus, the Panthers went regional. They picked a geographically based name, built a state-of-the-art stadium and hoped to draw from an area up to 4½ hours away. The Panthers' first two years were wildly successful.

With Nashville at a population of only about 600,000, the Oilers went with a statewide name. Like Carolina, they hope to draw fans from across a region that not only includes Tennessee, but also northern Alabama and southern Kentucky, as well.

And, likewise, the Oilers are getting a state-of-the-art stadium that will let them siphon off as much extra revenue as possible. As McClure says, "In the environment in pro football today, you have to have more money to have a quality team. The important thing is to be able to compete with the Dallases and San Franciscos and Miamis. You can buy a lot of Emmitt Smiths and Troy Aikmans and Michael Irvins."

But the Oilers will face challenges that the Panthers did not. First and foremost is the local competition. While Carolina goes ga-ga over college basketball, college football does not enjoy the same status. There is not much competition during football season.

It is very different in Tennessee. College football is king. Volunteer games are major social events. They regularly draw over 90,000. Everyone in the state, including Memphis, follows the team. Nationally, it is in the top three or four in terms of game-day atmosphere. To call following the Volunteers a religion may be to understate it.

Historically, pro football pushed aside college football in most big cities. It happened long ago in Chicago, Detroit, Houston, Miami, Dallas and New York. The situation may be different with the rabid SEC fans in Tennessee where traditions run deep and seem to be transferred genetically. No NFL team has ever gone face-to-face with such a direct challenge.

Another factor is that in those cities where the pro game beat college in the battle for fans, the transformation usually did not occur until the pro team became good. Seattle is a good current example where the Seahawks have never really made it and the Huskies are still the bigger draw.

Photo © The Associated Press.

Even in Carolina, after those two stellar seasons, empty seats could be seen in Ericsson Stadium the third season when the team did not play up to expectations. The Oilers rarely have played up to expectations and never have exceeded them. As they open in Nashville, they are a marginal playoff contender at best.

This leads to the next issue, which is whether the Oilers will be able to attract the free agents necessary to give them the kind of team they will need to keep the fans. They have put themselves in a position to have the money to do so. But it takes more. The best players want to win. The 49ers provide a good example. Free agents take less money to play for them because they know they will have a chance to win a Super Bowl.

The Oilers cannot make the same claim. They have always been about money first. Winning is secondary. Players know this. They also know about the mess getting out of Houston and all the problems in Memphis. The Oilers may be teetering on the edge of developing such a bad reputation that free agents will take less money just to avoid them.

It is too early to say. They have some selling points, starting with a nucleus of good young players in Steve McNair and Eddie George. Head coach Jeff Fisher also has a good reputation. Once the new stadium comes on line and they have a good permanent training facility, they will have even more to offer.

That returns the topic back to the fan base. If the Oilers reach out to their new fans just a little, something they have not yet fully committed themselves to do, they will probably get a warm reception that will last at least for a couple of seasons. At that point, they will need to have to produce on the field. If not, things might get a little sticky.

The Titans are supposed to remain in the Adams family after Bud's departure. Son-in-law and Executive Assistant to the President Thomas S. Smith has long been thought to be in line to take over. However, when Bud stepped down as president in 1999 he passed over Tommy (left) for former Vikings executive Jeff Diamond clouding the situation.

BIBLIOGRAPHY AND READING LIST

Bradshaw, Terry and Martin, Buddy. *Looking Deep.* Contemporary Books, 1989.

Carroll, Bob, Gershman, Michael, Neft, David, and Thorn, John, Eds. *Total Football: The Official Encyclopedia of the National Football League.* Harper Collins Publishers, 1997.

Glanville, Jerry, and Miller, J. David. *Elvis Don't Like Football: The Life and Raucous Times of the NFL's Most Outspoken Coach.* MacMillan Publishing, 1990.

Herskowitz, Mickey, Ed. *From Cannon to Campbell: An Illustrated History of the Houston Oilers.* Gulf Coast Graphics, Inc., 1979.

Kaplan, David, and Griffin, Daniel, Eds. *The Best of Bum. The Quotable Bum Phillips.* Texas Monthly Press, 1980.

Knox, Chuck, and Plaschke, Bill. *Hard Knox: The Life of an NFL Coach.* Harcourt, Brace, Jovanovich, 1988.

Matuszak, John, and Delsohn, Steve. *Cruisin' with the Tooz.* Franklin, Watts, 1987.

Miller, Patrick. *The Tyler Rose: The Earl Campbell Story.* Schuromil Productions, 1997.

Namath, Joe, and Oates, Jr., Bob. *A Matter of Style.* Boston: Little, Brown, 1973.

Namath, Joe Willie, and Schaap, Dick. *I Can't Wait Until Tomorrow ... 'Cause I Get Better Looking Every Day.* Random House, 1969.

Olajuwon, Hakeem, and Knobler, Peter. *Living the Dream: My Life and Basketball.* Little, Brown and Company, 1996.

Phillips, O.A., and Buck, Ray. *He Ain't No Bum.* Jordan & Company, 1979.

Ribowsky, Mark. *Slick: The Silver and Black Life of Al Davis.* MacMillan Publishing, 1991.

Smith, Bubba, and DeWindt, Hal. *Kill, Bubba, Kill.* Simon & Schuster, 1983.

Stabler, Ken, and Stainback, Berry. *Snake: The Candid Autobiography of Football's Most Outrageous Renegade.* Doubleday, 1986.

Stram, Hank, and Sahadi, Lou. *They're Playing My Game.* Morrow Books, 1986.

Tomjanovich, Rudy, and Falcoff, Robert. *A Rocket at Heart: My Life and My Team.* Simon & Schuster, 1997.

Twombly, Wells. *Blanda, Alive and Kicking: The Exclusive, Authorized Biography.* Nash Publishing, 1972.

INDEX

A

Abraham, Robert 177, 190, 196, 203, 213-14
Adams, Bud 11-15, 17, 20-25, 27-30, 32, 34-36, 38, 41-42, 45-54, 57, 59-64, 68-70, 73, 75-76, 78, 82-86, 90-91, 93-96, 98-100, 102, 104-06, 108-09, 111-12, 114-15, 118, 126, 134, 144, 146, 170-71, 181, 188, 194, 197, 199-01, 209-10, 213-17, 224, 226, 236-37, 239, 242-43, 246, 250, 252, 260-61, 265, 271-74, 280, 283, 285-86, 288-89, 291-92, 296, 298, 301-03, 309-14, 316-19, 323-24, 326-28, 331-32, 334-37, 339, 342, 344-47, 349-50, 353-54
Alexander, Willie 91-92, 97, 99, 101, 115, 126, 135-36, 145
Alexander, Les 314, 317-18, 331, 335
Allen, Patrick 189, 195, 203, 220, 226, 231, 244, 254, 262
Alm, Jeff 253, 260, 288, 291, 293
Arizona Cardinals 11-12, 17-18, 27, 30, 35, 59, 61, 87-88, 229, 350
Atlanta Falcons 69, 134, 218, 246, 255, 272, 292, 339, 357

B

Baker, Jesse 145, 147, 157, 160, 176-77, 183, 190, 195, 197, 203, 213
Baltimore Colts *See* Indianapolis Colts
Banfield, Tony 18, 22, 36, 40, 48, 65
Barber, Mike 119, 121, 125, 138, 140-42, 147, 153, 157, 161-62, 174, 176-77
Barrow, Michael 286-87, 289, 295, 298, 310, 319, 322, 327-28, 329, 338-39, 344, 348
Baugh, Sammy 34, 46-52, 55-56
Beathard, Pete 73, 75-79, 81-84
Bethea, Elvin 70, 78-79, 81-82, 84, 86- 87, 92, 94, 97, 99, 101-04, 106, 108-09, 115-16, 118, 121-22, 126, 128, 136, 140-41, 147, 156-57, 160, 169, 174, 176-78, 180, 183, 190-91, 224
Biles, Ed 113, 116, 130-31, 154, 159, 164, 171-82, 184, 237
Bingham, Gregg 100-01, 103, 106-07, 109, 116-17, 120, 128, 146, 157, 160, 165, 167, 170, 172, 174, 176-80, 183-84, 190, 195
Bishop, Sonny 47-48, 50, 55, 58, 70, 73, 77, 82, 84, 88
Bishop, Blaine 286, 294, 311, 322, 330-31, 338, 344, 348-49, 352, 355-56
Blanda, George 16-17, 19-27, 29-33, 35-40, 42-45, 47-52, 54-59, 61, 65-67, 69-70, 72-73, 76-77, 79, 82, 87, 89, 91, 102, 118, 163
Blanks, Sid 45, 48-50, 54
Bostic, Keith 182-83, 190, 195, 203, 223, 226, 233, 235
Boston Patriots *See* New England Patriots
Bowden, Joe 273, 289-90, 322, 338, 348, 356, 358
Boyette, Garland 65, 69-70, 73-74, 77-78, 82, 84, 88, 92, 94, 97, 101
Brazile, Robert 113, 115-18, 121-22, 128, 130, 135, 138, 140, 142, 147, 155, 157, 160, 163-64, 167, 174, 176, 180, 183-84, 190, 195
Bredesen, Phil 324-26, 328, 336, 346, 354
Breen, John 16-20, 22, 23, 25-27, 41, 61-62 67, 69, 85, 90, 92-93, 95-96, 98-100, 128
Brown, Bobby 21, 30, 43, 49, 60, 64, 66, 70, 89, 91, 178, 181
Brown, Gary 260, 262, 288, 292-95, 298-99, 308, 311, 322, 331, 337
Brown, Steve 182, 190, 195, 203, 207, 226, 239-41, 254, 260, 262
Brown, Willie 43
Buffalo Bills 30, 35-37, 49, 57, 94, 106, 108, 120, 136, 183, 194, 207, 212, 217, 232 240, 256, 277-78, 291, 309, 329, 350
Bugel, Joe 124-25, 139, 180, 184, 201
Burrough, Ken 90, 94, 97-99, 103, 106, 109, 115-16, 118, 122, 125, 128, 130, 135, 141, 143, 148, 150, 154, 157, 162, 173-74, 177, 183

C

Campbell, Earl 130-42, 145-50, 153, 155, 157, 161-65, 172, 174-80, 183-85, 188, 190-93
Campbell, Hugh 186-89, 192, 194, 196-97
Campbell, Woody 69-70, 73, 77-79, 82, 86
Cannon, Billy 17-19, 21-27, 29-33, 35-37, 39-40, 42-44, 46-47, 50, 60, 73, 131
Carlson, Cody 212, 226-27, 254, 257, 262, 275, 284, 286, 291, 296, 301, 305, 309-10, 312
Carolina Panthers 320-21, 325, 340, 359
Carpenter, Rob 123, 127, 130, 133, 135-36, 150, 161, 174-75, 194
Casper, Dave 135, 162-63, 173-74, 176-77, 179-80, 183
Caster, Rich 132, 135, 143, 149, 157, 159, 161-63, 173
Chandler, Chris 320-22, 327, 329-30, 338-41, 344, 357
Chicago Bears 11, 14, 19, 27, 83, 128-29, 162, 197, 205, 239-40, 275, 328, 357
Chicago Cardinals *See* Arizona Cardinals
Childress, Ray 195-96, 203, 208, 212, 223-24, 226-27, 230-31, 234, 239, 241, 251, 255, 258-59, 262-63, 267, 272, 275-77, 281, 288, 291, 293, 300, 310-11, 319, 322, 327-28, 337
Cincinatti Bengals 115, 117, 121, 127-29, 136-37, 146, 148, 174, 178-79, 197, 205-06, 221, 228, 230, 240-41, 255-56, 263, 274-75, 292, 309-10, 337-38, 339-40, 350, 356
Cleveland Browns 16, 33, 80, 93-94, 98, 102, 105, 108, 115, 118, 122, 127, 135-36, 147, 149, 161, 163, 174, 179, 192, 194, 197, 204, 206, 218, 220, 229-30, 232, 240, 242, 256, 265, 275-77, 292, 310, 327-28, 333-35, 349-50
Cline, Doug 18, 36, 40, 48, 55, 65-66, 69-70
Coleman, Ronnie 105, 107, 115, 117-18, 122, 127-28, 130, 135, 141, 145, 165
Collins, John 85, 87, 90, 92-93
Cook, Anthony 322-23, 330, 338, 347-48, 352, 356, 358
Culp, Curly 106, 108-09, 115-16, 118, 121, 126, 128, 130, 138, 140, 160, 162
Cutsinger, Gary 35-36, 40, 48, 51, 54-55, 60-61, 65, 67, 70, 82

D

Dallas Cowboys 15-16, 23, 27, 35, 41, 51-52, 54, 63, 67-68, 88-89, 92, 94, 96-97, 100-01, 103, 106-07, 113-14, 120, 124, 126, 129, 133, 148, 179, 190, 196, 204, 207,

227, 229, 239, 314, 320, 325, 350, 352
Dallas Texans *See* Kansas City Chiefs
Davis, Al 28, 35, 41, 43-44, 63, 67, 163, 215, 332, 334, 339, 342
Del Greco, Al 264-67, 275, 278-80, 293, 297, 338-39, 349, 356-58
Denver Broncos 17, 23, 31, 34, 36, 38, 43, 47-49, 51, 55, 65-66, 69, 72, 95-97, 102, 108, 121, 128, 149, 197, 221, 328, 335, 351
Dewveall, Willard 27-29, 32-33, 38, 44
Dickey, Lynn 91-94, 96, 98, 101-02, 105, 108, 119, 126, 163, 185
Dishman, Cris 225-26, 228, 240, 244, 254-55, 259, 262-63, 269, 272-73, 275, 280, 282, 294, 297-98, 302, 309, 311, 319-20, 322, 328, 337-39, 344, 348
Donaldson, Jeff 189, 192, 214, 229, 232, 254
Donnalley, Kevin 260, 281, 290, 305, 322, 338, 340, 348, 351, 355
Duncan, Curtis 212, 223, 226, 232, 244, 258, 267-68, 272, 274, 276-79, 281, 287, 294-95, 299, 308
Dyson, Kevin 355, 357

E

Eason, Bo 189, 192, 195, 203-05, 207, 214
Eatman, Irv 322, 325, 328, 330, 338, 348
Eddy, Jim 253, 260, 268-69, 272, 282-83

F

Farr, Miller 69-70, 73-74, 76-78, 81-84, 86-87
Fields, Angelo 159, 163, 165, 168, 177
Fisher, Ed 114-15, 118, 125, 133, 141, 146, 160
Fisher, Jeff 301, 308, 310, 319-22, 327-28, 331, 337-40, 342-45, 348-353, 355
Floyd, Don 18, 21, 24, 30, 33, 36, 40, 43, 48-49, 54-55, 65-66, 68, 70, 73, 76
Ford, Henry 304, 308-09, 322, 330, 338, 342, 348, 352, 355-56, 358
Foss, Joe 16, 18, 32, 34, 61, 63
Frazier, Charley 36, 48, 54-55, 57-58, 60, 62, 65, 67, 73, 76-77, 79, 82,
Frazier, Willie 48, 57-58, 60, 62, 70, 90, 92, 96
Fuller, William 204, 208, 212, 226-27, 230-31, 234, 244, 249, 257-59, 262-63, 267, 269, 272-73, 280-81, 285, 293, 296-300, 302-04, 309, 330

G

George, Eddie 337, 339, 341-42, 347-52, 355-56, 358
Gerela, Roy 70, 82-83, 86
Gilbride, Kevin 235, 244, 254, 261, 267, 272, 275, 286, 289, 290-91, 295, 297-98, 300-02, 310, 327, 340
Gillman, Sid 18-20, 24, 29, 32, 35, 37, 41, 44, 61, 80, 95, 100-12, 168
Givins, Ernest 202-03, 207, 211, 223, 226, 233, 240, 243-44, 251, 254-55, 258, 263, 265-69, 273, 275-76, 278-81, 287, 290, 292, 294-95, 298-99, 302, 311, 320
Glanville, Jerry 134, 189-90, 195-97, 199-204, 206-08, 211, 213-15, 218-25, 227-30, 232-36, 240, 242, 244-46, 255, 292, 301
Glick, Freddy 30, 36, 44, 50, 55, 57, 65-66, 69-70
Granger, Hoyle 60, 65-67, 70, 72-73, 75-77, 79, 81-83, 88, 90, 96-97
Gray, Leon 145, 157, 159-60, 163, 166, 168, 176-78, 183
Gray, Mel 320-21, 323, 330, 342, 350
Green Bay Packers 60, 68, 76, 119, 126, 163, 183, 204, 275, 322, 340
Grimsley, John 189, 203, 206, 208, 226, 229, 233-34, 249, 254, 257, 260
Groman, Bill 21, 24-26, 31-33, 38, 40, 43, 62, 65

H

Haik, Mac 78-79, 81-82, 86, 92, 96
Halas, George 11-14, 16, 18, 19-21, 25, 27, 35
Hardeman, Don 113, 115, 118-20, 122, 126, 131
Harmon, Ronnie 337-38, 342, 350
Harris, Jackie 355, 358
Hayman, Conway 114-15, 125, 133, 146, 160-61, 165
Hennigan, Charley 22-23, 25, 29, 31-33, 35, 38, 40, 43, 48-50, 54-55, 57-58, 66-67, 69
Herzeg, Ladd 171-72, 176-78, 181, 183, 187-89, 191-92, 194-95, 197, 200, 202, 204-06, 209-10, 215-18, 223-26, 228, 235-38
Hicks, WK 48, 55, 58, 65-66, 70, 73-74, 76, 79, 82-83, 87
Highsmith, Alonzo 211, 214, 218, 221, 225-26, 233, 239, 254-55
Hill, Drew 195-96, 203, 205, 207-08, 211, 223, 226, 228-29, 232-33, 239, 242, 244, 254-56, 258, 263, 267-69, 272
Hines, Glen Ray 60, 65-66, 70, 75, 78-79, 81-82, 84, 88, 91, 101
Hofheinz, Roy 28, 36, 53, 75, 78
Holmes, Kenny 344, 348, 352, 356, 358
Holmes, Pat 63-65, 70, 73, 77, 82, 92, 94, 99
Holovak, Mike 173, 182, 188-89, 200, 202, 225, 238-40, 243, 245, 249-50, 252-55, 260-62, 264, 272, 274-75, 283, 291, 301
Hopkins, Brad 286-87, 290, 295, 297-98, 309, 320, 322, 328, 338, 344, 348, 351, 356
Houston, Ken 69-70, 72-74, 76-77, 81-82, 84, 86, 92, 94, 96, 98-100, 183, 189, 201
Houston Sports Association (HSA) 28, 36, 53, 78, 214-15
Howfield, Ian 262-64
Hughes, Ed 38, 90-93, 95, 197
Hunt, Daryl 145, 174, 180, 183
Hunt, Lamar 12-15, 35, 38, 41, 61, 63, 68, 147, 160, 167
Husmann, Ed 30-31, 33, 35-36, 40, 54-56

I

Ivy, Frank "Pop" 30, 35-36, 40, 42-46, 51
Indianapolis Colts 11, 18, 61, 64, 69, 80, 85, 88-89, 95, 99, 102, 121, 147, 177, 197, 206, 220, 309, 356

J

Jackson, Steve 260, 264, 279, 294, 297-98, 305, 322, 330, 344, 348, 352, 355-56
Jacksonville Jaguars 321, 327, 339-40, 356-57
Jamison, Al 22, 25-26, 32-33, 37-38, 40, 42
Jancik, Bobby 35-36, 40, 48, 50, 55, 57, 65, 67, 70, 72
Jeffires, Haywood 211, 223, 232-33, 241, 244-45, 251, 255, 258, 263,

265, 267-69, 275-77, 279, 281, 291, 295, 298-300, 308, 310-11, 322, 328-29, 331, 335, 337
Jeppesen Stadium 14, 16, 23-24, 27, 29-31, 36, 38, 49, 61
Johnson, Billy "White Shoes" 105, 110, 115-119, 129-30, 132, 134, 136, 146, 160, 165, 349
Johnson, Charles 87-89, 92-93, 96, 102
Johnson, Richard 195-96, 226, 244, 254, 258-59, 267-68, 273
Joiner, Charlie 70, 82-83, 86, 88, 92-93, 97-99, 121, 193
Jones, June 134, 213, 223, 235-36, 254-55, 259
Jones, Sean 225-27, 230, 234, 242, 244, 248-49, 254-55, 257-59, 262-64, 266, 268, 272-76, 280-82, 288, 292, 295, 300, 302-03, 340

K

Kansas City Chiefs 14-17, 19, 22-23, 27, 30, 38-39, 41-42, 48, 52, 56, 60-61, 66, 68, 70, 72-73, 78-79, 82-83, 93, 99, 105-06, 123, 128, 134, 146, 162, 198, 204, 225, 228, 241, 256, 263, 273, 291, 297-98, 328, 338
Kiner, Steve 104-07, 109, 117, 128, 132, 137, 145
Klosterman, Don 28, 34, 35, 52, 59, 61-63, 65, 68-70, 72, 74, 81, 86, 89, 123, 152

L

Ladd, Ernie 28, 31-32, 37, 54, 61-67, 70, 73, 75, 77, 84-86
Lanier, Bob 313-14, 317-18, 323-25, 331-32, 334-35, 344
LA Raiders *See* Oakland Raiders
Largent, Steve 119, 122, 143, 147, 162, 193, 221
Lathon, Lamar 253-54, 260, 262-64, 267, 269, 275, 289, 292, 294, 298, 300, 308, 311, 320, 340
Lee, Jacky 18, 21, 27, 29-30, 38, 43-44, 48, 62, 66, 70, 72-73
Lemm, Wally 21, 28, 30, 32, 35-36, 46, 59, 61-70, 72-73, 77-78, 81-83, 85, 87-90, 201
LeVias, Jerry 70, 82-84, 86, 88-89, 91, 114
Lewis, Daryll 260, 262-63, 290-91, 309, 311, 322, 331, 338, 345, 348, 350, 352, 355, 358

Liberty Bowl 337
Luck, Oliver 177, 183, 185-86, 188
Lyles, Robert 189, 195, 203, 205, 208, 220, 226, 229, 236, 241-42, 244, 254-55, 262

M

Maggs, Don 202, 254, 286
Manning, Archie 178, 183 186
Maples, Bobby 52, 54, 58, 60, 65-66, 69-70, 77, 82, 88, 91, 97
Marshall, Wilber 286-87, 289, 291-92, 299
Martin, Carroll 21, 47-48, 51, 53, 55, 57, 59, 61
Matthews, Bruce 182-83, 190-92, 195, 197, 203-04, 207-08, 213-14, 218, 223, 233, 242, 244, 246, 249, 257-59, 262, 269, 273-74, 276, 281, 283, 287, 290-91, 298, 300, 309, 311, 320, 322, 329, 331, 335, 337-38, 340, 345, 348, 352, 355, 358
Matuszak, John 100-01, 104, 106, 165
Mauck, Carl 114-15, 118, 125, 139, 146-47, 150, 152, 154-55, 160, 167, 173, 177
McClure, Mike 286, 314-18, 324-25, 331, 336, 345-47, 354, 359-60
McDowell, Bubba 239, 244, 255, 265, 269, 273-75, 278, 280, 293, 300, 302, 320
McLane, Drayton 314, 316-17, 323, 325-27, 333, 335, 344
McNair, Steve 321-22, 324, 329, 331, 338-42, 344, 348-51, 355-57
Meads, Johnny 189, 195, 203, 208, 226, 241, 243-44, 256-57, 262, 265, 273
Miami Dolphins 63, 66, 69, 73, 76, 79, 82, 95, 97, 108, 116, 126, 137-38, 148, 174, 196, 206, 240, 263, 275, 340, 349
Mills, John Henry 286, 311, 322, 337, 342, 344
Minnesota Vikings 14, 69, 83, 103, 105, 107, 163-64, 183, 194, 207, 240, 254, 275, 327, 357
Mitchell, Leroy 70, 82, 83, 86
Montgomery, Glenn 239, 260, 290, 295, 302, 304, 311, 322, 337
Montgomery, Greg 225, 232, 244, 258, 262, 267-68, 279, 281-82, 300, 308
Moon, Warren 57, 69, 187-88, 191-92, 195-97, 203-08, 217-18, 220-23, 226-29, 232-33, 235-36, 239-45, 249, 251, 255-59, 261-65,

267, 269-70, 272-75, 277-79, 281-82, 285, 289, 291-92, 294-300, 302-03, 305, 311
Moore, Zeke 69-70, 76, 82-84, 86, 92, 99, 101, 115-16, 119, 121, 126, 132
Moriarty, Larry 182, 192, 194-95, 197, 203-05
Munchak, Mike 176-77, 182-84, 191-92, 195, 197, 204-05, 208-09, 213, 233, 244, 249, 255, 257, 258-59, 263, 267-69, 272, 281, 287, 294, 297, 300, 308, 345

N

Namath, Joe 42, 51-52, 54-55, 57, 66, 70, 73, 77, 79-80, 83, 85, 97, 123
New England Patriots 15-16, 24, 27-29, 31, 35, 37-38, 41, 43-44, 55, 60, 79, 82, 136, 139, 145, 162, 174, 178, 197, 228, 240, 259, 263, 271, 356
New York Jets 15-16, 23, 26-27, 34, 37-38, 42, 47, 49, 51-52, 55, 60, 63, 66, 79-83, 97, 106-07, 126, 148, 163, 255, 263, 267, 295, 311, 329, 340, 356
New York Giants 11, 18, 27, 51, 80, 174-75, 197, 261, 266, 350
New York Titans *See* New York Jets
Nielsen, Giff 131, 148, 150-51, 167, 172-73, 175-78, 183, 185-86, 188, 190, 206, 213, 227, 327
Noll, Chuck 52, 80, 158, 170, 203, 219-20, 222, 240, 272
Norton, Jim 22-24, 32-33, 36, 40, 44, 48, 50, 55, 57, 65, 70, 73-74, 76-77, 79, 82

O

Oakland Raiders 15, 23, 27, 29, 31, 38, 41, 43-44, 47-48, 52, 55, 60, 65, 69-70, 73, 76, 78-80, 82-84, 89, 93, 97, 102, 107, 118, 120, 128, 135, 148, 159, 161, 164-65, 191, 260, 262, 337, 349

P

Pardee, Jack 128, 146, 252-55, 261-62, 264-65, 268, 271-72, 275, 279-80, 283-84, 289-90, 293, 296, 299-300, 304, 310
Parker, Willie 69-70, 73, 77, 81-82, 88
Pastorini, Dan 91-95, 97-100, 102, 106, 109, 115, 117-18, 121-23, 125, 127, 129-30, 132, 134-36,

138-43, 146-49, 152-53, 155-59, 161, 164
Perry, Vernon 145, 150-53, 157, 160, 163, 174, 177, 182-83
Peterson, Bill 87, 95-102, 105
Phillips, OA "Bum" 103, 105-06, 109, 111-16, 118-37, 139, 141-43, 145-48, 151-52, 154-55, 158-59, 161, 166, 170, 172, 191, 254, 260, 291, 338, 349
Pinkett, Allen 202, 226, 232-33, 239, 242, 257, 262, 266, 268-69, 272
Pittsburgh Steelers 14, 45, 61, 64, 94, 105, 107, 109, 116-17, 127, 136, 140, 146, 149, 153, 161, 170, 175, 178, 183, 192, 196 255, 257, 265, 272-73, 275, 292-93, 306, 310, 327-28, 339, 350-351
Polsfoot, Fran 90, 113, 119, 193
Pritchard, Ron 70, 82, 86, 92, 97-98, 115

R

Reed, Alvin 69-70, 72, 76-78, 81-84, 86, 89, 92, 94, 97, 99
Reese, Floyd 255, 272, 300-01, 304-05, 307, 310, 319-22, 337, 343-45, 355
Reihner, George 123, 125, 127, 130, 136, 138, 145, 173
Reinfeldt, Mike 121, 126, 128, 135, 138, 147, 157, 160, 163, 174, 177, 180, 183, 190, 340
Renfro, Mike 131, 133, 138, 143, 148-49, 151, 153, 157, 160, 173-74, 177-78, 183, 190
Rhome, Jerry 51-52, 88, 92, 320-21, 330, 342-43, 351
Riley, Avon 173-74, 177, 183-84, 190, 196, 203, 206
Robertson, Marcus 260, 290, 292-93, 300, 308-10, 322, 327, 338-39, 345, 352, 355
Robinson, Eddie 273, 275-76, 281, 294, 298, 322, 337, 340, 356
Rooney, Art 12-14, 16, 170
Rozelle, Pete 17-18, 27, 34, 45, 52-54, 61, 63-64, 67, 69, 83, 86, 95-96, 127, 156, 170, 194, 215, 231, 250, 252
Rozier, Mike 189, 192, 194-97, 204, 206, 208, 217, 220-21, 223, 226, 232-33, 239, 244, 254-55, 262
Ryan, Buddy 197, 255, 284, 286, 289-90, 292-93, 295-98, 300-01, 303, 310-11, 341
Rymkus, Lou 18-25, 28-30, 33, 50, 52, 55-56, 61, 89

S

St. Louis Cardinals *See* Arizona Cardinals
Salem, Harvey 182-84, 190-91, 195, 202, 204, 208, 268
Sampson, Greg 96-97, 99, 101, 109, 115, 121, 125-26, 130, 144
San Diego Chargers 15-17, 19-20, 23-25, 27-29, 31, 34-35, 37, 357
Sanders, Chris 322, 328, 330, 338, 342, 348, 351
Schlinkman, Walter 21, 30, 46, 52, 55-56, 63, 90, 95, 105, 124
Seattle Seahawks 339, 350, 356
Slaughter, Webster 274, 277, 279, 281, 294, 299-300, 308, 310-11, 320
Smith, Al 212, 214, 223, 226, 229, 254, 258-59, 268-69, 276, 281, 288-89, 300, 310-11, 322, 327, 337-39
Smith, Bubba 115-16, 118-20
Smith, Doug 189-90, 202-03, 226-27, 229-30, 253-54
Smith, Tim 160, 174, 177, 183-84, 192, 195, 203, 213
Smith, Tody 100-02, 109, 120-21
Smith, Tommy 215, 360
Spence, Julian 22, 24-26, 29-30, 32, 36
Stabler, Ken 23, 57, 78, 123, 135, 158-61, 163, 165, 172-74, 176-78, 185
Steinberg, Leigh 187, 292, 312, 325
Steinkuhler, Dean 189-92, 195
Stemrick, Greg 114, 126-28, 147, 153, 160, 162-63
Stensrud, Mike 145, 147, 160, 167, 176-77, 183, 190, 195-96, 203, 207
Stepnoski, Mark 320, 331, 338, 340, 348
Stram, Hank 16, 19, 23, 30, 33, 38, 64, 67, 73, 80, 106
Studley, Chuck 183-85
Suggs, Walt 28-29, 36, 42, 55, 58, 67, 70, 77, 79, 81-82, 84, 88, 93, 96
Suman, Don 21, 28, 30, 34

T

Tagliabue, Paul 252, 260, 271, 287, 301, 315, 324, 326, 332-35, 353-54
Talamini, Bob 21, 25, 31-33, 40, 48, 50, 55, 58, 67, 70, 73, 75-78, 80
Taylor, Hugh "Bones" 47, 52-57, 59, 61
Thigpen, Yancy 355-57
Thomas, Rodney 322, 327-28, 331, 338, 351
Thompson, Ted 114, 121, 125, 127-28, 148, 340
Tolar, Charley 22-23, 33, 35-38, 40, 43-44, 46, 48-49, 51, 55, 57, 70
Towns, Morris 123, 125, 133, 137, 143, 146, 160, 177, 183, 190
Trull, Don 42-43, 45, 48, 55-57, 66, 70, 73, 78-79

W

Walker, Gary 322-23, 330, 338, 348, 352, 356, 358
Washington Redskins 46, 93, 100, 106, 116, 196, 229, 263, 286, 334, 350
Washington, Ted 101, 105, 109, 116-118, 121, 128, 132, 138, 160, 174, 177
Webster, George 69-70, 73-74, 77, 81-86, 88, 92-93, 97- 98
Werblin, Sonny 42, 47, 51, 63, 101
White, Lorenzo 225-26, 239, 241, 243, 254-55, 257-58, 262-63, 265, 267-69, 272, 274-76, 279, 281, 287, 291-92, 311
Williams, David 239, 276, 281, 288, 291, 295, 297, 320, 322, 328
Williams, Jamie 190, 192, 195, 205-06, 208, 217, 224, 226, 229, 235, 241, 282
Williams, Lee 262-263, 267-68, 272-73, 276, 281, 290, 302, 304, 308
Williams, Tom 87, 88, 124
Willis, Fred 98-99, 102-05, 108
Wilson, JC 131-32, 146, 160, 174, 177, 182-83, 190
Wilson, Ralph 15, 47, 63
Wilson, Tim 123-24, 133, 138, 161, 174, 177
Woolfolk, Butch 194-95, 197, 206, 213
Wortham, Barron 322, 330, 339, 348, 355-356
Wyche, Sam 221, 230, 241, 259, 263
Wycheck, Frank 322, 331, 338, 342, 351, 355, 357-58

Y

Young, Bob 92, 96, 159-60, 254, 290-91, 297, 309

Z

Zendejas, Tony 195-96, 198, 221, 231-32, 240-41, 244

ABOUT THE AUTHOR

John Pirkle is a third generation Houstonian and a graduate of Waltrip High School (1977), the University of Texas at Austin (1981) and California Western School of Law at San Diego (1989). He also spent six years as a trial attorney at the United States Department of Justice in Washington D.C. This is his first book.

Author photographs by Jennifer Haywood of Houston.

Visit the Sportline Publishing Web Site at:
www.sportlinebooks.com

To contact Sportline Publishing or the author of *Oiler Blues*, John Pirkle, send your Email to:

info@sportlinebooks.com

To order additional copies of *Oiler Blues: The Story of Pro Football's Most Frustrating Team*, send $19.95 (for the softcover) or $24.95 (for the hardcover) plus $3.00 postage and handling to:

Sportline Publishing
PMB A-16
3346 East T.C. Jester Blvd.
Houston, TX 77018

Trade Orders may be arranged through:

Midpoint Trade Books
27 West 20th Street
Suite 1102
New York, NY 10011
(212) 727-0190
(212) 727-0195 fax